Cyber Worship in Multifaith Perspectives

Mohamed Taher

The Scarecrow Press, Inc.
Lanham, Maryland • Toronto • Plymouth, UK
2006

SCARECROW PRESS, INC.

Published in the United States of America
by Scarecrow Press, Inc.
A wholly owned subsidiary of The Rowman & Littlefield Publishing Group, Inc.
4501 Forbes Boulevard, Suite 200, Lanham, Maryland 20706
www.scarecrowpress.com

Estover Road
Plymouth PL6 7PY
United Kingdom

British Library Cataloguing in Publication Information Available

Library of Congress Cataloging-in-Publication Data

Taher, Mohamed, 1955-
Cyber worship in multifaith perspectives / Mohamed Taher.
p. cm.
Includes bibliographical references and index.
ISBN-13: 978-0-8108-5257-0 (pbk. : alk. paper)
ISBN-10: 0-8108-5257-8 (pbk. : alk. paper)
1. Worship. 2. Religion—Computer network resources. 3. Internet—Religious aspects. 4. Cyberspace—Religious aspects. I. Title.

BL550.T34 2006
203'.802854678—dc22

2006018579

™ The paper used in this publication meets the minimum requirements of American National Standard for Information Sciences—Permanence of Paper for Printed Library Materials, ANSI/NISO Z39.48-1992.
Manufactured in the United States of America.

Contents

Preface

Cyber Worship in Multifaith Perspectives explores worship on the Net. It is not about 'everything you need to know' even on the subjects of faith & belief. This book is just about religious and spiritual experience under the rubric, cyber worship --worship as (Prayer, Praise, Scripture, Sacrament, Rituals, Confessions, Eucharist, Rites, Pilgrimages, Reflection, Contemplation, etc.) performed in cyberspace. The term 'Cyber Worship' includes variants, such as, religions-online, online-religions, religions on the Net, religions in the cyberspace, online worship, virtual worship, electronic prayer, cyber church, e-prarthana, cyber puja, cyber salat, cyber Hajj, cyber synagogue, cyber Minyan, so on and so forth.

Neither, cyber worship is a rival temple, nor multifaith a new religion. Here in a generic sense Multifaith is used to signify multiple faiths representing a unity in diversity. It includes first, mainstream religions & spirituality, and second alternative traditions of belief & practice. Alternative traditions, here include, alternative systems of belief religious practices, non-mainstream spiritualities, new age movements, non-traditional movements, paganism, non-conformists, cults, etc.

Drawing on over six years experience of Web services in Multifaith perspective, in this book I have attempted to provide a systematic catalog of services, products, processes, approaches, applications, and functions. Thus, one would find worship resources that are available on the Internet, viz., a) streaming RealVideo Salat from Mecca, Webcasts of Congregational service, Service via Webcam, click and pray digital rosaries, virtual puja, Real Confessions, 24X7 prayer, Online Funeral, Internet Grave, etc. and b) static symbols useful for desktop, e-mail prayer request, downloadable Salat practice software, learning how to develop an altar, receiving sacraments by snail mail, subscribing scripture by e-mail, so forth.

This book, therefore, explores, a critical yet largely unexamined facet of social capital, i.e., personal /communal, as well non-work related use of Internet in everyday life—irrespective of computer and its location: at home, in workplace, Internet café, cyber kiosk or on a palm top. Such a cyberspace may help in connecting with innernet (or soul, spirit, sacred space). Moving within the above parameters *Cyber Worship in Multifaith Perspective* facilitates a journey through visualizations of adoring, venerating, consecrating, and blessings. This exercise will aid in assessing how such resources are accessed, scattered, portrayed thereby enabling to compliment real world's worship pattern. As an outcome of this visual one could view the sociology of Internet, as well as, theology of those who are involved in connecting the virtual communitas—i.e., Wired Swamis, Rabbis, Imams, Monks, Pastors, as well e-Congregations of respective faiths / spiritualities / meditational sanghas.

This book is then a quick reference, among others, for two groups, viz., businesses and communities. Businesses will find competitive intelligence based on an integrated unique approach --(web site ranking, evaluating content, position analysis, link popularity, metadata, etc.) called Webmetrics. In other words, this Web measurement and analytics is applied to depict *supply* after dotcom burst and *demand* for sacred-space in a post 9/11 era. The primary purpose of such a knowledgebase, is to identify the hidden (albeit not totally mysterious) potential of e-multifaith market, and secondary is to offer a benchmark for return-on-investments and thereby examine future of the blessed bandwidth poised amidst 'now or never' business Webs. For believers as individuals or communities it has, a detailed pathfinder with Webwise maps, directories, tools (loaded with many freebies), as well technique assisting individual seekers; furthermore for congregation's it has interesting findings to consolidate energies in the vertical Web (find a cheaper ISP, or free Web analyzers).

In *Cyber Worship in Multifaith Perspectives* we finally have a book that gets beyond speaking about 'Web presence.' Navigating into deep Web it successfully nets faithful seekers, mediators and service providers. As against other Webquests that go horizontal, the book takes us into the vertical Web. Such a vertical surfing unfolds founding and funding stories of startling faith-based model temples meant for Internet-only worshipers. These temples are designed in a way or set to step-upon the Celestial Ladder with simple, fast, convenient, secure, one-click.

Preface

The netizens, without having to convert themselves, might convert their screen into a temple of worship, according to the profession of their original faith. Thus the screen can bring together the people of diverse faith and instil in them a kind of religious accommodation that we badly need today. Multifaith optics is more than ever essential, with diverse communities just looking for a bit or byte of tolerance among neighbours. Hopefully, this book will help in:

- building communication bridges,
- fostering a spirit of understanding, as well
- using a new set of lenses to view the common ground which demonstrates that all roads lead to the same G-d, Lord of the Universe.

Behind every activity, there is a source of inspiration. A book about cyberspace in a Multifaith context inevitably emerges from my personal and professional network. The foremost component of such a network comes from the accommodation imbibed by my father in particular and the entire family environment in general.
For all the cooperation, I am deeply indebted to Joseph Romain, Director Multifaith Information Services, Ontario Multifaith Council. I thank my colleagues for all their nice and kind help, viz., Liz Chapel, the CEO., Joann Rose, Ayanna Goddard, Joanne Rose, and Charmaine Saunders. I wish to sincerely thank the Board members of Ontario Multifaith Council, namely, Mr. Hari Chopra, Hindu Representative, Mr. Harsharan Singh Sikh Representative, Rabbi Ronald Weiss Jewish Representative, Dr. Ervad J Bagli Zoroastrian Representative, Mr. Prakash Mody, Jain Representative, and Ontario Multifaith Council's staff, Rev. Stuart Schroeder and Michael Skaljin, for their kind advice on taxonomies of the respective faiths.

Thanks are also to all whose feedback in the last few years augmented my ideas towards building the infobridges across diverse communities. In fact my acquaintances include representatives from a multiplicity of faith and cultural areas and I owe my gratitude to all of them. Salutes to the Technocratis, I mean my Web Gurus, whose support always comes synchronously, and these include Yusuf Mansuri, Yunus Mansuri, Abdurrahman Sait, and David keaveney. Special thanks are to Dr. Norman Horrocks, Dr. Sue Easun. Dr. Martin Dillon, Karen Gray, Jayme Bartles, and the team at the publishers' domain, and all these deserve high regards from me.

I would like to thank for understanding and support my loving family members: Ameena my wife, Amatul Momin, Hafsa Taher my daughters and son, Mohamed Salman. My sincere prayers are that our children and their progeny enjoy a successful life promoting harmony and peace among the humanity at large.

Dr. Mohamed Taher
Toronto
mt2222@yahoo.com
taher.cjb.net

Credits: Copyright Permissions

p. 18, Prayer Before Logging Onto the Internet; **p. 33**, Two Minute Daily Puja; **p. 33**, I-church - We are looking for a Web Pastor!; **p. 69-109**, Dublin Core metadata Editor to generate the tags; **p. 69**, World Prayers; **p. 69**, Kashi Ashram Tour; **p. 69**, Belief System Selector, **p.70**, What religion is the best?; **p. 70**, Godulike; **p. 71**, Trucker's Prayer Room; **p. 71**, Museums of World Religions; **p. 71**, Webcam Central: Cams by Category; **p.71**, Business Gets the message B2C: Religion; **p.72**, Blessed Bandwidth over the Internet; **p. 72**, *Taipei Times*; **p. 72**, Virtual Church of Benevolent Deities Inc.; **p. 73**, Kiosk,; **p. 73**, Online Wiccan Site; **p. 74**, Bashar: Web page design by Bashar Communication, Inc. Copyright by Darryl Anka. Copyright Reserved. Contact www.Bashar.org; **p. 74**, Cyber Shrine; **p. 74**, Tao Sanctuary; **p. 75**, Introduction / Ritual Begins here; **p. 75**, Adhiparasakthi Virtual Prayer Room; **p. 76, 78, 81, 90, 95, 100, 101, 103,** and **104,** Multifaith Information Manual, Toronto, Ontario Multifaith Council, 2000; **p. 76**, Temple of Mithras; **p. 76**, House of Worship; **p. 77**, Baha'is Deepening on the Internet; **p. 77**, Bahai-Virtual Tour (picture); **p. 77**, The Internet and the Covenant; **p.78**, Wat Thai Kusinara Chalermraj; **p.78**, Dragon Gate Temple; **p. 79**, Cyber Meditation: Daily Zen; **p. 79**, Meditation Hall Redesigned; **p. 80**, Seiwa-en's Baisn; **p. 80**, Zen; **p. 81**, Blessed Bandwidth; **p. 81**, Jesus Online; **p. 82**, Miraculous Winking Jesus Christ; **p.82**, Parish of Springfield: Virtual Meditation Room; **p. 83**, Online Confessions; **p.83**, Where Truth Hurts: Confession Booth; **p. 83**, Online Confession Box; **p. 84**, Father Max- Confess Now; **p. 84**, The Virtual Church; **p. 84,** and **284**, Cyber Worship; **p. 85** and **301**, Virtual Church of the Blind Chihuahua; **p. 85**, Requiem; **p. 85**, The Perpetual Web Rosary; **p. 86**, CyberChurch; **p. 86**, Porter; **p. 87**, Sacred Space: Jesuit prayer; **p. 87**, Experience Menlo; **p. 88**, Prayer Schedule for PopulationPrayer.com; **p. 88**, Internet Daily Chapel; **p. 89**, The shroud of Turin; **p. 89**, Prayers and Miracles 24 hours a day; **p. 89**, Saint Rose of Lima Virtual Prayer Room; **p. 90**, Alpha Church; **p.90**, Mahakali; **p. 91**, Eprarthana.com; **p. 92**, Confession / Arti; **p. 91**, E-Anjali; **p. 92**, Durga Pujas - Live Webcam Coverage from USA; **p. 92**, Prarthana; **p. 93**, The Hindu Kids Universe- Multimedia; **p. 93**, D/FW Hindu Temple Society; **p. 93**, Mataji's Ultimate Site- And Hindu Temple Links; **p. 94**, Virtual Temple; **p. 94**, Ganapati Bappa Moriya; **p. 95**, Blessings on the Net**;** **p. 95**, Lord Ayyappa of Sabarimala; **p. 95**, Sabarimala- Sree Ayyappan Temple; **p. 96**, Projek Cyber Mosque; **p. 96**, First Mosque on the Moon; **p. 96**, Salat Relay- snap shot; **p. 97**, Moon Sighting; **p. 96**, Glorious Month of Ramadhan; **p. 97**, Nisab Calculator Table's Page; **p. 98**, Zakat Calculation Page; **p. 97**, Zakat Calculation- Comprehensive Form; **p. 98**, Zakat Calculator; **p. 99**, Hajj- Movie and Hajj Illustrated; **p. 99**, The Noble Sanctuary; **p. 99**, Majalis; **p. 100**, Emam Reza (A.S); **p. 100**, Islamic Cemetery; **p. 100**, Online Graveyard, **p. 101**, Jain World; **p. 101**, Digital Religion/ Renewing Judiasm; **p.101**, Rabbi Bookman's Spiritual Work out; **p. 102**, Memorial Prayer; **p. 102**, Live Western Wall Camera at Aish; **p. 102**, On-line Gurudwara; **p. 104**, Entrance to Temple; **p. 105**, The Sun Circle Meditation Hall; **p. 105**, Yoga Everywhere; **p. 105**, Online Finger Meditation Tool; **p.106**, Circle Sanctuary; **p. 106**, Cosmic Mother Sharing Her Life with us; **p. 107**, Spirituality: Post a Prayer, **p. 107**, Minute Meditation; **p. 107**, Learning Meditation; **p. 138**, Welcome to the wild, wacky and wonderful world of Internet Spirituality; **p.141**, A Religious Experience: What is being done with the internet and where are we going?; **p. 145**, "Cyberworship: Are teens finding faith online"; **p. 148**, CyberFaith: How Americans Pursue Religion Online, Pew Internet.Org; **p.162**, My religious journey on cyberspace(refit.ucsm.ac.uk/articles/191jarvis.pdf); **p.163**, How to get to Heaven from the Internet; **p. 164**, "Does Allah Care about Copyright?"; **p. 168**, A Guide to Buddhist Memorial Service for lost information, Daioh Temple, Kyoto, Japan; **p. 169**, Religion: Heuristic Resources for Inquiry & Dialogue; **p. 187**, Cyber Worship Illustrated:: Examples of Online Worship; **p. 188**, Seven logical Consequences of Interreligious Dialoguing; **p. 205**, A Theology of Technology; **p. 218**, Pope John Paul II -- World Communications Day: Pope gives benediction to Internet; **p. 221**, Ethics Survey; **p. 247**, A Reappraisal of Typologies of New Religious Movements; **p.261**, Recent Reference Question; **p.265**, Guidelines for Church Website; **p. 272**, Report on Webmaster Survey; **p. 273**, Research Survey: Sikhs on the net; **p.275**, Islaam.com Survey; **p. 277**, Cyberworship Site Map [Eattheword.com]; **p. 278**,, Religious Resources;

Credits

p. 280, Spiritual Topics / Specific Religion [religioustolerance.org]; **p. 282**, Worship Map; **p. 285**, Denomination Taxonomy; **p. 304**, Key Functions of Religion, William Martin; **p. 293**, Beliefnet Site Map ; **p.295**, A Taxonomy of Religions according to their Hermeneutics of Fecal Occurrence; **p. 299**, Worship Web Links; **p. 300**, Religion Online; **p.301**, "Cyber Cemeteries and Virtual Memorials: Virtual Living Monuments as On-line Outlets for Real Life Mourning and A Celebration of Life," Hermann Gruenwald and Le Gruenwald, in *Making Sense of Death: Spiritual, Pastoral, and Perosnal Aspects of Death, Dying and Bereavement* (Amityville, Baywood, 2003) 113-114; **p. 316,** Google Page Rank Prediction; **p. 316**, Cynthia Says Portal (cynthiasays.com); **p. 316**, Link Popularity (linkpopularity.com); **p.324**, Church of Ireland Website Survey (ireland.anglican.org/survey/results.pdf); **p. 333**, Guidelines for Church Websites.

"If I had one thought I'd like to leave with you today, it would be like this: What we are creating is a fabric of intelligence: a supercomputing network that will weave the next human renaissance...Even 'virtual religion' will be possible, where individuals can participate in stimulated religious experiences from a variety of cultures and beliefs. Everything changes when we live inside a universal information continuum." -- [George Fierheller, Vice-Chairman, Rogers Communications, at the fifth Ian P. Sharp lecture, delivered at the University of Toronto, on October 7, 1993

Cyber Doors at a Glance: Religious / Spiritual Groups:

Press B

Baha'i	Buddhism	*Christianity*	**Hare Krishna**	*Hinduism*
Islam	Jainism	*Judaism*	**Native American Spirituality**	*Rastafarianism*
Sikhism	Wiccan Church	*Zoroastrianism*		

Press P for *PRAYERS*

Legend:
(You can customize your Key Board as per your faith / spirit's mind-map)
F1 Connect your computer for cyber worship: service, prayer, praise, meditation, yoga...
F2 Plan your transcendental web roadmap and destination
F3 Set your intentions to talk directly with the Sublime
F4 Retry (path may be busy): Control temptations to deviate
F5 Speak to a live representative of God: Press 1 for grace, Press 2 for solace, Press 3 for ...
F6 Download live audio, video via Real players, Windows Media ...
F7 Open the Gates of Alternative Traditions if you are looking
F8 Mainstream Traditions for the Contented
F9 Go Direct to Cyber heaven
F10 Exit from the trance

Press W for **Worship**

1

Cyber Worship Mapping Webwise: Noah, Abraham and Beyond

Spells:
This spell is designed to stop people from bothering you on the Internet! So if you have peskey people that are bothering you on the Internet try this little spell!!!

All you have to do is chant the following
"Mercury and cyber space
Stam your feet and start the chace. Boogies of the
'Net be gone Beware my magick CD rom.
I cleance, I clear, I scare away Don't come back
another day!"
www.angelfire.com/wizard/wicca/internetspell.html

How Do You Worship Your Gods?
We practice two types of magic, worship magic and mind magic. Note that we use the term 'magic' and not 'magick.' 'Magick' was thought up by politically-minded Craft practitioners who didn't want their religious practices trivialized nor confused with sleight-of-hand...
www.mysticwicks.com/showthread.php?t=367

1.1 Mapping Alternative Traditions Webwise

A. Online Cyber Worship

a. Rituals, Magic, Spells, Meditating, Circle Casting, Invoking & Evoking...

First Church of Shatnerology www.shatnerology.com	Online First Church of the Dome www.io.com/~maniac/church.html	Holy Shrine of Journey The Journey Webring http://holyshrineofjourney.com
Secular Web: Kiosk Infidels.org/www.secweb.org/ kiosk.asp	Spiral Goddess Grove Begin the Journey www.spiralgoddess.com/ SGGrove.html	Church Of Satan Satan Worshipping or Worshipping the Devil www.dpjs.co.uk/devil.html
Secular Web: Agora Informal place to gather & read www.secweb.org/agora.asp	Belief System Selector www.selectsmart.com/RELIGION	God-U-Like www.godulike.co.uk
Online Wiccan Rituals http://go.to/OnlineWiccanRituals	Cabal KaBob: DemonWorship On a stick – WebCams http://rj3.net/ckb/ webcam.shtml?zoom=y&order=3	Magick's Realm Spells, Blessings, Rituals... www.magicksrealm.f2s.com
Cult of the Almighty Dave http://home.earthlink.net/ ~dth/cult.html	Church of Juan Valdez Worship of Juan, The Burro, The Bean www.netcontrol.net/archives-98/ 1813034/index.shtml	Church of Gerbil – Canada www.angelfire.com/ ar/abootgerbils

Martian Wicca! www.iamawitch.com/articles/ article_0004.html	Altar in Space? www.iamawitch.com/articles/ article_0004.html	Virtual Worship www.iamawitch.com/articles /article_0004.html
The Last-Chance Cathedral & Discount House of Worship http://dragonet.com/allsaint	First Church of Wintermute http://gridley.acns.carleton.edu/ ~harrisws/wintermute	First Church of Jesus Christ, Elvis http://jubal.westnet.com/ hyperdiscordia/ sacred_heart_elvis.html
Bardic Beltaine www.paganlibrary.com/rituals_spells/ bardic_beltaine.php	A Basic Love Spell www.paganlibrary.com/rituals_spells/ basic_love_spell.php	Beltane www.paganlibrary.com/ rituals_spells/beltane.php
The Blot www.paganlibrary.com/ rituals_spells/blot.php	Candlemas (Imbolc) Ritual: 2 February - www.paganlibrary.com/ rituals_spells/ candlemas_ritual-2_february.php	The Care and Feeding of Online Rituals www.paganlibrary.com/ rituals_spells/ care_feeding_of_online_ritual.php
Casting The Circle www.paganlibrary.com/ rituals_spells/casting_circle.php	Casting the Circle www.paganlibrary.com/ rituals_spells/casting_circle_2.php	Casting the Circle http://www.paganlibrary.com/ rituals_spells/ casting_the_circle3.php
Spiritual Sisters of the Internet Café www.spiritualsisters.com	Church of Ravenstar Searose Faerie Tradition Witchcraft www.raven-star.org	Goddess temple online www.spiralgoddess.com
The Chaplet of the Holy Guardian Angel www.beastbay.com	The Church of Satan www.satannet.com	The Temple of Set www.xeper.org
Shri Adi Shakti The Kingdom of God HH Shri Mataji Nirmala Devi http://adishakti.org	Infinite Goddess – Embracing the Divine Mother www.goddess.ws •	Avatars of the Goddess www3.simpatico.ca/ chartreuse/ AvatarsOfTheGoddess/ JudeoChristian.htm
Church of Virus http://virus.lucifer.com	The Temple of the Bowie http://ugr8.ucsd.edu/Bowie/main.htm	SuperChurch www.superchurch.net
Maya Gods http://members.tripod.com/elpage6	Native American Prayers and Blessings www.angelfire.com/md/elanmichaels/ prayers.html	Native American Religion beliefs and rituals www.stormwind.com/common/ nareligion.html
Native American prayer www.barefootsworld.net/natpray.html	Wicca prayer www.soultospirit.com/ traditions/prayers/wicca_prayers/ wicca_prayers7.asp	Beltane Ritual www.paganlibrary.com/ rituals_spells/beltane_ritual.php
Cult of the Dead Cow www.cultdeadcow.com	Andersainism www.nada.kth.se/~asa andersianism.html	Church of all worlds http://yoyo.cc.monash.edu.au/ groups/eas/EASFrameset-5.html
Hubble Space Telescope Photo: 'The Eye of God' http://urbanlegends.about.com/ library/bl_eye_of_god.htm	Avatar Search www.AvatarSearch.com/index.html	Daily Guru Thoughts www.gurustu.com/daily/index.php
Candle Magic www.paganlibrary.com/ rituals_spells/candle_magic.php	Candle Blessing www.paganlibrary.com/ rituals_spells/candle_blessing.php	Blessing My New Home www.paganlibrary.com/ rituals_spells/ blessing_my_new_home.php
Belief System Selector www.selectsmart.com/RELIGION	Confessions of a cyber-god www.cyberlife-research.com/ articles/confessions.htm	Unitarian Universalists Browse common questions www.uunashua.org/100quest.html
Religions FAQ www.faqs.org/faqs/religions	Church of questions http://education.atu.edu/ people/sadams/blogger2/ 2002/08/03.html	God's FAQ www.godsfaq.com
Mythology FAQs www.faqs.org/faqs/mythology	Shamanism FAQs www.faqs.org/faqs/shamanism	Ashram Vidya Order Primordial Tradition www.vidya-ashramvidyaorder.org

Archangel Michael has a message for you www.ronnastar.com	The Raven Lodge www.shamana.co.uk	Wolf Lodge Robert Ghost Wolf and Wolf Lodge Shaman of the Metis People www.wolflodge.org
Runes & The Northern Mysteries Correspondence Course (Fee-based) www.aswynn.nuneschool.org/ correspondence.html	Online Coven Ritual Schedule Online Class Rituals www.paganclasses.com/ classschedule.html	Shinto Overseas Centers www.shinto.org/eng/overseas-e.htm
Aeclectic Tarot Browse 400 different Tarot & oracle decks www.aeclectic.net/tarot	Aleana's Sacred Flame www.msnusers.com/ AleanasSacredFlame	Tantra Ashram www.tantra.co.il/ashram/index.asp
Asiya's Shadows Qurater Calls While Casting a circle, call the four elements to Protect, Bless, Witness & Add power www.asiya.org/index2.html	Holidays: The 13 Lunar Eshats www.geocities.com/ circleofthelunarlight/ holidays.htm	World Prayers – Prayer Collective **Multifaith Practices** www.worldpyaers.org
Futahashira Shrine http://member.nifty.ne.jp/ 2hashira/futa_english/index.htm	Kannagara Jinja Shinto Shrine, Washington,USA. (Mie prefecture) http://kannagara.org	Cats Lair Temple & Seminary of Wicca www.geocities.com/ cats_lair_temple/ home.html
Futahashira Shrine - Shinto - http://f-shrine.com/english/index.htm	Den of ZaWolfSpirit www.angelfire.com/ mo2/ofwolfandman	Shamanic Ecstasy (ayahuasca, shamanic hallucinogens) http://deoxy.org/shaman.htm
Many Paths www.manypaths.com	Air Meditation www.paganlibrary.com/ rituals_spells/air_meditation.php	Metista Teachings and Techniques http://www.metista.com
Yule Chant Wiccans www.modernpaths.com/library/ prayer/ articles/f_lib_prayer_home_starhawk.html	Calendars from the Sky (Sun and Stars) http://webexhibits.org/calendars	The Ancient Call www.paganlibrary.com/ rituals_spells/ancient_call.php
Asylum on Web Cam www.asylumcam.com/allcams.htm	New Age Temple www.devotee.addr.com/temple/ index.htm	Sacred Circle Sanctuary www.goddess- statues.netfirms.com
Listen to Meditation www.vipassana.com/audio_files/ index.php	Angel healing temple & metaphysical store http://steppingstones.to	Read DAILY prayer (look for the button 'Click here')
Terra Transformations http://terraangel2002.tripod.com/ terratransformations	Isle of Avalon new age centers, UK. www.isleofavalon.co.uk	Conversations With God www.cwg.org
Tibetan Book of the Dead www.lib.virginia.edu/exhibits/ dead/index2.html	Sepher Yetzirah www.vermontel.com/~vtsophia/table.html	Conversations With God www.conversationswithgod.org
Enuma Elish www.sacred-texts.com/ane/enuma.htm	Corpus Hermeticum www.sacred-texts.com/chr/herm/index.htm	Nag Hammadi Texts www.gnosis.org/naghamm/ nhlalpha.html
Daily Tao http://nauticom.net/ www/asti/asti.htm	Taoism Initiation Page www.taopage.org	Taoism- Serenity Found www.geocities.com/ WestHollywood/Village/ 3200/intro.html
Taoism: The Temple of the Immortal Spirit translations, resources... www.thetemple.com	The Abode of the Eternal Tao www.abodetao.com	Tao of Pooh: An Introduction www.algoriths.com/ users/belascot/pooh.html
Taoist Texts www.clas.ufl.edu/users/ gthursby/taoism	Tao Te Ching www.chinapage.com/laotze.html	Read Tao Te Ching www.hm.tyg.jp/ ~acmuller/contao/laotzu.htm
Shinto Texts English translations: Yengishiki, Kojiki, Nihongi. www.sacred-texts.com/shi/index.htm	Confucian Texts www.sacred-texts.com/cfu/index.htm	Apple Tree Spell Book of Shadows www.paganlibrary.com/ rituals_spells/apple_tree_spell.php

Ethiopian Texts http://anes235-1.ff.cuni.cz/ ethiopian/INTRO.HTM	Corpus Hermeticum www.sacred-texts.com/chr/herm/ index.htm	Pistis Sophia www.webcom.com/~gnosis/ library/psoph.htm
The Egyptian Book of the Dead www.sacred-texts.com/ egy/bookdead.htm	1st and 2nd Books of Jeu www.webcom.com/ ~gnosis/library/bookss.htm	Gnostic Texts www.gnosis.org/library.html
Banishing and Casting www.paganlibrary.com/ rituals_spells/banishing_and_casting.php	Banishing The Circle www.paganlibrary.com/ rituals_spells/banishing_circle.php	Dead Sea Scrolls www.webcom.com/ ~gnosis/library/scroll.htm
Satanic Bible www.beyondweird.com/satanic-bible.html	Pagans Online www.pagansonline.com	Halloween online http://www.halloween- online.com/
Native American Prophecies www.crystalinks.com/ native_american.html	Online Covens Directory www.ariadnespider.com/ Witchcraft/Online_Covens/index.html	Halloween Web Cams www.halloweenwebcams.com
Teaching other faiths **Multifaith Perspectives** www.ifcmw.org/ resources/creative_models.pdf	Song of the Queen of Sheba from the Kebra Nagast (Rastafarians) www.modernpaths.com/ library/sacred/articles/ f_lib_text_home_kebra.html	Calendrical Bookmarks: Chinese, Japanese ... http://emr.cs.it.edu/ home.reingold/ calendar-book/ calendar-links.shtml
Ritual Blades Sowrds, Daggers & Armor http://ritualblades.com	Universal Calendar Calculator: Far East, Greek, Middle East, ... www.cf-software.com/other.html	Today's Calendar and Clock Page: Maya / Aztec, Chinese www.ecben.net/calendar.shtml
Gnosis Archive www.webcom.com/~gnosis/ search_form.html	Hershey's Chocolate Ritual www.angelfire.com/stars/ shiningonme/choclate.html	Sanctum: A sacred or holy place www.docstrange.com/ main/sanctum.asp
Three General Wonderful Prayer Affirmations www.prayandvisualize.com/ general_wonderful_prayer.htm	Release Fear, Anxiety, an Issue... Music While you Visualize (Real Audio / Streaming) Three General Wonderful Prayer Affirmations www.prayandvisualize.com/ release_fear_anxiety_an_issue.htm	A Prayer for Peace Three General Wonderful Prayer Affirmations www.prayandvisualize.com/ affirmations_main.htm
Prayer and Visualizations www.indigorecords.com/NewFaith/ prayer_and_visualization.htm		

B. Offline Cyber Worship

a. Know-How, Process, Procedures, Activity, Functions, Methods...: (Alternative Traditions, continued..)

Ask Claudia Psychic healer www.askclaudia.com	Have a Problem? / Need Advice Ask Dr. Berlee www.awomensjourney.com	Do you Believe in Magick (See side menu also) www.monmouth.com/ ~appleblossom/fire/index2.htm
Ask Why www.askwhy.co.uk	Send a Prayer Request for Virtual Worship	Do What Thou Wilt Shall Be the Whole of the Law. www.winternet.com/ ~blister/alchemy.html
Advice: Online answers to your questions www.catalystpoint.org/ multicastings/letters.html	Mythology FAQs www.faqs.org/faqs/ mythology	Have a question Dial [1-800-Ask-a-Priest]
Raving Atheist: Parody? http://ravingatheist.com/ archives/parody.html	Mythology and religion http://ancienthistory. miningco.com/msubmyth.htm	Theosophy Article: The Number Seven www.blavatsky.net/blavatsky/ arts/NumberSeven.htm
From Shirdi Sai to Satya Sai http://saionline.org/shirdi-sathya.html	Acharya Rajneesh www.hinduwebsite.com/masters.htm	Osho: The Book of the Secrets : a new commentary http://www.otantra.net/ oTantra/VBTv1/ chapter08.html

Terra Transformations http://terraangel2002.tripod.com/ terratransformations	Sorceryn www.sorceryn.com	Tattoos – Tribal Tattoos www.vanishingtattoo.com
Ogopogo – Myth or Fact www.seesya.com/index.htm	Parodier http://home.swipnet.se/ ~-52528/sidor/parodier.htm	Spirit Dimension http://spiritdimension.com
Taoism or Daoist www.edepot.com/religion.html	Chad Hansen's Chinese Philosophy (Taoist Interpretations) www.hku.hk/philodep/ch	Dao House...of discourses and dreams www.geocities.com/ dao_house/index
Daoism Depot collection of Tao Te Ching translations www.edepot.com/taoism.shtml	Heavenly Way http://home.nyc.rr.com/hsiaostemple	Taoism for Dummies (Flash required) www.geocities.com/tao4dummies
TaoWorks Village Find a Taoist near you, visit the village. www.taoworks.org	Taoist Mysticism www.digiserve.com/mystic/Taoist	Healing Tao USA Site www.healingtaousa.com
True Tao Home Page (teachings, stories and translations) www.truetao.org	The Tao House Modern semi-new-age semi-taoist eclectic view. http://gnv.fdt.net/~taohouse	Soul City www.soulcityinc.com
Taoism Page www.easternreligions.com/tframe.html	ALLFaiths Press®Shintoism http://interinc.com/Allfaiths/Shintoism	Pagan rituals and prayers for death www.globalideasbank.org/ ndw/NDW-6.HTML
Kami no MIchi - The Way of Kami On A Shinto priest www.csuchico.edu/ ~georgew/tsa/Kami_no_Michi_ToC.html	The "Interi" Shinto Homepage On life and death. www.geocities.com/Athens/8871	Green Pages www.oakgrove.org/GreenPages
Bantu customs (death / burial) http://lucy.ukc.ac.uk/ ERA/Ancestors/gluckman.html	Natives - Mayan rituals (death / burial) www.halfmoon.org/vision.html	American Natives - Lakota rituals http://dying.miningco.com/ library/weekly/aa032099.htm
Path Of The Feather Techniques of shamanic journeys... www.pathofthefeather.com	Shamanism and Animal Spirits www.geocities.com/ RainForest/4076/index1.html	Totems Animals and Familiars Native American shamanic practices. www.geocities.com/ Athens/8793/totems/totems.html
Native American Prophecies (a white psychic... named Z) www.crystalinks.com/ native_american.html	Summary of Native American Religions Religion of the Iroquois Nation, Dakota (Sioux) and Apache tribes http://are.as.wvu.edu/ruvolo.htm	Manuela Standing Woman Native American traditions www.geocities.com/ manuela_standing_woman/ MSW.html
The Bear's Byte Home Page Native American religion & tradition www.thebearbyte.com	United Tribal Spirits Inter-tribal Native American culture & spirituality http://unitedtribal.org	Universal Spiritual Teachings Native American spirituality & healing www.meshupeshu.com
Articles on Spiritual Heritage Native American www.bluecloud.org/religion.html	Native American Spirituality http://members.aol.com porchfour/religion/nativeam.htm	Windhorse Services Native American healers www.windhorz.com
A Glossary of Native Spirituality http://news.mpr.org/features/ 2003/08/18_gundersond_spiritualityterm	The Red Hummingbird Foundation, Inc. Teachings based on Native American prophecies www.redhummingbird.org/ purposes.html	Heart of Sky Maya religion and spirituality www.uwec.edu/academic/ curric/greidebe/hos/Spirit
Online Rituals at the Dance www.thedance.com/rituals	Glossary Religious Holidays www.pgcares.com/ interfaith_glossary.html	Human Devolution: A Vedic Alternative to Darwinism **Multifaith Perspective** www.humandevolution.com
Glossary of Religious Terms www.religioustolerance.org/ glossary.htm	Pagan / Wiccan Glossary http://paganwiccan.about.com/ library/glossary/blglossary.htm	A Pagan Glossary of Terms www.neopagan.net/ Pagan_Glossary.html
Neo-Pagan Research Links www.geocities.com/ mikerdna/neolinks.html	Glossary of Dissenters http://people.bu.edu/dklepper/ RN307/dissenters.html	A Wiccan Glossary www.ecauldron.com/ wiccaterms.php
Gibbon's Channeling Research site http://home.tiscali.nl/gibbon	Glossary of Pagan Terms & Festivals http://notendur.centrum.is/ ~snorrigb/feb5.htm	Rituals & Magick: Wiccan Information and Tutorials www.glasstemple.com/ basics/ritual.html

Creeds, Rules and Their Origins http://secretcircle.nightworld.net/crones/ crones3.htm	What is Wicca? www.ladyanne.com/whatiswicca.html	Magic – Learning the Basics www.angelfire.com/ok/ bobbiesues/ pg7magic.html
The Principles of Magick: The Art of Effective Invocation http://members.tripod.com/ Stormbringer777/ magic6.html	Witches have Eight Major Holidays Pagan Holidays and Festivals http://notendur.centrum.is/ ~snorrigb/feb5.htm	

b. Products, Resources, Materials...: (Alternative Traditions, continued..)

New Age Web Works Spiritual, Pagan, Psychic, Metaphysical, Alternative healthcare www.newageinfo.com	Alternative spirituality directory www.theorderoftime.com/ cyber/to/rs-file/altdir.html	Alternative directories www.theorderoftime.com/ cyber/to/rs-file/altdir.html
Resources for Reconstructionists and Traditionalist Heathens www.swordnshield.com	Alternatives Information http://www.alternatives.com	Esoteric Web Directory www.esotericlinks.com/ cgi-bin/ Linkmat.cgi?script=esotericism
Pagan search engine www.ariadnespider.com	UFO Seek – Witchcraft, Paranormal Search Engine www.ufoseek.com/Witchcraft	Esoterism – Mysticism Search Engine http://esoterism.com/links/ MYSTICISM
Witches Portal http://groups.msn.com/ TheWitchesPortal	Index: Witches of the World www.witchvox.com/xwotw.html	Alternative Health and Spiritual Directory www.godserver.com
Wicca gateway www.ariadnespider.com/Wicca	The_East gateway www.ariadnespider.com/The_East	Pagan gateway www.ariadnespider.com/Pagan
New_Age gateway www.ariadnespider.com/New_Age	Magick gateway www.ariadnespider.com/Magick	Gateway Rituals & Spells www.paganlibrary.com/ rituals_spells
Left_Hand gateway www.ariadnespider.com/Left_Hand	Occult Forum Index Discussion on paganism, witchcraft, Wicca, magic, spells, ritual www.occultForums.com	International Directory www.1spirit.com
MEME Update Cults on the Internet www.memecentral.com/ mu/mu0005.htm	Wiccan / Pagan Service Links List of On-line Services http://users.whtvcable.com/ adjatti/flow/vpslinks.html	Wicca Net www.wiccanet.com
Spiritual, Methaphysical & occult Resources www.primenet.com/ ~subru/Metaphysical%20Links.html	A to Z of Paranormal, Supernatural, weird & Unusual Phenomena (For a price) www.paranormality.com	Holy Smoke http://groups.msn.com/ TheWitchesPortal/ holysmoke.msnw
The Glass Temple Quality Wicca & Witchcraft Information www.glasstemple.com	Rituals / Spells' Directory www.paganlibrary.com/ rituals_spells	Wicca, Witchcraft, Neopaganism www.geocities.com/ shadowsofasiya/ linkswicca.html
Sarlo's Guru Rating Service **Multifaith Gateway** www.globalserve.net/ ~sarlo/RatingsP.htm	The Page of Unreason Destructive sects www.update.uu.se/~fbendz/pseudo	Alternative Market Place http://alternativemarketplace.com
Earth Spirits Emporium http://earthspirits.org	Essential Metaphysical Shop www.newageshops.com/mall.htm	Mystical Magickal Mall - www.newagereseller.com/ mysticalmagickalmall
Download Today's Best Sermons http://store.yahoo.com/ pttranscripts/index.html	Digital World www.geocities.com/~wtwilson3	Occultpedia www.occultopedia.com/ supernatural_satanism.htm
Like to join Soul Networking? www.dvostrukaduga.hr/page/ soulnet.htm	Circle of Souls Pagan Radio Network Pagan/New Age world-Fusion www.circleofsouls.net	Alternative web portal indexing sites www.spiral-web.com
Witches Chat Dot Com Getting the Palace Program to Join Us www.moonlitmagickparadise.com/ joinus.html	Interactive Relay Chat's Atheism About Religion www.irc.atheism.com	White Dragon – IRC Moots Welcome to # Pagan www.whitedragon.org.uk/irc.htm

Elfin Magical Diary (For a price) www.elfindiaries.co.uk	Basic Terms of Shinto www.kokugakuin.ac.jp/ijcc/wp/bts	Listening to Nature, Devas, Angels & Spirit Guides www.devas.org/start.htm
Medea's Chariot Internet Roadstop http://Nexus.MNIC.net/~rajchd	Spiritual Survival Handbook www.survivalmanual.com	The Vaults of Erowid human spirituality: directory www.erowid.org
Want a Nanny - (Download for free) Computer God software www.bluechillies.com	Pagan Top 100 www.pagansunite.com/pt100/list.html	Create your own Sacred Cyberspace (Spells & Rituals with Candles) www.circle-of-light.com/spells
Tao Webring www.webring.com/hub?ring=tao2	The Gods' Revival Award http://www.angelfire.com/ga/gentiles/AWARD.html	Blessed Bee Awards - Pagan Sites http://members.aol.com/brininsf/blessedb.html
Jinja & Shinto Jinja Online Network League. www.jinja.or.jp/english	Serious Links - Scepticism http://users.ox.ac.uk/~worc0337/serious/scepticism.html	Phenix Fire Pagans Promoting Religious Tolerance through Knowledge www.homestead.com/phenixfire/index.html
Annals of Improbable Research (AIR) Hot A.I.R www.improb.com	The Pagan Teaching Circle, Johnson State College www.angelfire.com/vt/paganteachingcircle/index.html	Facilitating personal growth http://onespiritproject.com
WebCity House of Worship **Multifaith Directory** www.webcityusa.com/worship.htm	Global Thinking About Religion & Spirituality www.homestead.com/tomharpur	Guide to Ancient Wisdom www.wisdomworld.org
Alternate Realities: links to: Wiccan, Pagan and Earth Religions sites www.esotericart.com/fringe/PaganLinks.htm	**Multifaith** - All Things Spiritual Directory www.allspiritual.com/MultiFaith.php3	Spell Kits, Magickal Oils, Incense, ETC.. www.1magickalapothecary.com/main.html
Pagan Worship, Devil Worship, The Devil is God www.paganworship.com	Universal Lodge http://home.eol.ca/~freemason/lodge/uxwhatis.htm	Saving Graves www.savinggraves.org/links/religious/
Innate - a fanlisting for Pagan faiths http://fan.500ml.org/paganism/	The Pagan Hierarchy http://seapagan.org/pagan-hierarchy	Strange Directory - paganism www.worldofalternatives.com/harmonics/links/paganism.html
Pagan Clergy http://groups.yahoo.com/group/pagan-clergy	"Pagan Places" A place to learn about paganism. http://www.pacificnet.net/~spectre/pagan.html	Neopaganism (sometimes Neo-Paganism) http://www.informationblast.com/Neopaganism.html
Cult3D Exporter http://www.cult3d.com/news/default.asp	Silent Inspiration. http://www.silentinspiration.com/downloads.html	What Neopagans Believe 5.6 or Neopagan Polytheology 101 http://www.neopagan.net/NeopagansBelieve.html ======
World Scripture: A Comparative Anthology of Sacred Texts - **Multifaith Resource** 4600 passages from 268 texts and 55 oral traditions www.euro-tongil.org/ws/index.html	The Pagan Net- Web Hosting www.paganlink.org/netstuff/Pagan_Networsking/Webcrafting/Hosting	Agayuliyararput: Our Way of Making Prayer: The Living Tradition of Yup'ik Masks http://www.si.umich.edu/CHICO/yupik/

C. Religions-Online / Online-Religions -

a. Home Pages of Religious and Spiritual Groups: (Alternative Traditions, continued..)

Holy Web log www.mindspring.com/~weblog	Miss monster home www.missmonster.com	Perl Monks - The monastery Gates for Perl devotees http://perlmonks.org
Ericka's Home page www.geocities.com/ericka_olofsen/index.html	Pagan Pride Project www.paganpride.org	Witches' League for Public Awareness www.celticcrow.com

The Goddess's Guild Were all are welcome Wiccans, Witches, Pagans, Christians, Satanists http://groups.msn.com/ TheGoddesssGuild	Suza Scalora www.myth.com/mythhtmlsite	Welcome to Radical Spirit www.radicalspirit.org
Avalonia: Wicca & Witchcraft www.avalonia.co.uk	The Modern Tradition of Witchcraft http://witch.drak.net/ tempest/witchery.html	Covenant of the Goddess www.cog.org
Maitreyan Order of Hsien Tao www.spirit-alembic.com	Center of Traditional Taoist Studies www.tao.org	Daoist Studies http://daoiststudies.org
MSB Academy: Taoism www.flowinghands.com/ mbs_htm/mbs.taoism.htm	Taoist Restoration Society www.taorestore.org	The Maitreyan Order of Hsien Tao Tantric-Alchemical-Kaballah: master Khiron www.spirit-alembic.com
Onisaburo Deguchi Omoto reform movement of Shinto. www2.plala.or.jp/wani-san/ODb_.htm	Shintoism Hub www.knowdeep.org/shintoism	International Shinto Foundation www.shinto.org/menu-e.html
Jinja Honcho: The Association of Shinto Shrines www.jinjahoncho.or.jp/en/ndex.html	GRACE Esoteric Training Center www.GRACEetc.com	Dance of the Deer Foundation www.shamanism.com
The Foundation for Shamanic Studies www.shamanism.org	Order of the White Lion www.orderofthewhitelion.com	U.S. Grand Lodge, Ordo Templi Orientis (Order of Oriental Templars) www.oto-usa.org/index.html
Kimbas Angels - angels and angelology http://kimbasangels.com	Multi Dimensions: conscious, unconscious and superconscious www.multidimensions.com	First Online Church of Bob www.modemac.com
Church of the Rainforest www.geocities.com/RainForest/1447	Virtual Church of the Blind Chihuahua www.dogchurch.com	Church of the SubGenius www.subgenius.com
Church of the Virus www.lucifer.com/virus	Nahziryah Monastic Community - Nazir Order of the Purple Veil www.nmcnews.org	Soul City: Pot Pourri www.soulcityinc.com
New Age practices www.newagepage.com	New Age Centers Isle of Avalon, Glastonbury, UK www.isleofavalon.co.uk	New Age Spirituality www.religioustolerance.org/ newage.htm
GRACE Esoteric Training Center www.graceetc.com	Empathy Online www.empathyonline.co.uk	Now Age www.sfheart.com/lovelight
Science of Wholeness www.scienceofwholeness.org	Angelspeake www.angelspeake.com	The Soul Element www.thesoulelement.com
Confucianism www.geocities.com/ Tokyo/Springs/6339/ Confucianism.html	Infidel Guy: Rational Radio and Debate www.infidelguy.com	SETI @ Home (Search for Extraterrestrial Intelligence at home) http://setiathome.ssl.berkeley.edu
Cybernetic Grove & Virtual Stone Circle www.neopagan.net	House of Satan www.houseofsatan.com	United Satanic Front (USF) www.geocities.com/ Athens/Parthenon/ 5947/usf.html
Rainsnow: Unite people on various spiritual paths www.rainsnow.org	Karinya for Body, Mind and Spirit www.karinya.com/notce1.html	Jonestown and Peoples Temple www-rohan.sdsu.edu/ ~remoore/jonestown/ contents.html
Cosmosofy – The Internet Universal Religion www.comosofy.org	Center for Duck Studies Priest, Popes, Quacks www.jagaimo.com/duck/ f_reading.html	The Church of the Profit$ http://home.epix.net/~jlferri/ profit.html
Okana's Web: Polish Paganism www.okana.org	Indian Paganism www.geocities.com/ indianpaganism/ index.html	Thuban: gnostic and hermetic writings http://pages.zoom.co.uk/ thuban/index.htm
Terra Mater International New Age inspired and Mother Earth centered movement (Native American religions) www.terramaterint.org	Utah Native American Church www.utah-nac.org	Walking Stick Foundation A nonprofit Jewish and Native American partnership ... indigenous spirituality. www.walkingstick.org

World Light Center Joyous & Glorious Ascension of People of our Planet www.worldlightcenter.com	White Mountain Education Association www.wmea-world.org	Bringing you into the darkness since 1993! www.darklinks.com
Earth Upliftment Network www.earthupnet.com	Exploration. Magick...Spirituality http://www.wisewayz.com	Pagan Awareness Network Australia www.paganawareness.net.au/ links.html
The Druid Grove (The Order of Bards, Ovates and Druid) www.obod.co.uk/obod	The Odinic Rite www.odinic-rite.org	The Pagan Federation www.paganfed.demon.co.uk
The British Druid Order www.druidorder.co.uk	Celtic Deities and Myths www.eliki.com/ancient/myth/celts	Asatru Folk Assembly www.runestone.org
Psychic service to the stars Spell caster, exorcist... www.angelfire.com/weird/ar/index.html	Cult – For Those Who Worship Waves www.surfcult.com.au/ new/html/frame.html	Mithraeum (Mithras) www.mithraeum.org
Lietuvos Romuva: Bbaltic faith www.romuva.lt	Northern Earth Mysteries www.northernearth.co.uk	Guild of the Grail www. guildofthegrail.cjb.net
Ancient latvian paganism www.pagan.drak.net/ wwcrew	Slavic Folklore/Mythos http://slavjanstvo.org/en	San Graal School of Sacred Geometry www.sangraal.com
Terra Firma" National Anarchism online www.terrafirma.rosenoire.org	November 9: traditionalism, fascism, nihilism www.november9.org	Temple 88: national-socialist / aryanist fraction of ONA http://temple88.cjb.net
International Third Position (ITP) www.itp.org	Third Position Collective www.thirdposition.net	Ananda Marga www.anadamarga.com
MysticWicks Online Pagan Community and Pagan Forums www.mysticwicks.com/ archive/index/t-38653	Pagan Educational Network Sponsors of the Charitable Fund www.bloomington.in.us/ ~pen	Pagan Webweaving www.hue.org/paganview
Bhakta Samaj of USA www.bhakta.com	Ananda Church of Self-Realization www.anandaseattle.org	Ananda Marga www.anandamarga.org
Unitarian Universalist Association UU Pagans www.cuups.org	Unitarian Universalist Association http://www.uua.org/ main.html	Thomas Jefferson Memorial Church Unitarian Universalist monticello.avenue.gen.va.us/ tjmc
Australian and New Zealand Unitarian Association www.anzua.org/	Famous Unitarian Universalists www.famousuus.com	International Council of Unitarian Universalists www.uua.org/icuu
Unitarian Universalist Buddhist Fellowship www.uua.org/uubf	Canadian Unitarian Council www.cuc.ca	The Southern Universalist www.athens.net/ ~wells/souniv.htm
Sai Baba Puttaparthi www.eaisai.com/baba	Largest Unitarian Universalist Communities Top Ten States with most UU members www.adherents.com/ largecom/com_uua.html	Religious Technology Center The Guarantor of Scientology's Future Scientology www.rtc.org/home.htm
Secret Societies www.inwd.com/ kmedeke/ cults.htm	Access New Age www.accessnewage.com	Foundation for Information about Societal Problems and Occult Tendencies www.stelling.nl/ simpos/simpoeng.htm
Scientology Parishioners Scientologists On-line http://on-line.scientology.org	Scientology: Global Organization Locator www.scientology.org/ world/worldeng/global	Scientology Home Page http://www.scientology.org
Landover Baptist Church www.landoverbaptist.org	Brahma's Homepage Virtual Installation in HTML www.geocities.com/ SoHo/Square/8956/ Brahma/opening.htm	NurelWeb Cults & Religion Website Academic Approach to the Study of Religion www.acs.ucalgary.ca/~nurelweb
Malkuth Tourism Club (on the road to enlightenment) http://malkuth.f2g.net	WiccaNet: Home of the Seekers Circle on the Web http://wiccanet.net/ seekers/index2.shtml	Institute for Astroenergetic Studies,Manjushri Mandala http://www.cybermonks.net

Amma's – A New World of Knowledge www.ammas.com	First Church of the Last Laugh (FCLL) http://saintstupid.com/menu.htm	Theologically Correct dot Com Ministries: Cults_and_New_Religions http://www.theologicallycorrect.com/resources/ Cults_and_New_Religions
DRESIANISM! A RELIGION FOR THE INFORMATION AGE! http://stealth.kirenet.com/~vastator/dresianism.html	Masons, Grand Lodge of Canada in the Province of Ontario, Freemasonry Lodge www.grandlodge.on.ca/framemain.htm	Scottish Rite of Canada Freemasonry, Masons and Masonry http://scottishritemasons-can.org
Society of Elder Faiths www.elderfaiths.org	Centre For Pagan Studies www.centre-for-pagan-studies.org/	The Church of the Grey www.churchofthegrey.com

1.2 Mapping Baha'i Webwise

A. Online Cyber Worship

a. Prayer, Praise, Scripture, Sacrament

Asylum on Web Cam www.asylumcam.com/allcams.htm	House of Worship Live Snapshot www.us.bahai.org/how/webcam.htm	Bahai Prayers for the PDA www.memoware.com
Bahai Prayers Online in text format www.ibiblio.org/Bahai/BWC-Etext/compilations/bahai.prayers/bp-eng-tx01	Baha'i Prayers www.sacred-texts.com/bhi/comp/bp06.txt	Bahai's Deepening on the Internet – Join Congregations at your local time using IRC tool (very Saturday) http://users.tebenet.nl/~kuijer-e/main.htm
Baha'i Devotions www.bahaidevotions.org/index.htm	Online Bahai Religious Texts www.hinduwebsite.com/general/etextsbahai.htm	Bahai Prayers for Peace www.peaceprayer.org/bahai.html
Voice A Vision • Post A Prayer Dare A Dream Multifaith Voices www.heartpath.com/hpcontent/voiceAvision.asp	Ancient Wisdom: Submit a Prayer Multifaith Voices www.awisdom.com/community/submit_prayer	Prayer Book Meditations, Adorations, Celebrations, Invocations Multifaith Prayers Multicultural Prayers www.prayforpeace.com/index.php
Bahai Texts http://bahai.com/writings	Uplifting Words (quotes by e-mail) www.upliftingwords.org	Bahai FAQs www.faqs.org/faqs/bahai-faith
The Kitab-i-Aqdas www.sacred-texts.com/bhi/aqdas.htm	The Kitab-i-Iqan (Book of Certitude) www.sacred-texts.com/bhi/iqa.htm	Sacred Texts www.sacred-texts.com/bhi/index.htm
Selections from the Writings of the Bab www.sacred-texts.com/bhi/bab/swb.txt	Epistle to the Son of the Wolf www.sacred-texts.com/bhi/esw.htm	Kitab-I-Aqdas: Glossary http://bahai-library.com/writings/bahaullah/aqdas/glossary.html
Bahai-Deepening http://users.tebenet.nl/~kuijer-e/announce.html	A Baha'i Pilgrimage (November 1996) www.manvell.org.uk/pilgrim/	Baha'i World Faith www.sacred-texts.com/bhi/comp/bwf.txt
Aerial Photo of Chicago Bahai Temple www.photography-plus.com/project/Bahai.htm	Virtual Baha'i tour www.einhanet.co.il/bahai/	Pilgrimage 159 BE http://omv.op.het.net
Pictures of Bahai Temples Delhi, Haifa www.planetware.com/sub/BAHAI.HTM	Bahai Temples Around the World www.abqbahai.org/Bahai%20temples/intro.html	Holy Places & Pilgrimages www.upliftingwords.org/pilgrimage.htm
Universal Calendar Calculator Middle East, Bahai www.cf-software.com/other.html	Today's Calendar and Clock Page: Bahai www.ecben.net/calendar.shtml	Work on the Mother Temple www.kingdom-project.org whats_hap/workon_how.html

World Prayers – Prayer Collective **Multifaith Practices** www.worldpyaers.org	Bahai Chant English / Persian… Listen sample from CD www.gollmer.net/chants/ english/start.htm	Slideshows of Bahá'í places of interest www.bahaindex.com/ modules.php? name=Content&pa=showpage&pid=65
Baha'i Kids Room - Prayer http://campus.fortunecity.com/ caltech/531/kids/prayers.html		

B. Offline Cyber Worship

a. Know-How, Process, Procedures, Activity, Functions, Methods… / Products, Resources, Materials…:(Baha'i cond..)

Popular Items at the Baha'i Faith Index www.bahaindex.com/ modules.php?name=Top	Ask - contact us: Bahai www.us.bahai.org/contact.asp	Ask your Question about Being a Baha'i www.askanowner.com/qa/ ask.asp?guid=&sid=1&lid= 12952&parent_level=12952
Ask A Question Joel Bjorling www.allexperts.com/ getExpert.asp?Category=2728	Ask A Question Bahai Faith - Ask a Question Here: www.allexperts.com/ getExpert.asp?Category=2728	Ask A Question Ross Campbell www.allexperts.com/ getExpert.asp?Category=2728
Internet and the Covenant www.bahaiworld.com/ conference/ca/unravel	Bahai Prayers www.bahaiprayers.org	Bahai Graphics Index (photographs, icons..) www.safnet.com/ bahai/graphics
Conversations with God www.us.bahai.org/ prayers/default.htm	Source for Baha'i materials www.special-ideas.com	Other resources - Digital World www.geocities.com/~wtwilson3
Glossary of Bahai Words www.uga.edu/ bahai/glossary.html	Glossary Religious Holidays www.pgcares.com/ interfaith_glossary.html	Glossary of Religious Terms www.religioustolerance.org/ glossary.htm
Vegetarianism and Bahai www.fragrant.demon.co.uk/ vegidiet.html	How to Build the Bahai Temple www.wurlington-bros.com/ BuildYour/howbahai.html	Bahai Radio www.bahairadio.org/ farsi/shortwave.asp
Spiritual Food www.uga.edu/bahai/ News/031399.html	The Coming of the Day of God http://members.aol.com/ adventarts/Day.html	Online book - Near-Death-Experience & the Baha'i Faith http://die.geocity.de/ spirit/LightAfterDeath.html
Islam and Bahai Faith: A Brief Guide www.safnet.com/ bahai/docs/islam1.html	H-Bahai, An H-Net Network A discussion forum for Shaykhism, Babism, Baha'i http://www.h-net.org/~bahai/	Graham's Framed Baha'i Pages (Information and reports on Baha'i) www.fragrant.demon.co.uk/ bahai.html
Baha'i Faith Index - Web Links: Your link to all things Baha'I (information in over 40 languages) www.bahaindex.com	Links to Bahá'í websites www.bcca.org/info/ links.html	WebCity House of Worship **Multifaith Directory** www.webcityusa.com/ worship.htm
Multifaith - All Things Spiritual Directory www.allspiritual.com/ MultiFaith.php3	World Scripture: A Comparative Anthology of Sacred Texts - **Multifaith Resource** 4600 passages from 268 texts & 55 oral traditions www.euro-tongil.org/ws/index.html	

C. Religions-Online / Online-Religions -

a. Home Pages of Religious and Spiritual Groups: (Baha'i cond..)

The Bab, Sayyid Ali Muhammad Shirazi http://bci.org/islam-bahai	Bahaullah. Mirza Hussayn Ali Nuri www.bahai.com/Bahaullah/glory1.htm	Shoghi Effendi, The Guardian www.warble.com/ Bahai/BasicFacts/basic5.html
Baha'i House of Worship http://web.bnc.bahai.org.au/	Bahai Computer and Communication Association http://bounty.bcca.org/~cvoogt	Baha'i Faith Pages from Skye www.breacais.demon.co.uk/ index.htm

Association of Baha'i Women (Scotland) www.manvell.org.uk/abw/	Naveed Foundation www.naveedfoundation.com	Association for Baha'i Studies (English-Speaking Europe) www. breacais.demon.co.uk/ abs/index.htm
The Orthodox Baha'i Faith - Mother Baha'i Council of the US http://www.rt66.com/ ~obfusa/council.htm	Baha'i International Community www.bic-un.bahai.org	The Baha'i World -- Official Site of the Baha'i Faith www.bahai.org
A Virtual Baha'i Community, Middle Tennessee http://home.talkcity.com/ SpiritCir/PyriteTCC/index.html	Bahais in the United States www.us.bahai.org	Bahais in India www.bahaindia.org
Spirituality Bahai's Home http://home.talkcity.com/ ParadiseDr/Spirituality-bahaifaith	Spirit Home Page Meditations on peace www.swtch.com.au/rjpare/spirit	Phoenix Online UK Baha'i Youth Site http://phoenix.warble.com
Sarwals' Home http://bahai.htmlplanet.com	Sina's Baha'i page www.sina.iwarp.com	Online Bahai Course http://farrid.20m.com/onl.htm
Phoenix Online - UK Baha'i Youth Site http://phoenix.warble.com	The Online Epicenter for Baha'i Youth www.bahaiyouth.com	Warriors of Virtue Baha'i Youth Workshop, Tucson, Arizona http://warriorsofvirtue.bigstep.com
Bosch Baha'i School www.bosch.org	Mottahedeh Development Services A Social and Economic Development Agency of the Baha'i Faith www.mdssed.org	Baha'i Training Institute Board for Scotland (ARCHIVE) www.manvell.org.uk/tis/
Louhelen Baha'i School Retreat and Conference Center www.louhelen.org	The Wilmette Institute US Baha'i National Center, offers both correspondence and residential courses http://wilmetteinstitute.org	

1.3 Mapping Buddhism Webwise

A. Online Cyber Worship

a. Prayer & Praise (Chanting, Samadhi Or Meditation):

Dragon's Gate Temple www.geocities.com/Tokyo Temple/9937/dg2.html	Cyber Puja -- Devotion www.mahindarama.com/ mbt/cybepuja.htm	Get Blessed Worli Buddhist Temple www.blessed-bandwidth.net/ worlibuddhisttemple/ worlibuddhisttemple.htm
Meet Buddhist Yogi C. M. Chen www.yogichen.org	Frequently Asked Questions about Access to Insight & About Buddhism www.accesstoinsight.org/faq.html	Dragon's Gate Temple's Question & Answer Dept. www.geocities.com/Tokyo Temple/9937/ques.html
Buddhist Temple www.geocities.com/ Tokyo/Temple/9937/ dg2.html	Buddhism Q & A www.geocities.com/ Tokyo/Temple/9937/ques.html	Buddhist Worli Temple http://blessed-bandwidth.net/ worlibuddhisttemple/ worlibuddhisttemple.htm
Instructions for Daily Dharma Practice (non-sectarian) www.heartlandsangha.org/daily.html	Confidential answers to your questions www.allexperts.com/ getExpert.asp?Category=948	Hand-washing basin (to enter shrine) www.outside-in.com/ seiwa-en/index2.html
Daigo Temple www.daigoji.or.jp/e/index.html	Hsi Lai Temple www.hsilai.org	Cyber View: Pannyavaro Should monks surf the Internet www.buddhanet.net/mag_surf.htm
Virtual Buddhist Temple: The White Path Temple www.mew.com/shin	Enmanji Buddhist Temple www.sonic.net/~enmanji	Hongwanji Buddhist Mission www.dot.net.au/hbma
Teishoin Temple www.win.or.jp/~kameno	West Covina Buddist Temple www.livingdharma.org	Dragon Flower Ch'an Temple www.bfm.org/zen

Buddhist Temple, Laos (Multimedia) http://encarta.msn.com/ medias_761551958/Laos.html	Dalai Lama's Advice on New Millennium http://mail.thu.edu.tw/ ~kings/GoodKarma2.pps	Search Buddhism www.buddhanet.net
Universal Calendar Calculator: Far East www.cf-software.com/other.html	Today's Calendar and Clock Page: Buddhist www.ecben.net/calendar.shtml	Singapore Buddhist Lodge www.amtb1.org.sg
Online Buddhist Center www.idsl.net/heather/ onlinebuddhistcenter/welcome.html	Insight Meditation Online Vipassana Bhavana, Satipatthana, ... www.buddhanet.net/insight.htm	Listen to Meditation www.vipassana.com/ audio_files/index.php
Tibetan Buddhist Practices www.geocities.com/Athens/Parthenon/7534	Kong Meng San Phor Kark See Monastery www.kmspks.org	Buddhist Instruction Retreat www.fundamentalbuddhism.com
Zen Meditation (interested in practicing?) www.mro.org/ zmm/zazen.shtml	Zen Mountain Monastery Doing a Retreat www.mro.org/zmm/retreats/index.html	Zen Mountain Monastery www.zen-mtn.org
Hosshinji Soto Zen Monastery www.semui.co.jp/hosshinji	Meditation: Meditative Cyberspace www.dailyzen.com/meditation.html	Novice Buddhist Monk at Entrance of Cave, Laos www.terragalleria.com/ theravada/laos/pak- ou/picture.laos4658.html
Buddhist prayer www.geocities.com/Tokyo/ Dojo/1299/buddha.htm	Namgyal Monastery Online www.namgyal.org	Welcome to Sanctuary www.worldpuja.org/ SANCTUARY/ROOMS/sanctuary.htm
Meditation @ Sounds True Listen Before You Buy www.soundstrue.com	Buddhist Meditation and Retreat Camps www.buddhafield.com/ fwbolinks.html	Buddhist Chant www.beliefnet.com/ story/81/story_8171_1.html
Middle Path, The http://sakya.faithweb.com/index.html	Meditation instructions www.buddhanet.net/ bn_audiodl.htm	The Grave of Montezuma www.angelfire.com/ nt/unknowngalaxy/page4.html
Tom's Tibetan Prayer The Ghandarva Experience www.worldpuja.org/ SANCTUARY/ROOMS/ghandarvart.htm	Plum Village www.plumvillage.org	Ocean of Merit www.namoguru.org
Buddhist Mysticism www.digiserve.com/ mystic/Buddhist	Prison Retreats www.gatelessgate.org/ prison/coleman/prison_retreats.htm	Browse the list of Temples www. Mandirnet.org/temple_list.html
The Baiman Buddhas Afghan Buddhas http://hss.fullerton.edu/ comparative/	Visit to the stupa: BOROBUDUR www.bergerfoundation.ch/Borobudur/E/	Dharma Centre Locator www.interlog.com/ ~daryl/dcl.html
List of Dharma groups and centers www.dharmanet.org	worldwide directory of Buddhist centers www.buddhanet.net	Buddhists, North America www.buddhistinformation.com
World Prayers – Prayer Collective **Multifaith Practices** www.worldpyaers.org	Mountains and Rivers Order www.mro.org/zmm/mro.shtml	Chanting (Audio) www.buddhanet.net/ bn_audiodl.htm
Buddhist- chant 1 www.manitobabuddhistchurch.org/ chants/chant1.ram	Buddhist- chant 2 www.manitobabuddhistchurch.org/ chants/chant2.ram	

b. Sacrament (Rituals): (**Buddhism continued...**)

Music of Tianjin, China www.nimbus.ltd.uk/nrl/ world/5416a.html	Temple, Japan (Audio visuals) www.terakoya.com/index_e.htm	Wat Thai Kusinara Chalermraj www.watthaikusinara.org
Temple bells, Korea www.kbs.co.kr/Expo96/ today/audio/part4/ index.htm	Tibetan mantras and chants www.emusic.com/albums/2149/	Tibetan nuns, pujas www.emusic.com/albums/2134/
The Kalachakra Mandala www.tibet.com/Buddhism/ kala1.html		

c. Scripture (Dharma, Teaching, Three Baskets, Inspirational Devotions): (**Buddhism continued...**)

Buddhist Texts http://www.sacred-texts.com/ bud/index.htm	Manitoba Buddhist Church - Scriptures www.manitobabuddhistchurch.org/ scriptures/3.htm	Zen Texts http://sunsite.unc.edu/zen
Dhammapada - Sayings of Buddha - Translated by J. Richards www.edepot.com/ dhamma2.html	Ehi-passika Venerable Buddharakkhita's translation of The Dhammapada. http://wsrv.clas. virginia.edu/~cam4z/	Read Dhammapada www.buddhanet.net/frames47.htm
Voice A Vision • Post A Prayer - Dare A Dream **Multifaith Voices** www.heartpath.com/ hpcontent/voiceAvision.asp	Ancient Wisdom: Submit a Prayer **Multifaith Concerns** www.awisdom.com/ community/submit_prayer	Prayer Book Meditations, Adorations, Celebrations, Invocations **Multifaith Prayers** Multicultural Prayers www.prayforpeace.com/ index.php
Electronic Buddhist Text Initiative www.human.toyogakuen-u.ac.jp/ ~acmuller/ebti.htm	Chinese Buddhist Canon Series www.buddhist-canon.com	Sayings of Buddha I - The Dhammapada - Buddhist Peace www.johnworldpeace.com/ buddha1.html
Turn the pages of Scripture The Diamond Sutra www.bl.uk/collections/ treasures/treasures.html	CyberSangha Buddhist Archives http://worldtrans.org/ CyberSangha/csindex.html	Online Dharma Libraries: Texts www.dharmanet.org/ files.html
Enlightenment? www.moksha.org	Gospel of Buddha http://filebox.vt.edu/ users/juwilson/ indiaunitplan/ comparison.html	Buddhist Reading Room www.buddhistreading.com
Jousenji Temple Cemetery, Japan (Webcam) www.jousenji.com/ main/javacam/yscam.html	Family Dharma Connections www.pulelehuadesign.com/ familydharma	Electronic Resources for Buddhist Texts www.geocities.com/ manjushri_2000/ buddhisttexts.html
Introduction to Theravada Hinayana (The Lesser Vehicle) www.ncf.carleton.ca/dharma		

B. Offline Cyber Worship

a. **Know-How, Process, Procedures, Activity, Functions, Methods.../ Products, Resources, Materials...:(Buddhism continued...)**

Download Ritual Objects www.potalaworld.com/ catalog/ritual/ritual.html	Insight Meditation Active Tutor (Download) www.buddhanet.net/ ac-instruct.htm	Om Mani Padme Hum The Meaning of the Mantra in Tibetan Buddhism www.dharma-haven.org/ tibetan/ meaning_of_om_mani_padme_hum.htm

Gateless Passage Nonsectarian http://villa.lakes.com/ cdpatton/index.html	Library of e-books www.buddhanet.net	Kalavinka Dharma World (nonsectarian) www.kalavinka.org
Life of Buddha in Pictures www.psych.csusi.edu/ psy344/buddhism.ppt	Salvation in Buddhism & Islam **Multifaith Dialogue** http://users.iafrica.com/ l/ll/lloyd/5-SpecialStudies/ Islam-Buddhism.html	Other resources - Digital World www.geocities.com/~wtwilson3
Asia Pacific Research Online http://www.ciolek.com	Kamat's Potpourri on Buddhism www.kamat.com/ kalranga/budhist/index.htm	Allspirit Selected Buddhist Writings www.allspirit.co.uk/buddhism.html
Digital Library for a Lay Theravada Buddhist www.accesstoinsight.org/ lib/bps/wheels/wheel206	Gateways to Buddhism DharmaNet International http://dharmanet.org	Surfing the Indranet: Lance Daybreak' Digital Dharma (Article) www. www.techgnosis.com/indranet.html
Prison Dharma Net www.prisondharmanetwork.org/ articles-colosi.htm	Buddhist Virtual Library http://www.ciolek.com/ WWWVL-Buddhism.html	Internet Guide to Pure Land Buddhism www.pitaka.ch/vlpl.htm
Buddhist links www.dabase.net/ budlinks.htm	Socially-engaged buddhism www.lotusmedia.org/ eb/resources.html	Shin Buddhism Network www.aloha.net/ ~rtbloom/shinran
The Temples of Orissa Buddhist http://ignca.nic.in/ orist016.htm	Engaged Buddhism www.igc.org/bpf/ineb.html	Basic Points Unifying the Theravada and the Mahayana www.serve.com/cmtan/ buddhism/Misc/Unify.html
Electronic Bodhidharma, Japan www.iijnet.or.jp/iriz	Digital Buddhism www.acmuller.net/ddb/ index.html	Digital Buddhist Library and Museum [Taiwan] http://ccbs.ntu.edu.tw/e-CBS.htm
Buddhist Cyberspace – Webmasters http://www.buddhistwebmasters.net/	Email via the Web www.fortibet.org	Buddhist studies www.ciolek.com/ WWWVL-Buddhism.html
Digital Buddha Vacana: Software www.geocities.com/ buddha_vacana/	Buddhist Software www.dharmanet.org/ multimedia.html	A Handful of Leaves: Free CD www.accesstoinsight.org/ cdrom/index.html
MoonPhase displays on system taskbar www.locutuscodeware.com/ moonphas.htm	Buddha - The Great Legend Vipassana Research Institute's Chattha Sangayana CD-ROM http://web.ukonline.co.uk/ buddhism/freebies.htm	Budsir: Cd-Rom Thai edition of the Pali Tipitaka and Atthakatha www.mahidol.ac.th/ budsir/budsir-main.html
Chattha Sangayana Tipitaka CD from V.R.I. www.tipitaka.org	Tibetan Computer Software www.tibet.dk/tibetan_clipart/ softlink.htm	Buddhist: Icons http://zen.dvdesign.com/icons.html
Buddhist Software http://zen.dvdesign.com/ software.html	Buddhist: Desktop Tips http://zen.dvdesign.com/tips.html	Buddhist Door Glossary Index www.tunglinkok.ca/9710/ sources/glossary.htm
Wings to Awakening: Glossary www.accesstoinsight.org/ lib/modern/thanissaro/ wings/glossary.html	The Buddhist Monastic Code: Glossary www.accesstoinsight.org/ lib/modern/thanissaro/bmc1/glossary.html	Glossary of Pali & Buddhist Terms www.accesstoinsight.org/ glossary.html
Glossary of Religious Terms www.religioustolerance.org/glossary. htm	Glossary Religious Holidays www.pgcares.com/interfaith_glossary.html	Buddhist ceremonies and funeral rights www.buddhanet.net/d_cermon.htm
Heavenly Way http://home.nyc.rr.com/hsiaostemple	Chinese Buddhist funeral ries www.buddhanet.net/cfuneral.htm	Buddhist funeral rites in thailand www.buddhanet.net/bfuneral.htm
Buddhazine www.tricycle.com	Search a Priest in Cybersangha www.buddhanet.net	Zen@metalab www.ibiblio.org/zen
Buddhism Depot www.edepot.com/ buddha.shtml	Buddhist Quote of the Moment... www.edepot.com/buddha.shtml	American Buddhist Articles non-dualistic www.heartlandsangha.org/new.html
Web Guide to Buddhist Studies www.uni-giessen.de/ ~gk1415/buddhiststudies.htm	Snow Lion - Internet Tibet Resources www.snowlionpub.com/	Sadhu! The Theravada Buddhism Web Directory www.parami.org/sadhu/

Vipassana Meditation www.dhamma.org	Basic Breath Meditation Instructions www.accesstoinsight.org/ lib/modern/thanissaro/ breathmed.html	Mahasati Meditation www.mahasati.org
Learn the Ritual Prayer www.bergerfoundation.ch/ Home/pelerins.html	Shambhala Meditation Center www.shambhala.org	Karma Triyana Dharmachakra, USA www.kagyu.org
Simhanada The Lion's Roar www.simhas.org	BuddhaNet: E-Books, Australia www.buddhanet.net/ebooks.htm	Cyber Monastry Eight Gates of Zen http://cybermonastery.dharma.net
Monastery store http://dharma.net/ monstore	"Pradaksina" ritual to walk around www.bergerfoundation.ch/ Home/pelerins.html	Buddhism Online Obon Festival www.livingdharma.org/ Living.Dharma.Articles/ BuddhismOnline-Toshi.html
WebCity House of Worship **Multifaith Directory** www.webcityusa.com/ worship.htm	Meditation and Buddhism Search www.sanatanadharma.net	The Sects of the Buddhists http://ccbs.ntu.edu.tw/ FULLTEXT/JR-ENG/tw.htm
Discussion of Buddhist Mysticism Audio Books www.najaco.com/books/audio_books	Christian Contemplation and Zen Enlightenment: Are They the Same? Comparative Perspectives http://www.innerexplorations.com/ewtext/cc.htm	Buddhist Perspectives on Other Religions: Past and Present Comparative Perspectives http://www2.bc.edu/~clooney/mak.html
Multifaith - All Things Spiritual Directory www.allspiritual.com/MultiFaith.php3	World Scripture: A Comparative Anthology of Sacred Texts - **Multifaith Resource** 4600 passages from 268 texts and 55 oral traditions www.euro-tongil.org/ws/index.html	

C. Religions-Online / Online-Religions -

a. Home Pages of Religious and Spiritual Groups: (**Buddhism continued**)

Mahayana (The Great Vehicle) Electronic Bodhidharma [Japan] www.iijnet.or.jp/iriz	Mahayana www.baus.org/baus/ budresou.html#mahayana	Nichiren Shoshu America www.cebunet.com/nst
Nichiren Buddhist Fellowship www.nichiren.org	Shingon Buddhist International Institute/HeavenEarth Net www.shingon.org	Kempon Hokke Kai www.concentric.net/ ~fujufuse/ hokkekai.htm
Soka Gakkai (Japan)--Official English Site http://sokagakkai.info	Nichiren Shu www.nichirenshu.org/ index2.htm	Soka Gakkai International (SGI)-USA www.sgi-usa.org
Institute of Buddhist Studies www.shin-ibs.edu	Soka Gakkai Malaysia http://www.sgm.org.my	Soka Gakkai International www.sgi.org
Mahayana Pure Land School www.geocities.com/ Tokyo/Pagoda/3570	Engaged Buddhism www.engagedpage.com	Socially-Engaged Buddhism www.lotusmedia.org/eb
Mahayana Pure Land School www.geocities.com/ Tokyo/Pagoda/3570	True Buddah School Net (w/ Tantrayana, Zen) www.tbsn.org	Buddhist Cultural Center Hinayana / (Theravada) http://www.lanka.net/bcc
Vipasana - Hinayana (Theravada) vipassana.com	Theravada Hinayana (The Lesser Vehicle www.baus.org/baus/ budresou.html#theravada	Khmer Buddhist Organization www.khmerbuddhist.org
International Buddhist Center Hinayana http://members.aol.com/ uparatana	Theravada Buddhism world.std.com/~metta/ index.html	Vipassana Research Institute www.vri.dhamma.org
International Meditation Centres (Sayagyi U Ba Khin) Hinayana www.webcom.com/ ~imcuk	Suan Mokkh www.suanmokkh.org	Vajrayana http://home.hkstar.com/ ~francish/index.html
Vajrayana Foundation Center www.vajrayana.org	Vajrayana www.baus.org/baus/ budresou.html#vajrayana	Tibetan Buddhism or Vajrayana Dharma Haven [USA] http://dharma-haven.org
Vajrayana Foundation Hawaii www.ilhawaii.net/~vfh/index.html	Rigpa International www.rigpa.org	UK Rigpa www.users.dircon.co.uk/ ~m-brook/Rigpa/index.htm
Japan Tibet Homepage www.twics.com/ ~tsgjp/jthpe.html	Dorje Shugden International Coalition www.he.net/~shugden	Palyul Foundation of Canada www.interlog.com/~palyul
Non-Sectarian www.baus.org/baus/ budresou.html#non_sectarian	Dharma Communications www.dharma.net/dchome.html	Non Sectarian DharmaNet International www.dharmanet.org
Chinese philosophy www.personal.monash.edu.au/ ~sab/index.html	Chinese Buddhism Resources www.baus.org/baus/ budresou.html#c_buddhism	IRIZ: The International Research Institute for Zen Buddhism at Hanazono University. http://iriz.hanazono. ac.jp/index.en.html
Buddhism in Canada www.buddhismcanada.com	Buddhist Association, USA. www.baus.org	Buddhist Door [Canada] http://tunglinkok.ca
Manjushri, the Buddhist online community www.manjushri.com	Philadelphia Buddhist Association www.philabuddhistassoc.org	Buddhist Association, Lehigh Valley www.balv.org
Hsi Lai Temple, International Buddhist Progress Society, USA www.ibps.org	Amitabha Buddhist Society of USA www.amtb-usa.org	Jade Buddha Temple, Texas Buddhist Association, Inc. www.jadebuddha.org
Buddhism City, Chinese www.buddhismcity.net	Mid America Buddhist Association www.econ.uiuc.edu/~wee/ MABA/index.html	American Zen Buddhist Temple - Vairocana Monastery www.evenlink.com/~azbtnews
Buddha Gate Monastery, USA www.media.mit.edu/~dc/canon	Mahabodhi Society of USA www.mahabodhi.org/index.html	Buddhist Astrology Site www.anchor-web.com/ Daka/astrology.html

The Refuge: A Sangha for the Skeptical Buddhist www.xmission.com/ ~mustard/sangha.html	Tantric Buddhism (scientific pantheism) http://members.aol.com/ Heraklit1/tantra.htm	Oxford Centre for Buddhist Studies www.cam.ac.uk/ societies/ buddha/ oxford_centre.html
His Holiness The Dalai Lama www.tibet.com/DL/ index.html	The 14th Dalai Lama www.dalailama.com	Center for Buddhist Studies http://ccbs.ntu.edu.tw

1.4 Mapping Christianity Webwise

> **Prayer Before Logging Onto the Internet:**
> Almighty and eternal God,
> who created us in Thy image and bade us to seek after all that is good, true and beautiful,
> especially in the divine person of Thy only-begotten Son, our Lord Jesus Christ,
> grant we beseech Thee that,
> through the intercession of Saint Isidore, bishop and doctor,
> during our journeys through the internet
> we will direct our hands and eyes only to that which is pleasing to Thee
> and treat with charity and patience all those souls whom we encounter.
> Through Christ our Lord. Amen. http://catholic.org/isidore/prayer.htm

A. Online Cyber Worship

a. Prayer:

CyberWorship www.cyberworship. freeservers.co.uk	Simultaneous Worship Service [Visioncast or SimulCast] www.biltmorebaptist.org	Worship Live - Audio/Video www.touchandchange.com/ artman/publish/cat_worship_0.shtml
ZChurch: A Real Church in a Virtual World – Interactive Worship http://zchurch.com	Sacred Sapce Daily Prayer Online www.jesuit.ie/prayer	Jesus Online http://adore.inetcam.com
Rev. Al's Cyberchurch www.angelfire.com/ct2/churches/ revalscyberchurch.index.html	Internet Daily Chapel http://patriot.net/~bmcgin /chapel.html	Augustine Day by Day www.artsci.villanova.edu/ dsteelman/augustine
Many Faces of Lutheran Worship View Video Clips www.elca.org/co mosaic/summer2001.html	Daily Fuel Nextwave Online Community www.nextwavefaithful.com/ dailyfuel.asp	Streaming video's Worship Services - Each Sunday www.esteroumc.com/ worshipsvcs.html
Peachtree Presbyterian Church - Live Webcast www.acswebnetworks.com/ quasar/isl/content/ channel.isl?channelid=- 1999998723&partnerid=1004	Sonrise Worship Center Glorifying God in Cyberspace www.writeanswer.org/Sonrise	Saint Michael's Church, Mumbai www.blessed-bandwidth.net/ mahimchurch/ mahimchurch.htm
Click on a prayer www.geocities.com/ Athens/Ithaca/9777/indexsmall.html	Papal Encyclicals Online Papal & Official Documents www.papalencyclicals.net	Revival Service [on a Web Cam] http://liveprayer.com
Amen Christian Online Church http://acolc.faithweb.com	Online Church for those with disabilities / infirmities http://members.tripod.com/ ~network7/CHURCH.htm	Introduction Service for Singles www. churchofchristsingles.com
Church Home on the Net (Voice Prayers) www.churchofthe.net	Faith Community Church Online Rediscover Your Faith www.FCCWaupaca.org	Internet Church Christian informational project www.church.kiev.ua

Church On the Net http://ChurchOnTheNet. Homestead.com/ ChurchOnTheNet.html	Prayer Schedule (you can pray with us all around the world) www.populationprayer.com prayer_schedule.html	Select a Mass www.rockies.net/~spirit/Charlene/ cathmass.html
Northeastern Pennsylvania Christian Internet Church www.geocities.com/ Heartland/Cabin/6664	Paws Of Love Christian Mission Christian internet church for pets www.skypoint.com/ members/zurich/p1.html	CyberChurch is a real church http://thecyberchurch.org
Prayer Directory www.catholic-forum.com/ links/prayer.htm	Select a Church Webcasts www.online-churches.net/ churches/web-casts.html	Revival (Cyberchurch) Full list of 40 videos (RealVideo Web TV) www.globalchange.com/ easter.html
Archangel Michael has a message for you www.ronnastar.com	Daily Devotions Lutheran Hour Ministries Online www.lhm.org/ dailydevotions.asp	Cyber Worship: Prayer Schedules http://members.aol.com/ Starchild0/Theology/ liturgy.html
First International Church on the Web www.ficotw.org	Virtual Diocese Diocese Without Borders (A Congregation with no physical location) www.partenia.org/eng/	Non-denominational www.24-7prayer.com/index2.php
Daily Psalms www.universalis.com	Virtual Prayer Room http://sabe.nlnet.co.uk/ prayer/proom/form.pl	Interested in running a 24-7 prayer room? www.missionteam.co.uk/ 24-7sa/background/ signup.htm
Daily prayer: morning www.universalis.com/ cgi-bin/display/lauds.htm	Daily prayer: evening www.universalis.com/ cgi-bin/display/vespers.htm	Daily prayer: night www.universalis.com/ cgi-bin/display/compline.htm
Worship Online (Streaming video) www.sugarcreek.net/ Multimedia/WorshipOnline.aspx	Internet Worship – 24/7 www.cathedralofhope.com/ worship247/index.php	Online Meeting for Worship (Quaker Worship Online) http://worship-quaker.org
First Church of Cyberspace www.godweb.org	Cyber-Church.com Bringing Christ to the web http://cyber-church.com	Cyber Church of the Web A CHURCH WITHOUT WALLS www.geocities.com/ Heartland/Hills/6838
St. John's Internet Church www.religionnet.com	Directory of Directories for Churches of Christ www.churchzip.com	Highland Church of Christ Web Connection www.highlandchurch.org/web.html
Not Proud Online confessions www.notproud.com/index.php	Real People, Real Confessions www.dailyconfession.com	Confessional Booth www.fear.gr
Welcome to BigChurch - Bringing people together in love and faith! http://bigchurch.com/ go/f4046.subprayer_0312	Wuzupgod – Contact God http://wuzupgod.com/ slogans/contact.htm	Virtual Confession Booth for Women www.herconfessions.com
1997 Catholic Internet Directory www.catholic-church.org/ cid/online.html	Join Weekly online Service (non-denominational) www.mb-soft.com/ cwalk/index.htm	Liturgy Planner Online (Paid subscription) http://members.tripod.com/ planningliturgy
Practical Prayerwalking www.waymakers.org/ prayerwalking.html	Gateway to the CyberTemple www.premamusic.com/ CyberTemple/index.html	Prayer Before Logging Onto the Internet www.catholic.org/ isidore/prayer.htm

The ABC of Faith Listen to … Accept. Believe. Confess. www.spirit-net.ca/ charlene/jesuslovesme.html	Plumbline Ministries – Prayer Anointed.net www.plumblineministries.org/ prayer	Prayer_door www.aiht.edu/doorways/ prayer_door.asp?adclfr=OVprayer
The Mantle Questions about Christianity www.garymills.org	Church for all Internet Church (Open to all believers) www.churchforall.org	Want to Talk to Someone about how to be saved Call 1-800-Need-Him or 1-800-633-3446
Questions? Let's Talk – Live tracts Via Email or instant messanger's: AOL / ICQ / Yahoo / MSN / Paltalk http://livetracts.com/talk.html	To Know how you can have a personal relationship with Jesus Christ call 1-888-NEED-HIM 1-888-JESUS-2000 www.knowhmonline.com	All Souls Prayer Network call or email to activate the network www.allsoulscatholicchurch.org/ ministries/prayer_network.htm
Have a question" Dial [1-800-Ask-a-Priest]	Click & Drive (Yahoo map) http://pages.prodigy.net/ gcarella.allsaintsvcny.html	Mass in transit www.liturgicalpublications.com/ mass_in_transit/ mass_in_transit.html
Prayer Chat Room www.c-chat.com/java/ prayer.php	Questions of faith www.explorefaith.org/ questions.html	Welcome to e-Prayer! www.globalprayeralert.org
Spiritual Counsel www.godfoucs.net counsel.htm	Ask The Pastor - Email any question about the Christian www.historictrinity.org/ questions.html	Consultant on Religions /Cults (Web cam of Don Dutkowski) http://imwhynotaskdpn. comrades.com
24-Hour Counselor www.lifeway.com	Quakers FAQ www.faqs.org/faqs/ Quaker-faq	Scientology FAQs www.faqs.org/faqs/ scientology
Circle of Light SoulMate Love, Opening the Hearts of Humanity www.circleoflight.net	Mormon Beliefs & Practices www.lds.index.org	Amen-online An Ecumenical project with prayers from four millennia http://amen-online.org
Sin, Suffering, Sorrow (Worship Ideas) www.worshipmap.com	Listen to Virtual Worship (Worship Service Excerpt) www.angelfire.com/tn/ fbaptist/virtualworship.html	Third Annual Christmas Eve Midnight Cyberservice http://lairdschapel.fathweb.com
Christian prayer examples http://members.tripod.com/ ~ALTAYR/Pray1.html	Prayers for Peace www.angelfire.com/ md/elanmichaels/ peace.html	Daily Mass-Multimedia Site www.themass.com/ default800.htm
Voice A Vision • Post A Prayer Dare A Dream **Multifaith Voices** www.heartpath.com/ hpcontent/voiceAvision.asp	Ancient Wisdom: Submit a Prayer **Multifaith Concerns** www.awisdom.com/ community/submit_prayer	Prayer Book Meditations, Adorations, Celebrations, Invocations **Multifaith Prayers** Multicultural Prayers www.prayforpeace.com/ index.php
Intercessory Prayer www.godfoucs.net prayer.htm	Prayers for peace - Jewish, Christian and Muslim **Multifaith Platform** salmanspiritual.com/ peace_prayers.html	Cyberbook of Traditional Prayers www.catholic.net/RCC/ Indices/Inspirations/Prayers.html
Heavenpoint cemetery photos & funeral (Partially in Chinese) www.heavenpoint.com	The Virtual Memorial Garden pictures, audio, video http://catless.ncl.ac.uk/vmg	Online-Funeral View live funeral services http://www.online-funeral.com/
Visit a Memorial http://virtual-memorials.com	Perpetual Memorials Electronic Memorials to the Departed (Paid service) www.memorials.com/	Online Memorials Shopping www.widgets.ws/Shopping/ DeathCare/OnlineMemorials
Virtual memorial www.angelsonline.com/ pagelist.htm	Ask a Funeral Question www.ofsa.org/ask_ofsa	The Internet Grave www.gotcha.com.my/igrave

How to Get to Heaven from the Internet http://fishthenet/ot/ heavenfrominternet.htm	Church of the East forwards the Yoga of Jesus **Multifaith Perspectives** http://Church-Of-The-East.org	g o t c h a ! I - g r a v e www.gotcha.com.my/igrave
Springfield Parish Virtual Meditation Room www.kerrypoet.utvinternet.com med/index.html	Meditation Groups Worldwide www.wccm.org/directgrps.html	Prayer of Salvation www.ficotw.org/salvaton.html
Infinite Goddess – Embracing the Divine Mother (Mother Mary) www.goddess.ws	Messages from Mary (Text format) www.olpg.org/ messages.htm	Listen to the Rosary, pray www.theworkofgod.org/ Devotns/Rosary/rosary.htm
The Seven Dolors of Mary www.thekolbegroup.org/ September7_the7sorrowsofMary.html	The Seven Dolors of Mary www.7dolors.com	Ambassadors of Mary Pilgrim Virgin Statue http://ambassadorsofmary.com
Adoration to the Blessed Sacrament (click on CD-ROM) www.theworkofgod.org/ Devotns/Euchrist/ Topics/adoratn.htm	The Porter: Your Monastic Guide Brother URL www.christdesert.org/ noframes/porter.html	Spiritual Renewal Center www.christdesert.org/ Dominican/index.htm
Couturier's 'Invisible Monastery' www.chemin-neuf.org/ chemins_neufs/n2/ prieres.html	Carmelite Spirituality www.carmelite.org/ heart.htm	Benedictine Spirituality www.procopius.org/ spirituality.htm
Net for God www.netforgod.org	French Spirituality www.ewtn.com/ library/Montfort/ Handbook/Frenchs.htm	Ignatian Spirituality http://web.lemoyne.edu/ ~bucko/V_SPIRIT.HTML
The Word Meditating and Praying Scriptures www.geocities.com/ zeke826/index.html	Meditation Modules www.virtualrosary.org/ modules.php	Monastic Chant (Audio) www.christdesert.org/ noframes/chant/chant.html
Daily Reflection www2.csbsju.edu/ cgi-bin/osb/ dose.pl?daily&dquote.txt&dquote	Praying each day www.prayingeachday.org/ reflect.html	Searching for God, online www.rediff.com/search/ 2003/feb/26god.htm
Online Retreat in everyday life www.creighton.edu/ CollaborativeMinistry/ cmo-retreat.html	The Novo-Tikhvin Women's Monastery www.sestry.ru/eng	A place for quiet contemplation [30 second prayer 30 second thought] http://vurch.com/
Retreat Association www.retreats.org.uk	Retreats / Monasteries http://uk.groups.yahoo.com/ group/CLEF/links	World Community for Christian Meditation www.wccm.org
Benedictine Monastery (North Carolina) www.Belmontabbey.org	Order of Saint Benedict www.osb.org	Saint Adrian of Canterbury (See Saints) www. Domestic-church.com
Asylum on Web Cam www.asylumcam.com	Search a monastry Click on a region of the world to find a monastery www.op.org/international/ english/Nuns/monasteries.htm	Read DAILY prayer (look for 'Click here') www. ficotw.org/salvaton.html
Bringing people together in love and faith (Free membership) http://bigchurch.com/ go/f4046.subprayer_0312	Apostleship of Prayer www.cin.org/ap	Plumbline Ministries! www. plumblineministries.org/ prayer
20-Day eCourse - FREE! 1,001 Ways to Use the Power of Prayer www.amazingprayers.com	Spiritual guidance for anyone seeking a path to God www.explorefaith.org	This is truly an awesome place to pray http://annointed.net/ ?OVRAW=Prayer&OVKEY =prayer&OVMTC=standard
Voluntary Worship – Public Prayer for Chaplains (Multifaith context) www.forces.gc.ca/chapgen/engraph	Chaplain's Corner International Association of Women Police www.iawp.org/chaplain/chaplain.htm	24 – 7 Jesus Church www.24-7jesuschurch.net

World Prayers – Prayer Collective **Multifaith Practices** www.worldpyaers.org	The Gateway Prayer Group. (subscription) www.calastrology.com/ gatpraygroup.html	Christian Prayer Book www.prayerbook.com/ Chaplets/chaplets.htm
Inclusive Worship Music www.rit.edu/~labdis/InclusiveWorship.html	Peace Prayer - Inclusive Prayers www.peaceprayer.org/inclusive.html	Holy Spirit Temple, Online http://our.homewithgod.com/ holyspirittemple
An Atlanta church broadcasting Sunday morning services -live with audio and video www.peachtreepres.org	e-Church Worship on line -Bringing Church To You- www.church-at-home.com/ pages/1/index.htm	DAILY BREAD www.augnet.org/AugustineSECTION3/ AugustinesImpact/OnPrayer/0112- DailyBread.html
Imagination & Visualization Prayer www.wf.quik.com/vancam/Prayer.htm		

Prayer & Praise

"Separate but Inseparable"

@ www.godfocus.net

b. Praise: (Christianity continued)

Digital Rosary (Pray with a bead) www.pathguy.com/rosary.htm	Rosary in different Languages http:// ourworld.compuserve.com/ homepages/234v432/ mirjam.htm	Rosary Center The Rosary Confraternity www.rosary-center.org
The Perpetual Web Rosary Select Latin / English http://cul.detmich.com/ rosary.html	Prayer, Praise and Promises A daily devotional www.virtualchurch.org/ prayerdev.htm	Ecumenical Rosary www.ecumenicalrosary.org
Christmas on the Net www.holidays.net/ christmas	Easter on the Net www.holidays.net/ easter	Days of Holy Week (Lent) www.cresourcei.org/ cyholyweek.html
The Original Free Multimedia Rosary And Prayer Network www.virtualrosary.org	Christian Fellowship Devotional www. Cfdevotionals.org	Praise portal http://praise.net/worship/ links
Christian Broadcasting Network's Watch Online www.cbn.org/the700club	Devotional Help www.disciple.org/ biblesearch/default.asp	Celebration of Praise and Worship www.skycrest.net/ servEast.html
Vatican Radio www.wrn.org/vatican-radio	Global Radio Network www.ewtn.com/wewn/index.htm	Trinity Broadcasting Live Audio www.tbn.org
Free MP3 Downloads www.mp3.com	Highest Praise Productions (Christian MP3 Resoruces) www.highestpraise.com	Christian Worship Online Baptist Broadcasts www.onlineworship.net
Spiritual Children's Music http://genres.mp3.com/music	The Brick Testament, illustrated bible www.thereverend.com/ brick_testament	Songs MP3 www.familyworship.org.uk/ songs.htm
Ignatian Spirituality in Music www.creighton.edu/ CollaborativeMinistry/ cmo-retreat.html	Christian Chant www.beliefnet.com/ story/81/story_8171_1.html	Whitfield Assembly of God Online - devotions (audio...) www.whitfieldassembly.org
Virtual Church RealAudio Hymns www.virtualchurch.org		

c. Scripture: (Christianity continued)

Search the Bible www.goshen.net	Audio Bible www.ficotw.org	Audio Bible Online www.Audio-bible.com/ Bible/Bible.htm

Thru the Bible in One Year In Ten minutes a day www.prayertower.net/ index.htm	Speaking Bible -Speed Bible Free HTML Bible www.htmlbible.com	Message(s) & Study The Gospel – Abbreviated www.worship-online.org/ message.html
Gospel of Judas http://earlychristianwritings.com/ gospeljudas.html	Signs Gospel http://earlychristianwritings.com/ signs.html	Lost Sayings Gospel Q http://earlychristianwritings.com/ q.html
Oxyrhynchus 1224 Gospel http://earlychristianwritings.com/ oxyrhynchus1224.html	Gospel of Mark http://earlychristianwritings.com/ mark.html	Gospel of Matthew http://earlychristianwritings.com/ matthew.html
Gospel of John http://earlychristianwritings.com/ john.html	Gospel of Luke http://earlychristianwritings.com/ luke.html	Epistle of Barnabas http://earlychristianwritings.com/ barnabas.html
Gospel of Thomas http://earlychristianwritings.com/ thomas.html	The Gospel of Salvation www.kingdom-gospel.com/ saved.html	Gospel of Barnabas http://barnabas.net
Infancy Gospel of Thomas http://earlychristianwritings.com/ infancythomas.html	Treatise on the Resurrection http://earlychristianwritings.com/ treatiseres.html	Gospel of the Hebrews http://earlychristianwritings.com/ gospelhebrews.html
Book of Thomas the Contender http://earlychristianwritings.com/ contender.html	Infancy Gospel of James http://earlychristianwritings.com/ infancyjames.html	Gospel of Truth http://earlychristianwritings.com/ gospeltruth.html
Gospel of Philip http://earlychristianwritings.com/ gospelphilip.html	Secret Book of James http://earlychristianwritings.com/ secretjames.html	Gospel of the Egyptians http://earlychristianwritings.com/ gospelegyptians.html
Apocryphon of John http://earlychristianwritings.com/ apocryphonjohn.html	Gospel of Mary http://earlychristianwritings.com/ gospelmary.html	Gospel of the Savior http://earlychristianwritings.com/ gospelsavior.html
Books of Jeu http://earlychristianwritings.com/ jeu.html	Gospel of the Ebionites http://earlychristianwritings.com/ gospelebionites.html	Gospel of the Nazoreans http://earlychristianwritings.com/ gospelnazoreans.html
Oxyrhynchus 840 Gospel http://earlychristianwritings.com/ oxyrhynchus840.html	Traditions of Matthias http://earlychristianwritings.com/ traditionsmatthias.html	Book of Elchasai http://earlychristianwritings.com/ elchasai.html
Testaments of the Twelve Patriarchs http://earlychristianwritings.com/ patriarchs.html	Coptic Apocalypse of Peter http://earlychristianwritings.com/ nhlapocalypsepeter.html	Odes of Solomon http://earlychristianwritings.com/ odes.html
Advanced Search of the Bible www.christ.com/Jesus	Scripture selection Virtual Christianity: Bibles www.internetdynamics.com/ pub/vc/bibles.html	Cyber Scripture Bible Gateway www.writeanswer.org/Sonrise/ bibles.htm
Book of Divine Worship (PDF / HTML formats) http://anglicansonline.org/ resources/liturgical.html	Bible www.bible.org	Bible Browser http://goon.stg.brown.edu/ bible_browser
Online Church with Bible Studies http://ChurchOnTheNet. homestead.com/ ChurchOnTheNet.html	Old Testament Apocrypha http://wesley.nnu.edu/ noncanon/apocrypha.htm	TLC Jesus, Promoting Unadulterated Word of God www.tlcjesus.org
Old Testament Pseudepigrapha http://wesley.nnu.edu/ noncanon/ pseudepigrapha.htm	Read The Book of Common Prayer 2004 www.ireland.anglican.org	New Testament Apocryphal Gospels http://wesley.nnu.edu/ noncanon/gospels.htm
Turn the pages of Scripture The Sforza Hours www.bl.uk/collections/ treasures/treasures.html	Turn the pages of Scripture The Sherborne Missal www.bl.uk/collections/ treasures/treasures.html	Special Text for Everyday Use: Cyberspace Churches of Christ www.coc.nu/when
Daily Readings Presbyterian Church http://horeb.pcusa.org/ search/dailyreadings.htm	Scripture Readings for up-coming weeks BCMHE Online Chapel www.campusfaith.org/pages/ Chapel.html	Online Bibles www.crchog.org
Quaker Writings people.delphi.com/ pdsippel/index.html	New Testament Apocryphal Acts http://wesley.nnu.edu/ noncanon/acts.htm	New Testament Apocryphal Apocalypse http://wesley.nnu.edu/ noncanon/apocalypse.htm

Urantia Book www.urantia.org/ detail.html#Titles	Search the Book of Mormon www.hti.umich.edu/ relig/mormon	Book of Mormons www.desertbook.com/ scriptures/ bom_home.html
Mormon Texts http://scriptures.lds.org	Excellent Exegesis Online (Free) (For any denomination) www.lectionary.org	Complete worship experiences based on the lectionary www.lumicon.org
Baptisma: Liturgy Resources www.textweek.com/ yeara/baptisma.htm	Audio Sermon Calvary Grace Fellowship Pentecostal www.faithandvision.bc.ca	Sermon Portal www. sermoncentral.com
Listen Sermon Christian Pulpit www.Talkingbible.com	Spiritual Life Church Sermons-English & Spanish www.spirituallifechurch.com	New Millennium Church Free Sermon & Prophesies www.newmillenniumchurch.net/ home/sermons.php
Free Sermons www.newmillenniumchurch.net/ home/sermons.php	Liberty Gospel Center Online church offering prayer, Biblestudy http://wakeup.to/theLord	Audio Sermon Host (For a price) www.audiosermonhost.com
Thought for the Week Worship / Communion ... WebChurch Sanctuary www.webchurch.org/ sanct.htm	Past Sermons Group B Sermon 11.. Digital Christianity http://users.chariot.net.au/ ~brucehan/index25.htm	Online Audio & Video Sermons www.heargoodnews.com
Transcript Audio Sermons www.christianity-x.com/ christianity-x/transcript.html	John Piper Sermons www.worshipmap.com/ sermons/piper-index.html	Sermons of St John Vianney (Text) www.theworkofgod.org/ Library/Sermons/ JdVianey/Sermons.htm
Sermons www.virtualchurch.org/ sermlist.htm#grace	The Skeptic's Annotated Bible www. skepticsannotatedbible.com	CyberChurch Broadcast Center www.thecyberchurch.org
Jakob Böhme On-line Manuscripts www.passtheword.org/ Jacob-Boehme	Sermon Search www.sermonhelp.com	Sermon Seekers www.sermonseekers.org
Computer-Assisted Theology: Internet Resources http://users.ox.ac.uk/ ~ctitext2/theology	The Tablet www.thetablet.co.uk	New World Translation www.towerwatch.com/Witnesses

Scripture & Sacrament

"Separate but Inseparable"

@ www.godfocus.net

d. Sacrements: (Christianity continued)

Virtual Church (entrance, rooms, sanctuary, closet...) www.virtualchurch.org	Holy Communion First Worship Service www.alphachurch.org/holycommunionwor2.htm	Lord's Supper Second Worship Service www.alphachurch.org/ holycommwor.htm
The Eucharist as Presence and Sacrament Worship of the Eucharist Outside of Mass www.therealpresence.org/ eucharist/pea/a2.html	Church of the Holy Sepulcher: Jerusalem – 3D Tour www.inisrael.com/ ipix/java/jer.htm	Search a Church www.christianity.net/ churchlocator
Virtual Tour of Jerusalem http://jeru.huji.ac.il/ md/vjt/sub2.html	Archdiocese of the Internet www.bromike.com	St. Mary's Chruch Tour www.educhurch.org.uk/ pupils/combs/stmarys.html
Sistine chapel www.christusrex.org/ www1/sistine/0-Tour.html	Virtual Church Kids! www.virtualchurch.org/ kids.htm	Shroud of Turin The Holy Face of Christ www.theworkofgod.org/ shroud.htm

Web cam of the Monks of Adoration Chapel www.monksofadoration.org/ chapel.html	Virtually Gracious www.cybergrace.com	Live Prayer from Church – audio www.raldioc.org/mass/mass.htm
Krena Prayer Amulet - Free http://store6.yimg.com/ I/calastrology_1760_398452	St. Thomas Community Church (non-denominational) Online celebration of the Lord's Supper http://members.tripod.com/ st.tcommchurch/home.html	Sweet Spirit Christian Church Virtual church, (non-denominational) www.sweetspiritchurch.org
Interactive XMASTREE www.xmas4all.net	Heavens Grocery Store www.geocities.com/jesusfouryou/ heavensgrocerystore.html	Gospel of John (Video Trailer) http://home.christianity.com/ 79261.html
Christmas Webcam Page http://users3.ev1.net/ ~hwillcox/cam.html	Email Santa or view Christmas Web Cam Portal www.emailsanta.com/ Christmas_WebCams.asp	Halloween Web Cams www. halloweenwebcams.com
Want to start a Tract Ministry? www.ficotw.org	Ceremony in Santa Claus Church www.dicoverturkey.com/ English/movies/default.htm	Study Guide for Congregations **(Multifaith Resource)** www.calchurches.org/ publication_pdfs/BBU-edition2.pdf
Create your own Sacred Cyberspace (Spells & Rituals with Candles) www.circle-of-light.com/spells	Scripture Union www.scripture.org.uk	Consecration Video Clip www.epischicago.org/Bishop/Consecration99/

B. Offline Cyber Worship

a. Know-How, Process, Procedures, Activity, Functions, Methods...: (Christianity continued)

Get Free Online Pastoral Counselling www.owlnook.com	e-Ask the Pastor www.crchog.org	Select a Pastor / Expert www.allspiritual.com ChristianExpertAdvice.php3
Catholic Experts www.ewtn.com/EWTN/ Experts/conference.htm	Ask Pastor Know-It-All - http://thor.prohosting.com/ ~pastor	Ask the Pastor - Answering questions about religion http://members.aol.com/ askthepastor
Ask an expert www.konig.org/ cidask.htm	Questions Answers- Browse www.gmaf.org/answers.html	Have a Question About Your Faith? Ask a Priest www.realfaithtv.org/ask.asp
Ask a Bible Specialist www.bibleinfo.com/ question.html	Ask a Pastor www.ssnet.org/c gi-local/cvv/pastor	Ask A Pastor www.askapastor.org
Ask the Pastor http://hometown.aol.com/ walts9/askthepastor/ home/index.html	Ask The Deacon www.geocities.com/ ~nickknight	Ask The Amish www.800padutch.com/ askamish.html
Ask A Priest www.manitobacatholic.net faith/ask/priest/2002-10	A Christian Counselor http://www.achristiancounselor.com/	Divining America Sharing your questions **Multifaith Issues** www.nhc.rtp.nc.us/ tserve/getback/getback.htm
Order of the mass www.theworkofgod.org/ Devotns/Euchrist/ guide.htm	Ask The Pastor www.historictrinity.org/ questions.html	The Sufism of the West (A comparison of Christian mysticism to Sufism) www.blaketashi.com
Parts of the Mass www.kerrypoet.utvinternet.com/ mass/menu.shtml	Daily Bread Gateway www.augnet.org/ AugustineSECTION3/ AugustinesImpact/ OnPrayer/ 0112-DailyBread.html	Charity categories www.maygodbless.com/ metromart/ charity_categories.htm
Donate Stock & Securities www.alphachurch.org/ donatelow.htm	Word Talks: Difference between the Scrolls & the Gospels www.wessleymission.org.au/ ministry/tra/2001/010527.html	Buddhist and Christians **Multifaith Path** www. heartlandsangha.org/ unity.html

End of Life Decisions Catholic Church www.elderweb.com/ default.php?PageID=839	Preparations for death - Catholic www.newadvent.org/ cathen/04660c.htm	End of Life Decisions Catholic Church www.elderweb.com/ default.php?PageID=839
End of Life Decisions Church of Jesus Christ and Latter Day Saints www.elderweb.com/ default.php?PageID=839	End of Life Decisions Episcopal Church www.elderweb.com/ default.php?PageID=839	End of Life Decisions United Church of Christ www.elderweb.com/ default.php?PageID=839
End of Life Decisions Presbyterian Church www.pcusa.org/pcusa/ ga210/ovt/98-50.html	End of Life Decisions United Methodist Church www.elderweb.com/ default.php?PageID=839	Internet Question Box www.cin.org/users/james/questioons
Wired With Christ Jesus.com www.wwcj.com	Internet Congregation 1999 www.religion-research.org/ RRAPaper1999.htm	Cyber-Church Project Evangel Praise Center www.evangelpraisecenter.org/ cyberchurch
Liturgical Year www.catholicculture.org/ lit/overviews/ lit_year_main.cfm	**A Multifaith Merry Christmas** www.raheelraza.com/ multifaith_xmas.htm	Christianity Without Christmas Eveyday Living www.tomorrow-ucg.org/ tv/p365.htm
Prayer Tower (non-denominational) How it Works www.prayertower.net/ How.htm	How to Start Campus Prayer Groups www.gocampus.org/ alliance/engage/ engage1-9.htm	In virtual heaven Concepts of convergence in digital and religious spaces Avatars, creation, spirit www.uni-paderborn.de/ ~bergerma/texte/ heaven.html
How to Plan 40 Days of Prayer and Fasting www.wesleyan.org/ ecg/40_days/how_to_pln.htm	From Jesus to Christ www.pbs.org/wgbh/pages/ frontline/shows/religion	Internet for Christians (IFC) http://ifc.gospelcom.net/
Martinus Luther www.bc.edu/bc_org/avp/ cas/ger/luther.html	Digital Luther www.martinluther.de	Martin Luther www.geocities.com/Vienna/ 1667/luther.htm
Glossary of Religious Terms www.religioustolerance.org/ glossary.htm	Glossary Religious Holidays www.pgcares.com/ interfaith_glossary.html	Fortes in Fide: Information for Traditional Catholics www.the-pope.com/ jmcnally.html
Theories of the Historical Jesus http://earlychristianwritings.com/ theories.html	Later Church Fathers http://earlychristianwritings.com/ fathers/	Telling the Digital Gospel www.next-wave.org/ sep00/digital.htm
What is inclusive Christianity www.auburn.edu/~allenkc/ interfaith/interfaith.html		

b. Products, Resources, Materials…: (Christianity continued)

Quaker Electronic Archive and Meeting Place http://www.qis.net/~daruma	Virtual Christian Gateway www.servehim.com	Cyber Christian Portal www.christianity.net
The First Christian Root Directory www.active-ss.com/ rootdirectory	Lutheran Links www.stpaulslutheran.com/ links.htm	Internet Christian Library Serving the Internet Community since 1993 www.iclnet.org
Roman Catholic Online Saints Index http:// saints.catholic.org/ index.shtml	Online Evangelism - Christian Search Engine www.fishthe.net	Cyber Church Gateway www.praize.com/engine/ Churches/Cyber-Churches
Christian Search Engine www.praize.com/engine	Search Engine for Roman Catholics www.everythingcatholic.com	Web Search http://search.crossdaily.com
Christianlinks www.christianlinks.com	Explore Christianity.com by Topic http://home.christianity.com/ topics	Netsites: Your Guide to the Net www.catholicvoice.com.au/ 175/links.htm
ACTS Christian Search Engine & Directory www.actschristian.com/a/	Catholic Online Search http://community.catholic.org	Christian Links Directory www.christpages.net

Christian Online Community www.colc.com	Search for Christian Sites http://kedesh.christianitytoday.com/ search/index.taf	Christian Internet Directory www.konig.org/links.htm
Christian Interactive Network http://search.cin.com	Christian Topsites http://online- churches.net/toplist/churches.html	Charity sites www.konig.org/ cidcharity.htm
1 Million Christian Links http://jamesablevins.com	Home of Best of the Christian Web http://www.botcw.com/index.html	All In One Christian Index http://allinone.crossdaily.com
Websites www.saintmarys.edu/ ~incandel/funweb.html	Cove of Catholic Links http://catholic.8m.com/ churches.htm	Mixing Monitors for Worship Sound Advice www. experiencingworship.com/ articles/sound/ 2001-6-Mixing-Monitors-for2-p4.html
The Mixing Console in Worship Sound Advice www.experiencingworship.com/ articles/sound/	Digital Juice - Sound Advice www.experiencingworship.com/ articles/sound/ 2002-8-Digital-Juice-.html	Creating Online Worship www.goodsoil.co.uk/ worshipOnline.asp
Heal Your Church Web Site Teaching, Rebuking, Correcting & Training in Righteous Web Design www.healourchurchwebsite.com	How to Start a Web-based Church www.ficotw.org/wbc.html	Ethos of a User-Friendly Church Site www.gospelcom.net/guide/resources/ southside.php
Webmaster Grab Bag http://ifc.gospelcom.net/ internet_tech/270/	Want a Nanny - (Download for free) Computer God software www.bluechillies.com	Worship Banners (Sale) www.realitycheckpress.com/ Gallery3.htm
Add 'Bible Verse of the Day' on YOUR Website! www.christ.com/ biblevotd/biblevotd.html	Design Altar http://web.media.mit.edu ~hlubinka/altarnation	Servanthood Design: A Ministry Serving the Graphics & Web Design Needs www.servanthooddesign.org
Make Palm Crosses www.bromike.com/easter/ palmcross.html	Guidelines for Church Websites http://ourworld.compuserve.com/ homepages/cphicks/tbcweb.htm	Christian ISP www.fish.co.uk
Free Web Development Service www.frommeyer.com/ free-services.html	Christian Web Site Webmasters www.christian-web-masters.com	Christian Web Hosting www.gracenet.org
A Christian ISP Service http://churchluk.net	Christian ISP Management View Web Cam www.ispmgt.com/webcam.php	Build a Free Church Website http://forministry.com
LORD of Hosts Gateway for Webservants www.christ.com/Jesus	Catholic Live ISP www.catholicweb.com/ cl_about.cfm	Your Christian Resource Community www.christiansunite.com
Build a Will & be billed www.buildawill.com	Catholic Internet Services, Inc. www. catholicinternetservices.com	Eucharistic Miracle: Betania, Venezuela www.monksofadoration .org/Betania.html
Ecumenism Webquest Evaluation. www. faithcentral.net.nz/ webquest/ecumenism/ evaluation.htm	The Eucharist Eucharist Miracles Resources http://eucharist.pray-with-the-heart.org	711 : Christian Directory http://search.711.net
Today's Calendar and Clock Page www.ecben.net/ calendar.shtml	Calendrical Bookmarks: Roman/Julian/Coptic (Solar), Ecclesiastical/Orthodox (Lunisolar) http://emr.cs.it.edu/ home.reingold/calendar-book/ calendar-links.shtml	Universal Calendar Calculator: Julian, Gregorian, Quaker Gregorian, Quaker Julian, Greek, Ethiopian, Coptic… www.cf-software.com/ other.html
Download Needs (Gadgets & Tech) http://channels/ netscape.com/ns.tech/ downloads.jsp	Religious Business Card with Scripture (for a price) www.thechristiancardstore.com/ oldfabucawis.html	Christian Bank Checks www.christianlinks.com/ ppc/ppc.php?act=12

A To Z Christian Internet Directory www.themissionary.net/ pages/index.html	Looking to give a unique Christmas gift? www.botcw.com/ 1634kjv/index.html	Church Buyers Guide www.christianitytoday.com/cbg
Pray Timer www.namb.net/ evangelism/prayer/ praytimer/default.asp	Download Praize Messenger www.praize.com/	Sources of Worship— Lectionary based Prayers http://desperatepreacher.org/ worship/
Download Today's Best Sermons http://store.yahoo.com/ pttranscripts/index.html	Download an Image www.christianshareware.net	Download Episcopalian icons (See software) www. pathguy.com/index1.htm
EPIC Software Assisting Praise, Worship & Ministry Through Technology www.epicsolution.co.uk	Computer GOD 1.00 (Security & Encryption Tool) (For a price) www.bluechillies.com/ details/14802.html	Worship Him Presentation Software for Churches www.worship-him.com
Adoration Worshipware Media 4 Ministry www.1shareware.com/ showprod.php?pid=6250	Worship aids - Mennonites www.mhsc.ca/ encyclopedia/ contents/W71ME.htm	Amish General Store (Anabaptist) www.amishgeneralstore.com
Methodist Hymn www.hymnsite.com	Videos & more www.guidinglightvideo.com	CD-ROMs www.christianbook.com
Cyber Hymnal Portal www.cyberhymnal.org	CD-ROMS (DBS) Bible, Talmud, Jewish Thought http://faculty.biu.ac.il/ ~barilm/dbs2e.html	Computer-Assisted Theology Internet Resources users.ox.ac.uk/ ~ctitext2/theology
WorshipCenter Pro (Sale) www.topshareware.com/ WorshipCenter-Pro-download-3886.htm	Guaranteed Prayers or Your Money Back (for a price) Prayers to screw your enemies Prayers for faith, Prayers for… www.parnau.com/jeff/pray.htm	Worship Planning Software Visual Liturgy www.vislit.com
Church 2000 – The Christian Information Source www.church2000.org	Song search Christian praise and worship music www.songquery.com	Church Computer Online www.ccug.org.uk/ LinksRes.asp? CATEGORY_N=11
Learn Gospel Music www.blackgospel.com	Worship Music Audio / Video / CD-ROM/ DVD www.worshipmusic.com	Sign up for weekly email from Pope John Paul II www. daughtersofstpaul.com/ johnpaulpapacy/meetjp/theman
Get the T-shirt Wear the Prayer www.24-7prayer.com/front-page.php	Free Stuff! (Worship Music) www.worshipmusic.com/ hunforgranop.html	Subscribe to e-Prayer Network www.crchog.org
Prayer Request Pages Directory www.praize.com/engine/ Prayer/Prayer_Request_Pages/ Index.html	Join the Pauline books & media mailing list http://lb.bcentral.com/ex/ manage/	V-Mail Online Information Form Web-based Tool (for a price) http://vineyardboise.safeserver.com
PrayerNet Browse / Request prayer www.churchnet.org.uk/ prayer/1.html	Praying the News www.socialholiness.com/ id33.htm	Get this Month's FreshPrayer www.waymakers.org/ freshprayer.html
e-Daily Bible Verse www.crchog.org	Subscribe daily Bible verse www.arcamax.com/ afpops/1285.htm	Scripture tools www.worshipmap.com/resources/ scripture/scripture.html
Word Alive Cyber Membership form www.wordalivechurch.org/ pages/cyber.htm	Desperate Preacher's gateway www.desperatepreacher.com	Christian Mission Opportunities Classified Directories www.missionfinder.org/ index.htm
Statistical abstracts of Churches of Christ Worldwide www.churchzip.com/ statisticalsummary.htm	Cyber-Church:Topia Directory (see under: society <Religion <Christianity<Churches) www.topiasearch.com	Click to find local Mass Times Or call: 1-800-Mass Times (1-800-627-7846) www.wriv.com/links.htm

UK Christians www.ukchristians.co.uk	UK Churches www.churchnet.org.uk/ ukchurches	Experiencing Worship Sound & Video [Worshiper & Worship Leader] www.experiencingworship.com
Sources for Spirtuality SpiritHome www.spirithome.com	Other resources - Spiritual Survival Handbook www.survivalmanual.com	Jesus Files Sources for worship & activities www.jesusfiles.co.uk
Quality Christian Education via the Internet www.goldenstate.edu	Sermon Writer Software (Free Sample) www.sermonwriter.com	Bible Training www.virtualbibleschool.com/ a3.htm
Online Evangelism Training www.gospelcom.net/bgc/iec/otoe	Free Online Bible Course http://www.start-page.net	Want more streaming video cybertracts, Bible studies, dial [1-800-TheWord]
Methodoloyg of Teaching **Multifaith Education** www.ifcmw.org/resources/ creative_models.pdf	World Wide Study Bible www.ccel wheaton.edu/wwsb	God's Word or God's Words? World Bible Translation Center www.wbtc.com/articles/ translation/god's_word.html
WebCity House of Worship **Multifaith Directory** www.webcityusa.com/ worship.htm	Northwest Churches and Synagogues www.webcityusa.com/ worship.htm	Websites for Church & Synagogue Libraries www.vchstrojans.org/Seminar- LibrariansWebsotes.pdf
Anointed Christian Links www.anointedlinks.com/links_a.html	Free Bible Software www.ficotw.org	Christian Info Directory across Canada www.christianinfodirectory.org
Lutheran Resources for Worship www.augsburgfortress.org	Anglicans:Liturgical Resource Portal http://anglicansonline.org/resources/ liturgical.html	Pastor's Index to the Web http://stuwww.tcu.edu/ ~jweaks/piw.html
Theology Library Christian Scriptures www.shc.edu/theolibrary/bible5.htm	Christian Contemplation and Zen Enlightenment: Are They the Same? Comparative Perspectives http://www.innerexplorations.com/ ewtext/cc.htm	Healing and recovery - Common Praise: The Taize Inspiration www.faithlinks.org/ viewarticle.asp?ID=333
All inclusive worship http://newsobserver.com/features/ story/3263922p-2917370c.html	Inclusive Worship, Camperdown Uniting Church http://vic.uca.org.au/cfm/goodnews/ inclusive_worship.htm	Family Inclusive Worship http://www.cey.angdon.com/ familyworship.htm
Inclusive worship, Inclusive Community http://ubcmn.org/page6.htm	sermon archives www.findthepower.com/ virtualchurch/index.htm	Living Sounds Online http://livingsounds.org
Astrology and Religion Nexus Multifaith Perspective www.findyourfate.com/ astrology/astrology-religion.htm	**Multifaith** - All Things Spiritual Directory www.allspiritual.com/ . MultiFaith.php3	...An interview with God. Not really, but still worth a look! www.interviewwithgod.com
Daily Reflection www2.csbsju.edu/cgi-bin/osb/ dose.pl?daily&dquote.txt&dquote	Inclusive Worship Celebration Planning Resources www.mccchurch.org/ oldintranet/worship6.htm	Teach Us to Pray Public Prayers for Services of Worship www.cresourcei.org/prayers.html
Paths: The Way of the Soul www.snark.ca/ano2.htm	Saving Graves www.savinggraves.org/links/religious/	Tools for Prophets in the Information Age http://ac.marywood.edu/skb/ prophets/resource2.html
Writing Prayers for Alternative Worship www.alternativeworship.org/ practice_writingprayers.html	Christianity Among the Religions of the World http://christianity.about.com/library/ weekly/aa031097.htm	"Worship or Entertainment" www.emmitsburg.net/tumc/ pastor_wade/ 2002/worship_entertainment.htm
Church: Worship— or Entertainment? www.pianomoods.com/ entertainment.html	WORSHIP IS NOT ENTERTAINMENT www.christianity-then-and-now.com/ html/ biblical_study_013.html	Worship or Entertainment? www.examiningthescriptures.com/ entertai.htm
Church of Ontology Invites You to Meaningful Worship www.usfreeads.com/ 126565-cls.html	Worship Software Comparison Chart www.churchmedia.net/software/ comparison.shtml	From Judaism to Christianity: Worship & Customs A Comparison of Two Religions http://library.thinkquest.org/C004351F/ Worship.htm
Jesus Internet Community For Priests, Nuns and Laypersons! www.jesusinternetcommunity. homestead.com/	World Scripture: A Comparative Anthology of Sacred Texts - Multifaith Resource 4600 passages from 268 texts and 55 oral traditions www.euro-tongil.org/ws/index.html	

C. Religions-Online / Online-Religions -

a. Home Pages of Religious and Spiritual Groups:

aa. Denominations: (Christianity continued)

National Association of Congregational Christian Churches http://www.naccc.org/	National Council of Catholic Bishops -- United States Catholic Conference http://www.nccbuscc.org	International Alliance Of Web-Based Churches www.ficotw.org/Alliance.html
Covenant Assembly Evangelical Alliance (non-denominational) http://god.ontheweb.com	Sources for congregations: Alban Institute www.congregationalresources.org	List of Online Churches and Denominations http://christiansnet.com/ drj/denomdir.html
Denominations Directory http://netministries.org/ denomlst.htm	The Anglican Church in America http://www.acahome.org	Anglicans www.church-of-england.org
Church of England (Official) http://england.anglican.org	Anglican Centre in Rome www.anglicancommunion.org/rome	American Baptist Churches www.abc-usa.org
Conservative Baptist Association of America http://www.cbamerica.org	Baptist Churches / Southern Baptist www.sbc.net	Seventh Day Baptist Churches www.inwave.com/7church/ 7church.html
Southern Baptist Churches www.io.com/~tarrytwn/SBC/ othersbc.htm	Seventh Day Baptist Churches www.inwave.com/ 7church/7church.html	Shouter Baptists (National Evangelical Spiritual Baptist Faith Intl. Center of Canada) http://shouterbaptist.org/ nav.html
Cooperative Baptist Fellowship www.cbfonline.org/indext.cfm	Southern Baptist Convention http://www.sbc.net/sbcsplash	Progressive National Baptist Convention www.pnbc.org
Free Methodist Church www.freemethodistchurch.org	Lutheran Church -- Missouri Synod http://www.lcms.org	Evangelical Lutheran Church in America http://www.elca.org
United Methodist Church http://www.umc.org	International Communion of the Charismatic Episcopal Church http://www.iccec.org	The Episcopal Church http://ecusa.anglican.org
Episcopal Orthodox Christian Archdiocese of America http://eoc.orthodoxanglican.ne	Presbyterian Church in America http://www.pcanet.org	Presbyterian Church (U.S.A.) http://www.pcusa.org
United Church of Christ www.ucc.org	Quakers www.quaker.org	Evangelical Friends International (Quakers) www.evangelical-friends.org
General Conference Mennonite Church www2.southwind.net/~gcmc	Anabaptist Mennonites www.anabaptists.org	The Mennonite Church www.mennonites.org
Jesus Radicals Anabaptist (Mennonite) www.jesusradicals.com	Conservative Mennonite Conference www.cmcrosedale.org	Christian Church (Disciples of Christ) www.disciples.org
Seventh-day Adventist Church http://www2.adventist.org	Seventh Day Adventist Churches www.adventist.org	The Brethren Church www.brethrenchurch.org
Church of the Brethren http://www.brethren.org	Brethren in Christ www.bic.church.org	Church of the United Brethren in Christ www.ub.org
Assemblies of God www.ag.org	Pentecostal Assemblies of the World International www.pawinc.org	Pentecostal Assembly of God www.paog.org
Pentecostal Holiness Church of Canada www.phcc.ca	Apostolic Church of Pentecost of Canada www.acop.ca	United Pentecostal Church International http://www.upci.org
Church of God in Christ www.cogic.org	Jehovah's Witnesses http://www.watchtower.org	Jehovah's Witnesses www.freeminds.org
Coptic Papal Residence Homepage http://www.copticpope.org	Greek Orthodox Archdiocese of America http://www.goarch.org	Russian Orthodox Church www.russian-orthodox-church.org.ru/en.htm
Orthodox Christian Page in America www.ocf.org/OrthodoxPage	Orthodox Church in America http://www.oca.org	Christadelphians www.christadelphian.org.uk
Christian Serbian Orthodox Church in Australia & New Zealand www.upis.com.au/spc/eng/	Ukrainian Orthodox Church of America http://www.uocofusa.org	The Wesleyan Church http://www.wesleyan.org

New Apostolic Church International http://www.nak.org	The Salvation Army http://www.salvationarmy.org	International Churches of Christ www.icoc.org/html/ whoset.html
The Coalition of Spirit-filled Churches www.spirit-filled.org	Churches of Christ www.churchesofchrist.org	Christian Reformed Church http://www.crcna.org
Mormons The Church of Jesus Christ of Latter-day Saints http://www.lds.org	Unificationism Rev. Sun Myung Moon www.unification.net	The First Church of Christ, Scientist Christian Science www.tfccs.com
The Moravian Church http://www.moravian.org	Christian & Missionary Alliance www.cmalliance.org	Reformed Church in America http://www.rca.org
Worldwide Church of God http://www.wcg.org	New Age Christianity http://home.connexus.net.au/~bbsite	Committee on Worship (COW) Church Worship Resources www.swedenborgianresources.org/ cow/about.html
United Church of God www.ucg.org	Progressive Christianity – Non-dogmatic forms for the Christian Faith www.tcpc.org	Universal Life Church Monastery **Multifaith Ordination** http://www.ulc.org
Official Site of Santa Claus www.officialsanta.com		

b. Congregations: (Christianity continued)

Official Web Sites of Religious Bodies www.wabashcenter.wabash.edu/ Internet/official.htm	Church's homepages www.disciple.org/ churches/default.asp	The Anglican Catholic Church www.anglicancatholic.org
Sandhurst Baptist Cyber-Church http://ourworld.compuserve.com/ homepages/ianinglis	Temple Baptist Church Online www.tbcplano.org	The Episcopal Missionary Church http://www.emchome.org
Reformed Episcopal Church/ Anglican Province in America http://www.recus.org	Orthodox Presbyterian Church http://opc.org	The Full Gospel Pentecostal Church International www.emmanueltemplechurch.com
Church of the Holy Ghost www.freeyellow.com/ members6/church-of-the-holy-ghost	Mother of God Church (Russian Orthodox Church) www.pomog.org	Saint John Coltrane African Orthodox Church www.saintjohncoltrane.org
Abbaye Notre Dame des Dombes www.citeaux.net/ elenchus/moines/24.htm	Christian Community Church http://christianchurch.netfirms.com	Word of Life Ministries www.wordoflifeministry.us
CyberChurch online connection ... church fellowship www.thecyberchurch.org	New Age Christianity http://home.connexus.net.au/ ~bbsite	Angle Cyber Church Membership via e-cell group www.angelcyberchurch.com
Christ Church Turnham Green www.christchurch-tg.org.uk	Chiswick Parish Church www.chiswickparishchurch.org	Ekklesia Theological think www.ekklesia.co.uk

c. Ministries: (Christianity continued)

Church Homepages www.webcom.com/~nlmnet/ xiancus1.html	Faith Communities Today Project http://fact.hartsem.edu/ denom/denom_list.htm	University of Pittsburgh Association of Chaplaincies (non-denominational) www.pitt.edu/~chaplain
Churches Together in England www.churches-together.org.uk	Anglican Chaplaincy in Belgrade www.anglicanbelgrade.faithweb.com	Common Worship Church of England www.cofe.anglican.org/ commonworship
US Episcopalian Missionary www.episcopalian.org	Cyber Home for all Baptists www.baptist.org	Progressive National Baptist Convention www.pnbc.org
Jesus Radicals Anabaptist (Mennonite) www.jesusradicals.com	UCC Fellowships of Reconciliation www.serve.com/ussfor	Anabaptists (Amish, etc.) www.faithfound.com/ browse.php?cat=4
The Cathars www.cathar.net	Catholic Pentecostal www.grarg.com/ ccc/faq/ccr/#mary	Jehovah's Witnesses http://www.watchtower.org

Candlelight Christian Ministries Christian Outreach Ministry www.jesus-ourlord.com	Community of Christ http://cofchrist.org	Christian Fathers www.newadvent.org/ fathers
Christian Internet Ministry www.christianministry.org/ac.htm	Internet Ministries http://webminister.com	Ecunet Online ecumenical community www.ecunet.org
Divine Word Missionaries www.divinewordmissionaries.org	Mapping Center for Evangelism and Church Growth www.mappingcenter.org	New Age Christianity http://home.connexus.net.au/ ~bbsite
Billy Field Ministries www.billyfields.com	Divine Mercy Supersite www.divine-mercy.com	The Aquarian Age Gospel of Jesus http:// reluctant-messenger.com/ aquarian_gospel.htm
Faith Community Church Online (rediscover your faith) www.FCCWaupaca.org	Hope4You Ministries http://personal.lig.bellsouth. net/lig/j/p/price69/hope4you.htm	Ekklesia Theological think www.ekklesia.co.uk
Faith & Reason Ministries Reconciling Christianity with Accepted Science www.faithreason.org	Walk By Faith Internet Ministry www.walkbyfaith.com	The Fatima Network Our Lady of Fatima Online www.fatima.org
TFP: American Society for the Defense of Tradition, Family and Property www.tfp.org	Prayer Book Society http://churchnet.ucsm.ac.uk/ prayerbook	Grace Life Ministries www.gmaf.org/ gracelife.html
Father Alexander: Orthodox Christian www.fatheralexander.org	Charles A. Coulombe: Christian and Monarchist www.thinline.com/ ~ccoulomb/index.htm	WRBC Evangelical Dance Ministry www.webspawner.com/ users/wrbcedance
Society of St. Pius V: Organization of traditional Catholic priests www.sspv.net	Ortodoxia Griega Tradicionalista http://orthodox.org.mx	The traditional Latin Mass www.traditionalmass.org
Sure Foundation Theological Institute www.virtualbibleschool.com/ a3.htm	The Veil: Contemplations in Catholic Tradition www.theveil.net	Ministry of Black Gospel Music www.blackgospel.com
Christian Way Former Christian Scientists for Jesus Christ www.christianway.org	Unofficial Infinite Way Prayer www.theunofficialinfiniteway.com/ prayer.html	American Institute of Holistic Theology www.aiht.edu/doorways/ prayer_door.asp? adclfr=OVprayer
Center for Social Holiness www.socialholiness.com	Committee on Worship (COW) Church Worship Resources www.swedenborgianresources.org/ cow/about.html	Stuart's Celtic Christianity www2.gol.com/users/stuart/ celthihs.html
RAPHA Christian Ministries www.rapha.org	Teens 4 Jesus Youth Ministries www.teens4jesus.org	St. Christopher website, Toronto (for diverse communities) www.stchrishouse.org/ index.htm
Christian Info Directory across Canada www.christianinfodirectory.org	Grief and Loss Resource Center www.rockies.net/~spirit/ grief/grief.html	Americans United for Separation of Church and State www.au.org
Universal Life Church Monastery **Multifaith Ordination** http://www.ulc.org	Official Site of Santa Claus www.officialsanta.com	

The internet church, or *i-church* , is intended to be a Christian community of the Church of England based in the Diocese of Oxford under the pastoral care of the Bishop of Oxford. Community membership will be open to people of all Christian traditions. Organised through an active web site, and led by an ordained or lay 'web pastor', its purpose will be:

- to provide a focus of Christian community for those who wish to explore Christian discipleship but who are not able, or do not wish, to be participant members of a local congregation.
- to provide an additional means of support to those who do not find all that they need within their own worshipping community
- to provide continuing connectivity with Christians who travel, either through their work or in their life-style, and who are not able to maintain relationships with a geographical Christian community

"I-church." http://www.i-church.org

1.5 Mapping Hinduism Webwise

A. Online Cyber Worship

a. Prayer:

Plain Talk about God:
Gandhi asking for Kriya Yoga initiation, the Fastest Path to God
http://karmawhammy.com/?OVRAW=God&OVKEY=god&OVMTC=standard

Mahatma Gandhi once visited one of the biggest libraries in London and asked the librarian: "What spiritual book is most often issued?" The librarian replied: "It is the Gita."
http://www.sivanandadlshq.org/religions/gita.htm

Two Minute Daily Puja

Each time when you say 'Samarpayami' (literally: I am offering), please offer two akataas to the LORD with love and devotion.
Akshatha is uncooked rice, if possible colored with kumkum , saffron powder, termaric and a little bit of water. Can be prepared well advance for a week and kept near the ALTAR
http://www.hindunet.org/day_as_hindu/puja/shortpuja.htm

Virtual Darshan – Ambe Mata www.ahmedabadcity.com	Virtual Darshan - Ganesh www.ahmedabadcity.com	Virtual Darshan – Hanuman www.ahmedabadcity.com
Durga Puja: Live Webcam coverage from USA www.durgapujas.com/ camview.htm	Digital Avatar www.charm.net/ ~nayak/avtar2.html	Puja International (under construction) http://cyberpuja.com/ pujaint
Virtual Darshan - Krishna www.ahmedabadcity.com	Prarthana: Online Hindu Temple Worship Service http://prarthana.com	Cyber Prarthana www.eprarthana.com
Virtual Poojas www.mantraonnet.com/member-vp.html	Siddhivinayak Temple, Mumbai http://blessed-bandwidth.net/ siddhivinayak/siddhivinayak.htm	Sri Sri Ravi Shankar Guruji http://blessed-bandwidth.net/ srisriravishankar/ srisriravishankar.htm
Suprabhatham (Audio, text, translation) www.balaji.net/html/a01suprabhatham.html	Surya Namaskar Salute to the Sun www.urday.com/surya.htm	24 Avtaar (Incarnation) www.urday.com/24.htm
Matsya www.namaste.it/ kundalini/ kundalini_eng/matsya.html	Vishnu as Matsya (Fish Incarnation) www.sanatansociety.com/ indian_art_galleries/harish_johari/ hj_go_vishnu_fish01_painting.htm	Matsya Avatar www.panchangam.com/matsya.htm
Hindu prayer http://home.earthlink.net/ ~tolp/hindpray.htm	Hindu Universe – Digital Prayers www.hindunet.org/ multimedia/digiprayers	Matsya Avatara http://matsya.nols.com
Aarti (Audio) www.hindukids.org/aarati.shtml	Aarti & Puja (Audio) www.hindunet.org/ puja/hindi.html	Virtual Temple www.umich.edu/~hindu/ temple/temple.html
Ganesh Temple Online www.ganeshtemple.org	Navratri, Celebrate the festival of Victory: Online Arti (Text in Hindi Script) http://www.webdunia.com/occasion/ nav_durga/onlineaarti.htm	Durga Temple Online www.durga.org
Sri Sri Ravi Shankar Guruji, Mumbai www.blessed-bandwidth.net/ srisriravishankar/ srisriravishankar.htm	Ram Temple Online www.ramtemple.org	Ingredients needed for Yajna www.scsmath.com/ n_comer/trove/ yajna_notes_items.html
Virtual Lakshmi www.eprarthana.com/ virtual/vlakshmi.htm	Virtual Shiva www.eprarthana.com/ virtual/vshiva.htm	Supreme Trio – Shiva www.char.net/~nayak/shiva.html

Virtual Anjali Durga Puja Mantra www.thepuja.com/arati.htm	Virtual Hanuman www.eprarthana.com/ virtual/vhanuman.htm	Virtual Krishna www.eprarthana.com/ virtual/vkrishna.htm
Virtual Amman www.eprarthana.com/ virtual/vamman.htm	Virtual Balaji www.eprarthana.com/virtual/vbalaji.htm	Lord Venkateswara www.balaji.net
Virtual Ganesh www.eprarthana.com/ virtual/vganesh.htm	Virtual Rama www.eprarthana.com/virtual/vrama.htm	Virtual Murugan www.eprarthana.com/ virtual/vmurugan.htm
Other Virtual Puja Rooms http://icarus.cc.uic.edu/ stud_orgs/religion/hindu/pujaroom.html	Lord Rama Rama is the 7th avatar of Vishnu www.umich.edu/ ~hindu/shrine/rama.html	Shri Hanuman Online www.hanuman.com
Mahadev's Site www.mahadev.org	Vaishnodevi www.vaishnodevi.com	Shirdi Sai Baba's Site www.saibabaofshirdi.net
Virtual Sai Baba www.eprarthana.com/virtual/vsaibaba.htm	Virtual Sri Sai Baba of Shridi (Slides – On Spot) www.shirdibaba.org/newhome/ index.html	Sai Baba Shirdi's Daily Artis (Audio) www.shirdibaba.org/ aartis/index.html
Sabrimala Sree Ayyappan Temple www.sabarigiri.org/sabarimala.htm	Virtual Ayyappan www.eprarthana.com/ virtual/vayyappan.htm	Lord Ayyappa of Sabarimal, Kerala www.ayyappan-ldc.com
Priest Talks www.durka.com/durka900.htm	Wireless Phones www.mobilehindu.com	Yoga instructor, Massachusetts www.focalpointyoga.com
How to Meditate? Guided Meditation with Swami Shuddhananda www.babalokenath.org/meditation	Listen to Swami (Ramakrishna Missionaries) www.sriramakrishna.org/real.htm	free meditation www.net-sightings.com/ meditation/free_meditation.htm
Prayer Book Meditations, Adorations, Celebrations, Invocations **Multifaith Prayers** Multicultural Prayers www.prayforpeace.com/index.php	Ancient Wisdom: Submit a Prayer **Multifaith Concerns** www.awisdom.com/ community/submit_prayer	Voice A Vision • Post A Prayer Dare A Dream **Multifaith Voices** www.heartpath.com/ hpcontent/voiceAvision.asp
Free Zodiac Match Test www.emode.com	Karma Removal Astrology www.astroved.com	Yoga (Video) www.sahajayoga.ca/video
Method of Meditation www.umich.edu/~hindu/ meditation/medimain.html	Enlightening Elastomeric Experiences http://latexmindresearch.tripod.com	Your Mediation Room (Login) www.cyberastro.com/ products/vedicremedy/ meditation.asp
Introduction to Vipassana Meditation www.sfhealth.org/vipbrochure.htm	Places of Pilgrimage www.pushtimarg.net/ English/Pilgrimage/places.htm	Meditating on A-U-M www.hinduismtoday.com/ archives/2003/4-6/16-17_vedas.shtml
Astrology On The Hour - Horary Chart http://astrologyonthehour.com/index1.htm	2004 Astro Forecast: Vedic Astrology Predictions http://hinduism.about.com/ cs/astrology/a/aa121503a.htm	Online Holy Calendar Find today's date and time (Astrologically auspicious?) http://mailerindia.com
Calendrical Bookmarks: Hindu (Lunisolar) http://emr.cs.it.edu/home.reingold/ calendar-book/calendar-links.shtml	Today's Calendar & Clock Page: Hindu & other Indian www.ecben.net/calendar.shtml	Know your Nakshatras (Lunar mansion … Hindu Zodiac) www.vedicprediction.com/ ?hop=4india
Allexperts Yoga Q&A www.allexperts.com/ getExpert.asp?Category=1762	Teacher finder www.yogabasics.com	One Stop Yoga Limited www.one-stop-yoga.co.uk
Yoga Anand Ashram Online www.santosha.com	Learn the Basics of Yoga www.soyouwanna.com/site/ syws/basicyoga/basicyoga.html	Yoga Directory www.yogadirectory.com
Gandhi Virtual Asram www.nuvs.com/ashram	Search an Ashram www.indiayogi.com/ content/yogipilgrim/default.asp	Shradhanjali (Memorial ?) www.biharonline.com/ shradhanjali/prayer.htm
Geeta Kutir: Haridwar www.geetakutir.com	Dhyana Ashram www.tamil.net/people/dhyana_ashram	HariHar Ashram: Haridwar www.hariharashram.org

Omkarananda Ashram: Rishikesh www.omkarananda-ashram.org	Pranavananda Ashram, Toronto www.pranavashram.com	Santhigiri Ashram Ashram of Karunakara Guru www.santhigiri.org
Sri Ganapati Sachchidananda Ashram: Trinidad www.dyc-tt.org	Kashi Ashram Tour **Multifaith Tour** www.kashi.org/tour.htm	Sant Shri Asaramji Bapuji www.ashram.org
Baradi The Holy Pilgrimage www.babalokenath.org/ Baradi.htm	Prayer4Peace.net A nonsectarian project to accumulate one billion Vajrasattva mantra www.prayer4peace.net	World Prayers – Prayer Collective **Multifaith Practices** www.worldpyaers.org
Let Me In Mataji's Ultimate Site www.mataji.org	Video Pravachanas www.pushtimarg.net/ English/Pravachana/ video%20pravachan.htm	

b. Praise: (Hinduism continued)

Krishna Bhajans www.bhajans.org/txt/ krishna/krishna_264_csx.htm	Pongal: Great Indian Thanksgiving! http://hinduism.about.com/ library/weekly/aa011001a.htm	Practice Reading Slokhas - Gajananam (Audio) www.panchangam.com/gaja.htm
Practice Reading Slokhas - Mooshika Vahana (Audio) www.panchangam.com/moosh.htm.htm	Practice Reading Slokhas - Guru Brahma (Audio) www.panchangam.com/guru.htm	Practice Reading Slokhas - Shaantaakaaram (Audio) www.panchangam.com/santha.htm
Practice Reading Slokhas - Shiva Stuthi (Audio) www.panchangam.com/shiv.htm	Practice Reading Slokhas - Uruvai Aruvai (Audio) www.panchangam.com/uruvai.htm	Practice Reading Slokhas - Yaakundendu (Audio) www.panchangam.com/yakun.htm
Practice Reading Slokhas - Ariru Thadanthozh (Audio) www.panchangam.com/ariru.htm	Tamil Slokas – Threading Ceremony (Upanayanam) www.panchangam.com/yajur01.htm	Learn the Mantra – Threading Ceremony (Upanayanam) www.panchangam.com/upan.htm
Gâyatrî Mantra **Multifaith Perspective** http://wahiduddin.net/ mantra/gayatri.htm	Gâyatrî Mantra (Graphic) www.magpage.com/~mcguffin/ gayatriyantrawith.jpg	Sai Baba chanting Gâyatrî Mantra (Audio) http://wahiduddin.net/mp3/ gayatri_baba_2.mp3
Gâyatrî Mantra (Transliterated) http://w3.gwis.com/~ajmani/gayatri.html	Sankirtan Sadguru, Devotional, Shastras.. www.iiramii.net	Telugu Bhakti Pages http://68.88.118.16/ telugupages/Devi/DurgaDurgastotras.htm
Mantras www.carnatic.com/ karmasaya/index.php?full=Mantra	Durga Puja on the Net Recipes of Puja www.pujaonthene.com/puja_recipes.htm	Durga Puja Puja Rituals www.bangalinet.com/durgapuja.htm
Moola Mantra Sri Lakshmi Kubera Yantra www.panchangam.com/dana.htm	Wedding Ceremony rituals www.panchangam.com/kalyaan.htm	Moola Mantra: Ganapathi Yanthram www.panchangam.com/gyant.htm
Vedic Mantras Audio http://puja.net	Variyar Swamigal www.hinduwebsite.com/ masters.htm	Sadhu Vaswani www.sadhuvaswani.org
Sri Madhavacharya www.hinduwebsite.com/masters.htm	Sri Yogananda www.hinduwebsite.com/masters.htm	Guru Raghavendra www.hinduwebsite.com/masters.htm
Adishankara www.hinduwebsite.com/masters.htm	Sri Ramanujacharya www.hinduwebsite.com/masters.htm	Jeddu Krishnamurthy www.hinduwebsite.com/masters.htm
Anandamayi Ma www.hinduwebsite.com/masters.htm	Sri Aurobinda www.hinduwebsite.com/masters.htm	Ramakrishna Parmahnasa www.hinduwebsite.com/masters.htm
Swami Prabhupada www.hinduwebsite.com/masters.htm	Ramana Maharishi www.hinduwebsite.com/masters.htm	Swami Rama Tirtha www.hinduwebsite.com/masters.htm
Maha-Lakshmi mantra chanting for worship www.sanatansociety.org/ indian_music_and_mantras/ mantras_mahalakshmi_mantra.htm	Ganesha mantra chanting for worship www.sanatansociety.org/ indian_music_and_mantras/ ganesha_mantra_invocation.htm	Swami Vivekananda www.hinduwebsite.com/masters.htm
Hindu Chant www.beliefnet.com/ story/81/story_8171_1.html	Hanuman Chalisa audio cassette or CD will be sent FREE www.hanuman.com	Links Related to Hanumanji www.mataji.org/chalisa.htm

c. Scripture: (Hinduism continued)

Hindu Texts www.hindunet.org/scriptures	Ramayana for children www.hindunet.org/ramayana	Virtual Ramayana www.hscc.net/ramayana
Bhajan Kirtan www.geocities.com/Athens/ Acropolis/4637	Bhajans (Devotional Songs) http://www.bhajans.org/	Puja and Bhajans www.hindunet.org/puja/
Ragas and classical music www.nimbus.ltd.uk/ nrl/wm_ra.html	Vedic Chanting Audio http://puja.net	Search for Bhajans www.hindunet.com/ search/search.cgi?Terms=bhajan
Gita (Audio) in Sanskrit www.bhagavadgita.org	Read Translated Gita www. iskcon.org/sastra/f_bg.html	Bhagavad Gita www.bhagavad-gita.org
Read Holy Gita www.the.gita.net	Digital Images of Gita Govinda http://ignca.nic.in/ img_0002.htm#Gita Govinda	GITA GOVINDA - Multimedia Project http://ignca.nic.in/ gita.htm
Everyday Sloka from Gita (Audio) www.geocities.com/Athens/ Acropolis/5294/indexhome.html	Listen the Verses of Gita in Sanskrit www.bhagavadgita.org	Hinduism: Scriptures http://hinduism.about.com/ library/weekly/extra/ bl-intro-scriptures.htm
Read Upanishads www.hindunet.org/upanishads	The Laws of Manu http://hinduism.about.com/ library/weekly/ extra/bl-lawsofmanu4.htm	Sri Brahma-samhita, TEXT 41 www.bvml.org/ SBS/3.html
Rig Veda (Audio, Sanskrit) http://frontpage.hindunet.org/ rigveda/audios/Default.htm	Swami Venkatesananda's translation of Vasistha's Yoga www.yogavasistha.com	Vedas & Upanishads (Transl.) www.san.beck.org/EC7-Vedas.html
Read Rig Veda www.yoga.com/raw/readings/ rig_veda.html	ISKCON Related Tape Ministries Hare Krishna RealAudio http://chantandbehappy.com/ ministries/index.htm	Bhakti Yoga (Sanskrit & English) www.bhakti.net/main.htm

d. Sacrament: (Hinduism continued)

Astrology Online (Horoscope) http://astrology.mantraonline.com	Video Clips The Hindu Way of Life Preperation for Divali: The Pooja www.visittnt.com/ ToDo/Events/Divali/Index.htm	Om: Symbol of the Absolute http://hinduism.about.com/ library/weekly/aa022200.htm
Tour of Adhiparasakthi Temple, Melmaruvathur (Tamilnadu) www.omsakthi.org/templevideo.html	Ganapati (Ganesh)Temple, India (Audio) www.siddhivinayak.org/ siddhivinayaknew/audios/index.htm	Browse the list of Temples www. mandirnet.org/ temple_list.html
Prasad to Krishna - Free www.ahmedabadcity.com	Prasad to Ganesh - Free www.ahmedabadcity.com	Prasad to Hanuman - Free www.ahmedabadcity.com
OM - Omshanti (animation) www.missouri.edu/ ~omshanti/newflash/index2.html	Sacred Symbols www.mantraonnet.com/ member-ss.html	Cow Worship The Whole Universe in the Holy Cow www.urday.com/cow.htm
Hindu Festival - Mini movie www.hindunet.com/ multimedia/digiprayers/f_index.html	Video Clips The Hindu Way of Life The Wider Appeal of Divali www.visittnt.com/ ToDo/Events/Divali/Index.htm	Images of Ganges River www.historylink102.com/ india/ganges-river-2.htm
Scientific Procedure of a Pooja or Hindu Ritual Hindu Astrology Center Jyotish Ashram www.swamiram.com/ pujaprocess.html	River Ganges in pictures www.sanatansociety.org/ india_travels_and_festivals/ ganges.htm	Images of Temple Deities www.geocities.com/ Athens/Delphi/2627/ page1.html
Images of Temples www.hindunet.org/ hindu_pictures/temples/ temples.html	Hindu Image Gallery www.geocities.com/ mohan_ayyar	Shiva Shakti Madalam Yantra, Mantra Tantra www.shivashakti.com

B. Offline Cyber Worship:

a. Know-How, Process, Procedures, Activity, Functions, Methods.../ Products, Resources, Materials...: (Hinduism continued)

Ask Rishi http://mailerindia.com	Send an Email to Pandit Mano Mohan Mukherjee http://vedicshastri.com	Ask Swami www.vedmandir.com/index.php
Submit Puja Request www.astroshastra.com/ services/pujarequest	FAQ's: Swami's Question of the Week www.vishnumandir.com	Yoga teacher directory www.yogasite.com
Saints and Sages of Kashmir http://kashmir.org/ religion.html	HinduNet Signature Merchandise www.cafeshops.com/hindunet2	Virtual Library – Vaishnava Texts www.floridavediccollege.edu/library.htm
Infinite Goddess – Embracing the Divine Mother (Lakshmi) www.goddess.ws	Baby names http://hinduism.about.com/ library/babynames/ bl-mbabynames-b.htm	Ganesha: The Elephant-God-All About the Zoomorphic Hindu D... http://hinduism.about.com/ library/weekly/aa083000a.htm
Sri Sukta Homam Puja Service – Order form www.saranam.com/Pujas	Sale of Temple Prasadams (Tirumala Tirupati Devasthanams) www.balaji.net/html/ a07prasadam.html	Search Hinduism www.hindunet.org
Mira Bai www.siddhayoga.org/ community/families/ tales_2000/mirabai/6.html	Tulsidas www.sivanandadlshq.org/ saints/tulsidas.htm	Basaveshwara www.itihaas.com/ medieval/basaveshwara.html
Tukaram www.neonblue.com/ tfs/tukabio.htm	Thyagaraju http://home.att.net/ ~s-prasad/tyagaraja.htm	Madam Blavatsky www.blavatsky.net/index.htm
Surdas www.itihaas.com/ medieval/surdas.html	Saiva Saints www.hinduwebsite.com/ siva/sivasaints.htm	Swami Dayanada Saraswathi www.aryasamajhouston.com/ htmdocs/daya.html
Siddha Yoga chanitng CDs www.bookstore.siddhayoga.org	Krishna Das's Chanting CD's www.krishnadas.com	Jai Ambe CD Kali Mandir, Calfornia www.kalimandir.org
View Chariot Festival in Toronto (photos) www.durka.com/durka000.htm	Eight Lectures on Yoga by Aleister Crowley www.mninter.net/~jmcmanus/yoga	Glossary of Yoga Darren's Cyber Ashram www.darrenmain.com/ pages/resources/yoga/glossary.html
Glossary of Religious Terms www.religioustolerance.org/ glossary.htm	Glossary of Hindu Terms www.digserv.com/mystic Hindu/glossary.html	Glossary of Sanskrit Terms www.hindunet.org/glossary
Digital Dharma www.hinduismtoday.com/ archives/2003/4-6/ 86-digital_dharma.shtml	Glossary Religious Holidays www.pgcares.com/ interfaith_glossary.html	Divali: Festival of Lights www.hindunet.org/HPG.pdf
The Puja Room Items for puja (ritual) for family and personal www.healthyplanetonline.com	Krishna Culture Online Vedic Store - http://krishnaculture.com	Krishna Software Inc. on Indian philosophy, religion, and culture www.krishnasoft.com
Rudraksha.com www.rudraksha.com	Puja Guide for Educators www.asia.si.edu/ pujaonline/puja/sitemap_1.html	"Pradaksina" ritual to walk around www.bergerfoundation.ch/ Home/pelerins.html
Basic Tenets http://hinduism.about.com/ library/weekly/extra/ bl-intro-tenets.htm	Worship Articles - Sells a variety of articles for puja. www.mysticworship.com	Yantra - Offers all types of Yantras, Shivling, and japamalas for worship. www.yantrashastra.com
Other resources - Spiritual life of Saints, Mystics, Gurus www.indiayogi.com/ content/indsaints/default.asp	Heavenly Way http://home.nyc.rr.com/hsiaostemple	Hindu last rites www.hindunet.org/last_rites
Hare Krishna Hard Core (article) www. techgnosis.com/hare.html	Hare Krishna – Audios http://realaudio.krishna.org	Interactive Bhagavad Gita (audio/visual) (for a price) www.mantraonnet.com/ shopping-multimedia.html
Shudh Bhojan (Pure Food) www.mantraonnet.com/ member-shudhbhojan.html	Ayurvedic Cooking ... http://cyberpuja.com/ vediccooking	Mnatra Portal www.mantraonnet.com/

Pooja Articles (Sale) www.mantraonnet.com/ shopping-pooja-articles.html	Spiritualism and Divine Life www.hinduwebsite.com/ divinelife/divineindex.htm	Bhanjan Portal www.bhajans.org/txt/ krishna/krishna_264_csx.htm
Build Your Bhajan Site www.hindunet.com/ memberscgi/community.cgi	Religious & Spiritual portal for Indians across the globe http://blessingsonthenet.com	Pictorial Exhibition of Devotion in India www.kamat.com/ indica/faiths/ bhakti/toc.htm
Wellness for Body and Soul www.self-realization.com	Yoga Centers India www.self-realization.com/ yoga/yoga_centers_india.htm	International Yoga Directory www.self-realization.com/ yoga_directory.htm
Download our Yoga Freeware Program www.self-realization.com/ yoga_software.htm	The Path of Devotion - Bhakti www.kamat.com/indica/faiths/bhakti	Yoga Movement www.yogamovement.com
Image Consecration (Read) www.asiasociety.com/ Essay.asp/EssayID=18	Hindu Electronic Networks www.hindunet.org/hindu_pictures/	Virtual India **Multifaith Digital Reality** http://india.projectmiso.net/ ashram/religion
Directory of Indian Temples www.templenet.com/about.html	Directory of Hindu sites www.hindunet.org	Hindu Resources Online www.hindu.org
The Temples of Orissa Hinduism - general http://ignca.nic.in/ orist017.htm	The Temples of Orissa Shaivism http://ignca.nic.in/orist018.htm	The Temples of Orissa Vaishanavism http://ignca.nic.in/orist019.htm
The Temples of Orissa Sun Worship in Orissa http://ignca.nic.in/orist020.htm	The Temples of Orissa Saktism in Orissa http://ignca.nic.in/orist021.htm	Sri Chaitanya Saraswat Math www.scsmath.com
Download an Image www.geocities.com/SoHo/Lofts/6834	Australian Hindu ISP www.hindunet.com.au	Directory of items in Category: Sathya Sai Baba http://groups.yahoo.com/ group/SaiBabaLeelas/message/ 995?source=1
Vastushastra Architectural concepts from Vedas www.projectpyramid.com/ vaastu_shastra.htm	Rahul Gajjar - vedic theory of anahata dhwani or sound without vibrations www.vadodara.com/co/rahulgajjar.htm	WebCity House of Worship **Multifaith Directory** www.webcityusa.com/worship.htm
Personal Worship Puja Hinduism http://alexa.herc.ru/mirrors/www.enteract.com/ jwalz/Eliade/118.html	SAIVITE VIRTUE – e-book www.himalayanacademy.com/books/ virtue/VContent.html	Islam & Hinduism Similarity of the Two Divine Messages **(Multifaith Perspectives)** www.atimes.com/atimes/ Front_Page/EL25Aa02.html
Bhakti Yoga The path of devotion www.nvcc.edu/home/lshulman/ Rel231/lectures/hindu/bhakti.htm	Astrology and Religion Nexus **Multifaith Perspective** www.findyourfate.com/ astrology/astrology-religion.htm	**Multifaith** - All Things Spiritual Directory www.allspiritual.com/MultiFaith.php3
Life-Cycle Rituals www.photius.com/religion/ india_life-cycle_rituals.html	World Scripture: A Comparative Anthology of Sacred Texts - **Multifaith Resource** 4600 passages from 268 texts and 55 oral traditions www.euro-tongil.org/ws/index.html	Welcome To Cyber Durga Puja (about the puja) www.intwebservice.com/ cybercafe/durga.htm
Ashtanga Yoga Mysore Blog www.yogaisyouth.com/blog/	Dharmapuri Laxmi Narasimha Swami Dharmapuri Narasimha Swamy's Cyber Darshan http://www.dharmapurishrine.org/	Om Sri Sai Jyotisha VidyaPeetham-Home Page http://www.onlinejyotish.com

C. Religions-Online / Online-Religions:

a. Home Pages of Religious and Spiritual Groups (Hinduism continued)

American Yoga Association www.americanyogaassociation.org	Akhila Bharatha Ayyappa Seva Sangham www.saranamayyappa.org	Ayyappa USA? Canada: www.ayyappan.com
Basava Samithi of Australasia www.users.bigpond.com/ onkar/basava	Foundation For World Awakening www.worldawakening.org	Haidakhandi Samaj www.babaji.org.uk

Hans Samelan Sabha: UK http://website.lineone.net/ ~yogs	Hare Krishna Movement (ISKCON) www.iskcon.org	Home Pages of Deities www.mantraonnet.com/ member-homepages.html
Hindu Mythology www.indianythology.com	Hare Krishna, ISKCON – Texas www.iskconhouston.org	Hindu Heritage Endowment www.hheonline.org
Kripalu Center for Yoga and Health www.vgernet.net/ kali/entrance.html	Isha Foundation Dhyanalingam (worship & meditation) www.ishafoundation.org/ dhyanalingam.htm	International Gita Society www.gita-society.com
Shri Kanchi Kamakoti Peetham., Tamil Nadu kamakoti.org	Kanchi Kamakoti Centre, California www.kanchikamakoticenter.org	Project Ganesh www.projectganesh.org
Shankara Kendra www.sankarakendra.20m.com	Shiva Vishnu Temple Cultural Centre, California www.livermoretemple.org	Shri Gaayatri Mandir http://shrigaayatrimandir.tripod.com
North American Sankethis (NASA) www.sankethi.org	Sri Yohamaya Bhuvaneswari Peetam http://jaibhuvaneswari.org	The Mother's Service Society, Pondicherry, India www.motherservice.org
Sri Venkateswara Temple Tirumala Tirupati Devasthanams www.tirumala.org	Shree SiddhiVinayak Temple, (Ganesh Temple) Mumbai www.siddhivinayak.org/main.asp	Sambodh Foundation www.sambodh.org
A Tribute to Hinduism Dedicated to Lord Ganesha Lord of Beginnings www.atributetohinduism.com index_old.htm	Shree Swaminarayan Mandir Hindu temple, UK www.swaminarayan-baps.org.uk	The Veda Mandir and Community Centre www. VishwaHinduParishad.co.uk
Sanatan Society for Scientific Spirituality www.sanatan.org	Sanatana Dharma World Congress of Ethnic Religions Multifaith Perspective www.wcer.org/members/sasia/ india/index.htm	SASTA-Sri Ayyappa Society of Tampa Inc. www.freewebz.com/ sasta
Natha: classical Yoga and Tantra www.natha.fi/index.html	Ramakrishna Ananda (Graham Ledgerwood) www.yogaworld.org	Shamdasani Foundation (Hong Kong) --Sai Baba of Shirdi-- www.saibaba-fund.org
Sri Chaitanya Saraswat Math www.scsmath.com	Sreemadbhagbad Gita Sangha www.gita-sangha.org	The Heart of Yoga Association www.heartofyoga.org
Anusara Yoga www.anusara.com	Satyananda Yoga www.satyananda.net	Yoga Supersite on Holisticonline.com www.holisticonline.com/ Yoga/hol_yoga_home.htm
Propogation of Yoga and Vedanta www.abhedashram.org	Vedic Heritage, New York www.vedicheritage.org	Vedanta Center: Atlanta www.eternalquest.org/ index.html
Satchidananda Ashram, Yogaville International Headquarters for Integral Yoga http://yogaville.org	Universal Society of Spiritual Love **Multifaith Perspective** www.ussli.org	Yoga Institutes http://india-tourism.com/ 713.0.html
Ayurvedic Natural Health Centre Goa www.healthandayurveda.com	Atma Vikasa Center of Yogic Sciences, Mysore http://indigo.ie/ ~cmouze/yoga_online/Mysore.htm	Adytam Vigan Satsang Kendra, Jodhpur www.the-comforter.org
Come 4 Yoga, Chennai www.come4yoga.com	Foundation of Pathanjala Yoga Kendra, Bangalore www.yogelements.com	Bharatiya Yoga Vidya Dham, Nasik www.yogavidyadham.org
Yoga Centers / Clinics /Colleges www.indiatouristoffice.org/ Culture/yoga.htm	Heavenly Gardens Chandigarh www.heavenlygardens.org	Health and Yoga, U.P., www.healthandyoga.com
Kriyayoga Fellowship Worldwide, U.P., www.kriyayoga-yogisatyam.org	Mahayog Academy, Nanital www.mahayog.com	Manoyoga, Hyderabad www.brahmavidya.tv
Matha Yoganandamayi Ashram, Chennai www.yoganandamayi.org	Mysore Mandala Yogashala http://mandala.ashtanga.org	Parmarth Niketan Ashram, Rishikesh,(Himalayas) www.yogashramrishikesh.com
Prana Holistic Health Centre, Pondicherry www.pranacentre.freeservers.com	Pranava Yoga Dhama, Karnataka www.mysoreyoga.org	Shree Bindu Sewa Sansthan, U.P. www.jaisiyaram.com
Siddha Yoga http://chsharma.tripod.com	Soul Searchers, Delhi www.angelfire.com/ blues/soulsearchers	Sri Matha Yoganandamayi Ashram, Chennai www.yoganandamayi.org

UWPDEM (Universal World Peace Divine Empire) www.uwpdem.org	Yog-Ganga Centre For Yoga Studies www.yog-ganga.com	Manav Dharam www.manavdharam.org
Western Asrology www.cyberastro.com/ products/vedicremedy/meditation.asp	International Website of Brahmakumari World Spiritual University www.brahmakumaris.org.in	Hinduism Today www.hindusimtoday.com
Hindu Universe www.hindunet.org	American Institute of Vedic Studies, Santa Fe www.vedanet.com	Arsha Vidya Gurukulam, Saylorsburg www.arshavidya.org
Hindu University of America, Orlando www.hindu-university.edu	World Association for Vedic Studies, New Orleans www.umassd.edu/indic/waves	Yoga Research & Education Center, Lower Lake www.yrec.org
International Cooperated Ayurvedic University www.eisra.nl/gb/icau.html	Florida Vedic College www.floridavediccollege.edu	Maharishi Vedic University www.maharishi.org
Oxford Centre for Vaishnava and Hindu Studies www.ocvhs.com/ocvhs/3/faculty	Vidyapeethas Rashtriya Sanskrit Sansthan www.sanskrit.nic.in/main vidyapeethas	Sri Sri Radha Rasabihariji International society for krishna consciousness. www.geocities.com/Athens/9686
Iyengar Yoga School of Toronto www.iyengaryoga.ca	Yoga Home page http://holistic-online.com/Yoga	Vedic University of America www.vedicvoice.com

1.6 Mapping Islam Webwise

A. Online Cyber Worship

a. Prayer (Salat, Dua, Ibadah, Rituals, Rites):

If you make the click rhyme with your heart as musical instrument, by using your four fingers of the right hand, except the thumb, (each finger appointed to a key), you may see that you can make it match your words, as an associate rhyme. If you imagine that many people across the world, are at the very same time making such rhyme, whispering "La ilah ila Allah", with you, just as you you can feel its beauty. nice. I was taught to say it with 5 parts. so here's a Cybermuslim

Testimony of Faith (cybershahadah):

La ila ha illa 'Llah
a s d f <space>
Muhammmma dun rasu lu 'Llah
; l k j <space>

recited at the time of rest on the qwerty keyboard. it occurs to me that this could be called the First Pillar of Cyberislam.
www luckymojo com/esoteric/religion/islam/ny200003cyberislam txt

Cyber Mosque, Malaysia http://cybermosque.mpsj. gov.my/index.html	How to Perform Salat (Audio / video) www.islamicity.com/ Mosque/salat/salat9.htm	Salat Demo (movie) www.islam.com/salat/salatfinal.html
Live Prayers www.liveislam.com/english.htm	Live Prayer from Haram (with English) www.kacst.edu.sa/en/stream/ Al-Majd%20TV.asx	Live Prayer from Haram Mosque www.saudiembassy.net/ RealVDO/live.ram
Daily Prayers From Madina Mosque www.islam.org/Live/TV2.ram	Prayer Timings www.islamicfinder.org/world.php	Browse Prayer FAQs (esp. Maliki School) www.guidinghelper.com/qna/salah.html
Universal Calendar Calculator: Middle East / Islamic www.cf-software.com/other.html	Calendrical Bookmarks Islamic (Lunar), Persian (Solar) http://emr.cs.it.edu/ home.reingold/calendar-book/calendar-links.shtml	Today's Calendar and Clock Page: Moslem, Persian &Parsi www.ecben.net/calendar.shtml
Online Muslim Matrimonial (Islamic Occasions Network) www.ezsoftech.com/omm/default.asp	Basic Pillars of Islam Audio, Text, … www.totel.net/~lgmz/pillars.htm	Shahadah First Pillar of Islam www.geocities.com/ mihrab786/Shahadah.html
Moon Sighting Online http://moonsighting.com	Embracing Islam www.geocities.com/ embracing_islam/index.html	Archived Taravih Salat www33.brinkster.com/ islamicards/down1.htm

Prayer Comparisons: Five Islamic Schools www.islam.org/ encyclopedia/chapter7/6.html	Prayer companions (mat, cap, and tasbih, miswak) http://www.strath.ac.uk/ Departments/SocialStudies/ RE/Database/Glossaries/ Islam/Salat.html	Compass Mobile Phone (Qibla pointer) (on sale) lge.com (#5300 compass) www.etechkorea.info/articles/20030921001.php
Prayer direction (Qibla) www.islamworld.net/qibla.html	Types of Prayer (Sunni) www.islam.com/ salat/typesofprayers.htm	Types of Pryaer (Shia) www.unn.ac.uk/ societies/islamic/ islam/pray.htm
How to Perform Prayer Second Pillar of Islam www.geocities.com/mihrab786/salah.html	Prayer made simple www.usc.edu/dept/MSA/ fundamentals/pillars/prayer	Learn how to pray (basics illustrated) http://oregonstate.edu/ groups/msa/books/prayer.html
Learn How to Pray Click or download Basics – Sheikh Ibn Baz http://english.islamway.com/ prayer/BegSound.htm	Learn How to Pray Click or download Advanced – Sheikh Ibn Baz http://english.islamway.com/ prayer/AdvSound.htm	Why Do Shia's Prostrate on Earth during prayers and join the prayers – FYI http://shia.org
Ablution (Wudu) Chart www.tazkiya.net/Library/Fiqh/Hanafi	Sufi prayer www.journeyofhearts.org/ jofh/kirstimd/sufipray.htm	Apply for Zakat www.zakatchicago.com/
Ramadan Third Pillar of Islam www.geocities.com/ mihrab786/Ramadan.html	Ramadan Index www.masnet.org/spirit.asp?id=602	Check Zakaat Nisaab http://jucanada.org
Calculate Zakat www.zakatchicago.com/	Zakat Questions www.zakatchicago.com/new/faq.asp	Cyber Zakath Pay Zakah Online http://islam.org/ contribute/iin/
Speak to Mufti (Imam) www.alinaam.org.za/spk2mft.htm	Dial-a-Fatwa 1-800-95-fatwa	Zakath Calculator Version 1.0 users.kfupm.edu.sa/MATH/kabir/zakat.htm
Browse Shia Question Bank www. al-shia.org/html/eng/q&a/ fehrest.html	Audio Fatwas http://hajirahfoundation.org/ audio_fatawas.php	Read-a-Fatwa www.islam-qa.com
Q & A http://islamhelpline.com/ askquestions.asp	Search-a-Fatwa www.fatwa-online.com	Q & A Ifta Department Jami'yyatul Ulama Canada Canadian Council Of Muslim Theologians http://jucanada.org
Check Minimum Mahr http://jucanada.org	Search Ismaili issues www.amaana.org/ismaili.html	New Fatwa This Week www.islamweb.net/web/ Fatwa.newthisweek?thelang=E
Check Mahr Fatimi http://jucanada.org	Sacrifice: Udhia/ Qurabani Online www.kind-hearts.org/udhia/u_form.asp	Fatwa Corner www.masnet.org/index_fatwa.asp
Hajj Supplications On Traveling for Hajj & Umrah www.islamonline.net/ English/hajj/2002/01/topic15.shtml	Hajj - Flash Map: The pilgrimage www.cnn.com/2004/WORLD/ meast/01/22/saudi.hajj/index.html	Hajj video clips www33.brinkster.com/ islamicards/down1.htm
Haj Movie (Urdu) www.sistani.org/html/ urd/manasek/haj-movie.html	Hajj (Pictures) Fifth Pillar of Islam www.ummah.net/hajj/pics	Haj at a glance www.ezsoftech.com/hajj/default.asp
Hajj Takbeer www.islaam.com/audio/misc/	Haj & Umra Illustrated (English) www.sistani.org/html/ eng/menu/5/amali.html	Hajj Talbiyah www.ummah.net/hajj/
Haji & Umroh –PesantrenOnline (Indonesia) www.pesantrenonline.com/haji.php3	Cyber Hajj http://openmysite.com/firmanallah/links/ Cyberhaj.html	Hajj Documentary Film www.islam.org/Video/cnn1.ram
Prayers for peace - Jewish, Christian and Muslim **Multifaith Platform** salmanspiritual.com/peace_prayers.html	World Prayers – Prayer Collective Multifaith Practices www.worldpyaers.org	Voice A Vision • Post A Prayer Dare A Dream **Multifaith Voices** www.heartpath.com/ hpcontent/voiceAvision.asp

Prayer Book Meditations, Adorations, Celebrations, Invocations:**Multifaith Prayers** Multicultural Prayers www.prayforpeace.com/index.php	Ancient Wisdom: Submit a Prayer **Multifaith Concerns** www.awisdom.com/ community/submit_prayer	

b. Praise (Darud, Qasida, Taarif, Salam, Naat, Vadhaif, Dhikr, Tasbeeh): (Islam continued)

Dua (Audio) www.islaam.com/audio/misc/	25 Duas from Holy Quran http://tariqnazir.tripod.com/ Islamic.html	Dua'a: Supplications by Imam Zain al-Abideen (A.S.) www.duas.org/sajjadiya/sajjadiya.htm
Supplication (Dua) http://muttaqun.com/ supplicationsframe.html	Listen Dua al-Qunoot http://toledomuslims.com Sounds/SoundDetail.asp?ID=7	Taravih Tasbih www.islamicacademy.org
Everyday duas (Arabic & English) www.themodernreligion.com/ basic/pray/duas.html	Al-Mathurat (Dua) Imam Nawawi's collection www.angelfire.com/ak/ PKPMS2/mahrat.html	Dua on WAP / Mobile Service: FAQs www.duas.org/wap/waphelp.htm
Dua's for Ramzan (Ramadhan) www.geocities.com/nohay/33/ramzan	Naat Shareef (Urdu, a few in Arabic- Audio) www.islamicacademy.org/ html/audio/Naat.htm	Birthday of the Prophet - Mawlid www.sunnah.org/ibadaat/ three_frameset.htm
Naat Shareef Urdu Panjabi Arabic Naats www.islamicacademy.org/ html/audio/Naat.htm	Dala'il-ul-Khayrat – Durood Shareefs Muhammad Sajad Ali Qadiri-Noshahi Presentation www.angelfire.com/pa2/durood	Mawlid al Naib www3.kumc.edu/diversity/ethnic_relig/mawlid.html
Naatsharif A City Of Ghulaman-e-Mustafa Urdu, Punjabi, Arabic, English http://naatsharif.com	Islamic Multimedia (Quran, Hamd, Naat...) www.minhaj.tv/new/index.minhaj	Qasida Burdah Shareef www.angelfire.com/pa2/durood
Salam and Darud – Eulogy www.madni.net/Darood/	Nasheeds - Islamic Songs English translations www.nasheedworld.com	Nasheed - Islamic Music Dawud Wharnsby Ali www.bismikaallahuma.org/ Archive/nasheed.htm
Live Majaalis of Imam Husain(A.S.) www.imamreza.net/eng/ services/i_site/classied.htm	Marsiya, Nauha, Majalis ... www.azadari.com	Karbala Online: Cyber Hussainiyah for Islamic Shia Recordings www.karbala.com/shiaindex.htm
Latest Nohay of 2003 www.shah-e-najaf.com/ nohay.htm	Qawwalli http://naatsharif.com	Serving Dawoodi Bohras Worldwide – Audio Archive (Quran, Naat, Qasida...) http://audio.mumineen.org
Music (Qawwali)- Sama www.vislink.it/stefanoleoni/ pagina_sama.htm	Qawwali with Classical Indian Music **Multifaith Music** http://makar-records.com/ siteus/frameecole.html	Qawwali: Music of the Sufis Nusrat Fateh Alik Khan www.hummomin.com/ qawali/nusrat.php
Zikr & Tasbi Index http://salmanspiritual.com/ prayers.html#index	Listen Live Majalis www.islamicentre.org	Qawwali: Music of the Sufis www.globetrekkertv.co.uk/ destination_guide/asia/ Pakistan/qawwali.php
Supplication (Dua) http://muttaqun.com/ supplicationsframe.html	Majalis 2004 Shean-e-Islam http://shean-e- islam.tripod.com/sheaneislam/	Qawwali - select the singer www.musicindiaonline.com/music/l/0400
Muslim Chant www.beliefnet.com/story/ 81/story_8171_1.html	Religious Media www.pakistanvision.com/site	JOIN ZIKR-ALLAH ONLINE! http://groups.msn.com/ AwarenessagainstourEnemy/ howtogetpaltalkandjoinzikrallahonline.msnw
Religious & Devotional Music /Qawwali www.bobsmusicindex.com/ ReligiousAndDevotionalEssay.html	Devotion www.islamunveiled.org/ eng/ebooks/mislam/mislam_spiri.htm	Ibn Arabi's Prayers – Direct mind www.digiserve.com/mystic/Muslim/ Ibn_Arabi/put_mind.html

c. Scripture (Quran, Hadith, Inspirational literature): (Islam continued)

Qur'anic Recitation Resource 40+ Qaris - 200+ recitations www.kitabullah.com	Listen Quran (Four Qira'ts – over 100 Qaris) http://islamweb.net/pls/iweb/audio.eqerraa_qaree	Learn Quran (Audio) www.arab2.com/quran/
Search the Quran (English Translation) www.soundvision.com/info/quran	Memorize Quran www.hummomin.com/quran/index.php	On-Line Audio Quran http://oregonstate.edu/groups/msa/quran/reciter/prog/huffaz_e.swf
Great Tajweed (English) www.abouttajweed.com	Memorize / Recite Multilingual Holy Quran www.equran.org/qrn/view/browse/txt/0008.html	Correct Way of Reciting the Holy Quran www.tadjweed.com/Isti3atha&Basmalah.htm
Recitation, murattal/tarteel style www.jebril.com/en/holy_quran/quran_london.htm	Quran Recitation www.islaam.com/multimedia/mak/	Listen Quran - Imam Sudais www.hamoislam.com/quraan.htm
Listen Quran - Qari Basith http://english.islamway.com/bindex.php?section=echapters&recitor_id=4	Turn the pages of Quran www.bl.uk/collections/treasures/quran/quran.html	Read a Translation of Quran www.netmuslims.com/quran/
Listen from more reciters http://english.islamway.com/sindex.php?section=erecitorslist	Quran index www.geocities.com/Athens/Delphi/4838/islam/quran.html	Text - Meccan / Madinan Surahs www24.brinkster.com/theislampage/quran/quran.html
Search Arabic Text www.islamicity.com/ps/default.asp?inc=PhoneticSearch.asp	Search Quran www.usc.edu/dept/MSA/reference/searchquran.html	Browse Quran http://lrhazi.com/quran/index.php
Roman Transliteration www.usc.edu/dept/MSA/quran/transliteration/	Thematic Quran Index www.quran.org.uk/ieb_quran_exegesis1.htm	Al-Quran Professional Web-based Version www.ekabakti.com
Transliteration (Audio) www.geckil.com/~harvest/quran	Summary of Recitations of each night's Taraweeh http://members.tripod.com/worldupdates/ramadaan/id137.htm	Test your skills in Transliteration http://transliteration.org/quran/Test/Test71.asp
English Translation, Quran – Yusuf Ali http://web.umr.edu/~msaumr/Quran	English Translation Quran – Marmaduke Pickthall http://wings.buffalo.edu/sa/muslim/quran/pickthall	English Translation Quran – Dr. T. B. Irving http://isgkc.org/translat.htm
English Translation Quran – E. H. Palmer www.sacred-texts.com/isl/palm/index.htm	English Translation Quran – Muhammad Asad www.geocities.com/masad02	Qur'an Subject Index www.usc.edu/dept/MSA/quran/quranindex.html
Multilingual Qur'an, Commentary, Searchable www.al-islam.org/quran	Other Translations Quran- www.quran.org.uk	Dictionary of the Qur'an www.emuslim.com/quran/lughat.asp
Web sites distorting the Qur'aan www21.brinkster.com/salafi/warning.html	Commentaries, Qur'an www.quran.org.uk	Comprehensive Qur'anic resource (Arabic) www.altafsir.com/IntroSrc.asp
Qur'an Manuscripts, digital http://faculty.washington.edu/wheelerb/quran/quran_index.html	Quranic Manuscripts www.islamic-awareness.org/Quran/Text/Mss/	Qur'anic Browser Engine and Resources (Passage lookup and Word search functions) www.al-quran.org.uk
Urdu & Arabic Quran Online Subject-Wise Quran www.softwarepk.com/quran/	Quran Network Shia Resource www.qurannetwork.com	Quran (Audio) Listen / download http://johnw.host.sk/quran.html
Quran Browser www.masnet.org/qur_browse.asp	Miracle Family of Quran www.ya-hussain.com/int_coll/others/qurankids/waziri/biography2.htm	Prophet Muhammad (PBUH) Final words to humanity (a video clip: 'The Message') the story of Islam movie www.islamicdatacenter.com
40 Hadith Qudsi www.geocities.com/~abdulwahid/hadith/qudsi.html	A new Ayah and Hadith every day http://magazine.al-islam.com	Hadith Collections – Mishkat al-Masabih www.jamiat.org.za/isinfo/mishkat.html

Hadith Collections – Shahih Bukhari www.usc.edu/dept/ MSA/fundamentals/hadithsunnah/bukhari	Dars-e-Bukhari (Urdu) www.hajirahonline.com/audio/ navalulrahman/Dars-e-Bukhari-100703.rm	Hadith Collections - Tirmidhi www.jamiat.org.za/ isinfo/tirmidhi00.html
Major Collections - Abu Dawood Hadith resources www.usc.edu/dept/ MSA/fundamentals/ hadithsunnah/ abudawud	Hadith Collections – Sahih Muslim www.usc.edu/dept/ MSA/fundamentals/ hadithsunnah/muslim	Hadith Collections - Muwatta of Imam Malik www.usc.edu/dept/ MSA/fundamentals/ hadithsunnah/muwatta
Thematic Index www.road-to-heaven.com/ hadith.htm	Search Hadith www.usc.edu/dept/MSA/ reference/searchhadith.html	Browse Hadith index - brief http://hadith.al-islam.com/ Baya
Hadith Scholar – Imam Nawawi www.nawawi.org	Sermons in Urdu (audio) http://hajirahfoundation.org/ sitemap.html	Khutba Online (Islamic Sermons - Audio) www.khutba.org
Search a Sermon Friday Sermon From Masjid al-Aqsa www.al-aqsa.org	Friday Khutba Online http://dar-us-salam.com/khutba/	Listen speeches of the Imam www.qaradawi.net (Arabic) www.geocities.com/ Athens/Acropolis/ 6808/products.html
Khutbah Jummah Cyber Mimbar www.muis.gov.sg/ websites/khutbah/ser-250521.asp	Friday Khutab www.angelfire.com/ ca/hasakr/friday.html	Questions and Answers http://shareeah.vze.com
Dawat-e-Islami - weekly live congregation and speeches www.dawateislami.net	Mufti Nawal-ur-Rahman's Friday sermons, Chicago (Urdu) http://hajirahfoundation.org/ sitemap.html	Mufti Taqi Usmani's Lectures (English) audio http://hajirahfoundation.org/ sitemap.html
Tasawwuf: Answers to Six Questions on Tasawwuf The Great Internet Debate www.sunnah.org/tasawwuf/ great_internet_debate.htm	Maulana Mannan Nadwi's Friday Sermon, Canada, (English) audio http://hajirahfoundation.org/ sitemap.html	Listen to Sunni Path Daily Guidance from the Beloved of Allah www.sunnipath.com
Dr. Jamal Badawi Islamic Teachings Channel 200 www.islamicity.com/ multimedia/radio/ch200	Virtual Inspiration (ilham) www.ahya.org/tjonline/eng/ 09/09Ghayb.html	Nahjul Balagha www.hyderi.org/ jamatlinks.htm
	Online Books – Islam www.najaco.com/books/	As-Sahifa Al-Kamilah Al-Sajjadiyya: The Psalms of Islam www.al-islam.org/sahifa

d. Sacraments (Muqaddas, Mutabarrik, Tabarruk, Aathar): (Islam continued)

View Haram Mosque (Mecca) www.allaboutturkey.com/mosque.htm	View Masjid Nabawi (Medina) www.iad.org/Madinah.html	View Masjid Aqsa – Dome of Rock www.aicpmultimedia.og/ html/Islamic_pictures-dome_of_rock001.html
Holy cities www.isesco.org.ma/ Palestine/Eng/doha/Part1.1.htm	Mecca www.rafed.net/ towns/english/maka.html	Medina www.rafed.net/ towns/english/madena.html
Islamic monuments http://ismaili.net/ ~heritage/mirrors/ imit/akahome.html	Pillars of Faith Mosque (Six Pillar Mosque) –Istanbul, Turkey (Search here) www. atla.com/digitalresources/ searcha.asp	World Mosque Gallery Download www.ipg.cwc.net/download.htm
View Mosque of Omar (Jerusalem) www.fortunecity.co.uk/ shangrila/las/454/ israel/templem.html	Search Mosque http://islamicfinder.com	Directory of Masjids in USA http://islamicity.com/orgs
Cybermosque – Your Da'wa Starts here www.promotingislamonline.com/ cybermosque.html	Online Guide to Al-Haram al-Sharif in Jerusalem www.noblesanctuary.com	Grand Mosque, Kuwait www.freekuwait.com/mosque

Mosques Around the world www.islamicity.com/Culture/ MOSQUES/Default.htm	Virtual Tour of a Mosque Lancashire Mosque www.lancashiremosques.com/ discovery_mosque_tour.asp	Tour Historical Sites around Makkah and Madina www.al-islam.org/ ziyarat/Saudi.htm
Prophets' Tomb (Green Dome in Madina) www.sunnah.org/ ibadaat/ziyara.htm	Mosque on the Moon www.alsahah.com/jamaz	Mosques www.islamonline.org/ English/ram2002/10/ topic06.shtml
Praying for the dead - Reciting Quran www.sunnah.org/ ibadaat/ funerals.htm	Online graveyard Islamabad, Pakistan www.islamabad.net/ graveyard	Virtual Funeral Prayer (Prayer in Absentia) article www.sunnah.org/fiqh janaza_ghaib.htm
Panlyurfa Dargah (Mavlud movie) www.dicoverturkey.com/ English/movies/default.htm	Mausoleum of Saint Hajiali, Mumbai www.blessed-bandwidth.net/ hajiali/hajiali.htm	Submit a prayer for the dead www.karbala-najaf.org
Whirling Dervish – Mevlevis (Sufi Music movie) www.dicoverturkey.com/ English/movies/default.htm	Rumi's Whirling Dervish (interested in Whirling?) www.sentient.org/rumi.html	Maulana Rumi's Masnavi www.intratext.com/ X/ENG0134.HTM
Miracle in Ajmer www.dargahajmer.com/ miracle27.htm	Sufi Retreat – Qanqah (Khanqah Imdadiya Ashrafiya) www.khanqah.org	Qanqah www.touregypt.net/ featurestories/khanqahbarquq.htm
Prayer alerts on Cell phone, Pager, PDA www.jannah.com/salatpager	Miracles of Islam www.islamicmiracles. faithweb.com	Friday Prayers (Juma) www. dar-us-salam.com/ khutba/Rules+guidelines.htm
Eid (Festival) Prayers www.usc.edu/dept/MSA/ fundamentals/pillars/ prayer/ Eid-Prayers_1.html	Sample Friday Prayer http:// muslim-canada.org/ fridaysermon.htm	Salat message on Pager (Hong Kong Residents) www.cyberpager.net/ default.asp

B. Offline Cyber Worship

a. Know-How, Process, Procedures, Activity, Functions, Methods…: (Islam continued)

Q & A Library Ahle Hadees.com www.quransunnah.com	Islam FAQs www.faqs.org/faqs/islam-faq/	All About Ramadan www.ramadan.co.uk
Q & A Library Ahle Hadees.com www.quransunnah.com	Islam FAQs www.faqs.org/faqs/islam-faq/	All About Ramadan www.ramadan.co.uk
Browse Q & A www.askislam.com/Practices/f	Ask Allamah www.qaem.org/allamah	Fatawas Regarding Women www.uh.edu/campus/msa/articles/ fatawawom/Content.html
Ask Islam http--hlms.org-Islam-Ask.htm	Ask-a-Fatwa www.islam.tc	Ask Sunni Imam www.ask-imam.com
Sheikh Abdulaziz Bin Baz (Browse Fatawas & Sermons) www.binbaz.org.sa/ aboutbinbaz1.asp	Shaikh Ibn Baz (Grand Mufti) (english resources) www.binbaz.co.uk	Answering-ansar www.answering-ansar.org
Jamia uloom-i-sharia Submit Questions by E-Mail www.shariah.tk	fatawa and legitimacy Questions www.muttaqun.com/ cgi-bin/lspro/lspro.cgi? hit_out=971950400	Browse FAQ;'s – Shia Context http://www.imamreza.net/eng/ services/i_site/classied.htm
Islam On Line: Fatwa Bank Search Fatwa by Title, Mufti, Topic www.islamonline.net/fatwa/ English/searchFatwa.asp	Islam – Questions and Answers www.islam-qa.com	Fatwa On Line www.fatwa-online.com
IslamiCity Q & A www.islamicity.com/qa	ISNA Q & A www.isna.net/Library/ fiqhqa/questions.asp	Fiqh Council of North America www.fiqhcouncil.org
Ask Imam www.irshad.org/ask.php	Fatwa Archive Select a Category www.islamtoday.net/englihs/ fat_archives/index.cfm	The Imam.com www.theimam.com
Ask the Jamiat's Imam www.jamiat.org.za/askjam.html	Ask Alima (Female Fatwas) www.hajirahfoundation.org /ask_alima.html	Submit questions by email www.islam-online.net
Question of Faith www.muslimgateway.com/ inspiration/questions	Quick Reference Guide Fiqh (Islamic jurisprudence) & other topics http://muslim-canada.org/ sitedex.htm	Need a Fatwa? Send e-mail now Jamia Nizamia, India www.jamianizamia.org/ jamia8.htm
Islam FAQ (Part 1/15): www.faqs.org/faqs/ islam-faq/part1	Q & A – (Browse) www.albalagh.net/qa	700 Questions & Answers posed by inquirers http://sultan.org/fordawa.txt
Dawah resources http://daawah.com	FAQ's Sufism www.republika.pl/ sufism/FAQ2.htm	To send Arzi (message) to Syedna Mohammed Burhanuddin (TUS) http://mumineen.org/araz.html
Q&A Library- Islam Q&A http://63.175.194.25/ index.php?ln=eng&dgn=3	Department of Dawwah, MJC www.hakimquick.com/ questions.htm	Fatwa / Laws (Browse / select) http://2muslims.com/ directory/Beliefs_And_Practices
Halal-Wa-Haram www.msifinancial.com/ disc1_frm.htm	Learn Ablution Wudoo of the Prophet www.qss.org/articles/ wudoo/wudoo_ToC.html	Soft drinks - Halal Contents www2.coca-cola.com/ contactus/faq/ ingredients.html
Fatwas on Vegetarianism www.islamicconcern.com	Permissible (Halal) Non-Permissible (Haram) www.themodernreligion.com/ HalalHaram.htm	Angles (General) www.islamia.com/ Angels%20&%20Jinn/ Angelsin.htm
Encouraging Good (Maroof) & Forbidding Evil (Munker) http://nvmsa.8m.net/ khutbahs/malshareef/ before_the_boat_drowns.htm	Islamic Advices http://members.tripod.com/ worldupdates/ contentstable/id16.htm	Wisdom of Idiots www.khamush.com/ sufism/idris_shah.htm

Tabligh spreads through the Internet (Dawa – Shia Approach) www.africafederation.org/ fedsamachar/march97_3.html	Tazkiyah - Purification via Ihsan www.muhajabah.com/ tazkiyah.htm	Islamic Tarbiyah www.daralislam.org/ programs/bring/tp.cfm
Ikram -e- Muslemeen www.al-madinah.com/ SixPointsTabligh/ikram.htm	Iman increases / decreases www.hizmetbooks.org/ Advice_for_the_Muslim/ wah-2.htm	Loss of Iman www.hizmetbooks.org/ Endless_Bliss_First_Fascicle/ b1-11.html
Striving for Educational & Cultural Awareness www.imam-alasr.com/ links.asp	Al-Islam and the Signs of the Last Days www.islam.tc/prophecies	Deen Or Dunya.com www.angelfire.com/ mo2/deenordunya
Islamic Concepts on Cultural Coexistence www.worlddialogue.org/ pdf/speech15.pdf	Some Guidelines for Unifying the Ummah Al-Istiqaamah www.sunnahonline.com/ ilm/istiqaamah/ feb1998_d.htm	A Brief Guide to Islamic Sects www.geocities.com/ defender_of_the_truth/ index.html
Maulana Rumi's Masnavi www.intratext.com/ X/ENG0134.HTM	The Sufism of the West (A comparison of Christian mysticism to Sufism) www.blaketashi.com	Concerning the Naqshbandiyya in Turkey www.haqq.com.au/~salam/cosan/ naqshis.html
Enneagram (personality types – Sufism) www.australiansuficentre.org/ enneagram.htm	Living Islam: Rene Guenon, multilingual www.abc.se/~m9783/trg.html	Islam & Yoga, Similarities **Multifaith Perspectives** www.penkatali.org/ yoga.html
Sir Muhammed Allama Iqbal www.allama-iqbal.htmlplanet.com	Sheikh Ahmad Kuftaro's Web Site www.kuftaro.org	Imaam-e-Aazam Abu Haneefah www.geocities.com/ ~abdulwahid/abuhanifah/al-imam.html
Islam & Christianity Similarities & Differences **Multifaith Dialogue** http://muslim-canada.org/ islam_christianity.html	Christianity & Islam No more differences than Thickness of a Twig **Multifaith Dialogue** http://muslim-canada.org/ michaelwolfe.html	God in Semitic Religions **Multifaith Perspectives** www.hildesheim.co.uk/ quickreference/ religion/semitic.html
Formless God in Monotheistic religions **Multifaith Traditions** www.kheper.net/ realities/Absolute/ Monotheistic-formless.html	Islamic Worship compared I **Multifaith Log** www.iad.org/PDF/WAMY8.pdf	Islamic Worship compared II **Multifaith Log** www.thetruereligion.org/god.htm
Muslims customs and Traditions www.understanding-islam.com/ related/sscategory.asp?scatid=32	Rubaiyat of Omar Khayyam www.okonlife.com	Islamic Poetry www.islamicedfoundation.com/ material.htm
All about Death (in Arabic) www.almawt.com	Funeral prayer (Janaza) http://oregonstate.edu/ groups/msa/ books/funeral.html	Death: Legal Aspects of Autopsy & Burial in the State of Washington www.idrismosque.com/ death.html
Muslim Cemetery www.idrismosque.com/ muslimscemetery.html	Funeral Homes www.idrismosque.com/ funeralhome.html	Funeral Rites: From Death Bed To Grave www.idrismosque.com/ burialprogram.html
Step By Step Illustrated Janazah Guide www.idrismosque.com/ janazahguide.html	Islamic death rituals www.understanding-islam.com/ rb/mb-108.htm	End of Life Decisions Islam www.elderweb.com/ default.php?PageID=839 Islamic Philosophy Online www.muslimphilosophy.com
Islamic Civilization http://cyberistan.org	Islam and America www.geocities.com/ WestHollywood/ Park/6443/America	Spirit of Muslim art www.calligraphyislamic.com/ research.htm
Islamic Informatino Line: Top Ten Myths About Islam www.islaminalaska.com/ toptenmyths.html	Islamic Architecture – Mosque Three Liturgical Structures: Masjid, Jami, Idgah http://library.thinkquest.org/ C0074851F/1.htm	Etiquette for Non-Muslim visiting the Mosque www.idrismosque.com

b. Products, Resources, Materials...: (Islam continued)

Software (some are free) www.rameez.net	Cyber Salat – Software www.jas.org.jo/~muneer	Al-Fajr dialer www;aliasoft.com/ islamboard/fajr.html
Qibla – Software www.jas.org.jo/~muneer	Prayer Times – Software www.jas.org.jo/~muneer	Sehri dialer www;aliasoft.com/ islamboard/fajr.html
Download Islamic tools @ Portal Masjid www.masjid.or.id/ download/download%20area.htm	Islamic Download .com www.geocities.com/ Athens/Agora/4229	Donate your Car for Dawa www.islamicity.com/ donate/cardonation/ Make_A_Difference.asp
Quran's Video www.interactiveislam.com	Download Islamic Videos http://lightuponlight.com	Islamic CD http://2muslims.com/ islamiccd.shtml
Islamic studies syllabus www.iberr.co.za/ topics3.htm	Al-Islah Publications www.everymuslim.com	Islamic Downloads www.netmuslims.com/ downloads
Sufi Glossary http:// essenes.crosswinds.net/ sufiglossary.html	Easy Dictionary of the Quran (Internet Version) Abdul Karim Parekh www.emuslim.com/ Quran/Lughat.asp	Glossary of Religious Terms www.religioustolerance.org/ glossary.htm
Shia Digital Glossary www.al-shia.com/html/eng/books/ contemporary/glossary.html	Islamic Glossary www.islamicity.com/ islamicglossary	Glossary of Islamic Terms www.islam101.com/ selections/ GLOSSARY0.html
Glossary Religious Holidays www.pgcares.com/ interfaith_glossary.html	Noor-e-Madinah Network www.nooremadinah.net/ main.asp	Islamic Video Library www.irf.net/irf/ aboutirf/middle/library.htm
Islamic Digital Library http://islamicdigitallibrary.com	Ahlul Bayt Digital Islamic Library Project www.al-islam.org/allah/ index.html	Scholars's of Islam's Library www.islaam.com/ Scholars.aspx?
Online Islamic Library of Dawat-e-Islami www.dawateislami.net/ services/library/default.asp?lid=p	Al-Islam Unity Encyclopedia www.1ummah.org/encyclopedia	Online Library www.youngmuslims.ca/ online_library/default.asp?section =Quran&orderid=title
Story of Islam DVD www.mpihomevideo.com	Salat CD Software SalatBase • http://islamicbookstore.com/ salatbasepc.html	Al-Islam Subject Index www.al-islam.org/index
Islamic Virtual Library www.islamicschool.net/ links.htm	Islamic Movies http://hem.passagen.se/ carlomar/video.htm	Islamic Freebies for your computer www.khadijasislamicresources.com/ computer.html
Internet-Based Learning in Malaysia: Islamic Law 2000 Conference www.bileta.ac.uk/00papers/ yaakub.html	Online Courses on Islam www.studying-islam.org	Islamic Education www.cie.org
Salvation in Buddhism & Islam **Multifaith Dialogue** http://users.iafrica.com/ l/ll/lloyd/5-SpecialStudies/ Islam-Buddhism.html	Study Arabic & Islaam Global directory www.allaahuakbar.net/ quran/study_Arabic.htm	Islamic Academy for Islamic Knowledge Learn Now in English-Urdu www.islamicacademy.org
On-line Arabic Classes www.arabacademy.com/main/ online/registrar.htm?part=74	Online Knowledge Tests www.islam101.com/ onlineTests/index.htm	Online Course on Islam www.islam101.com/ dawah/course101.html
Weekly Online Lesson www. rapidcityjournal.com/ nie/archives/2001/1211.html	Madrasas (Islamic Seminaries) Shia Resource http://www.madressa.net	Status of Islamic centres / Masjids in North America www.soundvision.com/ info/muslims/masjids.asp

Islamic Centers & Mosques http://abujasir.tripod.com/ Islamic-centers-mosques.htm	Step by Step Salat – DVD www.astrolabepictures.com/vaw0.html	ABIDANCE: Finding the Heart and Staying in it Download www.geocities.com/reachnin/abidance
Quran Translation Project www.islamicedfoundation.com/ quran.htm	Quran Super List (850 Sites) www.preciousheart.net/ Main_Archives/ Links_Folder/ SUPER_List_Quran.htm	Virtual Chat http:// chat.netmuslims.com
Web sites on Basic Beliefs in Islam www.glink.net.hk/ ~hikaya/islam.html	Multimedia resources - Sufism www.the-heart.net	Dua in-Car / Duaa al-Safar (Digital travel tool – On sale) www.dalma.com
Music & Musical instruments www.muhajabah.com/ music.htm	Arabian Music Select musician www.oud.gr/music_arabic.htm	Muslim Home Theater - Audio Video clips www.muslimgateway.com/library/av
Callers to Islam www.callerstoislam.org/links	Prayer and Mourning www.muslimgateway.com/community/prayer	Marriage video in Arabic www.benadir-islam.com
Download Adhan (Four choices) Audio www.islaam.com/audio/misc/	Download Adhan (Two choices) Audio www.muslimsonline.com/~ig/ islam/islamloads/wavs1.htm	Halal Serve: By the Community, for the Community http://halalserve.com
Create an Online Sacred Space (Paid service) http://gatekeepers.ca	Islamic ISP www.monstria.com	Free English Web Hosting for Muslims www.muslimtents.com
Muslim Access, Islamic ISP, USA. www.MuslimAccess.com	First Free Islamic Service Provider www.islamdirect.com	The communities online Free homepages www.muslimsonline.com
Free Islamic software http:// members.tripod.com/ worldupdates/contentstable/ id25.htm	Islamic ringtones www.textually.org/ringtonia/ archives/000705.htm	Muslim Networks Consortium www.duke.edu/web/ muslimnets/csmn_about.html
Template Adfunk Internet Solutions Article www.geocities.com/ unlimitedsearch/Template.htm	Islamic Clipart Downloads www.netmuslims.com/ downloads	A Guide to Develop a 12-month Personal Plan (Download) www.soundvision.com/Info/ development/annual.asp
Islam WebRing www.geocities.com/ Paris/7860/islamring.htm	Islamic symbols www. understanding-islam.com/ related/sscategory.asp?scatid=34	Image Gallery www.islamicedfoundation.com/ imagegallery/images.htm
Islamic Pictures & Slide Presentations http:// members.tripod.com/ worldupdates/contentstable/ id24.htm	Gregorian Hijri Dates Converter www.rabiah.com/convert	Find your Islamic Birthday www.islam.com. Islamicdates.asp
Islamic Screensavers Downloads www.netmuslims.com/ downloads	Islamic Date (South Asian) http://urdustan.com	Apparel & Hijab Gateway (See under Muslim Market Place) www.talkislam.com
Female Hiajb – Dress Code www.islamicgarden.com/ page1071.html	Islamic Veil http://niqaab.tripod.com	Hijab Collection (Sale) www.alhannah.com/hijab.html
Mubarak Cothing Company (Islamic dress, Kufi, Abayya...) http:// mubarakclothing .safeshopper.com	Islamic Stitches (With Quran / Hadith inscriptions) www.islamicstitches.com	Male Hijab – Dress Code www.muttaqun.com/malehijab.html
Directory of Islamic organizations www.latinodawah.org/ links/links5.html	Hajj and Umrah information http://hajj.al-islam.com	How to Perform the Rituals of Hajj and Umrah (Shaikh Salih Uthaimeen) www.iad.org/books/HAJJ.html
Fatwas on Hajj Fiqh of Hajj www.islamonline.net/ English/hajj/2002/01/Topic2.shtml	Haj & Umrah Comprehensive Information Portal www.the-webplaza.com/ hajj/index.shtml	Hajj booklet (Shia) Hajj Assistance Committee of North America Download http://hajj.org

Islamic Software & Organizations http://mrbasheer.tripod.com/ islam_links.htm	1000s Of Authentic Islamic References http://msapubli.com/ index.html	More than 430 free online Islamic books www.islammessage.com/ books/e/Bookslist.htm
Zabihah: Guide to Halal eating http://zabihah.com	Halal & Haram Directory www.angelfire.com/country/ balai/biro/halal.htm	Over 100 Free Islamic Books http://groups.yahoo.com/group/ alislaahpublications/files
Faith Kitchen www.muslimgateway.com/ sites/kitchen	Muslim Search Engines Gateway (esp. geographic) http://searchking.net/portal/ adilbookz/search2.html	BAHISHTI ZEWAR Heavenly Ornaments www.alinaam.org.za/ bahishti/bahishti.html
List of Some Trusted Sites www.islamic-knowledge.com/Guide/ Source.htm	Muslims Internet Directory www.2muslims.com/ directory	One step away from heaven Hadith & Quran based Guide www.road-to-heaven.com
Try Cyber Muslim Dhikr by typing ... www.luckymojo.com/ esoteric/religion/ islam/ny200003cyberislam.txt	Muslim Gateway: Faith Bazaar www.muslimgateway.com/ sites/shopping	Islamic Library (Al-Maktabah Al-Islamiyyah) - Online Library http://library.oneummah.net/ modules/mylinks/
Shia Web portal www.ksiaworld.com	Suggested Reading: Book List (for Women) Federation of Muslim Women, Canada www.fmw.org	Islamic world A List of Links http://195.37.93.199/hofheinz/ cyberislamlinks.html
Shia – Ithna Ashari – Portal http://al-shia.com/html/eng/index.htm	Shia – Ithna Ashari: Aalulbayt Library http://al-shia.com/html/eng/lib/up.htm	Islam and Interfaith Relations in South Asia www.islaminterfaith.org/ publications.html
Shia Search Engine www.shiasearch.net	List of Shia Organizations www.shia.org/organizations.html	Ahmadiyyah: Advanced Information J.I.McGrath mb-soft.com/believe/txw/ ahmadi.htm
Oneness of God, Brotherhood of Mankind The Quran www.twf.org/Library/God.html	Infography About Food – Halal www.infography.com/ content/090346286115.html	WebCity House of Worship **Multifaith Directory** www.webcityusa.com/ worship.htm
Islam & Hinduism Similarity of the Two Divine Messages **(Multifaith Perspectives)** www.atimes.com/atimes/ Front_Page/EL25Aa02.html	Astrology and Religion Nexus **Multifaith Dimension** www.findyourfate.com/ astrology/astrology-religion.htm	Mosques Around the World Hand painted representations of fourteen mosques by Chinese artist www.uah.edu/msa/mosques.html
Multifaith - All Things Spiritual Directory www.allspiritual.com/ MultiFaith.php3	Islam A – Z: Essentials of Faith & Belief www.modernmuslims.com/ essentials.htm	Direction for Kabah (Mathematical) From Anywhere www.islamworld.net/qibla.html
Prayer Times Delivered to You, Every Time http://members.tripod.com/ salaattime/main.htm	Prayer Programs: Free Downloads (Qibla programs, Prayer Times) www.idleb.com/directory/ computers_And_Internet/ Free_Downloads/ Prayer_Programs	Available Databases for Islam and The Koran Softwares http://216.234.166.68/ islamdat.html
Hidayah Onlnne Guidance according to Quran and Sunnah Hidayahonline.org	Paths: The Way of the Soul www.snark.ca/ano2.htm	Cyber Muslima http://www.modernmuslima.com/
Muslim Cemeteries in North America www.msa-natl.org/resources/ Cemeteries.html	ISLAMIC CEMETERY (DARUL SALAAM), San Jose CA www.islamicresearch.org/Pages/ cemetry.htm	List of Muslim Cemetaries http://muttaqun.com/ cemetaries.html
Saving Graves www.savinggraves.org/links/religious/	Muslim Funeral Guide www.iio.org/janazah/bur_1299.pdf	Prediction of Prophet Muhammad in Various Other Scriptures (Taurat, Bible, Parsi, Hindu, Buddhism) www.geocities.com/islamicmiracles
Udhiyah (animal sacrfice) http://www.witness-pioneer.org/ vil/Articles/ misc/udhiyah_ritual_in_islam.htm	PrayerMinder for the Palm www.sajda.com/PilotFlavor.html	IBaat SafeWeb (Safe Internet experience, filtered Internet access provider) http://safeweb.ibaat.com/index.php

World Scripture: A Comparative Anthology of Sacred Texts - **Multifaith Resource** 4600 passages from 268 texts and 55 oral traditions www.euro-tongil.org/ws/index.html	NEW Direct SMS for Prayer http://www.bilal-prayer.com/	The First ever shia urdu newspaper site http://nawa-e-islam.com/
Project: E-ISLAM A Virtual Environment for the Dissemination of a Real Islamic Museum http://pi.ijs.si/ ProjectIntelligence.Exe?Cm= Project&Project=E-ISLAM	Muslim Literary Society Online Texts www.muslimliterarysociety.com/ texts.htm	

C. Religions-Online / Online-Religions:

a. Home Pages of Religious and Spiritual Groups (Islam continued)

Prophet Muhammad's Biography http://muhammad.com	Prophet Muhammad's Mission www.muhammad.net	Major Events in the Life of Prophet Muhammad http://cyberistan.org/ islamic/milestonesp.html
The Imam Ali Home Page - A Sunni-Shia Dialogue www.imamali.i12.com	Ahl-ul-Bait (A.S.) World Assembly - Shia www.ahl-ul-bait.org	Biography of the Last Prophet of God www.prophetmuhammed.org
The Shia http://shia.org	Institute of Ismaili Studies www.iis.ac.uk	Aga Khan Development Network www.akdn.org
Aba Saleh Welcome To Yamahdi.Com http://momineen.org	Dawoodi Bohras www.malumaat.com	Progressive Dawoodi Bohras www.dawoodi-bohras.com/ content.htm
The Promised Mehdi (Mehdi-Al-Ma'ood) www.promisedmehdi.com	Ibn Abbas Institute - Alawi organization www.ibnabbas.org	Jafria Association of North America www.jana.org
Nation of Islam http://www.noi.org	Sunnah Organization www.islaam.org	Alevi Shia www.alevi.com
Black Muslims www.muhammadspeaks.com	Ahmadiyya Muslim Community http://www.alislam.org	Lahore Ahmadiyya Movement http://aaiil.org
Deendar Movement in India http://alhafeez.org/rashid/ deendar.html	Salafi Dawah in India www.salafi.ws	Cyber Murid: Ismaili Forum www.cybermurid.com/
International Islamic Propagation Center www.the-quran.org	Al Salaf www21.brinkster.com/salafi	Back To Quran and Hadith Movement www.angelfire.com/ak4/hafiz30/
Universal Sunnah Foundation www.usf.edu.pk	Monotheist www.monotheist.org	The Canadian Society of Muslims Sunni-Hanafi http://muslim-canada.org
The Revival Of Islamic Da'wah Center www.troid.org	International Society for Islamic Secularization (ISIS) www.secularislam.org	Qura'an and Sunnah Society of North America (QSSNA) www.qss.org
Muslim Peace Fellowship www.mpfweb.org	Tolerance Foundation www.tolerancefoundation.org	Dar al Islam Building Bridges with American Community & Among the Muslims of America www.daralislam.org
Muslim Pubic Affairs Council (MPAC) www.mpac.org	United Nation of Islam www.unoi.org	Nawawi Foundation www.nawawi.org
Muslim Council of Britain (MCB) www.mcb.org.uk	Islamic Awareness Page **Multifaith Directory** www.geocities.com/ WestHollywood/Park/6443	American Muslim Alliance www.amaweb.org
Fiqh Council of North America (FCNA) www.fiqhcouncil.org	Islamic Society of North America (ISNA) www.isna.net	Islamic Assembly of North America (IANA) www.iananet.org
Muslim American Society (MAS) www.masnet.org	Council on American-Islamic Relations (CAIR) www.cair-net.org	Islamic Circle of North America (ICNA) http://icna.org
American Muslim Council (AMC) www.amconline.org	Islamic Assembly of North America (IANA) www.iananet.org	United American Muslim Association www.fatihcami.org
Islamic Foundation of North America www.islamicedfoundation.com	Institute of Objective Studies www.iosworld.org	Islam with complete freedom www.oumma.com

Muslim Students Association (MSA) www.msa-natl.org	South American and Caribbean Muslim Organizations www.latinodawah.org/ links/links2.htm	Muslim American Society (WDM) www.wdmonline.com
Hispanic Muslims, Texas http://hispanicmuslims.com	Latino American Dawah Organization, Illinois www.latinodawah.org	Muslim Women's League (MWL) www.mwlusa.org
Bism Rabbik Foundation, Florida www.bismrabbik.org	Alianza Islamica, New York www.alianzaislamica.org	Centre for Islam & Science www.cis-ca.org
Islam and Human Rights Fellowship Program www.law.emory.edu/HR	KARAMAH: Muslim Women Lawyers For Human Rights www.karamah.org	The Corporation of World Healers www.geocities.com/ reachnin/cwh
Zakat Foundation of America http://www.thezakat.org/	Institute of Islamic Studies and Centre for Study of Society and Secularism http://ecumene.org/IIS/csss.htm	Muslim Family Network www.al-usrah.net
Islamic Halal Food Monitor of Canada www.ihfmcanada.org	IFANCA (Halal) www.ifanca.org	Al-maun Islamic food bank www.geocities.com/ tajah88/index.html
International Association of Sufism www.ias.org	Sufi Web resources http://world.std.com/~habib/sufi.html	Halal Food Bank, Toronto www.muslimwelfarecentre.com
Sufis Schools – Naqshbandis www.naqshbandi.org	Other Sufis www.oneummah.net/ tasawwuf/scholars.htm	Sufi Lineage (a Naqshbandi sample) http://sufischool.w.interia.pl/ thesilsila.htm
Sufi Schools - Ni'matullahi www.nimatullahi.org/ KN.HTM	Sufis Schools – Qadiri Rifai order www.qadiri-rifai.org	Sufis Schools – Chistis www.gharibnawaz.com
Sufis Schools – Tariqa Muridiyya http://freespace.virgin.net/ ismael.essop/index.htm	Sufis Schools – Zahuri www.zahuri1.direcon.co.uk	Sufis Schools – Qadriah (Audios / Videos) Abdul Qadir Al-Gillani www.algillani.com
Turkish Sufism - Turkish Sufism www.geocities.com/ koc_bulent	More Sufi orders www.chatlink.com/ ~mushtaq/links.html	Browse Sufi Orders http://homepages.haqq.com.au/ salam/sufilinks
Initiation (Jerrahi style) www.ashkijerrahi.com/ four_steps_and_seven_levels.htm	Allegiance (Bay't) http://erfan-gonabadi.com/ Publications/Bay_at/bay_at.html	Sufi saints www.soofie.saheb.org.za/ a_few_great_saints.htm
Hafiz Shirazi Online www.hafizonlove.com	Maktab Tarighat Oveyssi Shahmaghsoudi www.mtoshahmaghsoudi.org/	Hasan al Basri www.arches.uga.edu/~godlas/ sufismearly.html#Hasan
Abdul Qadr Jeelani http://algillani.com/ saq/index.shtml	Moinuddin Hasan Chishti www.sufiajmer.org/html/ khwaja_moinuddin.html	Rabia al-Adwiya www.jamiat.org.za/ women/hdRabia.htm
The Threshold Society & Mevlevi Order www.sufism.org/	Jalaluddin Rumi www.khamush.com	Maulana Rumi Online www.rumionfire.com/
Sufi Shrines in India www.j-morris.dircon.co.uk/ shrines_index.htm	The Egyptian Society for Spiritual and Cultural Research (ESSCR) www.esscr.org	More Sufi masters www.arches.uga.edu/ ~godlas/Sufism.html
Mausoleum of Saint Hajiali http://blessed-bandwidth.net/ hajiali/hajiali.htm	Sunni Sufis www.wponline.org/ vil/Books/AG_FIB/ch4.htm	Images Of Mazar (Tombs) Of Great Muslim Saints and Heroes http://members.fortunecity.com/ mist91/dervesh/saints/ MazarImages.html
Sufism, North America http://sufiorder.toronto.ca/ links.htm	Samarkand Sufism (swedish) www.samarkand.nu	Naqshbandiya Khanqah Alipur Sayyidan: Tomb of Sayyid Jamait Ali Shah www.nfie.com/khanqah.html
Cyber Sufism www.akusufi.com	as-Sunnah Foundation http://sunnah.org	Wahdat al Wujud http://muslim-canada.org/sitedex.htm
Farid-e-Millat Research Institute Quran, Hadith, Fiqh, Fatwa. Sirat www.research.com.pk/ home/fmri/index.minhaj	Belfast Mosque http:// belfastmosque.tripod.com/ otherlinks.htm	Islamic Cemetery (for a price) www.islamicresearch.org/ Pages/cemetery.htm

Peter Lamborn Wilson – Sufi situationist www.euro.net/mark-space/ PeterLambornWilson.html	Seyyed Hossein Nasr Foundation www.nasrfoundation.org	Welcome to School of Sufi Teaching, Poland www.republika.pl/ sufism/thesite.htm
Hadith Study Association www.ihsanetwork.org/ ihsan-home1.asp?lang=e	Islamic Internet Missionaries www.geocities.com/ Athens/Agora/6088/Index2.html	Imam Khomeini's (r.a) Home Page http://203.35.96.11/ khomeini/index-english.html
The Ibn 'Arabi Society www.ibnarabisociety.org	Emam Reza (A.S) Network www.imamreza.net/old/eng	Jamia Al- Azhar – Cairo www.alazhar.org/index3.htm
Aligarh Muslim University www.ac.in	The Islamic University of Gaza, Palestine www.iugaza.edu	Islamic Online University www.bilalphilips.com/iou
Darul Uloom Deoband, India www.darululoom-deoband.com	Darul Uloom Nadwatul Ulama, India http://nadwa.virtualave.net	Al-Madeena Research Foundation International www.al-madeena.com
International Islamic University, Malaysia www.iiu.edu.my	Foundation Khadimou Rassoul North America www.toubaislam.org	International Islamic University, Islamabad www.iiu.edu.pk
International Islamic University, Chittagong, Bangladesh www.iiuc.ac.bd	Islamic University of Riau (UIR Pekanbaru), Indonesia www.uir.ac.id	Islamic Home Schooling and Arabic Resources Online www.arabesq.com
Oxford Centre For Islamic Studies www.oxcis.ac.uk/main.html	Islamic Azad Univesity, Tehran Study online www.azad.ac.ir/azad/index.asp	Maktab-e-Rasool Institute of the Holy Prophet Mohammad's Teaching www.maktab-e-rasool.org
Islamic University Madinah al-Munawarah www.iu.edu.sa/english/ index.htm	Alrasool Islamic Center, Utah www.freewebs.com/ alrasoolcenter/audiovideo.htm	Organization of Islamic conference www.oicexchange.com
International Institute for the Study of Islam in the Modern World www.isim.nl	Online Course: Basics in Islam http://home.universalclass.com/ i/crn/8740.htm	Bibliotheca Alexandrina (Digital) Library of Alexandria, Egypt www.bibalex.org/newwebsite/ English/index.aspx
International Institute of Islamic Thought (iiit) www.iiit.org	Institute of Islamic Information and Education www.iiie.net	Idara-e-Jaaferiya www.molaali.com
Islamic Art and Architecture Organization www.islamicart.com	Islamic Trading Foundation www.islamist.org	Islamic Shia Ithna-Asheri Jamaat of Toronto www.jaffari.org
Tipu Sultan Advanced Study & Research Centre, India Darul Umoor http://darulumoor.ibc.co.in/ home1.html	Ask Buddha http://www.askbuddha.org/	Ask the Dalai Lama http://www.askthedalailama.com/

1.7 Mapping Jainism Webwise

A. Online Cyber Worship

a. Prayer (Prarthana, Puja, Seva):

Cyber Darshan www.jaindarshan.com	On-line Aarti of Bhagwan Mahavir www.webdunia.com	Jainism Simplified www.umich.edu/~umjains/ jainismsimplified/ jainsimp.html
Virtual non-violence www.wizard.net/ ~ethan/ahimsa.net	Yogeesh Ashram www.geocities.com/ Athens/3861	Jina and the Soul www.ops.org/scrtec/ india/jainism.html
Meditation and Yoga www.jainnet.com	Meditation in Scriptures www.terapanth.com/ impressions/ medit-script.htm	Jain Tirth Yatra Jain pilgrim places, India www.jaintirth.org
Voice A Vision • Post A Prayer Dare A Dream **Multifaith Voices** www.heartpath.com/ hpcontent/voiceAvision.asp	Ancient Wisdom: Submit a Prayer **Multifaith Concerns** www.awisdom.com/ community/submit_prayer	Prayer Book Meditations, Adorations, Celebrations, Invocations **Multifaith Prayers** Multicultural Prayers www.prayforpeace.com/index.php

World Prayers – Prayer Collective **Multifaith Practices** www.worldpyaers.org	Mangalayatan Jain pilgrimage center, UP, India www.mangalayatan.org	Shri Mahavir Jain Aradhana Kendra - Koba Pilgrim place of Lord Mahavir http://kobatirth.org

b. Praise (Stuti): (Jainism continued)

Jain Bhakti's, Puja's, Stuti's etc. www.atmadharma.com/ bhakti/bhakti.html	Inspirational Presentations www.jaina.org/ educationcommittee/ education_material	Religious Songs www.bhaktisangeet.com

c. Scripture (Shastra): (Jainism continued)

Search Scriptures www.angelfire.com/co/atmajyoti	Read a Scripture www.angelfire.com/co/atmajyoti	Audio Lectures www.atmadharma.com/ Audio/index.html
A Treatise on Jainism www.sacred-texts.com/jai/treatise.txt	Ten Virtues Of Monks www.sacred-texts.com/jai/10virtue.txt	Twelve Reflections or Bhavnas www.sacred-texts.com/jai/12bhavna.txt
Five Bodies and Eight Vargnas www.sacred-texts.com/jai/5bodies.txt	Fourteen Auspicious Dreams www.sacred-texts.com/ jai/14dreams.txt	Twelve Vows Of Layperson www.sacred-texts.com/ jai/12vows.txt
Meaning Of Ashta Prakari Puja www.sacred-texts.com/jai/8puja.txt	Nine Tattvas (Principles) www.sacred-texts.com/jai/9tatvas.txt	Atma Siddhi Shastra www.atmadharma.com/ external/atmsidhi.html
Six Universal Substances (Dravyas) www.sacred-texts.com/ jai/6substns.txt	Five Great Vows (Maha-vratas) www.sacred-texts.com/jai/5vows.txt	Akaranga Sutra www.sacred-texts.com/jai/akaranga.htm
Jainism in English & Gujarati www.geocities.com/haren_shah	Original Jain Literature translated www.atmadharma.com	Kalpa Sutra www.sacred-texts.com/jai/kalpa.htm

d Sacrament (Prashad): (Jainism continued)

Jain Temples, U.S. www.adherents.com/ largecom/templjain_statesUS.html	Donate a Shastra www.atmadharma.com/ donate/index.html	Browse the list of Temples www. Mandirnet.org/temple_list.html

B. Offline Cyber Worship

a. Know-How, Process, Procedures, Activity, Functions, Methods... / Products, Resources, Materials...: (Jainism continued)

Free Downloads inc. music! www.atmadharma.com/ downloads/downloads.html	"Pradaksina" ritual to walk around www.bergerfoundation.ch/ Home/pelerins.html	Download a Song www.jainworld.com
Q&A on Jainism www.jaina.org/ educationcommittee/education_material	Jainism Basics www.jaina.org/ educationcommittee/education_material	Jain Rituals and Holidays www.jaina.org/ educationcommittee/education_material
FAQ's About Jainism www.yja.org/faq.html	Principles of Jainism www.jaingyanprasar.com	Ahimsa - Nonviolence www.jaina.org/ educationcommittee/education_material
Jain Astrology www.jain-astrology.com	Search Jainism www.cs.colostate.edu/~malaiya/ jainhlinks.html	Life of Tirthankars www.jaina.org/ educationcommittee/education_material
Jain Institutions www.jaina.org/ educationcommittee/education_material	Jain Symbols www.jaina.org/ educationcommittee/education_material	Pictures of Mahavir Life www.jaina.org/ educationcommittee/education_material

Pictures-Sadhu Sadhvis www.jaina.org/ educationcommittee/education_material	Yantras of Bhaktambar Stotra www.jaina.org/ educationcommittee/education_material	Dreams of Trishala -Video files AVI www.jaina.org/ educationcommittee/education_material
Jain Festivals www.cs.colostate.edu/ ~malaiya/calendar.html	Jain portal http://terapanthsurat.com/jainlink.asp	Jain rituals Burial practices www.indiaritual.com/jain/j12.htm
Virtual Heritage Documented www.jainheritage.com	Jain Heritage Centres: A Historical Jain Portal www.jainheritagecentres.com	Terapanth Surat Jainism / Spirituality Gateway www.terapanthsurat.com/JainLink.asp
Jain Shala www.jainshala.com	Essence of Jainism - Original Jain Literature and Jain Logic www.atmadharma.com/ JAINHOME.html	Jain resource www.usao.edu/ ~usao.ids3313/ids/html/Jainism.html
Dietary code of practice amongst Jains (WVC 2000) www.ivu.org/congress/ 2000/jainism.html	Vegetarian food and Jain Conduct www.atmadharma.com/ vfjc/vfjcttl1.html	The Temples of Orissa Jainism http://ignca.nic.in/orist015.htm
List of Jain Books Open / downloads www.jainworld.com/ jainbooks/bookslist.htm	Jain Study Circle www.jainstudy.org	Jainism Potpourri www.kamat.com/ kalranga/jain/index.htm
Glossary of Religious Terms www.religioustolerance.org/ glossary.htm	JAINA Proposed Curriculum For Pathshala www.jaina.org/ educationcommittee/education_material	Jainism on the Internet www.jaina.org/ educationcommittee/education_material/
Glossary of Jain Religion Words www.terapanth.com/glossary_jaina.htm	Websites for Indian Terapanth www.terapanth.com/fabody.htm	Glossary of Sanskrit Terms www.hindunet.org/glossary
Glossary Religious Holidays www.pgcares.com/ interfaith_glossary.html	WebCity House of Worship **Multifaith Directory** www.webcityusa.com/ worship.htm	**Multifaith** - All Things Spiritual Directory www.allspiritual.com/MultiFaith.php3
World Scripture: A Comparative Anthology of Sacred Texts - **Multifaith Resource** 4600 passages from 268 texts and 55 oral traditions www.euro-tongil.org/ws/index.html		

C. Religions-Online / Online-Religions:

a. Home Pages of Religious and Spiritual Groups (Jainism continued)

Atmavallabh www.atmavallabh.com	Atmasiddhi www.atmasiddhi.com	Ahimsa www.ahimsa.com
Atma Dharma www.atmadharma.com	Jain Samaj http://jainsamaj.org	Jain Religion www.jaindharam.org
Digambar Jains www.digambarjain.com	Digamber Jain Site www.jinvani.com	Kushi's Kitchen http://vegsource.com/ vegcentral/links-cgi/jump.cgi?ID=772
Vegetarian Central http://vegsource.com/vegcentral/links	Vegetarian Society of Botswana www.ivu.org/vsb	International Vegetarian Union (IVU) www.ivu.org
Oswals - Origin and Development www.oswals.net	Jain International University Online University www.jainu.org	International Alumni Association of Shri Mahavir Jain Vidyalaya www.iaamjv.org/html/default.asp
International Mahavir Jain Mission, Blairstown, NJ www.imjm.org	Tamil Jain Page http://geocities.com/ athens/Crete/9810/index.html	Tamil Jains www.geocities.com/tamiljain
Jains www.jaina.org	Yogeesh Foundation International International Society for Human Unity www.geocities.com/Athens/3861	Jain Home page www.jain.ws
Jain Center of Northern California www.jcnc.org	Jain Center Of Greater Boston www.jcgb.org	Oshwal Jains in Canada www.oshwalscanada.org
Young Jains of America www.yja.org	Jains, Houston www.jain-houston.org	Jains in Germany www.jain-germany.de

Vision of a faithful:

> Jain Centers or Temples should all have a web site. Such a web site extends the reach of beyond the confines of the temple. All such sites should have some interactive components. They must be backed by volunteers who will answer questions, encourage people to visit or conduct guided tours if needed.
>
> Malaiya Yashvant. "Jainism on Internet." January 02, 2003
> http://www.jaina.org/educationcommittee/education_material/

1.8 Mapping Judaism Webwise

A. Online Cyber Worship

a. Prayer (Tefilah, rites, etc:):

> "Please God, help me cleanse the computer of viruses and evil photographs which disturb and ruin my work ... so that I shall be able to cleanse myself (of sin),
>
> ShlmoEliahu, Chif Rabbi, Safed, Israel.
> www.gnatoll.com/modules/news/article.php?storyid=127

Cyber Synagogue www.wnrf.org/ cms/cyberor.shtml	Temple Beth Tikvah online www.templebethtikvah.com/ sermon_september2002-3.shtml	'Place a Note in the Wall' See the Wall Camera www.aish.com or dial 1-800-505-PRAY
Click-Me Tour of the Synagogue http://scheinerman.net/ judaism/synagogue/ tour/index.html	THE SYNAGOGUE (illustrated) http://scheinerman.net/ judaism/synagogue/ synagogue.html	Voice A Vision • Post A Prayer Dare A Dream **Multifaith Voices** www.heartpath.com/ hpcontent/voiceAvision.asp
Prayers for peace - Jewish, Christian and Muslim **Multifaith Platform** salmanspiritual.com/ peace_prayers.html	Ancient Wisdom: Submit a Prayer **Multifaith Concerns** www.awisdom.com/ community/submit_prayer	Prayer Book Meditations, Adorations, Celebrations, Invocations **Multifaith Prayers** Multicultural Prayers www.prayforpeace.com/index.php
Cyber Seder www.emanuelnyc.org/ seder/seder.html	Sabbath Eve Broadcasts Temple B'nai Jeshurun www.tbj.org/broadcst.html	Worship Services Temple B'nai Jeshurun www.tbj.org/worship.html
Congregation Kadimah-Toras Moshe, Massachusets Ktm.shuls.net	Full Synagogue Web Cam tour www.hitchams.suffolk.sch.uk synagogue/full.htm	World's First Mobile Siddur www.jewish-wap.com
Prayers Online www.hamerkaz.com.au/ religion/prayref.asp	Blessings & Prayers www.thinkjewish.com/ walk.html	AskMoses - Live! http://moses1.askmoses.com/ search.html?new=1
Daily Thought: A Great Way to Start your Day www.chabad.org	Rabbi Bookman's Spiritual Workout www.betham-miami.org/ workout/	Chanukah Tunes from Torah Tots www.torahtots.com/holidays/ chanuka/maoztzur.htm
Haggadah audio www.cyber-kitchen.com/ holidays/passover/haggadot.htm	Jewish Music www.shamash.org/judaica/ rebshlomo/audio/index.html	Kaddish - prayer for the dead www.ou.org/yerushalayim/ kadish.htm

Liturgy (for concert) www.cduniverse.com/ productinfo.asp?pid=1173503&cart =164455617&style=music	Dot it yourself ''Cyber Minyan – A Rabbi's Spiritual Workout www.tbam.org/workout	Shabbat Candles www.uahcweb.org/ny/ tinw/ReligiousLiving/ ReligiousObjects/Shabbat.htm
The Mezuzah www.uahcweb.org/ny/tinw/ ReligiousLiving/ ReligiousObjects/Mezuzah.htm	The Shofar www.uahcweb.org/ny/ tinw/ReligiousLiving/ReligiousObjects/Shofar.htm	Shabbat Candle Lighting Times www.chabad.org/ calendar/candlelighting.asp
The Tallit www.uahcweb.org/ny/ tinw/ReligiousLiving/ReligiousObjects /Tallit.htm	Havdalah - Ritual and Objects www.uahcweb.org/ny/ tinw/ReligiousLiving/ ReligiousObjects/HavdalahRO.htm	Lulav and Etrog www.uahcweb.org/ny/ tinw/ReligiousLiving/ ReligiousObjects/LulavEtrog.htm
Chanukah Menorah www.uahcweb.org/ny/ tinw/ReligiousLiving/ ReligiousObjects/Menorah.htm	Kippah www.uahcweb.org/ny/ tinw/ReligiousLiving/ ReligiousObjects/Kippah.htm	Sukkah www.uahcweb.org/ny/ tinw/ReligiousLiving/ ReligiousObjects/Sukkah.htm
Tefillin www.uahcweb.org/ny/ tinw/ReligiousLiving/ ReligiousObjects/Tefillin.htm	Seder Plate www.uahcweb.org/congs/ny/ ny054/ReligiousLiving/ ReligiousObjects/SederPlate.htm	Menzuzah or Mezuzot Ritual guide for dedicating a Jewish Home www.rebgoldie.com/ Mezuzah%20hanging%20ritual.htm
World Prayers – Prayer Collective **Multifaith Practices** www.worldpyaers.org		

b. Praise: (Judaism continued)

Shabbat sounds and prayers (grace after meals) www.613.org/shabbat.html	Chanukkah Candle Lighting Blessings www.hamerkaz.com.au/ religion/prayer/chanukah.asp	Havdalah Home Ritual www.hamerkaz.com.au/ religion/prayer/havdalah.asp
Kaddish, Mourner's www.hamerkaz.com.au/ religion/prayer/kaddish.asp	Mezuzah, Affixing www.hamerkaz.com.au/ religion/prayer/mezuzah.asp	Shabbat Evening Home Ritual www.hamerkaz.com.au/ religion/prayer/shabbat.asp
Shema www.hamerkaz.com.au/ religion/prayer/shema.asp	Sukkot Blessing www.hamerkaz.com.au/ religion/prayer/sukkot.asp	Shabbat sounds and prayers (grace after meals) www.613.org/shabbat.html
The Transliterated Siddur http://members.aol.com/ jordanleew/siddur/	Praise resource www.tehillah.org	Shabbat Resouce www.yehud.com/Holidays/Shabbat/
Candle Lighting Times http://www.ou.org/ zmanim/Zmanim/ Candlelighting/default.htm	Candlelighting Times www.aish.com/candlelighting	Hebrew Words for Praise www.cyberworship. freeservers.co.uk/ hebrewpraise.htm

c. Scripture (Hebrew Bible, Midras,): (Judaism continued)

The Zohar - The Most Powerful Spiritual Tool www.kabbalah.com/k/ index.php/p=zohar/about	Purim story (Audio) http://holidays.net/ purim/reaudio.htm	Purim story (Slides) www.tzivos-hashem.org/ yomtov/purim/slideshow/ prmslshw.html
Torah www.uahcweb.org/ny/ tinw/ReligiousLiving/ ReligiousObjects/Torah.htm	Torah Reading www.613.org/dolgin.html	Divrei Torah www.shamash.org/tanach/dvar.html
Virtual Torah www.virtualjerusalem.com/ Torah/index.htm	Turn the pages of Scripture The Golden Haggadah www.bl.uk/collections/ treasures/treasures.html	Read Torah On Line www.torah.org
Torah - The Family Parsha http://aish.com/a/familyparsha/current.asp	High Holidays Messages ... www.usawebs.net/benyehuda/holidays.htm	

d. Sacrament: (Judaism continued)

Jewish Community Center of West Hempstead "Congregants only" online schedule www.myshul.com/pages/ congregants/congregants.asp	The faceted stained glass symbolizes G-d, the Torah and 12 Tribes www.myshul.com/pages/ ourwindow/window.htm	Synagogue Search www.maven.co.il/synagogues.asp
Online Memorial Service (Yizkor/ritual) http://yizkor.ort.org/ html/synagogserv.shtml		

B. Offline Cyber Worship

a. Know-How, Process, Procedures, Activity, Functions, Materials...: (Judaism continued)

Glossary of Hebrew Terms http://scheinerman.net/ judaism/synagogue/ glossary.html	Official Judaism Glossary http://uwacadweb.uwyo.edu/ religionet/er/Judaism/ JGLOSSARY.HTM	Glossary Religious Holidays www.pgcares.com/ interfaith_glossary.html
Glossary of Religious Terms www.religioustolerance.org/glossary.htm	Ask Jewish America www.jewishamerica.com/askus.htm	Ask / Read Answerline www.torah.org
Questions www.RabbiUSA.com	Learn About this Week's Parshah www.chabad.org/parshah/default.asp	Key Jewish FAQs www.chabad.org/library/ article.asp?AID=108385
Ask a Rabbi www.askarabbi.com	Ask Rabbi Anything www.hillel.org/hillel/Forums.nsf/ RabbiCyberstein	Ask The Rabbi www.chabad.org/tools/asktherabbi.asp
Answer the Rabbi! Question on the weekly sedra www.yakar.demon.co.uk/ psgate.htm	Sophia's Wisdom- Ask Madame Zohar www.sophiaswisdom.com/ ask_zohar.shtml	Go Ask A Rabbi http://jewish.com/ modules.php?name=askarabbi
Select a Rabbi / Expert www.jewish.net/links/ Ask_an_Expert/Ask_a_Rabbi/index.shtml	Bais Medrash Questions www.torah.org/qanda/answerline.php3	Ask Rabbi Questions www.torah.org/qanda/answerline.php3
Questions www.RabbiUSA.com	Ask Rabbi Anything www.hillel.org/hillel/Forums.nsf/ RabbiCyberstein	Universal Calendar Calculator: Hebrew www.cf-software.com/other.html
Judaism philo.ucdavis.edu/ Courses/RST23/ rst23homepage.html	Calendar of Jewish Holidays http://bnaibrith.org/caln.html	Hebrew Calendar www.hareshima.com/ CALENDAR/HebrewCalendar.asp
Today's Calendar and Clock Page: Jewish www.ecben.net/calendar.shtml	Calendrical Bookmarks Hebrew (Lunisolar) http://emr.cs.it.edu/home.reingold/ calendar-book/calendar-links.shtml	Holidays and Observances: The Books of the TaNaKh www.uahcweb.org/congs/ ny/ny054/ReligiousLiving/index.htm
Online Worship is Kosher (Article) www.augustachronicle.com/ stories/120796/jewish.html	Reform Orthodox Judaism, Compared www.pps.k12.or.us/ schools-c/pages/westsylvan/ student/religion/judaism_am/venn.htm	Orthodox Judaism http://judaism.about.com/library/ 3_intro/level1/bl_denom_ortho.htm
Virtual Synagogue Being Planned (Article) www.cjnews.com/ pastissues/01/jan25-01/front5.asp	End of Life Decisions Reform Judaism www.elderweb.com/ default.php?PageID=839	Orthodox Judaism End of Life Decisions www.jlaw.com/forms
Jewish Funerals www.jewish-funerals.org	End of Life Decisions Conservative Judaism www.elderweb.com/default.php?PageID=839	Judaism and death http://dying.miningco.com/ cs/judaismdeath
Clothes and Appearances Jewish Dress Demo Making Tsitsit www.rigal.freeserve.co.uk/ jewish/clothing/clothing.htm	Equipping you to Spiritually Survive www.survivalmanual.com	Are you ready for Y6K? www.innernet.org.il/archives/y6k.htm

b. Products, Resources, Materials…: (Judaism continued)

Full-service Jewish ISP www.realolam.com	Get Connected to the Jewish World with Yehoodee's Internet Service www.yehoodee.com/ISP~net.html	Jewish Internet Access www.thejnet.com
Develop database-driven Web sites www.shuls.net	CD-ROMS (DBS) Bible, Talmud, Jewish Thought http://faculty.biu.ac.il/~barilm/dbs2e.html	Free Downloads www.hamerkaz.com.au/free.asp
About WorshipWare http://members.tripod.com/~MummaD/About.html	Tools for Online Synagogue Management http://shamash.org/links/Computers/more2.shtml	Donate www.chabad.org/tools/donate/
Locate a synagogue, Select: Type, Style, Affiliation www.synagogues.com	**Multifaith Directory** www.yehud.com/cgi-bin/odp/yehudodp.pl?passurl=/Society/Religion	Jewish Subject Gateway www.maven.co.il/subjects.asp?S=117
Jewish resources center www.allthingsjewish.com	Directory of Messianic sites www.messianic.com	Jewish Studies Internet Directory jewishstudies.virtualave.net/index.shtml
Pesach Passover directory www.maven.co.il/subjects.asp?S=125	Directory of Jewish resources http://jewish.com	Directory, information & services www.yehud.com
Rosh Hashana Directory www.maven.co.il/subjects.asp?S=122	Yom Kippur Directory **www.maven.co.il**/subjects.asp?S=123	Portal directory to the Jewish world www.maven.co.il
Portal to the Jewish World www.jewishdirectory.com	Judaism 101 www.hamerkaz.com.au/religion/toc.htm	Jewish portal supersite www.zipple.com
The Jewish Internet Portal www.hareshima.com	Hebrew With Speech English Hebrew Talking Touch-Screen Dictionary www.shofarjudaica.com/e780t.html	Byado Kippot www.byadokippot.com
Kosher Mezuzahs Parchment Scrolls www.jewishcenter.co.il	Menorah and Hanukkah wall hangings www.arearugsforyou.com/Hanukkah_Collection.htm	Offering sterling silver atoras (neckbands) for talis. www.atoros.com
Tallit Handmade talitot made in accordance with Talmudic and Rabbinical law www.tallithandmade.com	Jewish Weaving www.jewishweaving.com	Ritual wear www.linda.salvay.com
Kosher-certified t-shirt style tzitzit www.neatzit.com	Women's shabbos robes www.larobes.com	Israel Tallit Store www.tallit.biz
Finders Kippahs http://finderskippahs.ca	Hats by Susan For Orthodox Jewish women www.hatsbysusan.com	Headcoverings by Devorah women's kippot, headscarves, and snoods. http://headcoverings-by-devorah.com/home.html
Egokippot Yarmulkes www.egokippot.com	Selling do-it-yourself kippah-beading kits www.geocities.com/beadakippah/beadakippah.html	Beith David An internet Torah learning center http://beithdavid.org
A Partners in Torah TOTALLY FREE. Click or call 800-STUDY-4-2 www.study42.org	Jewish Learning on IRC www.geocities.com/~alyza/Jwish.htm	Learning www.torah-bits.org/html/learning.html
ALEF - The Open Academy for Jewish Learning www.vbm-torah.org/alef.htm	Religious Living Online www.uahcweb.org/congs/ny/ny054/ReligiousLiving/index.htm	WebCity House of Worship **Multifaith Directory** www.webcityusa.com/worship.htm
Websites for Church & Synagogue Libraries www.vchstrojans.org/Seminar-LibrariansWebsotes.pd	Jewish Lessons for the Palm Pilot www.jewishcontent.org/pda/palm	Pocket P C Applications www.jewishcontent.org/pda/pocket-pc
Kabbalah Links www.geocities.com/koulourakia_girl/links.htm	**Multifaith** - All Things Spiritual Directory www.allspiritual.com/MultiFaith.php3	Saving Graves www.savinggraves.org/links/religious/
Tools for Prophets in the Information Age http://ac.marywood.edu/skb/prophets/resource2.html	From Judaism to Christianity: Worship & Customs A Comparison of Two Religions http://library.thinkquest.org/C004351F/Worship.htm	World Scripture: A Comparative Anthology of Sacred Texts - **Multifaith Resource** 4600 passages from 268 texts and 55 oral traditions www.euro-tongil.org/ws/index.html

C. Religions-Online / Online-Religions:

a. Home Pages of Religious and Spiritual Groups (Judaism continued)

Kosher Home www.kosher.com	HealthCare Chaplaincy Jewish Institute Kallah www.healthcarechaplaincy/educatio n_03_01.html	Masorti Foundation www.masorti.com
Congregations Movements www.hareshima.com/ Congregations/movements.asp	Congregations Orthodox www.hareshima.com/ Congregations/orthodox.asp	Congregations Conservative www.hareshima.com/ Congregations/conservative.asp
Congregations Reform www.hareshima.com/ Congregations/reform.asp	Congregations Reconstructionist www.hareshima.com/ Congregations/reconstructionist.asp	Congregation of Jews and Gentiles www.bnaichayim.com/ welcome.html
Messianic Congregations www.bnaichayim.com/links.html	The Union for Reform Judaism The synagogue arm of the Reform Movement http://www.urj.org	Reform Judaism http://rj.org
Union For Reform Judaism http://uahc.org/	Orthodox Union www.ou.org	Society for the Advancement of Judaism www.thesaj.org
United Synagogue of Conservative Judaism http://uscj.org	Association of Conservative rabbis www.rabassembly.org	Conservative Juaism www.jewish.net/links/ Synagogues_and_Movements/ Conservative/index.shtml
MBIC - Ministers Credentialing www. messianicbureau.org/mbima	AishDas Society Committed to providing meaning and emotion in Jewish practice. http://aishdas.org	ALEF - The Open Academy for Jewish Learning - Online www.vbm-torah.org/ alef.htm
Baal Shem Tov www.baalshemtov.com	ATID, the Academy for Torah Initiatives and Direction www.atidfellows.org	Akhlah: The Jewish Children's Learning Network www.akhlah.com
Bat Ayin Learning Institutions www.batayin.org	Beit Israel www.beitisrael.4t.com	Bet Modzitz http://modzitz.org
Not In My Name www.nimn.org	BiTS - Spreading the Wellsprings of Chassidus and Kabbalah www.torah-bits.org	Temple Israel of Northern Westchester, NY www.uahcweb.org/ congs/ny/ny054/
Ask a Rabbi - LiveChat live with a Rabbi or Chabad representatives online www.askMoses.com	Jewish Theological Seminary www.jtsa.edu	Congregation Yeshuat Yisrael A Messianic Jewish Congregation www.yeshuatyisrael.com/Services.htm
	Queen's Jewish Centre Qic.shuls.net	

1.9 Mapping Sikhism Webwise

A. Online Cyber Worship

a. Prayer (Ardas):

Cyber Gurudwara www.gurudwara.net	Cyber Darshan www.sikhpoint.com/cybergurudwara/	Sri Dashmesh Darbar http://blessed-bandwidth.net/ sridashmeshdarbar/ sridashmeshdarbar.htm
Sri Dashmesh Darbar, Mumbai www.blessed-bandwidth.net/ sridashmeshdarbar/ sridashmeshdarbar.htm	Audio Prayers www.sikhs.org/audio.htm	Daily Hukamnama www.sikhs.org/ hukam_listen.htm
On-Line Gurdwara Devotional Menu www.bedfordgurdwara.org.uk/ centre/gurdw.htm	RealAudio Discourses Beloved Satguru Guru Gobind Singh Sahib www.baisakhi1999.org/audio.htm	enter the Gurudwara www.saysatsriakal.com/index2.htm
Daily hukamnama www.sikhpoint.com	FAQs on Sikhism www.allaboutsikhs.com/ mansukh/index.htm	The Sikh-Faith Question Answer And Philosophy http://members.pgonline.com/ ~mpurewal/
Prayer Book Meditations, Adorations, Celebrations, Invocations **Multifaith Prayers** Multicultural Prayers www.prayforpeace.com/index.php	Ancient Wisdom: Submit a Prayer **Multifaith Concerns** www.awisdom.com/ community/submit_prayer	Voice A Vision • Post A Prayer Dare A Dream **Multifaith Voices** www.heartpath.com/ hpcontent/voiceAvision.asp

Yoga www.kundaliniyoga.com	Yogi Bhajan (Lectures) www.sikhnet.com/Articles	Yoga www.3ho.org/clients/kiit/gt/ Yoga.nsf/by+Name?OpenView
Learn Gurmukhi www.goldentemple.faithweb.com/ custom4.html	Most Sacred Sikh Shrines www.sikhs.org/gurdwara.htm	Browse the list of Temples www. Mandirnet.org/temple_list.html
Virtual Tour of the Golden Temple Complex www.sikhs.org/golden	Gurudwaras in USA http://gurudwara.faithweb.com/ GuruKirpa.html	Sikh Cyber Museum www.sikhcybermuseum.org
Sikh Temples Gurdwaras Worldwide in Pictures www.geocities.com/gurdwaraworld/ gurd1.html	World Prayers – Prayer Collective **Multifaith Practices** www.worldpyaers.org	Sikh-Seek Sikhism Web Guide www.sikhseek.com

b. Praise (Salah / Sift): (Sikkhism continued)

Gurbani audio clips www.sikhnet.com	Rosary of Divine Wisdom www.srigurugranthsahib.org/ rosary/index.htm	Melodius Gurbani Kirtan www.sikhvideos.org/?for=vid

c. Scripture (Bani): (Sikkhism continued)

Sikh Texts www.sikhs.org/ transl.htm	The Sikh Religion www.sacred-texts.com/ skh/tsr1/index.htm	Gurbani Search www.allaboutsikhs.com/ sggs/gursearch.htm
Gurumukhi Pronunciation guide www.sikhs.org/topics4b.htm	Daily Hukamnama www.sikhnet.com	Sikh Videos Gurbani Kirtan www.sikhvideos.org
Shri Guru Granth Sahib www.sacred-texts.com/ skh/granth/index.htm	Kirtan www.gurbani.org/kirtan.htm www.sikhs.org/english/frame.html	Sri Guru Granth Sahib [the Living Lord, the Eternal Guru] www.baisakhi1999.org/ srigurugranthsahib.htm

d. Sacrements (Prasad): (Sikkhism continued)

Sikh Seek www.sikhseek.com/ Gurdwaras/General/more2.htm	Search a Gurudwara www.gurudwara.net/ gurudwara/home.asp	Browse the list Gurdwaralist www.geocities.com/ gurdwaraworld/gurdwaralist.html
Gurudwara Central Jersey Sikh Association www.gurudwara-cjsa.org	Guru Gobind Singh Gurdwara, UK www.gobind-singh.org.uk	Sikh - picture gallery www.geocities.com/ Athens/Cyprus/8104/index.html
Gurbani Archive www.sikhnet.com/Gurbani	Photos of Ten Gurus www.goldentemple.faithweb.com/photo3.html	Religious Emblems www.sikhs.org/khanda.htm
Golden Temple – image www.goldentemple.faithweb.com		

B. Offline Cyber Worship:

a. **Know-How, Process, Procedures, Activity, Functions, Methods… / Products, Resources, Materials…: (Sikkhism continued)**

Submit questions - Gateway to Sikhism mailto:sewadar@allaboutsikhs.com	Ask Me a Question http://religion.lifetips.com/ Cat.asp_Q_id_E_57411	ASK SEEK KNOCK www.nijjhar.freeserve.co.uk/sikhism.htm
Ask A Question www.allexperts.com/ postQuestion.asp? Expert=39390&Category=949	Sikhism: Questions & Answers www.sikhcoalition.org/SikhismQA.asp	Ask questions : Sikhism www.allspiritual.com/cgi-bin/ Ultimate.cgi?action=intro
Virtual Sikhism Religious Cards www.greetsomeone.com/ cards/religion/sikhism/index1.shtml	Sikh Faith Question, Answer, and Philosophy http://members.pgonline.com/~mpurewal/	Find an Expert www.allexperts.com/ getExpert.asp?Category=949
Sikhism Resources on the Internet - 1 www.hinduwebsite.com/ sikhism/sikhlinks.htm	Find a Scholar Gianis Listing in UK www.bookagiani.com/Gianis_list.asp	Glossary of Religious Terms www.religioustolerance.org/ glossary.htm

Glossary of Religious Terms www.sikhs.org/glossary.htm	Glossary Religious Holidays www.pgcares.com/ interfaith_glossary.html	Sikh Calendar Gurupurbs www.sikhs.org/dates.htm
Sikhism Resources on the Internet - 2 www.hinduwebsite.com/ sikhism/sikhlinks2.htm	Sikh Primer (Beliefs and fundamentals) www.sikhs.org	Basic concepts of Sikhism www.hinduwebsite.com/ sikhism/glossary.htm
Rehat Maryada Sikh Links www.gurmat.com/sikh_links.html	Sikh Calendars www.gurbani.com/link-it/ default.asp?catid=8&cattitle=Sikh+Calendars	Vaisakhi www.clickwalla.com/ index.php?cid=114
Hindu-Sikh Relationship www.hindunet.org/alt_hindu/ 1994/msg00068.html	Famous Sikhs http://allaboutsikhs.com/person/	Sikh Studies Chairs www.sikhfoundation.org/ newsletter0703.asp
Abstracts of Sikh Studies www.sikhstudies.org/ SchRstVol.asp?VolCod=4	Do We Know Latest World Religious Guru- Sikh Canon's Doctrine? http://allaboutsikhs.com/ articles/art-053.htm	WebCity House of Worship **Multifaith Directory** www.webcityusa.com/ worship.htm
PRAYER It's Nature and Technique www.ruhanisatsangusa.org/ pray/pray_title.htm	sikhims portal www.allspiritual.com/Sikhism.php3	Download Images www.sikhs.org/other.htm
Become our Religion Guru at LifeTips.com http://religion.lifetips.com/ Cat.asp_Q_id_E_57411	Anand Karaj – A Union of Two Souls Sikh Wedding www.sikhs.org/wedding	**MultiFaith** - All Things Spiritual Directory www.allspiritual.com/MultiFaith.php3
Sikh Kids Learning to Tie Turbans at Gurdwara Sahib http://community.webshots.com/album/ 49623914NrtjTi	Download Banis for PDA www.sikhnet.com/s/BanisOnPDA	World Scripture: A Comparative Anthology of Sacred Texts - **Multifaith Resource** 4600 passages from 268 texts and 55 oral traditions www.euro-tongil.org/ws/index.html

C. Religions-Online / Online-Religions:

Home Pages of Faith / Spiritual Groups (Sikkhism continued)

Sikhism Homepage Ten Gurus www.hinduwebsite.com/ Sikhism/sikhindex.htm	San Jose Gurudwara www.sjgurdwara.org/	German Sikh Site www.sikh-religion.de
Khalistan Movement www.burningpunjab.com	Siri Singh Sahib www.yogibhajan.com	Sant Nirankari Mission www.nirankari.com
Sikh Media Action www.sikhmedia.org/ main.html	Khalsa Page www.worldkhalsa.com	Sikh Sabha, New Jersey www.sikhsabha.org
Unity of Man Sant Kirpal Singh **Multifaith Perspective** www.unity-of-man.org	West Coast Sikh Youth Alliance www.wcsya.org	3HO International Kundalini Yoga Teachers Association www.kundaliniyoga.com
3HO Healthy-Happy-Holy Organization (California) www.3ho.org	Sikhism Information - FUNDRAISER 2003 www.sikhnet.com/	Sikh Cyber Museum www.sikhcybermuseum.org/ People/Macauliffe.htm

1.10 Mapping Spirituality Webwise

A. Online Cyber Worship

a. Prayer, Praise, Scripture, Sacrament

Asylum on Web Cam www.asylumcam.com/allcams.htm	Prayer & Mourning www.modernpaths.com/r/m/prayer	Tangible Bridge between Heaven and Earth www.antahkaranah.com
Prayers & Reflections www.modernpaths.com/library/prayer	Prayer4Peace.net A nonsectarian project to accumulate one billion Vajrasattva mantra www.prayer4peace.net	The Prayer Room www.celestinevision.com/ prayerroom/gb.php
Free Online Inspiration Ananda Mission www.ananda.org/inspiration/index.html	Spirit Prayers Prayer Book http://spiritnetwork.com/indexprayer.html	Spiritual webcams www.integrativespirituality.org/ Spiritual_Webcams.htm

God-U-Like www.godulike.co.uk	Belief System Selector www.selectsmart.com/ RELIGION	Kabir online **Multifaith mystic of India** www.kabirweb.com
Spirituality @ Sounds True Listen Before You Buy www.soundstrue.com	Cosmic Cathedral The Cradle of your Heart www.ananda.org/inspiration/magazine/ yogananda/christmas1.html	Listen to Meditation www.vipassana.com/ audio_files/index.php
Cyber Shrine Japanese / English www.kiku.com/electric_samurai/ cyber_shrine	Heart Lights Ministry Online Spiritual Counseling www.heartlights.org	My Questions of Faith www.modernpaths.com/ r/i/questions
Spiritual Healing www.circlesanctuary.org/ healing/healing.html	Submitting a Healing Request www.circlesanctuary.org/ healing/spiritualhealing.htm	Selena Fox Telephone Consultations www.circlesanctuary.org/ healing/consult.htm
Mystic Fire Video www.mysticfire.com	Rational Mystic Sanctuary (reclaiming one's own lived experience) http://home.earthlink.net/ ~rationalmystic/door.htm	Circle of Light SoulMate Love, Opening the Hearts of Humanity www.circleoflight.net
Javanese Mysticism (Subud in particular, Translations of texts) www.xs4all.nl/~wichm/javmys1.html	GodConsciousness.com Mystical texts from around the world http://www.godconsciousness.com	Sacred Texts by Jane Hope www.modernpaths.com/library/ sacred/articles/ f_lib_article_sec_sacredtext.html
Sant Morari Bapu www.hinduwebsite.com/masters.htm	Sri Sathya Saibaba www.hinduwebsite.com/masters.htm	Sant Dariya Saheb www.hinduwebsite.com/masters.htm
Spirit Journeys www.spirituallightjourneys.com/	World Prayers – Prayer Collective **Multifaith Practices** www.worldpyaers.org	World Wide Online Meditation Center www.meditationcenter.com
Click on Garden to enter with video Welcome to Mediation Theraphy.com www.zenbodymind.com	Sanctum: A sacred or holy place www.docstrange.com/main/sanctum.asp	Prayer and Faith Healing http://1stholistic.com
Wisdom Rituals (Stillpoint Labyrinth) All in Good Faith – Educating Mind and Spirit www.worldreligions.ca/all_in_good_faith1.htm		

B. Offline Cyber Worship

a. Know-How, Process, Procedures, Activity, Functions, Methods.../ Products, Resources, Materials...: (Spirituality continued)

The Earth Ascension Times Phone/Personal Sessions with ZaKaiRan www.geocities.com/zakairan	Personal Sessions with Michael El Nour dial (1) 310 441 9333 www.antahkaranah.com/ article_sessions.htm	Sacred Merkaba Techniques www.merkaba.org
Glossary of Religious Terms www.religioustolerance.org/ glossary.htm	Glossary Religious Holidays www.pgcares.com/ interfaith_glossary.html	Metaphysical & Spiritual Glossary http://spiritnetwork.com/glossary
Defining Mysticism www.well.com/user/ elliotts/smse_index.html	Essential Information on the Mystical Experience www.bodysoulandspirit.net	Golden Mean http://TheGoldenMean.homestead.com
Church of Questions http://education.atu.edu/ people/sadams/blogger2/ 2002/08/03.html	Ask Archangel Michael Your Questions www.antahkaranah.com/ ask_frameset.htm	Faith Bazaar www.modernpaths.com/ r/s/shopping
Mysteries.Net www.mysteries.net	Mystic Sayings Collection www.mudmystic.com	Mystical World Wide Web www.mystical-www.co.uk
Spiritual Knowledge www.kisol.com	Mysticism (Evelyn Underhill) www.ccel.org/u/underhill/ mysticism/mysticism1.0.html	Learning Meditation www.learningmeditation.com/ getaway1.htm
Sumarah- A Study of the Art of Living (Javanese mysticism) http://tunggal.tripod.com/index2.htm	The Mystic (commercial offering of teachings, techniques) www.themystic.org	Observations on how to be content (Wally-Vladimir-Kuskoff on mysticism) http://members.surfeu.fi/wpk
Solism (Sol Mysticism) http://members.aol.com/ SolMystic/SOL/index.htm	Silvan's Glade Exploring mysticism in nature writing. www.geocities.com/vwaffle	Religious Corner (mystical and historical aspects of God) www.geocities.com/ dpv5716/index.html

Subud the Coming New Age of Reality (develop a true human character) www.subud.ws	Mysticism in World Religions www.digiserve.com/mystic	Soon You Will Understand... The Meaning of Life www.themeaningoflife.org
Empowerment 12 Steps www.circlesanctuary.org/ healing/empower.htm	Web Weavings – Services – San Luis Obispo (For a fee) www.catryce.com/Healing/Services.html	Other resources - Digital World www.geocities.com/~wtwilson3
From 'The Spiritual Cyborg' (Article) www.techgnosis.com/techgnois/ tgspirit.html	Snakes & Ladders: Floormaps of the Metaphysical Supermarket (Digital resources) www.techgnosis.com/snakes.html	Modern Paths: Rites & Rituals **Multifaith Perspectives** www.modernpaths.com/ library/rituals/
Death and Dying www.beyondindigo.com/ channels/topic.php/topic/33	Thoughtful Living Near Death Experiences www.ndeweb.com	Meditation Enlightening Elastomeric Experiences http://latexmindresearch.tripod.com
Near-Death Experiences www.mindspring.com/ ~scottr/end.html	Near Death Experiences and the Afterlife www.near-death.com	Observations on God, Life and the Human Journey Near Death Experiences www.observations.net
Thelemic Astrology www.thelemicgoldendawn.org/ files/astrology.htm	Qabalistic Magnetism www.a-m-h-r.org/aa/ qabalistic_magnetism.html	Exposing Modern Spirituality www.geocities.com/ the_theologian/content/homiletics/ spirituality.html
First Nations Spirituality (Aboriginal spiritual traditions of North America) www.aetheric.com/firstnations	Heart of Sky Maya religion and spirituality www.uwec.edu/academic/ curric/greidebe/hos/Spirit	Native American Spirituality (land-based spirituality, creation mythology and immanence) www.greenspirit.org.uk/ resources/NatAmerSpirit.htm
Listening to Nature, Devas, Angels & Spirit Guides www.devas.org/start.htm	Native American Lore Index www.ilhawaii.net/~stony/loreindx.html	Prayer Project www.celestinevision.com/ worldprayerproject.html
Native American Spirituality http://members.aol.com porchfour/religion/nativeam.htm	Articles on Spiritual Heritage Native American www.bluecloud.org/religion.html	Esoterism – Mysticism Search Engine http://esoterism.com/links/ MYSTICISM
A Course in Miracles www.modernpaths.com/ library/sacred/articles/ f_lib_text_home_course_miracles.html	The Sufism of the West (A comparison of Christian mysticism to Sufism) www.blaketashi.com	The Wild Divine Project www.wilddivine.com/banner.php
Spiritualist Churches New Zealand www.lighthousespiritualcentre.ca/ Churches/churchnewzealand.html	Spiritualist Churches Australia www.lighthousespiritualcentre.ca/ Churches/churchaustralia.html	Spiritualist Churches Great Britain www.lighthousespiritualcentre.ca/ Churches/churchuk.html
Spiritualist Churches World Wide www.spiritualistchurches.net	Spiritualist Churches in Canada www.lighthousespiritualcentre.ca/ Churches/churchcanada.html	Spiritualist Churches USA www.lighthousespiritualcentre.ca/ Churches/churchusa.html
Topics to Explore www.spirituality.com	Mediums World Wide www.worldwidemediums.com	Worldwide Spiritualist Directory www.lighthousespiritualcentre.ca/ Churchdirectory.html
WebCity House of Worship **Multifaith Directory** www.webcityusa.com/worship.htm	Other Spirit Sites www.spirit.com/slinks.html	Spirit and Leather www.weston.com/leather/leatherspirit.htm
Four elements basic to traditional meditation http://1stholistic.com/Meditation	Circle Dancing - Meditation & Prayer in motion www.bellaonline.com/articles/ art18085.asp	Cosmic Spirituality www.tomharpur.com
Renewing the Sacred Balance Supporting David Suzuki's Nature Challenge www.faith-commongood.net/ sacredbalance/index.asp	Leader Tools Growth Finder: Using The Internet to Diagnose Spiritual Health http://smallgroups.com/group_leader/ leader_tools/growthfinder.html	Respirit (I dreamed I had an interview with God) http://www.respirit.com/ Interview-with-God.html
A Spiritual Health Check Up Four Diagnostic Questions to Assess Spiritual Health www.abbc.org/ sermons_2002/2002_12_29_am.htm	**Multifaith** - All Things Spiritual Directory www.allspiritual.com/MultiFaith.php3	World Scripture: A Comparative Anthology of Sacred Texts - **Multifaith Resource** 4600 passages from 268 texts and 55 oral traditions www.euro-tongil.org/ws/index.html
Serenity Notebook www.geocities.com/Heartland/ Ranch/3721/serenity.html	Paths: The Way of the Soul www.snark.ca/ano2.htm	Talking With God www.americanswami.com/main/2004/04/ sunday_march_4t.html

	Spiritual Health Links www.getnoni.com/links66.html	

C. Religions-Online / Online-Religions:

a. Home Pages of Religious and Spiritual Groups (**Spirituality continued)**

The Aberdeen Spiritualist Centre http://freespace.virgin.net/ spiritualist.centre	Cowichan Spiritualist Church of Healing and Light http://members.shaw.ca/connieis/ spiritualist2.htm	Self-Realization Fellowship Paramahansa Yogananda www.babaji.org
Centre for the Souls Journey into Light www.healthypages.org/zannierose	Core Spirituality www.corespirituality.com	Integrative Spirituality www.integrativespirituality.org
Kaleidoskop Spiritualist Centre for Mediumship and Development www.kaleidoskop.org	Naniamo Christian Spiritualist Church www.lantzvillecomputers.com/ ChurchPageT.htm	Peace Worldwide [We preach among the fundamentalist muslims] www.pww.org.pk
REGNB?GEN [We are a spiritualist society, Sweden] www.spiritus.nu	The Spiritualist National Union www.snu.org.uk/index2.htm	Waterloo Spiritualist Church SNU www.kwest.pwp.blueyonder.co.uk/ WaterlooChurch.html
Subud International Cultural Organization www.subud-sica.org	Near Death Experience Research Foundation www.nderf.org	American Indian Religious Rights Foundation www.airr.org

1.11 Mapping Zoroastrianism Webwise

A. Online Cyber Worship

a. Prayer, Praise, Scripture, Sacrament

Cyber Temple www.zarathushtra.com	Images of Zoroaster http://sangha.net/messengers/ zoroaster.htm#Images of	Prayers & Fire-temples http://www3.sympatico.ca/ zoroastrian
Question Hotline www.geocities.com/ zoroastrianismtoday	Temple of Zoroaster http://sangha.net/ messengers/zoroaster.htm	Zoroastrianism/FAQ www.faqs.org/faqs/ zoroastrianism/FAQ/
The original Cyber-Temple www.zarathushtra.com/ z/temple/temple.htm	Zoroastrian Cyber-Temple www.zarathushtra.com/	The Cyber-Temple with the new Fire www.zarathushtra.com/ z/temple/temple2.htm
The Achaemenian Open Air Temple www.zarathushtra.com/z/ temple/temple3.htm	Ancient Wisdom: Submit a Prayer **Multifaith Concerns** www.awisdom.com/ community/submit_prayer	Voice A Vision • Post A Prayer Dare A Dream Multifaith Voices www.heartpath.com/ hpcontent/voiceAvision.asp
Priestly Services http://priest.yasna.com	Daily Rituals: Zarathustrian Assembly www.zoroastrian.org	Various Zoroastrian Fire-Temples www.iras.ucalgary.ca/ ~volk/sylvia/FireTemple.htm
Prayer Book Meditations, Adorations, Celebrations, Invocations **Multifaith Prayers** Multicultural Prayers www.prayforpeace.com/index.php	View Navruz www.dicoverturkey.com/ English/movies/default.htm	A word by word translation Avesta & Gatha www.zoroaster.com
Universal Calendar Calculator: Zoroastrian www.cf-software.com/ other.html	Avesta text www.avesta.org/avesta.html	Online Translations holy texts www.sacred-texts.com/zor
Gathas: The Divine Hymns of Zarathushtra Various Translations www.zarathushtra.com/ z/gatha/index.htm	Zoroastrian Holy Books (online translations) www.sacred-texts.com/zor	World Prayers – Prayer Collective **Multifaith Practices** www.worldpyaers.org
Zoroaster Temple at Grand Canyon National Park www.kbt.com/gc/gc_zoro.html		

B. Offline Cyber Worship:

a. Know-How, Process, Procedures, Activity, Functions, Methods, Materials ...Products, Resources, Materials...

(Zoroastrianism continued)

Farohar or Faravahar www.stanford.edu/ group/Zoroastrians/ faravahar.shtml	Basic Tenets www.ozemail.com.au/ ~zarathus/tenets33.html	Glossary of Zoroastrian Terms www.avesta.org/zglos.html

List of Parsi Dharamshalas of India http://ignca.nic.in/ bibzs005.htm	List of Parsi Anjumans of India http://ignca.nic.in/ bibzs004.htm	Ahura Mazda www.pantheon.org/articles/a/ ahura_mazda.html
Basic Zoroastrianism and the Teachings of Zarathustra www.hinduwebsite.com/ zoroastrianism/zoraindex.htm	Good Thoughts - The Zarathushtrian Assembly www.zoroastrian.org	Homage Unto Ahura Mazda www.zarathushtra.com/ z/article/dhalla/index.htm
Life of Zarathustra www.cybertrails.com/ babadas/Zarathustra.html	World Scripture: A Comparative Anthology of Sacred Texts - **Multifaith Resource** 4600 passages from 268 texts and 55 oral traditions www.euro-tongil.org/ws/index.html	Who Are The Zoroastrians? German-Persian Mythological connections www.ozemail.com.au/ ~zarathus/zor33.html
Zoroastrian Religion www.power.inms.nrc.ca/ bamji/zoroastrian.html	AltaVisions: All Zarathushti related material www.Zarathust.com	Firdowsi's Shahnameh on Interactive CDROM www.storymation.com/ shahnameh.html
Meher Baba Avatar of the Age http://davey.sunyerie.edu/ mb/html/	AHORAIAN Persian Empire, Zoroastrianism and Mithraism http://members.gnn.com/ areshtad/ahoraian.htm	The Shah-Namah or The Epic of Kings by Ferdowsi http://classics.mit.edu/ Ferdowsi/kings.html
Births, Deaths www.zoroastrian.net/BandD.htm	Astrology and Religion Nexus **Multifaith Perspective** www.findyourfate.com/ astrology/astrology-religion.htm	**Multifaith** - All Things Spiritual Directory www.allspiritual.com/MultiFaith.php3
	PersianDNA www.persiandna.com	

C. Religions-Online / Online-Religions:

a. Home Pages of Religious and Spiritual Groups: (Zoroastrianism continued)

The Zarathushtrian Assembly www.zoroastrian.org	O'Shihan Cultural Organization Home of Gatha Group www.oshihan.org	World Zoroastrian Organisation www.w-z-o.org
Zoroastrians of Shiraz http://shiraz.freeservers.com	Zoroastrianism and Mazdakism http://forums.delphiforums.com/ zoroastrianism1/start/	Zoroastrian Net Worldwide community centre. www.zoroastrian.net
Zoroastrianism and Yezidism www.knowdeep.org/ zoroastrianism	Spenta Mainyu' Beacon www.geocities.com/ spenta_mainyu	Zoroastrian Association of Western Australia Inc. www.webace.com.au/~zawa
Zoroastrian Association of South Florida http://zasf.org	Zarathustrian Association of New Zealand ZANZ www.zanz.org.nz	Zoroastrian Association, Western Australia www.zawa.asn.au
Zoroastrian Association of Greater New York ZAGNY www.zagny.org	Zoroastrian Association of Metropolitan Washington, Inc. ZAMWI www.nicom.com/~zamwi	Zoroastrian Association of Pennsylvania and New Jersey ZAPANJ www.zapanj.org
Zoroastrian Association of Houston Online www.zah.org	Zoroastrian Groups in North America www.fezana.org	Zoroastrian Association, Metropolitan Chicago www.zac-chicago.org
Zoroastrian Association, Greater Boston Area http://web.mit.edu/ zoroastrian/www/ZAGBA/home.html	The Baroda United Zoroastrian Youth Trust BUZY www.buzy.org	California Zoroastrian Center www.californiazoroastriancenter.org
The Singapore Parsi Association http://members.xoom.com/sinparsi	Parsis (India) www.vision-Divine.com	Zarathusti Business Network and Online Shopping Mall Promote www.zarathusht.com
Zoroastrian Education and Research Society ZERS www.zers.com	Zoroastrian Trust Funds of Europe, Inc. ZTFE www.ztfe.com	

2

Cyber Worship as-is On the Web

This chapter will bring live instances of how each faith group presents itself in performing Cyber Worship. The following chart represents the pattern reflecting one of the many ways in which online religion is operating on the Web.

- Log on and pray (or take a look)
- Read the Word (or listen, view, glance)
- Try to read in between the lines (or move towards religiousness or get transformed to a different mode)
- Ponder (or glance at the spiritual ladder)
- Meet others in a congregational set up (conferencing by video or audio)
- Find like-minded Cyber Worshipers (using chat, forums, etc.)
- Reduce distinctions (blur inter-religious or intra-religious divides)
- Get to the level of Knowing (reduce illusions) – share the so far hidden or private knowledge and make public all enlightenment
- Open the closed doors to reach the sublime directly (no bureaucracy, no hurdles) even adopt open source religion
- Give what is gained online, disseminate the experiences and facilitate sustainable development environments

2.1 Multifaith

"Multifaith is a wide variety of faith traditions presented simultaneously. Multifaith is not a religion, but an approach to living in a religiously and spiritually diverse world that respects the integrity of different faith traditions and promotes diversity.[52] It is not an attempt to convert people from one faith to another or to meld different beliefs and practices into a new faith."

Gathering of Light Multifaith Spiritual Fellowship,

www.gatheringoflight.com

"An attempt to initiate dialog, cooperation, and understanding among individuals of many different faiths. It is occasionally used as a synonym for "interfaith." Unfortunately, various religious groups define the term "faith" differently. For example, some conservative Christians regard a person who is not of their denomination to be from a different faith. Other conservative Christians would regard liberal Christians as being of a different faith. Still other Christians interpret "Multifaith" as involving other religions, as in a Christian-Jewish-Muslim exchange."

Glossary [A To M] of Religious Terms

http://religioustolerance.org/gl_c.htm

Table 2A.1 World Prayers

Title	World Prayers
Creator (author)	Jody Baxter
Subject or keywords	world prayers; prayer; prayers; prayer archive; prayer collection; prayer anthology; collection; collective; sacred verses; sacred; verse; database; collection; spiritual; spirituality; visionaires; divine; mysteries; inspiring; inspirational; inspired; adorations; adoration....MORE
Description	A multi-faith Prayer Collective for inspiration, education and healing.
Publisher	Mandala Net Design
Date	2004-3-1
Type	Text
Format	text/html, digital media || 16831 bytes
Identifier	http://www.worldprayers.org
Language	English

Voice Populi:

"A multi-cultural prayer collective attempting to gather the great prayer classics from spiritual traditions around the world into a common archive for the purpose of inspiration, study and cross cultural appreciation." http://www.conjure.com/religion.html

"Inspiring words of peace and spirit from various world religions." http://www.peacepilgrim.com/links1.htm

Table 2A.2 Kashi Photo Tour

Title	Kashi Ashram Tour
Creator (author)	Kashi Church Foundation
Subject or keywords	Kashi ashram; Ma Jaya Sati Bhagavati; Kali; tantra; hindu; Swami; Baba; Ramana Maharshi; kundalini; chakra; Hanuman; Mother; Goddess; God; Tibet; HIV; AIDS; service organization; pranayam; yoga; community; ganga; Ganges; spiritual; retreat; MORE...
Description	To provide information about our organization and to promote interfaith dialogue and acceptance. Praise and Prayer.
Contributor	Dhumavati, dhumavati@kashi.org
Date	2004-04-21
Type	Text
Format	text/html, digital media || 13682 bytes
Identifier	http://www.kashi.org
Language	English

Voice Populi:

"The Guru is Ma Jaya Sati Bhagavati. For more about her, and her ashram in Florida, go to http://www.kashi.org/" http://www.well.com/user/tomcarr/atlanta_buddhism.htm

"Homepage Mother Kali About Ma Ma's Teaching Ma's Kashi Ganga Gita Daily Prayer From Ma Books and Tapes River Paintings Ma's Sacred art Intensives and Retreats Kashi Schedule Kashi Tour River Fund River..." http://www.helpyourselfcentral.com/links/religionandspirituality.html

Table 2A.3 Religion Selector

Title	SpeakOut.com Religion Selector
Subject or keywords	TakeAction; About Us; Death Penalty; SelectSmart; Forum; VoteMatch; Gun Control; Race Relations; Gay Rights; SelectSmart.com; Contact Us; Privacy and Use Policies; SpeakOut.com; Issues; Education; Technology; Abortion; Animal Rights; Advertising information; .....MORE
Date	2003-11-13
Type	Text

Format	text/html, digital media || 56679 bytes
Identifier	http://speakout.com/activismtools/selectors/religion/

Voice Populi:

Here is a test that explores the match between your beliefs and religion: Religion Selector--you may or may not agree with its results. I took this test and it said that I am in exactly the right place for my beliefs.
http://www.uwsp.edu/education/lkirby/SelfKnowledge/Spiritual.htm

Ever wonder what religion your beliefs most closely correspond to? Try SpeakOut.com's religion selector.
http://noodle.pds.k12.nj.us/freedholm/Sacred/sacred_links.htm

Table 2A.4. What religion is the best?

Title	Our Findings; Fade To Black; Main Page; Consumer Reports Index; How We Scored; Fade To Black Magazine; Final Results
Subject or keywords	Our Findings; Fade To Black; Main Page; Consumer Reports Index; How We Scored; Fade To Black Magazine; Final Results
Publisher	Comcast Cable Communications, IP Services EASTERNSHORE-1
Type	Text
Format	text/html, digital media || 2328 bytes
Identifier	www.fadetoblack.com/ consumerreport/religion/finalresults.html

Voice Populi:

The concept of this site was to provide ideas, thoughts and comedy onto a different medium."
http://www.metagrid.com/subkat.php4?kat=m_42

"Leading the world to higher consciousness through mockery and cheap publicity stunts."
http://www.atheistalliance.org/internet/net_newsletters.html

Table 2A.5 God-U-Like – An Irreverent Look at the Faith Industry

Title	Godulike - An Irreverent Look at the Faith Industry
Subject or keywords	Agnosticism; Ahmadiyah Sect; Akan; Aleut / Inuit (Eskimo) Religion; Amish; Ananda Marga Movement; Anglicanism (Church of England); Anthroposophy; Anti-Cult Movement; Assemblies of God; Atheism; Australian Aborigine Religion; Baha'i Faith; Balinese Religion (Agama Tirtha); Bantu; Baptists; Batak Religion; Branch Davidian Sect; Buddhism; Bushman; Cargo Cults; Children of God; Christian Science; …MORE
Description	An Irreverent look at the Faith Industry
Type	Text
Format	text/html, digital media || 19714 bytes
Identifier	http://www.godulike.co.uk

Voice Populi:

"An irreverent analysis of over 100 religions."
http://dmoz.org/Society/Religion_and_Spirituality/

"Pick a god any god, and read all about him, er.. it, er.. her and every religion known to mankind"
www.jimithypagan.co.uk/links.htm

Table 2A.6. Trucker's Prayer Room

Title	Layover.com:
Creator (author)	Dr. D. Ghosh, layover.com
Subject or keywords	trucking job; truck driver job; truck driving job; driving job owner operator job; owner operator; trucking employment; truckers; trucking
Description	layover.com is a one-stop trucking resource providing information on all aspects of the trucking industry.
Type	Text
Format	text/html; charset=iso-8859-1, digital media || 24962 bytes
Identifier	http://www.truckingsites.com/chap/pc1.htm

Table 2A.7 Museums of World Religions

Title	Museum of World Religions
Date	2001-10-02
Type	Text
Format	text/html, digital media || 802 bytes
Identifier	http://www.mwr.org.tw/en-library/en.htm

Table 2A.8. Webcam Central: Cams by Category: Religion

Title	WebCam Central : Cams by Category : Religion
Subject or keywords	Italy; USA - Nevada; IslandCam Two; LocationCam; 770 LIVE; France; RandomCam; Add-A-Cam; Canada; Shop; webcam piazza e basilica di S.Antonio a Padova; Poland; USA - New_York; USA - Kentucky; 1st webcams of Jura in France; Catholic Community of St. Paul; Home; MyCams; Jim Holley; House of Worship, Evanston, Chicago IL; CategoryCam; Jesus Online; Privacy Statement; Add to MyCams; Search;
Type	Text
Format	text/html, digital media || 12636 bytes
Identifier	http://camcentral.com/category.asp?item=Religion

<u>Voice Populi:</u>
"cross-indexed listing of several hundred live WebCam sites on the Internet."
Yahoo Directory (http://dir.yahoo.com/Computers_and_Internet/Internet /Devices_Connected_to_the_Internet/Web_Cams/Web_Directories/)

Table 2A.9. Business gets the message B2C: Religion

Title	Business gets the message - B2C - Religion
Subject or keywords	mobile messaging; wireless messaging; SMS; MMS; EMS; short messaging service; short message service; text messaging; text messages; B2C; B2B; B2E; C2C; B2G; G2C; G2E; GSM; services; business; corporate; enterprise; uses
Description	A round-up of the latest interesting and innovative applications of mobile messaging
Type	Text
Format	text/html, digital media || 25637 bytes
Identifier	http://www.xiam.com/news/business-gets-the-message/b2c/religion.shtml

<u>Voice Populi:</u>

"Religion in your phone"
http://www.umtsworld.com/lastword/lw0026.htm

Table 2A.10. Religious Blessings over the Internet

Title	Blessed Bandwidth over the Internet
Creator (author)	British Satellite News
Subject or keywords	Internet, London, Video, Religions, Hindu, Sikh, Buddhist, Islam,
Contributor	Hisham Mohammed El-Hennawy
Date	2003
Type	Text
Format	text/html; charset=iso-8859-1, digital media || 24962 bytes
Identifier	http://www.bsn.org.uk/80256A17005C4834/(httpScripts)/3969168ECDA00A2280256DDE00353F7D?OpenDocument

2.2 Alternative Traditions

Table 2B0. The Taipei Times Online Saturday, April 8th, 2000

Cyber-worship

An official from the Tainan Mayor's office shows off the "EC Ma-tsu" Web site next to the statue of a god from Tien-hou Temple in Tainan. The new Web site allows worshippers to make online offerings and provides information on religious celebrations. <http://taipeitimes.com/chnews/2000/04/08/image/0000006270 >

Where is this actual temple? Whom does this cater to?

TA TIEN HOU (MATSU) TEMPLE, TAINAN, Taiwan
Ta Tien Hou Temple, also known as the Matsu Temple, was used as the palace of the exiled Ming prince Chu Shu-kuei until 1683. In that year, the Ching general Shi Lang had the palace converted into a temple devoted to Matsu, the Goddess of Mercy, who he gave the honorary title of Tien-hou, or "Queen of Heaven". The oldest official temple to Matsu in all of Taiwan, it faces west on a slope looking out to the old city wharf, such that the temple buildings rise majestically from front to back.[1] < http://www.tpg.gov.tw/tpaih/historic_e/history37.html > <accessed Aug 21, 2003>
[Note: One should not be confused with a similar name of a Temple in Texas[2] < http://www.virtualtourist.com/vt/d66da/4/f515/ >]

Table 2B. 1. Virtual Church of Benevolent Deities Inc.

Title	Virtual Church of Benevolent Deities Inc
Creator (author)	Heidi L. Nordberg
Subject or keywords	deities inc religion interfaith openness compassion peace satire spirituality postmodern ironic joy parody jester
Description	Homepage of the Virtual Church of Benevolent Deities Inc. To perform an ironic yet productive collapse between benevolent deities and the idea of a corporation, and to reawaken spiritual joy and laughter.
Publisher	Virtual Church of Benevolent Deities Inc
Contributor	VirusHead, virushead.net
Date	2004-02-19
Type	Text
Format	text/html, digital media || 9563 bytes
Identifier	http://www.virushead.net/bdi/
Language	English

Voice Populi:

Visit VirtuBene. You can pick up your share of stock, read the invocation, see some quotations of the jester prophets, and more
http://www.comedy-zone.net/links/Satirical_Humour/more35.html

"Virus jokes, help for ex-Jehovah's Witnesses, BabyBoo baby stuff for Mom and Dad, Religious Insight / Compassion Healing awards for your site, webmaster tools, original photographic ecards, charity clicks, web cams, search portal, consumer help, news in religion, vampire links, more."
http://www.enlightenment.com/ec/index.cfm?big_list=1&cat=Spirituality

Table 2B.2. Kiosk

Title	The Secular Web
Creator (author)	Various
Description	To defend and promote a naturalistic, nontheistic worldview
Publisher	Internet Infidels
Contributor	James J. Lippard, President Internet Infidels; jlippard@infidels.org
Date	Some portions updated daily, 2004
Type	Text
Format	Text/html, digital media
Identifier	www.secweb.org/kiosk
Language	English

Voice Populi:

"Popular pieces on issues of interest to nonbelievers"
http://mywebpages.comcast.net/daviwat/spirit.html

"The Secular Web promotes and links to sites and organizations that promote humanism, atheism and agnosticism"
http://members.verizon.net/~vze4m3yd/links.htm

Table 2B.3. Online Wiccan Site

Title	Online Wiccan Rituals
Creator (author)	Simovess; simovess@carolina.rr.com
Subject or keywords	Online; wicca; wiccan; rituals; pagan; witch; witches; spirituality
Description	We are an open online Wiccan Coven, however, we accept all who choose the Pagan paths. To bring education to those seeking knowledge on Wiccan or Paganism in general.
Publisher	InterLan Communications ILAN2-BLK
Contributor	Simovess
Date	2001-10-18
Type	Text
Format	text/html, digital media || 1087 bytes
Identifier	http://go.to/onlinewiccanrituals
Language	English

Voice Populi:
"An Open Online Coven for solitarians to join other in practice of spells, rituals, or celebrations"

http://owr.mytopsitelist.com/onlinewiccanrituals

"For those who are solitary or coven members who want to practice with other like-minded individuals. Online rituals through chat to bring strength in numbers and with the intent of making your own ritual work more successful."

http://www.mind-n-magick.com/search/html/Rituals_L2K_Passages/Rituals/

Table 2B.4. Bashar

Title	Portal3
Creator (author)	April Rierdan, President, april@bashar.org Bashar Communication
Subject or keywords	Bashar, multi-dimensional, hanneling, mediumship, psychic reading, psychics, extraterrestrials, metaphysics, UFOs, Area 51, alien abduction, higher self, spirit guides, spiritual healing, out-of-body, sacred geometry, ET contact, Darryl Anka, crop circles, psychic predictions, past lives, meditation, telepathy, karma, transformation, ascension, reincarnation
Date	2003-10-28
Type	Text
Format	text/html, digital media || 4991 bytes
Identifier	http://bashar.org/meditationrm/Portal3.html
Language	English
Voice Populi:	

"Multi-dimensional being, channeled through Darryl Anka, speaks on a variety of topics. Includes forums and events listings"
http://dmoz.org/Society/Religion_and_Spirituality/New_Age/Channeling/Channeled_Material/

"Channeling on topics such as reincarnation, karma, ascension, psychic predictions, spiritual healing, higher self, metaphysics, extraterrestrials, holistic health, success, relationships, etc"
http://www.thewildrose.net/links/channelling.html

"Bashar Tapes and Channelings - This is the official website of Bashar, channeled by Darryl Anka, a consistent source of expansive and loving communication since the early 1980s"
http://www.floweroflife.org/links.htm

Table 2B.5. Cyber Shrine

Title	Cyber Shrine
Subject or keywords	Shinto; Shrine; Japan; Japon; kami; amaterasu; susanoo; yamatotakeru; tenjin; inari
Description	photos of Shinto Shrine in Japan
Date	2004-01-12
Type	Text
Format	text/html, digital media || 14564 bytes
Identifier	http://www.kiku.com/electric_samurai/cyber_shrine/
Voice Populi:	

"CyberShrine has photos of several dozen shrines. You can get your omikuji fortune told here too!"
http://www.culture-at-work.com/jpnlinks.html

"This site has links to numerous photographs of Shinto shrines and torii (sacred arch or gateway) in Japan."
http://religiousmovements.lib.virginia.edu/nrms/shinto.html

"Photographs of Japanese Shinto Shrines, virtual fortune teller, links to twenty-seven other shrines"
http://www.seas.ac.uk/InfoEastAsia/Japan_for_Schools.shtml

Table 2B.6. Tao Sanctuary

Title	Welcome to TrueTao.org / Taoism.net
Subject or	Flash Intro; Enter Web Site; Enter with Music; TrueTao.org / Taoism.net, music, enter, web, site,

keywords	with
Description	Animal Nutrition, Music, Seminars
Publisher	The Pajo Group ARIN-PAJO2
Contributor	Derek Lin, dereklin@prodigy.net
Date	2003-09-14
Type	Text
Format	text/html, digital media || 1921 bytes
Identifier	http://www.Taoism.net
Language	English

Voice Populi:

"Good source of Taoist links, history, translations etc"
http://www.globalserve.net/~sarlo/Ratlinks.htm

"featuring I-Kuan Tao, Lao Tzu, Chuang Tzu, and other great philosophers. Site includes lineage, articles, stories, and map to the temple"
http://dir.yahoo.com/Society_and_Culture/Religion_and_Spirituality/Faiths_and_Practices/Taoism/

Table 2B. 7. Ritual Begins here

Title	CyberSamhain Introduction
Creator (author)	Mark Pesce, mark@playfulworld.com
Subject or keywords	Adam Madgett; The manifestation of the sacred ontologically founds the world; keep sacred silence; Introduction; ontos; The Ritual begins here; Teknos; the creation of a world necessarily implies the creation of a world-view
Publisher	United Layer, Inc. UNITEDLAYER-1
Type	Text
Format	text/html, digital media || 2724 bytes
Identifier	http://media.hyperreal.org/~mpesce/samhain/

Voice Populi:

The Hyperreal Media Archive, ...normally archives media-related material about "the history of electronic music, rave culture and their related memes"
http://www.nielsenhayden.com/makinglight/archives/002372.html

Table 2B. 8. Adhiparasakthi Virtual Prayer Room

Title	Adhiparasakthi Virtual Prayer Room
Creator (author)	webmaster@omsakthi.org
Subject or keywords	Om Sakthi Spiritual Movement Worship Page Virtual Prayer Room
Description	Virtual prayer room for devotees of the Om Sakthi Movement
Date	2000-03-04
Type	Text
Format	text/html, digital media || 848 bytes
Identifier	http://www.omsakthi.org/worship/prayer_room.html
Language	English

Voice Populi:

"A Religious tolerance cite promoting understanding through education"
http://www.earthmomma.homestead.com/EarthArt.html

"A philosophy which embraces all religions." This is an example of the current movement toward "religious tolerance." This group is a sponsor of the Ontario Consultants on Religious Tolerance.
http://www.bible-prophecy.com/religions.htm

Table 2B. 9. Temple of Mithras

Title	The Temple of Mithras
Creator (author)	Glyn Goodrick
Subject or keywords	TEMPLE, temple of mithras, roman army, Persia, museum, cult, cosmic egg, Hadrian's Wall, Zodiac, altars; nave, cult, mithras, frieze, roofs, domu, altars, worship, sculpture, columns
Description	Temple of Mithras now loading. Internally, each had an antechamber, a nave with raised benches along the walls, and a sanctuary with altars and the tauroctony. Against the nave walls there were clay benches faced with wickerwork and covered with a thick rendering of plaster.
Publisher	Lindsay Allason-Jones
Date	2000-03-15
Type	Text
Format	text/html, digital media || 756 bytes
Identifier	http://museums.ncl.ac.uk/archive/mithras/frames.htm
Language	English
Voice Populi:	

"Explore the ruins of the 3rd century temple to the Roman god Mithras at Carrawburgh on Hadrians Wall, and the reconstruction on display in the Museum of Antiquities at the University of Newcastle, through Virtual Reality." http://clerccenter3.gallaudet.edu/ClercCenter/Library/Team10.nsf/0/e7dc3a25cf4b894b852567a1006adec9?OpenDocument

"This site contains a wealth of information and pictures plus video images of one of the temples found at Hadrian's Wall." http://www.ngfl.ac.uk/edulinks/history.html

2.3 Baha'i:

	Basic Beliefs: ▪ The Oneness of God; the oneness of religion; and the oneness of humanity. ▪ The Purpose of religion is to unify humanity. ▪ All great religions and prophets are divine in origin. ▪ All great religions represent successive stages of divine revelation throughout human history. ▪ The eradication of racial and religious prejudice (Multifaith Information Manual, 2000)

Table 2C.1. House of Worship – Live Snapshot

Title	Baha'i's of the United States - House of Worship: Webcam
Subject or keywords	Live Snapshot; Click here; History; Events; Activities; Visitor Information; Baha'i House of Worship, automatic, image
Description	If you would like to update it sooner, please click the 'Refresh' or 'Reload' button on your browser. This image is automatically updated every 60 seconds
Date	2004-05-03
Type	Text
Format	Text/html, digital media || 35202 bytes

Identifier	http://us.bahai.org/how/webcam.htm

Voice Populi:

This site is the official U.S. web page. A more U.S. perspective.
http://www.nrvbahais.org/contacts.htm

The home page of the Bahá'í House of Worship in Wilmette, Illinois, providing information on all aspects of its operation and services. It even has a webcam!
http://www.planetbahai.org/library/lbhousesofworshipa.html

Table 2C.2. Baha'is Deepening on the Internet

Title	Welcome to Bahai-deepening
Subject or keywords	Baha'i Deepening; The Baha'i Academics Resource Library, online chat, dialogue,
Date	2001-09-07
Type	Text
Format	text/html, digital media || 15327 bytes
Identifier	http://users.tebenet.nl/~kuijer-e/main.htm

Voice Populi:

"Hosts a deepening for every Saturday for Bahai's and non-Bahai's-, on Bahai's topics, 4:00pm GMT on EFnet, IRC. The site has archives of past deepenings and the schedule of upcoming topics"
http://www.wunderdirectory.com/listings/dir/4/5127/Bah%C3%83%C2%A1'%C3%83%C2%AD/

"If not the largest, certainly one of the largest on-line depositories of Baha'i and Baha'i related documents"
http://www.manvell.org.uk/lynx/academic.htm

Table 2C.3. Bahai-Virtual Tour (picture)

Title	Bahai - Virtual tour
Subject or keywords	Bahai, virtual, tour, Ipix, Israel, project, virtual tour, Faith, cyber, online
Date	2003-03-06
Type	Text
Format	text/html, digital media || 2213 bytes
Identifier	http://www.einhanet.co.il/bahai/bahai1.html

Table 2C.4. The Internet and the Covenant

Title	Bahai - The Internet and the Covenant
Subject or keywords	Bahai, Faith, cyber, online, Internet, Baha'i, virtual, Message, conference
Type	Text
Format	text/html, digital media
Identifier	www.bahaiworld.com/conference/ca/unravel
Summary	**"The Covenant and the Internet: Implications for Baha'is of Online Communication"** Jennifer Flynn Clark - As many of us know, the Internet is a powerful and dangerous tool. Any kind of information can be found in a very short period of time; some of it useful and factual, some of it misleading and confusing. As Bahá'ís, it is particularly important to deepen on the use of this technology within the boundaries of the Covenant. This participatory session will explore the Internet and the Covenant in direct relation to one another, referring directly to a compilation of writings from the Universal House of Justice with specific guidance on this topic, as well as from additional Writings of the Guardian, Bahá'u'lláh and 'Abdu'l-Bahá. http://www.bahaiworld.com/conference/ca/unravel/2002/workshops.htm

http://www.bahaiworld.com/conference/ca/unravel/2002/THEINTERNETANDTHECOVENANT.ppt

2.4 Buddhism

Basic Teachings:

- The First Noble Truth – Dukkha, Ordinary existence is a State of Suffering.
- The Second Noble Truth – The Arising of Dukkha, Cause of Suffering.
- The Third Noble Truth - The Cessation of Dukkha, End of Suffering.
- The Fourth Noble Truth - The Path, Embracing the teachings of Lord Buddha.
- The Eight-Fold Noble Path (For Lay People only) (Multifaith Information Manual, 2000)

Table 2D 1. Wat Thai Kusinara Chalermraj

Title	Wat Thai Kusinara Chalermraj
Creator (author)	Anita Shu
Subject or keywords	Wat; Thai; Kusinara; Chalermraj; Mahavihar; Buddha; Buddhism; Religion; Religious; Tourism; Dhamma; Peace; Mahacetiya; Chedi; Shrine; Royal; Place; Worship; Reverence; Thailand; India; Kushinagar; Kusinara, MORE..
Description	This Thai Buddhist Temple, in the land of Buddhism, at the location of Lord Buddha's Nirvana at Kushinagar, is created from the project of returning Buddhism to the land of its origin.......MORE.
Contributor	Elizabeth Shu; office@watthaikusinara.org
Date	2001
Type	Text
Format	text/html; charset=ISO-8859-1, digital media || 14353 bytes
Identifier	http://watthaikusinara.org

Voice Populi:

"This Thai Buddhist Temple, in the land of Buddhism, at the location of Lord Buddha's Nirvana at Kushinagar, is created from the project of returning Buddhism to the land of its origin." http://www.healingintent.com/page1016.html

"This is the well-designed site of a Theravada temple in Kusinara, India" http://www.livingdharma.org/Links.html

Read More at: http://dir.yahoo.com/Society_and_Culture/Religion_and_Spirituality/ Faiths_and__Practices/Buddhism/SchoolsLineages__and_Sects/Theravada/Temples_and_Monasteries/

Table 2D 2 Dragon Gate Temple

Title	Buddhism online at Dragon's Gate Temple
Creator (author)	Rev. Hugh Ryunyo King; ryunyo@yahoo.com
Subject or	buddha; buddhist; buddhism; sukhavati; dharma; sangha; dukkha; bodhisattva; jodo shinshu;

keywords	buddhist temple;meditation; buddhist church; meaning of life; compassion; Nagarjuna; buddhist services; mahayana buddhism; pure land Buddhism
Description	Buddhism for the Buddhist who doesn't have access to a local Temple (or can't understand them). It was a photograph sent to us by Peng Yau Tan, of Singapore. Our purpose is to promote the study and practice of the Buddha's way. MORE
Publisher	DRAGON'S GATE TEMPLE, Member of Hongaku Jodo Association of Pure Land Buddhism
Type	Text
Format	text/html, digital media || 6429 bytes
Identifier	http://www.geocities.com/Tokyo/Temple/9937/dg2.html
Language	English

Voice Populi:

"An on-line Buddhist Temple. Buddhism online in plain english. Rev. Hugh Ryunyo King, minister"
http://www.religiousresources.org/directory/listing.php?listing_id=3842

Buddhism for the Buddhist who doesn't have access to a local Temple.
http://www.searchbug.com/directory.aspx/Society/Religion_and_Spirituality/Buddhism/Lineages/Pure_Land_and_Shin/

Table 2D 3. Cyber Meditation- Daily Zen

Title	Daily Zen Meditation
Creator (author)	Elana BlueStone
Subject or keywords	Zen Art © 2004 TrueBlueDesigns; PAST DAILY ZEN; SUBSCRIBE; Fu Shan-hui (487-659; GIFTSHOP; WELCOME; SHARE TODAYS QUOTE; MEDITATION
Description	Zen quotes from the philosphies of Zen, Buddhism, and Taoism. Send your greetings with zen cards, or enter the meditation hall and share this silent space with others around the world. Inspire, uplift and offer tranquility online
Contributor	Craig Jansen
Date	March 25, 2004
Type	Text
Format	text/html, digital media || 9068 bytes
Language	English

Voice Populi:

"An elegant haven of quotes that changes daily, inspiring artwork and a dash of h umor to keep it all in perspective."
http://www.ibiblio.org/zen/

"A unique and elegant environment. Profound contemplation of the day, inspiring artwork, seasoned with a dash of humor to en-lighten the day. Come visit this spacious haven steeped in Zen spirit."
http://www.buddhanet.net/l_zen.htm

Read More at http://www.brainhelp.co.uk/RelaxationZone.html

Table 2D 4. Meditation Hall

Title	meditation hall redesigned
Creator (author)	Heather Woollard
Subject or keywords	Guided; Meditation; View; Meditations: for kids; View Meditations: for adults; Listen to Buddhist Music; indfulness of Breath; Createyour own altar
Description	To provide Buddhist resources for families and individuals interested in and / or practicing Buddhism. Particularly, to provide families with resources that they

	can use to include children in their practice. Resource for Buddhist meditations, Buddhist study, practice ideas, Buddhist activities, Buddhist music, artwork, online games and poetry.
Contributor	Heather Woollard
Date	2004-02-18
Type	Text
Format	text/html, digital media || 2495 bytes
Identifier	http://www.idsl.net/heather/onlinebuddhistcenter/meditationhall.html
Language	English

Table 2D 5. Seiwa-en's Pathways

Title	outside/in
Creator (author)	Photography: Scott Anderson
Subject or keywords	Japanese Gardens; CD-ROMs; web site design; publishing; interactive design; outside-in; video; information landscaping; Information architecture; graphic design; photography; interior design; garden design; Seiwa-en; Koichi Kawana; Sen no Rikyu; Missouri Botanical Garden; City Garden; Portland Japanese Garden; Seattle Japanese Garden; Bloedel Reserve; Kubota Garden; Brooklynn Botanical Garden; Denver Botanic Gardens; Como Ordway Memorial Japanese Garden; garden web sites; Zen Buddhism; backyard gardens; scott anderson; garden web site design; bringing the outside-in
Description	Visit the Missouri Botanical Garden's online site.
Contributor	Jody Baxter, President, The World Prayer Project
Date	2002-06-11
Type	Text
Format	text/html, digital media || 2373 bytes
Identifier	http://www.outside-in.com/seiwa-en/home/body.html
Language	English

Voice Populi:

"You can undertake a "virtual tour" of Seiwa-en, maintained by the Missouri Botanical Gardens in St. Louis"
http://www.csuohio.edu/history/
japan/japan02.html

Table 2D 6. Zen – Do-NOT-ZZZ

Title	ZEN
Subject or keywords	webmaster@do-not-zzz.com
Date	2000-05-08
Type	Text
Format	text/html, digital media || 3551 bytes
Identifier	http:// www.do-not-zzz.com

Voice Populi:

"Master the basics of Zen without falling asleep."
www.memepool.com/Subject/Religion/

"Visually rich, funny, intuitive, basic introduction to Zen. Produced by Kodai-ji Temple, Kyoto, Japan. Requires Shockwave and a 4.0+ browser."
http://open.thumbshots.org/Society/Religion_and_Spirituality/Buddhism/Lineages/Zen

Table 2D 7. Blessed Bandwidth

Title	Blessed-Bandwidth.net
Creator (author)	Shilpa Gupta
Subject or keywords	net art; web art; art on the net; Tate modern uk; art; arts; shilpa gupta; India; mumbai; religion; beliefs; blessing; blessings; the blessing; worship; customs; ideology; prayers; religious beliefs; traditions; online; gods; prayer; bandwidth; internet cable; MORE...
Description	Get Instant Peace and Happiness, Net art project by Shilpa Gupta, at Tate Online,In a world divided by religion, see her visit various religious shrines with an internet network cable and get it blessed, Choose from hindu, islam, sikh, christian, buddhism, sri sri ravi shankar. Get blessed for instant peace and happiness, MORE....
Publisher	Tate Online
Type	Text
Format	text/html, digital media || 4571 bytes
Identifier	http://www.blessed-bandwidth.net/
Language	English

Voice Populi:

"TOO busy to fulfil your spiritual obligations? Fear not, for it seems help is at hand. An Indian artist, Shilpa Gupta, has created a website that offers online blessing for Hindus, Muslims, Sikhs, Buddhists and Christians" http://timesofindia.indiatimes.com/articleshow/290541.cms

"Shilpa Gupta's site lets visitors pick a religion and watch videos of computer cables being blessed at religious sites in her home city of Bombay, or Mumbai.........They are also invited to contribute to a confession diary - with sin ratings of low, medium, high or severe - and "look after and feed" a downloadable programme called God.exe" http://news.bbc.co.uk/2/hi/entertainment/3250203.stm

Affiliation:
Apparently, beginning today, you can be blessed through your Internet connection, and you'll even receive a certificate of blessing that you can print out on your very own printer
http://www.onreligion.com/article.php?story=20031107074837553

2.5 Christianity

Basic Beliefs – Anglican Church of Canada:
Christian belief has its origin in the doctrine of creation. The Incarnation of God in our Lord Jesus Christ is the ultimate act of creation. From this truth we see the whole created order as good. The presence of sin cannot be explained by its identification with the material order. Sin resides in the person and/or the collective, the community. The gift of reason gives rise to the possibility of sin.... (Multifaith Information Manual, 2000).

Table 2E 1. Jesus Online

Title	Adoration Chapel – iVISTA Main Page
Creator (author)	Rob Ludwig, Parish Administrator St. Martin of Tours Church, Louisville, KY 40202 ludwig@louisville-catholic.net
Subject or keywords	Intercam, adore, adoration, chapel, vts, virtual, online, church
Date	2004-02-27

Type	Text
Format	Text/html, digital media || 5809 bytes
Identifier	http://adore.inetcam.com/dynamicindex/cam0av.html
Language	English

Voice Populi:

Adoration Chapel Camera
http://louisville-catholic.net/webcams/webcam_main.shtml

JESUS ONLINE: Webcam of Adoration
www.rockies.net/~spirit/charlene/cathmass.html

Table 2E 2. Miraculous Winking Jesus Christ

Title	The Miraculous Winking Jesus
Subject or keywords	jesus; christ; jesus Christ, witness, miraculous, services, rev, come, rights, life, say
Description	Thousands flock to see The Miraculous Winking Jesus Christ who winks so that God would forgive us of our sins. Don't start your day without a wink from Jesus Christ. This site is NOT related to scientology. If you are fortunate enough to witness this image of Jesus Christ wink, please tell your friends and family about this miracle! On April 23 rd 1996, this picture of Jesus Christ miraculously winked at me.
Contributor	Jonathan C. Chance, adminn@WinkingJesus.com
Date	2004
Type	Text
Format	text/html, digital media || 1614 bytes
Identifier	http://www.winkingjesus.com
Language	English

Voice Populi:

"Will you be one of the fortunate ones who sees Jesus wink?" Says Ken Banner, Doctoral Student in Religious Studies at the University of Pennsylvania http://ccat.sas.upenn.edu/~kbanner/

Referred by The Final Frontier - The Armchair Pilgrims's Guide to Online Shines
http://www.mcauley.acu.edu.au/theology/Issue3/Elmer.htm

Table 2E 3. Parish of Springfield: Virtual Meditation Room

Title	Springfield Parish: Virtual Meditation Room
Creator (author)	Fr Aquinas T. Duffy; frduffy@eircom.net
Subject or keywords	prayer; meditation; healing; parish; parishes; dublin; ireland; catholic; irish
Description	A virtual meditation site with images, sound and prayer.
Date	2000-10-01
Type	Text
Format	text/html, digital media || 1062 bytes
Identifier	http://www.kerrypoet.utvinternet.com/med/index.html
Language	English

Voice Populi:

"A beautiful, peaceful place to go to on the 'net if you seek comfort and the words of Jesus. You can even click on the 'Personal Gospel' link so that Jesus is speaking directly to you"
http://www.myhelppage2.homestead.com/healingministry.html

Referred by: Wellsprings on the Web- Drawing from the wellsprings of Christian spirituality
http://www.wellsprings.org.uk/welworld.htm

Table 2E 4. Online Confessions

Title	Confession
Subject or keywords	ULC Store; Contact Us; Home; Forum; Become Ordained; Online Confession; Prayer Requests prayer, forgive, life, peace, thought, people, who, way, guilt, ordained
Description	If you don't want to write about your sins, you may enter an "X" to signify that you have thought about your sins and wish to turn from them and seek forgiveness: As you unburden yourself of past sins, remember to also forgive those who have wronged you. It is also a useful way to begin a commitment to a better life in the future.
Contributor	Brother Kevin Andrews, Pastor; Kevin@ulc.net
Date	May 19, 2001
Type	Text
Format	text/html, digital media || 6932 bytes
Identifier	http://www.ulc.net/confession.html
Language	English

Voice Populi:

Referred by Mark's Universal Life Church
http://www.mavn.us/mark/ulc.htm

"The Universal Church of Life will ordain you via the internet and with one click of the mouse will take visitors from miss or mister to a fully fledged minister."
-Says Hendon Times
http://www.hendontimes.co.uk/archive/display.var.127336.0.netting_yourself_virtual_absolution.php

Table 2E 5. Where Truth Hurts: Confession Booth

Title	Where The Truth Hurts - Confession Booth
Creator (author)	Patrick Jonston, docjohnston@alltel.net
Subject or keywords	Science & Med; Family & Homeschooling; ProLife; News & Views; Confession is Good for the Soul; Contact Dr. J; Photo Album; Articles & Tracts; Home; Who Are We; Theology; Confession Booth;
Description	Clicking on one of the icons below does not necessarily mean that you are confessing guilt, nor that you are being pardoned for the crime you have committed. The views represented in Confession Booth do not necessarily reflect the views of anybody but God. The Almighty hereby takes all responsibility if your feelings are hurt and your self-esteem demolished.)
Date	2004-03-30
Type	Text
Format	text/html, digital media || 8824 bytes
Identifier	http://www.wherethetruthhurts.org/confession.htm
Language	English

Voice Populi:

"If your self-loathing needs a boost and you're susceptible to Christian put-downs, then drop by the Johnston Family's confession booth"
http://www.jesusmuseum.com/archiveweek89.html

"Well the Ministry of the Johnston Family has been kind enough to give all us sinners a way to confess without really confessing. With just the click of a button you can confess, or not confess, to a list of the above sins."
http://www.surreally.net/vaspider/pazuzu/archives/2003_04.html

Table 2E 6. Online Confession Box

Title	Online Confession Box
Subject or keywords	Confession, sins, sorrow, online confession

Date	2002-11-09
Type	Text
Format	text/html, digital media || 8360 bytes
Identifier	www.p45.net

Table E 7. Father Max- Confess Now

Title	Father Max - Confess Now
Subject or keywords	Once???Twice????3 or More; Online Confession is Easy, Convenient, and Fun; What's New; Home; Photo Gallery; Site Map; Contact; Optional; Commandments Violated
Date	2002-11-09
Type	Text
Format	text/html, digital media || 8360 bytes
Identifier	http://www.enter.net/~jtmaru/frmax/frmax2.html

Table 2E 8. The Virtual Church

Title	3D foyer of the virtual church!
Creator (author)	P.F. (Simon) Measures - Web Shore; simon@teachingpages.co.uk
Subject or keywords	church; online; virtual; 3D; interactive
Description	This is the online experience of Harvest Field Church, Cheltenham, England. In the virtual realm we're here for you wherever you have internet access!
Date	2002-09-10
Type	Text
Format	text/html, digital media || 1829 bytes
Identifier	http://www.thevirtualchurch.com

<u>Voice Populi:</u>

3D Flash site includes prayer room, worship hall, chat lounge, Bible school, children and teens zone.
http://dmoz.org/Society/Religion_and_Spirituality/Christianity/Churches/Cyber-Churches/

"Better than graphics, though, is the experience you'll have as you go to the Main Hall and hear the sermon by Simon Measures of Cheltenham England or read devotions. Then you can go to the prayer room and post a prayer request or pray for someone else. You can go to the church office and leave or read comments or join the church."
http://www.thischristianlife.com/articles/featured0802a.html

Table 2E9. Cyber Worship

Title	CyberWorship
Creator (author)	Paul Vickers, paul@EatTheWorld.com
Subject or keywords	Christian, praise and worship, religion, hebrew, church, radical, heart of worship
Description	Cyberworship is a resource for those interested in learning more about Christian praise and worship. Let's get back to the heart of worship
Publisher	United Layer, Inc. UNITEDLAYER-1
Date	1999-11-17
Type	Text
Format	text/html, digital media || 11451 bytes
Identifier	http://cyberworship.freeserve.co.uk

Voice Populi:
Uses the Hebrew and Greek symbols as well as english letters. Great Word study of Old and New Testaments, including Worship and praise.
http://www.tehillah.org/index4.shtml

"Devoted to all things 'praise and worship'. Presently it contains a detailed Greek & Hebrew word study on the themes of Praise and Worship in the bible."
http://www.praise.net/worship/links/

Table 2E10. Virtual Church of the Blind Chihuahua

Title	Graveyard – VCBC
Creator (author)	J. A. H. Futterman
Subject or keywords	www.dogchurch.org; Mailroom; Scriptorium; In Memory of You; Giftshop; Graveyard; School; ; Forum; Home; Richard Daniel; Canine Funeral Service; Chapel; 1999. All rights reserved; DogPAC; J. A. H. Futterman; Copyright; Restroom; Send this page to a friend; VCBC
Contributor	John A. H. Futterman, PhD, scooper@dogchurch.org
Date	2004-02-22
Type	Text
Format	text/html, digital media || 10620 bytes
Identifier	http://dogchurch.org/graveyard/index.html

Voice Populi:
"Sounds funny, but it's not. Here's a guy who has baptized libertinism and skepticism, and wants to call it faith. No thanks."
http://www.gty.org/~phil/bookmark/fulllist.htm

"It will leave you laughing, either with religion, or at religion."
http://www.psychwww.com/psyrelig/links.htm

"It's sense of humor alone makes it well worth a visit. Beyond that we'll let John Futterman speak for himself. "This is," he writes, "a sacred place in cyberspace named in honor of a little old dog with cataracts, who barked sideways at strangers, because he couldn't see where they were" "
Read more at: http://www.aril.org/Christian.html

Table 2E11. Requiem

Title	Catholicireland.net - Requiem
Subject or keywords	Liturgy; Stories; back to catholicireland.net; Library; Contacts
Description	Personal accounts of coming to terms with the loss of loved ones Guides for funeral liturgy and for prayers for wakes and removals Reading resources to help with grief and bereavement issues
Contributor	Alan McGuckian SJ
Date	2004-03-16
Type	Text
Format	text/html, digital media || 1349 bytes
Identifier	http://catholicireland.net/pages/index.php?nd=50

Figure 2E 12. The Perpetual Web Rosary

Title	Perpetual Web Rosary
Creator (author)	Robert Roesser, Catholic United for Life, Southeast Michigan
Subject or keywords	Perpetual Web Rosary, web rosary, ongoing rosary, world-wide community, jesus, father, God, Glory be, Catholics, United for Life, Mother of God, death, Mary, Christ, Christian, hail

Description	As you say each prayer click within the rosary to advance to the next prayer. Spanish version | Italian version | French version | Vietnamese version Catholics United for Life If more than one person is participating at a time the number of prayers from all are added.
Date	2004
Identifier	http://www.mich.com/~buffalo/rosary.html
Language	English

Voice Populi:

"Ongoing online virtual Rosary sponsored by Catholics for Life. Includes Spanish version and French, as well as English"
http://www.nunshabits.com/links2.htm

"A web-based, perpetual Rosary. All the Rosary prayers are provided"
http://dmoz.org/Society/Religion_and_Spirituality/Christianity/Denominations/Catholicism/Prayer_and_Spirituality/Devotions/Marian/Rosary/

Table 2E 13. CyberChurch- evangelpraisecenter.

Title	CyberChurch
Subject or keywords	Webservant's Inn; Evangel Praise Center's; About Us; God's Plan for You; Kid Power; Tues 6 p.m. PST beginning March 12; Women; Home; Click Here; Click here; What We Believe; Christian Living; What is a Cyber-Church; Cyberchurch; Portal; Contact Us; These Doors Never Close; Evangel Events; Bible Study; Youth; Pastor's Desk; Daily Devotion; Teen
Date	2003-09-20
Format	text/html, digital media || 6495 bytes
Identifier	http://www.evangelpraisecenter.org/cyberchurch

Voice Populi:

"Weekly Bible studies, mp3 files of sermons and pastoral contact is available here."
http://www.ourownstories.com/god_loves_you.htm

"An Assemblies of God church online with Bible study, streaming sermons, pastoral counseling, prayer, chats and discussion"
http://www.crosssearch.com/Churches_and_Denominations/Online_Fellowships/93159.php

"Cyberchurch outreach of Evangel Praise Center includes streaming audio sermons and Bible studies, live chats, and pastoral contact"
http://zeal.com/category/preview.jhtml?cid=10047127

Table 2E 14. Porter

Title	Porter
Subject or keywords	Seeking God; the Guestmaster; Giftshop; the Giftshop; information; 1998 The Monastery of Christ in the Desert; Brother URL; Home; Chant; reservations; our life; The Porter; Light; your monastic guide; Porter; News; Monastic Studies
Date	2003-08-10
Type	Text
Format	text/html, digital media || 3318 bytes
Identifier	http://www.christdesert.org/noframes/porter.html

Voice Populi:
"The Monastery of Christ in the Desert Brother URL Is Your Monastic Guide. He is the Porter at the Monastery of Christ in the Desert, and it's his job to insure that you have an enjoy able tour of the monastery. Just pick the site you would like to visit from the list"
http://www.cedarnet.org/bles_sac/websites.html

"This site is a good resource for information on monasticism in general and the Rule of St. Benedict in particular. There are also good sections on chant, prayer, and the Desert Fathers. There are a few questionable authors offered in the bookstore, but the site as a whole is excellent."
http://www.catholicculture.org/sites/site_view.cfm?recnum=1597

Table 2E 15. Sacred Space: Jesuit prayer

Title	Sacred Space - the prayer site run by the Irish Jesuits
Creator (author)	Jesuit Communication Centre, 36 Lower Leeson Street, Dublin 2, Ireland.
Subject or keywords	prayer; pray; spirituality; spiritual; God; Spirit; Christ; Christian; Jesuit; Ignatius; Ignatian; devotion; scripture; bible; sacred; space; meditation; contemplation; communion; holy; divine
Description	Sacred Space is a prayer site, updated daily, which guides you through a ten minute session of prayer, centred on a passage of scripture chosen specially for the day.
Date	2004-04-30
Type	Text
Format	text/html, digital media || 12059 bytes
Identifier	http://www.jesuit.ie/prayer

Voice Populi:
Referred by Roman Catholic Archdiocese of Halifax, Nova Scotia, Canada http://www.catholichalifax.org/

A sign of the times, one of the best places to pray could be in front of your computer. This web site run by the Society of Jesus features a 10 minute prayer session each day, based on a short passage from Scripture.
http://www.cathud.com/info/

"Pray? At my computer? Try it!"
Says St. Joseph Catholic Community (http://www.stjosepheldersburg.org/)

Table 2E 16. Experience Menlo

Title	Welcome to Menlo Park Presbyterian Church / Silicon Valley
Subject or keywords	Special; Mission; Seminars; Servant; Village; Technologies; Women; Marriage; Children; Baptism; Trips; eStore; Oxygen; Design; Care; Discipleship; Serve; Cong; Kingdom; Info; Preschool; Senior; Kirk; Prayer; Missions; Adult; FOG; MORE...
Description	Menlo Park Presbyterian Church is a Christ centered church serving Silicon Valley and the world
Publisher	Hurricane Electric HURRICANE-1
Contributor	Brent James
Date	2004
Type	Text
Format	text/html; charset=ISO-8859-1, digital media || 27647 bytes
Identifier	http://www.mppc.org/more_about_menlo/Experience_Menlo
Language	English

Voice Populi:

"One would expect a large church in California's Silicon Valley to be technology-rich, and Menlo Park Presbyterian Church takes full advantage of electronic enhancement to enrich the music and worship experience of the congregation of 3,000."

http://www.beliefnet.com/story/136/story_13687_1.html

"Sermons by John Ortberg, formerly a teaching pastor at Willow Creek Community Church"

www.wennerdahl.com/pages/347860/

Table 2E 17. Prayer Schedule for PopulationPrayer.com

Title	Prayer Schedule for PopulationPrayer.com
Subject or keywords	Prayer for the Global ecology of the Earth; Prayer Subjects; Prayer for Global Peace.
Description	The following times apply to the time zone where you live, whether you live in China or Brazil, in Canada or in Australia, etc; 8:30 pm; The following prayer schedule has the times and subjects for which you can pray along with us all around the world; 8:15 pm; 8:45 pm; Prayer for the sick and suffering; Prayer for people in need; PopulationPrayer.com; We invite you to pray with your heart and soul, while doing so imagine other people around the world praying right along with you; The success of PopulationPrayer.com and its vision depends on you and everyone that is hoping for a better world.....MORE
Contributor	Graham
Date	2004-04-06
Type	Text
Format	text/html, digital media || 3707 bytes
Identifier	http://www.populationprayer.com/prayer_schedule.html
Language	English

Voice Populi:

PopulationPrayer.com is a prayer site devoted to worldwide prayer. Our goal is to have a portion of the Earth's Population praying together at the same time.

http://www.mychristianweb.com/guide/Reference/Worship/index.shtml

Referred by CrossSearch - an online directory of Christian websites

http://www.crosssearch.com/Reference/Prayer/85688.php

Table 2E.18. Internet Daily Chapel

Title	The Internet Daily Chapel
Creator (author)	Bill McGinnis, Director B,cgin@patriot.net
Subject or keywords	ETHICS; Featured Products; FEATURED PRODUCTS; reading Of The Scriptures; CONSULTING; POLITICS; Declaration Of Faith; bmcgin@patriot.net; The Birth Of Jesus Official Text; CLICKING HERE; Rev. Bill McGinnis, Director; Christmas Day; AUTOMOTIVE; www.InternetDailyChapel.org... MORE...
Description	To provide a complete Christian worship service online
Publisher	Abovenet Communications, Inc ABOVENET-4
Contributor	Volunteers
Date	2004-03-22
Type	Text
Format	text/html, digital media || 6832 bytes
Identifier	http://patriot.net/~bmcgin/chapel.html
Language	English

Voice Populi:
"A Complete Christian Worship Service Each Day" http://www.wsmcafe.com/new_users/0/8/08091159nbw/

"A daily worship service provided by Bill McGinnis at Gospelgate Christian Ministries, available by subscription or on the world wide web. Recommended."
Gospelgate Christian Ministries (http://www.iclnet.org/pub/resources/s-910.html)

Table 2E 19. The shroud of Turin

Title	Shroud of Turin - The holy face of Christ
Subject or keywords	The Work of God; The Shroud of Turin; www.theworkofgod.org
Description	Shroud of Turin - The holy face of Christ
Publisher	Accretive Technology Group, Inc. ANI-002
Date	2001-10-24
Type	Text
Format	text/html, digital media || 4077 bytes
Identifier	http://www.theworkofgod.org/shroud.htm
Voice Populi:	

"This is a Catholic information site from Australia"
http://www.priestsforlife.org/plgroups/generalchristianlinks.htm

Table 2E 20. Live Prayer.com

Title	Liveprayer.com, Prayer and Miracles 24 hours a day
Creator	Bill Keller
Subject	prayer; miracles; healing; finances; relationships; devotions; christian cards; christian; Jesus; testimonies
Description	Live Person Praying For Your Needs 24 hours a day. Visit The Miracle Center for Healing, Finances, and Relationships. Free Daily Devotional Sent To Your Email Box. Send Free Christian E-cards to your friends. Honor a Loved One on our Front Page!
Date	2004-03-08
Type	Text
Format	text/html, digital media || 18255 bytes
Identifier	http://liveprayer.com
Voice populi:	

"Daily devotional written by Bill Keller founder of LivePrayer.com which has webcasting of pastors and other volunteers praying over the Internet 24 hours a day, seven days a week. Join the hundreds of thousands who are blessed each day by these insights into the Word of God."
http://www.church2000.org/devotions/

Table 2E 21. Saint Rose of Lima Virtual Prayer Room

Title	Saint Rose of Lima Parish Home Page
Subject or keywords	Saint; Rose; Lima; Roman Catholic; Catholic; education; academic; religious; religious education; parish; New York; Rockaway; Rockaway Beach; spiritual
Description	This is the official site of Saint Rose of Lima Roman Catholic Church in Rockway Beach, New York. In addition to the parish information, this site offers its visitors religious education and academic information for spiritual and personal growth.
Date	2004-04-02
Type	Text
Format	text/html, digital media || 23918 bytes
Identifier	http://www.stroseoflimarb.org/index.html

Language	English

Table 2E 22. Alpha Church

Title	Alpha Church
Creator (author)	Rev. Patricia E. Walker
Subject or keywords	Alpha church, church, free bible, bible, free, worship, events, actions, spirituality, Christian global Church, Baptism, kids, prayer, jesus, Christ, Jesus Christ, "Jesus Christ, Jesus, Christ, Savior, Lord, God, church home, Holy Spirit, holy spirit, jesus, Christian church, cyber church,
Description	Alpha Church is a full on-line Christian global Church. Our Worship Services involve people of every age, race, and ability. You may Worship twenty-four/seven. Take Holy Communion, receive Baptism, be Married, and community chat with other people like you who are growing in their faith and understanding of Jesus Christ, our Savior. (Please note: if the Worship Service has pauses during the first playing, let it play through fully once, and the second time through will be pause free. Also, turn your sound volume to a medium level when viewing messages.) Prayer requests are usually distributed to church participants on a bi-weekly basis. Rev. Walker, our minister, starts to pray as soon as the request is received.
Date	2003-11-26
Type	Text
Format	text/html, digital media || 1850 bytes
Identifier	http://www.alphachurch.org
Language	English

Voice Populi:
"A full Christian community with traditional and contemporary worship services."
http://directory.google.com/Top/Society/Religion_and_Spirituality/Christianity/Churches/Cyber-Churches/

Affiliations: "A completely online, non-denominational church."
http://www.abqwebwomen.org/business.htm

2.6 Hinduism:

Basic Beliefs:

- A wide variety of beliefs held together by an attitude of mutual tolerance. All approaches to God are valid.
- Humankind's goal is to break free of this imperfect world and reunite with God.
- The soul reincarnates and transmigrates until reunion with God.
- Many Hindus are vegetarians as the killing of living creatures is not favored.
- One must perform his or her duties to God, parents, teachers and society

(Multifaith Information Manual, 2000)

Table 2F 1. Mahakali

Title	Lakshmi International – Hindu Deity devotional paintings
Creator (author)	Mark Rosen; mark@mahakali.com
Subject or keywords	Shiva, Krishna, Kali, Durga, Lakshmi, Rama Hanuman,Vishna, Subramanya, artikeya,hindu,deity,india,incense,lotus oil,paintings,yatra,divali,nataraj, paintings, artist, hindu,

	brahma, kali, ramayana, divine, vishnu, portraits, shri
Description	Devotional Hindu Deity paintings from India. Paintings on oil, silk and paper. Krishna paintings, Radha paintings, Radha Krishna paintings. Paintings of Krishna, Shiva, Kali, Ganesh, Durga, Lakshmi, Rama, Hanuman, Vishnu and many others in oil, silk and paper. Gallery of Deity paintings Order online with our secure shopping cart. The purpose of these web pages is to take you on a yatra (pilgrimage) to have holy darshan (vision) of different manifestations of Devi Mata ...MORE....
Date	2003
Format	Text, digital media 5900 bytes
Identifier	http://www.mahakali.com/yatra/yatra.htm
Language	English

Voice Populi:

"Go on a virtual yatra (pilgrimage). Along the way, you will learn about each Hindu temple, as well as stories about the gods. The site is dotted with pictures and sound files to enrich the 'journey.'"
http://www.milligan.edu/bible/pkenneson/hindu.htm

"Devotional Hindu Deity paintings from India. Paintings on oil, silk and paper ..."
http://jyotisha.00it.com/links/hinduism.html

Table 2F 2. Eprarthana.com

Title	EPrarthana.com - Offer Poojas/Archanas & Buy Religious Products > Poojas (Specific Purpose Poojas, Pooja for your Star, Fasting Days Pooja, Online Pooja,...) > Shopping (Music - Cassettes & CD's, Books, Arts & Crafts) > What's New - Saranam Ayyappa CD
Subject or keywords	Archana; Pooja; Purohit; Prohit; Religion; Spirituality; Poojai; Hindu; Chennai; Madras; South India; Tamil Nadu; India; Spiritual; Religious; Temple; Koil; Kovil; Ashram; Mandhir; Kanchipuram; Mandir; Aalayam; Deivam; Kadavul; Prarthanai; Prarthana; Offer; Prayer; Aayilyam; Anusham; Asuvathi; Avittam; Bharani; Barani; Hastham; Karthigai; Krithigai; Kettai; Masham; Magam....MORE
Description	EPrarthana is the only web site that allows you to order Pooja's / Archana's over the internet to more than 2000 temples in India.
Contributor	Nambi, nimbi@vsnl.com
Date	2004 May 4
Type	Text
Format	text/html, digital media || 49074 bytes
Identifier	http://eprarthana.com/virtual/vshiva.asp
Language	English (background prayer in Sanskrit)

Voice-Populi:

"Arrange Hindu Archanas over the Internet in any of over 2000 temples in India [through eprathana.com]"
http://www.hindu.org/temples-ashrams/

"Sumathi, who lives in India and works for the Bank of Madura, says that most of the employees start wirk only after doing ganpati pooja downloaded from e-prathana.com"
http://www.rediff.com/search/2003/feb/26god.htm
Referred by SAMACHAR -- The Bookmark for the Global Indian
http://www.samachar.com/religion/

Table 2F3. Confession/ Arti

Title	Online Aarti
Publisher	AO Technologies AOTECH
Contributor	A Zed Infocom Pvt Ltd Presentation
Type	Text

Format	text/html, digital media || 5384 bytes
Identifier	http://urday.com/onlineaarti.htm
Voice Populi:	

"Urday.com : is a spiritual web site with the sole purpose of promoting Sanatan Dharma and spreading its awareness among the masses. It has a panel comprising of prominent scholars.....who are ever ready to give appropriate advises to you as well as solutions to any kind of your problems."
http://www.hindu.org/teachers-orgs/identity/
"Live Chat with Panditji to solve your problems, providing Indian Astrology, know about ur future, and more"
http://www.allspiritual.com/Hinduism.php3

Table 2F 4. E-Anjali

Title	DurgaPuja 2000: Home
Subject or keywords	Movie; Music; Free E-mail; E-Anjali; GuruAnimation; Feedback; Women; Fashion; Cartoons; Home; Kids; Travel; Horoscope; Archives; Timeline; Recipe; Shop; Education; News; Online Parikrama; Books,
Description	Let us celebrate Durga Puja in a whole new way this year, and make the Pujas come alive with love, light and laughter in the hearts of one and all. it is a time for coming together, of reunion and rejuvenation, of the rebirth of our spiritual selves .
Contributor	webmaster@netguruindia.com
Type	Text
Format	text/html, digital media || 18484 bytes
Identifier	http://www.netguruindia.com/puja2000/anjali2.html
Voice Populi:	

"Click "e-Anjali" for an interactive virtual puja"
http://home.wlu.edu/~lubint/SoAsiaPage.htm

Table 2F 5. Durga Pujas- Live Webcam Coverage from USA

Title	Puja 2001 - A Global Competition to celebrate Durga Puja – Durgapujas along with Chaltabagan Sarbojonin - Live Webcam Coverage from USA
Creator	Dr. D. Ghosh
Subject or keywords	Durga, puja, durga puja, celebrate globally, puja parikrama, kolkata, anjali, recipe, ankur, bangla puja, music, India
Identifier	www.durgapujas.com
Language	English
Voice Populi:	

"You will surely feel nostalgic when you will watch the Flash movie at the site"
http://ajantrik.8m.net/www.htm

"Can send puja greetings, has a children's drawing contest. Also has a quiz and adda section."
http://www.prabasi.org/Activities/DurgaPuja2000/DP2000NetPuja.html

Table 2F 6. Prarthana

Title	Prarthana : Online Hindu Temple Worship Services - Pooja, Archana, Homam, Prarthana in Indian Temples Tirupathi, Guruvayur, Palani, Tirunallar in India
Subject or keywords	hindu temples; india online worship service; temple services india; online ganapathi homam; temples in india; eprarthana; balaji temple; tirumala tirupati; guruvayur; palani temple; tirunallaru;

	online prayer; hindu deities; hindu philosophy
Description	Prarthana offers online pooja,archana,homam, prarthana and other worship services in hindu temples in India
Date	2004-02-13
Type	Text
Format	text/html, digital media || 14219 bytes
Identifier	http://www.prarthana.com/

Voice Populi:

"Offers puja, archana, prarthana and homa at some of the most sacred temples in India"
http://www.hindu.org/temples-ashrams/

"You can send in mail orders for items such as music cassettes, CDs, religious books and pictures of deities."
http://www.timescomputing.com/20000823/sit1.html

Table 2F 7. The Hindu Kids Universe- Multimedia

Title	The Hindu Kids Universe - Multimedia
Subject or keywords	Hindu Kids; Aarati; Morning Prayer; Aum; om; Surya Nanaskar; Shlokas for Gods; Shlokas; Morning Prayer Shlokas; Namaskar Mantra; Peace Prayer; Shlokas for gods; Stotras; Goddesses Gauri; Goddesses Gayatri; Goddesses Kamakshi; Stotras on Goddesses; Goddesses Lalitha; Goddesses Laxmi; Goddesses Meenakshi; Other Goddesses; Goddesses Rajeswari; Goddesses saraswati; Stotras on Gods; Lord Vishnu; Lord Ganesh; MORE…
Description	Largest Hindu and Hinduism, Hindu Kids site on the net. Contains comprehensive introduction to Hindu dharma, complete text of 85 books, several scriptures, listing of Hindu temples around the world, newsgroup archives, information on Hindu culture, Hindu festivals, Hindu calendar, Hindu history, links to all known Hindu sites, a special section for kids and current events. Special sections on Jain, Sikh and Buddha dharma.
Publisher	American Digital Network ADN-WEST
Contributor	cbando@lynx.new.edu
Type	Text
Format	text/html; charset=ISO-8859-1, digital media || 7331 bytes
Identifier	http://www.hindukids.org/pray/aarati.html

Table 2F 8. D/FW Hindu Temple Society

Title	D/FW Hindu Temple Society ::: Online Puja ::: Shri Radha Krishna
Subject or keywords	Kamsa Chanoora Mardhanam; Upcoming Events; Vasudeeva Sutam Devam; Kids Korner; Links on Hinduism; Home; Monthly Activities; About the Temple; Become Member; Meet your Priests; Sub Committees; Aarati; Temple Hall; Krishnam Vande Jagadgurum; Community Services; Calendar; Deevaki Paramaanandam; Donation; Need Volunteers; Contact Us; Magazine: ARCHANA; Puja Services; Online Puja
Date	2003-05-22
Type	Text
Format	text/html, digital media || 14492 bytes
Identifier	http://www.dfwhindutemple.org/radhe_krishna.htm

Voice Populi:

"Serving Texas Hindus with pujas to Maha Lakshmi, Venkateshwara, Shiva, Ganesha, Kartikeya, Ayyappa, Ram Parivar, Durga, Srinathji, Vitthoba and Rukmini, Krishna & Radha, Hanuman, Dattatreya and Navagrahas."
http://www.hindu.org/temples-ashrams/

Table 2F 9. Mataji's Ultimate Site- And Hindu Temple Links

Title	Mataji's Ultimate Site- And Hindu Temple Links

Subject or keywords	mataji; ambaji; temple; gayatri; navratri; mandir; manavmandir; ahmedabad; india; amba; religion; gujarat; gujarati; ma; god; goddess; hindu religion; indian festivals; matadi; indian temple; spirituality; bhajan; kirtan; hindu religion ....MORE
Description	Beautiful Indian Goddess Mataji, Ambaji extends Blessings from Temple. Spiritual Experience. Links to Hindu God/Goddess. Click for Free Prasad. Listen Gayatri Chants
Publisher	Time Warner Telecom TWTC-NETBLK-16
Date	2003-08-14
Type	Text
Format	text/html, digital media || 8839 bytes
Identifier	http://www.mataji.org

Voice Populi:

"Beautiful Goddess Mataji Ambaji welcomes to Award winning website click to get free prasad."
http://www.ispsquash.com/Link_WorshipLinkPage.htm

"Describes the Hindu Goddess Mataji, also known as Ambajji who is known to be the source of divine energy"
Netscape Directory
http://h-207-200-81-7.netscape.com/Society/Religion_and_Spirituality/
Hinduism

"Take blessings from Manavmandir Ahmedabad and listen Gayatri chants."
http://ca.dir.yahoo.com/Society_and_Culture/religion_and_spirituality/faiths_and_practices/hinduism/deities/durga

Table 2F 10. Virtual Temple

Title	Virtual Temple
Creator (author)	Vasudeva Mahavisno, Department of Pathology, University of Michigan
Subject or keywords	Virtual temple, virtual, temple, meditation room, meditation, gallery, hindu, god, library, shrine
Description	Back to HSC mainpage
Date	12-May-1998
Type	Text
Format	text/html; charset=iso-8859-1, digital media || 1706 bytes
Identifier	http://www.umich.edu/~hindu/temple/temple.html
Language	English

Voice Populi:

"Go to Shrine link and click on the Parvathi link. (The entire site provides a good introduction to some of the important Gods and Goddesses)."
http://faculty.pittstate.edu/~knichols/goddess.html •

Referred by The Time magazine
http://www.time.com/time/interactive/religion/god.html

Table 2F 11. Ganapati Bappa Moriya

Title	Ganapati bappa Moriya
Subject or keywords	Virtual Darshan of Ganeshji; AhmedabadCity Home; Offer Free Prasad to Lord Ganesha; Gift Prasad for your family
Date	2000-12-18
Type	Text
Format	text/html, digital media || 3847 bytes
Identifier	www.ahmedabadcity.com/GaneshChaturthi/indexVD.htm

Table 2F 12. Blessings on the Net

Title	Blessings On The Net
Subject or keywords	Special; Other Links; About Us; Mini Sabarimalai; Greetings; Shopping; Help; Navagraha; A comprehensive portal on Indian culture providing value added services and products, catering to religious and spiritual needs of Indians across the globe; Temple Official Websites...MORE
Description	If you see a human face in the icon below then one of our Customer Service agents is online and available to chat or else click below for your feedback. All Rights Reserved BlessNet India Enterprises Pvt. Offer Online donation for Lord Shani Shani Temple More Info
Date	2001
Type	Text
Format	text/html, digital media || 53642 bytes
Identifier	http://blessingsonthenet.com
Language	English

Voice Populi:

"Offer On-line Puja and Donation at some of the famous temples in India through www.blessingsonthenet.com, a platform for temples in India to host their official websites. The website provides information on the Temples and Temple Deities, the History, Legends, Management,...offer donations/ book pujas to temple of your choice."
http://www.mmbayarea.org/Marathi-World/God%20On%20Web.htm

"A comprehensive portal on Indian culture providing value added services and products, catering to religious and spiritual needs of Indians across the globe.- features temples, tour packages, books, audio clips, pictures, art, and online puja offerings"
http://hinduwebsite.com/hinduismgenlinks.htm

Table 2F 13. Sabarimala- Sree Ayyappan Temple

Title	Lord Ayyappa of Sabarimala, Kerala, India
Creator (author)	P. Mohamkannan
Subject or keywords	swamy; swamiye; sharanam; sharanamayappa; hari; hariharan; hariharasudan; hariharasudhan; ayappaswamy; shabarimala; shabarigiri; pallikettu; vavar; ambalam; kshetram; lord; bhagwan; malikapurathamma; neythenga; MORE...
Description	Lord Shree Ayyappan of Sabarimala in Kerala and the procedure of visiting the hill temple is explained in the pages
Date	2004-04-02
Type	Text
Format	text/html; charset=UTF-8, digital media || 22687 bytes
Identifier	www.ayyappan-ldc.com/

Voice Populi:

"Lord Ayyappan of Sabarimala, Kerala - A complete guide to Sabarimala"
http://www.gis.net/~rajiv/hinduism.html
"offers introduction, background, austerities, pilgrimage information, temple opening dates, photo gallery, and more."
http://ca.dir.yahoo.com/Society_and_Culture/religion_and_spirituality/faiths_and_practices/hinduism/temples

Table 2F 14. Swamiye Sharanam

Title	Sabarimala Sree Ayyappan Temple
Subject or keywords	Sabarimala, austerities, makara, jyothi, events, history, route, pumba, erumeli, today, sabarigiri, SREE AYYAPPA TEMPLE, temple, kerala, lord parasurama, Ramayana, lord, lord ayyappa
Contributor	Prakash, Webmaster
Type	Text
Format	text/html; charset=ISO-8859-1, digital media || 8907 bytes
Identifier	http://www.sabarigiri.org/sabarimala.htm
Language	English (background prayer in Malayalam)

Voice Populi:
"Information on Lord Ayyappa and Sabarimala Sree Dharma Sastha Temple."
http://directory.google.com/Top/Regional/Asia/India/Kerala/Localities/Sabarimala/

2.7 Islam:

Basic Beliefs:

There are five pillars of Islam, They are:

- Declaration of Faith (Shahadah) – Declaring allegiance to God and Prophet Muhammad.
- Prayers (Salah) – establish prayers five times daily.
- Fasting (Saum) – Month-long fasting in the month of Ramadan.
- Charity (Zakah) – Pay annual charity.
- Pilgrimage (Hajj) – Journey to Mecca once in a lifetime.

(Multifaith Information Manual, 2000; www.omc.ca)

Table 2 G1. Projek Cyber Mosque

Title	Welcome to Projek Cyber Mosque MPSJ
Creator (author)	Toshiba
Subject or keywords	MPSJ; KSM; Earthmedia, projek, cyber mosque, mpsj, mosque, cyber
Date	2002-06-03
Format	text/html, digital media || 8842 bytes
Identifier	http://cybermosque.mpsj.gov.my/index.html

Table 2G 2. First Mosque on the Moon

Title	Arch. Khalid Aljammaz website
Creator (author)	Khaed M. Alijammaz; khaled@alijammaz.net
Date	2001-09-30
Type	Text
Format	text/html, digital media || 1108 bytes
Identifier	http://www.alsahah.com/jamaz/

Table 2G 3. Salat Relay- snap shot

Title	IslamiCity.com - Islam; The Global Muslim eCommunity
Subject or keywords	"Islam Allah God Religion Muslim Mohammed Muhammad Prophet Arab American Jesus Christianity Judaism Jew Catholic Real Audio Quran Hadith Imam Islam Islam Salat Interest Islamic Free Islamiyet
Description	A great information site about Islam and Muslims in text,audio and video. Also, a good reference for non-Muslims who are searching about Islam, Muslims, Prophet Muhammed(pbuh), other prophets (e.g. Jesus, Mousa) and religions (Christianity, Judaism, Buddism)
Type	Text
Format	text/html, digital media || 5548 bytes

Identifier	http://islamicity.com/m/mediadisplay

Table 2G4. Moon Sighting

Title	Moonsighting with Astronomy
Creator (author)	K. Shaukat; Shaukat@moonsighting.com
Subject or keywords	astronomy; new moon; new-moon; newmoon; moonsighting; moon sighting; moon-sighting; sighting; hilal; hilaal; helal; helaal; crescent; crescent moon; visibility; lunar visibility; crescent visibility; moon visibility; lunar calendar; islam; islamic calendar; Khalid Shaukat
Description	Where on earth earliest moonsighting is possible, using criteria developed by Khalid Shaukat
Type	Text
Format	text/html, digital media || 13719 bytes
Identifier	http://moonsighting.com

Voice Populi:

"Earliest visibility of moon across the globe, calculated by the latest criterion developed by Shaukat" http://www.cv.nrao.edu/fits/www/yp_planetary.html

"Moonsighting.com - detailed information about moonsighting and astronomy" http://www.zawaj.com/events/ramadhan_main.html

"Moonsighting with Astronomy - Where on earth earliest moonsighting is possible, calculated by criteria developed by Shaukat" http://www.universetoday.com/html/directory/moon.html

Table 2G5 Glorious Month of Ramadhan

Title	Glorious Month of Ramadhan
Subject or keywords	Sunni, Shi'i, Shi`a, Shia, Shi'ite, Shiite, Islamic, Shi'a, ahlul bayt, digital islamic library project, DILP, al-islam, Islam, Muslim, God, Allah, religion
Publisher	AT&T WorldNet Services ATT
Contributor	Ahlul Bayt DILP
Type	Text
Format	text/html, digital media || 5548 bytes
Identifier	http://www.al-islam.org/help/ramadhan
Source	http://www.al-islam.org/info/contact2.asp

Voice Populi:

"Info about Islam, beliefs, current and historical events and more." www.conjure.com/religion.html

Table 2G 6 Nisab Calculator Table's Page - Jami'yyatul Ulama Canada

Title	Jami'yyatul Ulama Canada, Canadian Council of Muslim Theologians (CCMT)
Subject or keywords	Arabs and Muslims Are Victims of Anti-Semitism; Nisaab Table; Links; About Us; Important Bulletin; www.jucanada.org; Dozens of abuse inquiries underway; Mahr Fatimi; Christians Massacre Hundreds of Muslims; J U Home; UM Financial (Islamic Financial Services - survey; Contact Us; Masajid; Read; Halal Foods; Contact Us; Youth Tarbiyyah Program; Cricket World Cup; Shariah Program; Weak, Saheeh, Dha'eef, Hasan, Mawdhoo; Fabrication Ahadith Explained...MORE
Date	2004-05-18
Type	Text
Format	text/html, digital media || 38445 bytes
Identifier	http://jucanada.org

Voice Populi:
"This is a non profit organization of Muslim Theologians (religious scholars). Its inception is to serve the socio-religious needs of the Ummah."
http://www.islamcan.com/cgi-bin/links/islamcan.cgi?action=view-links

Table 2G7 Zakat Calculation Page - Council of Islamic Organizations of Greater Chicago

Title	Z a k a t. C h i c a g o
Subject or keywords	Zakat Online; jewelry; Loans Given; Nisab and Rates; Categories of Wealth; Cows and Buffalos; Business; nisab; Apply for; Directions; Calculation; Nisab & Rates; Download Zakat; Web Site; Contact Us; Camels; zakat@ciogc.org; Minerals
Publisher	Potomac Networks POTOMAC-BLK1
Contributor	The Council of Islamic Organizations of Greater Chicago 330 E. Roosevelt Road, Suite G5, Lombard, IL 60184 Phone: 630-629-7490 Fax: 630-629-7492
Type	Text
Format	text/html, digital media || 16150 bytes
Identifier	http://www.zakatchicago.com/new/zakahN.asp

Voice Populi:
Referred by The Council of Islamic Organizations of Greater Chicago (www.ciogc.org)

Table 2G8. Zakat Calculation - Comprehensive Form – Islamic Foundation

Title	Zakat Calculation - Comprehensive Form
Subject or keywords	Zakat, calculator, calculations, form, islam, info, The Council of Islamic Organizations of Greater Chicago
Publisher	The Council of Islamic Organizations of Greater Chicago, 330 E. Roosevelt Road, Suite G5, Lombard, IL 60184
Type	Text
Format	Text/html, digital media
Identifier	http://www.zakatinfo.com/calc_comp.shtml
Language	English

Table 2G9 Zakat Calculator – Islamic Voice

Title	Zakat Calculator
Subject or keywords	The KFUPM FANS Group; Total Zakath amount to be paid; LESS : General Liabilities (other than deducted above; 9; Zakat on Cash and Bank Balances; Zakat on pure silver; Jewelry, House hold items made of silver etc; Zakath Calculator; mibuhari@ccse.kfupm.edu.sa; Business Stock; X. Liabilities; VII. Zakat on loans, Government bonds, provident funds, LIC Etc; IX. Zakat on Animals including poultry and fish farming; Zakat on Animal/Poultry/Fish Farming (Other than egg laying birds & milk yielding animals; Note….MORE..
Publisher	Islamic Voice
Date	2003-12-13
Type	Text
Format	text/html, digital media || 29866 bytes
Identifier	http://faculty.kfupm.edu.sa/MATH/kabir/zakat.htm

Table 2G. 10.Hajj- Movie

Title	haj-movie
Creator (author)	Hajj, movie, ali, personal, sistani.org, sistani
Date	2003-05-17
Type	Text

Format	text/html, digital media || 830 bytes
Identifier	http://sistani.org/html/urd/manasek/haj-movie.html

Voice Populi:

"Sistani.Org - Personal website of Ali Husaini Sistani"
http://www.theconnection.org/shows/2004/01/20040119_a_main.asp

Table 2G 11.The Noble Sanctuary

Title	The Noble Sanctuary
Subject or keywords	noble sanctuary; haram al-sharif; al-aqsa mosque; dome of the rock; muslim jerusalem; islam; muslim; jerusalem; muhammad; islamic architecture
Description	The history and significance of the Noble Sanctuary, Dome of the Rock and Al-Aqsa Mosque in Jerusalem.
Contributor	AQ Spiker, Webmaster
Date	2004-03-01
Format	text/html, digital media || 4045 bytes
Identifier	http://www.noblesanctuary.com
Language	English

Voice Populi:

"At the heart of Jerusalem is the Noble Sanctuary, Al-Haram al-Sharif, enclosing over 35 acres of fountains, gardens, buildings and domes. At its southernmost end is Al-Aqsa Mosque and at its centre the celebrated Dome of the Rock. The entire area is regarded as a mosque and comprises nearly one sixth of the walled city of Jerusalem."
http://www.kwsnet.com/religion.html
"This online guide is a tour of what's called the Temple Mount by Jews, the Noble Sanctuary by Muslims."
http://www.americanpressinstitute.org/content/3931.cfm

Table 2G 12. Majalis

Title	Majalis
Subject or keywords	www.yahusain.com; majalis; urdu; English, husain, USA, maulana, raza pasha, murtaza jaferi, india
Date	2004-03-16
Type	Text
Format	text/html, digital media || 14120 bytes
Identifier	http://www.yahusain.com/majalis.htm

Voice Populi:

"http://www.yahusain.com broadcasts live Urdu & English majlis from idera-Jaferia, located at Burtonsville, Maryland USA, at 8.30 PM Eastern TIME. Urdu majlis are recited by Maulana Murtuza Jaferi, and English majlis are recited by Maulana Raza Pasha. Both the Maulana's are from India."
www.shianews.com/hi/announcements/majaalis/index.php

Table 2G 13. . Emam Reza - Ziyarah

Title	Emam Reza (A.S.) Network || Emam Reza (A. S.)
Subject or keywords	Three-Dimensional Ziyarah; ; ; In the present programme the following thresholds can be viewed; Emam Reza (A. S; The lovers of Holy Ahlul Bayt(A.S.) and Imam Reza(A.S.) willing to visit live the holy shrine of Imam Reza(A.S.) in the holy city of Mashhad on Emam Reza(A.S.) Network by three-dimensional mean (VRML; Gowharshad Courtyard; Software Programme; are recommended to download the; Ziyarah; Home; Quds Courtyard; By this way they can perform the Ziyarah of the holy shrine of Imam Reza(A.S.) on internet through three-dimensional means; The Holy Burial Chamber; Cosmo Player
Date	2003-02-18
Type	Text
Format	text/html, digital media || 4817 bytes

Identifier	http://www.imamreza.net/old/eng/emamreza/ziyarat/3d.htm
Voice Populi:	
"Great islamic site" http://links.muslim-women.org/	

Table 2G 14. Islamic Cemetery

Title	Cemetry
Subject or keywords	Islamic Cemetery; ISLAMIC CEMETERY; Buried Marhomeen; Islamic cemetery and Monument (Dar-us-Salaam) House of; DEDICATION; ISLAMIC CEMETERY (DARUL SALAAM; Home; please recite Sura Fateha for Shaheed; DAR-US-SALAAM; Peace
Publisher	Islamic Research Association
Contributor	Syed Shah, Director, Islamic Research Association
Type	Text
Format	text/html, digital media || 8377 bytes
Identifier	www.islamicresearch.org/Pages/cemetry.htm
Voice Populi:	
Referred by www.convertstoislam.com/Sites/sites.html	

Table 2G 15. Online Graveyard - Islamabad

Title	World's First Online Graveyard - Islamabad Graveyard (Online Janazah)
Creator (author)	President@islamabad.net
Subject or keywords	Online Janazah From Islamabad Graveyard Guide | Search | Fa'tiha | Book (Urdu) After Death | Last Journey | Washing Ghusl | Dress | Map Janazah | Grave | Stay in Grave | Visit Grave | Method of Prayer | Virtual Tour Online Namaz-e-Janazah
Description	Asia's First City Graveyard portal on Internet with databases and services.
Publisher	GT Group Telecom Services Corp. –Eastern GTEAST-BLK-1
Contributor	info@islamabad.net, president@ islamabad.net
Date	2003-12-05
Format	text/html, digital media || 1422 bytes
Identifier	http://www.islamabad.net/graveyard
Language	English (Text on images in Arabic & Urdu)
Voice Populi:	
"A website working on gathering and displaying all sorts of information about 'Islamabad - The Beautiful' has come up with a unique idea to automate the Islamabad graveyard as the online data pertaining the cemetery has been made available on the internet." PakTribune.com: Pakistan News Service http://www.paktribune.com/news/index.php?id=41411 "…first online graveyard of Asia which can be accessed not only on the Internet but on the Wireless Application Protocol.….site offers a grave search facility, virtual tour of the graveyard, prayer guidance, guided map".. http://www.pakdef.info/forum/showthread.php?t=4906&goto=nextnewest	

2.8 Jainism

Basic Beliefs: Jainism rests on four "pillars"

- Ahimsa: Non-violence, ranging from an act of simple kindness to a comprehensive outlook of universal fraternity.
- Anekantavada: Principle of relativity, since truth has many aspects, and all viewpoints are tenable.
- Non-acquisition, or setting limits to one's desires so that one does not deny others.
- Karma: Deeds or actions, seen as something which accumulates according to one's thoughts and activities and which affects one's future lives. …

(Multifaith Information Manual, 2000; www.omc.ca)

Table 4H1 Jainworld

Title	Welcome to Jainworld- jain community, jainism, tirtha, prayers,? navkar mantra and more
Subject or keywords	Jain world; jainworld; jain-world; jaina; jainism; preksha; dhyan; mahaveer; shraman; philosophy; theology; religion; religious; ahimsa; JSG; non violence; organisation; muni; meditation; recipies; prayer; bhajans; kshmavani; digamber; swetamber; terapanth; acharya; sadhus; culture; tirthanker
Description	Combining the aspirations of JAINS around the globe and is being positioned to link various aspects of our lives like - religious, social, philosophical, cultural etc. Jainism. The Religion of this millenium
Date	2004-05-30
Type	Text
Format	text/html, digital media || 12093 bytes
Identifier	http://jainworld.com

Voice Populi:

"This web site combines the aspirations of JAINS around the globe and is being positioned to link various aspects of our lives like - religious, social, philosophical, cultural etc. cutting across all barriers. Objective is to complement the current work being done at various web sites to create a complete knowledge-base of authentic and original scripts and various commentaries on them. Special emphasis is on how this can help us in day-to-day life now and keep us ahead in the days to come." http://www.conjure.com/religion.html

2.9 Judaism

Basic Beliefs:

- Existence of one, indivisible, God by whose will the universe and all that it contains was created and continues to be maintained. (For more information on Beliefs, faith symbols, religious holidays and Practices refer: Multifaith Information Manual, 2000; www.omc.ca)

Table 2J1. Digital Religion/ Renewing Judiasm

Title	CBC Radio	Tapestry	Past Programs
Subject or keywords	Tapestry; CBC Radio; CBC; CBC Programs
Contributor	Marieke Meyer, MeyerM@toronto.cbc.ca, Producer, Tapestry CBC Radio One
Type	Text
Format	text/html, digital media || 18145 bytes
Identifier	http://cbc.ca/tapestry/archives/2003/081703.html

Table 4J2. Rabbi Bookman's Spiritual Work out

Title	Rabbi Bookman's Spiritual Workout
Creator (author)	Rabbi Bookman
Subject or keywords	parasha; INTRODUCTION; Our Hearts/Behavior; Our Minds/Torah; letting me know; Chumash; Meditation; Modeh Ani; Tanach; Sh'ma; D'var Torah; INSTRUCTIONS; Torah Reading; Our Spiritual Energy/Soul; WORKOUT; Our Bodies/Health; THE WORKOUT; The Daily Check-in with Self; The Torah Commentary; Tallit and Tefillin
Description	If you feel faint or light headed at any point during this workout, keep going and enjoy it! You are

	getting the full effect of what this workout has to offer; Torah Reading -- The page numbers direct you to The Torah Commentary, UAHC Press.. MORE..
Contributor	Helene Layne, Hlayne@tbam.org
Date	2003-10-07
Type	Text
Format	text/html; charset=ISO-8859-1, digital media || 7490 bytes
Identifier	http://www.betham-miami.org/workout/

Voice Populi:

"Rabbi Terry A. Bookman's Seven Minute Spiritual Workout This workout is designed to work on your connection to self and the Transcendent Power of the Universe we call God."
http://www.kcstar.com/standing/holiday/stories/2.htm
Referred by Union for Reform Judaism (http://www.uahc.org/search/srch.html)

Table 2J3. Memorial Prayer

Title	Yizkor/ritual - online Yahrzeit and memorial website
Subject or keywords	For female family & friends; Holocaust Prayer; Kaddish; Yizkor; Memorial Prayer; Memorials; Please choose a prayer; For male family & friends; terms & conditions; War Casualties Prayer; credits; Privacy Policy
Contributor	Angela Cutler, Internet Designer/ Administrator; Angela.Cutler@ort.org
Type	Text
Format	Text/html;charset=UTF-8, digital media || 3970 bytes
Identifier	http://yizkor.ort.org/html/memprayer.shtml

Voice Populi:

"Create a permanent memorial for your loved one, listen to Memorial prayers and use our Yahrzeit email reminder service"
http://bible.ort.org/
"Information about Jewish memorial customs can be found on the online Yizkor site, which also contains a memorial in the public section"
http://www.m-sampson.net/dad.html
"Online Yahrzeit email reminder service and memorial. Information on memorial customs, Memorial prayers in Hebrew, English with transliteration."
http://dmoz.org/Society/Religion_and_Spirituality/Judaism/Holidays_and_Observances/

Table 2J4. Live Western Wall Camera at Aish

Title	Live Western Wall Camera at Aish
Subject or keywords	Rabbi; Seminars; www.chanukahtoday.com; Aish; Russian; Click; Gedalia; Camera; HOME; www.jewishandjudaism.com; jewish; portion; Store; wall; WALL; Live; weekly; audio; Low; Spirituality; Kalman; site; e-mail; NuSpectra; Shraga; April; friend; www.UseTracker.com; Inc; rabbi; Society; Israel; studies; MORE..
Description	HOME | Society Today | Jewish World | Dating | Family | Spirituality | Jewish Literacy Holocaust | Western Wall Camera Live | Ask the Rabbi | Weekly Torah Portion | Holidays | Email Lists Jer. Site founded by Rabbi Kalman Packouz Editorial by Rabbi Kalman Packouz & Rabbi Shraga Simmons Torah teaches us how to maximize our pleasure and potential in life
Publisher	webmaster@aish.com, Old City, Jerusalem, Israel, POB 14149
Contributor	Nechemia Coopersmith
Type	Text
Format	text/html, digital media || 44640 bytes
Identifier	http://www.aish.com/wallcam
Language	English

Voice Populi:

"Check out Live images from the Western Wall, brought to you by Aish HaTorah."

http://www.shamash.org/trb/judaism.html / Referred by http://www.israelive.net/

2.10 Sikhism

Basic Beliefs:

- There is one God, whose name is truth eternal. Creator of all things, the all-pervading spirit. Fearless and without hatred, timeless and formless. Beyond birth and death. Self-enlightened. Known by the Guru's Grace.
- God is the supreme Guru, revealed as guide and teacher through the Word, contained in the Guru Granth Sahib.
- Humankind by nature is ignorant, misguided, and dominated by the evils of lust, covetousness, attachment to worldly things, wrath, pride and egotism. This results in a cycle of birth and rebirth. (Multifaith Information Manual, 2000)

Table 2K1. On-line Gurudwara

Title	Nanak Naam Centre Bedford Virtual Centre Gurdwara Index Page
Subject or keywords	Committee News; Visiting Raagis; FOCAL; Homepage; Sikhi Classes; Nanak Naam; Virtual Centre; The Committee; Visiting Gianis; Contacting; Site Search; Visiting Groups; Coming to Visit; SIKH CENTRE; Gurbani English; Aspects; Europe's new; Library; Notices; Bedford; Regular Services; Sikhism; Sangat Affairs, library, sikhism, interior, sikh, nanak, truth, khalsa, services, meditation, prayer; MORE…
Description	WaheGuruJi Ka Khalsa WaheGuruJi Ki Fateh - Wonderful Teacher The Realm of Purity…Wonderful Teacher The Resolution
Contributor	Tirath Singh, Educational Secretary
Date	2004-04-06
Type	Text
Format	text/html, digital media || 6659 bytes
Identifier	http://www.bedfordgurdwara.org.uk/centre/gurdw.htm
Language	English

Voice Populi:

"Information on the local Sikh Gurdwara, events and future projects"
http://directory.google.com/Top/Regional/Europe/United_Kingdom/England/Bedfordshire/Bedford/Society_and_Culture/Religion/
Referred by Standing Advisory Council on Religious Education (http://www.bedfordshire.gov.uk/BedsCC/SDedusit.nsf/Web%5CThePage/Bedfordshire+SACRE+-+Links+to+useful+websites)

2.11 Zoroastrianism

Basic Beliefs:

- The belief in one Supreme Creator – Ahura Mazda (The Omnipotent, Omniscient and Omnipresent Lord).
- Life is a struggle between good and evil.
- The importance of following the path of Asha (Righteousness), based on three fundamental guiding principles of Good Thoughts, Good Words and Good Deeds.
- The ultimate triumph of Good over Evil, leading to Perfection and Immortality at the Renovation. . [Multifaith Information Manual, 2000.]

Table 2M1. Entrance to Temple

Title	Entrance to Temple
Creator (author)	Shahriar Shahriari; s@ Shahriari.com
Subject or keywords	Zoroastrianism; Zoroaster; Zoroastrian; Zarathushtra; Zarathustra; Ahura Mazda; God; Angels; Prayers; Temples; CyberTemples; Cyber-Temples; Praying; Places of Worship; Churches; Sacred Fire; Worship
Description	The first Zoroastrian Cyber-Temple
Date	2003-10-07
Type	Text
Format	text/html, digital media || 13105 bytes
Identifier	http://www.zarathushtra.com/z/temple/index.htm
Language	English

Voice Populi:

"religious corporation established with the aim of studying and disseminating information on the Divine Message of Zarathushtra and promoting the Zarathushtrian Fellowship."
http://dmoz.org/Society/Religion_and_Spirituality/Zoroastrianism/

"Liberal Zoroastrians in Anaheim (Los Angeles) California, USA. Site includes information about degree programs in Zoroastrian studies at Spenta Graduate School which is affiliated with the Assembly"
http://www.clas.ufl.edu/users/gthursby/rel/z-aster.htm

2.12 Spirituality:

Spirituality in general has many diverse manifestations. In the following is one that represents indigenous traditions of the Americas. The Web sites that follow, in this section, may or may not represent this faith group.

Basic Beliefs – Native American Spirituality:

Traditional Native cultures are authentic and dynamic, fostering distinctive and sophisticated human development. A sense of identity and pride are rooted in established spiritual traditions and principles.

(Multifaith Information Manual, 2000)

Table 2N 1. The Sun Circle Meditation Hall

Title	Enlightenment.Com - Psycho-Spiritual Content Generating Community Infrastructure: Sun Circle Meditation Hall Welcome
Creator (author)	Lance Culp, Meditation Hall Host
Subject or keywords	Spirituality; Psychology; Consciousness; Psychospiritual; God; Meme; Life; Death; Meaning; Love; Happiness; Peace; Trance; Transformation; Health; Awareness; Humanity; Potential; Light; Transpersonal; Wilber; Zukav; What Works; Practice; Ritual; Magic; Esoteric; Help; Meditation; MORE..
Description	Innovative psychospiritual content generating community infrastructure
Publisher	Enlightenment.Com, Inc.
Contributor	Mark Hopkiss and Gabriel De Witt
Date	2004-04-20
Type	Text
Format	text/html, digital media || 5129 bytes
Identifier	http://www.enlightenment.com/solstice/
Language	English

Voice Populi:
"Serving the Spiritual and Economic Needs of Individuals & Organizations by 'Building a Living Community of Transformation and Interaction' "
The Psychospiritual Research Institute: psychospiritualresearchinstitute.com
"Resources and products for the spiritual seeker."
Open Directory Project http://open.thumbshots.org/Society/Religion_and_Spirituality/Enlightenment)

Table 2N 2. Yoga Everywhere

Title	Yoga Everywhere - Prayer pose
Subject or keywords	yogaeverywhere; yoga everywhere; yoga-everywhere; yoga on the keyboard; yoga at the keyboard; yoga on the computer; yoga at the computer; yoga; compassion; fitness; stress; stress release; stress reduction; relaxation; meditation; breath; breathe; breathing exercises; exercise; fitness; daily practice; daily routine; peace; energy; holistic approach; healing; tension reduction; mindful; happiness; stretches; stretching; anxiety; circulation; quiet mind; awareness; water retention; connection; asana; pranayama; metta; satsang; om; namaste; guru; yoga teacher; love; community; health; practice; Megassage; Megan Lurie McCarver
Description	Interactive yoga site with stretches and breathing exercises. Mindful approach to your physical, emotional and spiritual well being. Try it, it's fun!
Date	2003-04-21
Type	Text
Format	text/html, digital media || 10446 bytes
Identifier	http://www.yogaeverywhere.com/keyboard/keyboard_3e.html

Voice Populi:
"Site describes simple daily practices, including breathing exercises, meditation and a set of yoga stretches that can be done at the keyboard. Also online newsletter"
directory.google.com/Top/Society/Religion_and_Spirituality/Yoga/Practices/

Table 2N 3. Online Finger Meditation Tool

Title	Online Finger Meditation Tool
Subject or keywords	Labyrinth Locator; Labyrinth Events; Veriditas; www.tkffdn.org; Netscape Communicator; Microsoft Internet Explorer; To view this meditation tool you must have; Online Labyrinth; CD Available; Contributions; To hear the music you must have; Products; Shop for productsMORE...
Description	Now Veriditas is pleased to present to you a state of the art online finger meditation tool.

	Labyrinth Events Labyrinth Locator Products Online Labyrinth Facilitator Network Contributions About Veriditas™ We would like to thank the TKF Foundation for their contributions to the Online Finger Meditation tool.
Type	Text
Format	text/html, digital media || 16483 bytes
Identifier	http://www.gracecathedral.org/labyrinth/interactions/index.shtml

Voice Populi:

"Walk a 'virtual' labyrinth on-line West Linn Lutheran Church"
http://www.wllc.org/labyrinth.htm

s"Mouse the Labyrinth! Grace Cathedral makes it possible for us to walk the Labyrinth at our computer. Click for added text, music, level of inertia, and the icon of your choice to do the mazing."
http://www.saintgregorys.org/Pages/Links_Other.html

Table 2N 4 Circle Sanctuary

Title	Circle Sanctuary Website
Creator (author)	Kathryn Huxtable; kathryn kathrynhuxtable.org
Subject or keywords	enter, circle, shall, rights, contents, arising, supplied, not, all, incidental; pagan; wicca; Circle Sanctuary; witch; nature religion; occult; Druid; Selena Fox; Dennis Carpenter; witchcraft
Description	The Official Website for Circle Sanctuary including information about it's Pagan/Nature Religious practices. Circle Sanctuary shall not be liable in the event of incidental or consequential damages arising from the use of information supplied herein.
Date	2004
Type	Text
Format	text/html, digital media || 3304 bytes
Identifier	http://www.circlesanctuary.org

Voice Populi:

"CircleSanctuary.org is among the Internet addresses run by nature-worshipping pagans."
http://www.worldnetdaily.com/news/article.asp?ARTICLE_ID=29995

Table 2N 5 Cosmic Mother Sharing Her Life with us

Title	Cosmic Mother Meditation
Subject or keywords	Mystical; Psychic Tarot Readings; psychic readings; prayer room; mystical; holistic; alien; ufo; aromatherapy; psychic; readings; news; headlines; forum; chat; polls; art; freebies; web page design; brochure; business cards; greeting cards; post cards; forum; ascended masters; angels; stones; occult; readers; MORE
Description	Light Chamber's StrMyst Net Mystical, Holistic Center offers a large variety of site options; such as, intuitive tarot, psychic readings, dream analysis, aromatherapy, herbs, Angels, chat rooms, forum, psychic readings, prayer room, mystical, holistic, alien, ufo, aromatherapy, psychic, readings, news, forum, MORE..
Date	2003-08-20
Type	Text
Format	text/html, digital media || 6364 bytes
Identifier	http://www.lightchamber.org/Services/ MeditationRoom/moonwater.htm

Voice Populi:
"Lightchamber Mystical Shoppe - Offers a wide variety of metaphysical and mystical products and services. Also includes schedule of related workshops and events."
http://dmoz.org/Society/Religion_and_Spirituality/New_Age/Shopping/
"More than a Psychic Shoppe. Offering Mystical, Magical, New Age, Conscious Content of UFO's, Alien, Angel, Ascended Masters, God('s), Goddess, Aromatherapy, Herbs, Oils, Elixirs, Jewelry, Books, Clothing, Tarot, Tools and more content."
http://www.sayahda.com/pathways.html

Table 2N 6. Spirituality: Post a Prayer

Title	:rejesus - spirituality - post a prayer:::.
Subject or keywords	home; macromedia; site map
Description	Your candle will burn for 24 hours and any other visitor will be able to see your prayer and perhaps pray along with you. About this section This is the place where you can post a prayer for others to read, and take time to pray for other people who have posted here. Simply add your name and your prayer, click the tick button and place your candle on an empty holder
Date	2004-02-19
Type	Text
Format	text/html, digital media || 7712 bytes
Identifier	http://www.rejesus.co.uk/spirituality/post_prayer/index.html

Voice Populi:
"At www.rejesus.co.uk you can light a virtual candle and type in a prayer for others to see. The candle will remain for 24 hours"
http://www.lexden.org.uk/prayerlinks.htm
"'ReJesus.co.uk' has created a place where you can post a prayer for others to read, and take time to pray for other people who have posted a prayer...Click one of the animated candles to visit and light your own candle!"
http://www.stnicholaskenilworth.org.uk/prayers.htm

Table 2N 7. Minute Meditation

Title	Minute Meditations - a quiet spot in your busy day
Subject or keywords	Minute Meditations Roman Catholic daily inspiration Christian Sermons, Religion
Description	Minute Meditations offers daily inspiration; a quiet spot in your busy day. God is the God of the second chance....Being born again means that all that went before is not held against us. Though time is too precious to waste, it must never be thought that what was lost is irretrievable. Please, make a donation to support the Web ministry of the Franciscans.
Date	2004
Format	text/html, digital media || 17874 bytes
Identifier	http://www.americancatholic.org/Features/Minute/default.asp

Referred by:
1. Catholic Diocese of Richmond (http://www.diocric.org/)
2. Saint Mary's Catholic Church, Blacksburg, VA (www.stmarysblacksburg.org)
3. St. Patrick Church, Kennett Square, Pa. (http://www.rc.net/philadelphia/st_patrick/)
4. Shrine Parish of St. Bernadette (http://members.aol.com/stbernacc/)
5. Church of the Holy Trinity (http://www.holytrinityzoarohio.Org/links.html)

Table 2N 8. Learning Meditation

Title	Meditation Room
Subject or keywords	meditation; meditate; guru; realaudio; learn; peace; relaxation; relax; peaceful; light;

	instruct; education; holistic; therapeutic; cleanse; healing; heal; spirit; spirituality; stress; relief; guidance; guide; intuition; serenity; serene
Description	Visit our Web site and achieve conscious relaxation and stress reduction through meditation. RealAudio meditations allow you to listen, relax and achieve inner peace right on the Web.
Date	2002-12-12
Type	Text
Format	text/html, digital media || 11289 bytes
Identifier	http://www.learningmeditation.com/getaway1.htm http://www.learningmeditation.com/room.htm

"http://www.learningmeditation.com/ room.htm offers a variety of free meditations"
http://www.healingtheworld.net/meditation.htm
Referred by:
Holistic Health Gateway - Your Gateway to Enhanced Living www.holistichealthgateway.com
"Variety of guided meditation available on-line to help you relax and learn to meditate"
http://www.karma-net.com/stress.htm
"Try the following meditation extracted from the learning mediation web site, ...for a peaceful and relaxed mind"
http://www.girl.com.au/meditation.htm
"In the Meditation Room you will begin a journey into a new level of relaxation and awareness. Each meditation serves a specific purpose, depending on what you want to achieve. Choose freely and feel free to perform more than one meditation."
http://www.brainhelp.co.uk/RelaxationZone.html

3

Fast Track to Multifaith Resources for Cyber Worship: What's Hot

[Surf the Virtual Worlds, NOW,
if you are looking for Sacred cyberspace, acts, sites, rites, rituals, objects, and moments]:

How This Mind Map Was Consecrated

In compiling a quick map of the sacred route, the designer has made sincere attempts to pave the path with grace and hope of synchronicity. Per chance if any of the links fail to work, it may not be construed as an error in design (rather dead links or broken directions are a common place in cyberspace) and hence, forgive the trespasses. Furthermore, included here are shortcuts to the themes, including topers, best sites, models that can be adapted, and other types of divine routes. Most of these websites are randomly selected, and systematically listed, albeit these represent the best pearls in the deep Web.

Limitations of time and resources prevented evaluating these resources; it is for you as a reader, consumer, and prosumer to shake the bottle before use.

In order to keep the subject alive and continuously updated, up-to-date versions of the websites in this book are available on my website at http://taher.cjb.net.

Connection contemplation prayer experience
transcendental meditation

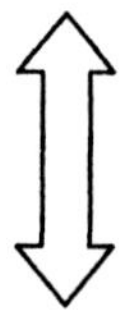

Satisfaction, Enlightenment Bliss, Nirvana

Transformation of mind, body soul into an altogether different
sphere or for furthering goal in the same path

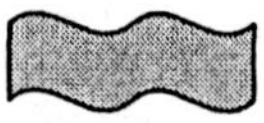

None of the above

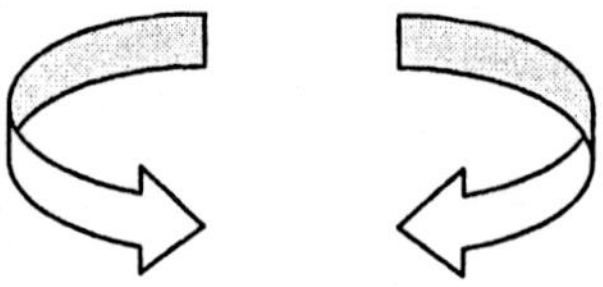

3.1 Ten step ready reference for every seeker

1. **Metanoia (initiate)**: Start your computer, get connected to the Internet {Be sure you have no viruses and bugs that otherwise deviate your holy activity, Amen}. A reference tool for beginners is Bruce Lawrence's *Complete Idiot's Guide to Religions Online.*

2. **Physical plane:** Is your browser up-to-date (most Web sites look at you if you have Internet Explorer 4.0 and above or at least Netscape 6.0); be sure you have audio, video, like Real Media, Window Media type devices. {Luckily these tools are mostly free, but some of their cookyware is an uninvited guest; May Almighty protect from spywares, Amen}

3. **The Focus:** So that you may take off smoothly and instantly, dedicate one window for Worship (you can have as many non-dedicated windows for your other activities) {May the Gates' fraternity grow to devise more doors and windows for your Cyber Worship, Amen}.

4. **The Path:** Select your Worship path from **Webwise mapped tables** in this book, or start googling for the website of mainstream religion/spirituality, or alternative traditions. {May the Lord increase your knowledge and get you towards the right path, Amen}

5. **The Medium:** Select the Worship site. Make sure you clearly understand and have selected right medium and right message. This precaution helps to avoid being lost in the maze or labyrinth, resulting from the traffic jam (on the biggest ever weird, wild, withering superhighway)

6. **Idea Plane:** Prepare your mind, mood and mode for Worship: Goal, mission, vision, and perceptions, all set to take off for a vertical flight (as against the horizontal/congregational form in traditional worship).

7. **The Message**: Load the Worship Page, confirm you are on the same wavelength and understand what the Web site is all about – authentic, reliable, credible, professional and most importantly meant to fulfill your desired goal: Worship (Not meant to turn you into games of chance).

8. **Setting the Angels:** (oops Angles!) That is, set all the required audio, video, text, and graphics in order to visualize the spectacular triangle – (a) seeker (b) Internet as a medium to reach (c) the penultimate destination: divine. Make sure you have fewer deviations, distractions and interruptions while you set off from the physical plane to the transcendental route.

9. **Direct, non-stop, to and fro**

Remember you come, click and conquer (or get conquered).

Why, because the clock's still ticking and the next click may lead you to:

10. **Pray:** Utter the Sacred Words, in the Name of (whatever comes to your mind) and Click to: {Pray, Hope and Trust you have a blessed journey, graceful companionship and safe landing back on the earth, Amen}

3.2 Cyber Worship in Multifaith: Top Pik-Wiks

- **What's new in Digital Religion? Listen to the audio discussion (the slant is towards Renewing Judaism):** www.cbc.ca/tapestry/archives/2003/081703.html
- **Whether my faith permits me to perform Cyber Worship (Message is the medium: online sometime for everyone. A Jewish point of view): Wired to the Kadosh Barukh Hu: Minyan Via Internet - A Responsum from the Committee on Jewish Law and Standards** http://learn.jtsa.edu/topics/diduknow/responsa/hatesh_internet.shtml
- **How much is the demand for online religion in Multifaith Perspective: Read the book or visit its Web incarnation (discover what is online, why you should be online, and how to get there): Give Me That Online Religion:** www.brendabrasher.com/online_religion.html
- **Where lies the resource on virtual religion?** www.religion-online.org
- **Why is it paying to be Webwise in your faith group: Andrew Careaga. "Cyber Congregations Go Fishing on the Net."** www.churchbusiness.com/articles/0a1.comp1.html
- **View the BBC virtual religions domain: "360 degree tour - places of Worship."** http://www.bbc.co.uk/leicester/360_images/places_of_worship_idex.shtml
- **When did e-prayer first begin?** www.globalprayeralert.org/_wsn/page2.html
- **Where can I find my Scriptures, Sacred text on the Net**: http://www.sacred-texts.com/

3.3 Top Cyber Worship Multifaith Websites:

- **Voice A Vision • Post A Prayer Dare A Dream - Multifaith Voices** www.heartpath.com/hpcontent/voiceAvision.asp
- **Ancient Wisdom: Submit a Prayer - Multifaith Concerns** www.awisdom.com/community/submit_prayer
- **Prayer Book: Meditations, Adorations, Celebrations, Invocations - Multifaith and Multicultural Prayers** www.prayforpeace.com/index.php
- **Prayers for peace - Jewish, Christian and Muslim - Multifaith Platform** http://salmanspiritual.com/peace_prayers.html
- **Church of the East forwards the Yoga of Jesus - Multifaith Perspectives** http://Church-Of-The-East.org
- **Voluntary Worship – Public Prayer for Chaplains (Multifaith context):** www.forces.gc.ca/chapgen/engraph
- **World Prayers – Prayer Collective, Multifaith Practices:** www.worldprayers.org
- **Study Guide for Congregations - (Multifaith Resource):** www.calchurches.org/publication_pdfs/BBU-edition2.pdf
- **WebCity House of Worship - Multifaith Directory:** www.webcityusa.com/worship.htm

3.4 State-Of-The-Art Reviews – Multifaith Perspectives:

- **Ron Csillag. "Virtual Synagogue Being Planned."** ***Canadian Jewish News*, 25 Jan 2001,** www.cjnews.com/pastissues/01/jan25-01/front5.asp
- **April Witt. "Jews Debate Whether Online Worship is Kosher – Technology @ Augusta"** www.augustachronicle.com/120796/jewish.html
- **Clark W. Woods. "A Religious Experience: What Is Being Done With The Internet And Where Are We Going?"** (Multifaith Vistas) www.speech.sir.com/academics/gibbs/students/busn6080-fl-2001-jbh/woods/woods.html
- **"Should Monks Surf the Internet?" (Buddhist Perspectives)** www.fengshuitimes.com/main/fst/default.asp?pg=268&cid=5
- **"In virtual heaven Concepts of convergence in digital and religious spaces Avatars, creation, spirit"** www.uni-paderborn.de/~bergerma/texte/heaven.html
- **Jay Rosen. "Journalism is itself a Religion: Special Essay on Launch of the Receiver." Press Think, 7 Jan 2004,** http://journalism.nyu.edu/pubzone/weblogs/pressthink/2004/01/07/press_religion
- **Inside Virtual India: A Sampling of faith on the Net:** http://india.projectmiso.net/ashram/ashram01.html
- **Compatibility Among (Some) Faiths: A New Perspective:** http://mb-soft.com/public/compat2.html
- **Steve Ayers, Did Someone Say Online Religion?** http://www.vu.union.edu/~concordy/19990923/sc2.html
- **Marty Beard, "Web's a big draw for believers and curious Religion bigger than auctions, stocks and dating,"** http://www.medialifemagazine.com/news2001/dec01/dec31/3_wed/news3wednesday.html
- **AsiaSource: AsiaTODAY - A resource of the Asia Society ... Reports Archive. Special Report Hinduism Online** January 03, 2001 www.asiasource.org/news/at_mp_02.cfm?newsid=39841
- **God of the Internet' is dead: Jon Postel - God.is.dead.com http://news.bbc.co.uk/1/hi/sci/tech/196487.stm**
- **"Is your God on the web,"** http://db.bbc.co.uk/gloucestershire/faith/2003/11/god_internet.shtml
- **Craig Smith, "Churches tackle cyber worship trend"** http://livesite.pittsburghlive.com/x/tribune-review/computing/archive/s_120374.html
- **Bill Broadway, "Internet puts world of religions, sects at your fingertips"** ***Washington Post Service*** www.miami.com/mld/miamiherald/2002/08/17/entertainment/3877649.htm?1c
- **Religion As A Cyber Society:** www.freeessays.cc/db/44/smu178.shtml
- **The Ruah Series - Netting the Faithful - Do.You.Jewhoo.?** www.sit.wisc.edu/~bnbarnes/Ruah%20Project/ four_jewhoo1.htm

- **The Ruah Series - Netting the Faithful - 3.0. Allah.alt.net.** www.sit.wisc.edu/~bnbarnes/Ruah%20Project/ three_allah1.htm
- **Pope to ping the faithful, Posted by: tragen on Wednesday, April 07, 2004** www.webwarrior.net/modules.php?op=modload&name=News&file=article&sid=4760
- **Mark Jones. "Preaching To The Convergence Choir – Digital Religion is Alive and Well, and Its Coming to a** Watch, Refrigerator, and Robo-Dog Near You." 17 Jan 2003. www.infoworld.com/article/03/01/17/030120opnoise_1.html (13 Feb 2004)
- **Stephen O'Leary, "Religion in the Digital Age,"** ***Online Journalism Review*****, 2000-03-24** http://ojr.org/ojr/business/1017965672.php
- **Brenda E. Brasher, "The Cyborg: Technological Socialization and Its Link to the Religious Function of Popular Culture,"** www.religion-online.org/cgi-bin/relsearchd.dll/showarticle?item_id=404
- **Practical Ministry Innovations** www.houseoffusion.com/cf_lists/index.cfm/method=messages&threadid=7994&forumid=4
- **Church offers prayer service to internet congregation: One of Britain's oldest churches has leapt into the 21st century by launching an online prayer service.** http://www.telegraph.co.uk/connected/main.jhtml;$sessionid$P2ZDE5XZGA5G5QFIQMFCFFWAVCBQYIV0?xml=/connected/2002/09/03/ecnepray03.xml&sSheet=/connected/2002/09/03/ixconn.html
- **Religion, the cyber way, January 11, 2001** http://www.hindu.com/2001/01/11/stories/09110655.htm
- **Helen T. Gray, "WORSHIP ON THE WEB: Religion sets its sites along information superhighway,"** ***The Kansas City Star*****, 05/18/01 22:15** http://www.kcstar.com/item/pages/printer.pat,fyi/3accaf37.518,.html
- **Finding Faith on the Web - A Chat with Internet Expert Tiffany Shlain** http://abcnews.go.com/onair/GoodMorningAmerica/chat_shlain_webfaith_001017.html
- **Religion News Blog: "Believers flock to online religion," Apr. 24 2003** www.religionnewsblog.com/ 3105-_Believers_flock_to_online_religion.html
- **"Cyberfaith,"** http://www.calvin.edu/news/clips/cyber.htm
- **The Church in Cyberspace: A Working List of Resources:** http://www.drury.edu/ess/church/disciples.html
- **Who's that knocking at your digital front door?**: http://holstonconference.com/thecall/archives/02-14-03/03_feb14_digital.html
- **Churches tackle cyber worship trend** http://livesite.pittsburghlive.com/x/tribune-review/computing/archive/s_120374.html
- **The Apostolic Cyberchurch: A Peek at the Future?:** http://www.ninetyandnine.com/Archives/20000221/cover.htm
- **Om Click Om** : http://www.rediff.com/search/2003/feb/26god.htm
- **Spiritualism online**: http://www.tribuneindia.com/2000/20001225/login/main10.htm
- **Richard Higgans, "Sold on spirituality,"** http://search.boston.com/globe/magazine/2000/12-3/featurestory2.shtml
- **Quentin J. Schultze, "Lost in the Digital Cosmos,"** http://www.religion-online.org/cgi-bin/relsearchd.dll/showarticle?item_id=2026
- **Lisa M. Bowman, "Spiritual sites attract larger flock," January 30, 2002,** http://news.com.com/2100-1023-826239.html
- **Taking In The Sites / By Sarah Wyatt, "Mourning the Dead in Cyberspace," August 18, 1997** http://commtechlab.msu.edu/Humans/heeter/PortalReports/NYTmournDead.html
- **Mike Penn, "The Morphing of Religious Practices,"** http://www.leaderu.com/critical/webreligion.html
- **Sara Reeder, "In The House of The Digital Gods: Meditations On The New Rituals of Cyberspace,"** http://earthportals.com/god.html
- **Jim Louderback, "Is service dead? Not yet. In fact, computers can dig up a real, live person to help you -- if you know where to look,"** http://www.usaweekend.com/01_issues/010520/010520techsmart.html

- **Andrew Careaga, "Embracing the cyberchurch,"** http://www.next-wave.org/dec99/embracing_the_cyberchurch.htm
- **Andre Careaga, "Cyber Congregations Go Fishing on the Net," Church Business, 10/2000** www.churchbusiness.com/articles/0a1comp1.html
- **Nidhi Taparia, "Hurry Om,"** http://www.indiaabroad.com/search/2000/dec/26god.htm
- **The Regents of the University of Michigan. Internet Public Library: Religion & Theology** http://www.ipl.org/div/subject/browse/hum80.00.00/

3.5 Top Contributing Scholars in the area of Cyber Worship, Ask-a-Specialist...

[Ps. Whom to ask? Looking for top movers and shakers? Profiles of experts in online-religion or religion-online, who can tell you the Net's worth, Net's gain, and so on]

Prof. Bruce B. Lawrence
Nancy and Jeffrey Marcus Humanities Professor of Religion, Duke University Department of Religion, 118 Gray Building, Box 90964, Durham, NC 27708
Email: bbl@duke.edu
www.duke.edu/religion/home/lawrence/lawrence.html
[Author, Complete Idiot's Guide to Religions Online]

Anastasia Karaflogka
Researcher, School of Oriental and African Studies, University of London
Email: a.karaflogka@blueyonder.co.uk
{researcher, taxonomy of Cyber Worship, special reference to ontology of rituals in cyberspace}

John Gresham, PhD
Associate Professor, Kenrick-Glennon Seminary & Paul VI Institute
http://sim74.kenrickparish.com
gresham@kenrick.edu
[responsible for the Web tool: Finding God in Cyberspace]

Steven Waldman
(Innovator / Online Believer, on Time's 100: The Next Big Wave), [founder of Beliefnet.com]
[Innovators (Steven Waldman)
A former magazine editor, he's the co-founder of Beliefnet.com, a religious website for people of all faiths. "Everyone talks about religion being a divisive force," he says. "Every day I see the opposite"
http://www.time.com/time/innovators/spirituality/profile_waldman.html

Lorne L. Dawson, Ph.D.,
University of Waterloo
E-Mail: ldawson@uwaterloo.ca
www.arts.uwaterloo.ca/~ldawson/lld.html

Dr. Gary R. Bunt
Lecturer in Islamic Studies,
University of Wales, Lampeter
http://www.virtuallyislamic.com
email: g.bunt@lamp.ac.uk
[author, Virtually Islamic, and Islam in the digital Age]

Debbie Herring
Research Scholar, Sheffield University Biblical Studies Department
Tutor, Oxford Brookes University Distance Learning theology courses
Tutor and course administrator at the Urban Theology Unit
Webmaster: www.cybertheology.net/
email: debbie@cybertheology.net
[researcher, cyber theology as it evolves]

Dr. Brenda E. Brasher
Department of Sociology, University of Aberdeen, Scotland, UK AB24 3QY
http: www.abdn.ac.uk/onlinereligion
e-mail: b.brasher@abdn.ac.uk
[author, Give Me That Online Religion]

Dr. Alan Godlas
Dept. of Religion, University of Georgia, Athens, GA 30602-1625
godlas@uga.edu
[Webmaster, www.arches.uga.edu/~godlas and www.uga.edu/islam]

Stephen D. O'Leary
Associate Professor, Annenberg School for Communication, University of Southern California, Los Angeles, California 90089-0281

[author, Religion Online: Finding Faith on the Internet, with Douglas E. Cowan]

Dr. Christopher Helland
Research Fellow, Gorsebrook Institute for Atlantic Canada Studies, Saint Mary's University, Halifax, NS, Canada B3H 3C3
chelland@SMU.ca
http://www.chass.utoronto.ca/~chelland/
[author, "Religion Online/Online Religion and Virtual Communitas" published in Religion and the Internet: Research Prospects and Promises]

Eileen Barker
Professor of Sociology with Special Reference to the Study of Religion, London School of Economics, Houghton St, London WC2A 2AE
e-mail: E.Barker@LSE.ac.uk
http://www.lse.ac.uk/collections/sociology/whoswho/barker.htm
[author, "INFORM: Bringing the Sociology of Religion to the Public Space" in Frontier Religions in Public Space, and has over 200 publications, which include the award-winning The Making of a Moonie: Brainwashing or Choice? and New Religious Movements: A Practical Introduction, which has been published in seven languages.]

Need another Expert to Ask (A sample):

*Witch Pagan Clergy Listings:
www.witchvox.com/vn/vn_index/clergy.html
*Have a Question About Funerals:
www.ofsa.org/ask_ofsa/index.cfm
*Judaism: Ask an Expert (Select your Rabbi):
http://slider-secure.vendercom.com/Society/Religion_and_Spirituality.htm
*Christian Expert Advice (Select your Pastor / Ministry):
www.allspiritual.com/ChristianExpertAdvice.php3
*Ask Imam (Select a source):
www.irshad.org/other/fatawa.php
*Ask the On-Line Pundits (Questions about Hinduism or Christianity, or the relationship between these two):
http://www.karma2grace.org/Webcomponents/FAQ/index.asp?det=58
*Ask the Rabbi - Rabbi David Wolpe
http://beliefnet.com/story/67/story_6718_1.html
*Ask the Imam - Sa'dullah Khan
http://beliefnet.com/frameset.asp?pageLoc=/story/86/story_8676_1.html&boardID=23270
*Ask the Lama - Lama Surya Das
http://beliefnet.com/author/author_75.html

*More: http://beliefnet.com/index/index_30001.html#advice

http://www.mille.org/people/CV-Oleary.html
Internet: soleary@rcf.usc.edu
[author, Cyberspace as Sacred Space]

Dr. T. Matthew Ciolek
Head, Internet Publications Bureau,
Research School of Asian and Pacific Studies (RSPAS),
National Institute for Asia and the Pacific,
Australian National University, Canberra, ACT, Australia
http://www.ciolek.com/PEOPLE/ciolek-tm.html
Email: tmciolek@coombs.anu.edu.au
tmciolek@ciolek.com
[author, Online Religion. In The Internet Encyclopedia]

3.6 Ask a User-Friendly Librarian to find Religious/Spiritual Tool in the Cyberspace:

- **Bahá'í Librarians and Information Professionals Network:** http://www.bcca.org/librarians/
- **Pagan Librarians (forum):** http://mailman.u.washington.edu/pipermail/libsup-l/1996-July/023176.html
- **Pagan Librarian Alliance for World Domination:** http://paganwiccan.about.com/cs/blogs/
- **Congress of Muslim Librarians and Information Scientists (comlis) (publications)**
  http://www.islam.gov.my/pai/t.htm
  http://www.lib.duke.edu/ias/NewBooks/Mideast/June_2003.htm
- **Lutheran Church Library Association:** www.lclahq.org
- **Middle East Librarians Association:** http://depts.washington.edu/wsx9/melahp.html
- **The Association of Christian Librarians:** http://www.acl.org/
- **The Association of Jewish Libraries:** http://www.jewishlibraries.org

3.7 World of Multifaith Websites – At Your Finger Tips

- **Multifaith Library, Ontario Multifaith Council for Spiritual and Religious Care:** www.library.omc.ca
- **Ontario Consultants on Religious Tolerance:** www.religioustolerance.org
- **Belief Net**: www.beliefnet.com
- **Adherents**: www.adherents.com
- **Faith and values**: www.faithandvalues.com
- **Multifaith.com**: www.multifaith.com/
- **MultiFaith - All Things Spiritual Directory**: http://www.allspiritual.com/MultiFaith.php3
- **MultiFaith - Spiritual Advantage Directory**: www.spiritualadvantage.com/MultiFaith.php
- **Multifaith and Religion Sites List**: http://www.conjure.com/religion.html
- **Multifaith Works Merchandise:** http://www.multifaith.org/Support/offer.html
- **MultiFaithNet Homepage: http://www.multifaithnet.org/**
- **Temple of Understanding Related Sites:** http://www.templeofunderstanding.org/links.htm
- **Category Prayer - ReligiousResources.org** http://www.religiousresources.org/directory/cat.php?cat_id=80
- **United Religions Initiative:** http://www.uri.org/
- **Across Boundaries Multifaith Institute:** www.acrossboundaries.net
- **Multifaith Ministries Education Consortium:** www.multifaithministries.org
- **Multifaith Voices for Peace and Justice:** www.multifaithpeace.org
- **Multifaith – All Things Spiritual Directory:** ww.allspiritual.com/Multifaith.php
- **Gathering of Life Multifaith Spiritual Fellowship:** www.gatheringoflight.org
- **Multifaith Council of NW Ohio:** www.multifaithcouncil.org
- **Multifaith, Interfaith Religious Educatino:** www.theinspirationstation.com
- **Interfaith and Multifaith Connections:** www.cuc.ca/interfaith_links.htm/
- **Multifaith and Multicultural Mediation Service**: www.educationaid.net/mmms.htm
- **Sandwell Multicultural, Multifaith Resource Collection**: www.thedirectory.org.uk/orgs/res_lewisham.html
- **Multifaith – Organizations**: www.paganpastoraloutreach.ca/multifaith/organizations.htm
- **Multifaith - websites:** www.paganpastoraloutreach.ca/multifaith/websites.htm
- **Multifaith Dialogue:** www.crescentlife.com/articles/multifaith_dialogue.htm
- **Multifaith Action Society:** www.multifaithaction.org
- **How A Multifaith Chaplaincy Program Operates:** www.correctionalchaplains.org/articles/01-02-2004.html
- **Multifaith.net:** http://www.multifaith.net/
- **Multifaith Worship - Boston College**: http://www.bc.edu/offices/campus-ministry/faith/multifaith/

- **LRCC - Spiritual and multifaith care [Cancer and treatment: Services for patients and families]:** www.lrcc.on.ca/cancer-and-treatment/spiritual-multifaith-care.xml
- **FFF - World Religions [A World of Many Faiths. ...]** www.faithfutures.org/multifaith.html
- **Multifaith Worship Opportunities:** www.clarke.edu/departments/campusministry/old/Multifaith%20Worship%20Opportunities.doc
- **Multi - Jewish and Muslim Women's Dialogue:** www.jewishcommunityaction.org/multi-faith.htm
- **Preston College - Multi-Faith Centre:** www.preston.ac.uk/pcsite/pages/multifaith.shtml
- **Multifaith Center - Orlando:** http://www.multifaith-orlando.com
- **Hospital Chaplaincy Gateway- Specialist resources [Specialist area...Multi-Faith and Cultural Resources]:** www.hospitalchaplain.com/htm/Resources-specialist/ multifaith.htm
- **Building -All Faiths Chapel:** http://uc.tamu.edu/buildings/chapel.htm
- **All Faiths!** http://www.allfaiths.us
- **USAF Academy Cadet Chapel All Faiths Room:** http://www.usafa.af.mil/hc/tafr.htm
- **RingSurf: tolerance of all faiths:** http://www.ringsurf.com/netring?action=info&ring=tolerance
- **All Faiths Are Equal:** http://www.freeindia.org/biographies/greatlkings/vikramaditya/page23.htm
- **"Uniting All Faiths"** http://www.rickross.com/reference/hom/hom2.html
- **Sri Pada: Sanctuary for all faiths:** http://sripada.org/nanayakkara.htm
- **The Golden Rule - It's True In All Faiths** http://members.aol.com/brininsf/golden.html
- **A community of believers of all faiths:** http://www.islamicity.com/awards/USAToday/USAToday.htm

3.8 Just-in-Time: Worship, Prayer, Meditation

- **Two Minute Short Puja (Hindu):** www.hindunet.org/day_as_hindu/puja/shortpuja.htm
- **15 minute Worldwide Simultaneous Prayer or Meditation with the Dalai Lama** for Peace and Non-violence http://www.tibet.ca/wtnarchive/2003/5/6_5.html
- **Two Minute Meditations: Worship** http://www.heartlight.org/two_minute/2m_980819_angels.html
- **Two-Minute Devotional - The Worship Show:** http://www.heraldoftruth.org/devo/20030811.html
- **Three-Minute Dramas for Worship:** http://www.rpinet.com/products/tmdw.html
- **Praying each day - From the De La Salle Brothers in the United Kingdom.** www.prayingeachday.org/reflect.html
- **Daily Prayer:** http://users.aol.com/prayerrx/
- **Prayers for Every Occasion. A site from a group of people in Santa Clara, California.** www.missionstclare.com/english/prayers/index.html
- **Fifteen Minutes of Daily Discipline: Rejoice 1 min., Review 5 min., Repent1 min., Resist, 1 min., Request 5 min., Recommit 1 min., Record 1 min:** www.retirementwithpurpose.com/fifteenminutes.html
- **1-Minute Daily Meditation , Daily Prayer - Roman Catholic** http://www.catholicroom.com/dailyfeatures/dailyprayer.htm

3.9 Sacred times for World Religions: Calendar for Festivals, Ceremonies, holy days ...

- **Diversity Calendar:** www3.kumc.edu/diversity/april.html
- **Interfaith Calendar:** http://www.interfaithcalendar.org/
- **INTERFAITH CALENDAR:** http://www.hamline.edu/~dkrueger/ifcalendar.html
- **Interfaith, Multifaith Religious Calendar of holidays** http://www.cheraglibrary.org/calendar.html
- **Interfaith Chapel - Religious Holy Day Calendar:** http://www.rochester.edu/chapel/holydays.html

- **NCCJ InterFaith Calendar:** http://www.nccj-chicago.org/calendar_03.htm
- **Jewish Calendar: Events and Holidays for Interfaith:** http://interfaithfamily.planitjewish.com/
- **Comparative-religion.com interfaith forums – Calendar:** http://www.comparative-religion.com/forum/calendar.php
- **Internation and Interfaith Calendar:** http://www.bendbahai.org/Interfaith.htm
- **Mystic Cowboy: January Interfaith Calendar:** http://mysticcowboy.org/archives/000102.html
- **Religious holidays from the many religions** http://www.multicultural.online.wa.gov.au/wppuser/eccru/homepage/links.html
- **Holidays and Special Days** Website **Directory** www.linkspider.org/KidsandTeens/PeopleandSociety/HolidaysandSpecialDays/
- **Relationships, Celebrations, and Traditions** http://www.educ.queensu.ca/~curr/units/Relation.pdf
- **Celebrating Holidays and Special Occasions on Websites** http://www.useit.com/alertbox/20021028.html
- **Omnigraphics - Days and Customs of** All Faiths http://www.omnigraphics.com/product_view.php?ID=566

3.10 Bibliographies, Infographies, Webliographies ... Multifaith Perspectives

[The following is a list of Multifaith resources, no attempt is made to evaluate their approaches, and hence don't consider this as a launch pad]

- **High Holy Links**: www.geocities.com/athens/delphi/5255/links.html
- **Philosophy in Cyberspace:** www.personal.monash.edu.au/~dey/phil/relig.htm
- **Ess, Charles. "Church in Cyberspace: A Working List of Resources."** www.drury.edu/ess/church/disciples.html
- **Religion Resources on the Interent:** www.sosu.edu/lib/subrel.htm
- **Cults on the Internet:** www.memecentral.com/mu/mu0005.htm
- **Resources for Studying Islam**, by Dr. A. Godlas: www.arches.uga.edu/~godlas/
  Internet Puts World of Religions, Sects at Your Fingertips:
  www.miami.com/mld/miamiherald/2002/08/17/entertainment/3877649.htm?template=contentModules/printstory.jsp
- **MetaReligion – Religious Tolerance Promoting Site**: www.meta-religion.com
- **World religions on the Web: A guide to some of the most helpful sites *C&RL News* (June 2002, Vol. 63 No. 6), by John Jaeger.**
  www.ala.org/Content/NavigationMenu/ACRL/Publications/College_and_Research_Libraries_News/Back_Issues__2002/June/World_religions_on_the_Web.htm
- **"The Digital Word: Internet Resources are Aids for the Deeply Devout"** www.digitalword.org/Pew.htm
- **Finding god n cybespace: A Guide To Religious Studies Resources On The Internet, by John L Gresham** http://sim74.kenrickparish.com/contents.htm
- **The Pagan Library**: www.paganlibrary.com/mylinks
- **Theology Library – Non-Christian Religions**: www.shc.edu/theolibrary/ncr.htm
- **Comparative Sites – Perspectives on Faith A Web Site for Inquiry About Religion**: www.bsu.edu/web/jcorbett/relig/compare.htm

3.11 Cyber Worship Webmetrics ... (Measuring the Visibility, pace, communication):

- **Measuring the Success of Seeds** (The formula is Impact = Ratings Seeds): http://worship.net/about/seeds_formula.asp
- **Namaste Unlimited World Prayer Project Statistics:** http://www.namaste-unlimited.com/Prayer/prayerstats.cfm
- **Statistics for Religious Life:** http://www.denison.edu/analog/ReligiousLife/
- **Survey.Net, Your Source for Information, Opinions & Demographics from the Net Community:** http://www.survey.net/rlg1r.html
- **Pew Internet & American Life Project:** http://www.pewinternet.org/reports/reports.asp?Report=53&Section=ReportLevel1&Field=Level1ID&ID=230
- **Usage Statistics for www,religion.no:** http://help.meg.nu/stats/religion.no/
- **Usage Statistics** for www.junbesh.com: **www.junbesh.com/logs/usage_200403.html**
- **Usage Statistics for Collaborative Ministry:** www.creighton.edu/stats/ColMin/usage_200312.html
- **Usage Statistics for religion.rutgers.edu:** www.rci.rutgers.edu/stats/web/religion.rutgers.**edu/**

3.12 The Web Awards – Religion

[Source: http://thewebawards.com/categories/religion.htm]

- **ALLfaiths Press** - http://interinc.com/Allfaiths/index.shtml
  Lists a variety of faiths]
- **The American Humanist Association** - http://www.infidels.org/org/aha
  Articles, essays, commentaries, lists, and bulletins]
- **Anglicans Online** - http://www.anglican.org/online/
  "The World's Largest Online Resource for the Anglican/Episcopal Community"]
- **Answers in Action:** http://answers.org
  Non-profit religious organization helping Christians to promote a better world]
- **Bible Gateway:** http://www.gospelcom.net/bible
  This is the ultimate Bible site. Great for research or plain inspiration]
- **Bible Quizzes:** http://www.islandnet.com/~hunter/quest00.htm
  So you think you know the Bible. Here is a great site to test your knowledge]
- **B'nai B'rith Interactive:** http://bnaibrith.org
  Dedicated to families, the community and the Jewish people of the world, this site is a growing repository of information]
- **The Buddha School Net:** http://www.tbsn.org/
  [This beautifully designed site offers a wealth of information regarding Buddhism]
- **CCM Online:** http://www.ccmcom.com/
  [This is the online version of the magazine dedicated to Christian music, events, and popular culture]
- **Christus Rex et Redemptor Mundi:** http://www.christusrex.org/
  [Visit some of the most beautiful works of art from churches all over the world without ever leaving your home!]
- **The First Church of Cyberspace:** http://www.execpc.com/~chender
  [Join their Sunday night Internet Relay Chat]
- **Gospel Communications Network:** http://www.gospelcom.net/
  [This is one of the best sites for Christian resources on the Web]
- **The Interfaith Alliance:** http://www.interfaithalliance.org
  [The purpose of The Interfaith Alliance is to promote the positive and healing role of religion in public life through encouraging civic participation, facilitating community activism, and challenging religious political extremism]
- **Word of Grace:** http://www.wordofgrace.org
  [An excellent site for the Word of Grace church in Mesa, Arizona]
- **The GODS' REVIVAL AWARD** is offered to webpages that promote the revival of the various pre-christian ("pagan"), polytheistic, ethnic Religions, Traditions and Ways of Everyday Life.
  http://www.angelfire.com/ga/gentiles/AWARD.html

3.13 Browser Wise Toppers: Miscellany

- **Best of the WEB Update- March/2002:** www.themediadesk.com/files5/bestupdate.htm
- **The best and worst of the web...** www.infidels.org/infidels/web.scan/1998/scan05.html
- **Best of Praise and Worship on the Web**
  http://innerc.mytopsitelist.com/jump.php?cmd=in&list_id=praisearchive&site_id=praisecharts
- **Worship On The Web:** http://www.urcwales.org.uk/synod/link/linkspage.htm
- **Worship on the Web:** http://www.links.net/www/worship.html
- **Finding worship on the Web:** http://www.crossroadsnews.com/jan02/frames/churchlinks.htm
- **Best Man Foot Worship on the Web!**
  http://www.tickling-feet.net/man_foot_worship.html
- **Worship on the Web:** http://www.cleardesk.co.uk/mellorvillage/worship.htm
- **Top 10 Religion Sites:** http://www.uga.edu/bahai/News/110400.html

3.14 Browser Wise Toppers – Islamic Sites

- **Top Ten Best E-Commerce Sites**
  http://www.islamonline.net/iol-english/dowalia/techng-15-12/techng3.asp
- **TOP 100 ISLAM SITES:**
  http://www.familytop100.com/relig_top100/islam_top100/
- **Muslim Minds Top Islamic Sites**
  http://web.archive.org/web/20030404050437/http://topsites.muslimminds.net/index.php?p=4
- **Opposing Views - Muslim Views Top Links**
  http://www.opposing-religious-views.com/Christianity_Muslim_Views.html
- **Muslim Top Links**
  http://www.discover-alabama.com/Society_and_Culture_Religion_Muslim.html
- **Muslim Top Sites**
  http://members.m4d.com/muslim/ffa/
- **Islam - Important Muslim Women Top Links**
  www.islam-directory.com/Social_Aspects_of_Islam_Women_in_Islam_Important_Muslim_Women.html
- **alt.muslim: The Top Ten Good News Stories Of 2003**
  http://www.blogit.com/Blogs/Blog.aspx/altmuslim/73781
- **Top Islamic Sites – Ranked**
  www.2muslims.com/directory/Cool
- **Islam Top 50: Top 50 Islamic Websites**
  www.islamtop50.com
- **Musalman Top 100 Islamic Sites**
  www.musalman.com/Top100/islamtop100_1.shtml

3.15 Browser Wise Toppers – Alternative Religions

- **TOP TEN REASONS WITCHES DON'T WORSHIP SATAN**
  http://tftb.com/deify/witchesdont.htm
- **DarkHorse Top 100**
  http://www.creativityweb.net/cgi-bin/darkhorsear/rankem.pl?id=virushea
- **MetaSpiritual Top100**
  www.listsitepro.com/cgi-bin/lsgold/lsgold.cgi?id=cassiel∓mp;click=1074881458

- **Wiccan/Pagan/Occultide Top 100 Sites**
  http://www.ultimatetopsites.com/religion/sylver6/
- **Top Ten Best Things About Being Wiccan**
  http://www.msu.edu/user/rohdemar/earth/Top10Things.html
- **Top Sites ~ The Wiccan Marie**
  http://www.geocities.com/ibwiccan/top.html
- **The Wiccan Marie Top Sites ~ Welcome ~**
  http://www.topsitelists.com/start/marie/
- **PAGAN - Pagan Top Links**
  http://www.pagan-links.com/
- **Pagan Top 100**
  www.pagansunite.com/pt100/list.html
- **2004 Top Gothic/Pagan/Wiccan Sites**
  http://topsitenet.com/cgi-bin/display.cgi?4461
- **Answering the Top 20 Questions Pagans Ask**
  http://www.gospelcom.net/uplook/pdfs/rs99_pagans.pdf
- **Top 100 Pagan Merchants**
  http://www.topsitelists.com/bestsites/kaylass/topsites.html
- **Wizard's Attic List of Top Pagan Sites Quick View**
  http://www.ultimatetopsites.com/religion/WizardsAtticList/quickview.html
- **Best of The Web Top Pagan Websites**
  http://www.geocities.com/pagan_crystal/banners.html

3.16 Browser Wise Toppers – Judaism

- **Top 100 Sites Network - Judaism**
  http://top100sitesnetwork.com/rev/Society/Religions/Judaism/
- **TOP 100: JUDAISM SITES**
  http://www.familytop100.com/relig_top100/jew_top100/
- **Christianity - Messianic Judaism Top Links**
  http://christianity-links.com/Denominations_Messianic_Judaism.html
- **Judaism - Judaism Top Links**
  http://www.judaism-links.com/
- **New Jersey - Judaism Top Links**
  http://www.cover-newjersey.com/Society_and_Culture_Religion_Judaism.html
- **Shamash's Jewish Links: Top 10 Rated**
  http://www.cover-newjersey.com/Society_and_Culture_Religion_Judaism.html
- **Opposing Views - Judaism Top Links**
  http://www.shamash.org/links/Ratings/
- **Judaism - Yiddish Top Links**
  http://www.judaism-links.com/Yiddish.html
- **The Jewish Agency For Israel: The Top Sites**
  http://www.jafi.org.il/top10/
- **The top 10 Jewish charities (January 26, 2001)**
  http://www.jewishsf.com/bk010126/sfacharitytop10.shtml
- **Messianic Jewish Top 100 Sites**
  http://www.messianic.com/top/
- **Top Picks: Judaism & Islam**
  http://www.globalengagement.org/issues/2001/10/judaism-islam-picks.htm

3.17 Browser Wise Toppers – Buddhism

- **Opposing Views - Buddhism Top Links**
  http://www.opposing-religious-views.com/Buddhism.html
- **faithfound.com : Top > More religions > Buddhism**
  http://www.faithfound.com/browse.php?cat=4314
- **Top Thai Sites: Thailand Buddhism, Meditation**
  http://www.topthaisites.com/Culture/buddhism.htm
- **Top Sites For Buddhism**
  http://topsitenet.com/religion/usa/4390/
- **Browse Top Level > Texts > Million Book Project > Buddhism**
  http://www.archive.org/texts/textslisting-browse.php?collection=millionbooks&cat=Buddhism
- **Knowledgerush.com Book Directory: top/Religion/Buddhism**
  http://www.knowledgerush.com/kr/jsp/db/directory.jsp?categoryId=84&categoryName=top%2FReligion%2FBuddhism

3.18 Browser Wise Toppers – Bahai

- **Bahai News - Top 10 Religion Sites**
  http://www.uga.edu/bahai/News/110400.html
- **Bahai Faith Top 100 Bestselling Books: Pamela Brode Baha'u ...**
  http://www.orientalia.org/books-./books-Bahai+Faith.html
- **Webeverything.co.uk > Bahai**
  http://www.webeverything.co.uk/directory/231139.html
- **The top bahai**
  http://clothing-store.apparel-find.com/bahai.html

3.19 Browser Wise Toppers – Jaininsm

- **Buy Jainism @ Top Selling Brands**
  http://www.topsellingbrands.com/shopping/type_browse/mode_12752.html
- **Buy The Jains (Library of Religious Beliefs and Practices) @ Top ...**
  http://www.topsellingbrands.com/shopping/asinsearch_0415266068.html
- **Society : Religion and Spirituality : Jainism :**
  http://www.website-hosts.org/dir/Society/Religion_and_Spirituality/Jainism/
- **Jainism Top 100 Bestselling Books: Helmuth Von Glasenapp ...**
  http://www.orientalgate.org/store-mode-books-page_num-8-input_string-Jainism-locale-us.html
- **The Jains (Library of Religious Beliefs and Practices) Top 100 ...**
  http://www.orientalgate.org/store-item_id-0415266068-search_type-AsinSearch-locale-us.html

- **Top/Society/Religion_and_Spirituality/Jainism**
  http://categoryweb.com/Top/Society/Religion_and_Spirituality/Jainism
- **Jainism Top 100 Bestselling Books: Maurice Lamm Houman Sarshar ...**
  http://www.orientalia.org/books-Jainism.html
- **Top 100 Sites Network - Jainism**
  http://top100sitesnetwork.com/rev/Society/Religions/Jainism/
- **Society > Religion and Spirituality > Jainism**
  http://www.webeverything.co.uk/directory/83862.html
- **Society - Religion and Spirituality - Jainism**
  http://www.undergrounds.com/tree.php3/catid=7253

3.20 Browser Wise Toppers – Hinduism

- **"Top hindu Websites"**
  Hinduism Today | May 1998
  http://www.hinduismtoday.com/archives/1998/5/1998-5-23.shtml
- **Hinduism - Meher Baba Top Links**
  http://www.hinduism-links.com/Spiritual_Personalities_Meher_Baba.html
- **HinduLinks Universe: Top 10 Rated**
  http://www.hindulinks.org/Ratings/
- **The Top 25 Hindu Websites**
  http://hindu.hypermart.net/
- **SpiritualMinds.com -Top Hindu Sites, Hinduism, Vedic Astrology ...**
  http://www.spiritualminds.com/hindusites.asp
- **SpiritualMinds.com -Top Hindu Sites, Hinduism, Vedic Astrology ...**
  http://www.spiritualminds.com/hindu.asp
- **Top Hindu / Indian / Sanskrit Baby Name Books**
  http://hinduism.about.com/cs/books/tp/aatp_babyname.htm
- **Top 6 Books on Hindu Marriage**
  http://hinduism.about.com/cs/matrimonials/tp/aatp_marriage.htm
- **Browse Top Level > Texts > Open Source Books > Hindu Rituals**
  http://www.archive.org/texts/textslisting-browse.php?collection=opensource&cat=Hindu%20Rituals
- **Hinduism - Gods and Goddesses Top Links**
  http://www.hinduism-links.com/Gods_and_Goddesses.html

3.21 Browser Wise Toppers – Christianity

- **Top Ten Indications that Your Worship Service May Be A Bit Too Relaxed!**
  http://graceland.gentle.org/topten/topnov98.html
- **Top 10 Series: Worship Collection: Vol. 1**
  http://www.carman.org/discography/albums/top_10.worship_1_2.html
- **Praise-Worship.Net : Top 5 Charts -**
  http://www.praise-worship.net/top5charts.htm
- **Christianity - Praise and Worship Top Links**
  http://christianity-links.com/Music_Styles_Praise_and_Worship.html
- **Top Christian directories and search engines to submit your web site**
  http://www.christiantopsites.com/
- **Tracy and Eric's Top 10 Worship Planning Reminders**
  Programme Resources: Connections 2000
  http://www.uccancamping.org/RES/PRO/HO10worshipplanideas.html
- **TOP TEN REASONS TO ATTEND OUR 6:00 P.M. SERVICE...**

http://www.belairpres.org/Welcome/Top_Ten.html

- **By the Rev. Mike Clark. Top 10 ways to find the ideal place of worship**
  http://latc.com/2000/02/02/special_sect/spiritua1.html
- **TOP 100 CHRISTIAN SITES**
  www.familytop100.com/relig_top100/christ_top100/

3.22 Browser Wise Toppers – Yoga:

- **The Top UK Yoga Websites, 2cYoga, 2c**
  http://www.2cuk.co.uk/yoga/
- **Yoga - Collection of Top Websites**
  http://www.search-it-all.com/related.aspx/Yoga
- **The Top UK Yoga Websites, Yoga 250 uk**
  http://www.250uk.co.uk/yoga/
- **Best yoga, kundalini, tantric, sikh, 3HO, vedic websites.**
  http://www.topsitelists.com/bestsites/kundaliniyogi/topsites.html
- **The Best Websites Online. ... Yoga Channel**
  www.baldegg.com/search/index.php/Society/Religion_and_Spirituality/Yoga/Practices/
- **Yoga Movement's Top Sites**
  http://www.yogamovement.com/links/topsites.html
- **Top 100 Yoga Tantra Veda Sites**
  http://www.topsitelists.com/edit.cgi?area=world&user=awareness
- **Top 10 sites for patna yoga ...**
  http://www.1-school.biz/topsites.php?q=patna+yoga+vidyalaya.+patna+school+
- **Top 10 sites for yoga meditation**
  http://www.1-medical.biz/topsites.php?q=yoga+meditation
- **Top 10 sites for yoga video**
  http://www.1-video.biz/topsites.php?q=yoga+video

3.23 Developing World Wide Worship Mindmaps – Survey, Tools, Responses…

- **Religion Selector: An Exploration of World Belief System:**
  www.speakout.com/activismtools/selectors/religion
- **Belief System Selector: An Exploration of World Religions**
  www.selectsmart.com/RELIGION
- **Ten Questions for Evaluating Corporate Worship:**
  www.sovereigngraceministries.org/pdf/conferences/worship/wl2001/evaluating_corporate_worship.pdf
- **"Bagley Baptist Form Mail Survey System." (Questionnaire)** www.bagleybaptist.freeuk.com/Survey.htm
- **Worship Survey**
  http://www.cumc-wf.org/worship_survey.htm
- **Jatinder Singh. "Sikh Internet Users Survey."** FormMail.to/cybersikhi or www.cybersikhi.com (2 Jan. 2004)
- **"Christian Online Resource Center Survey."** (Questionnaire)
  www.influencer4christ.com/survey/survey.php?opt=new (dead link 2 Jan. 2004)
- **Divining America: Sharing your questions - Multifaith Issues**
  www.nhc.rtp.nc.us/tserve/getback/getback.htm
- **WCC Worship Questionnaire**
  http://www.woodstockchristian.org/wccwq.html
- **Daily spiritual diary Questions**
  http://www.thedivinelifesociety.org/download/practicekarma.htm
- **How Well WORSHIP Questionnaire**

http://www.crcna.org/crmn/crmn_icym_worship.htm

- **Protection Environment Questionnaire for Houses of Worship: Multifaith Perspective**
  http://websurveyor.net/wsb.dll/14358/HoW-Security-Survey.htm
- **PROUT Indicators: Questions To Ask New Movements / Organizations ...**
  www.metafuture.org/Articles/PROUT%20INDICATORS.htm
- **Worship Team Questionnaire**
  http://www.goldcanyon.org/docs/questionnaire.doc
- **Ecumenism Webquest – Evaluation**
  www.faithcentral.net.nz/webquest/ecumenism/evaluation.htm
- **Worship Survey: MCC San Francisco A house of prayer for all people**
  http://www.mccsf.org/worship/survey/
- **Worship Survey Results -- May, 1999**
  http://www.jesusmcc.org/library/pastor07.html
- **Christian Prayer Survey**
  http://www.health-care-technology-llc.com/survey18.htm
- **EMSi Islamic Online Survey Respondents**
  http://www.datacards.com/kdm/kdm88237.htm
- **EMSi Jewish Online Survey Respondents**
  http://www.datacards.com/kdm/kdm88239.htm
- **EMSi Hindu American Online Survey Respondents**
  http://www.datacards.com/kdm/kdm97516.htm
- **EMSi Buddhist Online Survey Respondents**
  http://www.datacards.com/kdm/kdm88233.htm
- **Worship Survey**
  http://hopeonthenet.org/form.html
- **Innovative Worship Survey**
  http://stjohnsvandalia.org/worshipsurvey4.htm
- **Worship Survey: New Life Ministries**
  http://newlifeministries-nlm.org/online/worship_survey.htm
- **First Parish Church United, Westford, MA | Worship Survey**
  http://www.westford.com/firstparish/survey.shtml
- **Worship Satisfaction Survey**
  http://www.stmarksevanston.org/survey.html
- **A Prayer Survey**
  http://www.new-life.net/prayer02.htm
- **On our Knees : Prayer Survey Results**
  http://www.teal.org.uk/ep/onour.htm
- **House of Prayer Survey**
  http://www.centralcoastihop.net/form.html
- **EMSi Catholic Online Survey Respondents**
  http://www.datacards.com/kdm/kdm88235.htm
- **EMSi Protestant Online Survey Respondents**
  http://www.datacards.com/kdm/kdm88227.htm

- **Prayer Survey Reveals Interesting Trends**
  http://cbn.org/CBNNews/CWN/050302Survey.asp
- **Principal Concerns for prayer - Survey results: Projects**
  http://www.prayforspain.com/projects/index4.html
- **Prayer Survey (across five countries)**
  http://www.prayerguide.org.uk/prayer15.htm
- **Online Edition, Vol. VIII, No. 10: February 2003**
  Adoremus Survey Report - Lack of Reverence at Mass Tops Concerns
  http://www.adoremus.org/0203LiturgySurvey.html
- **The St. John Messenger: Worship Survey results**
  http://www.stjohnev.net/messenger/june2003/survey.html
- **Results of worship preferences survey**
  http://www.wcg.org/wn/99April/results_of_worship_preferences_s.htm
- **Worship 2003 Survey Results**
  http://www.salembaptist.net/nlcf/survey.html
- **Worship Survey Results**
  http://cmypage.com/rrumc/Survey/supplementalquestions.doc
- **Circular Church Worship Survey Results**
  http://www.circularchurch.org/WorshipSurveyResults.htm
- **EVALUATION OF THE WORSHIP SURVEY, 2002**
  http://www.christchurchblacksburg.org/newsletter/WORSHIPSURVEY2002.pdf
- **Worship Tops the List of Important Church-Based Experiences – Barna Research Group Survey**
  http://www.imaginations.ca/Worship%20True/worshipsurvey.htm
- **Self-Evaluation Tools - New Life Ministries**
  http://newlifeministries-nlm.org/online/self-assessment.htm
- **Mendon Presbyterian Church Worship Survey**
  http://www.mendonchurch.org/worshipSurvey.htm
- **Christian Worship Survey**
  http://www.praise.net/worship/survey/general/
- **Worship Survey - Door Creek Church**
  http://www.doorcreekchurch.org/worship/survey.htm
- **groovetastic-worship survey**
  http://members.diaryland.com/edit/showsurvey.phtml?name=groovetastic-worship

3.24 Spiritual Assessment : Tools, Techniques, Ports

- **Chaplain Service - Spiritual Assessment -**
  Joseph E. Quinlan All Faiths Memorial Chapel
  http://www.chillicothe.med.va.gov/chaplain3.html
- **Spiritual Assessment**
  http://www.jcaho.org/accredited+organizations/behavioral+health+care/standards/faqs/provision+of+care/assessment/spiritual+assessment+.htm
- **Spiritual Assessment - Audio / Video**
  http://www.geriatrics.umn.edu/SAT/spiritua.htm
- **A Spiritual Assessment**
  http://fumcrbrg.org/Spiritualassessment.htm
- **Spiritual Journey Growth Process: Self-Assessment Categories**
  http://www.fumcbirmingham.org/prayer/journey/sprtjny3.htm

- **Spiritual Assessment in Medical Practice.**
  http://www.findarticles.com/cf_dls/m3225/1_63/68547579/p1/article.jhtml
- **Toward Spiritual Assessment in Seventh-day Adventist Colleges and Universities**
  http://circle.adventist.org/browse/resource.phtml?leaf=2015
- **Spiritual Intelligence Assessment**
  www.spiritualassessment.com/spiritual_assessment.htm
- **Spiritual Pathway Assessment**
  http://www.fcogpunxsy.com/spiritual_pathway_assessment_tool.htm
- **How can I perform a spiritual self-assessment?**
  http://www3.mdanderson.org/patient/chaplaincy/self.htm
- **Leader Tools: GrowthFinder - Using the Internet to Diagnose spiritual Health**
  http://smallgroups.com/group_leader/leader_tools/growhtfinder.html

3.25 Navigate the Cyberspace if you are looking for Spirituality:

- **Next-Wave: Cyber-spirituality, more popular than eBay?**
  http://www.next-wave.org/jan01/Cyberspirituality.htm
- **Cyber-Spirituality on the Web**
  http://www.doublemirrors.com/dylan.html
- **Internet Spirituality**
  http://www.soulfoodministry.org/docs/English/InternetSpirituality.htm
- **Cybersociology #7: Dialogue on the Cyber-Sacred**
  http://www.socio.demon.co.uk/magazine/7/rossi.html
- **Would God Use Email?**
  http://www.pastornet.net.au/jmm/articles/9752.htm
- **On Acceptance of Cyber-Spirituality**
  http://members.aol.com/trnscndr/cyberspirituality.html
- **Internet Connection**
  http://go.studentz.com/my_life/internet_connection.htm
- **Time & Space in Cyberspace**
  http://www.abdn.ac.uk/onlinereligion/Chapter%20Three.htm
- **In the Company of Cyber-Seekers**
  http://www.lifeway.com/lwc/article_main_page/0,1703,A%253D155448%2526M%253D200243,00.html

3.26 Surf Cyber Meditation

- **Best online Meditation information**
  http://www.linkright.com/Meditation.html
- **Best Site Online. Meditation Technique**
  http://predictions.virtualave.net/witchcraft_karma.html
- **Transendental Meditation ! Best Site Online. Aquarius**
  http://gethoroscopes.bizhosting.com/transendental_meditation.htm
- **World Wide Online Meditation Center**
  http://www.meditationcenter.com/
- **Online Finger Meditation Tool**
  http://www.gracecathedral.org/labyrinth/interactions/index.shtml
- **Free Online Meditation Courses and Tutorials**
  http://www.docnmail.com/learnmore/meditation.htm

- **Melanie Online - Meditation Room**
  http://www.melaniegriffith.com/avalon/meditation_room.html
- **Prayer and Meditation Gems Online - Meditation Gems**
  http://home.att.net/~kdmrly/med.html
- **Buddhist Meditation: Insight Meditation Online, Vipassana Bhavana ...**
  http://www.buddhanet.net/insight.htm
- **Retreats Online - Meditation Retreats**
  http://www.retreatsonline.com/guide/meditation.htm
- **Welcome to Streets Online Meditation**
  http://www.streetsonline.co.uk/common/category.jhtml?CATID=cat1000885
- **Desktop Meditations - Online Meditation and Wellness Exchange**
  http://www.desktopmeditations.com/
- **The Mandala Project online meditation center**
  http://www.faystudios.com/index.mandala.cfm

3.27 Mystery Religions Revisited

- **Mystery religions page**
  http://www.belinus.co.uk/mythology/Mysteryreligions.htm
- **Paul and the Mystery Religions**
  http://www.probe.org/docs/mystery.html
- **Audio & Video tape - Masonic ritual and Ancient Mystery religions**
  http://www.ephesians5-11.org/catalog/dw-dbr.htm

- **The Mystery Religions**
  http://xx.acs.appstate.edu/~davisct/temenos/wisdom/mystery_religions.htm
- **Mystery religions early Christianity**
  http://www.geocities.com/intheword1/mystery_religions_early_christianity.htm
- **The Mystery-Religions**
  http://www.religion1.com/The_MysteryReligions_0486231240.html
- **Mystery Religions and Secret Societies**
  http://www.foxven.com/s-ona2.html
- **Esoteric Christianity**
  http://www.egodeath.com/bensonmysteryrels.htm
- **Mystery Religions in the Roman Empire**
  http://oncampus.richmond.edu/academics/classics/students/dave/Cults/
- **Common Elements Of Mystery Religions**
  http://www.idst.vt.edu/thbecker/mystrel.html
- **Christianity and the mystery religions (Particularly Mithraism) ...**
  http://www.unsolvedmysteries.com/usm243837.html

3.28 Magic & Religions in Cyberspace

- **Leyline Crossing: Magic Centered Religions**
  http://www.leyline.org/magic/religion/magiccenter.html
- **Egyptian Magic And Today's Religions**
  http://chitalnja.narod.ru/magick/egypt/21.htm
- **Religions of the World: New Pagan, Wicca, Magic**
  http://www.edunet.ie/resources/religioninfo/magic.html
- **AlmightyEulogy.com – The Official Homepage of Death / Black / Evil Metal band Eulogy:**
  www.alimightyeulogy.com

- **Myths-Dreams-Symbols: Exploring the Human Psyche**
  www.mythsdreamssymbols.com
- **Irish Magic, And Tuatha De Danaans**
  http://www.sacred-texts.com/pag/idr/idr18.htm
- **Magickal Dragon Dreams Top Pagan Sites - powered by List Site PRO**
  http://members.listsitepro.com/dragon/
- **Alternative Religions/Paganism/Magic**
  http://alternativemarketplace.com/pages/Alternative_Religions/Paganism/Magic

3.29 Quick Guide to Virtual tours / Pilgrimages:

- **Virtual Kashi – Multifaith Spaces**
  www.kashi.org/tour.htm (3 Mar 2004)
- **Virtual Tour of Jerusalem**
  http://jeru.huji.ac.il/md/vjt/sub2.html (3 Mar 2004)
- **Church of the Holy Sepulcher: Jerusalem – 3D Tour**
  www.inisrael.com/ipix/java/jer.htm (3 Mar 2004)
- **The Hindu Universe: Spiritual Tourism**
  www.hindunet.org/spiritualtourism (3 Mar 2004)
- **Virtual Baha'i tour:** www.einhanet.co.il/bahai/
- **Virtual Tour of the Golden Temple Complex**
  www.sikhs.org/golden
- **Click-Me Tour of the Synagogue** http://scheinerman.net/judaism/synagogue/tour/index.html
- **Full Synagogue Web Cam tour**
  www.hitchams.suffolk.sch.uksynagogue/full.htm
- **View Navruz:**
  www.dicoverturkey.com/English/movies/default.htm
- **Kauai's Hindu Monastery's Tour, Hawaii**
  http://www.himalayanacademy.com/hawaii/
- **Bhaktivedanta Manor Virtual Tour:** http://chantandbehappy.com/manorvirtual/index.htm
- **Vatican MuseumsOnline:** mv.Vatican.va/3_EN/pages/MV_Home.html
- **Walford Sikh Gurdwara (slide tour):** www.thegrid.org.uk/learning/re/pupil/sikh/inex.html
- **Lancashire Mosques - Virtual tour of a Mosque**
  http://www.lancashiremosques.com/discovery_mosque_tour.asp

3.30 Theology Sites: Comparative &/or Individual Perspectives:

- **Perspectives on Faith: A Web Site for Inquiry About Religion**
  www.bsu.edu/web/jcorbett/relig/compare.htm
- **Cybertheology: Theology In, Of and For Cyberspace**
  www.cybertheology.net
- **Theology & Pedagogy in Cyberspace II**
  http://faculty.garrett.edu/kalantzis/Conference2004/links/cybertheology.htm
- **Theology Web Site: Dedicated to the Online Theological Community – Just Shut Up and Believe Me**
  www.theologicalwebsite.com/index.shtml

3.31 Salvation-Wise Tools:

- **Cyber Salat - Software**: www.jas.org.jo/~muneer
- **Pager for Salat timings**: www.jannah.com/prayer
- **Pilot Yid**: www.pilotyid.com [a gateway to Kosher restaurants and Talmud selections, download on PDA]

- **Digital Rosary**: www.pathguy.com/rosary.htm [Pray with a bead]
- **Virtual Rosary**: www.virtualrosary.org [guided prayer, reflection, etc.]
- **Pal Talk**: www.paltalk.com/paltalk10/index.htm [Learn Scriptures: Bible, Torah by way of videoconference]
- **Jewish worship resources for the Palm Pilot**: www.jewishcontent.org/pda/palm
- **Download Banis for PDA (Sikhism)**: www.sikhnet.com/s/BanisOnPDA
- **Download an Image – Hinduism**: www.geocities.com/SoHo/Lofts/6834
- **Empowerment 12 Steps (Wiccans)**: www.circlesanctuary.org/healing/empower.htm
- **Synchronicity Collaborations - The Meditative Flute CD -Live Samples** http://www.synchronicity.org/Products/ProductDetails.aspx?productID=CMFCD&1=6&2=110&3=76
- **Promises of God – Palm Application that Lets You Look At What God Says About 18 Different Situations (Try for free):** www.pdatopsoft.com/software/item.php?pid=546

3.32 Worship / Service *Via* Camera (esp. WebCam or Web Camera):

- **Durga Puja**: www.durgapujas.com/camview.htm [Live Webcam coverage from USA]
- **Live Prayer from Haram Mosque**: www.saudiembassy.net/RealVDO/live.ram
- **Jousenji Temple Cemetery, Japan**: (Webcam) www.jousenji.com/main/javacam/yscam.html
- **Cabal KaBob: DemonWorshipOn a stick** - WebCams http://rj3.net/ckb/webcam.shtml?zoom=y&order=3
- **Halloween Web Cams**: www.halloweenwebcams.com
- **Spiritual webcams**: www.integrativespirituality.org/Spiritual_Webcams.htm
- **Christmas Webcam Page**: http://users3.ev1.net/~hwillcox/cam.html
- **Christmas Webcams Around the World**: www.emailsanta.com/Christmas_WebCams.asp
- **INTERACTIVE XMASTREE**: www.xmas4all.net
- **The Dome and Sacred Heart Basilica**: www.nd.edu/~webcam/domecam.shtml
- **Asylum cams**: (Asylum with Cats in cyberspace?) www.asylumcam.com
- **Webcam of The Monks of Adoration Chapel**: www.monksofadoration.org/chapel.html
- **Indian Matrimonial – India's Weding Webcast Interactive Source (For a price):** www.bharatmatrimony.com/webcast/webcast.shtml
- **The Daily Camera: Religion** http://www.dailycamera.com/bdc/religion/0,1713,BDC_2477,00.html
- **Eucharistic Chapel Cam** http://www.ccstpaul.com/index_chapel.htm
- **Adoration Cam** http://adore.inetcam.com/dynamicindex/cam0vo.html
- **Transfiguration** http://216.79.143.227/
- **Lordes Web Cam** http://www.lourdes-france.org/fr/frwcam.htm
- **Grotto** http://www.lourdes-france.org/gb/gbwcam.htm
- **Mass in Lordes** http://www.lourdes-france.org/gb/gbwcamm.htm
- **Water** http://www.lourdes-france.org/gb/gbwsigne.htm
- **Rosary Basilica** http://www.lourdes-patrimoine.com/gb/gbwcamb2.htm
- St. Martin of Tours Chapel http://louisville-catholic.net/webcams/chapelcam.html
- **St. Martin of Tours Sanctuary** http://louisville-catholic.net/webcams/sanctuarycam.html

3.33 Ten Commandments / Commitments' Faith-based:

- **Ten Commandments of Buddhism**
  http://www.olsommer.com/tsoh/textonly/buddhacom-t.html
- **Ten Commandments for Peace of Mind - How to attain at mental peace (Hinduism)**
  http://hinduism.about.com/library/weekly/aa060902a.htm
- **World Scripture - The Decalogue (Multifaith Perspectives)**
  www.unification.net/ws/theme014.htm
- **Ten Commandments and Commandments from other Religions**
  www.christainhistory.com/articles/ten_commandments.html
- **A Ten Commandments for Everyone**
  http://pw1.netcom.com/~cowdery/command.htm
- **The 10 basic principles of the Bahai faith**
  www.johnworldpeace.com/bahai1.html
- **The Assisi Decalogue for Peace**
  www.swanmore.freeola.com/thoughtfortheweek/thoughts/assisidecalogue.htm
- **The Code of Hammurabi**
  www.wsu.edu/~dee/MESO/CODE.HTM
- **The Ten Commandments: all points of view**
  http://www.religioustolerance.org/chr_10co.htm
- ***Which* Ten Commandments?**
  http://www.positiveatheism.org/crt/whichcom.htm

3.34 Best Practices in Information Technology – Ten Commandments Applied:

- **The Ten Commandments of HTML FAQ**
  www.visdesigns.com/design/commandments.html
- **The Ten Commandments for C Programmers (Annotated Edition)**
  www.lysator.liu.se/c/ten-commandments.html
- **PCWorld.com - The Ten Commandments of PC Security**
  www.pcworld.com/news/article/0,aid,113175,00.asp
- **Ten Commandments of Computer Ethics**
  www.brook.edu/its/cei/overview/Ten_Commanments_of_Computer_Ethics.htm
- **Ten Commandments for Success on the Net**
  www.fastcompany.com/online/03/command.html
- **The Access Web - The Ten Commandments of Access**
  www.mvps.org/access/tencommandments.htm
- **The Ten Commandments of Net Profits**
  www.profitzone.com/news1198.html
- **The Ten Commandments of Internet Marketing, web promotion, web ...**
  www.ecomhelp.com/ KB/web_promotion/kb_wpromo-the-ten-commandments-of-internet.htm
- **Lgendinc.com's Ten Commandments of Web Design**
  www.legendinc.com/Pages/MiscellaneousPages/HTMLCommandments.html
- **The Web Developers' Ten Commandments :: Komejo.com**
  http://www.komejo.com/writings/cmd3_2.php
- **Ten Commandments for good web page design**
  http://www.firstwebbuilder.co.uk/tencommands.html
- **Web Site Credibility: The Ten Commandments**
  http://www.onlineorganizing.com/Organizer_Article_Web_Site_Credibility.htm
- **Ten Commandments Strong Suggestions for Web-Based Digital Video**

http://bonfire.learn.unc.edu/zoo/03_info/ten_commands.pdf

- **The Ten Commandments Of Successful Web ...**
  http://idrl.crh-systems.com/x/site/
- **Ten Web Commandments**
  http://home.woh.rr.com/jimsjems/tencom.html
- **The Access Web - The Ten Commandments of Access**
  http://www.hammerdata.com/Newsgrp/lookupfields.htm
- **The Ten Commandments of Web Page Design**
  http://www2.uiah.fi/~jdevries/rethinking/
- **The Ten Web Page Commandments**
  http://www.profitzone.com/pznews/oct01-ten-commandments.html
- **Ten Commandments for hosting your web-site Free on ...**
  http://nettantra.com/webtools/ten.html
- **The Ten Commandments --- Travis Case Web Site**
  www.traviscase.org/Sermons/Ten_Commandments/TenCommandments.html
- **Ten Commandments of Sailormoon Website Creation**
  http://www.minki.net/fisheye/aq-comments.html
- **The 10 Commandments To Successful Search Engine Optimization**
  http://www.lilengine.com/print/search-engine-optimization/seo-commandments/
- **The 10 Commandments to Successful SEO**
  http://www.searchguild.com/article67.html
- **The Ten Commandments in the Quran (Compared with Bible's)**
  http://groups.msn.com/SubmissionToGodAlone/thetencommandments.msnw
- **Ten Commandments for Web Pages**
  http://home.woh.rr.com/jimsjems/tencom.html

3.35 Web-based Resources on Sacred Landscape (Sacrament, desecration, ...):

- **Sacred Landscape E-Mail List**
  www.netmasterinc.com/secrets/sacred_landscape.htm
- **Islamic Architecture** (Mosque and its liturgical structures)
  http://library.thinkquest.org/C007485F/1.htm
- **Mohamed Tajuddin Mohamad Rasadi. "The Design of Mosques as Community Development Centers from the Perspective of the Sunna and Wright's Organic Architecture."**
  www.art.ac.ir/conferences/Design/Mosque.htm
- "**Welcome to The Sacred Landscape**." (on sacred geometry: temple and shrine architecture).
  www.luckymojo.com/sacredland.htm
- "**Development Control Parameters for Non-Residential Development**." (includes Place of Worship & Institutional Developments).
  www.ura.gov.sg/circulars/text/dcd%20non-resi%20handbook%20_d0e12298.htm
- **"Worship 2000: Space for Worship ... Suited for Our Purpose."**
  www.elca.org/dcm/worship/
- Defining The Holy: Sacred Space In Medieval & Early Modern Europe ... Conference, 10 April 2003, University of Exeter
  http://www.ex.ac.uk/shipss/history/events/sacredspaceprog.pdf
- **Sacred Space Landscape Design (Interfaith)**
  http://www.sacredspacedesigns.com/
- **Geometries Of Power** (vastu and feng shui in context)
  www.govarch.dpws.nsw.gov.au/images/ss_09_geometries_of_power/Geo's%20of%20Power.pdf
- **Peter W Williams. Sacred Space in North America (Post 9/11 scenario)**

http://reo.nii.ac.jp/journal/HtmlIndicate/Contents/SUP0000003000/JOU0003000106/ISS0000017214/ART0000205240/ART0000205240.pdf

- **Clint Le Bruyne. "Worshipping God in the Everyday Spaces of Life: The Liturgical Life as Territorial Adventure."** http://thebigpicture.homestead.com/files/EverydaySpaces.html

3.36 E-Commerce and Cyber Worship – Compatibility, Competitiveness

- **Religious Insensitivity In Commerce & Industry**
  http://www.religioustolerance.org/com_inse.htm
- **Gods of Commerce - Religious sites**
  http://phillips.blogs.com/goc/2003/10/religious_sites.html
- **"+Commerce +Religious +aspects"**
  http://www.looksmart.com/r_search?key=%2BCommerce+%2BReligious+%2Baspects
- **Religion makes way for commerce**
  www.townonline.com/amesbury/news/local_regional/an_newmvboozesidems10172003.htm
- **Churches Get Online!**
  http://www.violetcollection.com/GetOnlineChurches.htm
- **Ministry Websites that Work: Today's Content Management Technology Makes it Easy to Keep Up With the Joneses.**
  www.churchbusiness.com/articles/321Feat1/html
- **6 Ways to Make Your Website Donor-Frinedly.**
  www.churchbusiness.com/articles/421high4/html
- **Soul for Sale on E-Bay.**
  http://www.ananova.com/news/story/sm_844462.html?menu=news.quirkies
- **Technology and Religion: An Interview with the Episcopal Church's Tom Ferguson.**
  http://www.technewsworld.com/perl/story/33078.html
- **Cyber Congregations Go Fishing on the Net.** By Andrew Careaga. Church Business 10/2000
  http://www.churchbusiness.com/articles/0a1comp1.html
- **"Religion Web Sites Surge Amid Spiritual Holidays And Extensive News Coverage, According To Media Metrix March 2002 Internet Ratings,"** [Two more religion sites break into the Media Metrix ratings for the first time] April 16, 2002,
  http://www.comscore.com/press/release.asp?press=277
- **Kevin Ferguson, "More churches turn to Web to raise funds," January 13, 2000**
  www.cnn.com/2000/TECH/computing/01/13/religious.e.commerce.idg/

3.37 Online-Religion/Spirituality: Are These Non-traditional Movements Here To Stay? Googling shows 'What is' and 'What may be':

- **Andrew Johnson, Salvatron 2000: Executive Summary, Sweet Fancy ...**
  ... Current web religions only provide part of the solution, such as supplemental spiritual materials and loony cults run out of shoddy one-bedroom walkups. ...
  www.sweetfancymoses.com/johnson_salvatron.htm
- **Cyberculture Religions**
  ... They're about a dime a dozen, and finding them is usually quite easy; just do a Yahoo search on cyber religions. You'll likely get a long page of glut. ...
  www.geocities.com/athens/delphi/5255/cyber.html
- **Defining Cyberpunk**

... 1984 has come and gone, but, soon enough, cyberpunk may be here. The motifs of cyberpunk: Posthumanism: artificial intelligence; cyber-religions; cyberspace; ...
www.cyberartsweb.org/cpace/scifi/cyberbib/ Essays/DefiningCpunk.html

- **A Dynamical, Evolutionary Perspective On Attention Capture**
  File Format: PDF/Adobe Acrobat - View as HTML
  ... Religions change, the US constitution changes, governments change, national boundaries change, technology changes, and specializations (eg, issues, theories ...
  www.psych.utah.edu/psych3130/attention.pdf
- **HTA Conference 2004: Technology and Religion | Kairosnews**
  ... The age of spiritual machines and the technologies of transcendence. Cyber-religions and the impact of the Internet on religion. ... http://kairosnews.org/node/view/3646
- **Humor - Simply Pets Directory: ... Negro de Disastre.". The Highly Unorthodox Temple Of Herman - The latest in a long line of bunny cyber-religions. Pray to Herman, the ...**
  www.simplypets.com/pet-directory/Pets/Rabbits/Humor/
- **Internet Religions of the World**
  Multifaith Course of study
  http://www.mc.maricopa.edu/~ladelia/rel_243%20Internet.htm
- **Interfaith: Religion and Beliefs for an Internet Generation**
  http://members.aol.com/porchfour/religion/religion.htm
- Internet Religion
  ... Pure cyber-religions are emerging, like"Transhumanists," who believe in eternal life through "uploading" their brains onto the Internet. ...
  www.wordtrade.com/religion/religioninternetR.htm
- **The Last Wizards - Technology's Spiritual History - Electric Gaia ... spaces and buildings. It should also be noted that one could now witness the creation of specific cyber-religions. Though many are ...**
  www.lastwizards.com/ pages/modules.php?name=News&file=article&sid=13 -
- **One of those strange and interesting cyber-religions. ...**
  www.clas.ufl.edu/users/gthursby/rel/featured.htm
- **Open Directory - Recreation: Pets: Rabbits: Humor**
  ... Negro de Disastre."; The Highly Unorthodox Temple Of Herman - The latest in a long line of bunny cyber-religions. Pray to Herman, the ...
  dmoz.org/Recreation/Pets/Rabbits/Humor/
- **Patterns of Diffusion and Religious Globalization**
  ... The American TV-Home Churches provide one important example and the extreme Internet religions mentioned above are others. Church of Scientology. ...
  www.abo.fi/comprel/temenos/temeno32/rothsten.htm
- **Religious Education: ... BUBL: 200 Religion (links). Virtual or Cyber-Religions. Copyright: IN-TELE. If you have any questions regarding this web contact [IN-TELE at Essex]. ...**
  intele4.essex.ac.uk/main/religiou.htm
- **Religious Studies Featured Sites: ... First International Church of Christian Yoga with online bookstore**
  http://home.earthlink.net/~kriyayogi/
- **Religious Traditions and Cults - AZ. Advaita Vedanta, advaita ...**
  www.self-improvement-personal-development.com/ p_reltra.html
- **Research Guides: Philosophy ... scriptures. A Guide to the Best Religious Studies Resources on the Internet Religions throughout the world are linked here. This ...**
  www.lib.jmu.edu/philosophy/internet.html
- **Search Results for futurist thinkers frontier future science ...**
  ... 22. Thinkers.Net Talk Menu, 75%. Living Rethinking Life Urban Wilderness, Living on The Internet Religions Fantastic Frauds or Spiritual Quest? ...

www.ethologic.com/sasha/links/futurist.html

- **Spiritual Surfers: Transcript**
  ... But there'll be hundreds of Internet congregations, thousands of Internet religions springing up like mushrooms all over the place and so, although there might ...
  www.godweb.org/transcript.html
- **Virtual Religions**
  http://www.clas.ufl.edu/users/gthursby/rel/virtual.htm
- **Virtual Gumshoe-Investigative Resources Available on the Web Cults**
  Cults and Organizations. Altar Of ... sects, etc. Cults Large Index of Cults; The Cult Controversy From the Washington Post; CULTS 'R US; ...
  www.virtualgumshoe.com/gator207.htm
- **Working the web: Cults**
  Cults. Creating a cult is a cakewalk, says Clint Witchalls. All you need are a few ideas, an audience and access ...
  www.rickross.com/reference/general/general530.html -
- Cults on the Web -- Oh, my!
  The Heaven`s Gate suicides naturally gave TV news pundits somethingto carp about this past weekend. ... Cults on the Web -- Oh, my! ...
  www.usatoday.com/tech/columnist/cc0331a.htm
- **Cults - Web Guide - People in Action**
  Cults - Message Board. People in Action - Web Guide Cults
  peopleinaction.info/**cults**/ -
- **Web Links For Cults, Sects, and New Religions**
  ... CESNUR. Cults and New Religious Movements. INFORM. ... Religious Movements Homepage. Social Psychology of Cults. Society for the Scientific Study of Religion. Syzygy. ...
  faculty.washington.edu/kitts/cultlinks.html -
- **Cults website.Cults online**
  ... Antichrist, 666, Rapture, Tribulation, Revelation. Research Cults At Questia Questia online library offers more than 70,000 books and journal articles. ...
  www.egeeart.com/Cults.htm -
- **Information on non-Catholic cults web page.**
  ... The linkbelow is intented to deepen your understanding of other dangerous, non-Catholic cults. ... 2000 - 2010 Suggestions for this web page are appreciated. ...
  www.cpats.org/InformationOnCults.cfm
- **Cults Opposing Views Web Directory**
  Cults Opposing Views Web Directory. Cults Opposing Views Web Directory. In Google web directory...
  www.repertoire-sites.com/index.php/Society/Religion_and_Spirituality/ Opposing_Views/Cults/
- **BBC Online - Cult - The Hitchhiker's Guide to the Galaxy**
  ... h2g2Talking Point h2g2 on unhelpful technology Douglas Adams' last Radio ProjectRadio 4 Hitchhiker's Guide to the Future DNA LinksDouglas Online Other Adams ...
  www.bbc.co.uk/**cult**/hitchhikers/ -
- **Web surfers prefer blessed to undressed- religious cults and sects**
  Web surfers prefer blessed to undressed- Religion News Report about religious cults, sects, and alternative religions. Religion News ...
  www.apologeticsindex.org/news1/an011227-18.html
- **Experts: No Proof of Satanic Cults :: Wytches' Web :: uk based ...**
  ... Online Shop. Pagan and spiritual gifts and supplies. (5% discount for Wytches' Web members.). Bookstore. ... Experts: No Proof of Satanic Cults Posted by: WebWytch. ...
  wytchesweb.net/print.php?sid=1953 –

3.38. Need more paths to find online resources?

[source: http://www.tblc.org/spl/collection]

200 Religion: general resources
Seminole Library's Online Guide to Religion; SPC Online Library Religion Resources; Voice of the Shuttle Religious Studies; Finding God in CyberSpace
200 Religion: education and research
BUBL Link Religion Education & Research; Hartford Institute for Religious Research; American Religion Data Survey.
210 Philosophy and theory of religion
Philosophy of Religion; BUBL Link Sources;
290 Comparative and religions other than Christianity
The Religious Movements Homepage Project; Ontario Consultants on Religious Tolerance; Virtual Religions Index.
292 Greek & Roman mythology
Greek Mythology; Ancient Greece on the Web; The Perseus Digital Library
293 Norse & Celtic mythology
Germanic Mythology ; Asgard; King Arthur
294.3 Buddhism
BUBL Link Buddhism Resources; Resources for the Study of Buddhism; Tricycle Buddhist Review; Librarian's Index to Internet Buddhism
294.4 Jainism
Jain Students Group at the University of Michigan;Jainism for All; Jain Principles Traditions and Practices; Jainworld
294.5 Hinduism
Manas: Religions of India; Hindu Philosophy; Hinduism Links; Hinduism for Schools; Elements of Hindu Devotion; A Study of the Hindu Religion
294.6 Sikhism
Sikhism Home Page; Essays on Sikhism; SikhNet
295 Zoroastrianism
Avesta -- Zoroastrian Archives; World Zorastrian Organization; Zarathushtrian Assembly.
296 Judaism
Judaism & Jewish Resources; Judaism 101; Reform Judaism; Chabad.org;
Jewish Theological Seminary of America; Shamash--The Jewish Network The Jewish Virtual Library.
297 Islam
Introduction to Islam; Resources for Studying Islam; The Islamic Interlink; A Sh'ite Encyclopedia; Sistani.org; Islam 101
297.93 Baha'i Faith
The Baha'i World; An introduction to the Baha'i Faith
299 Other Religions
The Church and School of Wicca
299.16 Druids, Celtic Religions
The Druid Grove
299 512 Confucianism
The Analects of Confucius; Essentials Readings on Chinese Philosophy
299.514 Taoism
Daoism Depot; Taoism Information Page
299.561 Shinto
Shinto Sacred Texts
299.73 Native American Religions
Native American Religion; Native American Spirituality.
299.936 Scientology
Church of Scientology; Secrets of Scientology; Religious Movements- Scientology

4

Navigating the Deep Sacred Space via Experiences of the Wise

Two different types of content is included in this chapter. First, there are articles by scholars and navigators in the field. These articles review the state-of-the-art of Cyber Worship. Specialists and others will find this of great value in understanding the paths and in visualizing the future trends. Second, are the efforts of the Web gurus who know how and where to find a needle in the hay stack. What these gurus have done is developed effective and efficient ways of harnessing the wild web. Such best practices include, here, are in the form of Website maps, Web indexes, taxonomies, and techniques that help organize the semantic Web.

4.1. Welcome to the wild, wacky and wonderful world of Internet spirituality

By the Rev. Dr. Sandra Bochonok
Revsandyb@aol.com
Preached February 3, 2002 at www.kuuf.org
http://www.soulfoodministry.org/docs/English/InternetSpirituality.htm

Welcome

Welcome to the wild, wacky and wonderful world of internet spirituality. Trying to describe internet spirituality reminds me of an ancient Hindu parable about six blind men trying to describe an elephant. The first blind man, touching the elephant's side, determined it was a wall. The second man, clinging to the tusk, concluded it was a spear while the third man, stroking the trunk, thought it was a huge snake. The fourth man, holding a leg, concluded it was a tree and the fifth man, clutching an ear, decided it was a fan. The sixth man, grasping the tail, was convinced he held a rope. Each described the elephant from his limited perception; each lacked the ability to see the larger picture.

So what is the larger picture of cyber spirituality? Taped to my computer desk is a faded comic that reads: "Desperate? Confused? Visit www.god.com for all your spiritual needs!" Who among us has not received humorous emails like the one I received the other day that read, "stop what you're doing for the next 60 seconds and if you really believe in prayer, send this email prayer to 10 friends if you want good luck to come your way." I must confess that I have a favorite email prayer taped on my refrigerator door: "Dear God, so far today I've done pretty good. I haven't gossiped or lost my temper. I haven't been greedy, grumpy, rude, selfish or over-indulgent. I'm very proud of that, thank you! But in a few minutes, God, I'm going to get out of bed and from then on, I'm gonna need all the help I can get. Amen." Another personal favorite is the story of a young mother helping her child say her prayers before bedtime. As the little girl recited the Lord's prayer, she made an innocent mistake. Rather than pray to be delivered from evil, she asked to be delivered from email.

Community.com

The internet is often called the information superhighway. Some argue it is a "solution waiting for a problem". Yes, it is the world's largest library. But many overlook the 'Net's astonishing ability to bring people together. Each individual with access can keep in touch with family and friends, get breaking news and discuss its implications, use the incredible search engine resources for research, comparison shopping and more. It is a medium of mass communication that is also intensely personal and interactive. Through the 'Net, we can ask for and offer advice, share ideas and get feedback while discovering new knowledge. We can meet new people and make valuable contacts, all the while improving our computer and writing skills. The internet can be compared to sitting at the local coffee shop. People sit at the table, talk and listen. You can send a letter to one or hundreds through email. It is a powerful spiritual companioning tool.

The internet truly came of age in 1998. Its growth has been phenomenal and has given hundreds of millions of people the opportunity to be online and communicate through a new medium. Its influence is clearly felt in politics, education, business and media. These interactive services make our lives easier and more convenient.

How it is integrated into people's lives will define this century. Already the 'Net has quickly become a global medium that is as central and valuable to our lives as the telephones of the 1920s and the television in the 1950s. The majority of consumers who have been online for three years or more now view this medium as a necessity to their lives. Almost every culture and nation now use it. Every age group is significantly involved from young school children to elderly users. People who live overseas without running water manage to get online and suddenly their world comes very close to our own.

If the blind men in the Hindu parable struggled to describe an elephant, just imagine them describing the internet. It's an incredible electronic maze, and it is an information superhighway. Perhaps most importantly, it is a community builder. The 'Net brings like-minded people together. Chances are you will find a community somewhere on the web. Groups who have often been excluded or who feel rejected by religion are finding spiritual community online. Deep friendships develop and it is not uncommon to hear people talking of their electronic soul mates.

People who have been reluctant to write a traditional letter, postcard or note are spending hours writing electronic letters (email) to pen pals around the world, sharing their faith experiences and favorite websites of spiritual hospitality and generosity, helping people pray with a simple click of the computer mouse.

7/24/365

It was Mae West who said, "Too much of a good thing is always wonderful!" All the good things of the internet have launched a wonderful global spiritual revolution affecting hundreds of millions of people. It occurs 7/24/365. The 'Net never sleeps and abounds with virtual lurkers and searchers, who eagerly explore the million plus existing websites dedicated to faith, religion and every kind of spirituality practice imaginable.

Internet evangelists from every imaginable DOC (Deity of Choice) eagerly share their faith through email, personal and church and denominational websites, with thoughtfully placed hyperlinks, while they send e-cards, virtual meditations, and participate in various list discussions and chat rooms.

1 in 4

Religious experts who study trends estimate approximately 70% in the United States of America are now online. The December 2001 issue of Yahoo.com magazine revealed that 1 in 4 adults in North America now uses the internet for religious and spiritual expression. According to George Barna (www.barna.com), 1 in 6 use the 'Net as their only spirituality resource. Amazing but true.

Just the other day while at a dance class in a local community center, a college student struck up a conversation with me. He began sharing some of his career dreams and aspirations before asking about the kind of work I did. I told him I was an internet pastor. He asked what that meant. It means that I live locally but work globally. The world is my parish. The student's eyes grew large as he excitedly shared that his father had no religious background of any kind, but constantly searched the internet for spiritual answers to his many questions.

God.com

With a click of the mouse, we can surf to a Roman Catholic reading room, leap over to an Orthodox Jewish discussion group and then visit a live online meeting with a Zen Buddhist group. And while we are at it, let's email a prayer to God through a virtual Jerusalem, a cyber Sistine chapel and through the WebPages of some of the great cathedrals around the world. Cyber pilgrims surf to Mecca and Mount Meru, the Vatican and many other holy places and experience profound, life changing moments of transformation in the process.

Miss church? No problem. Consider using a cyber church. Simply download a sermon, devotional, homily or meditation of your choice. Want to experience a few minutes of daily spiritual wisdom from other faiths? Visit a website such as www.beliefnet.com and request a daily inspirational email that can be Hindu, Muslim, Buddhist, Christian, a reading from Torah and/or the Bible and do not forget the wisdom from the Dalai Lama.

Confession has always been good for the soul. Many are eagerly trying digital confessions. Just fill in the blanks. The Confession Booth (http://anter.learning.cs.scu.ed/priest.html) make this easy for all seekers and you don't even have to be Roman Catholic to use it.

Digital Priest: And what is it you wish to confess?

Response: I committed the following sin:

(Murder) (Adultery) (Sloth) (Lust) (Avarice) (Deception) (Gluttony) (Pride) (Anger) (Covetousness) (Misplaced Priorities)

People are searching for spiritual insights and the 'Net can provide many answers. More than 10,000 world religions are represented online. Christianity alone has more than 33,000 denominations and there are so many websites from religious organizations, individuals, local churches that it can be overwhelming to the casual seeker.

Cybersalvation

Cybersalvation is today's virtual reality. "I found God through the internet" is an increasingly heard testimony. While some debate if the internet can save souls, it must be recognized as a rapidly growing movement. God.com is today's reality. Cyber evangelism is occurring globally in every major faith tradition and spiritual inclination. New technology is empowering people of faith to share ancient spiritual wisdom and Beauty (www.geocities.com/russian_icons/trinity.htm,www.geocities.com/russian_icons/theotokos.htm> and www.geocities.com/russian_icons/savior.htm) as well as culturally relevant outreach (www.seekerschurch.org) .

People who formerly sat in front of their televisions or went out for a social drink now surf the 'Net. Many have never darkened the door of a church, temple, synagogue or mosque. But they sample internet churches, spirituality chat and prayer rooms, searching web pages for religious information and spiritual companions. Each faith tradition is eager to share their interpretation of an online gospel. Everybody believes in something and that something is on the World Wide Web.

Spiritual hospitality, generosity and sanctuary through soulfoodministry.org

As international seekers explore and sample various websites, one quickly notices every website is different in approach, theology and practical spiritual practices. Globally, people are in search of websites offering spiritual hospitality, generosity and sanctuary. Quality content can transform lives while we search for meaning during our faith journeys (http://soulfoodministry.org/docs/English/FJ1.htm).

I confess to being a technically challenged minister who is blessed to work with a dream team of technically gifted, big hearted, dedicated volunteers. Through our combined efforts, Soulfoodministry.org is a gracious presence in cyberspace. We have been online since 1998 and serve virtual visitors from more than 102 countries. We offer a variety of devotional materials that strive to help our visitors feel closer to the Sacred. It is our goal to equip, energize, empower and encourage all who come to us and we represent a growing, global voice of faith.

Cyber pilgrims browse and download Spanish, French, Portuguese, Russian and English meditations and other spiritual resources written by a variety of international authors. Some visitors print off materials and share them with friends and family who are offline. I've known people on other continents who share hard copies of our reflections with those hospitalized or with others who are in prison. Many forward email copies of the devotionals and they circulate the world, stimulating electronic conversations about the Sacred. When America was attacked on September 11, 2001, a spiritual response was posted before the dust from the rubble cleared in an effort to offer comfort and solace for virtual readers. Visitors email various prayer requests to a trusted confidential prayer team (prayerteam@mccdc.com). These saints pray for the strange and the stranger alike in a variety of languages and situations. Even those who do not believe in prayer will email the prayer team "for a little extra help from the Big Guy in the sky." Some cyberpilgrims have actually traveled to my home from the other side of the world for moments of face to face conversation after a relationship is established.

Most of all, I have noticed that people are hungry for materials that help them feel closer to God. Archbishop Desmond Tutu once said, "If I do not spend a reasonable amount of time in meditation early in the morning, then I feel a physical discomfort. It is worse than having forgotten to brush my teeth." In my experience as an internet pastor, I can only conclude there are many around the world who would agree with the Archbishop as they use the internet as a vital part of their daily spiritual meditations.

God and pornography

There is a notable dark side to the 'Net that offers a great deal of crude and offensive matter. God and pornography can be found with equal ease. The internet has been called the world's largest library. Like any library, there are certain materials unsuitable for children. Because of the anonymity of cyberspace, it is easy to lurk and search unsavory websites. Our sexuality and spirituality are closely connected and it would behoove the wise to avoid cyber-porn, which is highly addictive and can lead to destructive behaviors. Because of the easy availability of pornography, no child should ever be allowed to surf, or explore the 'Net without accountability and adult supervision. There are many sexual predators and criminals in the cyber city who aggressively evangelize on the internet.

The internet and children

Children along with adults actively date through the internet. The church has a remarkable opportunity to be culturally relevant. Today's techno-savvy under-16ers have a new venue for exploring teen idols, puppy love and fantasies. Our kids are online looking for someone to communicate with. They like to get email. They post messages looking for cyber boyfriends and girlfriends as preteens. "Hi! I am looking for a cyber boyfriend! I am ten. I have brown hair and brown eyes. I love swimming, playing basketball, and think kittens are adorable! If you want to be my cyber boyfriend, email me." Help your children find web sites such as cyberkids.com, teentalk.com and cyberteens.com. These provide social sites and are easily found through large search engines such as yahoo and others. Falling in love is a spiritual experience. At the very least, let us offer safe guidelines for cyber dating for our young charges to reduce risky behaviors.

Wise youth pastors, religious educators and parents would do well to lead their children in participating in various chat and online communities.

Many teens are more technically adept than their spiritual leaders and are thrilled to participate in developing and maintaining their church web page and cyber youth outreach if given a change. Consider inviting the teens in your church to participate in such contemporary outreach and offer them an opportunity to teach the adults in their lives.

Some virtual realities and cautions while exploring 'Net spirituality

One of the most frequent questions in cyberspace is "Who are you?" "Where on the planet do you live?" In virtual reality you can be anyone you want to be. And anyone can publish materials and claim to be a theologian on the internet. A word to the wise—do not believe everything you read or everyone you meet.

Using the internet is as easy as using the telephone. But be very careful with confidentiality, privacy and veracity issues. The internet is as private as a postcard. Emails can be forwarded. We also leave electronic cyber footprints. Email is stored by internet providers and can be retrieved and traced to senders and receivers. Think twice before pouring out your problems to complete strangers online. Share with care. There is tremendous vulnerability in cyberspace. One of the most frequently heard statements I read in emails are: "I don't even know you and I'm telling you about my pain."

And our humanness imagines what people look like and what kind of persons they are. Our words represent our electronic voice. Psychological dependencies and codependencies can develop. Emails may confuse people with unfamiliar local idiom and language nuances. Transference and counter-transference issues can be easily experienced in email. For other issues and challenges in cyberspace outreach, you are cordially invited to use http://soulfoodministry.org/docs/GeneralConfJuly99.htm as a resource.

Summary

The internet is here to stay and is full of cyberpilgrims searching for enlightenment in the world of cyber spirituality. On Sunday mornings some people go to church. Many others simply turn on their computers.

I cordially invite you to use www.soulfoodministry.org as part of your journey. The internet is an amazing resource that needs to be experienced. Enjoy your surfing. Share with care. Teach your children cyber low risk behaviors. And may your Deity of Choice bless you with great electronic soul friends as you explore spirituality websites, chat rooms and virtual chapels.

****

4.2 A Religious Experience: What is being done with the Internet and where are we going?

By Clark W. Woods

www.speech.sir.com/academics/gibbs/students/busn6080-f1-2001-jbh/woods/woods.html

Introduction

What is religion? How can an individual's need for religion or spirituality be satisfied or enhanced by technology? In order to answer these and other questions, one must take a step back and briefly look at the long history of religion and how technological advances have affected it in the past.

Religion is not an easy thing to define. It does not fit easily into a neat box to be taken out whenever needed. To illustrate this, let us look at some quotes that attempt to define religion or the religious experience. British mathematician and philosopher Alfred North Whitehead defines it as what people do with their solitude (Online Religion 10). This definition would imply that one's religion is a private matter best experienced alone. However, Karl Marx takes a much grimmer view on religion when he states, "religion is the sigh of the oppressed creature, the heart of a heartless world, and the soul of soulless conditions. It is the opium of the people." (Definitions of Religion) As a society, we do not care for this definition, but it is nevertheless one view and must be considered when looking at an international forum such as the Internet. Finally, A Christian centered view of religion can be obtained from the Bible itself in James 1:27. Religion that God our Father accepts as pure and faultless is this: to look after orphans and widows in their distress and to keep oneself from being polluted by the world. (NIV) This view obviously suggests that religion is much more than a solitary experience or a fantasy made up to appease the masses. It all but mandates a physical community performing services to its community.

In mankind's long history, no one religion has ruled the hearts and minds of all people. Instead, it has been a consortium of beliefs that co-existed. Certainly, these religions have been shaped by events in our past. While it is not documented, it is clear that many of the ancient religions were influenced by natural events such as comets or earthquakes. In more recent times, one can see that easily available knowledge has certainly influenced Christianity. The advent of print allowed Martin Luther to spawn the protestant revolution by calling into question the teachings of the established order in the church (Online Religion 14). He literally published more information than the church and reached others as a result. While they have not had as profound an impact, radio and television also have had their influence on the religious experience. Slowly, congregations have come to expect a more polished service to resemble their television viewing experience. However, their impact has not been as large as the printing press because massive capital must be expended to pay for the television airtime.

The Internet is a fairly new technology that is used to disseminate information to the public and allows one to do this with a minimal capital investment making it a potent tool for change. Much of this change has already been demonstrated by the business world, but it yet has to truly be experienced by the religious world. How is the Internet being used today by various religions, and how is it likely to affect the future of that and other religions? This paper will attempt to look at some the sites in existence and answer these questions.

Traditional Religions

Most of the more established religions have a presence on the web. That presence can range from an attempt at a full worship experience to a bare bones site with only names of the clergy and a schedule of events. For the purposes of this paper, traditional religions refer to those with a history of an established physical presence at one or several locations. Specifically, the religions discussed in this paper will be Hinduism, Buddhism, Islamic, Judaism, and Christianity. Furthermore, the Christian category will be broken into smaller groups to attempt a fair representation of this highly fragmented religious segment.

Hinduism

The striking thing when visiting any site associated with the Hindu religion is the similarities of each site. Perhaps the best example of a typical site is www.hindunet.org/. Great pains are taken to explain the religion to anyone who visits the site. Yet there seem to be many opportunities for the practicing Hindu to utilize the site as well. For example, the site is linked to a calendar of events as well as a list of all physical sites for worship temples. This and other sites take this one step further allowing one to worship online. One can interact by clicking on a site for a Digital Avatar, download an image of a Shiva, or download several images to view in rapid succession. While this may not entirely replace the worship experience of the Temple, it can be utilized as a temporary measure while in an office or home setting. The Hindu sites seemed to have the least representation online yet the most useful information and services for its users. Also striking was the similarity of all of the sites visited. It seemed as though there was a great amount of organization between the sites.

Buddhism

Like Hinduism, most of the sites dedicated to Buddhism are very similar; however, there is a slight range in the level of the user they are trying to reach. Some of the sites are for practicing Buddhists and offer online temples to assist in meditation and resources to network. An example of such a site is http://www.edepot.com/buddha.html. While some general information is available, one can see that the primary focus of this site is to be a service to practicing Buddhists. Another site is http://www.buddhanet.net/. This site appears to serve the entire spectrum of users. It offers anything from beginning mediation classes and online worship, to a directory for other local Buddhist organizations. Much like the Hindu sites, there are striking the similarities between the Buddhist sites. Most of the sites have links to the other sites, all of which seem to espouse very similar ideologies. One must wonder whether this apparent unity is a result of planning or a result of fewer sites devoted to these religious practices.

Islamic

Unlike Hinduism and Buddhism, there are a significant number of sites devoted to the Islamic faith. With this increase seems to come an added diversity to the sites. One item that seemed odd about these sites was that none seemed to have the resources to locate local places of worship. This universal lack is curious and probably deserves further research in the future. The diversity of the remaining sites is tremendous. Some such as http://www.ummah.org.uk/what-is-islam/index.html and http://www.al-muslim.org/ offer basic explanations of the Islamic faith and religion. These sites obviously are geared toward the novice. Other sites offer information for networking with others. A good example of this is the site http://www.ummah.net/. It offers information on everything from events to Islamic owned shops. Still another site offers a tour of a Mosque complete with the prayer room. This site (http://isfahan.anglia.ac.uk/barsian/monar.html) is incredible in its ability to deliver grand images and to allow the user to roam freely using directional arrows. It is unclear whether this site is merely educational or is intended to allow one to enter the prayer room for worship. Nevertheless, it is an incredible experience on its own merits. Finally, there are sites that are akin to the apocalyptic Christian sites. They appear very fundamental and have a sense of urgency regarding the conversion to the Islamic faith. An example of such a site is http://www.islamworld.net/. While it offers general information, it also urges the reader to convert without delay since delay could cost you eternity. Taken as a whole, these sites definitely offer a wide range of material on the Islamic faith.

Judaism

Like the Islamic sites, the larger number of sites devoted to Judaism tends to increase the diversity. Once again, it seems that the sites offer a wide range of opportunities for the reader. For very basic information regarding the religion, one can go to a site such as http://www.jewfaq.org/. This site gives the doctrine and dogma concerning the faith but little else. Still other sites offer similar information while expanding on topics. For example, http://www.jewishpeople.net/ expands on this by offering a networking service for the Jewish people while offering such extras as kosher recipes. The site http://www.jewishpath.org/ is geared toward an individual that is practicing the Jewish faith. The content is a collection of prayers and study materials. Finally, there are sites that are devoted to relationships between the Jewish Religion and other religions. An example of this type of site is http://www.jcrelations.net/index.htm. This site is devoted to the relationship between Judaism and Christianity and furnishes articles and excerpts from conferences worldwide. These examples are merely some of the diverse range of materials on Judaism available. In fact, there is a search engine devoted entirely to Judaism at http://www.maven.co.il/subjects.asp?S=111. As stated earlier, it seems that as the number of sites offered grows the diversity of their offering grows as well. This will become even more obvious in the next section on Christianity.

Christianity

Christianity has the greatest number and by far the most diverse offering of sites. This diversity tends to focus more on the agenda of a single group at the expense of communicating the underlying doctrine of Christianity. Differences are magnified in order to draw distinctions between the web sites of different organizations or individuals. This practice is less common in the more established religions; however the sheer number of small sects vying for members makes this practice appear rampant among the Christian sites. Furthermore, none of the established denominations offer any method to practice worship online. Instead they are content to offer informational content and point users to physical locations. To more completely explore these Christian sites, each paragraph below will examine smaller sub groups such as the Catholics or Protestants.

The Catholic Church has been influential since the earliest days of Christianity. Therefore it would stand to reason that the Church would be well represented on the Internet. There are many sites devoted to Catholicism but the main site comes directly from the head of the Catholic Church, The Vatican. The site http://www.vatican.va/ is a voice for the Vatican itself. On it, one can find links to messages from the Pope to archives and other records. Another unique feature of this site is links to many of the famous works of art in the Church's possession. One can browse and look at photos of many famous works of art including the Sistine Chapel. The architects of this site are an order of Benedictine Monks in the desert in New Mexico (Online Religion 80). Like many other orders, they have utilized their talents in service to the Church. However, they have taken this service one step further and have created a site for their own monastery (http://www.christdesert.org/). On it, one can view the grounds and even reserve a cabin for a religious getaway. Other abbey's have similar pages for example http://web.ukonline.co.uk/worth.abbey/homepage.htm. Finally there are some sites that are devoted entirely to women's religious issues. For the most part, the sites that this links to are orders of both Catholics and Anglicans nuns. An example of such a site is http://www.geocities.com/Wellesley/1114/. These sites offer women everything from basic dogma to reservations for accommodations. As a result, these sites tend to be the most organized and useful of the Christian sites. In addition, there seems to be a direct correlation between the size of the organization and the ability to provide a cohesive web presence.

Many sites are offered by several of the Protestant religions. The Southern Baptist religion offers basic tenants for Christianity and the Southern Baptists service through http://www.sbc.net/sbcsplash/. This site offers news as well as a search engine for local congregations. While one can use the site to locate the various local congregations and their schedules, it does not link to any local church web sites. The United Methodists offer a site at (http://www.umc.org/). Much like the Southern Baptist's site, this site is well organized and shares information from news to dogma. One difference is that the local congregation lookup does link to existing local web sites. For example, the United Methodist site will link to a local site in Arkansas (http://www.nwafumc.org/index.html) allowing one to more fully explore the church before coming to the physical location. Outside the sites of the Southern Baptists and Methodists the national web presence of the other denominations falls off quickly. Other Protestant religions that have a presence include the Lutheran's (http://www.lutherancentral.com/) and the Quakers (http://websyte.com/PositiveChurch/). Outside the United States the Eastern Orthodox have a presence at (http://www.valamo.fi/valameng.html). Finally, there is the fragmented voice of various open denominations throughout the country. While they do not have the financial capital of many of the larger denominations, many manage to build a nice web site. For example, a church in Los Gatos, CA called Calvary has a web site at http://www.calvarylosgatos.org/ that conveys the church calendar, as well as posting the transcripts of the sermon (Internet Church 143). Collectively, the Protestant sites have fragmented pieces of information focusing less on Christianity as a whole and more on the individual dogma or physical location information.

Yet another sub group of the Christian faith is the Apocalyptic Evangelists. All of the Apocalyptic Evangelist sites convey a sense of urgency. They foretell of the coming judgement of Christ and attempt to quote scripture or point to events to support their arguments. One such site (http://www.hurstlinks.net/virginmary/) offers that the site's founder has seen the ghost of Mary and it has foretold of the end of the world. The site is complete with photos of the ghost and quotations of scripture designed to scare one into belief. Another site from a once famous televangelist, Jack Van Impe, is http://www.jvim.com/. While this site offers more information than the one regarding the Virgin Mary, it still centers on the theme that we are living in the end times and appeals readers to repent immediately. One curious fact of these sites and the other apocalyptic sites is that while they urge immediate repentance, they do not have any mechanisms in place to connect their users with local ministries to continue their growth.

Reference Materials

The sole purpose of some sites is to serve as a reference site. One site (http://www.fontbonne.edu/libserv/fgic/fgic.htm) strives to serve all religions with numerous links to other sites and links to reference materials. All major religions appear to be represented. In addition there are links to numerous papers comparing and contrasting the different religions. As discussed earlier, many of the Hindu, Buddhist, Islam, and Judaism sites supply source materials while many of the Christian sites do not. Separate sites serve that need. A site at http://www.ccel.org/ is an example with links to many items other than the bible such as the World Encyclopedia of Christianity. Another site (http://www.virtualchurch.org/index.htm) has many additional items not found in many other sites. For instance, this site offers children's stories and Christian music and hymns. Finally, a popular site for a study guide for the Bible is the Bible Gateway (http://bible.gospelcom.net/bible). It offers the ability to look up Bible verses in various translations and even provides a search engine for key words to aid in verse lookup for lesson preparation.

Cults

The Internet is also home to many cults. Some are more familiar than others, and many may debate whether an organization should be considered a cult. For example we are all familiar with the Mormons (http://www.lds.org/). Not only is this a good example of a web site, but it is also an example of an established religion that is considered a cult by many texts. Other cults are less familiar. In this category, one must list the growing number of celebrity sites that may or may not openly proclaim their worship. An example of a site that does not seem to be in operation any longer is a site paying homage to Keanu Reeves. This site although playfully makes remarks referring to Keanu as Jesus incarnate and the followers of this site as "the dudes" (Online Religion 132). Finally, one can see the sheer number and diversity of these sites at http://www.kassiber.de/cults.htm, which is a search engine, devoted to these diverse cults.

Non-Traditional Religions

The last category to be explored is those sites that espouse new religions. Two such examples of this are http://www.cosmosofy.org/ and http://www.cyberosophy.com/. Both of these hold themselves out to be new and enlightened religions for today's world. Similar sites hold themselves out to be online churches. One site, http://www.kenwinstoncainepresents.com/spiritmedicine.htm, is more orientated toward spiritual medicine and herbal technique, while another site (http://www.godweb.org/index1.html) makes every attempt to be a resource for one to attend a traditional service on line. The authors' claim that the "church" is always accessible and always there when needed for comfort. Only the individual can decide whether or not this fills the need of religion and that decision will largely rest on one's definition of religion as discussed in the introduction.

Conclusion

Online religion is catalyst for and a direct result of the changing environment. As the Internet continues to expand it brings with it a flood of new spirituality from new and old sources. One's experience at these sites can range from information aimed at encouraging one to visit a physical location to total online worship. In the introduction the question of how are the current sites likely to affect the future of online religion was posed. Certainly, each site offers a unique blend of information and services. As the envelope continues to be pushed the answer to that question lies directly with society. What will society allow and in what direction will the external forces for change be applied? Will society accept the definition of religion as proposed by Alfred North Whitehead in which religion is a solitary matter, or will the definition of religion from James 1:27 in which the burden is placed on the individual to help the oppressed of society become the dominant view? The answer to this question will directly influence whether future sites will be geared toward information and resources or toward a total worship experience. Whatever the outcome it seems certain that the influence of the Internet is likely to be as profound as the printing press was to the early Christians. In closing, let us ponder the words of Philo of Alexandria who stated, "Religion is nothing other than the turning of a purified soul to the true God." (http://www2.canisius.edu/~mcdermot/relig.html) Perhaps, this is the simplest and most complete definition of all.

****

4.3 Cyberworship: Are Teens Finding Faith Online?

Cara Baker

http://www.beliefnet.com/story/8/story_806.html

Teens can do just about everything online: shop, get help with homework, keep up with old friends and make new ones, listen to music, check out the latest videos and much, much more. They can even feed their souls as more teens turn to the Internet to explore faith and spirituality.

Currently 4 percent of teens say they use the Internet for religious or spiritual experiences, according to a study published April 20, 1998 by Barna's Research Group of Ventura, Calif.But teens aren't just talking and reading about faith and religion online. They're worshiping online. One out of six church-going teens surveyed by Barna predict within five years they'll use the Internet as a substitute for their current church-based religious experience.

"Our research indicates that by 2010 we will probably have 10 percent to 20 percent of the population relying primarily or exclusively upon the Internet for its religious input," says Barna Research Group President George Barna in a press release. "Those people will never set foot on a church campus because their religious and spiritual needs will be met through other means--including the Internet."

Will Online Religion Cause Us to Crave Human Contact?

"I think Barna's got a hold of a profound half truth," says church historian, author and futurist Leonard Sweet, president and dean of the Theological School at Drew University. "The problem is there is another half…I want to suggest the whole cyberworship phenomenon actually will create the exact opposite and more people will want a hands on, high touch, real life worship experience. I think Barna's right. More and more--especially natives to cyberculture--will increasingly find spiritual needs addressed and met to some degree online, but at the same time, that will create a hunger in them for authentic, real community."

"I think you always need to come to church and be with people of like faith, but there's nothing wrong with watching a video from a church service online," says Brian Garrison, youth pastor at World Harvest Church in Canal Winchester, Ohio. "But it should never replace Sunday worship, or Wednesday night or youth service for that matter. Kids need social interaction."

Quentin Schultze, Professor of Communication at Calvin College and author of "Internet for Christians" says teens are searching for answers to major life questions with the freedom and anonymity the Internet provides.

"Cyberworship is not changing the face of religion," Schultze says. "Perhaps 'cyberseeking' is. The Net has made it incredibly easy for people to 'check out' different religions and even to correspond with members of various religious groups. The anonymity of online seeking, along with the scope of available information, have facilitated widespread spiritual quests through cyberspace. Oddly enough, what appears to be a mass medium, seems to be much more like a very personal medium when it comes to spiritual seeking."

What Worship Online Looks Like

New age sites like www.spiritweb.com cater to those seeking alternative spiritual paths. Approximately 10 to 15 percent of visitors to SpiritWeb are teens, estimates Rene Mueller, SpiritWeb's webmaster.

"SpiritWeb tries to form a place where people can reflect upon personal experience--mystical approach to spirituality such as meditation, etc.--and realize that the actual spirituality is formed within the individual," Mueller says. "It doesn't require an established religion to relate one's personal experiences of divinity. This is the aim of the site--not preaching, not convincing, but to provide a place just to acknowledge this."

Cyberchurches or virtual churches, often ministries of Christian churches, allow visitors to experience a virtual church service by interacting with the web site. Some churches provide online counselling or prayer support, others "webcast" their services.

Christian sites like www.writeanswer.com provides a "Sonshine Worship Service" made up of several segments, each with a prayer, Scripture and lyrics to a hymn or chorus and follows up with text to a sermon. "Please sing along just as if you are at church," the web site encourages.

Does Online Interaction Lack "Messy Reality"?

Rabbi David Wolpe of Sinai Temple in Los Angeles, Calif., sees the Internet as a useful tool for communication and studying, but not worship.

"The Internet can be a useful tool to learn and connect to others," Wolpe says. "The danger is that you won't put yourself, your heart or your life--that you won't fully commit them to God and the tradition, which is bottom line what the tradition asks of us. In some ways it's too glitzy and too easy. Human interaction in all its messy reality is what a religious community is about. Pushing a button is not enough."

Jewish communities use the Internet for online studying, but there isn't much evidence of "cyberworship" yet.

"To my knowledge, worship on the web is not a factor in Jewish life right now--but I could be surprised," says Greg Weinstein, chair of the Internet Committee for the Knoxville Jewish Federation. "Typically, worship in Judaism requires 10 or more appropriate people to congregate together (in traditional branches). However, study and learning is considered important. In this context, the web could be a major factor. This is why you see [even] the most restrictive, conservative sects use the web for communication."

Islam and the Internet

Like Judaism, Islam places high importance on congregating, making personal online worship not ideal. Shahid Athar, clinical associate professor at Indiana University School of Medicine writes in his essay, "Roles of a Mosque in a Muslim Community": "...a Muslim can pray at home and his home is his mosque where he can live a comfortable Islamic life with himself and his family. However, we must remember that Islam is a religion to be practiced collectively. Never in the Quran does Allah address Muslims as 'believer,' but always as 'believers'. Thus we are supposed to pray collectively in a congregation and participate in other acts of worship like fasting and hajj together."

"While Muslims do pray individually, there is also a very important communal sense in Islam that might be lacking or might be expanded by the Internet," says Raymond Weiss, Vice President for Academic Affairs at Northwestern College.

Is Buddhism Branching Out Online?

Other religions, such as Buddhism and Hinduism, are active online, but their philosophies don't lend to online "worship" like Christianity. Ken O'Neill, involved in Buddhism since 1965, with an MA from the Institute of Buddhist Studies in Berkeley, Calif. says, "There's a lot of Buddhist activity online, e-lists and chat rooms permitting a kind of cybersangha to emerge. But Buddhists have nobody to worship since they aren't an anthropomorphic mythology as the Zarathustra tradition and its mythological derivatives in Jewish xian and Islamic traditions."

P. Ravi Sarma, trustee, the Hindu Temple of Atlanta, Ga., and chairman of the Humanitarian Activities Committee of the Hindu Temple says: "Hinduism does not require one to go to a temple and generally there are no required weekend services to attend. Many Hindus have a sanctum or a prayer room at home."

What's It All Mean and Where Is Worship Going?

Whether or not teens go to the Internet for worship, most agree the Internet is a great tool for communication.

"I have heard from some that have had ministries with people from all over the country and there is a group of students that get online at 10 p.m. each night to discuss a topic and they invite their non-Christian friends to participate," says Dale Gustafson, high school pastor at Calvary Church in Los Gatos, Calif. "They have had a lot of success with this because their friends can be anonymous if they like. I think this kind of fellowship will continue to grow, but I'm not sure how it will affect those who are currently going to church. I can see a generation of young people who come to know the Lord through Internet ministries and simply rely on it for growth and fellowship."

"I think there are so many values and virtues to it," adds Sweet. "Teens look at it as a place to connect--connecting with each other and peers and with God. The kinds of connections available are global connections. So the possibilities of connecting with people from around the world is wonderful."

The future of religion on the web will depend on how religious organizations utilize the web, Sweet says.

"If it doesn't establish presence and power in web space, it won't have a future," Sweet says.

****

4.4 CyberFaith: *How Americans Pursue Religion Online*

Principal author: Elena Larsen, Research Fellow
Lee Rainie, Director
Pew Internet & American Life Project, 1100 Connecticut Avenue, NW – Suite 710
Washington, D.C. 20036
202-296-0019
http://www.pewinternet.org/

A. DECEMBER 23, 2001

Executive Summary

28 million Americans have used the Internet to get religious and spiritual information and connect with others on their faith journeys. We call them "Religion Surfers."

- 25% of Internet users have gotten religious or spiritual information online at one point or another. This is an increase from our survey findings in late 2000, which showed that 21% of Internet users – or between 19 million and 20 million people – had gone online to get religious or spiritual material.
- More than 3 million people a day get religious or spiritual material, up from 2 million that we reported last year.
- For comparison's sake, it is interesting to note that more people have gotten religious or spiritual information online than have gambled online, used Web auction sites, traded stocks online, placed phone calls on the Internet, done online banking, or used Internet-based dating services.

The September 11 terror attacks compelled millions of Internet users to turn to religious issues and concerns online.

- ***41% of Internet users, many of whom had never considered themselves online spiritual seekers, said they sent or received email prayer requests.***
- ***23% of Internet users turned to online sources to get information about Islam. Presumably, most of them considered this to be information-gathering activity rather than spiritual activity.***
- 7% of Internet users contributed to relief charities online.

The most popular online religious activities are solitary ones. Most Religion Surfers treat the Net as a vast ecclesiastical library and they hunt for general spiritual information online. However, they also interact with friends and strangers as they swap advice and prayer support.

- **67% of Religion Surfers have accessed information on their own faith.**
- 50% have sought information on other faiths.
- Religion Surfers appear to be more comfortable *offering* spiritual advice online than *requesting* it: 35% have used email to offer advice, while 21% have sought advice in an email.
- 38% of Religion Surfers have used email to send prayer requests. The practice is far more common among congregation members (42%) than non-members (12%).

Within the Religion Surfer population, variations in religious devotion, history, and affiliation play a role in determining what activities attract individuals.

Religion Surfers' online practices can be studied from several viewpoints, based on their offline activities and history. Four patterns of practice highlight different groups: Active Religion Surfers use the Internet in different ways from less-active Religion Surfers; religious converts use the Internet in different ways from faith loyalists who remain with the religion in which they were raised; religious outsiders use the Internet in different ways from insiders who consider themselves in the mainstream of their communities; and church or temple members use the Internet in different ways from non-members.

- The most active online Religion Surfers (those who go online at least several times a week for spiritual material) are also the most active offline participants in their faiths.
- Those who have converted from the religion in which they were raised are more likely than those who have not to be active Religion Surfers (33% vs. 24%).
- Religious outsiders are particularly interested in using the Internet to meet others of their own faith and share items of religious interest. Outsiders are those who see themselves as a minority, who say they have few people of the same religion in their local communities, or who say they have faced discrimination due to their beliefs.

A table listing the things Religion Surfers do online can be found on page 13 of this report.

For Religion Surfers, the Internet is a useful supplemental tool that enhances their already-deep commitment to their beliefs and their churches, synagogues, or mosques. Use of the Internet also seems to be especially helpful to those who feel they are not part of mainstream religious groups. About 27% of Religion Surfers attribute to the Internet at least some improvement in their faith lives. Religion Surfers are optimistic about the Web's potential to improve the religious life of others, while at the same time they are fearful of the Internet's ability to do harm to others by making heretical or cult-inspired material so easily accessible.

- 15% of Religion Surfers say their use of the Internet has made them feel more committed to their faith, and 27% say it has improved their spiritual life to at least a modest degree.
- 35% believe that the Internet has a "mostly positive" effect on the religious life of others. And 62% of Religion Surfers say that the availability of material on the Internet encourages religious tolerance.
- 53% of Religion Surfers fear that the Internet makes it too easy for fringe groups to promote themselves in ways that can harm people.

Religion Surfers are distinguished from other Americans by their religious devotion, rather than conventional demographics. They take their faith seriously in the offline world and use online tools to enrich their knowledge of their faith and to practice their devotions.

- 81% of Religion Surfers describe their religious faith as "very strong," compared to 61% of the general public who said in a March 2000 Gallup poll that religion was "very important" in their life.
- 74% of Religion Surfers attend religious services at least once a week. Polls such as the General Social Survey, Gallup, and the National Election Study show that 26% to 39% of Americans attend religious services every week.
- 86% of Religion Surfers pray or meditate at least once a day. By comparison, 54% of all Americans say they pray that often, and 23% say they meditate every day.

Many Religion Surfers think key spiritual resources are more easily available online than offline.

- **64% of Religion Surfers believe that the Internet provides easier access to religious study and educational materials than they can otherwise find offline.**

- **Nearly half (44%) believe that the Internet provides easier access to prayer and other devotional materials than they can otherwise find offline.**
- **Non-members of religious organizations rely on the Internet to find resources that members of actual congregations are likely to find in their faith communities.**

Acknowledgements
Creating a survey that addresses the experiences of diverse religious backgrounds is no easy task. In addition to our survey team at Princeton Survey Research Associates, we would like to thank the following individuals for their contributions:
John Peterson, FaithandValues.com
Paul Edison-Swift, Evangelical Lutheran Church of America
Natalie Goldfein, Synagogue Transformation and Renewal
David Zemel, Charles and Lynn Schusterman Family Foundation
Izolda Trakhtenberg, Wild Moon Studios

Main Report

Introduction: Are Internet users singing out for that online religion?
As early as 1996, "Time" magazine documented a rich world of online religion sites.[1] It started with the Monastery of Christ in the Desert in remote New Mexico. The depiction of that natural beauty and peace that pervades the monastic landscape was expected. The image of robed monks mastering HTML code and jerry rigging an Internet connection through solar panels and a single cell-phone line was not. It illustrated a new world of spiritual place, time, and practice.

This site (http://www.christdesert.org/pax.html) is only one example among thousands demonstrating how people of faiths both mainstream and esoteric can find something for themselves online. Whether they need advice on fine points of canonical law, special music for a service, ideas for devotional study, material for a religious class, support in prayer, or simply a spirited debate that they cannot introduce in their own circle of friends, they can find it all in the glow of an Internet-connected monitor. The Web allows the faithful wide access to resources and links, and it offers the doubtful or curious a safe place to explore. It is a favorite venue for those rejecting mainstream religions to revive ancient faiths. It allows for Luther-esque defiance of the reigning powers, as demonstrated by exiled Roman Catholic bishop Jacques Gaillot who has established an online "diocese without borders."[2] The richness of the landscape creates a lush spiritual plain that is explored here in a survey of how online Americans use religious and spiritual material online.

In a survey from August 13-September 10 this year, the Pew Internet & American Life Project found that about 28 million Americans, or 25% of the Internet population, visit religious cyberspace, with more than 3 million seeking spiritual material on any given day. This is an increase from a survey finding by the Project in late 2000, showing that 21% of a smaller overall population of Internet users had gone online to get religious or spiritual material. At that time about two million people were using such Internet material on any given day. We call these online Americans "Religion Surfers."

Some may find comfort in the fact that spiritual browsing is a more popular online activity than online gambling, which has only been sampled by about 5% of the Internet population.[3] The act of searching for spiritual material online has also been done by more Americans than have traded stocks or bonds or mutual funds online, or done online banking, or participated in online auctions, or used Internet-based dating services, or placed phone calls online.

The variety of sites available to them appears boundless. They range from denominations and branches with large constituencies to sites posted by individuals in veneration of their deities. They run the gamut from multi-faith, multi-service sites such as Beliefnet.com and FaithandValues.com to sites set up for specific faiths and purposes, such as introducing singles of the same religion.

The popularity of religious Web sites raises an important issue about the extent to which Religion Surfers view themselves as *practicing* religion online. Religious observance is by nature both solitary and communal, and the contribution of the Internet to that space can be confusing. On the one hand, the Internet could be seen as an electronic prayer book, an aid to personal devotion, or a reference guide to spiritual issues without being an actual part of religious observance. On the other hand, an Internet site could be a "place" where people come together, either to chat or to pray or even worship with people around the globe who may be at the same site at the same time.

Demographer George Barna believes that eventually the Internet will fundamentally change the nature of worship among Christians. In his surveys of both adults and teenagers he has found marked interest in online sources of religious inspiration, and believes that by the end of the decade, millions of individuals with no faith community will take to practice and worship on the Web. But he also warns that "millions of others will be people who drop out of the physical church in favor of the cyberchurch."[4]

Religion Surfers are deeply devout *The percent of Religion Surfers who say these activities are very important to them*	
Solitary meditation or prayer	85%
Volunteering to help others	71%
Regular worship or prayer	70%
Conversation with fellow worshipers	69%
Group celebration of holidays	55%
Small group study	50%
Spending time in nature	45%
Regular confession	44%
Speaking with clergy or other advisors	43%
Going online for religious information	13%

Source: Pew Internet & American Life Project Religion Surfers Survey, July 24-August 15, 2001. N=500 and margin of error is ±4%.

The Pew Internet & American Life Project turned to online Religion Surfers to explore Barna's ideas, to get a sense of the things people do online when it comes to spiritual practices, and to learn how they think those activities affect their faith.

The audience is varied – most combine their online life with that of their own religious communities, seeking fuller comprehension and experience of their faiths. Some have long ago left their churches, synagogues, or temples, but still use the Internet to pursue their own spiritual needs. Some have changed faiths and seek out new information. Some feel isolated for their beliefs, and find communion with others in cyberspace where they cannot find it in their own neighborhoods. Many have mixed evaluations of the powers of the Internet. Many see it as a useful supplemental tool in their faith life, especially because it allows them access to additional spiritual information and resources. And they think that online spiritual material can be a force for good because it helps people of faith find each other more easily and because the availability of such material encourages religious tolerance. But they also worry that there is too much sacrilegious material online and that fringe groups can exploit Internet tools to damage others. The picture is as rich and varied as religious life itself.

This report is the first in a two-part study of religion and the Internet. This report is based on the results of a telephone survey of 500 adults who had told us in previous surveys that they sought out spiritual or religious Internet sites. It represents as closely as possible a random sample of all adult Internet surfers in the nation. The second part will be an online survey that will be open to all who care to participate, and in which we particularly hope to encourage the participation of religious minorities. For information on how to participate, write to religion@pewinternet.org.

Part 1: Defining the Religion Surfers

On the whole, Religion Surfers are present in all segments of society. They are fairly evenly spread out among men and women, blacks and whites, various age groups, and various economic and educational-attainment levels.[5] Unlike many other online activities, the act of getting religious or spiritual information online is not strongly related to an Internet user's level of experience. In many other activities, online experience correlates to higher level of participation in the activity – such as getting news online, or purchasing goods online, or doing work-related research online. This is not the case with Religion Surfers.

The Religion Surfers we surveyed parallel the religious profile of the American population at large. Christianity predominates among American Religion Surfers, but the group also includes a mix of religious minorities such as Unitarians, Baha'I, Taoists, and Pagans.

However, the intensity of religious devotion of Religion Surfers distinguishes them from the general population. Some 81% of online Religion Surfers describe their commitment to faith as "very strong," compared to only 19% of the population as a whole.[6] Furthermore, they say they back up these claims in practice; 74% of Religion Surfers attend religious services at least once a week, compared to estimates ranging from 26%-39% of the general population.[7] And 86% of Religion Surfers pray or meditate at least once a day, compared to 54% of all Americans.

Faith profile of online Religion Surfers

	Religion Surfers	*Religiously-affiliated US Population**	*Total US Population**
	%	%	%
Christian	91%	89%	77%
No affiliation	1.8%	*	14%
Jewish	1.6%	1.6%	1.4%
Buddhist	1.6%	0.6%	0.5%
Muslim	0.6%	0.6%	0.5%
Other religion	3%	7.3%	6.3%

Source: Pew Internet & American Life Project Religion Surfers Survey, July 24-August 15, 2001. N=500 and margin of error is ±4%.

**American Religious Identification Survey, 2001, shown at http://www.gc.cuny.edu/studies/key_findings.htm*

The traits that shape Religion Surfers

The most interesting differences among Religion Surfers appear when they are asked about aspects of their religious history and their spiritual practices. A few distinct groups emerged whose patterns of belief and surfing presented different pictures of faith online. These are:

- Active Seekers, those who spend the most time tracking down religious or spiritual content;
- Converts, those who have adopted a different faith than that in which they were raised;
- Community Members, those who belong to a congregation or worship group; and
- Outsiders, those who are acutely aware of belonging to a religious minority, and who may have felt discrimination based on their beliefs.

The groups are not mutually exclusive; there is some overlap among them. Still, we find that the distinctions provide useful ways to examine the differences in the Religion Surfer population.

Active Seekers: 27% of the overall Religion Surfers population

"Active Seekers" are those who log onto the Internet to get religious material daily or at least several times per week. By contrast, less active Religion Surfers access religious material on average less than once a week. The Active Seeker group is diverse – it runs the gamut on age, income, race, education, and Internet experience.

Active Seekers have incorporated Internet-related devotion into lives that are already richly devout. They are more likely than less-active Religion Surfers to describe their religious commitment as "very strong" (88% vs. 78%). They are more likely to belong to a church or other religious community (90% vs. 82%) and more likely to spend time at that church. Fully 65% of Active Seekers claim to be "very involved" in their places of worship, and 58% attend religious services more than once a week. Only 33% of those who are less active online attend so often. In addition to participating heavily in communal life, Active Seekers practice private prayer and meditation more often than others. Fully 70% pray at least once a day, compared to 53% of less active seekers praying that often.

Active Religion Surfers are also more likely to classify as "very important" seven out of ten items in our list of spiritual practices, including prayer, worship, volunteering, small group study, confession, conversations with spiritual advisors, and even going online for religious purposes.

These patterns show those who are already highly devout and have Internet access are likely to transfer their devotional interests to their surfing habits. While we cannot speculate on what makes any individual devout, we have found that Active Seekers are more likely than the rest of the Religion Surfer population to have converted from the faith in which they were raised (44% vs. 33%).

Converts: 36% of the Religion Surfers population

Converts are those who now practice a faith different from that which they practiced at age 16. Conversions include those within a larger faith, say a Protestant Christian who becomes chrismated (anointed with oil to mark their reception into the church) into the Orthodox Church, as well as complete changes of tradition, such as a Catholic who turns to Buddhism. The opposite of a Convert is someone we call a Faith Loyalist – that is, a person who has stuck with the faith tradition in which she was raised. As with Active Seekers, Converts largely mirror the demographic attributes of those who have remained with their original faiths

Converts are more likely than Faith Loyalists to belong to a non-Christian religion (14% to 5%). This tendency to be outside of the mainstream may explain why Converts are more likely than Faith Loyalists to see themselves as Religious Outsiders, by a margin of 19% to 8%.

Converts surf for religious material somewhat more frequently than Faith Loyalists, and are especially appreciative of the Internet's ability to provide quick access to educational resources. Fully 71% of Converts say it would be easier for them to find such resources online than offline.

Converts' devotion across a range of practices appears mixed. Converts are more likely than Faith Loyalists to say they have a strong religious commitment (84% vs. 79%) and are more likely to attend services more than once a week (47% vs. 36%) despite being less likely to belong to a formal church or religious group (79% vs. 89%). However, Converts are also more likely than Faith Loyalists to have used the Internet to look for a new congregation by a margin of 19% to 11%. Convert and Faith Loyalist alike are committed to the practice of individual prayer and meditation, 85% of each professing to do so at least once a day.

Active Seekers are very devoted to their religion

Percent who say this element of their faith life is "very important" to them

	Active Seekers N=136*	*Less-Active Seekers** N=364*
The things Active Seekers feel more strongly about		
Solitary meditation or prayer	93%	82%
Regular group worship	81%	66%
Volunteer work to help others	80%	67%
Small group study	64%	45%
Speaking with clergy or other advisors	60%	39%
Regular confession	55%	39%
Going online for religious material	27%	9%
Practices appreciated more equally between active and less-active surfers		
Group celebration of holidays	54%	56%
Spending time in nature	48%	43%

Source: Pew Internet & American Life Project Religion Surfers Survey, July 24-August 15, 2001. N=500 and margin of error is ±4%.

** Active Seekers go online at least several times a week for religious information*

*** Less-Active Seekers go online less frequently*

Finally, Converts are more likely than Faith Loyalists to have provided spiritual advice via email. Each group is equally likely to have sought spiritual advice via email.

Members: 84% of the Religion Surfers population

Members are those who belong to a church, synagogue, temple, or other formal worship group. Members are overwhelmingly women, by a 61% to 39% margin. They are more likely than non-members to find spiritual practices to be "very important" except for "spending time in nature," where non-members beat them out 63% to 41%.

Differences between church members and non-members in their approach to online material

The percent who say it is easier to do these things online rather than offline

	Non-members N=75	*Members N=421*
Find religious resources	77%	62%
Find volunteer opportunities	31%	14%
Find people who share their faith	28%	15%
Look for a new church or temple	23%	12%
Participate in spiritual discussions	18%	9%
Conduct worship	9%	3%

Source: Pew Internet & American Life Project Religion Surfers Survey, July 24-August 15, 2001. N=500 and margin of error is ±4%.

Church Members surf for religious material slightly more often than non-members. Members are more likely than non-members to be Christian (95% vs. 72%). By contrast, non-members are more likely to belong to faiths that may not be familiar to many Americans; 10% of non-members belong to "some other religion" than Christianity, Judaism, Islam, or Buddhism.

Non-members are more likely than Members to have used the Internet to look up information on faiths other than their own (61% to 48%), and, ironically, to look for a new church or congregation (24% to 12%). Members, on the other hand, are more likely to use the Internet for activities that might be more comfortable for those already in religious communities – such as giving spiritual advice, planning religious activities, and making prayer requests.

Religious Outsiders: 12% of the Religion Surfers online

In a country in which 89% of the religious population considers itself Christian, there are bound to be people who feel their faith puts them outside of the mainstream. Given the diversity of Christianity, many "minority" Christians might also feel disaffected. We classified a group of "Religious Outsiders" based on responses to three questions: whether they feel their religion is widely accepted in this country, whether there are many people of their own faith in their communities, or whether they believe they have run up against religious discrimination. Those who provided responses that showed some level of alienation in two out of three of those questions were placed in the Outsider category.

Religious Outsiders span all ages, races, education and income levels. They are less likely than Insiders to be Christian, but still, 74% of Outsiders say they are Christian. Our sample included 15 members of faiths other than the major Western religions, 73% of whom considered themselves outsiders. By contrast, only 8% of Christians consider themselves Outsiders.

Outsiders and insiders are surprisingly similar. They profess commitment to their faiths equally (about 80% of each group claims "very strong" faith), and are equally likely to consider "very important" most of the spiritual practices we asked about. Outsiders are less likely than insiders to belong to a formal congregation (66% vs. 87%). It is not surprising, then to note that formal group worship is less important to Outsiders than to insiders (57% vs. 72%). In addition, Outsiders are more likely than insiders to extol the virtues of spending time in nature (64% vs. 42%).

Religious Outsiders are slightly more likely than insiders to find it easier to interact with clergy (12% vs. 7% for insiders) and find others who share the same faith (24% vs. 16% for insiders) online than offline. However, the majority of Outsiders (76%) still find it easier to connect with clergy offline than online. And 59% of Outsiders say it is easier to meet with people of the same faith offline than online.

Part 2: What Religion Surfers do online

Religion Surfers are a spiritually well-rounded group who incorporate into their spiritual lives communal and individual activities, formal and informal practices. The most valued spiritual activities to Religion Surfers are individual prayer (85%), volunteer service (71%), communal worship (70%), and informal conversations with friends (69%). By contrast, the importance to them of going online for religious material is relatively low, with only 13% considering it "very important" to them.

Whether or not online content and activities contribute materially to their spiritual life, however, Religion Surfers still have favorite Internet-based activities. Active Seekers in particular like to explore various online materials, and are more likely than any other group to have participated in most types of online activity or practice.

Activities of online Religion Surfers

The percentage of Religion Surfers who have ever …

Looked for information about their own faith	67%
Looked for information about another faith	50%
Emailed a prayer request	38%
Downloaded religious music	38%
Given spiritual guidance via email	37%
Bought religious items online	34%
Planned religious activities via email	29%
Gotten idea for religious ceremonies online	28%
Subscribed to a religious listserv	27%
Downloaded sermons	25%
Gotten ideas for ways to celebrate religious holidays	22%
Sought spiritual guidance via email	21%
Gone online to find a new church	14%
Participated in religious chat rooms	10%
Played spiritual computer games	5%
Participated in online worship	4%
Taken an online religious course	3%
Used a faith-oriented matchmaking service	3%

Source: Pew Internet & American Life Project Religion Surfers Survey, July 24-August 15, 2001. N=500 and margin of error is ±4%.

Reference and study

Religion Surfers enjoy perusing religious topics, and the Internet remains a browser's dream. The top uses by Religion Surfers are simply to find information on their own faith or another one. Almost all non-Christians (96%) report seeking information on their own faiths. In this predominantly Christian country, the Internet may well be the most fruitful and convenient source of information on other religious traditions.

Among Religion Surfers, men are more likely than women to have used the Internet as a reference, 73% vs. 62% for researching their own faiths, and 57% to 46% for researching other faiths. Men are also twice as likely as women to have sought out sermons or other instruction online, 35% to 18%. While online religion courses would fit into this category of study, they are not yet popular. There are many plausible reasons for this, not the least of which might be that 85% of Internet users in America have slow dial-up modems that could make online coursework difficult and frustrating. It is far easier to simply browse at one's convenience on topics of interest.

Social activities

Old-fashioned face-to-face socializing is much more appealing to Religion Surfers than tech-aided interactions with others that are related to faith. Among the five least-used activities among Religion Surfers, three are largely social: online chat, playing faith-oriented computer games,[8] and using a faith-oriented matchmaking service.

In a different sense, however, the very nature of seeking religious material online appears to be a social one. Half of Religion Surfers have recommended a site to a friend or relative, and these recommendations are primary sources of favored sites. Some 44% of those who have a single favorite site learned of it from a friend or relative, rather than from their own searching. And 63% of Religion Surfers with a favorite site pass the URL along. However, while favorite sites may bounce around existing social networks, they do not serve to create new ones. Only 15% of those with favorite sites report using them to meet new people.

Advice and support

Those willing to seek advice or assistance can often find help online. Religion Surfers are quite generous. When asked about the support capabilities of the Web, they were far more likely to have reported giving faith-oriented advice (37%) than asking for it (21%). Women are more active than men in both seeking and giving advice.

Some 38% of Religion Surfers have used email to request prayer assistance. Online, one can put out prayer requests to close friends within one's own congregation,[9] to total strangers who volunteer their prayer time at Web sites, or to strangers who come together in online prayer circles to request prayers from and post them for each other. Congregation members are over three times as likely (42% vs. 12%) to have emailed prayer requests, suggesting that this intimate kind of interaction might be most practiced within existing communities.

The value of listservs

Advice manuals for creating successful Web sites stress repeatedly the need to keep content fresh and interesting. One means of providing regular fresh content is to provide a listserv. Religion Surfers can sign up for daily devotional material or updates from religious news services. Nearly one in three (27%) Religion Surfers are signed up to some sort of listserv, but it is particularly popular among Active Seekers. As stands to reason, Active Seekers are more likely than all others to have taken part in the activities we asked about, but in no other activity is the difference between Active Seekers and Religion Surfers as a whole so large. With almost half of Active Seekers subscribing to some form of religious listserv, they stretch 20 percentage points ahead of all Religion Surfers as a whole.

Active Seekers are the most likely to have done most spiritual activities online

	Active Seekers	*Less Active Seekers*
Look for information about their own faith	76%	63%
Give or receive faith-oriented guidance	51%	29%
Subscribe to a faith-oriented listserv	46%	20%
Get ideas for religious ceremonies	39%	24%
Get ideas for religious holidays	29%	19%
Find a new church or congregation	22%	11%
Participate in faith-oriented chat rooms	16%	8%
Participate in online worship	9%	2%

Source: Pew Internet & American Life Project Religion Surfers Survey, July 24-August 15, 2001. N=500, Margin of error is ±4%.

Spending money, tuning in

Online shopping and downloading music are two popular activities in the general Internet world. Shopping may be more of a secular activity online than a favorite pastime of Religion Surfers: 55% of all Internet users have purchased something online, whereas only 34% of Religion Surfers have clicked "head to checkout" for religious items. But music, whether sacred or worldly, enjoys equal appreciation among groups. Some 38% of both the Internet population as a whole and Religion Surfers in particular have listened to online music, and over half of young people (18-29) in both groups have done so.

Contributing money

It is hardly a revelation that Religion Surfers contribute to their places of worship. Fully 92% of them have done that. However, only a few have actually used the Internet to make contributions. Just 7% of Religion Surfers have made donations to a religious organization they found online. And only a fraction of that small group (14%) has actually made the contribution online.

Part 3: A case study of the most recent time Religion Surfers went online for spiritual purposes

Getting started

In addition to asking respondents about their general use of the Internet to get religious and spiritual information, we also asked a series of questions about the most recent time they went online for such information. We have used this technique in other research to try to understand more fully the kinds of information people seek, the strategies they use to find the information that matters to them, and their satisfaction with Internet tools in getting them the material they want.

In our sample of 500 Religion Surfers, 9% of them had looked for religious or spiritual information via the Internet on the same day we reached them, 26% had gone online for such information within the past week, 29% had made the search within the past month, 26% had made the search in the past six months and 9% had performed the search more than six months ago.

Not surprisingly, the people who had searched quite recently for information (those who searched within the past week) very closely match the profile of our Active Seekers in their enthusiasm for their faith, their involvement with their places of worship, and their personal prayer practices.

What Religion Surfers did online in their most recent Internet session

The percent who said they logged on to ...	
Find educational or devotional materials	40%
Find general information about a religious faith or tradition	29%
Communicate with people in their church	11%
Give or receive faith-oriented support	8%
Do something for some other reason related to their faith	7%
Find churches, religious schools, or other faith-based organizations	4%
Engage in prayer or worship services	3%
Look up religious songs, download music, or listen to spiritual music	2%
Purchase religious items	1%
Browse out of curiosity	1%
Find news about religious issues	1%
Don't know/refused to answer	3%

Source: Pew Internet & American Life Project Religion Surfers Survey, July 24-August 15, 2001. N=500 and margin of error is ±4%.

Why they went online

The substantial majority of these Religion Surfers were trying to get information, rather than using the communication features of the Internet to interact with fellow church members or others who are interested in spiritual issues. A strong plurality of the respondents were doing searches related to their personal spiritual growth.

Three-quarters of these Religion Surfers (76%) went to three or fewer sites in their most recent online quest.

Religion Surfers' favorite sites

One significant finding is that the Religion Surfers who say they have a favorite spiritually-oriented Web site were different kinds of searchers than were those who didn't have a favorite site. In general, 42% of Religion Surfers said they have a favorite place on the Web, while 55% said they tend to go to different sites in their spiritually-related searches.

In their most recent search, 39% of our respondents said they went to a familiar place online, while the rest either went to search engines like Google or Yahoo (36% did this), or a more general site such as the AOL home page or MSN.com (15% did that), or a religious portal (4% did that). Those who had a favorite site were more likely to have gone online in the last week than those who have not found a favorite cyberspot (40% to 33%). And those who have bookmarked or remembered a favorite Web site were more focused in their time online: 60% went straight to their favorite site, while 49% of those without a favorite site begin their searches at a major search engine.

There was no dominant pattern to the favorite sites Religion Surfers identified. The 208 respondents who said they had a favorite site identified more than 100 different sites as their favorites – some of the sites were focused on one denomination or institution, some were ecumenical, some were devout, some seemed more skeptical, some were commercial, some were tied to religiously oriented organizations, some were oriented towards religious approaches to social and political issues, some focused exclusively on ecclesiastical matters, and some included religious material amidst a wide array of secular content.

Overall, 55% of the respondents said their favorite site was affiliated with a particular religious or spiritual group that they belong to and 42% said their favorite site did not have that kind of personal affiliation. And every one of those who said the site was connected to a group they belonged to also report that they belonged to the group *before* they found the site. In other words, at least for those we call Religion Surfers, use of the Internet does not lead them to join a new faith-based organization or group as much as help them connect better with organizations to which they already belong. This is different from our findings related to many secular kinds of communities. We have found that use of the Internet has led people to join groups that they didn't belong to before they started using the Internet.

How they found their favorite sites

Word-of-mouth and offline marketing are the major ways that people have found a favorite spiritually oriented Web site. Fully half of those who have such a site (46%) say they found out about it from a family member or friend or in a church publication or bulletin. Another 31% say they saw an advertisement for the site or found it through TV, radio, or a magazine. Just 18% say they found their favorite site during an online search or chanced upon it while browsing the Web.

The features of Religion Surfers' favorite sites

The percent who say their favorite site...

	Has this feature and they use it	*Has this feature, but they don't use it*	*Does not have this feature*	*Don't know or refused to answer*
Information about their own faith or religion	67%	13%	18%	2%
Information about social issues important to people who share their faith	44%	20%	26%	10%
Guided meditations, devotions, or other material for personal prayer	41%	20%	29%	10%
Books, music or other religious material for sale	35%	38%	21%	7%
Information about different faiths or religions	16%	13%	66%	5%
Interactive prayer requests and responses	15%	24%	48%	13%
Chat rooms and bulletin boards	12%	27%	43%	18%
Regular online worship services	5%	8%	74%	13%

Source: Pew Internet & American Life Project Religion Surfers Survey, July 24-August 15, 2001. N=500 and margin of error is ±4%.

Did Religion Surfers find it easy or hard to get what they wanted online?

More than half of these Religion Surfers (56%) said it was very easy to find the information they wanted and another 32% said their search was somewhat easy to perform. Only 10% expressed some frustration with the difficultly of doing what they wanted to accomplish online.

We have asked similar questions of several other kinds of Internet users and have found roughly similar results. Those who belong to communities online (communities of all types, not just those that have a religious component), those who get health information online, those who used the Internet to get information about the terror attacks on America on September 11, and those who use government agency Web sites report similar levels of satisfaction or facility in their recent attempts to use the Internet for those purposes. For instance, 80% of those who use government Web sites say they accomplished what they wanted in their most recent effort to use such sites.

Part 4: Religion Surfers evaluate the impact of the Internet

A matter of faith

Studies in all areas have tried to get at the issue of whether the Internet *qua* Internet has powers that can change people. Concerns have arisen (and been challenged) as to whether Internet use fosters social isolation. The Southern Poverty

Law Center, a group which defends victims of hate crimes, watched with alarm as the number of hate sites on the Web seemed to skyrocket. Then it determined that more damage came out of the social interaction in offline discussion groups and rock concerts, rather than from static Web sites themselves.[10] In this report, we look at a slippery question indeed – can the Internet significantly affect a person's religious life?

The answers we got from Religion Surfers are both expected and quizzical. Not surprisingly, for Religion Surfers Internet browsing itself fell far behind traditional offline practices of prayer, worship, and service to others in the evaluation of the importance of spiritual practices. Few (2%) said that the Internet was a major aspect of their practice of faith. Nonetheless, some Religion Surfers attributed improvement in their spiritual life to their use of the Internet. Many more said they thought that use of the Internet could influence the spiritual lives of others.

Assessing the Internet's benefits

The percent of Religion Surfers who say each activity is done more easily online than offline

Find educational or study materials	64%
Find prayer or devotional resources	44%
Find people who share your beliefs	17%
Pursue volunteer opportunities	17%
Participate in spiritual discussions	10%
Interact with clergy and advisers	7%
Participate in religious services	4%

Source: Pew Internet & American Life Project Religion Surfers Survey, July 24-August 15, 2001. N=500 and margin of error is ±4%.

The power of prayer

One primary area of religious practice that might be affected by Web resources is prayer. Fully 85% of Religion Surfers said that that private prayer and meditation were "very important" to their spiritual life and almost half of Religion Surfers said they found prayer resources more readily available online than offline. Nonetheless, it would appear that those who rely on the Internet for prayer resources do not see themselves as "practicing" prayer online, any more than someone using a prayer book might see the book as a medium of prayer. The means are external, the practice internal – and that might explain why even the most devout users of online resources did not feel that the Internet was critically important to their faith life.

Even if a spiritual practice is not altered by the Internet, the availability of online resources may have other effects. Some people recognize how seeking of spiritual material online has increased their own commitment to their faith, and even more people believe that the Internet can provide some beneficial effects. One in six Religion Surfers (15%) say that online resources have contributed to their own faith commitment, and 27% said it had improved their spiritual life to at least a modest degree.

The impact on themselves

Not surprisingly, the Active Seekers were the most enthusiastic proponents of the spiritual benefits of the Internet. Some 26% of them said their use of the Internet increased their commitment to their faith – that is a rate 9 percentage points higher than the Religion Surfers group as a whole, and 16 percentage points higher than less active Religion Surfers. The most active Religion Surfers also showed a marked difference in recognizing the benefits to their spiritual life, with 46% citing some improvement, compared to 20% for the rest of the Religion Surfer population.

There is probably a two-directional effect taking place here. Netizens with strong religious beliefs would naturally be drawn to faith-oriented sites, and would derive benefits from such sites that would bring them back online for more. Religious sites would have to be rather exceptional to draw and sustain the attention of those with only a marginal interest in matters of faith. Also, as Active Seekers tend to be highly involved in offline religious activity, their online activities may simply serve to complement their interest in their flesh-and-blood faith communities.

It makes sense that Active Seekers would realize the most marked benefits from their online activities. It would appear intuitive that the Internet would do a lot for Religious Outsiders, those isolated in their communities who need only log on to meet their confederates worldwide. However, this group does not appear to be particularly lonely. About one in four Outsiders say it is easier for them to meet people of the same faith online, which is greater than the one in six religious insiders who say the same, but it does not seem a particularly high figure. Nor do Outsiders appear to need the Internet more than Insiders in any of the other aspects of study or practice we asked about.

Rather, the most enthusiastic beneficiaries of the Internet are those who do not belong to a congregation of worshipers. Non-members as a whole are less likely to describe themselves as having a "somewhat" or "very" strong commitment to their faiths (81% vs. 99%) but they are by no means less interested in the state of their souls. The Internet appears to provide for them many of the benefits of a congregation. Non-members are almost twice as likely as members to find it easier to meet people of the same faith online than off. They are also more likely to rely on the Internet than offline resources for reference materials, faith-oriented conversations, prayer resources, worship, speaking with clergy, and finding volunteer opportunities. And they are more likely to have sought out a new congregation (24% to 12%), even if they have not yet found one.

The impact on others

Interestingly, a notable portion of Religion Surfers appears quite optimistic about the effect of the Internet on others. Over one in three (35%) believed it has had a "mostly positive" effect on the religious life of others. Fully 62% of Religion Surfers believe that the availability of material on the Internet "encourages religious tolerance." Outsiders are less likely to share this rosy outlook. Still, almost half of them (47%) agree with it. And 86% of all Religion Surfers believe that the Internet helps people find others who share their religious beliefs.

But Religion Surfers also worry about undesirable material on the Web. Nearly two-thirds (64%) believe there is too much material on the Internet that is sacrilegious. Christians in particular worry about the amount of sacrilegious material available online. By the same token, 53% of Religion Surfers agree "it is too easy for fringe religious groups to use the Internet to hurt people." The belief that Internet content alone can lead to harm or benefits for viewers appears to exist in Religion Surfers, but may not be limited to them. It echoes long-running debates in this country over sex, violence, and commercialism in television programming.

The Internet and spiritual communities

In addition to the potential benefits and harms that the Internet poses to individuals, the evidence suggests that the Internet helps improve the workings of spiritual communities. In contrast to the 27% of individuals who claim their spiritual lives have been improved through the workings of cyberspace, 83% of congregations who participated in our study last year reported that their Web sites and use of email had helped the spiritual life of the congregation either some or a lot.[11] By creating better ties within a pre-existing community, by creating a Web presence, and by facilitating discussions that can be difficult to hold in other settings, congregations tightened bonds within their groups, re-established connections with former members, and in some cases, expanded their missions on a global scale. These are communal benefits. Web sites may not create new communities, but communities can create vibrant Web presences that redound to the benefit of their members.

Those who don't belong to a congregation are more likely than congregation members to cite some benefits from their online spiritual searches

The percent who say it is easier ...

	Non-members	*Members*
To access reference materials online than offline	77%	62%
To learn about volunteer activities online than offline	31%	14%
To meet people of the same faith online than offline	28%	15%
To participate in faith-oriented conversations online than offline	18%	9%
To speak with clergy online than offline	15%	6%
To participate in worship online than offline	9%	3%

Source: Pew Internet & American Life Project Religion Surfers Survey, July 24-August 15, 2001. N=500 and margin of error is ±4%.

Although we found that there are some spiritual things that Religion Surfers prefer to do online, we found little to support the theory that the Internet will take the faithful out of their churches and temples. While it may provide significant benefits to those who pray and do faith-related studies, use of the Internet does not appear to be as strong in forming new religious communities.

Meanwhile, the Internet brings a variety of benefits to different Religion Surfers. To those already highly engaged in their faiths and with a predilection for surfing, the Internet provides material that reinforces faith and surfing habits alike. To those highly engaged in their faith communities it brings new possibilities for members to work together, and reinforcing bonds that make the community strong. To those who remain outside of religious communities but want to pursue their spiritual needs, it provides resources for private practice and, to those who desire it, a safe place to explore re-entering a community of faith.

Methodology

This report is based on several surveys of Americans about their use of the Internet. The overall figures about the size of the Religion Seeker population comes from a survey of 2,247 American adults (18 and over) between August 13-September 10, 2001. Some 1,135 of them are Internet users. For results based on the total sample, one can say with 95% confidence that the error attributable to sample and other random effects is plus or minus 2 percentage points.

A more in-depth survey was given to 500 persons who have told survey takers at Princeton Survey Research Associates that they had ever gone online for religious or spiritual information. The telephone interviews among those 18 and older were conducted by Princeton Survey Research Associates between July 24, 2001 and August 15, 2001. For results based on the total sample, one can say with 95% confidence that the error attributable to sample and other random effects is plus or minus 4 percentage points. In addition to sample error, question wording and practical difficulties in conducting telephone surveys may introduce some error or bias into the findings of opinion polls.

Interviews for this survey were completed from a pre-screened sample of Internet users who in past surveys identified themselves as Internet religious or spiritual information Religion Surfers. Once the household was reached, interviewers asked to speak with the individual who had recently completed a telephone survey. Once the targeted person was on the phone, they were asked a few screening questions to make sure that they had ever gone online to look for religious or spiritual information.

At least 10 attempts were made to complete an interview at every household in the sample. The calls were staggered over times of day and days of the week to maximize the changes of making contact with a potential respondent. Interview refusals were re-contacted at least once in order to try again to complete an interview. The final response rate for the callback portion of the survey is 66%.

---

1 "Finding God on the Web" *Time Magazine*, 12/16/96.

2 See http://www.partenia.org/eng

3 August 13-September 10, 2001 tracking survey of the Pew Internet & American Life Project

4 "Internet's Religious Applications Getting Noticed" http://cyberatlas.internet.com/big_picture/demographics/article/0,1323,5901_772091,00.html

5 Pew Internet and American Life Project August 13-September 10, 2001 Tracking Survey

6 19% figure taken from the 1998 General Social Survey in response to the question "To what extent to you consider yourself a religious person?"

7 1998 General Social Survey, 2000 National Election Study

8 Many online faith-oriented games are multi-player role-playing games, and thus constitute social rather than individual activity.

9 Our report on Internet use in congregations, "Wired Churches, Wired Temples" (http://www.pewinternet.org/reports/toc.asp?Report=28) showed that 18% of responding congregations provided a place on their Web site for members to enter prayer requests, and that an additional 22% hoped to do so in the future.

10 "Hate On-Line: Reevaluating the Net" Intelligence Report, Summer 2001, pp. 54-55.

11 "Wired Churches, Wired Temples" at http://www.pewinternet.org/reports/tocasp?Report=28

****

4.5 My Religious Journey in Cyberspace: Re and ICT Working Together

Colin Jarvis, R.E. Today, AUTUMN 2001

http://web.archive.org/web/20030609221147/http://refit.ucsm.ac.uk/articles/191jarvis.pdf

It all began as a flyer sent to my school's RE department, 'A (paid) term off school courtesy of the Farmington Institute, Oxford'. It sounded too good to be true so I made further enquiries. After an interview at Lancaster University in February 1998 I learnt a few days later that I was in line for a long summer holiday followed by an even longer autumn term doing my favourite thing, messing about on computers – bliss!

To be fair, I was going to have to do some work to earn my Farmington sponsored keep, so I set about doing some planning for it. My idea was quite simple: as all RE teachers know, it is often very difficult to take large groups of pupils to visit places of worship as part of their RE education. Why not do the visit myself, photograph it, produce resources to be used during the 'visit', put it all on the Internet and allow the pupils to take a virtual tour of a mosque, synagogue or wherever? Now, I know that looking at a computer screen is vastly inferior to actually being in a gurdwara but if there isn't a gurdwara within travelling distance of your school, it's difficult to explore the building other than by using textbooks. I wanted to develop something that was interactive to a ertain extent (taking into account the limits of HTML and modem connection speeds!), where the pupils could click on something and a door would 'open'.

My first job was to contact local faith communities in and around Preston and arrange to photograph their places of worship. This all went amazingly easily and, armed with my school's digital camera, I visited three churches, a gurdwara and a Hindu temple in the first two weeks of my term. All the religious leaders were incredibly helpful, especially in the gurdwara – here, in a small terraced house in a rather rough area of Preston, I was treated to a meal, and a demonstration of the musical instruments used during worship. I was also encouraged to come back to show my photographs.

I chose to study three churches: a typical Anglican church, a Methodist church, and a Roman Catholic church. In the back of my mind was my own teaching experience of trying to show to the pupils the difference between liturgical and non-liturgical worship, and where the emphasis in worship lies for these different denominations. Hence I make a point of emphasising the position and size of the pulpit and the font in the Anglican and Methodist churches. A glossary is used to define important words and this can be accessed within the website by clicking on the word in question.

All the tours begin by clicking on a door. This takes you to a shoe rack, for example, in the Hindu temple. From there the tour usually takes you to the main building, except in the case of the mosque where the place for performing *Wudu* is shown. Moving the mouse around a picture reveals 'hotspots' (the cursor changes to a hand). The hotspots point to significant places in the building; clicking on these 'zooms' in on the feature and describes it in more detail.

Each tour ends with a worksheet that can be printed out and completed by the pupils. This will test their understanding and allow them to further develop their understanding by perhaps designing their own church interior taking into account the needs of the worshippers.

The website was finished about halfway through my Farmington term and I remember with great excitement when the disks I had been carrying were copied onto the server at REXS's offices in St. Martin's College, Lancaster. I remember asking, 'Is it now live?' It was, and it was a strange feeling knowing that anyone in the world could now access my work, if they knew where to look! The site was linked to the RE-XS site in their world religions section, and I couldn't resist the opportunity to log onto a computer, connect to the Internet and see my pages on the screen.

What was I to do with the rest of my term? I now had the Internet bug so I set about designing two other websites, one to take the pupils on a virtual pilgrimage in different religions and the other to explore how rites of passage are celebrated in religion. It was during the development of the latter website that I became aware of the tremendous power of e-mail. I found the website for the Yad Vashem Holocaust museum and decided to e-mail them to request further information; I was amazed to find that a reply came 20 minutes later giving me the information I needed. It made me wonder how in the world I would do the same thing using more conventional means of communication, and how long it would take.

My Farmington term was a wonderful experience – it gave me time to think, time to explore and time to evaluate. I heartily recommend it!

4.6 How To Get To Heaven From The Internet

http://www.fishthe.net/ot/heavenfrominternet.htm

All of us at one time or another in our lives have had to stop and ask someone for directions. Maybe we were looking for someone's house. Or maybe we were looking for the right road or street. Whatever the situation, all of us know what it is like to be in unfamiliar surroundings without a clue as to how to get to our destination.

Well, one of the most widespread, but untrue religious teachings of our day is that there are many roads that lead to God. If men are sincere, we are told, it does not matter which path they travel. In the end, they will all reach the same destination. A pretty picture, but not a true one. You see, there is a world of difference between trying to find the right house and the way to Heaven.

Jesus Christ spoke of two roads open to us: One is a broad road that leads to final destruction. On this broad road are many travelers, perhaps enjoying themselves, but thinking little about their destination. The other road is a straight, narrow pathway. The narrow way has fewer travelers, but it leads to God and eternal life.

How can you be sure which road you are really on? The answer can be found in the Bible.

In John 14:6, Jesus said, I am the Way, the Truth and the Life. No man comes to the Father but by me."

Jesus did not claim to show a way to God. He declared that he was the only way to God. "No one comes to the Father except through me", He said. In other words, Jesus claimed that He was the only way to a personal relationship with His Father, God.

Jesus made another unique claim, "I am the Truth ...". In other words, Jesus was saying He was the only truth about the way to God.

Also Jesus said, "I am the life ...". In 1 John 5:12 we read, "He that hath the Son hath life, and he that hath not the Son of God hath not life."

Eternal life is given only to those who believe that Christ died to pay the penalty for their sin and that He rose again from the dead.

Did you know that the Bible says that God has an inheritance waiting for you—the gift of everlasting life, but you have greatly offended Him by your sin? You cannot receive the inheritance until you make peace with Him. If you are self-righteous, and think you are a "good" person and don't need to repent, ask yourself if you have ever "lusted" for another person? God considers that to be adultery of the heart. Have you ever hated? The Bible says you have committed murder in your heart. Have you used God's name in vain? Then you are a blasphemer. Have you honored your parents, kept the Sabbath holy, always put God first, made a god to suit yourself (called idolatry) or been covetous (greedy)? On Judgment Day, you will be found to be guilty.

Despite all of our sins, Jesus suffered on the cross for us. He took our punishment. We broke the Law, He paid our fine, rose from the dead and defeated the power of the grave. All you have to do to receive the inheritance of everlasting life and avoid Hell is genuinely repent (apologize to God) and trust the Savior. Will you:

A. Be offended by such a thought, keep your pride and angrily leave this web site and end up in Hell?

B. Doubt the credibility of the Bible and refuse to investigate it any further?

C. Humble yourself, tell God you are sorry for your sins, trust Jesus with your eternal well-being, then read the Bible daily and obey what you read?

How can you get to Heaven from the Internet? The same way you get to Heaven from any other place, city or town in the world. You must receive Christ as your Savior. God is not willing that any should perish. He loves you. He is calling you to ask Christ to save you so you might become one of His children.

The Bible says in Romans 10:9, "If you confess with your mouth that Jesus is Lord and believe in your heart that God raised Him from the dead, you will be saved."

Nobody else can save you. Trust Jesus Today!

1. Admit you are a sinner.
2. Be willing to turn from sin (repent).
3. Believe that Jesus Christ died for you, was buried and rose from the dead.
4. Through prayer, invite Jesus into your life to become your personal Savior.

What to Pray:

Dear God, I am a sinner and need forgiveness. I believe that Jesus Christ shed His precious blood and died for my sin. I am willing to turn from sin. I now invite Christ to come into my heart and life as my personal Savior.

If you prayed this pray and meant it please fill out the below form and let us know, then tell someone else. You can call one of these numbers and tell them what Jesus has done for you: 1-888-NEED-HIM or 1-888 JESUS 2000.

If you accepted Jesus Christ as your own personal Savior then you will want to do the following:

1. Read your Bible every day to get to know Christ better.
2. Talk to God in prayer every day.
3. Be baptized, worship, fellowship, and serve with other Christians in a church where Christ is preached and the Bible is the final authority.
4. Tell others about Christ.

What is Necessary To Go To Heaven?

If you would like to ask questions about how you can come to know Jesus Christ personally via e-mail - click here

Questions? Let's Talk

If you would like to ask questions live about how you can come to know Jesus Christ personally

"Whoever acknowledges me before men, I will also acknowledge him before my Father in heaven.~ Matthew 10:32

If you just received the FREE gift of salvation by trusting Jesus Christ as your savior, or you are a new Christian, we would like to pray for you and send you some information to help you in understanding your new life in Christ. Please note that no one will visit you, and if you are under age 13 you must ask permission from your parents before filling out this form. (If you would like us to pray for you and send you the FREE information, please fill out the form at the link mentioned above)

****

4.7 Does Allah Care About Copyright?

Daniel Perrin

http://cseserv.engr.scu.edu/studentwebpages/Dperrin/Dperrin_FinalPaper.htm

Introduction

Illegal software (pirated, illegally copied, etc) in the Middle East is a rampant problem. It is estimated that 74% of software in Lebanon is illegal, while 37% of software in Israel is illegal[1]. The lack of intellectual property laws has been sited for the problem; even with these laws being introduced it might not resolve the issue. Though joining the World Trade Organization (as many Middle Eastern countries have recently done) forces the countries to officially recognize copyright law will this affect the citizen's view of copyright? Religion is a fundamental part of the Middle East with some countries laws derived from religious text. I believe by analysis of religious texts and law I can hope to gain perspective into the views on software piracy. I will focus on Jewish law and Islamic Fatwas. Once the religious perspective on copyright is derived I will analysis if the religious perspective holds up to general ethical analysis. My goal is not to judge (e.g. say copying of software is wrong therefore those who copy software are bad), but rather gain insight into the religious perspectives towards software piracy.

Fatwa - A legal opinion or ruling issued by an Islamic scholar.

Halacha – the root of Halacha in Hebrew translates to "Way" or "Path". The meaning of Halacha is the application of the Law (Torah) to everyday living.

Jewish Law (Torah)

'Torah' has the following meanings[2]:

1. A scroll made from kosher animal parchment, with the entire text of the Five Books of Moses written in it by a sofer [ritual scribe]. This is the most limited definition.
2. More often, this term means the text of the Five Books of Moses, written in any format, whether Torah scroll, paper back book, CD-ROM, sky-writing or any other media. Any printed version of the Torah (with or without commentary) can be called a Chumash or Pentateuch. However, one never refers to a Torah Scroll as a Chumash!
3. The term 'Torah' can mean the entire corpus of Jewish law! This includes the Written and the Oral Law, which

includes the Mishna, the Midrash, the Talmud, and even later day legal commentaries. This definition of Torah is probably the most common among Orthodox Jews. Usually you can figure out which definition is being used by the context.
For the context of this paper definition 3 will be used.

Jewish law can be viewed in two parts. The first part is the actual law itself, the Torah. The second part is Halacha, the application of the Law (Torah) to everyday living[3]. There is nothing in the body of the Torah that deals directly with intellectual property. Even rights of Authorship are not directly covered. In Halachic rulings there is a right of publishers. Due to the large cost of outlaying (preparing of the presses) for a work, there was granted time limited exclusive publishing rights[4]. The amount of time for exclusive rights was an area of great debate. Normally the rights were granted for three to twenty five years. Applying the right to publishing to software introduces a complex model.

Rights of Authorship can be derived from four principles[5]

1. The Rule Of Benefit and Loss – One who derives benefit and the other suffers loss is liable.
2. "Hasagat Ge'vul" – the legislation promulgated to prohibit the encroachment upon the economic and commercial rights of others.
3. “Dina De'Malchuta Dina" -- the law of the land is law.
4. “Shiur” – Retention. It is possible for a seller to sell an item to a purchaser, yet to retain certain aspects of ownership for himself

In an attempt to better understand the right of publishing let us apply to a concrete example. Imagine Microsoft has been given time limited exclusive rights to publish Windows 95©. The time limit is three years. The obvious application of Halachic material would mean Microsoft is the only company that could distribute Windows 95© on physical media. Microsoft would also be protected from other companies distributing the material in a non-physical way (e.g. over the internet). This is due to Microsoft being protected due to it being the first to incur the cost of publishing; the root for the reason to give exclusive rights still applies. After three years any other company or individual could start distributing Windows 95©. There is no direct right of authorship so Microsoft would no longer have rights to control distribution of Windows 95©.

Publisher rights have a firm hold in Halachic material. The rights of authorship can also be derived. These rights come from different Halachic rulings. By careful analysis of the ruling different relations to software can be found. These relations deal with both the final product and for the source code.

The Rule of Benefit and Loss can be applied to rights of software piracy. The pirate derives benefit from selling of the illegal (copy of) software and causes loss (for the legal holder of software). Though this is almost the same as publishing rights. If a software programmer made an algorithm for which he could sell the results, and someone else copied the algorithm (and sold the results) then the Rule of Benefit and Loss could be applied. The original programmer suffers loss of income when someone else uses the algorithm and sells the results. This does not fully cover the software copyright issue. What if no benefit is derived but only loss? "Hasagat Ge'vul" covers the issue when there is no benefit and only loss. This is due to prohibiting encroachment on the economic rights of others. This means that even if one distributed the copied algorithm for free (i.e. no benefit to oneself), it would still encroach on the original author’s economic rights to be able to sell the results of the algorithm. Thus the case of no benefit just loss is covered.

“Dina De'Malchuta Dina" has only limited application to software piracy. It would apply to case where Jewish law did not directly cover an issue. An example of this would be modification of software by a third party. Hence there is not benefit or loss (no loss of income for the original author), but if the law of the country prohibited such third party modifications then from a Jewish law perspective this law of the land would apply. This gives a country sensitive context for software laws and cannot form a general rule.

“Shiur” is the rule of retention. What is remarkable about this rule is that it covers such things as software licensing. The root of the law is that an author can retain rights even to items the author has sold. This would mean software could be sold to an individual and though the individual owned a copy of the software he or she does not have the right to install it on multiple computers. The author (programmer) has retained the right to determine the computers on which the software is installed.

There is no direct assertion in the Torah of protection of software copyright (or even authorship rights). Though by analysis of Halachic rulings it becomes clear there is a foundation for protection of software. This protection is formed by general principles that have applications outside the area of copyright ("Hasagat Ge'Vul" has its origins in fishing rights). Since these principles have been applied outside the area of the original rulings then applying them to software copyright is justified.

Islamic Law

For Islamic Law there has been direct comment of copyright issues. The Fatwa "Is There a Copyright Law in Islam" finds that copyright can be directly recognized. Islamic clerics view copyright as a contract. Allah says in the Qur'an, "O you who believe, fulfill the contracts."6 Thus a Muslim should fulfill the contract of a copyright. This would mean that the Muslim would need to enter into the contract. It is not clear to me how this can apply when there has been no acceptance of the contract, nor contract presented.

To better deal with this issue examination of the Fatwa "Copying CDs and Computer Programs that Have Copyrights" gives additional direction. Using three principles7:

(1) *"Muslims are to honor their agreements* (with others)";

(2) "*A Muslim's wealth is forbidden for others to use without his permission;*" and,

(3) "*Whoever is the first to acquire a mubaah (something lawful to acquire) is entitled to keep it"*

A Sheikh `Abd Al-`Azeez Ibn Baz finds it against Islamic principle to copy copyrighted material. Though there are times when it is permissible to copy copyrighted material. The first is in the case there is no protest from the holder of the copyright. This would fall under the category of freeware software where a copyright is held and restrictions could be placed on selling of the program. But there is no objection to giving away (i.e. allowing copying of the program). The second exception deals with Educational purposes. If the software is not affordable or not attainable (e.g. not sold in that country) then copying is all right. This is derived from:

"But he who is driven by necessity, neither craving nor transgressing, it is no sin for him. Lo! Allah is Forgiving, Merciful." (Al-Baqarah: 173)8

As can be seen the reason for copying was pure and is thus permissible. The last case where copying of software is permissible looks at copyright as money.

"Copyright is like money, which no one is permitted to take except through Shari`ah-based contracts. This is the case whether the owner of these programs is a Muslim or non-Muslim individual, or a Muslim or non-Muslim state. However, if a non-Muslim state is engaged in fighting Muslims, it is permissible to take their property as spoils of war", Dr. Mahmoud `Akam.9

This leads to copying of software where the copyright is held by warring country as all right. This loosely explains some of the attitudes towards US copyrights. If the individual Muslim feels that the US (a non-Muslim state) is fighting any Muslims (i.e. at war) then it is all right to copy the US software.

Though the software copyright issues have been directly dealt with through the Fatwas, it leaves a murkier picture then the Jewish law. This is due to the many exceptions placed upon the copyright laws. It is easy to justify copying of copyrighted materials from many non-Muslim countries that are at war (e.g. fighting Muslims, battling terrorism by cracking down on Muslim groups, etc.).

Utilitarian Analysis

Only some of the Jewish principles hold up to utilitarian analysis. Protection of publishing rights protects the publisher while leaving those wishing to acquire the material at the mercy of the publisher to sell the material at an affordable price. Thus is would be greater good to allow the material to be published by competing publishers thus giving those wishing to acquire the material a better chance to afford it. It could be argued that without the protection of the publisher no material would be available since it would not be viable for a publisher to stay in business (thus the protection serves the needs of the people wishing to acquire the material). I feel this argument is not viable since this would mean that in any case where a monopoly did not exist no business could exist. The Rules of Authorship only protect the author. If it could be proved that without protection of the author that authorship would dwindle, then from the utilitarian perspective it would be in the greater good to protect the author. There is a clear indication that some software would never be developed with some copyright protection. Though there are groups who develop software for free, the users of this software are usually technical people. Without easy to use software like Windows or Mac OS a majority of the population would not be able to operate a computer. Thus for the greater good it is better to allow Rules of Authorship.

Islamic law does not fall easily into utilitarian analysis. The Fatwas support protection of computer software. Some of the reasons for support like honoring of a contract seem to be for the greater good. The Fatwas have even added exceptions, which appear to be for the greater good. A student who could never purchase the software should be given the right to use it. There is no harm to the copyright holder (since the student could not purchase it in the first place), and for those with true needs who cannot obtain the software legally are allowed to use it (again for the greater good). The exception for war with non-Muslims is difficult to analyze from the utilitarian perspective. There is not always a greater good in war. The actions taken ultimately show allegiance to one's country, religion, etc. Thus the greater good is not a consideration, nor will I analyze these actions during war from a utilitarian perspective.

Duty-Based Analysis

Most of the Jewish principles for copyright are based on duty. The protection of publishers had its base in the duty to keep publishers viable so religious works could be published. This duty to the publishers has a root in the duty one would have towards their religion. The duty to protect publication of Jewish religious works appears pure to me, so I feel this holds up to deontological analysis. Applying this to a software publisher is more complex. Why would the user of software have a duty to protect the publisher of that software? Is this duty doing something for societies greater good? Is this duty one the user agreed too? I don't think the protection is for societies greater good, but I do think the user entered into an agreement. Hence the user by use of the software has introduced a duty to the publisher. The rights of authorship do not hold up as well. It adds a duty to all individuals to protect the author or software developer. The end user has no contract with the author or software developer.

Islamic Fatwa on copyright is Duty-Based. It raises a larger question on duty towards religion versus duty towards the outside world. Many of the duties are conditional which complicates the analysis. The Islamic Fatwas fall far from one Kant could accept. But instead falls directly into a prima facie duty as W. D. Ross could appreciate. For Software Copying this is the ordering of duties that I see.

1. One should better one's self
2. Protect contracts with those of the Muslim faith
3. One at war with one Muslim is at war with all Muslims and should be treated as such.
4. Though shall honor contracts.

Below is a chart that describes when it is OK (Not OK) to copy.

Reason For Violating Copyright	Holder Of Copyright (i.e. country)	Is War Present	OK, Not OK to Copy	Reason
Educational	Does Not Matter	Does Not Matter	OK	1
Non-Educational	Islamic	Does Not Matter	Not OK	2,4
Non-Educational	Islamic	Yes	Not OK	2
Non-Educational	Non-Islamic	No	Not OK	4
Non-Educational	Non-Islamic	Yes	OK	3

It is important to remember that the educational copying is permissible only if other options of legally obtaining the software are not possible. It seems that the Islamic Fatwas though complicated due to multiple duties being present still hold up to duty-based analysis.

Conclusion

Analysis of Jewish law does not explain the high rate of Software Piracy in Israel. The law finds that copying of software is not acceptable. Only parts of the law hold up to ethical analysis while showing that protectionism is the basis of much of the law. The Islamic Fatwa on copying of software holds up to both utilitarian and deontological analysis. While the ordering of duties could be questionable it is clear that the Fatwa was designed with duty in mind. It becomes clear that by the Fatwa illegal software copying in Muslims countries will persist until the countries having the copyrighted material copied come to peace with Muslims. The educational copying of software as outlined by the Fatwa seems acceptable due to at the heart of the principle no harm is being done (i.e. no software sale is lost due to no software sale being possible). The problem with the analysis of software piracy for Islamic countries is the lack of statistics on the origin of the software. Only with this knowledge could evaluation be done to see if the Islamic countries are following the Fatwa.

Endnotes

1 – Business Software Alliance (BSA), Eighth Annual Piracy Study, BSA
2 – Unnamed committee, Torah and Halachic Authority, Web Faq. (3.1)
3 – Unnamed committee, (3.1)
4 - Rabbi Israel Schneider, Jewish Law and Copyright, Jewish Law (Part 1)
5 - Rabbi Israel Schneider, (Part 2 and Part 3)
6 - As-Salamu, Is There a Copyright Law in Islam (2002)
7 - As-Salamu, Copying CDs and Computer Programs that Have Copyrights (2002)
8 - As-Salamu, Copying CDs and Computer Programs that Have Copyrights (2002)
9 - As-Salamu, Copying CDs and Computer Programs that Have Copyrights (2002)

Bibliography

As-Salamu, Copying CDs and Computer Programs that Have Copyrights (March 26, 2002) http://www.islamonline.net/fatwa/english/FatwaDisplay.asp?hFatwaID=35108 (accessed May 25, 2003)

As-Salamu, Is There a Copyright Law in Islam (August 24, 2002) http://www.islam-online.net/fatwaapplication/english/display.asp?hFatwaID=79181 (accessed May 25, 2003)

BSA, Eighth Annual Piracy Study. 2003, http://www.bsa.org/globalstudy/2003_GSPS.pdf (accessed June 06, 2003)

Hizb ut-Tahrir, Protection of intellectual property: Its reality and its Shar'i rule (not dated) http://www.mindspring.eu.com/intellectualproperty.htm (accessed May 25, 2003)

Parshat Bamidar, Is Online File Trading Kosher?, Jerusalim Center of Technology (not dated), http://www.besr.org/dvartorah/bamidbar.html (accessed May 25, 2003)

Rabbi Israel Schneider, Jewish Law and Copyright, Jewish Law (2003), http://www.jlaw.com/Articles/copyright1.html (accessed May 25, 2003)

Unnamed Committee, Torah and Halachic Authority, May 31, 2003, http://www.faqs.org/faqs/judaism/FAQ/03-Torah-Halacha/preamble.html (accessed June 06, 2003)

****

4.8 A Guide to Buddhist Memorial Services

www.thezen.or.jp/index.html

A Buddhist Prayer for Lost Information

Daioh Temple of Rinzai Zen Buddhism (Myoshin Temple Sect) has enjoy a 400 year long history and tradition of teaching the word of the Buddha. As we step into the 21st century, a spiritual void has been created and the need for religious guidance is more apparent than ever before. As a means of filling this void, we, at Daioh Temple, have decided to propagate the teachings of Buddha through the use of the Information Highway. And to start, it is our intention to hold the first ever buddhist service on the Internet.

What is this "Information Service"? Not to long ago before the computer was invented, people recorded important matters by committing them to paper through the use of a pen and ink. As we enter the 21st century, however, most of the knowledge gained presently is through the use of electronic-aided devices, whether they be televisions, radios or PCs. To recognize this great transformation of knowledge and the effort that was required to see it through, an "Information Service" will be held.

After the effort of transforming all this knowledge into electronic information has been completed, is it enough then to say that we are finished? And from there, can we truly make effective use of that which we have created? Sometimes, the answer is "no". To provide an example, there are many 'living' documents and softwares that are thoughtlessly discarded or erased without even a second thought. It is this thoughtlessness that has drawn the concern and attention of Head Priest Shokyu Ishiko. Head Priest Ishiko hopes that through holding an "Information Service" and by teaching the words of Buddha, that this 'information void' will cease to exist.

The procedures for carrying out the "Information Service" will be as listed below.

1. A 'REAL' buddhist service for lost information will be held at Daioh Temple in northwest Kyoto, Japan.
2. Teachings of the Buddha will be provided via the Internet.

3. The teachings on the Internet will be provided through a 3D site, "Jomoh Temple", which was constructed by Daioh Temple, Kyoto, Japan.
4. Daioh Temple can readily construct memorial statues/monuments on the temple grounds in Kyoto for those concerned parties.
5. Virtual "Jomoh Temple" , with it's principle diety of worship being Manjusri Bodhisattva, the god of wisdom and intellect, is not discriminatory against other buddhist sects or other religions from placing 'information pages' on its homepage.

The "Information Service" will be held this year and every subsequent year on October 24th at Daioh Temple in Kyoto, Japan. As the principle unit of the computer is the kilobyte (1024), it only seemed logical to hold the service on the 24th day of the 10th month. A special paper charm produced by Daioh Temple and made of silk called "*Sankenshi*" will be offered to all those who attend the service. It is also possible to order the charm via the "Jomoh Temple" homepage.

The virtual, 3D homepage of "Jomoh Temple" will go on-line on April 8th, the date believed to be the birth of the Buddha.

* What is "*Sankenshi*"?

Sankenshi is a piece of 100% silk produced by silkworms that have been genetically engineered for over 20 years by Head Priest Ishiko. Head Priest Ishiko is a graduate of Kyushu University with a doctorate in agriculture. He is world-renouned for his research with silkworms.

****

4.9 Religion: Heuristic Resources for Inquiry and Dialogue

Robert Merikangas, M.L.S., Ph. D.
rm30@umail.umd.edu
http://www.owlnet.rice.edu/~soci430/outlines/functions.html

This list of questions and related annotated bibliography is intended to support inquiry and conversations concerning religion and the diversity and unity of believers and non-believers, and also common actions for the betterment of humankind and our environment.

Introduction: This resource should be interactive and dynamic, constantly growing and changing. Reources are given as examples, but we hope that they are good ones. Web sites will be given when possible and appropriate, but the sources may be in any format: books, periodicals, reports, Web sites, etc. Send comments and suggestions. Current edition: November 25, 1998.

THE QUESTIONS AND RESOURCES

Suggested general questions we could ask ourselves: What has helped us to learn about our own faith traditions and communities, and what has helped us to learn about others? What forms of dialogue have been of value, and what issues are most in need of respectful dialogue in these times? What concerns for the well-being of others should drive our efforts to reach common ground for action?

Q-What are some general sources to use to learn about religion?

General encyclopedias, such as the *Britannica*, are useful, but especially see the encyclopedias dealing particularly with religions:

Encyclopedia of Religion
Encyclopedia Judaica
Encyclopedia of Islam
New Catholic Encyclopedia
Biallas, Leonard J. *World Religions: A Story Appoach.* Mystic, CT: Twenty-Third Publications, 1991.
The story approach makes this work different and valuable.
There are numerous textbooks, such as:
Ludwig, Theodore M. The Sacred paths: *Understanding the Religions of the Word.* Upper Saddle, NJ: Prentice Hall, various editions.

There are a number of specialized encyclopedias, such as:
Encyclopedia of Religion and Society. Ed. William H. Swatos, Jr. Walnut Creek, CA: Sage/Altamira Press, 1998.

Q-How can we monitor current scholarly discussions and reflect on them?
The best way to keep up with current discussion about religion and its meanings in culture and people's lives is from the current periodicals. We can use indexes and databases to search, but browsing is a good way to see what is happening. Some titles in McKeldin Library for browsing (note that the UnCover Reveal service will send tables of contents to you by e-mail):
Church History
Journal for the Scientific Study of Religion
Journal of Church and State
Journal of Ecumenical Studies
Journal of Feminist Studies in Religion
Journal of Religion
Journal of theAmerican Academy of Religion
International Journal for Philosophy of Religion
Parabola: The Magazine of Myth and Tradition
Religion and the Arts
Religious Education
Religious Studies
Review of Religious Research

Q-What are some good ways to monitor the current books?
Numerous publications report on current books, such as *ABPR*, and the UnCover Reveal service, but a good way to scan current books on religion, with abstracts, is by *Religion Studies Review* with the subtitle "A Quarterly Review of Publications in the Fied of Religion and Related Disciplines."
Another way to monitor the current books on religion is by scanning the periodical *Publishers Weekly*, especially the periodic issues devoted particularly to religious books. For example, see:
Bibles and sacred texts, October 12, 1998.
Special supplement, August 17, 1998, on spiritual fiction and books on prayer (and religion bestsellers, p. 31).

The current book shelves in local religious book stores also give access to recent publications.

The major religious publishers will give their catalogs.
Called the big 3: Thomas Nelson, Word, Zondervan.
Affiliated with churches: Abingdon Press, Augsburg Fortress, Brethren, Cowley, Ignatius Press, Orbis Books, Westminster/John Knox,.
Non-affiliated: Bear & Company, Crossroad, Eerdmans, HarperSanFrancisco, Paulist Press, Seervant.
Jewish tradition: Jewish Publication Society, Ktav.
Eastern tradition: Shambhala, Snow Lion.
For a good overview of publishers see:
Farry, Mike. *The Directory of Publishers in Religion*. Atlanta: Scholars Press, 1997.

Q-What would be some good periodicals to scan to see what is happening and what is being discussed about religion and within faith communities today?
Here is a short list; add your own:
America [Catholic weekly, published by the Jesuits]
The Christian Century
Christianity and Crisis
Commentary
Commonweal
First Things

Moment: The Magazine of Jewish Culture and Opinion
National Catholic Reporter [lay publication, offers social as well as church perspective]
Tikkun: A Bimonthly Jewish Critique of Politics, Culture, and Society

Q-What organizations might be useful for learning about current religious issues in the United States?
Americans United for Separation of Church and State.
http://www.au.org
They publish *Church & State.*

Q-What societies and organizations might be sources of scholarly knowledge and resources?
We can use our encyclopedias of organizations to find them, but here are some lists:
--American Academy of Religion.. --Members of the Council of Societies for the Study of Religion: American Society of Missiology, Association of Professors and Researchers in Religious Education, Catholic Biblical Association, Catholic Theological Society of America, College Theology Society, National Association of Baptist Professors of Religion, North American Academy of Litrugy, North American Association for the Study of Religion, Society for Buddhist-Christian Studies, Society of Christian Ethics.
--Ecumenical: North American Academy of Ecumenists, Christians Associated for Relationships with Eastern Europe, Graymoor Ecumenical and Interreligious Institute, World Conference of Religion and Peace, World Congress of Faiths, Headquarters of Won Buddhism.
--Others: Religious Education Association, Religious Research Association, Society for the Study of Myth and Tradition, Society for the Scientific Study of Religion, Institute on Religion in an Age of Science.

Q-What organizations might be resources on ecumenical activities and interreligious cooperation?
See as an example of organizations and publications, the issues of *Explorations,* from the American Interfaith Institute and the World Alliance of Interfaith Organizaions.
A book: *Sharing Shalom: A Process for Local Interfaith Dialogue between Christians and Jews.* Eds. Philip A. Cuningham and Arthur F. Starr.
Consultation on Church Union (1962-)
Global Congress of the World's Religions (1980-)
National Conference of Community and Justice (formerly National Conference of Christians and Jews) (1928-)
National Council of Churches.
http://www.ncusa.org
North American Academy of Ecumenists
World Conference on Religion and Peace
World Congress of Faiths
World Council of Churches
In the DC area, the Interfaith Conference of Metropolitan Washington has programs.
http://www.interfaith-metrodoc.org
For overviews on interfaith activities, see:
Braybrooke, Marcus. *Pilgrimage of Hope: One Hundred Years of Global Interfaith Dialogue.* New York: Crossroad, 1991.

Q-What is the place of religious studies in the university curriculum?
Since the University of Maryland does not have a religious studies program, but might well have one at some time, it might be worth investigating the state of religious studies. It is an area not without controversy, as might be expected. However, many colleges and universities have departments of religion or religious studies, offering majors or concentrations.
"Religion," chapter 10, pp. 169-183, of *Reports from the Fields: Project on Liberal Learning, Study-in-Depth, and the Arts and Sciences Major.* Volume 2 of *Liberal Learning and the Arts and Sciences Major.* Washington, DC: Association of American Colleges, 1991.
"This report focusses on the student: What should an undergraduate expect to gain from a concentration in the study of religion." (p. 171).

For current discussions on religious studies, see the *Journal of the American Academy of Religion.* For example, see the 1996 presidential address by Lawrence E. Sullivan in the Spring 1998 issue, and the article by Ivan Stenski, "Religion, Power, and Final Foucault," in the Summer 1998 issue (with responses and rejoinders).
For a good overview of the academic politics and controversies concerning the study and teaching of religion, see:
Allen, Charlotte. "Is Nothing Sacred? Casting out the Gods from Religious Studies," *Lingua Franca: The Review of Academic Life*, 6:7 (November 1996), 30-40.
She portrays the disagreements and hostilities between the AAR and the more recently founded North American Association for the Study of Religion (NAASR). The latter group sees the study of religion as a social science, not part of the humanities. Allen:
"In fact, the typical university religion department is a disciplinary hodgepodge in which faculty hiring -- and the course catalogs -- are governed mostly by the department head's idea of a varied array of religious traditions and theories." (pp. 34-35.)
Wiebe, Donald.*The Politics of Religious Studies.*New York: St. Martin's Press, 1998.
One of the main participants in the politics gives his overview in this collection of essays.
Wentz, Richard E. "Point of View: The Hidden Discipline of Religious Studies," *Chronicle of Higher Education*, Oct. 1, 1999, A72.
Pals, Daniel L. *Seven Theories of Religion.* New York: Oxford University Press, 1996.
A good introduction to the different approaches.
Penaskovic, Richard. *Critical Thinking and the Academic Study of Religion.* Atlanta: Scholars Press, 1997.

Q-What about sources about religion on the Internet?
We provide some links here, in all categories of this Diversity database, and generally in the category, "Meta-sites."
Q- What resouces are there for teachers of religion?
There are many books and journals and as, but a good single-source for discussion is the book by Nash:
Nash, Rober J. *Faith, Hype and Clarity: Teaching about Religion in American Schools and Colleges.* New York: Teachers College Press, 1999.

Q-What does the Internet mean in people's religious lives?
Zaleski, Jeff. *The Soul of Cyberspace: How New Technology is Changing Our Spiritual Lives.* New York: HarperEdge, 1997.
The Library of Congress subject headings for this book open up directions for further reading:
Religion -- computer network resources
Internet (computer network) -- religious aspects
Cyberspace -- religious aspects
Cobb, Jennifer. *Cybergrace: The Search for God in the Digital World.*New York: Crown, 1998.
A reviewer, Keith Devlin indicates that this book, which began as an article in *Wired*, has kernels of provocative thought, but thinks that Cobb should "learn to distinguish between genuine science and pseudoscience, both of which she tosses around with uncritical abandon..." (*Washington Post*, June 4, 1998, p. B5.
Davis, Erik. *Techgnosis: Myth, Magic, and Religion in the Information Age.*New York: Harmony Books, 1998.
Many churches are making use of the Internet. See:
Murray, Steven M. *A Guide to the Internet for Churches and Pastors.* Nashville, TN: Discipleship Resources, 1998.
A doctoral dissertation studies religion in cyberspace:
Wyndham, Michael Adair. Cyberchurch: Christian Community in Cyberspace. Sountern Baptist Theological Seminary, 1996.
Bedell, Ken. "The Extent and Nature of Religion on the Internet." May 1998.
www.religion-research.org/report1.htm

Q-Sacred books are vital to many religions: how can we find and read them?
We provide links to some Internet texts in the section "Reading Room." For those who prefer print, there are many compilations as well as complete editions of sacred books. Here are some examples of general compilations:
Novak, Philip. *The World's Wisdom: Sacred Texts of the World's Religions.* New York: HarperSanFrancisco, 1994.
The chapters are: Hinduism, Buddhism, Confucianism, Taoism, Judaism, Christianity, Islam, Primal Religions.

Ballou, Robert Oleson. *The Viking Portable World Bible.* New York: Viking, 1972. The cataloging reports: "The gist of each of the world's eight most influential religious faiths, as revealed by their basic scriptures."
Smart, Ninian, and Richard B. Hecht, eds. *Sacred Texts of the World: A Universal Anthology.* New York: Crossroad, 1982.
Serinity, Young, ed. *An Anthology of Sacred Texts by and about Women.* New York: Crossroad, 1993. Sources: Judaism; Christianity; Islam; Ancient Near East, Greece, and Rome; Northern European paganism; Shamanism and Tribal Religions; Hinduism; Buddhism; Confucianism; Taoism; Alternative Religious Movements.

Q-What other kinds of writings are needed for understanding the core beliefs of a religious tradition?
Creeds, catechisms.
Encyclopedia of American Religions: Religious Creeds. Detroit: Gale Research, 1988.
Catholic Church. *The Catechism of the Catholic Church.* Vatican City: Libreria Editrice Vaticana, 1994.
Commentaries, theological treatises, stories, autobiographies, manifestos, etc.

Q-If we distinguish between the general worldviews of religious people and the working out of the implications of worldviews systematically as theologies, how do we find the theologies?
Religious traditions offer extensive historical and present-time theological works, in which thinkers try to connect faiths to contemporary thinking and cultures, with implications for action in moral theologies or moral guidelines for practice. Religion-sponsored universities and theology schools teach these works and traditions. Programs for the preparation of teachers and clerics are many, and the syllabi of their courses would represent what is considered essential and important.
Q-What is the relation between philosophy and theology?
This is an age-old question, with a vast literature in every tradition.
Kerr, Fergus. *Immortal Longings: Versions of Tramscending Humanity.* Notre Dame, Indiana: University of Notre Dame Press, 1998.
Kerr examines the thought of some contemporary or recent thinkers, including Martha Nussbaum, Martin Heidegger, Luce Irigaray, Iris Murdoch, and Charles Taylor.
Rouner, Leroy S., ed. *Knowing Religiously.* Notre Dame, IN: University of Notre Dame Press, 1985.

Q-What are some of the major theological questions to investigate in the study of religions?
We might list: the meaning of salvation, the existence of an afterlife, the way life is to be lived, the position taken in relation to the pluralism of religions, the need or not to belong to a specific religion.

Q-Religions have sacred spaces and places which we might visit or hear or read about: what about them?
Kedar, Benjamin Z., and R.J. Zw. Werblowsky, eds. *Sacred Space: Shrine, City, Land.* London: Macmillan, 1998.
Proceedings from a conference held in Jersualem in 1992. From the introduction: "Landscape -- whether macro-cosmography or local geography -- is shaped, in the very act of our perceiving it, by our mindscape." (p. 10)
Chidester, David, and Edward T. Linenthal, eds. *American Sacred Space.* Bloomington: Indiana University Press, 1995.
In the *Religion in North America* series. Varied essays, from the Christian home to Mount Rushmore.
Brockman, Norbert C. *Encyclopedia of Sacred Places.* Santa Barbara,CA: ABC-CLIO, 1997.
An alphabetic list of articles, with a list by religious tradition and by country. For a sacred place such as Jerusalem, there are articles on Christian sites, Islamic sites, Jewish sites. One category is New Age sites. Mention is also made of the UNESCO World Heritage List of Cultural Sites. Many sites are the focus of pilgrimages by thousands and millions, such as as Mecca, Medina, Santiago de Compostela, and Lourdes.
In the Washington area there are many religious buildings, places of worship, burial grounds, and there are also sacred gardens, including, at least:
Franciscan Monastery gardens
Biblical Garden at the Washington Hebrew Congregation
Khalil Gibran Park (on Massachusetts Avenue)
For a Web site, by Martin Gray, of sacred places:
Sacred Places.
http:///www.sacredsites.com/

Q-How can we learn about religions from their rituals?
We can attend rituals and liturgies when they are open to visitors and when we are invited to special occasions. Rituals include regular prayer and worship services, and rituals for life events and transitions, such as being initiated into the community, getting married, death and burial. Some rituals celebrate and memorialize events in the history of the faith community. How do we learn about the meanings of the rituals?
Eisen, Arnold M. *Rethinking Modern Judaism: Ritual, Commandment, and Community.* Chicago: University of Chicago Press, 1998.
The author is a professor in the Department of Religious Studies at Stanford University. This study gives extensive treatment of changing practices and interpretations of rituals.

Q-What can we learn from religious clothes, vestments, and symbols?
People often wear clothing and symbols mandated or recommended by their religious traditions or particular religious communities. We can inquire into their histories and meanings.
We note as an example the exhibit at the Philadelphia Museum of Art until April 6, 1999: "Church Vestments and Emdroideries from the 14th through the 18th Century."

Q-What might we learn and should we learn from the history of religion and of religions, of churches?
Origins and spread, corruptions and renewals?
Splits and fragmentations, reunions?
Interreligious and ecumenical efforts and dialogues?
Heretics, apostates?
Bromley, David G., ed. *The Politics of Religious Apostasy: The Role of Apostates in the Transformation of Religous Movements.* Westport, CT: Preager, 1998.
Fundamentalisms?
The Fundamentalism Project. Edited by Martin E. Marty and R. Scott Appleby. Chicago: University of Chicago Press, 1991-
Ideas?
Contemporary Religious Ideas: Bibliographic Essays. Ed. G. Edward Lundin, Anne H. Lundin. Englewood, CO: Libraries Unlimited, 1996.

Q-Are cults different from religions?
Note: The Library of Congress reflects usage and uses different subject headings.
Should we label some groups, such as the Branch Davidians, cults, and call others religions? What about religion and "superstition" or "paganism"? Are cults religions we don't like? Or do we need to focus on actions we disagree with? Here is a good short article that raises the issues:
Strenski, Ivan."Lessons for Religious Studies in Waco? *Journal of the American Academy of Religion*61 (1993), 567-574.
Strenski refers to the statement by religious leaders after the Waco incident, published in the *Los Angeles Times,* May 8, 1993, page B4. They "warned that government efforts to define a cult would prove dangerous to religious liberty" and stated: "History teaches that today's cults' may become tomorrow's mainstream religions."
Allen, Charlotte. "Brainwashed! Scholars of Cults Accuse Each Other of Bad Faith," *Lingua Franca: The Review of Academic Life,* 8:9 (Dec./Jan., 1999), 26-36.
Allen gives a quick picture of the controversies, but ends by writing that "exchanges among cult scholars show signs of becoming more collegial." (p. 36)

Q-What issues arise concerning missions, conversion attempts, and proselytizing by religious communities?
In 1999, the publication and dissemination of resources by the Southern Baptists for the conversion of Jews and Hindus has created controversy. For example, see:
Rosin, Hanna. "Southern Baptists, Expanding Effort, Target Hindus for Conversion," *Washington Post,* Oct. 21, 1999, A19.
The movement of Jews to Christianity often causes conerns and controversies, whether or not active programs are carried out, such as activities by "Jews for Jesus."

See the study:
Harris-Shapiro, Carol. *Messianic Judaism: A Rabbi's Journey through Religious Change in America.* Boston: Beacon Press, 1999.
Some of the reaction to this book is reported in:
Dorfman, John. "Kosher for Christ," *Lingua Franca*, 9:6 (Sept. 1999), 21-23.

Q-What are the practices of "cults" that are problematic?What is the situation at the University of Maryland
The issue of cults has been frequently raised on college campuses. See the article in the UM *Diamondback*, October 8, 1998, p. 1: "Cults on Campus: Faith: Local Religious Officials Warn of the Dangers of Cults."
See the issue of *The Faculty Voice*January 1995, with the article" "Chaplains strive to counter influence of cults on campus," an interview with Chaplain Beth Platz.
The campus officials have given attention to providing literature warning students of the dangers from coercive practices by religious groups.
Maryland Cult Task Force : cti.itc.virginia.edu/~jkh8x/soc257/cultsect/mdtaskforce.htm
For a list of religions, cults, and new religious movements created by the Christian group called Watchman, which is a "Christian response to cults and new religious movements," see their Web site:
Watchman.
http://www.watchman.org

Q-How and why is the history of spirituality different from the history of religion?
Certainly spirituality and religion are closely interconnected, but treatises often deal with one or the other explicitly. For example, there are studies cataloged as "spiritual life -- history" rather than as the history of religion. See the series: World Spirituality.
Spirituality and the Secular Quest. Edited by Peter H. Van Ness. New York: Crossroad, 1996. Chapters cover a wide variety of spirituality-connected topics.
Wuthnow, Robert. *After Heaven: Spirituality in America since the 1950s.*Berkeley: University of California Press, 1998. A good introduction to the present scene, with a distinction between a focus on dwelling and a focus on seeking.
See the feature on "Spirituality in America" in the Sept/Oct 1998 issue of *Tikkun: A Bimonthly Jewish Critique of Politics, Culture, and Society.* One of the articles is "Ban the Word Spiritual'" by Rami Shapiro.
Bouyer, Louis. *History of Christian Spirituality.* 3 vols. New York: Seabury Press, 1963- .

Q-What is the role of prayer in religions?
Carmody, Denise lardner, and John Tully Carmody. *Prayer in World Religions.*Maryknoll, NY: Orbis Books, 1990. "Cursory as our survey of some of the major world religions has been, it makes clear the omnipresence of prayer. Prayers of petition, thanksgiving, adoration, sacrifice, and much more have filled the minds and hearts of people the world over. Where has this imperative to pray come from, and what does it imply for the current encounters among the world religions?" (p. 147).

Q-Whose stories, whose narratives should we listen to and learn from in seeking to understand religions?
We need to learn about the founding figures and prophets of the religious traditions -- how?
Hospital, Clifford G. *Breakthrough : Insights of the Great Religious Discoverers.* Maryknoll, N.Y. : Orbis Books, 1985. An example of a general introduction.
Of course, there are a vast number of works about individual "religious discoverers," such as Jesus the Christ.
We may also want to learn about the lives of martyrs, prophets, saints, leaders, teachers, mystics, reformers, etc.

Q-Why is it that the recognition of saints' in one faith community may lead to controversies with another?
For an example, see the canonization of Edith Stein, a Jew who converted to Catholicism, in 1998.

Q-Why and how should we listen to the faith stories of each other?
See *The Washington Post*, on the Saturday Religion page, beginning August 1, 1998, for faith stories. "Today the Religion Page begins sharing a selection of "Faith Stories" we recently solicited from readers. The range of personal journeys reflects what religious scholars say is an increasing trend toward spiritual "transformation," the movement from one belief to another. The Post received more than 130 stories by the July 10 deadline -- some testifying

to a lifelong search, others recounting emotional traumas that drove the writers from belief to disbelief or from one religion to another. We found Christians who became Jews, Jews who became Christians, Protestants who became Catholics and Catholics who became Muslims. Some returned to the faiths of their childhoods; others discovered a spiritual home in Neo-Paganism, the Baha'i faith, Buddhism, Quakerism or Mormonism. A few found a faith in God outside of any organized religion. "(August 1, p. B9) For the texts on the Web, search "Major Newspapers" in Academic Universe, with search terms: faith stories.

Q-What are some of the most significant or widely read spiritual autobiographies?
Some examples: what would you add?
Confessions of St Augustine.
The Seven Storey Mountain by Thomas Merton.
An Interrupted Life, the diaries of Etty Hillesum.
The Pillar of Fire, by Karl Stern, an example of a story of conversion.

Q-What do studies tell us about young adults and faith and religion today?
Beaudoin, Tom. *Virtual Faith: The Irreverent Spiritual Quest of Generation X.* San Francisco: Jossey-Bass, 1998.
A good overview.
Hoover, Brett. *Losing Your Religion, Finding Your Faith.* New York: Paulist Press, 1998.
Another treatment of faith journeys of the young as they mature.
Cimino, Richard, and Don Lattin. *Shopping for Faith: American Religion in the New Millenium.* San Francisco: Jossey-Bass, 1998.
Publisher describes a theme: "They show how spiritual experience will replace religious doctrine as the driving force in the free market of faith, how Baby Boomers and GenXers will rediscover traditional faith, and how megachurches and small groups will provide new homes for spiritual seekers."

Q-What do polls and surveys tell us about religion in Americans' lives, especially on campuses, today?
On campus, the University New Student Cenus for 1997-1998 reported on "Religion in Incoming Freshman Students' Lives." "Forty-seven percent of the 3271 respondents indicated that religion was imprtant in their lives and only 27% that is was not."
In the 1998-1999 University New Student Census the Religious Preferences of the freshman class (2400 respondents) showed from the survey: Catholic 28%, Jewish 16%, Other 15%, no preference 14%, Protestant 11%, atheist 4%, Hindu 2%, Islamic 2%, Buddhist 1%, no answer 5%.
The Gallup polls and other polls and surveys report on the belief in God and on religious participation in the United States.

Q-What has been reported about religion at the University of Maryland campus?
See the Campus Resources section of this Religion database. The index to the *Diamondback* in McKeldin Reference collection gives sources on religion. A good article appeared in the spring 1998 issue of the alumni magazine, *College Park*: "Keeping the Faith: The Challenge of Belief in a Secular Temple." (see link in Media) Letters to the editor in the Summer 1998 issue added information, especially about the Orthodox christians (letter by Patricia Jenkins, p. 4).

Q-What are some of the issues and topics of religious concern on the UM campus?
The practice of religion by students in relation to the practices of parents.
The conversion to another religion.
Pressure from "cults."
Community service for the needy.
Activities in student religious centers.
Celebrations of religious holidays and feastdays.
Interfaith dating and marriage.

Q-What are the opportunities for a career in religion?
In the Career Guide issue of the *Diamondback* of October 7, 1998, Elaine Albenda interviewed campus chaplains about careers in religious ministries.

See the Ministry Connection under Resources and Reference Centers in this database, and the *Chronicle of Higher Education* for academic positions.

Q-What is the significance of conversion in religious life and life in general?
Chelewinsky, Zdzislaw. *Search for Maturity: Personality, Conscience, Religion.* New York: P. Lang, 1998.
Walter Conn and many others have written extensively on conversion.

Q-What are our general models of personal moral development? Do we endorse the movement toward altruism, prosocial behavior, compassion, responsibility for others? What do the student affairs professionals contribute to the vision of ethics and education?
Kegan Robert. *In Over Our Heads: The Mental Demands of Modern Life.* Cambridge, MS: Harvard University Press, 1994.
A quite challenging and comprehensive study of development of great relevance to education.
Guthrie, David S., ed. *Student Affairs Reconsidered: A Christian View of the Profession and its Contexts.* Lanham, MD: University Press of America, 1997.
In one chapter, editor Guthrie reports that "we contend that the development of wisdom is the ultimate purpose of student learning, regardless of institutional setting. So, what do we mean by developing wisdom? We offer that growing in wisdom consists in establishing and reestablishing connections among three interrelated processes: remembering, discerning, and exploring." (pp. 53-54).
Q-In what ways does a religious worldview affect how we see and judge the world, the ways of the world, and the ways we should live, either in conformity with our culture or in a countercultural movement against it?
Rounder, Leroy S, ed.*Knowing Religously.* Notre Dame: University of Notre Dame Press, 1985.
A variety of philosophical perspectives, aware that a philosophy of religion is itself a part of religious knowing.

Q-What are the mystical traditions, and how are they expressed, especially in poetry?
See the histories of mysticism.
We can learn much from the poetry from religious traditions, such as:
Psalms of David
Rumi: *The Essential Rumi.*Translated by Coleman Barks. San Francisco: Harper, 1995.
St John of the Cross
See the section on Poetry and Religion.

Q-How do the humanists and others relate to the world religions by offering alternatives?
In the Religious Organizations section of the Gale *Encyclopedia of Organizations* you will find a number of alternatives to religions, such as atheist groups and humanist organizations. Examples of humanist groups:
American Ethical Union (and Washington Ethical Society)
American Humanist Society
International Federation of Secular Humanistic Jews
In the Washington area there is Machar: The Washington Congregation for Humanistic Judaism. On a flyer they report: Judaism of the natural, rather than the supernatural; Judaism of the human, rather than of the divine. In an invitation to an event on Sept. 14, 1997, they say: "You'll have a most unorthodox time."
At the University of Maryland and other campuses the atheists are advancing their organizations. See:
Nussbaum, Emily. "Faith No More: The Campus Crusade for Secular Humanism," *Lingua Franca* 9:7 (October 1999), 30-37.
Note the Campus Freethough Alliance (CFA).

Q-What are questions about the relations between religion and the human sciences?
Helminiak, Daniel A.*Religion and the Human Sciences: An Approach via Spirituality.*Albany: State University of New York Press, 1998.
The theologian and psychologist uses the work of Bernard Lonergan to provide an alternative to the widely read work of KenWilbur on religion.

Q-What are our questions about the relations between religion and mental health?

Koenig, Harold G. *Handbook of Religion and Mental Health.* San Diego: Academic Press, 1998.
From the back cover: "The book describes how religious beliefs and practices relate to mental health and influence mental health care. It presents research on the association between religion and personality, coping behavior, anxiety, depression, psychoses, and successes in psychotherapy and includes discussions on specific religions and their perspectives on mental health."

Q-How do values, including religious values, enter into the counseling situations?
Hall, C. Margaret. *Identity, Religion, and Values: Implications for Practitioners.* Washington, DC: Taylor and Francis, 1996.
Hall offers scenarios for counselors who want to allow or encourage consideration of the values and religious faiths of students.

Q-What are our questions about the relations between science and religion?
Wilson, Edward O. *Consilience: The Unity of Knowledge*. New York: Knopf, 1998.
Wilson seeks to find and show connections between the evolution of human qualities and moral behavior.
Theology Today, the October 1998 issue (vol. 55, no. 3), offers seven articles on "theology and science in conversation."
The Harvard University Center for the Study of World Religions is publishing an 11-book series on religion and ecology beginning in 1998. The first ones are *Buddhism and Ecology* and *Confucianism and Ecology.*
Overman, Dean L. *A Case Against Accident and Self-Organization.* Lanham, MD: Rowman & Littlefield, 1997.
Overman wrote this book in reaction to an article which reasoned from scientific theories that "individuals are free to select their own purposes and goals without regard to any standard" (p. xvii) Overman discusses the mathematical probabilities of the observed increasing complexity of the biological world and the possibilities of life arising from accidental or chance events.
Current discussions may be found in many places. Some examples:
Zygon: Journal of Religion and Science. This scholarly quarterly gives many perspectives on the current thought.
Current periodicals give reports on the discussions, such as the cover story, "Science Finds God" in *Newsweek*, July 20, 1998.
Newspapers also report publications and discussions. See, for example, the articles on the religion page (C8) of the *Washington Post*, June 13, 1998, "Bridging the Gap," and "A Scientist's Observations on Religion."
The issue of the campus *Faculty Voice* in Nov. 1998 has an article/book review about science in relation to postmodernism and religious thought by Stephen Brush.

Q- What about connections between religion and health?
Brown, Chip. *Afterwards, You're a Genius: Faith, Medicine, and the Metaphysics of Healing.* New York: Riverhead, 1999.
Sloan, R.P., E. Bagiella, and T. Powell. "Religion, Spiriutality, and Medicine," *Lancet*, 353 (Feb. 20, 1999), 664-667.

Q-What about connections between technology and religion?
In addition to the many books and articles, see the Web site:
Reconnecting.
http://www.reconnecting.com

Q-How might we learn about the connections between religion and the arts, such as music, theater, painting, architecture, literature?
Jackson, Philip W. *John Dewey and the Lessons of Art.* New Haven: Yale University Press, 1998.
See especially the section "spirituality of art-centered experiences."
See the Religion and Art section of this database.

Q- What about music?What about religious music?
Frith, Simon.*Peforming Rites: On the Value of Popular Music.* Cambridge, MA: Harvard Univerity Press, 1996.
Can we not only enjoy music, but also converse about its values and make judgments? Frith: "The importance of value judgments for popular culture thus seems obvious, but it has been quite neglected in academic cultural studies." (p. 8)

Sullivan, Lawrence E., ed. *Enchanting Powers: Music in the World's Religius Traditions.* Cambridge, MA: Harvard Center for the Study of World Religions, 1997.

Q-What about religion and the search for ultimate meaning in the films we make and watch?
We might gather a list of films which seek to provide stories and experiences of the search for meaning or the trials and joys of living in faith communities. We could watch these together and discuss them. See the film section of this database.

Q-As with films, we might experience and reflect on television programs: which ones?
Television provides access to films, and also creates its own stories, even about nuns and angels, even of a Catholic parish ("Nothing Sacred"). What do studies show about the inclusion of the religious dimension on the lives of TV characters in general?

Q-How could we learn about religion and dance?
Many religions incorporate dance in their liturgies and celebrations. Whirling dervishes have toured American cities.
The Jewish Avodah Dance Ensemble "pioneered in the development of dance midrash" and offers workshops to "explore the Talmud through movement improvisation." (Avodah Dance Ensemble, 243 5th St. #9, Jersey City, NJ 07302)
Tucker, JoAnne, and Susan Freeman.*Torah in Motion: Creating Dance Midrash.*Denver, CO: A.R.E. Pub., 1990.
Q-How do religions call on the members of their faith communities to practice their faith in action? What are the moral expectations?
The moral obligations and expectations of believers are complex, and range from general commandments to specific prescriptions, and there are great variations in moral codes, moral theologies, and recommended decision making processes and specific actions.
Many questions about religions and personal and social conduct and practice can be connected to the Ten Commandments, generalized as:

> Honor parents and authorities: obey legitimate authority and the laws, work for democracy and the end of political oppression.
> Do not kill. Work for nonviolent solutions and the end of wars and violence.
> Do not commit adultery. Live out good practices in all sexual relationships.
> Do not steal. Work for economic justice and for the good of the poor.
> Do not lie. Be honest in interpersonal relationships.

Clearly, each of these general areas opens up wide spaces for dialogue. What should I do, and what should I try to stop you from doing, and what good actions should I encourage you to do? And how do or do not religious traditions and reflections help us in these decisions?

Q-What is our situation in terms of diversity and pluralism in ethics and values?
Hesselgrave, Ronald P. *Public Ethics for a Pluralistic Society: Contrasting Visions of America's Religious and Moral Foundations.* San Francisco: International Scholars Publications, 1998.
This personal study raises many of the important issues in the historical context.

Q-Are there ways we can reach a consensus on common values?
Bok, Sissela. *Common Values.* Columbia: University of Missouri Press, 1995.
Bok provides a good basis for dialogue in these lectures and essays. Her project: "I suggest, in this book, that we look for a limited set of values so down-to-earth and so commonplace as to be most easily recognized across societal and other boundaries. To the extent that they are acknowledged as common and respected as such, they can provide a basis from which to undertake the dialogue and collaboration now needed. But they must also be so clear-cut as to offer standards for critiquing abuses --including those perpetuated either in the name of universalist political, religious, or moral doctrines or in that of ethnic, religious, political, or other diversity." (p. 1) She offers a short list of approaches for discussion concerning possible common values:

"1. The United Nations World Conference on Human Rights, held in Vienna in June 1993. 2. The World Parliament of Religions, assembled in Chicago in August 1993. 3. *Veritatis Splendor*, Pope John Paul II's encyclical, published in the fall of 1993. 4. The Report of the Commission on Global Governance, Our Global Neighborhood, issued in February 1995." (p. 28)

Bell, Wendell. "Universal Human Values," pp. 171-227, in *Values, Objectivity, and the Good Society* , volume 2 of *Foundations of Futures Studies* . New Brunswick, NJ: Transaction Publishers, 1997.

Bell points out the "limits of cultural diversity and relativism" and provides resources in support of "the core values of (a) knowledge, (b) evaluation itself, (c) justice, and (d) cooperation. (p. 172) He gives lists of universal or near-universal human values which have stood the test of time, and adds "there is a need for further inquiry and worldwide discourse exploring the question of what human values are the most appropriate." (p. 227) In a later chapter he asks: what human values ought to be changed? As a futurist, he gives special attention to concerns for future generations.

Huddleston, Lauren. "Morals, Ethics, and Common Values: Building a Base."*Futures Research Quarterly* 14, 1 (Spring 1998), 87-100.

A report summarizing the efforts of futurists in a meeting to build a base of values for humankind.

Prospects for a Common Morality . Edited by Gene Outka and John P. Reeder, Jr. Princeton, NJ: Princeton University Press, 1993.

The essays reflect the current debates on the possibility of a cross-cultural morality: "some essays defend and others attack the prospects." (p. 4) The editors compare the positions and summarize the agreements and disagreements, primarily in relation to the Enlightenment paradigm.

Q-Is pluralism in our values itself a value?

Rescher, Nicholas. *Pluralism: Against the Demand for Consensus.* Oxford: Clarendon, 1993.

A prominent philosopher promotes the value of pluralism.

Marty, Martin E. "The Valuings of the Public Scholar," *Soundings*, 80,2-3 (Summer/Fall 1997), 265-287.

The prominent theologian and historian states that "the public scholar, in distinction from the scholar who functions in public, values and welcomes pluralism and the pluralistic encounter." (p. 265)

Q-How do we incorporate what we have learned and should learn from the life and wisdom of Rev. Dr. Martin Luther King, Jr. in our educational institutions?

What about the need to cross boundaries?

Thelen, David. "Becoming Martin Luther King, Jr.: An Introduction," *The Journal of American History* 78,1 (June 1991), 11-22.:

"Better than any other American, King embodied the projected the dream of creating a world in which people and ideas could travel as far and intermingle as freely as they wanted without hindrance from laws and customs erected to keep them apart. While some leaders achieve greatness by making an original discovery in their fields or by contributing to the well-being of their particular cultures, King built his fame on the borders where -- as Bernice Reagon puts it -- people must straddle cultures. He tried to draw separate worlds together by building borderlands between them where people and ideas could mingle instead of collide. . . . Leaders who work at borders between worlds must face in two directions, demanding that people in the dominant culture listen to voices they have excluded while telling people from the excluded culture that they must express their cries for justice in ways the dominant culture can accept." (p. 15)

Q-How do civility and self-discipline enter into our conversations about learning together?

Carter, Stephen L. *Civility: Manners, Morals, and the Etiquette of Democracy.*New York: Basic Books, 1998.

Carter connects civility to religion and the moral norms of the community.

Q-What are the possibilities of a global ethic based on common values of the world religions?

Braybrooke, Marcus. *Stepping stones to a Global Ethic.* London: SCM Press, 1992.

Kung, Hans, and Karl-Josef Kuschel. *A Global Ethic: The Declaration of the Parliament of the World's Religions.* New York: Continuum, 1993.

Kung has been one of those taking the lead in urging the need for a global ethic. See the more recent study next.

Kung, Hans. *A Global Ethic for Global Politics and Economics.* Trans. By John Bowman. New York: Oxford University Press, 1998.

Knitter, Paul F. *One Earth Many Religions: Multifaith Dialogue and Global Responsibility.* Maryknoll, NY: Orbis, 1995.

From Hans Kung's foreword: "Dialogue loses all moral credibility if it remains only on the level of the intellectual or the spiritual, detached from the social misery and the physical and psychic sufferings of so many millions of persons." (p. x)
Studies such as the following may be found under the subject heading: Religious ethics -- comparative studies.
Explorations in Global Ethics: Comparative Religious Ethics and Interreligious Dialogue. Edited by Sumner B. Twiss and Bruce Grelle. Boulder, CO: Westview Press, 1998.
Dialogues among scholars, artists, and participants in global issues have been documented and could be used to generate further conversations. For example:
Myers, Ched. *Who Will Roll Away the Stone? Discipleship Queries for First World Christians.* Mayknoll, NY: Orbis, 1994.
An example of the challenge of liberation theology and American issues of rich and poor to American values. Myers raises the issue of reparation.
Divisive Barbarity or Global Civilization: The Ethical Dimensions of Science, Art, Religion, and Politics. Fourth International Dialogue on the Transition to a Global Society. Edited by M.L. Bradbury and Suheil Bushrui. Bethesda, D: University Press of Maryland, 1996.
Value questions and global ethics are emphasized in this collection of papers.

Q-What might spirituality contribute to the role of values in education?
The concept of "spiritual heritage" has been found useful for dialogue and teaching. For example:
Bushrui, Suheil. *Spiritual Heritage of the Human Race.* Rockport, ME: Oneworld Publications, 1997. A related publication, "Retrieving Our Spiritual Heritage: A Challenge of Our Time," was published by the Center for International Development and Conflict Management at the University of Maryland in 1994.
Groome, Thomas H. *Educating for Life: A Spiritual Vision for Every Teacher and Parent.* Allen, Texas: Thomas More, 1998.
Groome, perhaps the best known Catholic religious educator, offers a vision for all, "regardless of their religious background or affiliation or, indeed, the social context of their educating." (p. 11) .His treatment of a "reasonable wisdom" is particulary good.

Q-Is it useful to speak in terms of spirituality as a general goal for education?
Mott-Thornton, Kevin. *Common Faith: Education, Spirituality, and the State.* Brookfield, VT: Ashgate, 1998.
A study from the U.K.

Q-How does spirituality connect with education in specific ways?
Kane, Jeffrey, ed. *Education, Information, and Transformation: Essays on Learning and Thinking.* Upper Saddle River, NJ: Merrill, Prentice-Hall, 1998.
See several essays in particular, those by David E. Purpel, and the section on "spiritual intelligence" by Howard Gardner.
Foehr, Regina Paxton, and Susan A. Schiller, eds. *The Spiritual Side of Writing: Releasing the Learner's Whole Potential.*Portsmouth, NH: Heinemann, Boynton/Cook, 1997.
This work "has to do with helping teachers and students discover ways to access the inner and transcendent spiritual power inherent in human beings." (p. ix)

Q-Can schools reach a consensus on values?
In the United Kingdom a systematic effort was made to identify common values that could be used in education:
Teaching Right and Wrong: Moral Education in the Balance . Edited by Richard Smith and Paul Standish. Stoke on Trent, England: Trentham Books, 1997.
The National Forum for Values in Education and the Community provided a statement of values on which they found consensus. They also pointed out:
"Agreement on the values outlined below is compatible with disagreement on their sources. Many believe that God is the ultimate source of value, and that we are accountable to God for our actions; others that values have their source only in human nature, and that we are accountable only to our conscience."
"Agreement on the values is also compatible with different interpretations and applications of these values." (p. 11)

Q-Could we use the Golden Rule for agreement on values?

Wattles, Jeffrey. *The Golden Rule*. New York: Oxford University Press, 1996.
This work provides the basis for conversations about the role of the Golden Rule in our values.
Topel, John, S.J. "The Tarnished Golden Rule (Luke 6:31): The Inescapable Radicalness of Christian Ethics," *Theological Studies*, 59 (1998), 474-485.
Topel claims the full mutuality of the Golden Rule is unique to Jesus: do we agree?
Etzioni, Amitai. *The New Golden Rule: Community and Morality in a Democractic Society*. New York: BasicBooks, 1996.
Etzioni, a leader of the communitarian movement, offers methods for moral dialogues and sharing core values.

Q-Is there any agreement on wisdom (moral wisdom, practical wisdom, practical reason) as a primary goal of education? Could it apply at all levels, and not just in higher education?
Bereiter, Carl, and Marlene Scardamalia. *Surpassing Ourselves: An Inquiry into the Nature and Implications of Expertise*.Chicago:Open Court, 1993.
Going beyond their studies of expertise and creativity, the authors present a picture of active wisdom as an objective of education. "If creative experts are just experts who have learned from being more venturesome, wise expects are just experts who have learned from exercising more concern with human values and far-reaching consequences." (p. 235)
Maxwell, Nicholas. *From Knowledge to Wisdom: A Revolution in the Aims and Methods of Science*. New York: Blackwell, 1984.
Wisdom: Its Nature, Origins, and Development. Edited by Robert J. Sternberg. New York: Cambridge University Press, 1990.
These books, by Anderson and Allan, support essential conversations about practical wisdom, what Anderson calls practical reason and Allan calls moral practices.
Anderson, Charles W. *Prescribing the Life of the Mind: An Essay on the Purpose of the University, the Aims of Liberal Education, the Competence of Citizens, and the Cultivation of Practical Reason*. Madison: University of Wisconsin Press, 1993.
The quote on the cover from Alasdair MacIntyre makes a strong claim, which I would support: "No university president, provost, or dean should be allowed to hold office until he or she has passed an examination on this book."
Allan, George. *Rethinking College Education*. Lawrence: University Press of Kansas, 1997.
Allan's reflections on the purposes of higher education challenge us to go beyond the university as a resource center; he argues that "the essence of a college should lie in something other than its purposes, I want to propose that its essence should be a matter of its and its society's moral practices." (p. 134)
Note: there are a number of Web sites dealing with wisdom. One place to begin is:
Wisdom Page.
http://www.cop.com/info/wisdompg.html

Q-What can we learn from the examples of moral heroes?
Kidder, Rushworth M. *Shared Values for a Troubled World: Conversations with Men and Women of Conscience*. San Francisco: Jossey-Bass, 1994.
Parks Daloz, Laurent A., and others. *Common Fire: Lives of Commitment in a Complex World.* Boston: Beacon Press, 1996.
Chapter themes: connection, complexity, community, compassion, conviction, courage, confession, commitment. They "designed a study in which we conducted interviews over a period of several years with more than one hundred people who had sustained long-term commitments to work on behalf of the common good, even in the face of global complexity, diversity, and ambiguity." (p. 5)
Wuthnow, Robert. *Acts of Compassion: Caring for Others and Helping Ourselves.* Princeton, NJ: Princeton University Press, 1991.
Wuthnow gives examples of responsible people, and how they understand themselves.
An example of a collection of "saints" as models for our time:
Ellsberg, Robert. *All Saints: Daily Reflections on Saints, Prophets, and Witnesses for Out Time.* New York: Crossroad, 1997.

Q-How do we include assessment of education concerning values in our general assessment methods?

The American Association for Higher Education, in its Assessment Forum, provides many resources and examples. One example is the FIPSE-supported study for church-related higher education:
Taking Values Seriously: Assessing the Mission of Church-Related Higher Education.
http://www.gospelcom.net/cccu/news/assess.html

Q-Do we teach who we are? How do we hold ourselves accountable? Does our faith affect our teaching?
Drake, Susan. "Confronting the Ultimate Learning Outcome: We Teach Who We Are." In *Restructuring for Integrative Education: Multiple perspectives, Multiple Context* s, ed. By Todd E. Jennings, pp. 39-51. Westport, CT: Bergin & Garvey, 1997.
"It is impossible to teach a value-free curriculum, for we teach who we are." (p. 45) "Do we have a moral purpose? Do we teach with heart? Do we really care about the students who have been entrusted to us?" (p. 46)
These books by master teachers support conversations about the moral nature of the practice of teaching:
Palmer, Parker J. *The Courage to Teach: Exploring the Inner Landscape of a Teacher's Life* . San Francisco: Jossey-Bass, 1998.
Palmer asks us to confront the fears that prevent our making the connections we need.
Brookfield, Stephen D. *Becoming a Critically Reflective Teacher.* San Francisco: Jossey-Bass, 1995.

Q-What price are professors willing to pay when acting based on their convictions? What risks?
Should a university stand for the common good and rights of the people or the government or the corporations if there is a conflict? At what risk?
Whitfield, Teresa. *Paying the Price: Ignacio Ellacuria and the Murdered Jesuits of El Salvador.* Philadelphia: Temple University Press, 1995.
The United States was involved in these events. What do we think?
*Towards a Society That Serves Its People: The Intellectual Contribution of El Salvador's Murdered Jesuits.*Edited by John Hassett and High Lacey. Washington, DC: Georgetown University Press, 1991.
The picture of the ethical role of the university in these writings may serve as a challenge to North Americans.

Q-How do we see service learning as connected to the goals for moral education?
Jacoby, Barbara, and associates. *Service-Learning in Higher Education: Concepts and Practices.* San Francisco: Jossey-Bass, 1996.
Overview, with chapter on connections with student learning and development, and the importance of being reflective. Jacoby is at the University of Maryland.
Rhoads, Robert A. "In the Service of Citizenship: A Study of Student Involvement in Community Service," *The Journal of Higher Education*, 69,3 (May/June 1998), 277-297.
Rhoads gives good access to the literature on service learning and community service, and documents an effect on "democratic citizenship and fostering more caring selves" (p. 285).

Q-What is the place of the right of free exercise of religion in the American democracy?
Evans, Bette Novit. *Interpreting the Free Exercise of Religion: The Constitution and American Pluralism.*Chapel Hill: University of North Carolina Press, 1997.
Deals with issues and cases which help us to interpret the Establishment Clause and the Free Exercise clause in the Bill of Rights.
Noonan, John T. Jr. *The Lustre of Our Country: The American Experience of Religious Freedom.*Berkeley: University of California Press, 1998.
Scholar and judge, Noonan "demonstates historically that the free exercise of religion paves the way for basic freedoms." (Sullivan)

Q-What are the connections between religion in the public schools and character education?
See Web site:
Finding Common Ground: A First Amendment Guide to Religion and Public Education.
http://www.fac.org/publicat/cground/default.html
See especially:
Character Education in Public Schools by Charles C. Haynes.

www.fac.org/publicat/cground/ch14_1.html

Q-What roles do religious or church-related schools play?
Dwyer, James G. *Religious Schools v. Children's Rights.* Ithaca, NY: Cornell University Press, 1998.
Dwyer has a concern "that millions of children in this country are presently attending schools whose pedagogical practics harm them in serious ways."(p. 178)

Q-What are some of the issues involving public schools and religion?
Jurisnski, James John. *Religion in the Schools: A Reference Handbook.* Santa Barbara, CA: ABC-Clio, 1998.
Mott-Thornton, Kevin. *Common Faith: Education, Spirituality, and the State.* Brookfield, VT: Ashgate, 1998.
A list:
School vouchers.
Prayer in schools.
Reading the Bible.
Writing about religion or one's faith in a paper.
Celebration of religious holidays.
Singing religious songs.

Q-Organized religion has often attempted to influence and even censor cultural works, including books, works of art, films, television, etc. What do we think of these efforts?
Bald, Margaret. *Banned Books: Literature Suppressed on Religious Grounds.* New York: Facts on File, 1998.
A general survey, giving the circumstances of specific incidents.

Q-How well do the schools and colleges bring ethical considerations to bear on their studies of media such as television?
Many works are highly critical of American television. What do schools do with such works? An example:
Baker, William F., and George Dessart. *Down the Tube: An Inside Account of the Failure of American Television.* New York: BasicBooks, 1998.
They call their chapter especially on television for children, "*Kinderfeindlichkeit*, pervasive hostility toward children. Provocative?
What about the issue of violence in the media?
Bok, Sissela. *Mayhem: Violence as Public Entertainment.* Reading, MA: Addison-Wesley, 1998.
Bok offers analysis and ways to deal with our dilemmas concering violence in the media. What role should educational institutions play?

Q-How can we converse about making ethical and valued-based judgments about intervening in other peoples lives? What should the state and others do to those they care about, for their own good?
VanDeVeer, Donald. *Paternalistic Intervention: The Moral Bounds of Benovolence.* Princeton, NJ: Princeton University Press, 1986.
Kultgen, John. *Autonomy and Intervention: Paternalism in the Caring Life.* New York: Oxford University Press, 1995.
Sher, George. *Beyond Neutrality: Perfectionism and Politics.* New York: Cambridge University Press, 1997.

Q-What kinds of conversations might we have about ways to influence the personal behavior of others? What paradigms are there other than the pro- and anti-abortion debates on intervention? Policies on the use of drugs? Are there public standards for behavior, and ways to influence that behavior?
Sullum, Jacob. *For Your Own Good: The Anti-Smoking Crusade and the Tyranny of Public Health.* New York: Free Press, 1998.
How does the anti-smoking movement compare to other movements?
Clor, Harry M. *Public Morality and Liberal Society: Essays on Decency, Law, and Pornography.* Notre Dame: University of Notre Dame Press, 1996.
Clor notes: "As readers are no doubt aware, the appropriate posture of the civic community toward virtue and vice is a perennial and intensely debated topic." (p. 1) He offers considerations useful for conversations on the "public morality."

The American Civil Liberties Union has challenged some religious persons and groups: "Right now, extremists have captured a dangerous amount of government power. And they want to use that power to force you to conform to their idea of person morality. To do this, they need to change the Constitution and eradicate many personal freedoms you take for granted. They believe that by forcing you to behave the way they think you should behave, or nation will once again be the moral' one they remember' from the 1950s." (From a mailing in Nov. 1998, with a National Citizens' Survey on Civic Morality)

Q-What are some specific issues involving religion in the United States these days?
Following are a number of specific areas, as examples.

Q-Religion and public education?
Statement of Common Purpose Among Religious Communities Supporting Family Involvement in Education was a "document written in 1994 by leaders from 30 religious organizations representing approximately three-fourths of religiously-affiliated Americans". See: Partnership for Family Involvement in Education. http://pfie.ed.gov

Q-Religion and prisons?
McConnell, Elizabeth Huffmastser, and Laura J. Moriarty.*American Prisons: An Annotated Bibliography.*Westport,CT: Greenwood Press, 1998.
See the index under "religion in prison" for entries.
Q- Religion and homosexuality?
Olyan, Saul M., and Martha C. Nussbaum, eds. *Sexual Orientation and Human Rights in American Religious Discourse.* New York: Oxford University Press, 1998.

Q-How well does the press cover religious news?
Hoover, Stewart M. *Religion in the News: Faith and Journalism in American Public Discourse.*Thousand Oaks, CA: Sage, 1998.
Shepard, Alicia C. "Out of Control," *American Journalism Review*, 20:8 (October 1998), 20-28.
The story of Ralph Cipriano and his reporting on the Archdiocese of Philadelphia.
For one of the few television shows covering religion, on Sunday at 12:30 pm, see: Religion and Ethics Newsweekly.*http://www.wnet.org/religion/home.html*

Q-What kinds of emotions are brought into our conversations about the common good? How are emotions part of our visions of education and morality?
Dunlop, Francis. *The Education of Feeling and Emotion*. London: George Allen & Unwin, 1984.
Dunlop gives a good justification and also methods on the education of emotion.
Callahan, Sidney. *In Good Conscience: Reason and Emotion in Moral Decision Making.* New York: HarperSanFrancisco, 1991.
Callahan gives good coverage of the role that emotions play in morality.

Q-If the dominant American emotional style is being cool, what is the place in education for moral outrage? Are we even willing to show and discuss our emotions?
Stearns, Peter. *American Cool: Constructing a Twentieth-Century Emotional Style*. New York: New York University Press, 1994.
This social history provides access to general questions about emotions and judgments.
Mestrovic, Stjepan G. *Postemotional Society.*Thousand Oaks, CA: Sage, 1997.
Mestrovic's analyses, in this and his other sociological works, raise good questions about our ability to go beyond "nice" to serious ethical, emotional judgments and then to action.

Q-How should schools and colleges raise issues of social justice and ethical issues concering the environment? Many books, and specifically some books on education, challenge educators to deal with issues of social values: how should be meet and discuss these challenges? How do we go beyond "respect and responsibility" to deal with

controversial issues such as peace and nonviolence, justice and the political economy of a democracy, and the priority of a sustainable economy and ecology?

How could or should schools and colleges deal with books such as the following, which raise value-laden issues on a global scale?Are American teachers and students willing to converse about perspectives critical of the past and present policies of the U.S.A.?

Barber, Benjamin. *Jihad vs. McWorld.* New York: Times Books, Random House, 1995.

Martin, Hans-Peter, and Harald Schumann. *The Global Trap: Globalization and the Assault on Prosperity and Democracy.* Translated by Patrick Camiller. London and New York: Zed Books, 1997.

Bowers, C.A. *Educating for an Ecologically Sustainable Culture: Rethinking Moral Education, Creativity, Intelligence, and Other Modern Orthodoxies.* Albany: State University of New York Press, 1995.

Bowers, C.A. *The Culture of Denial: Why the Environmental Movement Needs a Strategy for Reforming Universities and Public Schools.* Albany: State University of New York Press, 1997.

"Science Undermines the Meta-narratives that are the Basis of Moral Authority." (Section heading, p. 43). This work challenges educators to examine their taken-for-granted cultural assumptions and to help their students to do so.

French, Marilyn. *Beyond Power: On Women, Men, and Morals.* New York: Summit Books, 1985.

French's extensive treatise provides material for discussions of power and the critiques of social patterns of domination by feminism. "But it is possible to live with an eye to delight rather than to domination. And this is the feminine morality." (p. 542)

Q- How significant are the connections between religion and peacemaking and pacificism?

Smock, David R. *Perspectives on Pacifism: Christian, Jewish, and Muslim Views on Nonviolence and Internation Conflict.* Washington, DC: United States Instiute of Peace, 1995.

Lawrence, Bruce B. *Shattering the Myth: Islam Beyond Violence.* Princeton, NJ: Princeton University Press, 1998.

Q-How well do we teach peacemaking and "getting along"?

Hutchinson, Francis P. *Educating Beyond Violent Futures.* New York: Routledge, 1996.

Provides goals and resources for education for peace and sustainable futures.

Levin, Diane E. *Teaching Young Children in Violent Times: Building a Peaceable Classroom.* Cambridge, MA: Educators for Social Responsibility, 1994.

Includes many materials for teaching.

Paley, Vivian. *You Can't Say You Can't Play.* Cambridge, MA: Harvard University Press, 1992.

Inspiring process of helping students change the culture of play and school work.

Rothman, Jay. *Resolving Identity-Based Conflict in Nations, Organizations, and Communities.* San Francisco: Jossey-Bass, 1997.

Rothman provides what he calls the ARIA framework.

Q-Are educators willing to foster conversations about the conflicts between individualism and a community orientation?

Beyond Individualism: Toward a Retrieval of Moral Discourse in America. Ed. By Donald L. Gelpi. Notre Dame, IN: University of Notre Dame Press, 1989.

Lappe, Frances Moore. *Rediscovering America's Values.* New York: Balantine Books, 1989.

Q-Is it useful to study the traditions of radical rhetoric as well as the mainstream American public address?

Darsey, James. *The Prophetic Tradition and Radical Rhetoric in America.* New York: New York University Press, 1997.

Q- Religion and American politics: what connections?

Benson, Peter L., and Dorothy L. Williams. *Religion on Capitol Hill: Myths and Realities.* New York: Oxford University Press, 1986.

Corbett, Michael, and Julia Mitechell Corbett. *Politics and Religion in the United States.* New York: Garland, 1999.

Greenwalt, Kent. "Religious Convictions in Public Life," *Report of the Institute for Philosophy and Public Policy,* 16:1 (Winter 1996), 6-10.

Q- How are religions and religious activists related to social change?

Harris, Frederick C. *Something Within: Religion in African-American Political Activism*. New York: Oxford University Press, 1999.
Adams, David K., and Cornelius A. van Minne, eds. *Religious and Secular Reform in America: Ideas, Beliefs, and Social Change*. New York: New York University Press, 1999.
Swatos, William H., Jr. and James K. Wellman, Jr., eds. *The Power of Religious Publics: Staking Claims in American Society*. Westport, CT: Praeger, 1999.
Kulick, Bruce, and D. G. Hart, eds. *Religious Advocacy and American History*. Grand Rapids, MI: William B. Eerdmans Pub., 1997.

Q- Religious rights around the world?
MOST Clearinghouse on Religious Rights (UNESCO) *http://www.unesco.most/rr1.htm*

Q- Religion and organizations: what connections?
Demerath, N.J., and others. *Sacred Companies: Organizational Aspects of Religions and Religious Aspects of Organizations.* New York: Oxford University Press, 1998.

****

4.10 Cyber Worship Illustrated: An Example of Cyber Worship

by Prof. Scott Douglas Adams[4]:

Asynchronous
Within this category a few sites can be found. They model a traditional order of worship and basically transplant the form in the online context. Printed text, music, and real audio push information at the worshiper. These web sites more than prove what online worship should not become. Even if the web pages were well done, nothing is improved or added to the world of worship by such creations. The medium is not fluid; it is boring; and it is awkward. The only advantage of this system is that a worshiper can come when s(he) wishes. Please look at these pages and click on their buttons to get a "online worship experience."

> Full service:
> http://internetchurch.oaktree.net/ (inactive link, Sept 1, 2003)
> http://www.cyberspacembchurch.org/worship.shtml (inactive link, Sept 1, 2003)
>
> Word centered, music centered, devotional web sites
> http://adams.patriot.net/~bmcgin/chapel.html (link accessed on Sept 1, 2003)

Synchronous not real time. These are prayer-based web sites that use the power of the web in order to get the word out in a simple medium and offer an opportunity for the "worshiper" to respond with a need or with a prayer. Though the theology of these web sites is quite extreme the method is useful. A church with an online presence could connect with its parishioners and with the broader community. *Prayer chains and prayer circles* that enhance weekly worship enforce the *8th day of worship services.* Again these web sites are *extreme* but fun to watch. The design of these pages and the use of other media is quite *scary*, but that is another discussion.

> http://amightywind.com/menu.html (inactive link, Sept 1, 2003)
>
> http://whstone.com/worship/ (inactive link, Sept 1, 2003)

Synchronous
These types of worship services would entail a full worship service that maintains an order of worship in real time through either a chat room or video conference over the internet or some communication medium. These may exist in some places, but I was unable to find one. This type of worship service could enhance the normal worship service in a local congregation. It would offer some worshippers that were away the *opportunity to attend* their *local congregation* and *feel present* in their own community. A prearranged time would be set like any worship service. The problems with this type of service have been clearly outlined above, yet question as to the value of this service could still be debated. Even if a person would were to stumble in during the service or was not part of the church community, this medium could serve as a pastoral

worship service, an evangelizing worship service to the wider community of the world. There are some redeeming qualities to this type of service but traditional forms and orders should help to keep the proper focus. From the definition above this would still not be considered corporate worship.

http://www.execpc.com/~chender/index1.html (inactive link, Sept 1, 2003)
http://www.geocities.com/~drybones21/main.html (inactive link, Sept 1, 2003).

Combination
web forms for prayer, email or pastoral care
parts of worship services or
Uses chat rooms, addresses for prayer
Lots of text for devotional life.
Uses Multi-media sound video or images for worship or personal devotion.

****

4.11 Seven Logical Consequences of Interreligious Dialoguing: Taxonomy of Praxis Possibilities

Anton Karl Kozlovic
School of Humanities
The Flinders University of South Australia
Email: Anton.Kozlovic@flinders.edu.au
www.uni-marburg.de/religionswissenschaft/journal/mjr/kozlovic2.html

Abstract: Despite the incredible amount of literature written about interreligious dialoguing, scant critical attention has been devoted to mapping out the potential logical consequences of the enterprise. This is regrettable, especially given the high hopes many expect to achieve through participation. The critical literature from various traditions was reviewed using textual criticism as the analytical lens. Seven logical outcomes were subsequently identified and explicated herein using the following taxonomy. Namely: (a) nothing happened, (b) understanding, (c) insightfulness, (d) tolerance, (e) conversion, (f) frustration, and (g) defection. It was concluded that the a priori understanding of these potential outcomes would significantly moderate future delegate expectations. In addition, professional awareness of the range, depth and contours of these dialogic consequences had important ramifications for both participant preparation and event organisation. Practical suggestions for dealing with various impediments were proffered as appropriate. Further research into this important praxis area was recommended.

Introduction

It is becoming increasingly self-evident that "religions no longer live in splendid isolation from each other" (Fredericks, 1998, p. 171). As such, this means that refusing "dialogue today could be an act of fundamental human irresponsibility--in Judeo-Christian terms, a sin" (Swidler, 1990, p. 14). So, it is not too surprising to find that much time and energy has been devoted in the recent past to official dialoguing activities throughout the world. For example, the Roman Catholic-Classical Pentecostal dialogue ran for approximately seventeen years (Sandidge, 1992) while the Roman Catholic-Lutheran dialogue lasted thirty years (Brunett, 1999). Given this incredible investment in time and energy, what outcomes can one legitimately expect from the enterprise? Despite the incredible amount of literature written about interreligious dialoguing, scant critical attention has been devoted to exploring the possible logical outcomes of all this work, and especially documented in one convenient spot. This academic deficiency was deemed in need of urgent repair. Consequently, the substantive critical literature from various traditions was reviewed, and integrated into the text to enhance narrative coherence (albeit, with a strong reportage flavour), using textual criticism as the analytical lens. This precursory investigation revealed seven logical possibilities worthy of explication. Namely: (a) nothing happened, (b) understanding, (c) insightfulness, (d) tolerance, (e) conversion, (f) frustration, and (g) defection. The following is a brief explication of each of these outcome possibilities.

Consequence #1 - Nothing Happened: Real or Imagined?

Overlooking for the moment that dialogue can beget more dialogue, one of the first claimed results for an event is that "nothing happened." After all, as Stanley J. Samartha (1981, p. 9) pointed out: "No dialogue can ever be automatically successful" nor:

> ...can we forget that the discovery of truth is not inevitable. The possibility of error, distortion, and confusion are present in situations of dialogue as in any human situation. There is no guarantee that all dialogues will automatically lead the participants into fuller truth (p. 14).

Broadly speaking, "nothing happened" is a logical possibility; neither side gained nor lost anything during the process. In practice however, this response is unrealistic. Dialoguers **do** change as a result of expose to knowledge and experience. Even no progress in the short-term is **a** result that will change expectations, attitudes and future participant behaviour in the long-term. Nor should this "nothing happened" response be dismissed automatically just because it is only a logical possibility. It is a useful pragmatic point to make to those faiths, especially new ones or ones inexperienced in dialoguing who fear contamination or conversion, and where a "the-others-weren't-affected-so-why-don't-you-try-it" style of pre-dialogue argument could be proffered for anxiety reduction reasons.

Eventually, the notion of nothing happening in the short-term can be widened to accommodate the notion of mutual transformation in the long-term. On the other hand, if the dialogue devolved into two monologues, then in reality, nothing constructive did happen; but then it would not be a dialogue (Kozlovic, 2003), whether true or otherwise! Nor would the opportunity for it present itself very soon because of this communications collapse and associated mistrust. As Norman Solomon (1991, p. 38) bluntly argued: "Missionizing undermines confidence and trust. If Christians target Jews in their "missions," there will be no dialogue; Christians will be talking to themselves, for no Jew will willingly stay to listen." This general stance is obviously antithetical to the goal of the dialogue enterprise. Religious dialoguing is **not** institutionalised proselytization or covert evangelism designed to change one's religious allegiance, nor is it a sublimated adjunct of religious colonialism in the form of spiritual-cum-institutional imperialism.

Consequence #2 - Understanding the Other and the Dialogic Process

Official dialoguing shows how religions feel, behave and think on various issues during the act of exchanging information, and so one ""of the more obvious results of this kind of formal dialogue is the death of mythologies." Ignorance on each side about the Other is removed and a broader understanding of each other is obtained" (Sandidge, 1992, p. 243). This is always a useful first step towards understanding and growth. However, it is important to realise that understanding the Other does **not** necessarily mean agreeing, approving, or supporting the position of the Other. After all, one may understand, but not necessarily condone ritual sacrifice, or when Jesus Christ dealt positively with the adulterous woman (John 8:1-11 KJV) he was not recommending the life style! As the Lutheran World Federation and World Council of Churches put it: "Entering into dialogue does not mean that one supports or ascribes to the ideas or activities of the other. And dialogue does not mean that all will agree. The creative tension of mutual critique is also a part of dialogue" (Brockway & Rajashekar, 1987, p. 177). Nor can it be "expected that one renounce one's faith in order to understand another religion. If interreligious dialogue is at all possible, it is not by renouncing all proclamation, commitment, and confession" (Krieger, 1993, p. 351).

Contrary to popular belief, true dialogue is not "a form of compromise on truth" (Mitri, 1995, p. 23) and it "does not portend capitulation but interreligious understanding and the lessening of tensions" (Saliba, 1993, p. 78). Nevertheless, dialogue does involve "a continuing process of learning and re-education" (Braybrooke, 1993a, p. 108), especially since dialogue "with ecumenical partners also elicits internal dialogue with Churches" (Brunett, 1999, p. 305). Indeed, the modern American witch Marion Weinstein (1991) considered such educative exchanges to be an essential prerequisite for her pagan appreciation of holism. As she argued:

> I believe deeply in the enrichment of cross-fertilization and the sharing process of spiritual traditions, rather than total superimposition of one tradition on another. I have begun to glimpse the riches of certain African and Native American magical traditions -- to name but two -- which have nourished my own work and outlook. I suspect that these traditions would be helpful to many spiritually deprived, "rational" types in the West. For me, "holistic" (which is as good a word as any for the thought-mode of occult work) means "all-inclusive"; to deny any aspect of one's own cultural heritage, or to deny the existence (in potential) of any other cultural heritage, is not holistic. It is a screening-out process -- "rational," sequential, linear and limiting. "Holistic" does not mean *either/or*, it does not mean *instead of*, or *in denial of*, or *in replacement of*. It means *all-together*" (pp. 264-265).

To use Karl Barth's words in a positive, revisionist way, "to dialogue with other religions was to howl with wolves (*'heulen mit den Wolfen'*)" (Narchison, 1998, p. 61). Therefore, the greater (wolf pack?) exposure to spiritual cross-fertilisation through mutual dialoguing, the greater the information transmitted and received, and hopefully the greater the opportunity for deeper understanding. This process can create greater thirst for knowledge and even explicit calls for it, as has been reported in the past:

> As we came towards the end of the three-year project people commented that they had learnt not only about other faiths, but so much more about their own beliefs and practices by having to explain them to others. Many felt a sense of loss at the thought that mutual cooperation and learning was coming to an end. As one Muslim phrased it: "We have learned to understand and trust one another; is it not possible to continue doing so?" (Hall, 1987, p. 29).

One is impelled to state an emphatic 'Yes!' And then quickly proclaim: "The symposium will end...but the dialogue must go on" (Pereira, 1987, p. 276) just as Imre Miklos, Minister for Ecclesiastical Affairs in the Hungarian government did after the Budapest 1986 Catholic-Marxist Dialogue. This sort of spontaneous practical result supported Maura O'Neill's (1990, p. 104) claim that dialogue "is a commitment. The more one engages in it, the greater is the perspective and the goal" (and assuming it was true dialogue, not confrontational debate).

There are of course many benefits to be gained from dialoguing. For example, Fr. Thomas Keating (1993) reported how his encounter between Buddhist, Hindu, Islamic, Jewish, Native American, Protestant, Roman Catholics, Russian Orthodox and Tibetan Buddhists resulted in his group becoming more cohesive, honest and relishing the event. As he claimed:

> We were surprised and delighted to find many points of similarity and convergence in our respective paths. Like most people of our time, we originally expected that we would find practically nothing in common. In the years that followed we spontaneously and somewhat hesitatingly began to take a closer look at certain points of disagreement until these became our main focus of attention. We found that discussing our points of disagreement increased the bonding of the group even more than discovering our points of agreement. We became more honest in stating frankly what we believed and why, without at the same time making any effort to convince others of our own position. We simply presented our understanding as a gift to the group (p. 108).

That very act can help participants understand the process better because dialogue "is first a practice (and a difficult one) before theories on dialogue or conclusions on the results of dialogue are forthcoming" (Tracy, 1990, p. 76). Having experienced it in a visceral way, participants can relish the opportunity to learn from their encounters and feed this understanding back into the next one, as well as forward their fruits onto their own congregations. However, exactly what will be learnt is unclear:

> ...some will ask, where will it all lead? History is open-ended; interreligious dialogue, just begun, is open-ended. What the future will bring the Christian religion, we do not know. And what the future will bring the non-Christian religions, we do not know (Kung, 1988, p. 250).

Indeed, a "truly dialogical relationship has no other purpose than itself. Dialogue is the end of dialogue" (Lochhead, 1988, p. 79). However, there are at least two ways it can legitimately end. As Paul Mojzes (1989a, p. 206) put it: "one cannot speak of the "death" of dialogue, unless the partners decide to eliminate one another by warfare, or unless one or both of them should vanish as viable life styles." If war occurs, then dialogue *per se* has drastically failed. If religions vanish, then they have been consigned to the dustbin of history to be rediscovered, raked over and argued about by future archaeologists, historians and religionists, as currently happens with Ancient Egyptian religion.

Consequence #3 - Insightfulness into One's Own Faith and Sharing it with Coreligionists

The very act of participants conversing with other faiths can have positive personal benefits. The many "who have pioneered the search for good relations between religious communities...have found that learning about other religious traditions has helped them appreciate their own more deeply" (Braybrooke, 1993b, p. 120). In a synergistic fashion, "the power of encountering the deep faith of a religious person from another tradition has the potential of unleashing a search for one's own spiritual roots and yearnings" (Boys, Lee & Bass, 1995, p. 265). How? Because dialogue "helps any careful thinker to rediscover one's own identity. Sometimes, indeed, only such dialogue can help one discover that identity - as if for the first time" (Tracy, 1994/95, p. 109). Therefore, to ""understand" another religion in the full sense of the word can only be possible -- and responsible -- when it leads us to a more complete understanding of our own tradition, that is, when the dialogue strengthens, deepens, and completes our own faith on all levels" (Krieger, 1993, p. 353). It can do this because:

> ...as awareness expands, human life intensifies, moving toward the bursting of all bounds--for which all religions and other worldviews have specific terms: for example, *moksha* or liberation (Hindu), *nirvana* or "reality" (Buddhist), *basileia theou* or reign of God (Christian). It is that Omega point of total awareness toward which all human life tends (Swidler, 1990, p. 71).

This phenomenon of rediscovery, strengthening and deeper appreciation was proudly proclaimed by the Christian Donald Swearer (1977, p. 20) when he said: "my involvement in the study and teaching of Buddhism has enlarged and deepened my own particular faith stance." For Revd. Paul A. Crow Jr. (2000, p. 96), his "life and understanding of the Gospel and the church were transformed" when he chose to study and then worship with the Orthodox Church. Personal religious growth was also proudly proclaimed by M. Darrol Bryant (1990, p. 20). She confessed that: "my encounter with men and women of other faiths led to a revitalization of my own faith." This positive phenomenon was also evidenced by Mary C. Boys. She proudly claimed that: "I simply cannot imagine being Catholic without being engaged with Protestants and Jews: They challenge me to new ways of understanding and proffer occasions for "holy envy," yet paradoxically deepen my own religious commitments" (Boys, Lee & Bass, 1995, p. 272). By "holy envy" she meant "experiencing something so profound in the beliefs, rituals, polity or practices of another tradition that one wishes his or her own community of faith also had (or practiced) it" (p. 273).

Such faith-stance growth can occur in two basic ways. Firstly, the participants are forced to understand their own beliefs better when intellectually challenged by competing belief systems. Especially, if Paul Mojzes' (1978, p. 11) 19th ground rule is applied, namely: "Challenge one another to be faithful to your own search for truth." This was also Revd. Crow Jr.'s (2000, p. 96) advice to those wanting to pursue the ecumenical vision as a vocation. He suggested that they: "Select some sectarian person and engage them for six months in constructive dialogue and heated debate about God's call to visible unity, diversity, and evangelization." However, before doing so officially (as opposed to unofficially, privately, personally), participants should be quite knowledgeable to start with to fulfil competency criteria (Kozlovic, 2001). Such challenges will no doubt spur on participants to do more exhaustive homework and so they will end up knowing more about the Other, which is always a useful step in the understanding process. Indeed:

> It may be that what my dialogue partners will speak of is their experience of that same reality that I know in Jesus Christ as God. If so, fine; I have much to learn from them. But it may be that they will speak of something else, something of which I am even less well informed. If so, I must listen all the more intently. I will have all the more homework to do afterwards in integrating what I learn with what I thought I knew. I will need to revise not only my theology but, perchance, my metaphysics. But surely that is nothing against this approach. Surely Christians must be as open to revising metaphysics as to revising theology (Cobb Jr., 1988, p. 97).

Secondly, dialoguers can understand their own faith better by seeing it mirrored from different perspectives not previously considered. Precisely because of the mindset which is automatically inherited when learning one's own faith in its traditional religious packaging (akin to professional blindness). Therefore:

> Through interreligious, interideological dialogue we will come to know better our own religious, ideological selves with all their consistencies and contradictions, their admirable and abhorrent aspects. Our dialogue partners will serve as mirrors for us, showing us our true selves. Such a prize alone is worth the price of frustration in dialogue (Swidler, 1988b, pp. 26-27).

This prized mirroring is similar to understanding a religious tradition historically, sociologically, anthropologically, psychologically, philosophically etc. The answer is not so much wrong, just different. And the more differences one gets the more comprehensive is the understanding of the totality of the religion, which can quickly exceed its traditional conceptualisation. As Avery Dulles (1992) argued:

> My own involvement in ecumenism over the past forty years has led me to cherish other values. I have acquired a deeper realization of how much the Catholic Church has to contribute from the wealth of its own heritage. At the same time I have gained an enormous respect for the other churches that have venerable traditions of their own. The Orthodox, I have found, possess an immensely rich heritage of Trinitarian and sacramental piety handed down from the Eastern fathers. They have a sense of spiritual communion (or *koinonia*) that supplements and partly corrects the more legalistic approach characteristic of the West. From Lutherans and other Protestants I have learned the spiritual power of a theology of the word of God that is capable of completing and balancing the more sacramental vision of the Catholic and Orthodox churches (pp. 192-193).

In a sense, this is the religious application of the social scientist's triangulation methodology, that is, where there is "strength in the converging of weaknesses" (Williamson, Harp & Dalphin, 1977, p. 84). Or it is the equivalent of the psychologist's figure-ground perception concept (Adams, 1973). Where, for example, a black background is needed before one can truly appreciate a contrasting white foreground figure, and where white on white (or black on black) would make the figure indistinguishable. Indeed, Christian theology itself can be in peril if dialogue is eschewed. How? Because:

> Many theologians have concluded that theology cannot continue to be made in isolation from an interior dialogue with other religious traditions, that in fact the future of Christian theology lies in the deepest possible assimilation of the spirit and findings of other religions. The data from non-Christian religions has become an essential element for theological reflection... (Richard, 1981, p. 2).

Overall, dialogue requires "a willingness to be persuaded that reality might not be exactly what we thought, and that there could be some truth for us yet to learn" (Peters, 1986, p. 885). Besides, each "tradition has its blind spots. Yet by genuinely dialoguing with people deeply rooted in different faith traditions we might look for a moment through their eyes and see what our own blind spot prevents us from seeing. And this is sheer joy" (Shapiro, 1989, p. 37). Of course, this sheer joy needs to be shared, as embodied in Leonard Swidler's (1983) 2nd dialogue commandment. Namely:

> Because of the "corporate" nature of interreligious dialogue...it is also necessary that each participant enter into dialogue not only with his partner across the faith line - the Lutheran with the Anglican, for example - but also with his coreligionists, with his fellow Lutherans, to share with them the fruits of the interreligious dialogue. Only thus can the whole community eventually learn and change, moving toward an ever more perceptive insight into reality (p. 2).

Raimundo Panikkar (1975) argued for the same thing in his I:9 principle:

> No inter-religious dialogue can yield any fruit unless it is (at least logically and anthropologically) preceded by an intra-religious dialogue within the partners themselves...only those who can critically undergo an internal dialogue within themselves are ready for religious dialogue (p. 408).

This is one good reason why the French Bishops (Murphy, 1978, p. 150) required their dialogue participants to debate amongst their brothers in the faith (Guideline 4). Then of course, "Interreligious dialogue is also intrareligious dialogue" (Mitra, 1986, p. 122) because "Interreligious dialogue focused on justice [for example] promotes intrareligious dialogue concerning ultimate and penultimate values" (Suchocki, 1987, p. 160). Therefore, in principle, one should not tolerate limits on gaining insights, or in sharing the good news of the dialogue to all interested parties if desired and appropriate.

Consequence #4 - Tolerance and an Increase in the Public Good

During the act of listening, dialoguers are inherently forced to be tolerant of competing belief systems because they need to know what is being said fairly, accurately and correctly **before** they can respond appropriately. Patience and attentive perception during dialoguing:

> ...involves tolerating, that is, accepting, enduring, bearing, putting up with; it involves acceptance in the sense of refraining from any strong reaction to the thing in question; it is half-hearted, an attitude towards something

> that is not liked, loved, respected, or approved of; and it is often, though not always, understood as a praiseworthy act or virtue (Newman, 1982, p. 6).

Tolerance is thus a practical consequence because the participants are also Sources and Receivers within a transactional model of human communication (DeVito, 1991; Kozlovic, 2003). They become tolerant because of either the fear of getting-as-good-as-they-give, and/or a desire to be treated in a fair, principled way because this is the way **they** want to be treated (i.e., mutual respect given in a reciprocal manner). Thus, one of the biggest barriers to dialogue is quickly demolished. However, tolerance does not mean giving in, which is a useful point to stress to the more anxious faiths/religions/ participants. Also:

> ...the importance of interreligious dialogue is not to reach common convictions on the basis of meta-religious criteria, but to achieve an attitude of mutual respect, of mutual willingness to listen and to learn, of mutual readiness to cooperate for the well-being of all humankind in spite of our differences on the touchstones of reality (Mulder, 1989, pp. 209-210).

This was also the third criteria of Scott Daniel Dunbar's (1998, p. 456) four essential criteria for interreligious dialogue. Namely, "a mutual attitude of respect and open-mindedness, implying a willingness to learn and grow from the other." By cultivating this tolerance-inspired, open-minded mutual respect, many wonderful cooperative ventures can be achieved. For example:

> Improved interreligious relations have resulted in a number of ways for Christians to join with others in the promotion of peace, justice, and the common good. Thus, a public spirituality has emerged that characterizes those who have crossed religious lines to join in special projects to negotiate the end to war, to apply moral pressure for nuclear disarmament and an end to violence as a political and social method, and to meet the needs of those who are oppressed, impoverished, and underprivileged (Borelli, 1993, p. 552).

Not only is dialoguing a significant force for societal good, but it must transcend itself to keep on doing public good otherwise stagnation sets in. Dialogue allows one to understand the Other better while learning the skills of cooperation and enriching one's faith/religious/ideological stance. In this way, dialoguing is an instrument of social change that needs to keep sharpening its tools if it is to stay pointed and relevant.

Interestingly, Robert Traer (1993, p. 115) saw dialogue as the means for fostering the legal, ethical and spiritual quest for truth and religious freedom. How? Because to "pursue the truth, without standing up for the rights of others to pursue the truth in their own ways, as religious communities and individually within those communities, would be to reduce freedom to privileged piety." This attitude fits in nicely with Prof. Michael Pye's (2001, p. 5) advocated concept of "soft" dialogue, namely, dialogue that is "gentle, patient, imaginative and creative, leaving many questions open for future consideration." Therefore, if dialoguers' tools are not kept pointed and relevant, if the pursuit of truth and religious freedom is abandoned, and if "soft" styles of dialogue are not actively encouraged, then the consequences can be disastrous. As Prof. Mallam Ishaq Oloyede reminded his fellow conference delegates: "the only alternative to dialogue is conflict; if you believe dialogue is bad, war is worse" (quoted in Blombery, 1991, p. 30)! On the other hand, it appears that for some Fundamentalists, war may be a preferable option to their biggest and repeatedly expressed fear, namely, the spectre of conversion (Dhalla, 1989, p. 39; Klenicki, 1984, p. 102).

Consequence #5 - Conversion: How to Ameliorate the Fear?

Although De Silva claimed in his 1st dialogue aspect that dialogue "does not in any way diminish full and loyal commitment to one's own faith, but rather enriches and strengthens it" (quoted in Samartha, 1981, p. 59), this claim is not strictly true. Dialogue **can** be like that, and for many, it **is** like that, but for others, dialogue poses a serious challenge. Not surprisingly, sympathy, tolerance and being truthful to oneself, to the Other and to God can seriously disturb believers' predetermined faith commitments and related loyalties. How? Because:

> ...we may find the very foundation of those things we cherish most deeply shaken in ways we did not anticipate and do not want. Many a theological student has become involved in study of and conversation with other faith traditions only to find him - or herself uprooted and disconnected from previously sustaining elements of Christian faith (Smith, 1991, p. 72).

Such an exposure can nurture strong pro-Other feelings and tempt believers to convert, a phenomenon that Sarah Cunningham (1987, p. 11) referred to as "co-optation." This is an occupational hazard for interreligious dialoguers and akin to the Human Resource Manager who after giving a staff course on career planning, follows his own advice and leaves his own company for greener pastures.

Indeed, many conversion accounts exist within the literature (Carmel, 1968; Gruss, 1979), and it is a potential outcome openly conceded by many dialoguers. For example, Philip H. Hwang (1989) argued:

> ...we must admit the genuine possibility for us to be converted to other religions. If we are really open-minded and honestly acknowledge the similarities and differences between religions, in the due process of time, it is quite possible to come to believe that the religions of other people are somehow much better than ours in many ways...one must be willing to be converted, and risk all the consequences. Unless, we seriously entertain this sad thing, yes it is a sad possibility, we will not have a genuine dialogue (p. 13).

Or as David J. Hesselgrave (1978, p. 227) flippantly put it: "about all one can lose in interreligious dialogue is *face* and *faith*." For professed true believers, loss of their faith is something to really fear, and which dialogue organisers should address by stressing that this is **not** the explicit intent of dialoguing (even if it is a potential outcome). For example, Jean-Claude Basset (1992) boldly asserted in his 10th rule:

> ...dialogue should not coerce anybody into renouncing his or her convictions, even missionary. Instead it should offer a space where everybody may give witness to one's living faith, with its certainties, questions and expectations. To renounce envy for the spiritual and social strengths of other communities, rejoicing at their deficiencies and difficulties, and even more so, not attempting to subvert their destiny, rules out neither emulation in human solidarity, nor the quest for truth (p. 39).

Similarly, Paul Mojzes (1978, p. 11) stated in his 24th ground rule that: "You must not try to convert your partner, or the dialogue may turn again into a monologue." Indeed, a "fundamental ground rule for any dialogue between Christians and Jews must be this: there can never be a question of Christians attempting to convert Jews to Christianity" (Cox, 1989, p. 121). Instead, true "interreligious dialogue must deepen and purify all religions and, in a certain sense, preserve their uniqueness" (Krieger, 1993, p. 353).

Unfortunately, some dialoguers believe otherwise. As one Christian said: "Our aim will be that the Muslim should be converted to faith in Jesus Christ...[on the grounds that] he may well despise the lack of sure faith implied by a form of dialogue which does not seek to convince and convert him" (Goldsmith, 1982, pp. 120-121)! Its Muslim equivalent is just as worrying: "Thanks to your democratic laws [Christian] we will invade you: thanks to our religious laws [Islamic] we will dominate you" (Bernardini, 2000, p. 53)! During the three-day Budapest 1986 Catholic-Marxist Dialogue: "One thing was clear to the Catholics: their partners in dialogue wanted to remain Marxists; they were not ready to abandon metaphysical materialism or atheism" (Pereira, 1987, p. 275). Nor should they be expected too if they were not convinced otherwise by faith, logic or God!

Fortunately, there are many useful strategies to ameliorate the fear of conversion. Firstly, be frank about such conversion possibilities, and point out that in well run dialogues the event organisers will be addressing the problem. Secondly, by asking participants to invoke the power of their own protective deities for comfort and security (e.g., God, Archangel Michael, Krishna, Sai Baba) with appropriate scriptural recitations if needed. For example, for Christians, reminding them of Matthew 18:20 (KJV): "For where two or three are gathered together in my name, there am I in the midst of them" keeping a watchful eye out. Thirdly, by repeating Ted Peters (1986) logical argument:

> Yes, it is quite likely that dialogue will change our minds. But there is absolutely nothing to fear on this score. If the God in whom we believe is in fact the creator and reconciler of the cosmos, then there is no truth - if it be genuine truth and not just partisan propaganda - that we could ever learn that could possibly lead us away from God (p. 885).

This tactic is highly recommended. Fourthly, if more support is needed, then a useful strategy is to point to the need for a common meeting ground. Put another way: "While neither partner is out to "convert" the other, the element of conversion in this sense of metanoia must be there in the heart of both. It is in this sense that we see the dialogical process as 'creating one heart'" (Coff, 1989, p. 210). In fact, the Christian M. Thomas Thangaraj (1991) saw mutually beneficial conversion as a necessity for *missio ecclesiae*, but one which also needed to contain elements of responsibility and regard for the Other. As he argued:

> The church will and should continue to bear witness to the love of God expressed in the life, ministry, death, and resurrection of Christ; but it can do so only in a setting of mutual witness, allowing our partners in dialogue to witness to us regarding their experience and vision of the mighty and salvific acts of God. Similarly, conversion will have to be defined as a two-way traffic wherein we are all converted to and by each other, which is different from an understanding of conversion as contributing to church growth (p. 175).

In short, conversion is positively characterised as a means of creating Coff's (1989, p. 210) "one heart," the soft form of positive conversion. Fifthly, Arvind Sharma (1998) posited the following argument for the anxious believers:

> In a dialogical situation...truth is indivisible - I have it, but you may have it too. In order for both of us to share it, if both of us have it in some sense, it must find a place *in-between* us. I do not have to go over to your side; you do not have to come over to my side; it is still indivisible and it can still be shared but by perambulation (from side to side) rather than transition (from one side to another) (p. 36).

That is, the spaces betwixt faiths/religions where one can safely meet. Sixthly, for those still fearful of conversion, another tactic is to point to the method of the Permanent Council of the French Bishops for forestalling potential loss of faith (Murphy, 1978, p. 150). Namely, to debate the different options and social commitments amongst brothers in the faith within the Church (Guideline 4). And secondly, to intellectually apply themselves to the renewal of their faith, and the knowledge of the word of God, within the Church (Guideline 5).

Curiously, Paul Mojzes (1989b, p. 4) noted how this fear of conversion plus love for the Others' truths prompted some religionists to adopt both religions. "Some people are so fundamentally affected by their experience with two or more religions that they feel justified in regarding themselves as adherents of more than one religion (not a novel experience in the Orient but increasingly commonplace in the West)." This "dual religious citizenship" (Jochim, 1995, p. 36) was formally evidenced by Charles Wei-hsun Fu (Taoist/Buddhist), Raimundo Panikkar (Catholic/Hindu/Buddhist), and Bibhuti S. Yadav (Hindu/Buddhist) as documented in Leonard Swidler's (1988a, pp. 254-256) *Toward a Universal Theology of Religion.* Dom Bede Griffiths is another prominent example of dual religious citizenship. Originally a Benedictine monk of Prinknash Abbey and then Prior of Farnborough Abbey in England, he went to India in 1955 to help found Kurisumala Ashram, a monastery of the Syrian rite in Kerala. However, he was soon dissatisfied with his original religious tradition and so sought a fusion between Judaic and Vedic revelations, which he described in *The Marriage of East and West* as follows:

> I had begun to find that there was something lacking not only in the Western world but in the Western Church. We were living from one half of our soul, from the conscious, rational level and we needed to discover the other half, the unconscious, intuitive dimension. I wanted to experience in my life the marriage of these two dimensions of human existence, the rational and intuitive, the conscious and unconscious, the masculine and the feminine. I wanted to find the way to the marriage of East and West (Griffiths, 1982, p. 8).

He did this by courageously crossing formal faith lines and searching for his lost half. Indeed, it could be argued that Charles Wei-hsun Fu, Raimundo Panikkar, Bibhuti Yadav and Dom Bede Griffiths are the human embodiments of interreligious dialogue. They also appear to be interreligious equivalents of the Hindu saint Ramakrishna whose:

> ...hunger for experience of the Divine led him to try various religions. As a Hindu he practiced yoga and worshipped in the spirit of bhakta (that is, he sought God through faith and devotion); he in turn became a Jain, a Buddhist, a Muslim, and a Christian. As a Shakta he experienced Brahman; as a Muslim he experienced God as Allah; as a Christian he knew God in Christ (Christian, 1973, p. 436).

It was a very instructive form of personalised revelatory ecumenism.

Consequence #6 - Frustration: Suppressed Desire?

Whatever the dialogue journey, one is going to be frustrated and experience religious angst at some point along the way. For example, Fundamentalists (e.g., Jehovah's Witnesses, Mormons) may be disappointed that their biblically based words of wisdom did not result in the Other's faith transformation. That is, they did not see the light, a literal expectation of other Fundamentalists who only need to feel the Holy Ghost (via glossolalia?) to expect instantaneous conversion, and/or to attribute it to the sinners' acceptance of Jesus Christ as their Lord and Saviour (e.g., Christian Revivalism). In a very real sense, even if unarticulated or unconscious, direct or indirect, they expect the words to have mystical or quasi-mystical properties which can trigger conversion experiences, to be "born again" (John 3:3 KJV). Or at least to protect them as evidenced by Christians who recite *The Lord's Prayer*, Hare Krishna's who chant the *Maha-mantra*, or Swami Muktananda's and Swami Sivananda's devotees who sing the *Om Namah Sivaya* mantra to disperse negativity. In fact, every major religion has sacred words of power (Crowley & Crowley, 1991), and which can be effectively integrated into official dialogue events as stress reducers and anxiety comforters as appropriate.

Regardless of whether this mystical conception of born-again dialogue has any ontological reality within official dialogue events, it may still be a dangerous attitude. Why? Because any expectation of instantaneous faith change triggered by words is not dialogue *per se*. Rather, it is a deliberate (surreptitious?) conversion attempt, and thus a gross violation of both Jean-Claude Basset's (1992) 10th decalogue item and Paul Mojzes' (1978) 24th ground rule which expressly forbids conversion attempts. Indeed, such an expectation is itself an indication of a profound misunderstanding of the human-human dialogic process (Kozlovic, 2003), and an indication of an organisational error, namely, poor personnel selection (Kozlovic, 2001). Dialogue participants who purposely behave like this, as opposed to letting it happen "naturally," should not have been selected as official delegates. Interestingly, the evangelical Christian, Virginia Ramey Mollenkott (1987) offered the following useful comments to those offended by proselytising Fundamentalists:

> The best advise I can offer to people who are disturbed by fundamentalist attempts to proselytize is to publicize broadly and repeatedly the distinction between psychological manipulation, materialistic inducement, and unethical coercion on the one hand, and simple communication of the facts of one's spiritual journey on the other (p. 63).

When such unobtrusive-looking, faith-based conversion attempts fail, then these same Fundamentalists may begin to feel personally inadequate in getting their religious points across and/or in failing to get a positive outcome for the Lord. However, this phenomenon may not be limited to just Fundamentalists. All dialoguers at some point are going to feel less than content about their performances. And then attribute this to some personal defect or past failing; as indicated by Eric Sharpe's (1992, p. 232) teaching tale about the ginger tom cat and its fearful memory of him. Nonetheless, it is to be expected, judged accordingly, and dare it be said, event organisers should not pussyfoot around the issue.

Participants may feel inadequate and frustrated because, in the dialogue context, they can no longer rely upon the following old argument form: "we-believe-in-X-because-we-are-Y-and-that-is-what-Y's-believe-in." Other delegates may not be impressed by this circular logic. Yet again, such an attempt would be the result of a misunderstanding of the non-conversion nature of the dialogic process, and of ignoring the basic point that no faith/religion/ideology has a monopoly on truth. Indeed, Paul Mojzes' (1978, p. 11) 24th ground rule is useful to recite here. Namely: "Neither's truth is absolute. Each partner needs the Other in order to get a more complete picture of the truth. Monopoly in thought leads to sluggishness in thinking and to the perversion of truth." Or as it was artistically expressed by the mystical poet Kahlil Gibran (1979, p. 66) in *The Prophet*: "Say not, "I have found **the** truth," but rather, "I have found **a** truth" [my emphasis].

For the philosophically inclined, Marcus Braybrooke's (1993a, p. 107) comment echoing the *neti-neti* tradition of Hinduism is proffered: "The Divine transcends our human thought and language and this involves a recognition of the relativity of all religious language and symbols. This "forbids any one religion from having the 'only' or 'final' word.""
For participants inclined to using fiction to nourish their faith then the following Idries Shah's (1973) Sufi teaching story *The Blind Ones and the Matter of the Elephant* is recommended:

> Beyond Ghor there was a city. All its inhabitants were blind. A king with his entourage arrived near by; he brought his army and camped in the desert. He had a mighty elephant, which he used in attack and to increase the people's awe. The populace became anxious to see the elephant, and some sightless from among this blind community ran like fools to find it. As they did not even know the form or shape of the elephant they groped sightlessly, gathering information by touching some part of it. Each thought he knew something, because he could feel a part. When they returned to their fellow-citizens eager groups clustered around them. Each of these

> was anxious, misguidedly, to learn the truth from those who were themselves astray. They asked about the form, the shape of the elephant: and listened to all they were told.
> The man whose hand had reached an ear was asked about the elephant's nature. He said: 'It is large, rough thing, wide and broad like a rug.' And the one who had felt the trunk said: 'I have the real facts about it. It is like a straight and hollow pipe, awful and destructive.' The one who had felt its feet and legs said" 'It is mighty and firm, like a pillar.' Each had felt some part out of many. Each had perceived it wrongly. No mind knew all: knowledge is not the companion of the blind. All imagined something, something incorrect (p. 25).

Feelings of inadequacy or frustration may exist because dialoguers looked at only **part** of the truth, which did not match the other parts of the truth, which their dialogue partners examined. Of course, this may also be an administrative function of the complexity of the topic, the number of participants involved, and the time available for such discussions.

Frustration can also arise because the dialogue has failed to meet the concerns of the participants, however conceived. For example, Letty Cottin Pogrebin's black-Jewish women's group petered out within two years, despite Maura O'Neill's (1990) thesis that women dialoguing together to avoid androcentric biases would achieve some form of feminist utopia. Or at least to help compensate for Ursula King's (1998, p. 43) complaint about female invisibility, marginalisation and exclusion which resembled "what the French call '*un dialogue des sourds*' (a dialogue of the deaf)." When Letty asked an ex-member why people stopped coming to the black-Jewish dialogue she was curtly told:

> "You Jews have to stop acting like God's chosen people," she barked, her eyes hard and angry. "The world doesn't revolve around you. Relations with Jews are not a priority for most African-Americans; our main concern is *survival*""... In other words, blacks worry about their actual conditions and fear for the present; Jews worry about their history and fear for the future (Pogrebin & Hutchinson, 1994, p. 220).

However, this frustration source can be attributable to the administrative failure of not setting a mutually beneficial agenda, and then not ensuring its ongoing relevance and maintenance throughout the course of the dialogue. This is also an apt reminder that "post-patriarchal dialogue" (King, 1998, p. 52), in this gender exclusivist way, is not an automatic panacea for feminist ills.

As an important corollary of the above problems, feelings of inadequacy can manifest themselves as personal depression and/or devalued self-esteem for letting down the faith/religion/ideological team. After all, the "sheer psychological difficulty for some Christians of entering into such a dialogue in depth should not be underestimated" (Sharpe, 1977, p. 142). However, Paul Mojzes' (1978, p. 11) 15th ground rule is of some comfort here, namely: "Do not assume that the conclusions reached are final. There will always be a need for continual dialogue regarding these views." Not surprisingly, feelings of frustration can elicit violent impulses from even experienced, knowledgeable and respected dialoguers, such as Prof. Harvey Cox (1989, p. 98). He toured Jerusalem and engaged in an informal conversation with an independent American Christian evangelist who had just recounted a phantasmagoric end-time scenario. As he reported: "I was appalled. A strange impulse to reach out and strangle my new unsought acquaintance rose in me, then subsided." Admittedly, it was an informal conversation, but one can imagine similar feelings arising during formal dialogues (e.g., Peters, 1986, p. 883). Prof. Cox's (1989) solution of allowing the violent impulse to subside seems a wise first step, whatever the situation.

Frustration and religious angst may also arise out of the fear of syncretism (i.e., the fusing of all the world religions) or the fear of indifferentism (i.e., ignoring the basic distinctive elements of each faith). However, they have to be balanced against the positive gains made. Syncretism and indifferentism may just be another way of saying "progress;" especially for those religions that found a way around their old theological stalemates (e.g., the Uniting Church formed from three different denominations). As De Silva argued in his 2nd dialogue aspect: "Dialogue, far from being a temptation to syncretism, is a safeguard against it, because in dialogue we get to know one another's faith in depth. One's own faith is tested and refined and sharpened thereby. The real test of faith is faiths-in-relation" (quoted in Samartha, 1981, p. 59).

For intrareligious dialoguers aiming for an ecumenical vision, then Revd. Crow Jr.'s (2000, p. 96) advice is pertinent. Namely, "Practice patience, perseverance, spiritual tenacity, and confidence in God's power to renew and reconcile God's people." Or as Arnold D. Hunt (1975) put it: "The Christian engaged in dialogue has to *trust the Holy Spirit* and believe that the outcome is in God's hands." For those Christians still frustrated, then the following rationale is advocated:

> A simple, overarching, organic, world religion-ideology is not the goal of interreligious, interideological dialogue. Rather, the goals could be said to be three: (1) to know oneself ever more profoundly; (2) to know the other ever more authentically; (3) to live ever more fully accordingly (Swidler, 1988b, p. 26).

This statement could form the motto, credo and mission statement of the religious dialogue enterprise. Of course, this does **not** mean that dialoguing is not subjected to potentially unsavoury problems, it is, but as Brockway and Rajashekar (1987) advised:

> Church groups should discuss, though not be discouraged by, potential local problems that may arise from dialogue with people of new religious movements: will it imply an endorsement of the group and/or its activities? Will it merely provide an easy forum for the mission of the new religious movement? (pp. 177-178).

Even if these suspicions are true, although it may initially provide a superficial veneer of respectability-by-association, and a platform for doctrinal dissemination, it will not be able to sustain it if the inherent nature of the message is defective. Indeed, for the suspicious, what better way to reveal deficiencies than by listening to it straight from the proverbial horse's mouth. After all, to be fair and rational, one must first listen then consider before passing judgment. Nor does it mean that dialoguing is immune from being used for unsavoury purposes; that view would also be naive. Why? Because:

> ...one must not forget the political motives or purposes of the dialogue. This may be to gain a greater measure of religious or political freedom, to obtain political support for specific measures, especially those unpopular and not so easily achievable without the support of the other, and so forth. Sometimes such purposes are not primary and often they are part of the "hidden agenda." When political motives emerge as the primary purpose of the dialogue, the chances are that no real dialogue will take place or that it will soon deteriorate. The fate of the dialogue often depends on oscillating political contingencies (Mojzes, 1989a, pp. 202-203).

Whether these contingencies turn out to be important factors in any particular dialogue or not, there is always the distinct possibility of failure because the Other's (perceived?) (mis?)behaviour has generated unsavoury consequences.

Consequence #7 - Defection and Beyond: Confirmation of the Worst?

This problem is an extension of the above-mentioned conversion and frustration fears, but with far more devastating consequences, namely, the failure of "conceptual *ahimsa* where religious differences are communicated without harm" (Dunbar, 1998, p. 462). For example, Christians may conclude that New Religious Movements (NRM) are some form of evil incarnate. Thus dismissing the whole dialogue enterprise as "'New Age thinking', seeing behind it 'a neo-Hindu-Buddhist plot' for the 'spiritual takeover' of the West" (Ariarajah, 1998, p. 14). This view can result in a deterioration of relations between faiths (and the dialogue organisers). The decline may start as a person-to-person dispute, but it can inevitably translate into a religion-to-religion dispute with the equally inevitable rebuffs. The reporting of this "failure" being relayed to coreligionists and further polluting their minds with anti-dialogue, and anti-religious sentiments about the Other. For example, an informal meeting occurred between Jehovah's Witnesses and Orthodox Christians which was reported to the Orthodox congregation as follows:

> Recently I had an encounter with a young woman from the cult of the Jehovah's Witnesses. She came to my office ostensibly to ask some questions about the Orthodox faith with an Orthodox friend of hers. She then promptly proceeded to lead me through the New World mistranslation of the Bible trying to prove to me that the Kingdom of God was a future situation in which Christ would establish His rule over the earth and we would all live in Paradise. Eventually I asked her a question - 'Have you experienced the kingdom of God?' She did not know what I was talking about. How irrelevant is a gospel which has nothing to say about the existential concerns of humanity which is only concerned with speculation about the future state - even the Marxists can do better than that (Bozikis, 1999, p. 4).

Regrettably, the Revd. Anastasios Bozikis was very unkind and uncharitable by character assassinating both her and the Jehovah's Witnesses (JWs) faith. He did this by:

(a) Using the negative, emotionally loaded word "cult" to describe her faith/religion.

(b) By comparing JWs to "Marxists" (i.e., religionists with non-religionists).
(c) By being derogatory and inferring that she/JWs were less competent than atheists.
(d) By (unnecessarily) ridiculing the JWs sacred text, the *New World Translation of the Holy Scriptures* by calling it the "New World mistranslation of the Bible."
(e) By suggesting that the JW "gospel" was "irrelevant" (not to JWs!).
(f) Because a young (brave?, curious?) woman (possibly academically mismatched compared to the Revd.) was (supposedly) stumped by a (tangential?) question.
(g) Even if true, it was unfair because she was seeking scriptural answers rooted in the Bible as opposed to the Reverend's non-scriptural, existential reply (for oneupmanship reasons?).
(h) Which (unfairly) indicated to the Revd. that the JW religion was (supposedly) invalid.
(i) And by (unnecessarily) inferring that this woman had a covert mission against the (misogynist?, affronted?) Revd. instead of an obviously keen desire to debate a scriptural point in his offices (i.e., his home turf) in the company of a fellow Orthodox (but not JW) companion.

If this was the type of response at the level of informal interreligious communications, one wonders what interreligious stress could be generated at the official dialogue level?! Nor is such a worrying scenario of contempt restricted to immature, new or foreign religions and their devotees. For example, Allan R. Brockway (1987) was secretary for Christian-Jewish relations in the World Council of Churches. He reported how an essentially nonreligious, *a*-theological criteria prevented interreligious dialogue with a New Religious Movement. As he reported:

> A case in point is the Unification Church, which has undertaken the most extensive program of inter-religious dialogue now existing in the world. To date, we have not accepted the oft-repeated invitation to participate in the dialogue it sponsors, but, on the contrary, have shied away from it almost to the extent of being unwilling to speak with Unification members. The operative criterion for this functional decision seems to have been a negative evaluation of some of the practices of the Unification Church, including (but not limited to) the identification of the Unification organization, Causa, with right-wing dictatorships in Latin America; the conducting of multiple marriages; and "brain-washing" in recruitment… (pp. 3-4).

Although there were dialogical concerns about Revd. Sun Myung Moon's Moonies (Moss & Chryssides, 1986), and their faith was the subject of numerous exposes (Streiker, 1978), at least Brockway had courageously acted. Firstly, by acknowledging the fact of their less desirable behaviour. Secondly, by realising that each religion had and still has its obnoxious elements. Thirdly, by identifying the need to discuss the matter with each other. And fifthly, by developing ways to make better decisions about similar New Religious Movements in the future. Cult/NRM scholar J. Gordon Melton (2000) came to a similar realisation. As he confessed:

> Several approaches have dominated our response to New Religions over the past generation. Overwhelmingly, of course, we have simply ignored them. They have not been taken seriously as religious communities, and their leaders have not been seen as thinkers with a worthy perspective. Why waste time with shallow amateurs? With a Karl Barth, a Karl Rahner, or a Carl Henry to read, why would we ever pick up a book by an Aleister Crowley, L. Ron Hubbard, or Maharishi Mehesh Yogi? It has been much easier to keep the wickedest man in the world, a mere science-fiction writer, or the giggling guru at arms length. In doing so, we miss the fact that many who have read their writings had found them to be quite mature, if unconventional, thinkers (p. 93).

Then of course there is the problem of the suppression and/or subversion of issues during dialogues. For example, Sr. Ann Gillen (1987) reported her disenchantment at the Copenhagen 1980 United Nations Conference on Women. As he complained:

> In my opinion and from my perspective, Western groups, including those from the United States and Israel, came ready to dialogue; the opposing coalition came determined not to dialogue but to dominate - both at the official meetings and at the Almager nongovernmental-organizational meetings. They came better prepared for that purpose, with their "goon squad" tactics. So, Copenhagen was a painful experience in power and powerlessness. As a woman of faith, I shared in the frustration of women who saw their hopes for the agenda subverted. In a special way I shared in the powerlessness of Jewish and Ukrainian women, both minorities scorned by the powerful at Copenhagen (p. 137).

It was a situation that Sr. Gillen attributed to anti-Semitism, and the desire to censor the stories of Soviet-generated suffering and oppression (in which case the goon squad tactics were easily identifiable trademarks). Regrettably, censoring dialogues runs the danger of isolating individual dialogues from each other, and of losing sight of the precious indivisibility of the interfaith movement (Meyer, 1991, p. 281).
Another stage in this deterioration process is the public denouncement of the Other's faith. For example, Juliet Sheen (1994) reported how in Geneva 1984 she attended a United Nations Seminar on encouraging understanding, tolerance and respect for religion and belief when:

> A vehemently anti-semitic address by the Saudi Arabian delegate shocked the Seminar delegates. He was quoting from materials about the medieval blood libel which he had learned in theology in university and had never questioned ...his deluge of century-old hate... (p. 16).

For a more public denunciation, one need only recall Revd. Ian Paisley's Pope-heckling, Anti-Christ accusations, and the deliberate, loutish disruption of ecumenical services, and the associated placard parades (Bruce, 1986, pp. 215, 216, 228). Despite years of contact with the Roman Catholic Church, this particular Free Presbyterian still had grave difficulties and brought shame upon himself and his faith before the whole world. From a public relations perspective, such behaviour is a disaster for the Free Presbyterians. However, it was a godsend for the Roman Catholics who repeatedly showed calmness, magnanimity and maturity while under fire, as well as toughness and organisational competence in dealing with Revd. Paisley in his obnoxious mode.
Although not as dramatic, Colin Brown (1992, p. 3) reported how some anti-intellectual Fundamentalists counter-attacked using a variety of biblically based passages. Such as: "'*Beware lest any man spoil you through philosophy and vain deceit, after the tradition of men, after the rudiments of this world and not after Christ.*' (Colossians 2:8)." However, the huge range of possible scriptural retorts was not documented. The one good thing about virulent opposition however, is that it can quickly burn itself out: "Presumably no one who has responded negatively to that exposure...is bothering to be engaged in further, on-going dialogue" (King, 1990, p. 122). Indeed, if such negative delegates persisted then it is another indication of organisational failure in weeding out such undesirables (Kozlovic, 2001).

Another unfortunate characteristic of denouncers is their frequent failure to find out what exactly triggered their wrath and then the means of resolving it. For example, during the Nairobi 1975 World Council of Churches' Fifth Assembly: "Serious confrontation between delegates did take place. There were some who considered "non-Christian" religions as demonic and were opposed to any kind of dialogue or efforts at seeking community with them" (Samartha, 1981, p. 51). Fortunately, the victims of this abuse were nonplussed and exhibited professional poise, tolerance and quick-wittedness far in excess of their detractor's behaviour:

> The missiologist who described all non-Christian religions as demonic missed the chance of personally meeting these "non-Christian" guests to discover and perhaps battle with "demonic" elements in them. At least one of the guests [comprising of Buddhist, Hindu, Jewish, Muslim & Sikh representatives] expressed disappointment that no one among those who talked loudest about proclamation actually came to him or others personally to proclaim the love of God in Jesus Christ (Samartha, 1981, p. 57).

Far worse than disillusioned participants avoiding future dialogues is to deliberately oppose the Other. One has only to look at some Iranian Muslim's perceptions of America as Satan incarnate, and their numerous attacks (polemical, physical and deadly) to see this regrettable possibility in action. Disillusionment can also manifest itself as increased proselytising activity, and faith reinforcing behaviour of the type demonstrated in Festinger, Riecken and Schachter's (1956) study of UFO cult believers.

Of course, proselytising activity is not necessarily a direct result of dialoguing, but the possibility of a faith/religion/ideology using the dialogue for political gain is potentially there. Paul Mojzes (1989a, pp. 202-203) warned about his, while Sara S. Lee (1991, p. 189) nervously reported: "Needless to say the recent desecration of Torah scrolls in a Brooklyn synagogue reinforces Jewish fears of anti-Semitism and reminds all of us that such fears are certainly not groundless." Then there are the conflicts that result directly from interreligious dialoguing itself. For example:

> It happened at a recent interreligious gathering. At the other end of the building, in the meditation room, some members of our group were learning Zen techniques while the rest of us sat in the Gothic chapel waiting for mass to begin. Suddenly a commotion broke out in the chancel. A Catholic priest from Tibet had grabbed the microphone and was shouting something about Jesus Christ being the "only way, the truth and the life!" A couple of other priests chased him around, trying to grab the microphone. Then two men leaped out of the pews and joined the melee. I thought to myself. "Yes, now I see that religious wars are possible. When the attackers found they couldn't bodily throw the interloper out without losing every sense of dignity and decorum, the presiding priest asked us all to leave and announced the mass would be held in another room. Most left. I stayed, and so did a dozen others. We listened to the priest's impassioned rebuke. We were selling out our Christian faith, he said. The very fact that we were conversing with "Buddhist idolators" was evidence that we had lost our commitment to the Christ of God "who alone can bring us out of darkness into the light." To conclude, he bowed and prayed for our souls (Peters, 1986, p. 883).

One imagines that such wayward guests are comparatively rare, but nonetheless, it does indicate that dialogue organisers need to be prepared for many possible contingencies. Another regrettable manifestation of dialogue participation is when the religion's members begin to loose faith in their own representatives, and then nastily turn on them:

> Often those who have pioneered the search for good relations between religious communities have faced misunderstanding and even hostility in their own faith community. They have been accused of compromising or "watering down" the distinctive beliefs of their own religious traditions (Braybrooke, 1993b, p. 120).

Prof. Harvey Cox (1989, p. 17) was keenly aware of this possibly. As he reported: "One of the risks [of dialoguing] is running the possibility of being viewed by one's coreligionists with suspicion or distrust." Indeed, "people in any religious tradition who are committed to dialogue often find themselves upbraided as turncoats by their own brothers and sisters" (Cox, 1989, p. 2). For example, Methodist minister Revd. Paula Niukula was considered:

> ...a great man who had done so much to try and promote dialogue and understanding among the various religious and racial groups in Fiji. [However, for]...his efforts he even had at times to suffer being ostracised by some members of his own Church who felt he was going too far in his outreach to people of other faiths (Ahern, 1998, p. 3).

However, Prof. Cox's (1989, p. 18) solution to the problem was, in principle, simple. Namely: "Perhaps the most unexpected thing I have learned in the dialogue with people of other religions is how important it is for me to keep in touch with those of my own faith community who remain suspicious and fearful of that dialogue." Unfortunately, this solution is not always effective if politicking was involved, for as Leonard Swidler (1990) noted regarding a Christian-Marxist dialogue:

> One notorious example on the Christian side was that of Salesian priest Guido Girardi, who for his continued dialogue with Marxists was fired from the Salesian University in Rome and in September 1977 was expelled from the Salesian Society. A similar fate overtook Roger Garaudy, Milan Machovec, Adam Schaff, and scores of other Marxist scholars. Dialogue was obvious perceived by the power brokers as an activity dangerous to them--and correctly so (p. 177).

Coreligionist contact is indeed important, but to avoid future unsavoury incidents, the dialoguer's congregation should be regularly briefed and debriefed per dialogue (if only as a courtesy gesture), and by consciously deciding to eschew politicking. However, even sharing one's insights about religious Others has its inherent dangers. As Kenneth Cracknell (1987) reported:

> I am...utterly lost for a response when I, or any other fellow-Christian, am reproached for sharing in a meeting organized by the Unificationists or Scientologists, or for visiting and accepting the hospitality of Rajneeshies or Hare Krishna devotees. Our very being there is a form of authentic witness... (p. 164).

Fortunately, his subsequent logical argument provided another potential solution to the problem:

> For Christians to draw boundaries and establish frontiers over which neither they nor their fellow-Christians have to pass seems to me morally and theologically wrong. Some urge for example that to talk to members of NRMs [New Religious Movements] "gives them credibility", but I hear this as the sub-ethical language of diplomacy; others speak of rubbing shoulders with heretics, but I hear this as the language of the Inquisition; others fear the contamination of the "demonic", but I know this is to under-rate the expulsive power of the Holy Spirit; others suggest that NRMs need "prophetic denunciation" but such denunciations may well prevent us from hearing what God might be wishing to say to us through such movements… We cannot talk with people who have no wish to talk with us, but where ever there are those who would enter into dialogue with us, we cannot refuse. There are no limits to be set to dialogue (p. 165).

This advice also makes good rational, academic sense.

Conclusion

Clearly, there is more to religious dialoguing than first meets the eye! An *a priori* understanding of the above logical possibilities, practical outcomes and potential solutions would significantly moderate delegate expectations for future events. Professional awareness of the range, depth and contours of these dialogic consequences would also have important ramifications for both participant preparation and event organisation and hopefully lead to more fruitful engagements. After all, to be forewarned is to be forearmed. Therefore, the sooner the profession acknowledges these outcome contours, and actively encourages dialogue participation (Kozlovic, 2002), the more successful will future events become. In addition to enhancing the interpersonal growth of participants, and lessening the chances of stagnation, decay or death of the entire enterprise. Further research into this important praxis area is warranted, highly recommended and certainly long overdue.

References

Adams, N. (1973). Figure-ground perception. In L. Batten & A. Storz (Eds.), *Psychology encyclopedia* (p. 99). Guilford, CT: Duskin Publishing.

Ahern, D. (1998). Interfaith search. *The Far East: Mission Magazine of the Columban Fathers*, **80**(2), 2-3.

Ariarajah, S. W. (1998). The impact of interreligious dialogue on the ecumenical movement. In J. D. May (Ed.), *Pluralism and the religions: The theological and political dimensions* (pp. 7-21). London: Cassell.

Basset, J.-C. (1992). Decalogue of dialogue. *Current Dialogue*, **23**, 35-39.

Bernardini, G. G. (2000). Difficulties of dialogue with Islam (1). *Christ to the World*, **45**(1), 53-55.

Blombery, 'T. (1991). Unity in diversity? Some impressions of the WCC 7th Assembly, *Australian Religion Studies Review*, **4**(1), 24-31.

Borelli, J. (1993). Interreligious dialogue. In M. Downey (Ed.), *The new dictionary of catholic spirituality* (pp. 550-553). Collegeville, MN: The Liturgical Press.

Boys, M. C., Lee, S. S., & Bass, D. C. (1995). Protestant, Catholic, Jew: The transformative possibilities of educating across religious boundaries. *Religious Education*, **90**(2), 255-275.

Bozikis, A. (1999). Communicating the faith: Reflections on Orthodox evangelism. *The Orthodox Messenger*, **10**(6/7-8/9), 4-8.

Braybrooke, M. (1993a). A pilgrimage of hope. In J. D. Beversluis (Ed.), *A sourcebook for the community of religions* (pp. 104-109). Chicago: The Council for a Parliament of the World's Religions.

Braybrooke, M. (1993b). A study guide for interreligious cooperation and understanding. In J. D. Beversluis (Ed.), *A sourcebook for the community of religions* (pp. 111-115, 117, 120-124). Chicago: The Council for a Parliament of the World's Religions.

Brockway, A. R. (1987). With whom do we dialogue? *Current Dialogue*, **12**, 3-4.

Brockway, A. R., & Rajashekar, J. P. (Eds.). (1987). *New religious movements and the churches*. Geneva: WCC Publications.

Brown, C. (1992). Witness or dialogue? Christian fundamentalists at bay. *Australian Religion Studies Review*, **5**(1), 1-5.

Bruce, S. (1986). *God save Ulster!: The religion and politics of Paisleyism*. Oxford: Clarendon Press.

Brunett, A. (1999). The harvest and the challenge: The ecumenical vocation on the threshold of the third millennium. *One in Christ: A Catholic Ecumenical Review*, **35**(4), 299-312.

Bryant, M. D. (1990). Interfaith encounter and dialogue in a trinitarian perspective. In P. C. Phan (Ed.), *Christianity and the wider ecumenism* (pp. 3-20). New York: Paragon House.

Carmel, A. I. (1968). My chosen people. In B. Dixon (Ed.), *Journeys in belief* (pp. 37-47). London: George Allen and Unwin.

Christian, J. L. (1973). *Philosophy: An introduction to the art of wondering.* San Francisco: Rinehart Press.

Cobb Jr., J. B. (1988). Toward a Christocentric Catholic theology. In L. Swidler (Ed.), *Toward a universal theology of religion* (pp. 86-100). Maryknoll, NY: Orbis Books.

Coff, P. (1989). One heart - monastic experience and interreligious dialogue. In M. D. Bryant & F. Flinn (Eds.), *Interreligious dialogue: Voices from a new frontier* (pp. 207-210). New York: New Era/Paragon House.

Cox, H. (1989). *Many mansions: A Christian's encounter with other faiths.* London: Collins.

Cracknell, K. (1987). Dialogue with new religious movements? In A. R. Brockway & J. P. Rajashekar (Eds.), *New religious movements and the churches* (pp. 157-167). Geneva: WCC Publications.

Crow Jr., P. A. (2000). When the ecumenical vision becomes a vocation. *Mid-Stream: The Ecumencial Movement Today*, **39**(1-2), 89-100.

Crowley, B., & Crowley, E. (1991). *Words of power: Sacred sounds of East & West.* St. Paul, MN: Llewellyn.

Cunningham, S. (1987). A meeting of the minds. In V. R. Mollenkott (Ed.), *Women of faith in dialogue* (pp. 9-16). New York: Crossroad.

DeVito, J. A. (1991). *Human communication: The basic course* (5th ed). New York: Harper Collins.

Dhalla, H. B. (1989). Interreligious dialogue: A Zoroastrian perspective. *Dialogue & Alliance*, **3**, 37-44.

Dulles, A. (1992). *The craft of theology: From symbol to system.* New York: Crossroad.

Dunbar, S. D. (1998). The place of interreligious dialogue in the academic study of religion. *Journal of Ecumenical Studies*, **35**(3-4), 455-469.

Festinger, L., Riecken, H. W., & Schachter, S. (1956). *When prophecy fails: A social and psychological study of a modern group that predicted the destruction of the world.* Minneapolis, MN: University of Minnesota Press.

Fredericks, J. L. (1998). Interreligious friendship: A new theological virtue. *Journal of Ecumenical Studies*, **35**(2), 159-174.

Gibran, K. (1979). *The prophet.* London: Heinemann.

Gillen, A. (1987). A rationale for coalition building. In V. R. Mollenkott (Ed.), *Women of faith in dialogue* (pp. 127-142). New York: Crossroad.

Goldsmith, M. (1982). *Islam & Christian witness: Sharing the faith with Muslims.* Downers Grove, IL: InterVarsity Press.

Griffiths, B. (1982). *The marriage of East and West.* London: Collins.

Gruss, E.C. (1979). *We left Jehovah's Witnesses -- a non-prophet organization. With the testimonies of converted Jehovah's Witnesses.* Phillipsburg, NJ: Presbyterian and Reformed Publishing.

Hall, M. (1987). Ecumenics and interfaith dialogue: An interfaith methodology. *Current Dialogue*, **13**, 28-31.

Hesselgrave, D. J. (1978). Interreligious dialogue - biblical and contemporary perspectives. In D. J. Hesselgrave (Ed.), *Theology and mission* (pp. 227-240). Grand Rapids, MI: Baker Book House.

Hunt, A. D. (1975). *Christ and the world's religions.* Adelaide: Christian Life Curriculum.

Hwang, P. H. (1989). Interreligious dialogue: Its reasons, attitudes & necessary assumptions. *Dialogue & Alliance*, **3**, 5-15.

Jochim, C. (1995). The contemporary Confucian-Christian encounter: Interreligious or intrareligious dialogue? *Journal of Ecumenical Studies*, **32**(1), 35-62.

Keating, T. (1993). An experience of interreligious dialogue. In J. D. Beversluis (Ed.), *A sourcebook for the community of religions* (pp. 106-108). Chicago: The Council for a Parliament of the World's Religions.

King, S. B. (1990). Toward a Buddhist model of interreligious dialogue. *Buddhist-Christian Studies*, **10**, 121-126.

King, U. (1998). Feminism: The missing dimension in the dialogue of religions. In J. D. May (Ed.), *Pluralism and the religions: The theological and political dimensions* (pp. 40-55). London: Cassell.

Klenicki, L. (1984). Jewish-Christian dialogue. Jewish view. In L. Klenicki & G. Wigoder (Eds.), *A dictionary of the Jewish-Christian dialogue* (pp. 100-103). New York: Paulist Press.

Kozlovic, A. K. (2001). Who should be allowed to participate in official interreligious dialogues? A review of issues. *Marburg Journal of Religion*, **6**(2), 1-11. [http://www.uni-marburg.de/religionswissenschaft/journal/mjr/kozlovic. html].

Kozlovic, A. K. (2002). Three tactics for encouraging newer faiths to participate in interreligious dialoguing. *Quodlibet: Online Journal of Christian Theology and Philosophy*, **4**(2-3), 1-9. [http://www.quodlibet.net/kozlovic-dialogue. shtml].

Kozlovic, A. K. (2003). A human communication approach to interreligious dialogue. *Australian Religion Studies Review*, **16**(1), 49-74.

Krieger, D. J. (1993). Communication theory and interreligious dialogue. *Journal of Ecumenical Studies*, **30**(3-4), 331-353.

Kung, H. (1988). What is true religion? Toward an ecumenical criteriology. In L. Swidler (Ed.), *Toward a universal theology of religion* (pp. 231-250). Maryknoll, NY: Orbis Books.

Lee, S. S. (1991). An educational perspective on interreligious dialogue: a Jewish view. *Religious Education*, **86**(2), 184-196.

Lochhead, D. (1988). *The dialogical imperative: A Christian reflection on interfaith encounter*. London: SCM Press.

Melton, J. G. (2000). Emerging religious movements in North America: Some missiological reflections. *Missiology: An International Review*, **28**(1), 85-98.

Meyer, H. (1991). Dialogue, bilateral. In N. Lossky, J. M. Bonino, J. Pobee, T. Stransky, G. Wainwright & P. Webb (Eds.), *Dictionary of the ecumenical movement* (pp. 280-281). Geneva: WCC Publications.

Mitra, K. (1986). Exploring the possibility of Hindu-Muslim dialogue. In L. Swidler (Ed.), *Religious liberty and human rights in nations and in religions* (pp. 109-123). Philadelphia: Ecumenical Press.

Mitri, T. (1995). Patient dialogue, urgent dialogue. *Current Dialogue*, **28**, 21-26.

Mojzes, P. (1978). The current status of the Christian-Marxist dialogue and suggested guidelines for conducting dialogue. In P. Mojzes (Ed.), *Varieties of Christian-Marxist dialogue* (pp. 3-14). Philadelphia: The Ecumenical Press.

Mojzes, P. (1989a). The what and the how of dialogue. In M. D. Bryant & F. Flinn (Eds.), *Interreligious dialogue: Voices from a new frontier* (pp. 199-206). New York: New Era/Paragon House.

Mojzes, P. (1989b). Universality and uniqueness in the context of religious pluralism: An introduction. *Journal of Ecumenical Studies*, **26**(1), 1-7.

Mollenkott, V. R. (1987). An evangelical perspective on interreligious dialogue. In V. R. Mollenkott (Ed.), *Women of faith in dialogue* (pp. 61-73). New York: Crossroad.

Moss, L., & Chryssides, G. (1986). Patronage or propaganda in interreligious dialog. *Update: A Quarterly Journal of New Religious Movements*, **10**(1), 10-14.

Mulder, D. C. (1989). Dialogue and syncretism: Some concluding observations. In J. Gort, H. Vroom, R. Fernhout & A. Wessels (Eds.), *Dialogue and syncretism: An interdisciplinary approach* (pp. 203-211). Grand Rapids, MI: William B. Eerdmans.

Murphy, F. J. (1978). Milestones of Christian-Marxist dialogue in France. In P. Mojzes (Ed.), *Varieties of Christian-Marxist dialogue* (pp. 139-151). Philadelphia: The Ecumenical Press.

Narchison, J. R. (1998). Theological education for pluralism in India. In J. D. May (Ed.), *Pluralism and the religions: The theological and political dimensions* (pp. 59-74). London: Cassell.

Newman, J. (1982). *Foundations of religious tolerance*. Toronto: University of Toronto Press.

O'Neill, M. (1990). *Women speaking, women listening: Women in interreligious dialogue*. Maryknoll, NY: Orbis Books.

Panikkar, R. (1975). Editorial: Inter-religious dialogue: Some principles. *Journal of Ecumenical Studies*, **12**(3), 407-409.

Pereira, A. J. (1987). Catholic-Marxist dialogue in Budapest. *Vidyajyoti Journal of Theological Reflection*, **51**(6), 264-276.

Peters, T. (1986). A Christian theology of interreligious dialogue. *The Christian Century*, **103**(30), 883-885.

Pogrebin, L. C., & Hutchinson, E. O. (1994). A dialogue on Black-Jewish relations. In F. L. Pincus & H. J. Ehrlich (Eds.), *Race and ethnic conflict: Contending views on prejudice, discrimination, and ethnoviolence* (pp. 219-226). Boulder: Westview Press.

Pye, M. (2001). The study of religions and the dialogue of religions (Shukyogaku to shukyotaiwa). *Marburg Journal of Religion*, **6**(2), 1-6. [http://www.uni-marburg.de/religionswissenschaft/journal/mjr/kyoto.html].

Richard, L. (1981). *What are they saying about Christ and world religions?* New York: Paulist Press.

Saliba, J. A. (1993). Dialogue with the new religious movements: Issues and prospects. *Journal of Ecumenical Studies*, **30**(1), 51-80.

Samartha, S. J. (1981). *Courage for dialogue: Ecumenical issues in inter-religious relationships*. Geneva: World Council of Churches.

Sandidge, J. L. (1992). Dialogue, Roman Catholic and Classical Pentecostal. In S. M. Burgess, G. B. McGee & P. H. Alexander (Eds.), *Dictionary of Pentecostal and Charismatic movements* (pp. 240-244). Grand Rapids, MI: Regency/Zondervan.

Shah, I. (1973). *Tales of the Dervishes: Teaching-stories of the Sufi masters over the past thousand years. Selected from the Sufi classics, from oral tradition, from unpublished manuscripts and schools of Sufi teaching in many countries.* St. Albans: Panther Books.

Shapiro, R. M. (1989). Moving the fence: One Rabbi's view of interreligious dialogue. In M. D. Bryant & F. Flinn (Eds.), *Interreligious dialogue: Voices from a new frontier* (pp. 31-40). New York: New Era/Paragon House.

Sharma, A. (1998). Towards a theory of dialogue. *Current Dialogue*, **32**, 36-38.

Sharpe, E. J. (1977). *Faith meets faith: Some Christian attitudes to Hinduism in the nineteenth and twentieth centuries.* London: SCM Press.

Sharpe, E. J. (1992). The limits of interreligious dialogue. *Mission Studies: Journal of the International Association for Mission Studies*, **9**(2), 228-235.

Sheen, J. (1994). Interfaith initiatives and the preparation of a world report on freedom of thought, conscience and religion or belief. *Australian Religion Studies Review*, **7**(1), 16-21.

Smith, J. I. (1991). Globalization in theological education: implications for interreligious dialogue and ecumenical understanding. *Quarterly Review: A Scholarly Journal for Reflection on Ministry*, **11**(2), 61-75.

Solomon, N. (1991). Themes in Christian-Jewish relations. In L. Klenicki (Ed.), *Toward a theological encounter: Jewish understandings of Christianity* (pp. 16-42). New York: Paulist Press.

Streiker, L. D. (1978). *The cults are coming!* Nashville: Abingdon.

Suchocki, M. H. (1987). In search of justice: Religious pluralism from a feminist perspective. In J. Hick & P. F. Knitter (Eds.), *The myth of Christian uniqueness: Toward a pluralistic theology of religions* (pp. 149-161). Maryknoll, NY: Orbis Books.

Swearer, D. K. (1977). *Dialogue: The key to understanding other religions.* Philadelphia: The Westminster Press.

Swidler, L. (1983). The dialogue decalogue: Ground rules for interreligious dialogue. *Journal of Ecumenical Studies*, **20**(1), 1-4.

Swidler, L. (Ed.). (1988a). *Toward a universal theology of religion.* Maryknoll, NY: Orbis Books.

Swidler, L. (1988b). Preconference paper: Interreligious and interideological dialogue: The matrix for all systematic reflection today. In L. Swidler (Ed.), *Toward a universal theology of religion* (pp. 5-50). Maryknoll, NY: Orbis Books.

Swidler, L. (1990). *After the absolute: The dialogical future of religious reflection.* Minneapolis: Fortress Press.

Thangaraj, M. T. (1991). Toward a dialogical theology of mission. In S. G. Davaney (Ed.), *Theology at the end of modernity: Essays in honor of Gordon D. Kaufman* (pp. 161-176). Philadelphia: Trinity Press International.

Tracy, D. (1990). *Dialogue with the other: The inter-religious dialogue.* Louvain: Peeters Press.

Tracy, D. (1994/5). Roman Catholic identity amid the ecumenical dialogue. In J. H. Provost & K. Walf (Eds.), *Catholic identity* (pp. 109-117). London: SCM Press.

Traer, R. (1993). Religious freedom. In J. D. Beversluis (Ed.), *A sourcebook for the community of religions* (pp. 114-115). Chicago: The Council for a Parliament of the World's Religions.

Weinstein, M. (1991). *Positive magic: Occult self-help* (rev. ed.). Custer, WA: Phoenix.

Williamson, J. B., Karp, D. A., & Dalphin, J. R. (1977). *The research craft: An introduction to social science methods.* Boston: Little, Brown and Company.

First published in Marburg Journal of Religion

****

4.12 A Theology of Technology: Raising the Theological Questions

Written Scott Rodin, Manfred Brauch, Marsha Brown-Woodard, Donna Hailson, Ron Sider, and Phil Ellmore

http://www.ebts.edu/theologyoftechnology.htm

The Revolution that is E-Learning

E-learning - schooling via electronic, informational technology - is revolutionizing the field of education, dramatically altering the roles of teachers, students, and educational institutions.

Witness what is or what may soon be:

Human educators replaced by software-based simulated teachers. Paper documents replaced by voice-activated tablet-like computers. Pen to paper notebooks replaced by online notebooks. Number 2-penciled exams replaced by electronic exams and human graders replaced by e-raters, essay-grading software.

At the time of this writing, teachers and students already participate in cyber field trips visiting distant sites through the use of technology. They engage in videoconferencing, consult searchable databases, and check on homework, test scores and the latest news via class websites. Students receive counsel from virtual mentors, unravel virtual mysteries via computer simulations, self-fashion a host of virtual identities, and role-play in ever-changing virtual cityscapes and communities.

Following graduation, these individuals will then go on to serve in ministry settings where the uncharted 'wired world' of informational technology is revolutionizing everything from Sunday worship services to Bible translation to Christian entertainment.

In Dallas, Texas, 8,200 congregants can be accommodated in the 900 by 900-foot sanctuary of the Potter's House. The facility is larger than two football fields combined. An overflow area holds another 3,500 people. "Within the sanctuary, 200 pews provide power and data terminals so worshipers can download sermon notes, PowerPoint presentations, and Bible passages. Altar attendants armed with personal digital assistants [like Palm Pilots and Pocket PCs] collect prayer needs and new-member data to download into the church server." Two 26 by 20 foot digital video projectors anchor the 150-foot stage where the pastor speaks to his congregation. The sermon is translated via wireless headphones into one of six languages.

As for other churches: according to *Christianity Today,* "about 60 percent have developed websites in the last three years" but most of these "are little more than glorified maps listing driving directions and service times." This situation is changing, however - and rapidly. Many churches are "starting to recognize the Web's potential to streamline office work and provide up-to-date information to large numbers of people." Some of these sites are now beginning to give high priority to developing youth materials for online distribution. Weekly Bible study materials, interactive games, chat rooms and quizzes about Bible passages are popping up on church websites around the country.

According to *Wired Churches, Wired Temples: Taking Congregations and Missions into Cyberspace,* which contains the results of a 1,300-congregation survey conducted by the Pew Internet and American Life Project, a 'broad scope' of online activities is already present in American congregational life. "Homilies, maps and prayer requests are posted, worship services are Webcast, new members recruited, college-level theology courses offered, reports from mission fields (one from Siberia!) filed, online gatherings for young people hosted, and homework assigned for confirmation classes. Some congregations have 'Ask the Pastor' e-mail services. Others have a FAQ (Frequently Asked Questions) page on their Web site."

Those who wish to forego or supplement a visit to the local brick and mortar church are now opting to go online - on the computer - to visit gospelcom.net, an alliance of more than 300 Christian ministries proclaiming the gospel of Christ in cyberspace to more than 219 nations and territories. At that website, one can be e-vangelized (hear the gospel or read the gospel online). One can also participate in Christian e-commerce; consult searchable Bibles and subject directories; engage in online devotions and Bible studies; and review parenting tips and other online guidance for life's challenges.

For the field missionary, it is also a whole new world. An article in the February 10, 2001 issue of *Christianity Today* contrasts how different ministry is for today's Wycliffe Bible Translators from what it would have been for their counterparts 50 or even 20 years ago.

Today, missionaries have access to email so communication that once took two to five months now takes minutes and hours. 'Translators' Workplace,' a CD-Rom with more than 200 resource books and 37 versions of the Bible now replaces a bulky library.

"'Shoebox,' a software program saves, translators years of time by cataloging and cross-referencing their lexical, grammatical and cultural notes." The "Acoustic Speed Analyzer Program," another software program, records sound waves in exquisite detail. It even has a function that displays the mouth position a speaker must create to produce specific vocalizations. What once required mailing cassettes to sound laboratories back in the US can now be completed in minutes." "CARLA," which stands for 'Computer Assisted Related Language Adaptation,' "automatically translates documents among a family of dialects." And Personal Digital Assistants such as pocket PCs and Palm Pilots, allow translators to call up Scripture while in the field and to reference it with those they are seeking to reach with the gospel.

Technology is also combining with theology to produce a new generation of theme park. Witness the Holy Land Experience, a $16-million, 15-acre 'living Biblical museum,' located between Walt Disney World and Universal Studios which welcomed nearly 20,000 visitors in its opening week in February 2001.

The theme park is described in a press kit as 'a wholesome, family-oriented educational and entertainment facility . . . [recreating] the city of Jerusalem and its religious importance between the years 1450 BC and 66 AD (through the Old and New Testaments, from Genesis through Revelation).'

Via replicated landscapes and architecture, dramatic enactments, multi-media presentations and more, visitors are transported to a bustling first-century Jerusalem street market; a wilderness tabernacle replete with 'the Shekinah Glory effect;' the sun-scorched Qumran caves; the Via Dolorosa (the street that Jesus trod on his way to Calvary); and the tranquil garden tomb wherein Jesus was buried. Off a Plaza of the Nations is also a six-story-high Temple of the Great King, where - in the 'Theater of Life' - guests view a film ('The Seed of Promise') which depicts everything from the Creation to the Second Coming of Christ. From there, it is on to the world's largest indoor model of first-century Jerusalem and then, perhaps, to the 120-seat buffeteria -- the Arabian-themed Oasis Palms Café -- where one can order a 'Thirsty Camel Cooler' or a 'Goliath Burger.'

Some critics view this venture as a 'Disneyfication' of the biblical message while others suggest that such an experience may generate interest in Christianity and, in doing so, inspire worship of the God of Christianity.

Such innovations on the web, in the church, on the mission field, and in popular culture demand that contemporary seminary educators address the potential impact of technology not only in the brick and mortar classroom and the virtual learning environment but in the wider world of ministry as well. Web and e-wire presuppositions and values necessitate a deciphering and decoding of the morality of technology and the nature of self-identity and interrelationships suggested by this technology. Because the computer has become more than 'tool and mirror,' because there are serious challenges to face in the realm of the virtual - in the e-world -- a theology of technology is essential.

As Brent Waters, of the University of Redlands, reminds us: the Christian theological perspective is crucial in the contemporary environment for "when knowledge is removed from an interpretive framework and technical means are confused with moral ends, the future is devoid of wisdom that goes beyond survival for its own sake. In a world being formed in a scientific and technological image, we need to preserve a theocentric perspective . . . At the very least, the church needs to consider carefully the scientific and theological contours of our present age, so that it may order its service of God in a faithful manner."

Those committed to analyzing the theology of technology are finding that constant innovation, instantaneous access to information, immediate gratification, entertainment and efficiency are the life-shaping values of technic ("the whole cluster of purposes, assumptions, and practices revolving around technology").

In the catalogue of technic, "knowledge is numerical, i.e., *quantitative* and quantifiable" and people and the products of their labor tend to be depersonalized. Technic lifts "*process* over *substance*" and asserts that "nothing can be known in the sense of 'once and for all.'" "Real useful knowledge," is said to reside in "*experts* or 'expert systems.'" Technic evidences a trend toward a "*meritocracy* based on *symbolic/analytic*, i.e., technical skills" so that "a person's worth is related directly (even solely) to the economic value of his specialized technical proficiencies and job success. The conviction that human beings share a common condition in their relationship to their Creator no longer carries much force."

The Fading Line Between Humanity and Technology

The ethical dimensions involved in the creation of new technologies plead for attention when one reads the disturbing musings of Ray Kurzweil, prolific inventor and author of *The Age of Spiritual Machines*. Kurzweil calls upon his readers to "imagine a world where the difference between man and machine blurs, where the line between humanity and technology fades, and where the soul and the silicon chip unite."

He writes: "Neuroscientists from the University of California at San Diego have found what they call the God module, a tiny locus of nerve cells in the frontal lobe that appears to be activated during religious experiences . . . When we can determine the neurological correlates of the variety of spiritual experiences that our species is capable of, we are likely to be able to enhance these experiences in the same way that we enhance other human experiences."

Before 2030, Kurzweil predicts, machines will be produced which will proclaim Descartes' dictum, "I think, therefore I am." These "[m]achines, derived from human thinking and surpassing humans in their capacity for experience, will claim to be conscious, and thus to be spiritual . . . They will believe that they have spiritual experiences. They will be convinced that these experiences are meaningful . . . Twenty-first century machines - based on the design of human thinking - will do as their human progenitors have done - going to real and virtual houses of worship, meditating, praying, and transcending - to connect with their spiritual dimensions."

And, he adds, "the technology to communicate between the electronic world and the human neural world is already taking shape. So we will be able to directly feed streams of data to our neural pathways. Unfortunately, that doesn't mean we can directly download knowledge . . . knowledge involves millions of connections; so our knowledge structures are not localized. Nature didn't provide a direct pathway to adjust all those connections, other than the slow conventional way."

Looking ahead to 2009, Kurzweil predicts that computers will play a central role in all facets of education:

> [At that time] the majority of reading is done on displays, although the 'installed base' of paper documents is still formidable. The generation of paper documents is dwindling, however, as the books and papers of largely twentieth-century vintage are being rapidly scanned and stored. Documents circa 2009 routinely include embedded moving images and sounds. Students of all ages typically have a computer of their own, which is a thin tabletlike device weighing under a pound with a very high resolution display suitable for reading. Students interact with their computers primarily by voice and by pointing with a device that looks like a pencil. Keyboards still exist, but most textual language is created by speaking. Learning materials are accessed through wireless communication. Intelligent courseware has emerged as a common means of learning . . . [and distance learning] is commonplace.

By 2019, he asserts, most learning will be accomplished through software-based simulated teachers or, if the educator is human, he or she will be accessed at a distance and will have more the role of mentor or counselor rather than traditional teacher. By 2029, Kurzweil suggests humans will learn primarily via virtual teachers and widely available neural implants which will be employed to improve memory and perception as, he believes, it still will not be possible, at that time, to download knowledge directly.

Thus, in Kurzweil's catalogue of present and approaching 'technic,' the attainment of knowledge appears to be configured as connections and structures. Spirituality then is simply a matter of mechanics, of inserting the right program or locating the right nerves to tease. Meaning is finally an 'installed base' wherein the soul and the silicon chip do indeed unite, where the line between humanity and technology does indeed fade.

The Major New Challenge to Theology

The "major new challenge to theology," according to David H. Hopper, author of *Technology, Theology, and the Idea of Progress*, is the potential "ability of technology to offer and inculcate another definition of the human." David O. Berger goes a step beyond Hopper to perceive an even greater threat in the potential for technology "to replace our faith in and need for God with a neverending stream of goods, cures, conveniences, and entertaining diversions."

David J. Wood echoes Marshall McLuhan's concerns over "the discarnate life" of the human being who, via electronic technology, is "freed from flesh" and "capable of instant transportation anywhere." Wood sees a need for individuals to gather "in time and space in order to pray, sing, confess, pass the peace, break bread, preach, baptize, and read Scripture." This incarnational engagement, Wood asserts, is "the witness we [Christians] bring to a world captivated as it is with the discarnate life."

The implications for the body, mind and spirit carried within the 'discarnate life' is also a concern for those within the fields of psychology and sociology who worry about the "eroding boundaries between the real and the virtual, the animate and the inanimate, the unitary and the multiple self." These perspectives further help to inform some of the questions that must be addressed by contemporary theologians.

From the Vantage Points of Psychology and Sociology

In *Life on the Screen: Identity in the Age of the Internet,* Sherry Turkle, of the Massachusetts Institute of Technology, observes the world being formed by 'online life' from the vantage point of psychology and sociology. Her particular concern centers on what happens to human identity in the new culture of simulation and downloads.

While appreciating the computer as 'tool' -- in such functions as account-keeping and communications - and 'mirror' - in its role as a medium on which to project ideas and fantasies - Turkle expresses some worries over what she identifies as 'eroding boundaries' in cyberspace. She writes:

> We are learning to live in virtual worlds. We may find ourselves alone as we navigate virtual oceans, unravel virtual mysteries, and engineer virtual skyscrapers. But increasingly, when we step through the looking glass, other people are there as well . . . In cyberspace, we can talk, exchange ideas, and assume personae of our own creation. We have the opportunity to build new kinds of communities, virtual communities, in which we participate with people from all over the world, people with whom we converse daily, people with whom we may have fairly intimate relationships but whom we may never physically meet . . . [We are in the business of] constructing identity in the culture of simulation . . . [wherein we find] eroding boundaries between the real and the virtual, the animate and the inanimate, the unitary and the multiple self . . . [and all of this is evidence of] fundamental shifts in the way we create and experience human identity.

These new 'postmodern' ideas on the nature of human identity, she argues, are characterized by such terms as "'decentered,' 'fluid,' 'nonlinear,' and 'opaque.'" They contrast with modernism, the "world-view that has dominated Western thinking since the Enlightenment. The modernist view of reality is characterized by such terms as 'linear,' 'logical,' 'hierarchical,' and by having 'depths' that can be plumbed and understood . . . The modernist computational aesthetic promised to explain and unpack, to reduce and clarify." Turkle asserts that this "culture of calculation" is being replaced by a "culture of simulation" which is concerned not with "calculation and rules" but with "simulation, navigation, and interaction."

She continues:

> When we step through the screen into virtual communities, we reconstruct our identities on the other side of the looking glass. This reconstruction is our cultural work in progress . . . At the same time that we are learning to see ourselves as plugged-in technobodies, we are redescribing our politics and economic life in a language that is resonant with a particular form of machine intelligence. In government, business, and industry, there is much talk of distributed, parallel, and emergent organizations, whose architecture mirrors that of computer systems. This utopian discourse about decentralization has come into vogue at the same time that society has largely become increasingly fragmented. Many of the institutions that used to bring people together - a main street, a union hall, a town meeting - no longer work as before. Many people spend most of their days alone at the screen of a television or a computer. Meanwhile, social beings that we are, we are trying (as Marshall McLuhan said) to retribalize. And the computer is playing a central role . . . Our rootedness to place has attenuated. These shifts raise many questions. What will computer-mediated communication do to our commitment to other people? Will it satisfy our needs for connection and social participation, or will it further undermine fragile relationships? What kind of responsibility and accountability will we assume for our virtual actions? . . . The Internet has become a significant social laboratory for experimenting with the constructions and reconstructions of self that characterize postmodern life. In its virtual reality, we self-fashion and self-create. What kinds of personae do we make? What relation do these have to what we have traditionally thought of as the 'whole' person? . . . Why are we doing this? Is this a shallow game? . . . an expression of an identity crisis . . . Or are we watching the slow emergence of a new, more multiple style of thinking about the mind?

In her book, Turkle dissects the psychological and sociological implications of virtual life: how the anonymity of most Multi-User Domains (MUDs) provides room for individuals to express unexplored parts of themselves; how play factors into the building of identity; how virtual experiences may and may not facilitate self-knowledge and personal growth and how the boundaries of role-play may become blurred in the virtual scape. She gives further attention to the issues of intimacy, multiple identities, and on-line gender swapping, netsex, deception, and the loss of the real.

The contemporary theologian will need to unpack these issues as well to develop a theology of technology that considers the implications for the broad categories of self-identity, group identity and institutional identity; the nature of community and interrelationships; the nature of language; the role of image; the reality of reality; and the nature of the human, the machine, and the divine.

Raising the Theological Questions

David O. Berger suggests that there are at least three issues of primary relevance to be considered when seeking to construct a theology of technology. (He cites these along with their related clusters of questions): *1. "Communications technology and the proclaiming of the Word.* Is the visual image so prevalent in modern communications taking precedence over the word? If so, what does that trend entail? Are all and any means of communication suited to and appropriate for the proclamation of the gospel? For religious education? How do we distinguish? How do we judge and choose? . . . *2. Aspects of technic which pose challenges to faith, Biblically based ethical principles, or human relationships and community . . . more attention must be focused on the positivism (paradoxically a kind of secular gnosticism) which often underlies technic.* An example: Given adequate hard data, i.e., quantitative data, and the means for processing and disseminating the information [it is believed by many today] the cognoscenti can resolve virtually any personal, social, or global problem. Surely this prevailing technological mindset has theological ramifications, and it is found in many guises and in many contexts, including church administration. Also, in this regard, computer technology itself raises fundamental questions about what it means to be human. What is thought, and how does it relate to emotions, to beliefs? Is programming common to computers and human beings? How do computers and television affect the intellectual, emotional, and spiritual development? . . . How do modern technologies affect Christian community? *3. Nuts and bolts - the function of technology in theological and religious education . . .* [A]ny curricular planning must consider the significant cultural and theological issues raised by modern technic as well as the use of technologies in the proclamation of the Word and in church polity . . . Finally, the place and function of learning technologies in theological education requires careful, critical attention."

Some additional questions before us are these:

- How does one discern truth and reality in the web-world?
- How does the new technology undermine or enhance our need for relationship and community?
- Are we in danger of replacing character development with virtual identity construction?
- When does role playing in virtual reality cross a line to the substitution of the virtual for the real?
- How does one maintain personal integrity when creating multiple virtual identities?
- How does the sophistication of virtual reality undermine both a belief in truth and an ability to recognize truth?
- How does one sort through the onrush of created and manipulated images?
- How does one handle the juxtaposition of connection online against the increasing personal detachment such connection engenders?
- How can theological educators help their students and the wider Church unpack the potentials and dangers in technology?

As Berger reminds us, one must not take for granted the positive features of technology as it will be tainted by the sin of those who develop and use it. Technology, thus, "requires constant vigilance and prudent decisions in its use. Some contemporary writers, e.g., Jacques Ellul, go one step farther and assert that technic embraces a philosophy inherently inimical to humane and spiritual values. That is, technology is not neutral."

If he is correct and technology is not neutral, the Christian must exercise great caution upon entering the web and must certainly be informed by a solid theology of technology. Such a theology must begin with a consideration of the nature of God and the nature of humankind and must address how the Church should approach technology and how technology may be used to follow after God's purposes and to advance the kingdom of God.

In the following pages, we will be concerned most specifically with beginning to delineate a practical theology of informational technology for instruction. We will begin with a section on theological perspectives and will then provide a list of the shoulds and should nots of technology. Further on, we will explore some of the practical implications and concrete applications of technology in the realm that is theological education.

We do all of this convicted by the knowledge that "in a world being formed in a scientific and technological image, we need to preserve a theocentric perspective" for we believe that the church must "consider carefully the scientific and theological contours of our present age, so that it may order its service of God in a faithful manner."

Raising the Theological Questions | Creating a Theological Context | Living out the Practical Implications | Invitation and Contact Information

---

A Theology of Technology: Creating the Theological Context

Truth and Knowing

Christians confess that God has revealed himself and his purposes in both the world of nature and the history of redemption. Through study of the world of nature, we receive general revelation about God and the marvelously complex world created by God. Through study of the Bible, that discloses the long history of redemption from Eden to the eschaton, we receive God's special revelation.

Both forms of revelation offer important knowledge and information about God. But the triune God, in whose image persons are made, longs for us not only to know about God, but also to be in right personal relationship with God. And God has revealed himself to us in Jesus Christ, that in Christ we might have personal, intimate and sufficient knowledge of and fellowship with God. This fellowship is the fruit of the work of the Holy Spirit who transforms us as receivers of the revelation of God. That is, we are changed that we might hear and see what can only be heard with new ears and seen with new eyes. This work of transformation within us is an act of grace that enables us to participate in the intimate relationship with God for which we were created and redeemed.

The truth of who we are lies in the greater truth of who our Creator is and why we are the product of his creative work. Therefore, 'knowing the truth' is only possible within the redeemed relationship we have with God in Jesus Christ. Knowing only the facts, the words, the rituals, the symbols and even the experiences of religion is not the same as this personal encounter and intimate relationship made possible by the Incarnation, life, death and resurrection of Jesus Christ.

Therefore, in the field of Christian ethics, including our use of information technology, it is critical that we understand the difference between knowledge about another and a personal encounter that opens us up to another, whether that be in our relationship with God ourselves, our neighbor or the wider creation. Facts, words, symbols and even experiences that remain detached from true relationship are never substitutes for the personal encounter with God in Jesus Christ. Personal encounter is necessary for real knowledge and for real truth to be found.

Jesus proclaimed himself to be *the way* to the Father, and therefore as the unique revelation of the heart of God and God's intention for his creation. Jesus proclaimed himself to be *the truth,* and therefore the source of knowledge of the will of God in and for our lives. And Jesus proclaimed himself to be *the life,* and therefore the creator, sustainer and definer of the quality of life intended for us from creation.

In all of our pursuits for clarity and direction in ethical matters, we must seek our answers within an ongoing encounter with the One who is the way, the truth and the life. We begin in faith, and seek after understanding. We begin with what is known and with what is certain in Jesus Christ and move from there to seek answers to the contemporary issues of our day. We must always make this right start if we are to discern truly God's guidance for these times.

The *Imago Dei* in Creation

Scripture affirms God as Creator of all that is. It also affirms that creation has great value on the basis of the divine pronouncement, "behold, it is very good!" (Genesis 1:31).

Being created in the image of a Trinitarian God means immediately that we are created in and for relationship. There are four levels of relationship that define us as God's creation. First is our relationship with God that includes prayer, worship, obedience, piety, holiness, reverence and rest. Second is our relationship with ourselves which includes physical and emotional health, self-control, and self-worth. Third is our relationship with our neighbor, which includes our family, marriage, and friendships and the qualities of sacrificial love, reconciliation, genuine fellowship, accountability, compassion, advocacy and presence. Fourth is our relationship to creation itself which includes environmental care and the responsible use of our time, talents and treasures. All four areas of our created reality are pronounced 'good' at creation.

Humanity, created in the image of the Creator God, has been entrusted with the mission of exercising responsible, creative stewardship over and within the creation. In this way we image God's creativity. This stewardship guides and limits all we do including our accumulation of scientific knowledge through the exploration 'of the things that have been made'. This includes our pursuit of and use of knowledge in the development of information technology. The limitations of stewardship require that we use all that is discovered, including information technology, to support, strengthen, and enrich human life and to continue to shape the world around us in keeping with the divine purpose for human wholeness and the goodness of the entire creation.

This human activity and creativity is always defined by the One in whose image we have been created. Therefore it is not a detached, independent creativity that can use any measure of success or 'common good' as a gauge for its creative work. Instead, our creativity and exploration are defined by our Creator. The goodness of what we create is determined by its ability to bring glory to our Creator. Why would we choose to create if not to glorify the One who created us and gave to us the skills, intelligence and will to create as a reflection of our Creator God?

Because all of our creative work is to glorify God, there is a spiritual dimension to all we create. Can then any product of our creative work be truly neutral? If in obedience to God we create to bring Him glory, doesn't our work have this positive spiritual dimension? If, under the influence of sin, we create to bring dishonor to God, to destroy His kingdom and injure our neighbor, our world or ourselves, then won't what we create also embody this negative spirituality? Again the value of our creative work is determined by our Creator who created us and all the cosmos for a spiritual purpose, namely, for relationship with God and therefore,for the glory of God. For this reason we must understand that there is a spiritual ethos to the works of our hands, either for evil or for good.

Our creative work in information technology then is guided, directed, and modified by the creativity of the God we know in Jesus Christ. The ethics of creativity, of innovation and technological advance must be guided by the creative activity we find in this God. Therefore it must spring from right motives, move ahead with a godly purpose and be set within the limits of holiness and a commitment to the building up of the kingdom of God.

The *Imago Dei* as Fallen

All four relationships were also broken in the fall and marred by sin. Scripture affirms that the sin of humanity manifested in the rejection of creaturely limitation and a denial of our dependence upon the sovereign God, results in the distortion of God's good creation at all four levels.

Our relationship with God is broken bringing the sentence of death upon us. Our relationship with ourselves is broken causing us to seek self-worth in alien definitions of success, pleasure, power and dominion. Our relationship with our neighbor is broken breeding hatred, prejudice, and the history of 'man's inhumanity to man.' And the creation itself lies polluted under its inhabitants and the creation "groans in travail" (Romans 8:20-22) longing for its liberation from its bondage to human sin.

These biblical truths reveal that the exercise of responsible stewardship of the created order, when marred by the distorting, twisting reality of sin, fails to accomplish the Creator's good purposes for human wholeness and the shaping of the environment in support of that wholeness. Therefore, the Christian community must always seek to discern how human creativity-including the accumulation of scientific knowledge and its employment in the development of information technology-has been distorted by human sin. It must also discern how the use of the fruits of that creativity have incorporated things which are contrary to God's purposes for human wholeness and the well-being of creation.

Our history on this side of Eden is indelibly marked by our attempted usurpation of the role of God. By trying to play God ourselves, we continually create God in our own image, according to our own likeness. And that always leads us to seek to control, to dominate and exploit. This ambition to dominate and control without the counterbalance of holistic mutuality is what Frederick Ferre′ referred to as the control syndrome. For Ferre′, "The control syndrome is what has brought mankind to its present perilous condition." William Stahl comments,

> "Matching our desire to master nature with our need to master our neighbor, modern society has been built upon economic and political dominance hierarchies which ignore reciprocity and holism, see competition and greed as virtues, countenance limitless exploitation, and are continuously at war or preparing for war."

He concludes, "We have enormous power but very little sense of direction. We are masters without meaning." We have become in Max Weber's words, "Specialists without spirit, sensualists without heart; this nullity imagines that it has attained a level of civilization never before achieved."

The result is the loss of the truth that is only found in Jesus Christ. In this denial of our created reality as God's beloved creatures, and in our rejection of the intimate fellowship that defines this reality, we have "exchanged the truth of God for a lie, and worshiped created things rather than the Creator" (Romans 1:25). Our society bears witness to our propensity for idolmaking. We substitute illusions and idols for reality at all four levels of relationship.

Information technology has, for some, become a powerful new idol. It is the icon of the 'religion' of technological advance. Information technology becomes an idol when it promises power, sovereignty, transformation, advancement and even utopia. This is what Stahl refers to as technological mysticism - the faith in the universal efficacy of technology. For Stahl, technological mysticism 1) is a form of social action, 2) is never a neutral instrumentality, and 3) has a tradition. "Every technology is enmeshed in a web of values... Like a religion, technological mysticism 'binds together' core values into a coherent, if implicit (and often unexamined) set of beliefs and rituals... We increasingly come to identify who we are by and through the machines we use."

Information technology also becomes an idol when it provides pseudo-relationships through virtual experiences and detached encounters that are antithetical to the truth of our existence as God's creation. In this idolatrous form, information technology promises genuine fellowship in its confusion of the exchange of information with the forming of relationships. Whenever our use of information technology takes on this idolatrous form, we know we have forsaken the truth of our existence and exchanged it for a lie that will always fail to satisfy.

In another form, information technology becomes an idol when we see it as a false expression of our freedom. George Grant cautions that modernity has stripped us of orders and guides that defined and limited our understanding and use of freedom. In the past, freedom was measured and defined by these orders, however, "as freedom is the highest term in the modern language, it can no longer be so enfolded. There is therefore no possibility of answering the question, freedom for what purpose?" Stahl comments, "If our freedom has no purpose external to itself, it must of necessity become technique. By understanding the world only as object, something apart from ourselves, we create the necessity for a method by which to know and control it. Our reason becomes instrumental, an account of means rather than ends. To be free in the modern world is therefore to practice technology." He concludes, "We may have freedom. We may have the power and control that technology gives us. But we do not have a system of meaning."

Whether as technological mysticism, as a false sense of relationship or as a usurpation of the sense of genuine freedom, information technology under the influence of sin can take an idolatrous form. Taken to its limits, it will demand our devotion, define our 'reality' and ultimately, lead us away from the one who is the way, the truth and the life.

The *Imago Dei* as Redeemed

Our relationships in all four areas are redeemed in Christ. Christian faith affirms that in the Incarnation-the historical event of Jesus Christ's life, death and resurrection-God has acted to make all things new, to bring about a new creation in which the distortion and brokenness of the old order is overcome, to redeem human life from its bondage to sin, and to liberate the entire creation from its bondage to decay.

The goodness of the Creator's creative work is reaffirmed in the Incarnation. According to Arthur Holmes, "despite the marring effect of evil, nature is not intrinsically evil. If God so values the creation that he gives himself to it in the Incarnation, becoming flesh as a Galilean carpenter, then we too should prize the good possibilities that it holds for human learning and culture and well-being."

The Gospel declares that in Jesus Christ the reign of God-God's sovereignty over and in creation-has broken into the world in a new way in order to reclaim it for the accomplishment of God's created intention. In Christ, we are called and empowered to participate in the embodiment of God's reign in all areas of human life-including the development and use of information technology.

In the work of Jesus Christ our relationships at all four levels have been redeemed and are now given back to us as gifts to be stewarded. Therefore our reality as the body of Christ is to seek wholeness and holiness in all of these areas of our lives. This is the work of the Holy Spirit. The Spirit opens our eyes to see these relationships as they were created to be. We see ourselves as children of the gracious God who brought us back to himself. We see ourselves as God's beloved creation, worthy of loving ourselves as God loves us, and secure in our place in God's creation. We see ourselves as neighbors called to be reconcilers, peacemakers and life-givers to one another. And we see ourselves as caretakers, nurturers and stewards of God's creation for his glory. The Holy Spirit not only opens our eyes to this new reality, but invites and empowers us to participate in the wholeness that is ours in Jesus Christ.

In our creative use of information technology, this relational wholeness must be our end goal and our guiding principle. We must ask about information technology's contributions to improving our ability to create whole, reconciled, holy and edifying relationships in each area. Our theology must ask about information technology's effects on every area of our lives including genuine community, on discipleship, on personal piety, on worship, on human dignity, on creation care, on marriage and family, on obedience, on reconciliation, on caring for the poor, on overcoming sin and on advancing justice.

As creatures created in the image of a Triune God, we must critique any technological 'advance' that diminishes, denies or destroys relational wholeness and holiness at any of these levels. Our ethical response to the use of information technology is an extension of our understanding of who we are as the children of God. It is derived from our understanding of why we were created and what sin has done to everything we are and everything we do. And it is focused on the new creation we have become in Christ.

Words, Images and Embodiment

This emphasis on relational wholeness is especially important in considering how information technology uses words and images. Information technology-as transmitter of information, ideas, beliefs, and values-depends for its validity on the truthfulness of words. Scripture affirms the centrality of the Word in God's relation with the world. It is in and through God's Word-truth itself-that an intelligible world is brought into existence, God's people are sustained and redeemed, and God's purposes for the creation and human community are disclosed. As we accurately retrace the Creator's fingerprints in the world of nature, we acquire incomplete but important truth about the world. Truthful words are essential for human wholeness.

Because sin has marred God's good creation, however, words have the power not only to lift up, heal, build up, encourage, sustain, create, and give life, but also to distort reality, tear down and destroy, divide and demean, debase and wound. The ability to discern what is true, what is *real* becomes increasingly challenging in a sinful world. Words are signifiers, metaphors of our experiences. Indeed, "There is no separation between our experience and our language." The use of words as a means to embody our experiences require that there be not only a signifier, but also that which is signified, and an interpreter. The interpreter is the community whose collective voice gives definition and meaning to that which is signified.

Therefore, according to Robert Bellah, "symbols are neither subjective or objective but relational." The more information technology has the power to offer convincing but distorted and false pictures of reality, the more destructive its potential becomes. And therefore, the more Christians need the communal discernment of the Christian community to help distinguish illusion, however seductive, from truth and reality. This validation of truth that emerges from the Christian community differs fundamentally from the post-modern idea that truth is actualized only and completely in and through the local community. The difference lies in the referent for that validation. For the Christian community, the truth that is validated is mediated to us in Jesus Christ through the Holy Spirit. It is never the truth *of the community,* but always it is God's truth spoken and heard in the community. That this happens, that it is genuinely and actually God's Holy Word that is heard and spoken in the Christian community is accepted by faith.

In postmodern thought, there is no referent for the truth established by the community. It is its own referent, and therefore its truth has no more validity than that of any other community. Yet it is seductively powerful as when the Internet becomes that community that validates what is true, what is real, what is to be believed, and therefore what is to be trusted and followed. In this way, the Internet can become both the signifier and the interpreter, and thus creates its own truth for its followers.

Further, in biblical perspective, God speaks his word and lives his word. Jesus is God's word spoken to the world and lived in the world. For human wholeness to be sustained, both the spoken and the embodied word are essential. Human communication, the lifeblood of wholeness-in-community-and consequently the use of information technology, must be characterized by both of these dimensions of the word.

Through an abuse of information technology we empower words and symbols beyond their logical limits. We allow disembodied words to take the place of true relationships. We have, according to Stahl, "become blind to our own metaphors, confusing our figures of speech with the ways things are." As a result, we allow detached experiences fueled by words and illusions to substitute for genuine encounter and fellowship - or conflict. We can fight battles, have sex, travel the world, propagate hatred, lie, evangelize, live out fantasies, search for a church, date, buy and sell, marry and be eulogized without ever encountering another person face-to-face. Words, images and illusions are the media. Where and when such words, images and illusions deny our created reality and exchange genuine relationships with disembodied data and digital images, we have again created our own gods in our own images.

The positive side of this is found in the employment of information technology for the furthering of the kingdom of God, kingdom values and the strengthening of the relationships we have with God, ourselves, our neighbor and creation. Where information technology strengthens relationships, furthers meaningful dialogue, increases understanding, facilitates reconciliation, promotes healing and justice, spreads the gospel, builds disciples, educates, motivates, and enables the work of God's people and the ministry of the Holy Spirit, then it is to be valued and employed. However, even here we must never confuse the words for genuine experience. We were created for relationships, which are experiential in their very nature. The exchange of words and metaphors without the interpretation of human experience in community will never lead us to truth, to genuine fellowship, to reconciliation and to the values of the kingdom of God. If this clear warning is heeded, information technology can be an effective tool for the Christian and for the church.

The consideration of the use of any form of information technology must acknowledge both the creativity of the human spirit which is a reflection of our creation in the image of a creating God, and the devastating effects of sin that mar that image at every level of human existence. Therefore, our ethics must start with an understanding of God, humanity, sin and redemption that have been revealed to us uniquely and sufficiently through God's self-revelation to us in Jesus Christ. From there we must consider the effect of any information technology on the Spirit's ongoing work of redemption, reconciliation and restoration of our lives at all four levels of relationship. Where information technology supports, encourages, enables, furthers and enhances that work, it should be celebrated as another tool to be used for the glory of God. Where information technology is used in any way against the movement and work of the Spirit for the upbuilding of the body of Christ, the advancement of the gospel and the furthering of the kingdom of God, it must be rejected and, where possible, converted into a tool for God's good purposes.

Raising the Theological Questions | Creating a Theological Context | Living out the Practical Implications | Invitation and Contact Information

---

Living out the Practical Implications

A central understanding for Eastern Seminary is the essential nature of personal relationships and wholeness within those relationships. This includes relationships with God, self, others, the created order. Therefore our use of information technology for teaching and learning must seek to affirm and enhance these relationships. The use of information technology in our classrooms and other ministry settings should be encouraged when it:

- Enables people to communicate more effectively.
- Facilitates a deeper knowledge of God, self, others, and creation.
- Builds community between teachers and learners.
- Democratizes power by allowing equal access to information and knowledge.
- Connects teachers and learners to the wider Christian community.
- Increases awareness of the multiplicity of contexts for ministry.
- Helps teachers and learners to cross cultural barriers and create better understanding of other cultural distinctives.
- Helps teachers and learners to reach their full potentials.
- Assists in creating personal and community balance.
- Reflects godly stewardship in the appropriate acquisition and use of information technology.

These assume that information technology can prove to be a positive force for theological education and practical ministry. But these same uses, in certain circumstances, might actually encourage the relational separation we wish to avoid. Because such use may separate people from genuine community, the use of information technology in our classrooms and other ministry settings should be discouraged when it:

- Isolates people and/or serves as a substitute for relationships.
- Replaces reality with pseudo-reality.
- Becomes an end in itself.
- Promotes dependency.
- Abandons previously revealed and accepted truth simply because it is not new nor as powerful.
- Centralizes power by hindering equal access to information and knowledge.
- Fosters a pursuit of the "latest and greatest" technology over the pursuit of truth.

- Manipulates people through powerful appeal to the emotions through a manufactured sensory experience while abandoning authentic spiritual encounter.

At this point in the Seminary's understanding of information technology this list of 'shoulds' and 'should nots' creates more questions than answers as to the actual use of information technology for teaching, learning, and ministry. It seems clear that certain uses can easily enhance relational wholeness. Such uses include:

- web-based classrooms, 'chatrooms' or 'bulletin boards' to stimulate teacher-learner interaction;
- posting of internet links to pertinent information;
- use of multiple presentation styles; electronic submission of course work through e-mail;
- inclusion of streaming video;
- posting course notes on a class web-site;
- use of the web to explore otherwise inaccessible material;
- real-time video conferences with authors, theologians, missionaries, others;
- Web-based research.

However, for a teacher, learner, or congregation member who is predisposed to avoid genuine community these technologies can easily become a means to isolation. This is not a new problem caused solely by an increased use of information technology, but it will require a new type of awareness. Will we be able to recognize this danger as it occurs and will we be equipped to appropriately address it when it does?

In addition, classes and individuals can now take virtual tours both in and out of the classroom. Imagine historical tours of biblical communities, up-to-date information from archeological expeditions, experiences of various styles of worship, the chance to 'talk' with figures like Martin Luther King, Jr. and St. Augustine. The possibilities for such technology are staggering.

But, who will program the Jesus of virtual reality? How will a virtual John Calvin respond to the astute theological student's question? The writings and movies of 'historical fiction' are already blurring history. How will things become in virtual reality and how will our classrooms and churches be equipped to help Christians distinguish 'real' reality from its 'virtual' counterpart?

Managing and interpreting information will take on new importance in an information technology-rich classroom environment. Instructors, eager to broaden and enhance communication with and among his/her students through extensive use of e-mail, chatrooms, may find themselves with far too much information to which to respond. Such an information flow will require teachers and learners to readjust their thinking about writing and responding to writing.

Interpreting data will also take on new meaning. Formally, information was generally made available through the filter of publishers, pastors, and educators. In a more or less agreed-upon exchange, it was expected that these trusted sources would provide accurate, high quality information to the public. In an information technology-rich world, individuals have the opportunity and are expected to seek their own information through on-line resources and other media. New skills are needed to discern what constitutes quality material.

As a seminary, we are committed to the value and worth of each individual and as such we need to be careful that our use of information technology does not create a type of caste system with a clear division between those who have access and those who do not. If classes are going to require Internet research, it is necessary that each student in that class have access to the Internet. This issue must go beyond access to include training. Each student must know how to use the necessary technology required to succeed in that class. At its heart, access to information technology is an issue of justice.

In a similar manner, for faculty to teach in this technologically rich environment they must have access to necessary equipment and must be adequately prepared to use that equipment. This includes affiliate and adjunct faculty who may not have the hardware, software, or training needed to incorporate successfully information technology into their class. Enabling this access will, in all likelihood, require additional staff, equipment, and time.

Faculty will be vulnerable to inappropriate critique as they use new technology and students will need to remember not to judge faculty members' subject expertise based on their technological ability.

Where Do We Go From Here?

Our Seminary mission is to prepare and equip students for leadership in the Church. Pastors and church leaders will leave the Seminary and find themselves as messengers of the Gospel in the midst of a technologically-obsessed, fast-paced, ever-changing world. It is essential that their ministry preparation include a familiarity with the promises and dangers of information technology. This knowledge must be informed, at least in part, through the seminary's use of information technology, and may also need to include more intentional work in a variety of classes.

- Pastoral Care classes will need to examine Internet addiction and its destructive effect on individuals and families.
- Theology and Ethics classes will focus on how information technology can increase the level of both good and evil in the world.
- Worship classes will cover the issues surrounding the use of all forms of information technology including presentation software, video, and projection equipment for worship.
- Biblical Studies classes will identify web sites that provide teaching helps for Biblical interpretation and understanding.
- Structure and Context of Ministry courses will include working with a church administration database, and will teach students how to access demographic information to better understand the neighborhoods surrounding their churches.
- Through Continuing Education seminars, on-line courses, and workshops it may be necessary to create forums to discuss areas of church life that are impacted by information technology, i.e. 'worship wars', cyber-hate, discerning the truth in an information age, e-vangelism, establishing church web-sites, and discipleship and information technology.

It is essential that the Church develop its own voice on information technology. Seminary professors, pastors and church leaders must be able to raise ethical questions about individual and corporate use of information technology and learn to hold persons and churches accountable for its use. This kind of prophetic voice must emerge from a solid theology.

The possibilities for effective, transformational ministry in this age are tremendous. But, as is often the case, great potential for good is accompanied by great potential for peril. It is unwise for the seminary, or the Church to embrace blindly all that information technology offers. It is equally unwise to reject information technology out of fear or ignorance. Through critical examination we seek to discard those things related to information technology that lead us away from God, self, others and the created order, and embrace that which is consistent with our understanding of God and His redemptive work in the world.

Bibliography

Dawn J. Grubb, "Wired for the World: Digital dogma has Potter's House churchgoers plugging in to God's word," Science and Spirit, January/February 2001, 30.

"Not Just for Visitors," Christianity Today, February 19, 2001, 17.

James P. Wind, "Crossing the Digital Divide: New Forms of Community on the Virtual Frontier," Congregations, May/June 2001, 9.

"Not Your Grandfather's Mission Field," Christianity Today, February 10, 2001, 58-59.

A basic definition of theology flows from the word's Greek roots (theos, God, and logos, speech): discourse about God. A more detailed definition is provided by Millard Erickson who identifies theology as "that discipline which strives to give a coherent statement of the doctrines of the Christian faith, based primarily upon the Scriptures, placed in the context of culture in general, worded in contemporary idiom, and related to issues of life." See Erickson, Christian Theology (Grand Rapids: Baker, 1986), 21. Technology is defined broadly as "the body of knowledge available to a civilization that is of use in fashioning implements, practicing manual arts and skills, and extracting and collecting materials." The Greek roots for the word are teckne, skill, and logos, speech. Thus, technology is, fundamentally, a discourse about skill. See: The American Heritage Dictionary of the English Language, 3rd ed. (Boston: Houghton Mifflin, 1992), 1843.

Brent Waters, "Truth and Virtue in a Scientific and Technological Age," Prism, 1991, (6:2), 21-22.

See David O. Berger, "The Theology of Technology and Vice Versa," Concordia Journal 19 (4), October 1993, 323.

****

4.13 Pope John Paul II -- World Communications Day May 12, 2002

http://op.org/domcentral/comday.htm

REUTERS
Pope gives benediction to Internet
By Reuters
May 13, 2002, 7:35 AM PT
Pope John Paul II is putting his faith in the Internet.
In his weekly address at St. Peter's Square on Sunday, the 81-year-old Pontiff said: "I've decided, therefore, to propose a big new theme for this year: 'The Internet--a new forum for proclaiming the Gospel.'" The leader of the world's Roman Catholics didn't say how much he practices what he preaches--for instance, whether he surfs the World Wide Web. He doesn't have his own e-mail address. But the Vatican does have an active Web site, the pope sent his first message over the Internet last year, and there's talk that he is searching for a patron saint for Internet users. " Recent progress in communications and information have presented the church with unheard-of possibilities for evangelism," he said.

"We shouldn't be afraid to put to sea in the vast ocean of information," he went on. "If we do so, the good news can reach the hearts of the men and women of the new millennium." In the past, the pope has said the Web should be regulated to stop depravity in cyberspace. Sunday, he gave it his unwavering blessing. "We have to become part of this modern and ever more finely woven web of communication with realism and confidence, convinced that, if it is used competently and with due responsibility, it can offer a sound opportunity for the dissemination of the word of the Lord."

Taken together, the pope's latest thoughts were a big step forward from January, when in his last comments on the Internet he emphasized its potential for harm, going so far as to say it could demean human dignity. "Despite its enormous potential for good, some of the degrading and damaging ways the Internet can be used are already obvious to all," he said at the time. Those comments raised the hackles of Internet die-hards who are generally against any form of censorship and any view that cyberspace should in any way be policed for content. The Roman Catholic Church has traditionally adapted to discoveries through the ages, from the Renaissance to the invention of printing presses and the Industrial Revolution. The Vatican has extensive media interests, with its own publishing house, a radio station, missionary news agency, television channel and newspaper.

ZENIT
http://www.zenit.org/english/
Pope Asks the Church to Navigate the Internet [2002-05-12]

ZENIT - The World Seen From Rome
Code: ZE02051204
Date: 2002-05-12
Pope Asks the Church to Navigate the Internet
On World Communications Day

VATICAN CITY, MAY 12, 2002 (ZENIT.org).- John Paul II invited the Church to "put out to sea" in evangelizing the world with the help of Internet. As the faithful in Italy and other countries today celebrated the solemnity of the Ascension, the Pope noted that the Church was also observing World Communications Day. He invited Catholics to use the Internet for spreading the message about Christ. "The Redeemer constitutes for the faithful the anchor of salvation and comfort in the daily commitment to the service of truth and peace, of justice and freedom," the Holy Father explained from the window of his study as he addressed pilgrims gathered in St. Peter's Square to pray the midday Regina Caeli. "In fact, we have to confront the realities of this world every day," he said. Among these realities, he declared, the media play a key role. That is why, he said, he selected Internet as the theme for this year's Communications Day. "The most recent advancements in communications and information have put the Church in front of previously unheard-of possibilities for evangelization," the Pope exclaimed.

The theme for the Holy Father's message for World Communications Day was "Internet: A New Forum for Proclaiming the Gospel.". "We must enter into this modern and every more replete communications network with realism and confidence," the Holy Father said, "convinced that, if it is used with competence and conscientious responsibility, it can offer useful opportunities for spreading the Gospel message." "There is no need, therefore, to worry about putting out to sea in the vast informational ocean," he added. "One can also reach the heart of men and women of the new millennium through the Good News itself." The Pope cautioned, however, "we must never forget that the secret of every apostolic action is, first of all, prayer." He insisted, "While we prepare to celebrate next Sunday the solemn feast of Pentecost, we, with Mary, invoke the Holy Spirit to instill in Christians a renewed missionary push and to guide the steps of humanity along the path of solidarity and peace."

PAPAL MESSAGE

PONTIFICIUM CONSILIUM DE COMMUNICATIONIBUS SOCIALIBUS

MESSAGE OF THE HOLY FATHER
FOR THE 36th WORLD COMMUNICATIONS DAY
THEME: "Internet: A New Forum for Proclaiming the Gospel"
Sunday, May 12, 2002

Dear Brothers and Sisters,

1. The Church in every age continues the work begun on the day of Pentecost, when the Apostles, in the power of the Holy Spirit, went forth into the streets of Jerusalem to preach the Gospel of Jesus Christ in many tongues (cf. Acts 2:5-11). Through the succeeding centuries, this evangelizing mission spread to the far corners of the earth, as Christianity took root in many places and learned to speak the diverse languages of the world, always in obedience to Christ's command to preach the Gospel to every nation (cf. Mt 28:19-20).

But the history of evangelization is not just a matter of geographic expansion, for the Church has also had to cross many cultural thresholds, each of which called for fresh energy and imagination in proclaiming the one Gospel of Jesus Christ. The age of the great discoveries, the Renaissance and the invention of printing, the Industrial Revolution and the birth of the modern world: these too were threshold moments which demanded new forms of evangelization. Now, with the communications and information revolution in full swing, the Church stands unmistakably at another decisive gateway. It is fitting therefore that on this World Communications Day 2002 we should reflect on the subject: "Internet: A New Forum for Proclaiming the Gospel".

2. The Internet is certainly a new "forum" understood in the ancient Roman sense of that public space where politics and business were transacted, where religious duties were fulfilled where much of the social life of the city took place, and where the best and the worst of human nature was on display. It was a crowded and bustling urban space, which both reflected the surrounding culture and created a culture of its own. This is no less true of cyberspace, which is as it were a new frontier opening up at the beginning of this new millennium. Like the new frontiers of other times, this one too is full of the interplay of danger and promise, and not without the sense of adventure which marked other great periods of change. For the Church the new world of cyberspace is a summons to the great adventure of using its potential to proclaim the Gospel message. This challenge is at the heart of what it means at the beginning of the millennium to follow the Lord's command to "put out into the deep": Duc in altum! (Lk 5:4).

3. The Church approaches this new medium with realism and confidence. Like other communications media, it is a means, not an end in itself. The Internet can offer magnificent opportunities for evangelization if used with competence and a clear awareness of its strengths and weaknesses. Above all, by providing information and stirring interest it makes possible an initial encounter with the Christian message, especially among the young who increasingly turn to the world of cyberspace as a window on the world. It is important, therefore, that the Christian community think of very practical ways of helping those who first make contact through the Internet to move from the virtual world of cyberspace to the real world of Christian community.

At a subsequent stage, the Internet can also provide the kind of follow-up which evangelization requires. Especially in an unsupportive culture, Christian living calls for continuing instruction and catechesis, and this is perhaps the area in which the Internet can provide excellent help. There already exist on the Net countless sources of information, documentation and education about the Church, her history and tradition, her doctrine and her engagement in every field in all parts of the world. It is clear, then, that while the Internet can never replace that profound experience of God which only the living, liturgical and sacramental life of the Church can offer, it can certainly provide a unique supplement and support in both preparing for the encounter with Christ in community, and sustaining the new believer in the journey of faith which then begins.

4. There are nevertheless certain necessary, even obvious, questions which arise in using the Internet in the cause of evangelization. The essence of the Internet in fact is that it provides an almost unending flood of information, much of which passes in a moment. In a culture which feeds on the ephemeral there can easily be a risk of believing that it is facts that matter, rather than values. The Internet offers extensive knowledge, but it does not teach values; and when values are disregarded, our very humanity is demeaned and man easily loses sight of his transcendent dignity. Despite its enormous potential for good, some of the degrading and damaging ways in which the Internet can be used are already obvious to all, and public authorities surely have a responsibility to guarantee that this marvellous instrument serves the common good and does not become a source of harm.

Furthermore, the Internet radically redefines a person's psychological relationship to time and space. Attention is rivetted on what is tangible, useful, instantly available; the stimulus for deeper thought and reflection may be lacking. Yet human beings have a vital need for time and inner quiet to ponder and examine life and its mysteries, and to grow gradually into a mature dominion of themselves and of the world around them. Understanding and wisdom are the fruit of a contemplative eye upon the world, and do not come from a mere accumulation of facts, no matter how interesting. They are the result of an insight which penetrates the deeper meaning of things in relation to one another and to the whole of reality. Moreover, as a forum in which practically everything is acceptable and almost nothing is lasting, the Internet favours a relativistic way of thinking and sometimes feeds the flight from personal responsibility and commitment.

In such a context, how are we to cultivate that wisdom which comes not just from information but from insight, the wisdom which understands the difference between right and wrong, and sustains the scale of values which flows from that difference?

5. The fact that through the Internet people multiply their contacts in ways hitherto unthinkable opens up wonderful possibilities for spreading the Gospel. But it is also true that electronically mediated relationships can never take the place of the direct human contact required for genuine evangelization. For evangelization always depends upon the personal witness of the one sent to evangelize (cf. Rom 10:14-15). How does the Church lead from the kind of contact made possible by the Internet to the deeper communication demanded by Christian proclamation? How do we build upon the first contact and exchange of information which the Internet makes possible?

There is no doubt that the electronic revolution holds out the promise of great positive breakthroughs for the developing world; but there is also the possibility that it will in fact aggravate existing inequalities as the information and communications gap widens. How can we ensure that the information and communications revolution which has the Internet as its prime engine will work in favour of the globalization of human development and solidarity, objectives closely linked to the Church's evangelizing mission?

Finally, in these troubled times, let me ask: how can we ensure that this wondrous instrument first conceived in the context of military operations can now serve the cause of peace? Can it favour that culture of dialogue, participation, solidarity and reconciliation without which peace cannot flourish? The Church believes it can; and to ensure that this is what will happen she is determined to enter this new forum, armed with the Gospel of Christ, the Prince of Peace.

6. The Internet causes billions of images to appear on millions of computer monitors around the planet. From this galaxy of sight and sound will the face of Christ emerge and the voice of Christ be heard? For it is only when his face is seen and his voice heard that the world will know the glad tidings of our redemption. This is the purpose of evangelization. And this is what will make the Internet a genuinely human space, for if there is no room for Christ, there is no room for man. Therefore, on this World Communications Day, I dare to summon the whole Church bravely to cross this new threshold, to put out into the deep of the Net, so that now as in the past the great engagement of the Gospel and culture may show to the world "the glory of God on the face of Christ" (2 Cor 4:6). May the Lord bless all those who work for this aim.

From the Vatican, 24 January 2002, the Feast of Saint Francis de Sales
JOHN PAUL II
http://www.vatican.va/holy_father/john_paul_ii/messages/communications/documents/hf_jp-ii_mes_20020122_world-communications-day_en.html

4.14 Ethics Survey
Answers to 55 Questions Submitted by Arthur Dobrin

by Dianne Bradford, Fiona Missaghian, Udo Schaefer and Robert Stockman
Compiled by Jonah Winters.
http://bahai-library.com/?file=winters_ethics_Survey.html

Terms:

Abdu'l-Bahá (1844-1921): Eldest surviving son of Bahá'u'lláh and his designated successor; regarded as being the perfect "Exemplar" of the Bahá'í Faith and the first of two infallible interpreters of Bahá'u'lláh's revelation.
Báb, The (1819-1850): The Prophet-Forerunner of the Bahá'í Faith; seen as a "bridge" of sorts between the Islamic revelation and the Bahá'í revelation.
Bahá'í: lit. "Of Bahá," i.e. Bahá'u'lláh. A follower of the religion revealed by Bahá'u'lláh.
Bahá'u'lláh (1817-1892): lit. "Glory of God." The Prophet-Founder of the Bahá'í Faith and the Manifestation of God for this era; the author/revealer of the core teachings of the Bahá'í revelation.
Guardian, The: honorific of Shoghi Effendi
Manifestation: A Prophet of God in any age, e.g. Christ, Buddha, Muhammad, and The Báb. "Minor" prophets such as Isaiah or Amos are not manifestations. The Manifestations are not God descended to earth, but rather perfect human reflections of the divine, such that the face of God as reflected in the Manifestations can be regarded as God Himself.
Shoghi Effendi (1897-1957): Grandson of Abdu'l-Bahá. Protector and "Guardian" of the Bahá'í Faith, and second of two infallible interpreters of Bahá'u'lláh's revelation.
The Universal House of Justice: Supreme elected administrative body of the Bahá'í Faith, consisting of a nine-member committee acting as a single executive voice. First elected in 1963, its seat is in the Bahá'í World Centre in Haifa, Israel.

Some prefatory comments:

I. All writings and texts quoted below can be found online at the Bahá'í Academics Resource Library, http://bahai-library.com. Full citations have not been provided; write to Jonah Winters, contact@bahai-library.com, for further information about any text cited here. This survey itself has been posted online at http://bahai-library.com/essays.
II. By common Bahá'í convention, extracts from the writings of the Bahá'í Faith's primary figures (The Báb, Bahá'u'lláh, Abdu'l-Bahá, and Shoghi Effendi) have been italicized. Extracts from the writings of the Universal House of Justice and their agencies (including the Notes to the *Kitab-i-Aqdas* where quoted below) have not been italicized.
III. A few respondents expressed their concern that the following 55 ethics questions might not be neatly answerable in a Bahá'í context. Reasons for this vary, but some primary objections have been:
   a. From a Bahá'í perspective, many of the answers to these questions would require a degree of contextualization rather than a blanket 'yes or no,' 'this or that' answer. This is best expressed in a letter from the Universal House of Justice dated June 1988:

> The Universal House of Justice does not feel that the time has come for it to provide detailed legislation on subjects such as abortion, homosexuality and other moral issues.... [I]n most areas of human behaviour there are acts which are clearly contrary to the law of God and others which are clearly approved or permissible; between these there is often a grey area where it is not immediately apparent what should be done. It has been a human tendency to wish to eliminate these grey areas so that every aspect of life is clearly prescribed. A result of this tendency has been the tremendous accretion of interpretation and subsidiary legislation which has smothered the spirit of certain of the older religions.
>
> On behalf of the Universal House of Justice to an individual, 5 June 1988

While the same could be said of other religions, in the Bahá'í Faith context is also informative in light of the Faith's fundamental tenet that certain religious truth itself is relative. This is expressed in the Faith's teaching of the "Progressive Revelation" of certain religious truth; God sends his Manifestations to each people and each time as they are needed, and no Revelation is final. The Revelations thus differ in many points of context and cultural relevance. The core spiritual teachings of all religions, though, are universal and unchanging. (For more on the Faith's relativism, see http://bahai-library.com/articles/relativism.html.) Future Bahá'í law, when universalized and globalized, may thus sometimes have to focus on the spirit of the law rather than its letter.

However, the Bahá'í Faith also teaches that ethical conduct can be universalized. Certain beliefs and actions are considered as wrong and immoral regardless of the historical context. But individuals are not necessarily capable of determining on their own which laws have contextual versus universal application. Bahá'ís are thus very conscientious about adhering as closely as possible to the written word of the Bahá'í Faith, its extensive body of sacred text left for the community by the Faith's Central Figures.

In a certain sense, making ethical determinations is a requirement for and mark of maturity. The human race is slowly but presently coming of age, the Bahá'í Faith teaches, and the capacity to discern ethical behavior is becoming a capability and responsibility of all believers. As the Universal House of Justice continued in the above letter, there are

> ...area[s] of the application of the laws [which are] intentionally left to the conscience of each individual believer. This is the age in which mankind must attain maturity, and one aspect of this is the assumption by individuals of the responsibility for deciding, with the assistance of consultation, their own course of action in areas which are left open by the law of God.
>
> (ibid.)

b. Besides the relativity of religious truth, the Bahá'í Faith also contains a certain relativity of historic truth. Authorized teachings of the Bahá'í Faith go back to the advent of the revelation of the Báb, 1844. Authorized interpretations of Bahá'í Teachings then extend to the death of Shoghi Effendi, 1957, and still inform present-day legislation of the Universal House of Justice. In that 150 years Bahá'í history has spanned place as well as time, with its Manifestations [prophets; see definition above] living in and revealing from Iran, Iraq, Turkey, and Palestine/Israel, and its authorized interpreters living in or speaking in England, Egypt, continental Europe, North America, and Israel. Some Bahá'í texts might have contextual but not universal relevance. Descriptions of specific ethical teachings must sometimes be described contextually and could be misleading when generalized. Examples include teachings on war, the treatment of apostates, martyrdom and suicide, genetic engineering, and bigamy.

c. The Bahá'í Faith is a very text-centered religion, in no small part because the tens of thousands of extant writings from its five central authorities (The Báb, Bahá'u'lláh, Abdu'l-Bahá, Shoghi Effendi, and the Universal House of Justice) contain guidance on thousands of topics. A corollary of this is that the three latter authorities were/are very careful only to interpret or legislate within the sphere of teachings left by their respective predecessors. By extension, present-day Bahá'ís and the Universal House of Justice refrain from extrapolating from precedents and hence avoid ruling on or offering interpretations about issues not previously addressed. Therefore, if any of the following answers lack clearly supporting quotations, they should be considered individual interpretation only and might or might not accurately represent Bahá'í teachings.

Introduction:

From Dr. Udo Schaefer, "On the Difficulty of Dealing with Ethical Questions," a chapter from "*In A Blue Haze: Smoking and Bahá'í Ethics*" (Prague: Zero Palm Press, 1997), online at http://bahai-library.com/books/bluehaze:

> The question of whether a certain behaviour is permitted or prohibited, good, evil, or neutral, is a question of ethics. A Bahá'í who wants to know how to act in a given situation, will begin by turning to his conscience, and since this has been formed by the revealed Word, to the Scripture, i.e. the sum of the Writings of Bahá'u'lláh and the authoritative interpretations of 'Abdu'l-Bahá and Shoghi Effendi. What might appear to be self-evident for every religious person is not necessarily so, as we shall shortly see.
>
> Today the presentation of concrete ethical standards has become problematic in our society. Certainly, the highest ethical values in the Bahá'í Revelation, the love of one's neighbour and of all humanity, or the cardinal virtue of justice, are sure to meet with approval. One can agree to these highly abstract values without having to commit oneself to

changing any patterns of everyday life. However, when it comes to assessing actual everyday behaviour affecting one's own self, especially when it comes to prohibitions, irritation can set in quickly.

The Bahá'ís are living in this society and are influenced by the prevalent ways of thinking whether they want to be or not, and in this society, thinking in moral categories is becoming more and more unfashionable. Many people are unaccustomed to it. To many it seems increasingly questionable that there should be such things as rigid norms and unalterable duties which unequivocally state what should or should not be done. This is concomitant with the decay of religion and the resulting erosion of the Christian value system.

In many parts of the world morality, called an "honourable form of stupidity" by Friedrich Nietzsche, has not only lost its general binding force but also its self-evident importance and is actually seen by many as a kind of stupidity. It has largely disappeared from everyday speech and is almost only used with an ironical undertone. A person who maintains moral points of view is considered a "morality apostle", with whom no one wants any interaction. This is evident in political discussions or in talk shows on television where interlocutors are admonished, for God's sake not to moralise. Especially in regard to so-called "social fringe groups" (criminals, social outcasts, prostitutes, drug addicts, homosexuals) or on the issue of abortion one should kindly refrain from any moral approach whatsoever. Persons who fail to do so disqualify themselves, exposing themselves as Pharisees and die-hard reactionaries. This process of "demoralisation" began with sociology; how far it has already spread can be seen by the semantic cleansing of our language, which bans the use of all terms that might hold any moral reproach.

Of course, Bahá'ís do not think that way. Experience with these issues shows, however, that they often have similar feelings, which is not surprising in this social climate. Therefore, a person presenting ethical demands and thus drawing an ideal of humanity "in light of which one's own everyday existence fails a thousandfold", is easily suspected of affectations or insincerity by being a moralist, a hell-and-brimstone preacher, as well as by violating the cardinal norm that prohibits self-righteousness. Self-righteousness is a distorted form of righteousness. According to Confucius the self-righteous are "the spoilers of morals." They were frequently and uncompromisingly rebuked by Bahá'u'lláh even as He praised the truly righteous, "well is it with the righteous that mock not the sinful, but rather conceal their misdeeds". When someone uses the pretext of moral responsibility to scrutinize commonly accepted social norms of behaviour, isn't that person preoccupied with the faults and sins of others? In the end, doesn't such a person violate the imperatives of his or her own ethics?

If this were the case, it would actually be totally inadmissible to be concerned with Bahá'í ethics, which as in all religions do make up a substantial part of our theology. However, we are not dealing here with a specific individual's unique and personal behaviour, but rather with abstract human behaviour. And to judge this behaviour in the abstract is not only permissible, but imperative, since God's Book is the "unerring Balance" "in which all who are in the heavens and all who are on the earth are weighed", through which "truth shall be distinguished from error". At a time "when no man knoweth how to discern light and darkness or to distinguish guidance from error", we are challenged to reflect what our duties are, whether certain ways of acting, accepted or disputed in society, are permitted or prohibited. How else could we then accomplish the task which 'Abdu'l-Bahá defined in a prayer: "to refute what is vain and false" and "to establish the truth"?

Udo Schaefer

THE 55 QUESTIONS

General

---

1. What does it mean to be a good person?

Submission under God's command is considered "good", but it needs to be pointed out also that this implies to follow (the most recent of) God's Messengers, Bahá'u'lláh. Bahá'u'lláh says:

> ***The source of all good is trust in God, submission unto His command, and contentment with His holy will and pleasure.***
> *Tablets of Bahá'u'lláh*, Words of Wisdom, pp. 153-155

Our duty to the Covenant of Bahá'u'lláh is first recognize the Manifestations of God and follow their teachings, from which goodness follows:

> *The first duty prescribed by God for His servants is the recognition of Him Who is the Dayspring of His Revelation and the Fountain of His laws, Who representeth the Godhead in both the Kingdom of His Cause and the world of creation. Whoso achieveth this duty hath attained unto all good; and whoso is deprived thereof hath gone astray, though he be the author of every righteous deed. It behoveth every one who reacheth this most sublime station, this summit of transcendent glory, to observe every ordinance of Him Who is the Desire of the world. These twin duties are inseparable. Neither is acceptable without the other...*
> Bahá'u'lláh, *The Kitáb-i-Aqdas*

Some Bahá'ís believe that striving towards social good would also define what a good person is, and many Bahá'ís have dedicated themselves to social improvement. Ultimately, according to Bahá'í teachings, only God and His Messengers know what is the right and good thing to do, since only God has the "complete picture," hence the command to submission. God demands that His people strive towards the social good.

Bahá'ís also believe that being good or being an ethical person has consequences for this world and the world beyond, so the ethical teachings of the Bahá'í Faith have a spiritual and "other-worldly" dimension as well. One needs to keep this in mind when asking why one should be good etc. Being an ethical person is strongly connected with the purpose of existence: know God through His Messengers and follow the laws.

----

2. Why be good?

1) By divine command. Bahá'u'lláh says:

> *... Live ye one with another, O people, in radiance and joy. By My life! All that are on earth shall pass away, while good deeds alone shall endure; to the truth of My words God doth Himself bear witness....*
> *The Kitáb-i-Aqdas,* Par. 70, pp. 44-45

Other reasons include:

2) Universal Eschatology: Because God knows what is good for His people and He only wants them to be happy, content and to live a life in peace.

3) Individual Eschatology: Because everyone's station after death will depend on one's goodness in this world (and of course God's acceptance

4) Purely for Love for God (Ultimate and most selfless reason).

'Abdu'l-Bahá, Bahá'u'lláh's appointed Successor and authorized Interpreter of His words, says:

> *... And the honor and distinction of the individual consist in this, that he among all the world's multitudes should become a source of social good. Is any larger bounty conceivable than this, that an individual, looking within himself, should find that by the confirming grace of God he has become the cause of peace and well-being, of happiness and advantage to his fellow men? No, by the one true God, there is no greater bliss, no more complete delight*
>
> *Secret of Divine Civilization*, pp. 2-3

----

3. Is it possible to be a good person and not be a member of your religion?

Yes, especially if one is a member of another of God's religions, which the Bahá'í Faith regard as all authentic; "The holy Manifestations Who have been the Sources or Founders of the various religious systems were united and agreed in purpose and teaching" ('Abdu'l-Bahá, *The Promulgation of Universal Peace*)

Abdu'l-Bahá even encouraged people to become "true Christians":

> *Thou didst begin thy letter with a blessed phrase, saying: 'I am a Christian.' O would that all were truly Christian! It is easy to be a Christian on the tongue, but hard to be a true one. Today some five hundred million souls are Christian, but the real Christian is very rare: he is that soul from whose comely face there shineth the splendour of Christ, and who showeth forth the perfections of the Kingdom; this is a matter of great moment, for to be a Christian is to embody every excellence there is. I hope that thou, too, shalt become a true Christian.*
> *Selections from the Writings of 'Abdu'l-Bahá,* http://bahai-library.com/writings/abdulbaha/swab/4/sec-16.html

While one can be good without being a Bahá'í, there is a great advantage to recognizing the truth of Bahá'u'lláh's Teachings. For example, say there existed a book series, and the first book in the series with all of its sequels contained the answers to all of the questions you could ever have. Now say you find one of these books. It could be one of these books that was already owned by a family member or one you came across unexpectedly. You read the book and realize what a treasure it is. You might even seek out and read some of the earlier books in this series because this one is so exciting and you hope for more sequels as well. But either because you don't know that there exists another sequel in this wonderful series of books or because you have been convinced by others that this book which you read is the last book of the series, you don't even look for any other sequels.

Now, since each sequel in the series summarizes or restates the answers found in all of the previous books, not going back to read any of the previous books in the series may not hurt you; although you would miss out on the beauty and excitement of these books by not reading them. However, since each book contains more of these answers than any of the ones previously written, not reading these sequels means that there are answers on which you are missing out.

The Revelation of God is like that series of books. As humanity matured as a race, a greater measure of God's Revelation was revealed through each succeeding Manifestation. To reveal too much too early would be to give the people more than they could handle. Therefore the Revelation of God's Will and mysteries was revealed slowly and progressively according to the capacity of the people of the time to receive it. Bahá'u'lláh's Revelation contains the fullest measure of God's Revelation thus far given to humanity. Therefore, to miss out on Bahá'u'lláh's Teachings is to keep yourself from knowing as much as you can about the mysteries of God, God's Will for humanity, and the solutions for the world's problems--solutions given by God Himself through Bahá'u'lláh. In addition, Bahá'u'lláh has clearly written that He is not the last of God's Manifestations/Messengers either. So, in a few centuries we can expect another sequel to the Books of the Revelation of God.

Ultimately, though only God can decide who is "good" and who is not. Until we face Him nobody can say for sure if He accepts our acts, even if we think they are good and even if they are in accordance with Bahá'í law.

----

4. Is it possible to be a good person and no longer believe in your religion? I.e., can an apostate be a good person?
Yes, but one does not fulfill the purpose of one's creation. As earlier quoted from the *Kitáb-i-Aqdas,* Bahá'u'lláh says:

> *The first duty prescribed by God for His servants is the recognition of Him Who is the Dayspring of His Revelation and the Fountain of His laws.... Whoso achieveth this duty hath attained unto all good; and whoso is deprived thereof hath gone astray, though he be the author of every righteous deed.*
> *The Kitáb-i-Aqdas*, Par. 1, p. 19

However, the Bahá'í teachings also emphasize that "One's beliefs are an internal and personal matter; no person or institution has the right to exert compulsion in matters of belief." (Universal House of Justice, private correspondence April 4 2001). As explained by Abdu'l-Bahá, "*The Cause of God hath never had any place for denouncing others as infidel or profligate, nor hath it allowed anyone to humiliate or belittle another.*" (http://bahai-library.com/uhj/takfir.html)

----

5. Is there a difference between religious requirements and morality?

God is the source of all good and His commandments help distinguish between right or wrong. The standards of morality are established by Religion and they are renewed with the appearance of each Manifestation of God. Therefore, what religions require of their followers is the utmost in morality

'Abdu'l-Bahá says:

> *The real bond of integrity is religious in character, for religion indicates the oneness of the world of humanity. Religion serves the world of morality. Religion purifies the hearts. Religion impels men to achieve praiseworthy deeds. Religion becomes the cause of love in human hearts, for religion is a divine foundation, the foundation ever conducive to life. The teachings of God are the source of illumination to the people of the world. Religion is ever constructive not destructive. Japan Will Turn Ablaze*, p. 43

----

6. What is the source of ethics?

God, as announced through God's Messenger for this Age. 'Abdu'l-Bahá says:

> *... The divine religions embody two kinds of ordinances. First, there are those which constitute essential, or spiritual, teachings of the Word of God. These are faith in God, the acquirement of the virtues which characterize perfect manhood, praiseworthy moralities, the acquisition of the bestowals and bounties emanating from the divine effulgences - in brief, the ordinances which concern the realm of morals and ethics. This is the fundamental aspect of the religion of God, and this is of the highest importance because knowledge of God is the fundamental requirement of man. Man must comprehend the oneness of Divinity. He must come to know and acknowledge the precepts of God and realize for a certainty that the ethical development of humanity is dependent upon religion. He must get rid of all defects and seek the attainment of heavenly virtues in order that he may prove to be the image and likeness of God... As God is loving and kind to all men, man must likewise manifest loving-kindness to all humanity. As God is loyal and truthful, man must show forth the same attributes in the human world. Even as God exercises mercy toward all, man must prove himself to be the manifestation of mercy. In a word, the image and likeness of God constitute the virtues of God, and man is intended to become the recipient of the effulgences of divine attributes.'*
> *Promulgation of Universal Peace*, pp. 403-404

----

7. Can someone be a good person and be an atheist?

Yes, since the morality brought by God's Messengers eventually becomes the standard for society. However, they are depriving themselves of attaining the purpose of their creation "to know and worship God." Someone who does the same thing as a religious person would do, but just does not believe in God, may be a good person in that he or she produces good for this world, but the purpose of his or her creation was not fully fulfilled.
The short obligatory prayer of Bahá'u'lláh, which many Bahá'ís recite daily, says:

> *I bear witness, O my God, that Thou hast created me to know Thee and to worship Thee. I testify, at this moment, to my powerlessness and to Thy might, to my poverty and to Thy wealth.*
>
> *There is none other God but Thee, the Help in Peril, the Self-Subsisting.*
> *Prayers and Meditations by Bahá'u'lláh*, # CLXXXI

Further, it is possible that religion may at times be itself bad and immoral (however, presumably the following quote doesn't contrast religion with *atheism,* i.e. actual disbelief in God):

> *Religion should unite all hearts and cause wars and disputes to vanish from the face of the earth, give birth to spirituality, and bring life and light to each heart. If religion becomes a cause of dislike, hatred and division, it were better to be without it, and to withdraw from such a religion would be a truly religious act. For it is clear*

that the purpose of a remedy is to cure; but if the remedy should only aggravate the complaint it had better be left alone. Any religion which is not a cause of love and unity is no religion. All the holy prophets were as doctors to the soul; they gave prescriptions for the healing of mankind; thus any remedy that causes disease does not come from the great and supreme Physician.
'Abdu'l-Bahá, *The Promulgation of Universal Peace*,
http://bahai-library.com/writings/abdulbaha/pt/3/sec-2.html

----

8. How do you decide what is right and what is wrong?

By the standards of religion. As it has ever been, God tells humanity what is right and what is wrong through His Manifestations, teachings which we learn and internalize largely through prayer and meditation. It is no different with Bahá'u'lláh. He, Himself, affirms:

We have, under all circumstances, enjoined on men what is right, and forbidden what is wrong. He Who is the Lord of Being is witness that this Wronged One hath besought from God for His creatures whatever is conducive to unity and harmony, fellowship and concord. By the righteousness of God! This Wronged One is not capable of dissimulation. He, verily, hath revealed that which He desired; He, truly, is the Lord of strength, the Unrestrained.
Epistle to the Son of the Wolf, pp. 38-39

About the Laws which He has revealed at God's bidding, Bahá'u'lláh says:

Think not that We have revealed unto you a mere code of laws. Nay, rather, We have unsealed the choice Wine with the fingers of might and power. To this beareth witness that which the Pen of Revelation hath revealed. Meditate upon this, O men of insight!

The Kitáb-i-Aqdas, Par. 5, p. 21

In addition, a certain amount of testing is also a part of each Revelation. Again turning to Bahá'u'lláh's Writings, we read:

... from time immemorial even unto eternity the Almighty hath tried, and will continue to try, His servants, so that light may be distinguished from darkness, truth from falsehood, right from wrong, guidance from error, happiness from misery, and roses from thorns...

The Kitáb-i-Iqan, p. 8

----

9. Why do bad things happen to good people?

The Bahá'í Faith offers a number of responses to this question. These include that suffering produces personal growth; that suffering need not prevent happiness, for one can be joyous in the midst of severity; that some people bring suffering upon themselves through their neglecting to follow the teachings of the Prophets; and finally that the reason for some suffering might only be known to God.
Tests and trials make us stronger.

Not until man is tried doth the pure gold distinctly separate from the dross. Torment is the fire of test wherein the pure gold shineth resplendently and the impurity is burned and blackened. At present thou art, praise be to God, firm and steadfast in tests and trials and art not shaken by them.
Selections from the Writings of 'Abdu'l-Bahá, http://bahai-library.com/writings/abdulbaha/swab/4/s

Shoghi Effendi, 'Abdu'l-Bahá's appointed successor and Guardian of the Bahá'í Faith, wrote:

> *... As long as there will be life on earth, there will be also suffering, in various forms and degrees. But suffering, although an inescapable reality, can nevertheless be utilised as a means for the attainment of happiness. This is the interpretation given to it by all the prophets and saints who, in the midst of severe tests and trials, felt happy and joyous and experienced what is best and holiest in life. Suffering is both a reminder and a guide. It stimulates us better to adapt ourselves to our environmental conditions, and thus leads the way to self improvement. In every suffering one can find a meaning and a wisdom. But it is not always easy to find the secret of that wisdom. It is sometimes only when all our suffering has passed that we become aware of its usefulness. What man considers to be evil turns often to be a cause of infinite blessings..*
> *Unfolding Destiny*, p. 434.

The Guardian also wrote:

> *...the world is full of suffering. Bahá'u'lláh tells us that the deeper are the furrows it digs into our very being, the greater will be the fruit of our life and the more enhanced our spiritual development. All the Saints that shine in the history of society had to pass through tribulations. Their form was various but their effect has always been the same, namely, the purification of our heart and soul for receiving the light of God.*
> Quoted in *Lights of Guidance*, No. 678, p. 204.

----

10. Is there a difference between a religious offence and a moral/secular offence?
Since we learn what is moral from religion, the two are inextricably entwined, and an offense in one is also reflected in the other. However, the Bahá'í Faith does recognize a distinction between certain public and private ethical behavior; if a Bahá'í drinks at home he has only God to judge, but if he drinks in public he harms the Faith. Similarly, the Faith recognizes that non-Bahá'ís do not and are not expected to follow all Bahá'í laws. Again with the case of drinking, the Faith does not chastise or judge the consumption of alcohol by those who do not follow them. http://bahai-library.com/uhj/alcohol.html
It is always most unfortunate when Bahá'ís of long standing, and even members of institutions at the national level, partake of alcoholic beverages, thus damaging themselves, harming the good name of the Faith in the eyes of non-Bahá'ís, and setting a bad example for the rank and file of the believers.
Of course, the Assemblies should not pry into the lives of individual believers; but in the case of any Bahá'í who blatantly violates the law, he should be counseled

----

11. Who enforces the moral rules of your religion?
The individual is responsible to enforce the rules of his/her own personal religious laws (prayers, fasting, pilgrimage, charity), and the observance or non-observance of these laws is between the individual and God. As for the other social laws which protect and guide the community at large, Bahá'u'lláh has established the institution of the House of Justice as follows:

> *The Lord hath ordained that in every city a House of Justice be established... It behoveth them to be the trusted ones of the Merciful among men and to regard themselves as the guardians appointed of God for all that dwell on earth. It is incumbent upon them to take counsel together and to have regard for the interests of the servants of God, for His sake, even as they regard their own interests, and to choose that which is meet and seemly.*
> *The Kitáb-i-Aqdas,* Par. 30, p. 29

Bahá'u'lláh has also set forth ordinances which helps to provide the Houses of Justice with the funds they will need to care for those under their jurisdictions. Of these Houses of Justice Bahá'u'lláh also says:
...Verily have We made [them] a shelter for the poor and needy... (*The Kitáb-i-Aqdas*, Par. 48, p. 37)
At present there is only one House of Justice established in the world, the Universal House of Justice, which deals with the world-wide affairs of the Bahá'í Faith, and has made itself available to world leaders for consultation as well. Indeed, several of the leaders and governments in the world have already availed themselves of this priceless guidance based

upon Bahá'u'lláh's teachings offered by the Universal House of Justice. National and local Houses of Justice at the present time go by the name of Spiritual Assemblies. (see further explanation in *Tablets of Abdu'l-Bahá vol. 1* p. 6; also Robert Stockman's *Bahá'í Faith in America vol. 2* note 139, p.448) These "Local Spiritual Assemblies" and "National Spiritual Assemblies" run the affairs of the community and enforce moral behaviour in the rare cases that such enforcement is necessary (e.g., by repeated and egregious public behavioral offenses). Enforcement comes first in the form of patient counselling to make sure the individual is familiar with Bahá'í law, and in the most egregious cases culminates in the retraction of the believer's voting rights and other aspects of community participation.

The Universal House of Justice explains the process:

> The Universal House of Justice feels that it is vital, for the sound development of the Cause of God in those communities where there remains any doubt among the friends as to the importance of obedience to [Bahá'í] law, that the National Spiritual Assemblies ensure that all believers are clearly informed of it. Of course, the Assemblies should not pry into the lives of individual believers; but in the case of any Bahá'í who blatantly violates the law, he should be counselled, assisted to overcome the habit, warned repeatedly of the consequences of continued disobedience, and ultimately, if he does not respond positively, be deprived of his administrative rights.
> online at http://bahai-library.com/uhj/alcohol.html

----

12. Should the moral rules of your religion apply to everyone?

When Bahá'u'lláh wrote His books with laws and teachings He did not think that they will only benefit His followers, but the whole planet, that they in fact have the purpose to unite the whole world and enable it to live in peace. But of course everybody has the freedom to choose.

Since the morality brought by God's Messengers eventually becomes the standard for society, they will inevitably apply to everyone eventually. About the Laws which He has revealed, Bahá'u'lláh says:

> *They whom God hath endued with insight will readily recognize that the precepts laid down by God constitute the highest means for the maintenance of order in the world and the security of its peoples. He that turneth away from them is accounted among the abject and foolish. We, verily, have commanded you to refuse the dictates of your evil passions and corrupt desires, and not to transgress the bounds which the Pen of the Most High hath fixed, for these are the breath of life unto all created things. The seas of Divine wisdom and Divine utterance have risen under the breath of the breeze of the All-Merciful. Hasten to drink your fill, O men of understanding! They that have violated the Covenant of God by breaking His commandments, and have turned back on their heels, these have erred grievously in the sight of God, the All-Possessing, the Most High.*
> *The Kitáb-i-Aqdas*, Par. 2, pp. 19-20.

----

13. What role should religion play in secular society?

Religion should serve the spiritual and social needs of all those willing to accept such help and where it is allowed by secular laws. It is an indispensible part of society. Again we turn to the Writings of 'Abdu'l-Bahá for clarification of the role and importance of religion to society:

> *... Religion is the light of the world, and the progress, achievement, and happiness of man result from obedience to the laws set down in the holy Books. Briefly, it is demonstrable that in this life, both outwardly and inwardly the mightiest of structures, the most solidly established, the most enduring, standing guard over the world, assuring both the spiritual and the material perfections of mankind, and protecting the happiness and the civilization of society - is religion.*
> 'Abdu'l-Bahá: *Secret of Divine Civilization*, pp. 71-72

Use of Force

----

14. Is killing ever justified?

Yes, if justice warrants it, such as in cases of self-defense and criminal justice. In the endnotes added to the English translation of the Kitáb-i-Aqdas, where further explanation and clarification can be found regarding some of its passages, is written:

> *... Shoghi Effendi in a letter written on his behalf has also indicated that, in an emergency, when there is no legal force at hand to appeal to, a Bahá'í is justified in defending his life...* Anonymous, *The Kitáb-i-Aqdas*, Notes Section, Note 173, p. 241

Abdu'l-Bahá explains in more depth:

> *There are two sorts of retributory punishments. One is vengeance, the other, chastisement. Man has not the right to take vengeance, but the community has the right to punish the criminal; and this punishment is intended to warn and to prevent so that no other person will dare to commit a like crime. This punishment is for the protection of man's rights, but it is not vengeance; vengeance appeases the anger of the heart by opposing one evil to another. This is not allowable, for man has not the right to take vengeance. But if criminals were entirely forgiven, the order of the world would be upset...*
>
> *The communities must punish the oppressor, the murderer, the malefactor, so as to warn and restrain others from committing like crimes. But the most essential thing is that the people must be educated in such a way that no crimes will be committed; for it is possible to educate the masses so effectively that they will avoid and shrink from perpetrating crimes, so that the crime itself will appear to them as the greatest chastisement, the utmost condemnation and torment. Therefore, no crimes which require punishment will be committed.*
> *Some Answered Questions, #77*

There is no explicit statement on euthanasia yet. The Universal House of Justice has said that it is "*a matter which the Universal House of Justice will have to legislate.*" Until they do, "*decisions [in these matters] must be left to the consciences of those responsible.'*" (*Lights of Guidance*, pp. 291-292)

----

15. Is war ever justified?
Yes, if in defense of the innocent. Where one state rises against another, all other states are to rise to defend the attacked. Bahá'u'lláh says:

> "Should one king rise up against another, all the other kings must arise to deter him. Arms and armaments will, then, be no more needed beyond that which is necessary to insure the internal security of their respective countries.
> *Epistle to the Son of the Wolf*, p. 31

Peace is of course preferable. Bahá'u'lláh says:

> "*... They must put away the weapons of war, and turn to the instruments of universal reconstruction. Should one king rise up against another, all the other kings must arise to deter him. Arms and armaments will, then, be no more needed beyond that which is necessary to insure the internal security of their respective countries.*
>
> *Epistle to the Son of the Wolf*, pp. 30-31

Abdu'l-Bahá summarizes how to avoid war:

> *To remedy this condition there must be universal peace. To bring this about, a Supreme Tribunal must be established, representative of all governments and peoples; questions both national and international must be referred thereto, and all must carry out the decrees of this Tribunal. Should any government or people disobey, let the whole world arise against that government or people.*

Selections from the Writings of 'Abdu'l-Bahá, http://bahai-library.com/writings/abdulbaha/swab/4/sec-203.html

----

16. Is violence against innocent people justifiable?
No. The Universal House of Justice has written:

> 'The use of force by the physically strong against the weak, as a means of imposing one's will and fulfilling one's desires, is a flagrant transgression of the Bahá'í Teachings. There can be no justification for anyone compelling another, through the use of force or through the threat of violence, to do that which the other person is not inclined.

'Abdu'l-Bahá has written:

> *O ye lovers of God! In this, the cycle of Almighty God, violence and force, constraint and oppression, are one and all condemned.*
>
> Quoted in letter from the Universal House of Justice, reprinted in *The American Bahá'í,* November 23, 1993, pp. 10-11

----

17. Can someone be a conscientious objector?
In our faith it is not allowed, though we can seek to serve in a non-combatant role. We are to obey just governments. Shoghi Effendi states:

> *Our position as Bahá'ís is not that we won't obey our Government or support the country if attacked, it is that we do not believe in, or wish to take part in, killing our fellow-men. We are not conscientious objectors at all; we will serve, but wish, as there is a provision in the law in the U.S.A. covering our attitude, to be classified as non-combatants. If you need to consult on this matter, you should refer to the N.S.A., as this question continually arises, and they can give you advice which will be the most accurate and applicable to present conditions.*
>
> *Lights of Guidance*, No. 1352, p. 407

----

18. Is force justifiable against children?
Regarding the disciplining of children, 'Abdu'l-Bahá says:

> *... Whensoever a mother seeth that her child hath done well, let her praise and applaud him and cheer his heart; and if the slightest undesirable trait should manifest itself, let her counsel the child and punish him, and use means based on reason, even a slight verbal chastisement should this be necessary. It is not, however, permissible to strike a child, or vilify him, for the child's character will be totally perverted if he be subjected to blows or verbal abuse.*
>
> *Selections from the Writings of 'Abdu'l-Bahá,* No. 95, p. 125

The Universal House of Justice emphasizes just how important this is:

> Among the signs of moral downfall in the declining moral order are the high incidence of violence within the family, the increase of degrading and cruel treatment of spouses and children, and the spread of sexual abuse. It is essential that the members of the community of the Greatest Name take the utmost care not to be drawn into acceptance of such practices because of their prevalence. They must be ever mindful of their obligations to exemplify a new way of life distinguished by its respect for the dignity and rights of all people, by its exalted moral tone, and by its freedom from oppression and from all forms of abuse.

From a letter online at http://bahai-library.com/uhj/violence.women.html

----

19. Is force justifiable against a spouse?

Again, this depends on the circumstances. A wife defending herself against an abusive husband would be allowable if such force is in self-defense and no other options exist.

The Universal House of Justice has written:
For a man to use force to impose his will on a woman is a serious transgression of the Bahá'í Teachings. 'Abdu'l-Bahá has stated that:

> *'The world in the past has been ruled by force, and man has dominated over woman by reason of his more forceful and aggressive qualities of body and mind. But the balance is already shifting; force is losing its dominance, and mental alertness, intuition, and the spiritual qualities of love and service, in which woman is strong, are gaining ascendancy.*
>
> Bahá'í men have the opportunity to demonstrate to the world around them a new approach to the relationship between the sexes, where aggression and the use of force are eliminated and replaced by cooperation and consultation. The Universal House of Justice has pointed out in response to questions addressed to it that, in a marriage relationship, neither husband nor wife should ever unjustly dominate the other, and that there are times when the husband and the wife should defer to the wishes of the other. If agreement cannot be reached through consultation, the couple should determine exactly under what circumstances such deference is to take place.
>
> 'From the Pen of Bahá'u'lláh Himself has come the following statement on the subject of the treatment of women:...
>
> *'No Bahá'í husband should ever beat his wife, or subject her to any form of cruel treatment; to do so would be an unacceptable abuse of the marriage relationship and contrary to the Teachings of Bahá'u'lláh.'*
> From a letter online at http://bahai-library.com/uhj/violence.women.html

----

20. Is suicide ever justifiable?

Our religion forbids suicide, but there have been many Bahá'í martyrs who knowingly went to their deaths.
One reason not to commit suicide is because of the harm it can do to the spirit. Shoghi Effendi says that

> 'Suicide is forbidden in the Cause. God Who is the Author of all life can alone take it away, and dispose of it in the way He deems best. Whoever commits suicide endangers his soul, and will suffer spiritually as a result in the other Worlds Beyond.... '
> *Lights of Guidance*, No. 677, p. 204

There was one prominent Bahá'í, Nabil, who drowned himself shortly after the death of Bahá'u'lláh in 1892. However, his action is neither condemned nor viewed as a role model. Shoghi Effendi explained that "Nabil's suicide was not insanity but love. He loved Bahá'u'lláh too much to go on in a world that no longer held Him." (*Unfolding Destiny,* Page 406)

----

21. To what extent is martyrdom acceptable?

Martyrdom is permitted if it is not done at one's own hands and is inflicted solely by others without solicitation, when, solely on account of our religious beliefs, others put us to death. We are to try to prevent this from happening, but we should not seek to save our life by denying our faith.

Martyrdom is one of the highest stations to which we can attain. Bahá'u'lláh says:

> *This is a Revelation, under which, if a man shed for its sake one drop of blood, myriads of oceans will be his recompense. Take heed, O friends, that ye forfeit not so inestimable a benefit, or disregard its transcendent station. Consider the multitude of lives that have been, and are still being, sacrificed in a world deluded by a mere phantom which the vain imaginations of its peoples have conceived.*
>
> *Gleanings from the Writings of Bahá'u'lláh*, sect. III, pp. 5-6.

However, martyrdom does not necessarily mean literally being killed for one's Faith. Those who sacrifice themselves by devoting their lives to teaching the Faith are equally martyrs. Martyrdom is also characterized by the high degree of detachment and sacrifice shown by the martyr. We have been told by the Universal House of Justice that what the Cause of God needs at this time are living martyrs. Even as 'Abdu'l-Bahá has stated:

> *... Martyrdom is the supreme test of belief. Great martyrs will arise in this Cause in the years to come. A believer is sometimes called upon to suffer a living martyrdom.*
> Quoted in *Ten Days in the Light of Akka,* Julia Grundy, p. 5.

The meanings of early Bahá'í martyrdom are discussed in depth in Jonah Winters' thesis "Dying for God: Martyrdom in the Shí'í and Bábí Religions," at http://bahai-library.com/theses/dying.

----

22. Is it right to kill an innocent person in order to save the life of another?

This is not allowable in most circumstances. It might be permissible in the case of an abortion of a fetus which endangers the life of the mother or in cases at times of tragedy when a choice must be made who receives medical attention first, etc. The Universal House of Justice says:

> Abortion and surgical operations for the purpose of preventing the birth of unwanted children are forbidden in the Cause unless there are circumstances which justify such actions on medical grounds, in which case the decision, at present, is left to the consciences of those concerned who must carefully weigh the medical advice in the light of the general guidance given in the Teachings...
> *Lights of Guidance*, No. 1155, p. 345

----

23. Is capital punishment acceptable; if so, for what offenses?

As an act of justice, capital punishment for murder is permitted, though life imprisonment is an acceptable alternative: "The law of Bahá'u'lláh prescribes the death penalty for murder and arson, with the alternative of life imprisonment." (Anonymous: *The Kitáb-i-Aqdas*, note 86, page 203-204).

The reason for such punishment must be understood to be corrective, not retributive. It is understood to have a cathartic result on the soul of the criminal and in taking away his life he will not have to pay for his crime in the next world. The above note continues:

> In His Tablets Abdu'l-Bahá explains the difference between revenge and punishment. He affirms that individuals do not have the right to take revenge, that revenge is despised in the eyes of God, and that the motive for punishment is not vengeance, but the imposition of a penalty for the committed offence. In *Some Answered Questions,* He confirms that it is the right of society to impose punishments on criminals for the purpose of protecting its members and defending its existence."
>
> ibid.

Having said this, capital punishment will only be enforced in a future Bahá'í society when humanity has "reached a much higher point of evolution," not in the society that we are living in now. It cannot be said in advance how a future Bahá'í society will apply which punishments to which types of offenses:

> The details of the Bahá'í law of punishment for murder and arson, a law designed for a future state of society, were not specified by Bahá'u'lláh. The various details of the law, such as degrees of offence, whether extenuating circumstances are to be taken into account, and which of the two prescribed punishments is to be the norm are left to the Universal House of Justice to decide in light of prevailing conditions when the law is to be in operation. The manner in which the punishment is to be carried out is also left to the Universal House of Justice to decide.
>
> ibid.

Finally, arson in the above is not necessarily meant as an offense resulting in capital punishment:

> In relation to arson, this depends on what "house" is burned. There is obviously a tremendous difference in the degree of offence between the person who burns down an empty warehouse and one who sets fire to a school full of children.
>
> ibid.

Science and Medicine

----

24. Under what circumstances, if any, is abortion allowable?

Abortion is considered morally wrong if it is done only to take the life of the unborn and not to save another life; abortion might be permitted in cases where the doctor and family involved decides it is necessary to save the life of the mother, in which case it is left to them to decide.

The Universal House of Justice says:

> Abortion and surgical operations for the purpose of preventing the birth of unwanted children are forbidden in the Cause unless there are circumstances which justify such actions on medical grounds, in which case the decision, at present, is left to the consciences of those concerned who must carefully weigh the medical advice in the light of the general guidance given in the Teachings. Beyond this nothing has been found in the Writings concerning specific methods or procedures to be used in family planning. It should be pointed out, however, that the Teachings state that the soul appears at conception, and that therefore it would be improper to use such a method, the effect of which would be to produce an abortion after conception has taken place.
>
> *Lights of Guidance*, No. 1155, p. 345

Regarding the case of rape, the Universal House of Justice says:

> One of the most heinous of sexual offenses is the crime of rape. When a believer is a victim, she is entitled to the loving aid and support of the members of her community, and is free to initiate action against the perpetrator under the law of the land should she wish to do so. If she becomes pregnant as a consequence of this assault, no pressure should be brought upon her by the Bahá'í institutions to marry. As to whether she should continue or terminate the pregnancy, it is left to her to decide on the course of action she should follow, taking into consideration medical and other relevant factors, and in the light of the Bahá'í Teachings ...
> Quoted in *The American Bahá'í*, November 23, 1993, pp. 10-11

----

25. Are autopsies allowable; if so, under what circumstances?

Autopsies are not forbidden, but proper respect to the body must be given and the autoposy must be followed by a proper burial according to religious law. The Báb explains the importance of treating the dead body with respect:

> *As this physical frame is the throne of the inner temple, whatever occurs to the former is felt by the latter. In reality that which takes delight in joy or is saddened by pain is the inner temple of the body, not the body itself. Since this physical body is the throne whereon the inner temple is established, God hath ordained that the body be preserved to the extent possible, so that nothing that causeth repugnance may be experienced. The inner temple beholdeth its physical frame, which is its throne. Thus, if the latter is accorded respect, it is as if the former is the recipient. The converse is likewise true.*
>
> *Therefore, it hath been ordained that the dead body should be treated with the utmost honour and respect.."*
>
> *Selections from the Writings of the Bab*, The Persian Bayan, V, 12, p. 95

----

26. Are there rules about body modification e.g. tattoos, cosmetic surgery or amputations?

There are no specific injunctions against them, but moderation should be observed. One is not to become a cause of displeasure to others, as pertains to one's dress and appearance.
On a similar subject, the Guardian has written:

> *Regarding Bahá'í women using facial make-up: individuals are entirely free to do as they please in such purely personal matters. As Bahá'ís are enjoined to use moderation in all things, and to seek the Golden mean, the National Spiritual Assembly can, if it deems it necessary or advisable, counsel the believers to use moderation in this respect also.*
>
> Shoghi Effendi: *Dawn of a New Day*, p. 193

Most especially, nothing should be done that would be harmful to one's body. Bahá'u'lláh says:

> *... Beware of using any substance that induceth sluggishness and torpor in the human temple and inflicteth harm upon the body. We, verily, desire for you naught save what shall profit you, and to this bear witness all created things, had ye but ears to hear.*
>
> *The Kitáb-i-Aqdas,* Par. 155, p. 75

----

27. Are transfusions allowed?

Transfusions are not prohibited. Indeed, we are instructed to seek and follow the advice of a competent physician when healing is needed. 'Abdu'l-Bahá says:

> *According to the explicit decree of Bahá'u'lláh one must not turn aside from the advice of a competent doctor. It is imperative to consult one even if the patient himself be a well-known and eminent physician. In short, the point is that you should maintain your health by consulting a highly-skilled physician.Selections from the Writings of 'Abdu'l-Bahá*, No. 135, p.156

----

28. Should extraordinary means be used to prolong life?

29. Should family and/or patients have the right to end suffering?

Extraordinary means to extend a life may be permissible with a doctor's advice and if it is not a cause of injustice. Regarding euthanasia, the Universal House of Justice has written:

> We have received your letter of March 18, 1974 in which you ask for the Bahá'í viewpoint on euthanasia and on the removal of life support in medical cases where physiological interventions prolong life in disabling illnesses. In general our teachings indicate that God, the Giver of life, can alone dispose of it as He deems best, and we have found nothing in the Sacred Text on these matters specifically but in a letter to an individual written on behalf of the beloved Guardian by his secretary regarding mercy killings, or legalized euthanasia, it is stated:
>
> "...this is also a matter which the Universal House of Justice will have to legislate."
>
> Until such time as the Universal House of Justice considers legislation on euthanasia, decisions in the matters to which you refer must be left to the consciences of those responsible.
>
> *Lights of Guidance*, pp. 291-292

----

30. Does anyone have the right to hasten death?

As a general principle, individuals are not to arrogate to themselves the responsibility for determining who may live. The Universal House of Justice has written: '... In general our teachings indicate that God, the Giver of life, can alone dispose of it as He deems best ... (*Lights of Guidance*, pages 291-292)

There are, of course, some exceptions: e.g. when abortion is necessary to save the life of the mother, or in the case where a criminal has incurred the death penalty. However, appropriate action in both cases must be decided by competent doctors and courts, respectively. Any other exceptions will have to be legislated by the Universal House of Justice as the issues arise.

----

31. In the case of conjoined twins when both will die if nothing is done to separate them but only one will live (and the other die) if the operation takes place, is the killing of one acceptable in order to save the life of the other?

The Bahá'í Faith has no explicit statement on this. The principle of preservation of life above all else would certainly apply, but how it would be applied would depend on the situation.

----

32. Is genetic engineering permissible?

There is no broad statement on this in the Bahá'í writings or legislation. The Universal House of Justice has written:

> The House of Justice has not found anything specific in the Bahá'í writings concerning the ethics of genetic engineering on human tissue, including foetal tissue, and on possible means of biologically creating replacement limbs and organs for human beings. It regards it as premature to give consideration to these matters and to their spiritual consequences. For the present, believers confronted with such issues are free to come to their own conclusions, based on their knowledge of the pertinent Bahá'í teachings. online at http://bahai-library.com/uhj/reproduction.html

The ethics of certain aspects of genetic engineering are thus left up to the individual. As the House recently clarified in response to a question about stem-cell research,

> For the present, believers faced with questions about them are free to come to their own conclusions based on their knowledge of the Bahá' i teachings on the nature and purpose of life.
>
> online at http://bahai-library.com/uhj/stem.cells.html

----

33. Is the theory of evolution compatible with your religion?
Yes, in its broad strokes the Bahá'í Faith accepts the theory of evolution. This fits in with the principle that science and religion each have their sphere of truth, and neither sphere can overrule the other sphere's authority. If a religion issues a teaching or ruling on a purely scientific fact which is contrary to the informed contemporary scientific consensus, then Bahá'ís are to accept the scientific explanation.
Speaking specifically about evolution, Abdu'l-Bahá explained;

> *[M]an, in the beginning of his existence and in the womb of the earth, like the embryo in the womb of the mother, gradually grew and developed, and passed from one form to another, from one shape to another, until he appeared with this beauty and perfection, this force and this power. It is certain that in the beginning he had not this loveliness and grace and elegance, and that he only by degrees attained this shape, this form, this beauty and this grace. There is no doubt that the human embryo did not at once appear in this form... Gradually it passed through various conditions and different shapes, until it attained this form and beauty, this perfection, grace and loveliness.*
>
> *Some Answered Questions,* section 47

Having said that, the Bahá'í Faith does not accept certain metaphysical extrapolations of evolutionary theory. For example, Abdu'l-Bahá explains that, though changing in outward form, the human identity has remained distinct from that of the animal.

> *[Man's] aspect, his form, his appearance and color change; he passes from one form to another, and from one appearance to another. Nevertheless, from the beginning of the embryonic period he is of the species of man--that is to say, an embryo of a man and not of an animal; but this is not at first apparent, but later it becomes visible and evident. For example, let us suppose that man once resembled the animal, and that now he has progressed and changed. Supposing this to be true, it is still not a proof of the change of species. No, as before mentioned, it is merely like the change and alteration of the embryo of man until it reaches the degree of reason and perfection. We will state it more clearly. Let us suppose that there was a time when man walked on his hands and feet, or had a tail; this change and alteration is like that of the fetus in the womb of the mother. Although it changes in all ways, and grows and develops until it reaches the perfect form, from the beginning it is a special species.*
>
> *Some Answered Questions,* p. 193

Shoghi Effendi offers a bit of clarification:

> *We cannot prove man was always man for this is a fundamental doctrine, but it is based on the assertion that nothing can exceed its own potentialities, that everything, a stone, a tree, an animal and a human being existed in plan, potentially, from the very "beginning" of creation. We don't believe man has always had the form of man, but rather that from the outset he was going to evolve into the human form and species and not be a haphazard branch of the ape family.*
>
> *Arohanui: Letters to New Zealand,* No. 75, p. 85

----

34. Are environmental concerns part of your religious ethic?
Yes, the Bahá'í Faith believes not only that this world is important for our development, but also that it has been entrusted to our stewardship. Therefore, care must be taken to preserve and better our physical environment. Shoghi Effendi says:

> *... For it is only through such divine precepts that the world can obtain peace and tranquility, and become an environment within which man can spiritually progress and attain his noble destiny.* Shoghi Effendi: *Light of Divine Guidance* Vol.1, No. p. 46

Moderation is again a key principle to achieving this end. Plant and animal species, many of which are important to our physical health and well-being, will not become endangered or extinct if moderation is exercised in how we use them and their environment. For example, regarding hunting, Bahá'u'lláh says:

> *... Take heed, however, that ye hunt not to excess. Tread ye the path of justice and equity in all things. Thus biddeth you He Who is the Dawning-place of Revelation, would that ye might comprehend. The Kitáb-i-Aqdas,* Par. 60, pp. 40-41

----

35. Do animals have any moral standing?

No, but Bahá'ís are exhorted to treat animals with the utmost respect. Bahá'u'lláh writes: *"Burden not an animal with more than it can bear. We, truly, have prohibited such treatment through a most binding interdiction in the Book"* (*Kitáb-i-Aqdas,* para. 187).

However, animals lack spiritual susceptibilities, are ignorant of divine religion, and have no knowledge of God. They thus do not have their own morality. This is discussed more fully online in Arthur Dahl's "The Bahá'í Attitude towards Animals" at http://www.bcca.org/ief/ddahl01a.htm

Though hunting is permitted, Bahá'u'lláh gives this warning:

> *... Take heed, however, that ye hunt not to excess. Tread ye the path of justice and equity in all things. Thus biddeth you He Who is the Dawning-place of Revelation, would that ye might comprehend. The Kitáb-i-Aqdas,* Par. 60, pp. 40-41

Bahá'ís are also not required to be vegetarians. However, Abdu'l-Bahá did state that humanity would gradually turn away from a meat-based diet and begin to rely much more heavily on fruits and grains. When asked "What will be the diet of the future?" Abdu'l-Bahá answered:

> *Fruit and grains. The time will come when meat will no longer be eaten. Medical science is only in its infancy, yet it has shown that our natural diet is that which grows out of the ground. The people will gradually develop up to the condition of this natural food."*
>
> *Ten Days in the Light of Akka,* online at http://bahai-library.com/books/tendays/words.html

Abdu'l-Bahá explains that we should regard harmful animals, not as ethically impure, but as pragmatically harmful; justice then requires that we treat harmful animals with less tolerance but be fully loving to the peaceful animals:

> *Most human beings are sinners, but the beasts are innocent. Surely those without sin should receive the most kindness and love - all except animals which are harmful, such as bloodthirsty wolves, such as poisonous snakes, and similar pernicious creatures, the reason being that kindness to these is an injustice to human beings and to other animals as well. If, for example, ye be tender-hearted toward a wolf, this is but tyranny to a sheep, for a wolf will destroy a whole flock of sheep. A rabid dog, if given the chance, can kill a thousand animals and men. Therefore, compassion shown to wild and ravening beasts is cruelty to the peaceful ones - and so the harmful must be dealt with. But to blessed animals the utmost kindness must be shown, the more the better. Tenderness and loving-kindness are basic principles of God's heavenly Kingdom. Ye should most carefully bear this matter in mind.*
>
> *Selections from the Writings of 'Abdu'l-Bahá,* No. 138, pp. 159-160

----

36. Does your religion predict an end of time? If so, when will that be and what will the world be like for humans?
This question could refer to three different issues: (a) the Big Bang; (b) a metaphysical beginning and ending to temporality itself, or (c) the Day of Judgment. The Bahá'í Faith affirms (a) via its emphasis on the primacy of science to solve scientific questions; it teaches that the metaphysics of (b) has no clear scientific answer; and it affirms the reality of and explains (c), the Day of Judgment. I'll explain further:
A) Big Bang:
Little need be said about this. The scientific consensus on the reality of the Big Bang and subsequent cosmology/planetary genesis is so broad and detailed that Bahá'ís accept it as scientific fact. However, this does not mean that Bahá'ís necessarily accept all metaphysical meanings physicists might express about their theories.
B) Beginning and ending of time itself:
There will not be an end of time. 'Abdu'l-Bahá says:

> *... For example, by present consideration we say that God is the creator. Then there must always have been a creation.... Therefore, God has no beginning and no ending; nor is His creation limited ever as to degree. Limitations of time and degree pertain to things created, never to the creation as a whole. They pertain to the forms of things, not to their realities. The effulgence of God cannot be suspended. Foundations of World Unity,* p. 53

Having said that, Bahá'í metaphysics also recognize that concepts such as the finiteness or infiniteness of time are just that -- metaphysical concepts only. In the "Tablet of Wisdom," Bahá'u'lláh explained:

> *As regards thine assertions about the beginning of creation, this is a matter on which conceptions vary by reason of the divergences in men's thoughts and opinions. Wert thou to assert that it hath ever existed and shall continue to exist, it would be true; or wert thou to affirm the same concept as is mentioned in the sacred Scriptures,* [i.e., that time had a beginning in Creation] *no doubt would there be about it, for it hath been revealed by God...*
>
> *That which hath been in existence had existed before, but not in the form thou seest today. The world of existence came into being through the heat generated from the interaction between the active force and that which is its recipient. These two are the same, yet they are different. Thus doth the Great Announcement inform thee about this glorious structure."*
>
> *Tablets of Bahá'u'lláh,* online at http://bahai-library.com/writings/bahaulláh/tb/8.html

C) Day of Judgment:
As for what many believe to be the Day of Judgement, the Day of God, or the Day of Resurrection, Shoghi Effendi says:

> *'Concerning the meaning of "Resurrection": although this term is often used by Bahá'u'lláh in His Writings, as in the passage quoted in your letter, its meaning is figurative. The tomb mentioned is also allegorical, i.e. the tomb of unbelief. The Day of Resurrection, according to Bahá'í interpretation, is the Judgement Day, the Day when unbelievers will be called upon to give account of their actions, and whether the world has prevented them from acknowledging the new Revelation.*
>
> *'The passage in Bahá'u'lláh's Tablet in which He explains the Sura of "The Sun" should not be interpreted literally. It does not mean that after the Day of Resurrection praise and peace will cease to be vouchsafed to the Prophet. Rather it means to the end of time, i.e. indefinitely and for all times." Dawn of a New Day*, pp. 79-80

Indeed, this Day of God comes whenever a new Manifestation appears in the world. Bahá'u'lláh says:

> *It is evident that every age in which a Manifestation of God hath lived is divinely ordained, and may, in a sense, be characterized as God's appointed Day...." Gleanings from the Writings of Bahá'u'lláh,* Sect. XXV, p. 60)

However, the appearance of the next Manifestation of God, and therefore the next Day of God, is not for many years to come. Bahá'u'lláh says: " *Whoso layeth claim to a Revelation direct from God, ere the expiration of a full thousand years, such a man is assuredly a lying impostor. ...*" (*The Kitáb-i-Aqdas*, Par. 37, p.32) As for humanity's immediate future: following the periods of test and travail that invariably precede paradigm-shifting growth, Shoghi Effendi quotes Bahá'u'lláh:

> *' "The winds of despair," writes Bahá'u'lláh, as He surveys the immediate destinies of mankind, "are, alas, blowing from every direction, and the strife that divides and afflicts the human race is daily increasing. The signs of impending convulsions and chaos can now be discerned, inasmuch as the prevailing order appears to be lamentably defective." "Such shall be its plight," He, in another connection, has declared, "that to disclose it now would not be meet and seemly." "These fruitless strifes," He, on the other hand, contemplating the future of mankind, has emphatically prophesied, in the course of His memorable interview with the Persian Orientalist, Edward G. Browne, "these ruinous wars shall pass away, and the 'Most Great Peace' shall come.... These strifes and this bloodshed and discord must cease, and all men be as one kindred and one family." "Soon," He predicts,"will the present-day order be rolled up, and a new one spread out in its stead." "After a time," He also has written, "all the governments on earth will change. Oppression will envelop the world. And following a universal convulsion, the sun of justice will rise from the horizon of the unseen realm." "The whole earth," He, moreover, has stated, "is now in a state of pregnancy. The day is approaching when it will have yielded its noblest fruits, when from it will have sprung forth the loftiest trees, the most enchanting blossoms, the most heavenly blessings." "All nations and kindreds," Abdu'l-Bahá likewise has written, "...will become a single nation. Religious and sectarian antagonism, the hostility of races and peoples, and differences among nations, will be approaching when it will have yielded its noblest fruits, when from it will have sprung forth the loftiest trees, the most enchanting blossoms, the most heavenly blessings." "All nations and kindreds," Abdu'l-Bahá likewise has written, "...will become a single nation. Religious and sectarian antagonism, the hostility of races and peoples, and differences among nations, will be eliminated. All men will adhere to one religion, will have one common faith, will be blended into one race, and become a single people. All will dwell in one common fatherland, which is the planet itself."* Shoghi Effendi: *The Promised Day is Come*, pp. 116-117

Behavior

----

37. Is sex outside marriage permissible?

No. Bahá'u'lláh forbids adultery in the *Kitáb-i-Aqdas*, His Book of Laws:

> "*Ye have been forbidden to commit murder or adultery, or to engage in backbiting or calumny; shun ye, then, what hath been prohibited in the holy Books and Tablets.*" (*The Kitáb-i-Aqdas*, Par. 19, p. 26)

He then sets the penalty for it:

> *God hath imposed a fine on every adulterer and adulteress, to be paid to the House of Justice: nine mithqals of gold, to be doubled if they should repeat the offence. Such is the penalty which He Who is the Lord of Names hath assigned them in this world; and in the world to come He hath ordained for them a humiliating torment. Should anyone be afflicted by a sin, it behoveth him to repent thereof and return unto his Lord. He, verily, granteth forgiveness unto whomsoever He willeth, and none may question that which it pleaseth Him to ordain. He is, in truth, the Ever-Forgiving, the Almighty, the All-Praised.* Bahá'u'lláh, *The Kitáb-i-Aqdas*, Par. 49, p. 37

In the endnotes section of the *Kitáb-i-Aqdas*, it is written:

> 'The Arabic word "*zina*", here translated as "adultery", signifies both fornication and adultery. It applies not only to sexual relations between a married person and someone who is not his or her spouse, but also to extramarital sexual intercourse in general. One form of "*zina*" is rape. The only penalty prescribed by Bahá'u'lláh is for those who commit fornication (see note 77); penalties for other kinds of sexual offence are left to the Universal House of Justice to determine.' Anonymous, *The Kitáb-i-Aqdas*, Notes Section, Note 36, p.181

----

38. Is sex only for procreation?
No, though procreation is one major reason for sex within marriage. Bahá'u'lláh writes:

> ... *Enter into wedlock, O people, that ye may bring forth one who will make mention of Me amid My servants. This is My bidding unto you; hold fast to it as an assistance to yourselves. The Kitáb-i-Aqdas*, Par. 63, p. 41.

However, the Bahá'í Faith also recognizes the sex impulse, and that there is a place for that in the lives of the individual. The Universal House of Justice quotes the Guardian as follows:

> *'The Guardian has clarified, in letters written on his behalf, that "The Bahá'í Faith recognizes the value of the sex impulse," and that "The proper use of the sex instinct is the natural right of every individual, and it is precisely for this very purpose that the institution of marriage has been established."'* The Universal House of Justice, from a Message dated January 24, 1993, reprinted in *The American Bahá'í*, November 23, 1993, pp. 10-11

----

39. Is masturbation allowed?
It is discouraged. Shoghi Effendi wrote:

> *The Bahá'í Faith recognizes the value of the sex impulse, but condemns its illegitimate and improper expressions such as free love, companionate marriage and others, all of which it considers positively harmful to man and to the society in which he lives. The proper use of the sex instinct is the natural right of every individual, and it is precisely for this purpose that the institution of marriage has been established. The Bahá'ís do not believe in the suppression of the sex impulse but in its regulation and control. Lights of Guidance,* No. 1156, p. 345.

However, it is also a matter Bahá'ís are encouraged not to dwell unduly on. The Universal House of Justice says,

> You should remember, however, that [masturbation] is only one of the many temptations and faults that a human being must strive to overcome during his lifetime, and you should not increase the difficulty you have by over-emphasizing its importance.... Be vigilant against temptation, but do not allow it to claim too great a share of your attention. You should concentrate, rather, on the virtues that you should develop, the services you should strive to render, and, above all, on God and His attributes, and devote your energies to living a full Bahá'í life in all its many aspects." *Lights of Guidance,* No. 1220

----

40. Is genital sex the only morally permissible type?
The Bahá'í Faith has no explicit statement on this. Bahá'u'lláh did expressly forbid *liwat,* but there is some disagreement on the exact meaning of this Arabic word. It almost exactly translates as Sodomy, in that the word *liwat* means "the

crime of Lot," i.e. the escapee from Sodom. However, just as the English word "sodomy" has multiple legal meanings, so did *liwat.* Its application to the Bahá'í context has yet to be clarified by the Universal House of Justice. More detail is found at http://bahai-library.com/conferences/sex.aqdas.html

.Shoghi Effendi provides some general principles:

> *On the question of sex the Bahá'ís are, in most of their fundamental views, in full agreement with the upholders of traditional morality. Bahá'u'lláh, like all the other Prophets and Messengers of God, preaches abstinence, and condemns, in vehement language, all forms of sexual laxity, unbridled licence and lust. The Bahá'í standard of sex morality is thus very high, but it is by no means unreasonably rigid. While free love is condemned, yet marriage is though not forced, to perform. Sex instinct, like all other human instincts, is not necessarily evil. It is a power which, if properly directed, can bring joy and satisfaction to the individual. If misused or abused it brings, of course, incalculable harm not only to the individual but also to the society in which he lives.*"6 April 1936 *Unfolding Destiny*, pp. 434-435

----

41. Are there moral codes regarding dress and hairstyles?

Moderation and courtesy in dress and appearance must be practiced, so as not to offend. Regarding the hair, Bahá'u'lláh says:

> *Shave not your heads; God hath adorned them with hair, and in this there are signs from the Lord of creation to those who reflect upon the requirements of nature. He, verily, is the God of strength and wisdom. Notwithstanding, it is not seemly to let the hair pass beyond the limit of the ears. Thus hath it been decreed by Him Who is the Lord of all worlds.*
> *The Kitáb-i-Aqdas*, par. 44, p. 35.

The exact meaning of these statements has not yet been defined, e.g. what it means for hair to "pass beyond the limit of the ears."

----

42. Is transvestism immoral?
43. Is homosexuality immoral?
44. Should gay marriages be recognized by the state?

While there is no statement on transvestitism, Bahá'í teachings as conveyed by the Universal House of Justice do discuss transexuallity. Both homosexuality and transsexuality are considered immoral:

> *No matter how devoted and fine the love may be between people of the same sex, to let it find expression in sexual acts is wrong. To say that it is ideal is no excuse. Immorality of every sort is really forbidden by Bahá'u'lláh, and homosexual relationships he looks upon as such, besides being against nature.*
> From a letter written on behalf of the Guardian, March 26, 1950

In practice, though, it's regarded more as a handicap than a moral failing, especially if it's the result of a treatable psychological disorder.

> A number of sexual problems such as homosexuality and transsexuality can well have medical aspects, and in such cases recourse should certainly be had to the best medical assistance. But it is clear from the teaching of Bahá'u'lláh that homosexuality is not a condition to which a person should be reconciled, but is a distortion of his or her nature which should be controlled and overcome. This may require a hard struggle, but so also can be the struggle of a heterosexual person to control his or her desires.

From a letter of the Universal House of Justice, cited in *Messages from The Universal House of Justice 1968-1973*, p. 110-111

Part of the reason for this emphasis on "normal" sexuality is given as an endnote to the English translation of the *Kitáb-i-Aqdas,* which also explains why the state must not recognize gay marriage:

> *The Bahá'í teachings on sexual morality centre on marriage and the family as the bedrock of the whole structure of human society and are designed to protect and strengthen that divine institution. Bahá'í law thus restricts permissible sexual intercourse to that between a man and the woman to whom he is married.*
> Anonymous, *The Kitáb-i-Aqdas*, Notes Section, Note 134, p. 223

----

45. Should all people have equal rights under the law even if they engage in immoral behavior?
If the immoral behavior is determined to be criminal by secular law, then those convicted of such should lose some or all of their rights. But as long as behaviour is not criminal or harmful to society, justice is the right of every individual, without prejudice of any kind. However, if the immoral behaviour is itself considered a crime, then the individual is then subject to the penalties set for that crime if convicted, just as every other individual is subject to the same laws and incurs the penalties for breaking a law.

----

46. Is it immoral to have more than one spouse at time?
Bahá'u'lláh officially limited the number of wives a man might have from four -- the prevailing Muslim standard as prescribed by Muhammad -- to two but encouraged only one. He states:

> *God hath prescribed matrimony unto you. Beware that ye take not unto yourselves more wives than two. Whoso contenteth himself with a single partner from among the maidservants of God, both he and she shall live in tranquillity....* Bahá'u'lláh, *The Kitáb-i-Aqdas*, Par. 63, p. 41

However, Abdu'l-Bahá clarified that, by conditioning bigamy upon justice, Bahá'u'lláh was in practice allowing only one wife; fully equal justice would not be possible in a marriage of two women to one man. An endnote to the Kitáb-i-Aqdas quotes Abdu'l-Bahá:

> *'Know thou that polygamy is not permitted under the law of God, for contentment with one wife hath been clearly stipulated. Taking a second wife is made dependent upon equity and justice being upheld between the two wives, under all conditions. However, observance of justice and equity towards two wives is utterly impossible. The fact that bigamy has been made dependent upon an impossible condition is clear proof of its absolute prohibition. Therefore it is not permissible for a man to have more than one wife.'*
> *The Kitáb-i-Aqdas*, Note 89, pp. 205-206

----

47. Is divorce acceptable?
Divorce is provided for in Bahá'í law, but is highly discouraged except in cases where reconciliation is impossible. Bahá'u'lláh says:

> *Should resentment or antipathy arise between husband and wife, he is not to divorce her but to bide in patience throughout the course of one whole year, that perchance the fragrance of affection may be renewed between them. If, upon the completion of this period, their love hath not returned, it is permissible for divorce to take place. God's wisdom, verily, hath encompassed all things.*
>
> *The Kitáb-i-Aqdas*, Par. 68, pp. 43-44

However, it must be observed that divorce was seen as only a last-resort option. In the next paragraph, Bahá'u'lláh continued:

> *Truly, the Lord loveth union and harmony and abhorreth separation and divorce. Live ye one with another, O people, in radiance and joy. By My life! All that are on earth shall pass away, while good deeds alone shall endure; to the truth of My words God doth Himself bear witness. Compose your differences, O My servants; then heed ye the admonition of Our Pen of Glory and follow not the arrogant and wayward.* ibid, p. 44, #70

Regarding its prevalent practice in Western society, Shoghi Effendi wrote:

> *There is no doubt about it that the believers in America, probably unconsciously influenced by the extremely lax morals prevalent and the flippant attitude towards divorce which seems to be increasingly prevailing, do not take divorce seriously enough and do not seem to grasp the fact that although Bahá'u'lláh has permitted it, He has only permitted it as a last resort and strongly condemns it. Lights of Guidance* #1309

----

48. Are the roles played by men and women a moral issue?

Their roles are largely a consequence of nature, but their equality is an indisputable religious, and therefore moral, fact. 'Abdu'l-Bahá says:

> *'In this divine age the bounties of God have encompassed the world of women. Equality of men and women, except in some negligible instances, has been fully and categorically announced. Distinctions have been utterly removed.' That men and women differ from one another in certain characteristics and functions is an inescapable fact of nature; the important thing is that He regards such inequalities as remain between the sexes as being 'negligible'.* Quoted in a "Women, A Compilation"; *Lights of Guidance*, No. 2102, p. 622

----

49. Are men and women separate but equal?

Yes, though Abdu'l-Bahá explains that women excel men in some categories and men excel women in other categories.

In the Introduction to *The Kitáb-i-Aqdas* is found this statement:

> *... That men and women differ from one another in certain characteristics and functions is an inescapable fact of nature and makes possible their complementary roles in certain areas of the life of society; but it is significant that Abdu'l-Bahá has stated that in this Dispensation "Equality of men and women, except in some negligible instances, has been fully and categorically announced.* Anonymous, introduction to *The Kitáb-i-Aqdas,* p. 7

However, Abdu'l-Bahá also explains that the world's gradual equalizing of male and female roles will give the impression of a femininization of society, as the once-underrepresented feminine ideals and attitutes take equal place with masculine ones.

> *The world in the past has been ruled by force, and man has dominated over woman by reason of his more forceful and aggressive qualities both of body and mind. But the balance is already shifting--force is losing its weight and mental alertness, intuition, and the spiritual qualities of love and service, in which woman is strong, are gaining ascendancy. Hence the new age will be an age less masculine, and more permeated with the feminine ideals--or, to speak more exactly, will be an age in which the masculine and feminine elements of civilization will be more evenly balanced.* Abdu'l-Bahá, quoted in *Bahá'u'lláh and the New Era,* 1976 U.S. edition, p. 156

----

50. Is the use of drugs and/or alcohol allowable?

No, unless proscribed by a competent doctor. A letter from the Universal House of Justice writes:

> ...One of these ordinances is the clear prohibition in the Writings of Bahá'u'lláh of the consumption of alcoholic drinks. This has been explicitly revealed in His Most Holy Book, the Kitáb-i-Aqdas. He states, "*It is inadmissible that man, who hath been endowed with reason, should consume that which stealeth it away. Nay, rather it behooveth him to comport himself in a manner worthy of the human station, and not in accordance with the misdeeds of every heedless and wavering soul* http://bahai-library.com/uhj/alcohol.html

Abdu'l-Bahá explains the harmful effects of drugs:

> *As to opium, it is foul and accursed. God protect us from the punishment He inflicteth on the user. According to the explicit Text of the Most Holy Book, it is forbidden, and its use is utterly condemned. Reason showeth that smoking opium is a kind of insanity, and experience attesteth that the user is completely cut off from the human kingdom. May God protect all against the perpetration of an act so hideous as this, an act which layeth in ruins the very foundation of what it is to be human, and which causeth the user to be dispossessed for ever and ever. For opium fasteneth on the soul, so that the user's conscience dieth, his mind is blotted away, his perceptions are eroded. It turneth the living into the dead. It quencheth the natural heat.* http://bahai-library.com/writings/abdulbaha/swab/4/sec-130.html

Shoghi Effendi explains that these prohibitions apply to all drugs:

> *[The Bahá'í Faith] requires total abstinence from all alcoholic drinks, from opium, and from similar habit-forming drugs:* http://bahai-library.com/writings/shoghieffendi/adj/2.html#20

----

51. Should prayers be allowed in public schools?

There is no statement on this, nor a clear principle I can think of that would shed light on this. There is the statement that "spiritual education is the light of the world of humanity and that its absence in the world is darkness itself," but extending this to cover prayer in school would be a stretch. The Bahá'í Faith does support the current separation of church and state.

----

52. Should the state subsidize religious schools or programs?

The state is not obligated to do so. However, it would be in the best interests of the state to do everything possible to see that all receive not only education that trains the mind, but also the spiritual education, which includes morals, that religion is so ideal for teaching. About the importance of religious and moral education, 'Abdu'l-Bahá says that "*spiritual education is the light of the world of humanity and that its absence in the world is darkness itself.*" (*Promulgation of Universal Peace*, p. 331)

'Abdu'l-Bahá also comments on the education of children and the importance which their training in morals has to society:

> *Training in morals and good conduct is far more important than book learning. A child that is cleanly, agreeable, of good character, well-behaved - even though he be ignorant - is preferable to a child that is rude, unwashed, ill-natured, and yet becoming deeply versed in all the sciences and arts. The reason for this is that the child who conducts himself well, even though he be ignorant, is of benefit to others, while an ill-natured, ill-behaved child is corrupted and harmful to others, even though he be learned. If, however, the child be trained to be both learned and good, the result is light upon light.*

> *"Children are even as a branch that is fresh and green; they will grow up in whatever way ye train them. Take the utmost care to give them high ideals and goals, so that once they come of age, they will cast their beams like brilliant candles on the world, and will not be defiled by lusts and passions in the way of animals, heedless and unaware, but instead will set their hearts on achieving everlasting honour and acquiring all the excellences of humankind. Selections from the Writings of 'Abdu'l-Bahá,* No. 110, pp. 135-136

However, any state-subsidized religious school would not be able to indoctrinate into politics:

> *Politics are occupied with the material things of life. Religious teachers should not invade the realm of politics; they should concern themselves with the spiritual education of the people; they should ever give good counsel to men, trying to serve God and human kind; they should endeavour to awaken spiritual aspiration, and strive to enlarge the understanding and knowledge of humanity, to improve morals, and to increase the love for justice.*
>
> *This is in accordance with the Teaching of Bahá'u'lláh. In the Gospel also it is written, 'Render unto Caesar the things which are Caesar's, and unto God the things which are God's '.* 'Abdu'l-Bahá: *Paris Talks*, pp. 158-159

----

53. Is the food a person eats a religious and/or moral concern?

We are taught to respect the gift of the body we have been given by the Creator. However, there are few restrictions regarding one's diet: alcohol is forbidden, as are the results of some hunting practices. Regarding the latter, in the Questions and Answers Section of *The Kitáb-i-Aqdas,* Bahá'u'lláh clarifies the passage regarding hunting as follows:

> *[Concerning hunting] He saith, exalted be He: "If ye should hunt with beasts or birds of prey" and so forth. Other means, such as bows and arrows, guns, and similar equipment employed in hunting, are also included. If, however, traps or snares are used, and the game dieth before it can be reached, it is unlawful for consumption.*
>
> Bahá'u'lláh, *The Kitáb-i-Aqdas,* Questions and Answers Section, No. 24, p. 115

As to the food of the future, when asked what this would be, 'Abdu'l-Bahá said:

> *Fruit and grains. The time will come when meat will no longer be eaten. Medical science is only in its infancy, yet it has shown that our natural diet is that which grows out of the ground. The people will gradually develop up to the condition of this natural food.*
>
> quoted in *Ten Days in the Light of Akka, Julia Grundy, pp. 8-9*

Food does become a religious matter during the period of the Fast. This is March 1 - March 20 each year, during which time Bahá'ís refrain from all food and water from sunrise to sunset and are to use their hunger to help meditate on the meaning of the body and of the spirit.

----

54. Is gambling allowed?

No, Bahá'u'lláh forbids gambling in the following paragraph from His Book of Laws: "*Gambling and the use of opium have been forbidden unto you. Eschew them both, O people, and be not of those who transgress.*" (*The Kitáb-i-Aqdas,* Par. 155, p. 75)
This is elaborated in the endnotes to the Aqdas:

> The activities that are included in this prohibition have not been outlined in the Writings of Bahá'u'lláh. As both 'Abdu'l-Bahá and Shoghi Effendi have indicated, it is left to the Universal House of Justice to specify the

details of this prohibition. In response to questions about whether lotteries, betting on such things as horse races and football games, bingo, and the like, are included under the prohibition of gambling, the Universal House of Justice has indicated that this is a matter that will be considered in detail in the future. In the meantime, the Assemblies and individuals are counselled not to make an issue of these matters and to leave it to the conscience of the individual believers.

The House of Justice has ruled that it is not appropriate for funds for the Faith to be raised through lotteries, raffles, and games of chance.

Bahá'u'lláh, *The Kitáb-i-Aqdas,* endnote #169

----

55. Is smoking allowed?
Yes, though tobacco only, and yet it is highly discouraged. 'Abdu'l-Bahá says:

> *But there are other forbidden things which do not cause immediate harm, and the injurious effects of which are only gradually produced: such acts are also repugnant to the Lord, and blameworthy in His sight, and repellent. The absolute unlawfulness of these, however, hath not been expressly set forth in the Text, but their avoidance is necessary to purity, cleanliness, the preservation of health, and freedom from addiction.*
>
> *Among these latter is smoking tobacco, which is dirty, smelly, offensive - an evil habit, and one the harmfulness of which gradually becometh apparent to all. Every qualified physician hath ruled - and this hath also been proven by tests - that one of the components of tobacco is a deadly poison, and that the smoker is vulnerable to many and various diseases. This is why smoking hath been plainly set forth as repugnant from the standpoint of hygiene... [I]n the sight of God, smoking tobacco is deprecated, abhorrent, filthy in the extreme; and, albeit by degrees, highly injurious to health. It is also a waste of money and time, and maketh the user a prey to a noxious addiction. To those who stand firm in the Covenant, this habit is therefore censured both by reason and experience, and renouncing it will bring relief and peace of mind to all men. Furthermore, this will make it possible to have a fresh mouth and unstained fingers, and hair that is free of a foul and repellent smell. On receipt of this missive, the friends will surely, by whatever means and even over a period of time, forsake this pernicious habit. Such is my hope.*
>
> *Selections from the Writings of 'Abdu'l-Bahá,* pp. 147-148

****

4.15 A Reappraisal of Typologies of New Religious Movements and Characteristics of the Unification Church

(Original publication in The Journal of Unification of States)
Yoshihiko Masuda

http://www.uts.edu/OLD/reappraisal.html

If we want to have an enlightened discussion on the Unification Church (UC) or any new Religious Movement (NRM), *1* we must acquire a clear under-standing of typological concepts and terms. Sometimes scholarly discussion of NRMs suffers from typological ambiguity and confusion (e.g., various concepts of cults). Misunderstand-ing of the UC has been made worse by ignorance of typological terms and concepts, which are intellectual tools to distinguish and to articulate the characteristics of religious groups from a comparative perspective. I am convinced that clarifying typological conceptuali-zations and categories is a prerequisite to an enlightened discussion of the UC or of any religious group.

In this paper, we will review and reappraise contemporary typologies of NRMs presented by the following scholars: 1) Robert Ellwood, 2) David Aberle, 3) Charles Glock and Robert Bellah, 4) Dick Anthony, 5) Frederick Bird, 6) Barbara Hargrove, 7) Frances Westley, and 8) John Lofland and James Richardson. In introducing each typology, we will examine how scholars identified, or would have identified, the UC in applying each typology. As a Unificationist, I am ever desirous of criticizing some scholars' erroneous characterizations of the UC and appreciating other scholars' helpful identifications. It is important for Unificationists to be aware how the church is characterized in scholarly works and to offer articulate critiques of misleading analyses.2

1. Ellwood's Typology

In *Religious and Spiritual Groups in Modern America*, historian of religion Robert S. Ellwood introduced many NRMs in America by organizing them into six categories primarily on the basis of their historical origins.3 The following are his six categories, his elegant phrases to sum up each category, and the religious and spiritual groups Ellwood classified in each category:

1) Groups in the Theosophical and Rosicrucian Traditions: "New Vessels for the Ancient Wisdom"
The Theosophical Society in America, The Full Moon Meditation Groups, Anthroposophy, Rosicrucianism, Modern Gnosticism, The "I Am" Movement, The Liberal Catholic Church
2) Spiritualism and UFO Cults: "The Descent of the Mighty Ones"
The Spiritualist Church, Giant Rock Space Convention, Understanding, Inc., Amalgamated Flying Saucer Clubs of America, The Aetherius Society
3) Initiatory Groups: "The Crystal Within"
Gurdjieff Groups, The Prosperos, Scientology, Abilitism, Builders of the Adytum, The Church of Light
4) Neo-Paganism: "The Edenic Bower"
Feraferia, Church of All Worlds, Ceremonial Magic and Witchcraft, Satanism
5) Hindu Movements in America: "The Ganges Flows West"
The Ramakrishna Mission and Vedanta Societies, The Self-Realization Fellowship, The Maharishi Mahesh Yogi's Transcendental Meditation Movement, International Sivananda Yoga Society, The International Society for Krishna Consciousness
6) Other Oriental Movements: "The East in the Golden West"
Western Zen, Esoteric Buddhism in America, Nichiren Shoshu of America, The Baha'i Faith, The Lovers of Meher Baba, Subud, The Unified Family

Ellwood classified the American UC in the 1960s, which its members used to call "The Unified Family," as one of the Other Oriental Movements.4 He also described it as one of the rare non-Western Christian cults in America.5

In his Introduction to an annotated bibliography entitled *New Religious Move-ments in the United States and Canada*, Ellwood revised his earlier classificatory scheme and presented nine categories to classify the NRMs.6 Based largely on the historical and geographical origins of the NRMs, the nine are as follows:

1) Theosophical, Rosicrucian, Gnostic
2) New Thought
3) Spiritualist/UFO Groups
4) Occult/Initiatory Groups
5) Neo-Paganism and Its Allies
6) Eastern Religions I: From India
7) Eastern Religions II: From East Asia
8) Eastern Religions III: From Islamic Countries
9) Christian Movements

It is noteworthy that Ellwood classified the UC as among the Christian Movements. When we consider the UC's historical origin and theological tenets, it is certainly fair to classify the UC as a group belonging to a Christian family.

Ellwood's nine categories for classifying the NRMs make his scheme less reductionistic than many of the sociological typologies of NRMs that employ a very small number of categories-frequently two or three.7 This is, however, a typology for those who are interested in the location of the historical hometown of the NRMs from the East. On the basis of their historical origins, eastern religions are divided into those stemming from India, from East Asia, and from Islamic countries. Sociologists of religion who are inter-ested in understanding a NRM's social role in its current host society tend to find this typology inadequate. Many historians of religions, however, appreciate this typology because it presents an accurate classifying scheme for NRMs on the basis of historical and theological data.

2. Aberle's Typology

Anthropologists have also contributed to the classification of social and religious movements. David F. Aberle in his book *The Peyote Religion among the Navaho* presented one of the most influential classifications among them.*8* According to Aberle,

Social movements may be classified by reference to two dimensions. One is the dimension of the locus of the change sought. The other is the dimension of the amount of change sought. As to locus, a movement may aim to change individu-als or some supra-individual system-the economic order, the technological order, the political order, the law, a total society or culture, the world, or indeed the cosmos. As to amount of change, movements may aim at total or partial change. These two dimensions give rise to four types□c9.

Utilizing these two dimensions, Aberle presented the following four types of social movements: 1) *transformative movements*, which aim at a total change in supra-individ-ual systems, 2) *reformative movements*, which aim at a partial change in supra-individual systems, 3) *redemptive movements*, which aim at a total change in individuals, and 4) *alterative movements*, which aim at a partial change in individuals. Because Aberle clearly acknowledged that religious movements constitute one class of social move-ments, we will be allowed to present Aberle's typology of social movements as a typology of NRMs as well. It is illustrated in Figure 1.

Figure 1: Aberle's Typology of New Religious Movements*10*

		Locus of Change	
		Supra-individual	Individual
Amount of Change	Total	Transformative	Redemptive
	Partial	Reformative	Alterative

A number of scholars applied Aberle's typology of social movements to their studies on NRMs.*11* Bryan Wilson referred to Aberle's typology in his *Magic and Millennium.12* In *"Moonies" in America*, David Bromley and Anson Shupe discussed Aberle's classification as a framework to understand the Unification movement.*13* Keith Roberts in his textbook also discussed Aberle's typology in the section on the NRMs.*14*

Following Aberle's typology, Bromley and Shupe identified the Unification movement as a "transformative" movement that aims at a total change in the supra-individual system. In fact, they called it "a world-transforming movement." I have acquired, however, certain reservation about their identifying the Unificationist move-ment as a "transformative" movement on the basis of Aberle's typology.*15* It appears to me that Bromley and Shupe underestimated the UC's efforts for a total change of indi-viduals-an aspect of a redemptive movement. In my view, the Unification movement attempts to bring about a total change of individuals and subsequent to or almost simultaneously with a total change of supra-individuals (culture and social structures). Aberle's category of the "redemptive movement" does not fit the Unification movement well, not because the UC is indifferent to the total change of individuals, but because movements in that category are assumed to be rather indifferent to changing the culture and social structures. Neither category is totally appropriate for the Unification movement, which is concerned with both.

In contrast to Bromley and Shupe's emphasis on the "supra-individual" world-transforming goals and activities of the Unification movement, Joseph Fichter found the UC essentially evangelistic and individualistic in its strategy of building the Kingdom of God on earth.*16* Even though the *CAUSA Lecture Manual* might be assumed to be evidence for the movement's world-transforming goals, the thrust of its content is rather more in agreement with Fichter's analysis than with Bromley and Shupe's.*17* In my view, however, Fichter's description of the UC somewhat underestimates the significance of its supra-individual "transformative" or "reformative" activities.

One must be fully aware that Aberle's typology presents so-called "ideal types" or pure types. Ideal types are not labels, but yardsticks to understand reality. Therefore, as Aberle himself cautioned, real movements always have a combination of elements from different types.*18*

3. Glock and Bellah's Typology

In *The New Religious Consciousness*, Charles Glock and Robert Bellah's celebrated book on NRMs in the San Francisco Bay area, they provide us with a three-fold classification of the NRMs:*19*

1) New Religious Movements in the Asian Tradition
2) New Quasi-Religious Movements
3) New Religious Movements in the Western Tradition

Although these categories are too simple to constitute a systematic typology, this three-fold classification is a commonsensical and convenient one. Tipton followed it in his research, selecting a typical NRM from each of these three categories (The Living Word Fellowship, Erhard Seminar Training [est], Pacific Zen Center) as subjects for his study.*20*

Strangely enough, Glock and Bellah's book did not include any research on the UC, despite Lofland and Stark's prior extensive research on it in the San Francisco Bay area and tremendous controversies about the UC in the mid-1970s.*21* Apparently, Glock and Bellah's classification was determined not inductively but deductively. The three-fold classification was decided first, and then nine representative NRMs-three of the most typical NRMs for each of the three types-were selected afterwards. However, the UC is not a representative type of any of Glock and Bellah's three categories. In light of its *geographical* origin from Korea, the UC is somewhat close to the "NRMs in the Asian Tradition"; on the other hand, in light of its *theological* origin, because its teachings are unmistakably based on the Judeo-Christian tradition, it is one of the "NRMs in the Western Tradition." If we were compelled to choose just one type among the three in classifying the UC, it would be "NRMs in the Western Tradition." Yet because of its Korean roots, the UC is not a typical example of NRMs in that category. Glock and Bellah's threefold classificatory scheme is too simple to deal with syncretic or eclectic NRMs such as the UC.*22*

4. Anthony's Typology

One of the most systematic and influential typologies of NRMs was formul-ated by Dick Anthony. He first introduced his typology in *Sociological Analysis* in 1978, revising it in later years.*23* It was originally developed as a device for summarizing his team's research into the mental health effects of the new religions.*24* We will begin by discussing his first presentation of the typology, where it became widely known and influential.

Viewing the contemporary emergence of NRMs as rooted in a normative break-down or value crisis, Anthony classified NRMs into *dualistic* and *monistic* movements in accordance with their different responses to increasing moral ambiguity. In this classi-fication, dualistic movements "reaffirm elements of traditional moral absolutism," whereas monistic movements "affirm relativistic and subjectivistic moral meaning systems."*25* Anthony noted the characteristics of dualistic and monistic movements as follows:

Dualistic movements such as "Jesus movement" groups and neo-Pentecostal groups can be viewed as articulating a fervent protest against relativistic and "permissive" trends in American culture through the strident reaffirmation of theocentric ethical dualism□c

Monistic or "eastern" mystical groups in America tend to project a vision of the universe in which there is an ultimate metaphysical unity or "oneness" which dissolves polarities and imparts an ultimately illusory or epiphenom-enal quality (Maya) to the material world□c Such [monistic] movements are thus often asso-ciated with notions of immanence and conceptions of divinity or ultimate reality as a depth of self.*26*

Furthermore, in his early typology Anthony subdivided contemporary American dual-istic religious movements into (a) "neo-fundamentalist (e.g., 'Jesus movement') groups" and (b) "revisionist syncretic movements." It is noteworthy that Anthony and his team classified the UC as a typical dualistic movement of the latter type, calling it "fiercely Manichaean."*27*

Anthony also advocated a systematic sub-typology of monistic movements by focusing on the means to monistic enlightenment from two different perspec-tives: *technical* versus *charismatic* approaches to spiritual realization and *one-level* versus *two-level* conceptualizations of consciousness expansion.*28* Technical movements employ standardized and repetitive "techniques" which can be taught and which are regarded as instrumental in acquiring the enlightenment. Charismat-ic movements, on the other hand, "seek□c enlightenment through veneration and emulation of leaders who are regarded as exemplars of advanced consciousness." Put differently, in such charismatic movements, "a personal devotional relationship to a 'master' is considered more spiri-tually vital and meaningful than the practice of standardized techniques."*29*

The Anthony typology's second variable involved a distinction between "one-level" and "two-level" conceptualizations of how to attain enlightenment. One-level monistic movements regard the monistic vision as having existential and experiential validity for its believers as soon as they are converted to it as a worldview. Therefore, members of these one-level movements regard themselves as already "having achieved a state of enlightenment towards which others are evolving." They make no distinction between immediate and ultimate levels of monistic truth. Accordingly, Anthony and his team noted that one-level monistic movements generally lack explicit ethics of self-denial or self-sacrifice, and that some scholars' critiques of NRMs as "narcissistic" and "socially complacent"*30* "may apply primarily (though not exclusively) to one-level monism."*31*

Two-level monistic movements, on the other hand, make a distinction between immediate wisdom and the ultimate monistic consciousness characteristic of an ad-vanced and rare stage of spiritual evolution. Devotees of these two-level movements see not only those outside their own movements but also themselves within the move-ments as being on a "lower level" of spiritual awakening. Consequently, they are likely to accept "moral prohibitions" appropriate to their lower level of consciousness as a necessary condition in order to reach the higher level of consciousness. Therefore, Anthony noted that the teachings of these two-level movements provided their believers with a rationale for self-discipline and moral restraint.

Combining charismatic versus technical and one-level versus two-level vari-ables, Anthony and his team thus generated four subtypes of monistic movements. Accordingly, they presented their classification of NRMs in contemporary America as follows:

1) Dualistic movements
a) Neo-fundamentalist movements
Alamo Foundation; Children of God
b) Revisionist syncretic movements
Unification Church
2) Monistic movements
a) One-level technical movements
Erhard Seminar Training, TM, Scientology, Nichiren
Shoshu
b) One-level charismatic movements
Manson Family, Mel Lyman's American Avatar Cult, Allan Noonan's Messiah's One World Crusade, OM cult
c) Two-level technical movements
Hare Krishna, Integral Yoga, Tibetan Buddhist groups, Zen groups, Yogi Bhajan [3HO]
d) Two-level charismatic movements
Meher Baba, Baba Muktananda, Bubba Free John, Maharaj-Ji

Robbins, Anthony, and Richardson noted that "the one-level versus two-level and the technical versus charismatic distinctions also have some value in typing *dualistic* groups and movements."*32* Agreeing with their note, I stated in my earlier evaluation of the Anthony typology in 1987 as follows:

I believe that to subdivide dualistic movements by these two variables would make the typology more comprehensive. This would contribute to the under-standing of salient characteristics of the UC. As indicated by Anthony et al., neo-Pentecostalism may be classified as a technical movement since glossolalia or baptism of the Holy Spirit is a standardized process for their salvation. We can also see that dualistic charismatic movements are guided by what Weber called "ethical prophets" in contrast to monistic charismatic movements that are cen-tered on "exemplary prophets." In this scheme of classification, neo-fundamen-talist groups that emphasize "justification by faith," "salvation by the blood of Jesus," or "immediate 'once and for all' redemption" may be classified as one-level movements. In contrast, those groups that emphasize paying the cost of discipleship and the future attainment of "sanctification" or "perfection" subse-quent to conversion may be viewed as two-level movements.33

As I recommended, Anthony later advocated classifying not only monistic groups but also dualistic groups by the same criteria. The revised Anthony typology assesses all NRMs along three dimensions: 1) its metaphysics in terms of monism or dualism, 2) its central mode of practice in terms of technical or charismatic type, and 3) its interpretive sensibility in terms of unilevel versus multilevel (previously called one-level versus two-level) sensibility. The new Anthony typology is illustrated in Figure 2:

Figure 2: The Anthony Typology*34*

	Monism	Dualism
Multilevel	Charismatic Multilevel monistic charismatic groups	Multilevel dualistic charismatic groups
	Technical Multilevel monistic technical groups	Multilevel dualistic technical groups
Unilevel	Charismatic Unilevel monistic charismatic groups	Unilevel dualistic charismatic groups
	Technical Unilevel monistic technical groups	Unilevel dualistic technical groups

In this revised typology, Anthony and Ecker classified the UC as "a unilevel, dualistic, charismatic movement."[35] Here, I strongly disagree with their classification of the UC as a unilevel movement. In my assessment, the UC is most definitely a multi-level movement. Its emphasis is not on instantaneous redemption, but on "paying indemnity" throughout one's life until attaining the goal of perfect unity of mind and body and an ideal family. Even then, one must keep on walking the path of self-sacrifice until completing the mission of the "Tribal Messiah." Thus, the UC encourages each member to practice self-discipline and self-sacrifice in order to reach complete unity with God, first in himself or herself on the individual stage, second in his or her blessed family on the family stage, and third in his or her tribal or clan community on the tribal stage. Moreover, in each stage the member is to "pay indemnity" in order to go up step by step in terms of relations with God, from the level of "servant of servant" to "servant" to "adopted son" to "real son" and so on to complete unity with God. This is the gist of what Reverend Moon has repeatedly taught UC members: "we need to pass the eight stages of restoration of indemnity vertically and horizontally."[36]

As for its metaphysics, it must be noted that the ideology of the UC deviates considerably from strict dualism. I regard Anthony and Robbins's labeling of the UC as "fiercely Manichaean"[37] or "extreme exemplary dualism"[38] as too hyperbolic to be an accurate description. The UC's most authoritative textbook, Exposition of the Divine Principle, predicted the coming in the near future of the peaceful unified world centered on God, after the struggles between the forces of good and evil have come to an end.[39] In particular, the seemingly dualistic struggle between democracy and communism was never more than provisional.

After repeatedly predicting the collapse of the communist world in our time, in 1990 Reverend Moon went to Moscow, delivered a speech in the Kremlin, and embraced then President Gorbachev. In 1991 he also visited North Korea, spoke in its Parliament, and embraced Kim Il-sung. Though some people regarded his embracing of communist leaders as a sign of change in Unification theology, I regard it as a sign that the leaders of the communist world had softened towards Reverend Moon's teach-ing. Reverend Moon has consistently preached that people should forgive and love their enemies. It was not so difficult for communist leaders, especially in their weak-ened condition and fearful of revenge by their enemies, to endorse his philosophy of forgiveness, true love, and social unity.

On the question of dualism, Eileen Barker's description of Unification theology is more careful and accurate than is Anthony and Robbins's. Barker noted:

> As well as the "soft dualism" of complementarity, Unification theology also exhibits an almost Manichaean dualism of the competing forces of good and evil. I say "almost Manichaean" because in Unification theology the forces of good and evil have not got an eternal character.40

James Beckford also critiqued of Anthony and Robbins, cautioning them against uncritically bundling the UC with Western fundamentalisms into the class of dualistic movements. Beckford noted.

If the distinction between eastern religious movements and fundamentalist movements has any heuristic value in helping to generate understanding of the sociological distinctiveness of the Unification Church it probably lies in the fact that the Rev. Moon's movement combines the two extreme types within itself. I am reluctant to accept that it can be meaningfully classified without severe qualification with any other kinds of Christian fundamentalist groups. And there are no fewer problems in likening it unreservedly to other eastern movements. It is a hybrid.41

Presenting another taxonomy of NRMs, which is less systematic than the above, Anthony and Robbins also referred to the dualistic NRMs that synthesize political and religious themes as *civil religion sects*. In contrast, monistic apolitical NRMs were divided into "eastern mystical movements" (e.g., Zen Buddhism, Meher Baba) and quasi-mystical therapeutic movements or "human potential movements" (e.g., est, Scientology).*42*

Anthony and Robbins pointed out the UC as the best example of the civil relig-ion sect.*43* I have no basic objection to their calling the UC a typical civil religion sect, insofar as their meaning of civil religion lies within the bounds of what was originally proposed by Robert Bellah in his seminal essay "Civil Religion in America," which did not attach any negative connotation to the concept of civil religion.*44* My objection lies rather in their description of the UC under that rubric, which was preoccupied with an analysis of affinity between the UC and American civil religion, especially its degener-ate type. Therefore, they failed to recognize the fact that the UC has promoted a pro-phetic type of not only American but also *global* civil religion.*45*

As Robbins noted, the Anthony typology contains "an explicit normative focus involving the discrimination of 'authentic' from 'inauthentic' paths to transcendence."*46* Particularly through its distinction between unilevel and multilevel movements, it offers a diagnosis whether or not a particular NRM is likely to lead to destructive social and psychological consequences. I agree with Robbins that the unilevel versus multi-level distinction is "really the key critical dimension of the [Anthony] typology."*47* I appreciate the unilevel versus multilevel distinction, despite Anthony's erroneous clas-sification of the UC as a unilevel movement, because I agree with Anthony's judgment that unilevel-type movements can be harmful to their believers' spiritual growth.

5. Bird's Typology

Canadian sociologist of religion Frederick Bird also saw the emergence and growth of NRMs as a response to the contemporary moral dilemma. Bird's thesis was that these movements tend to encourage among their adherents "reduced feelings of moral accountability" or "enhanced feelings of innocence."*48*

Bird developed a classification of NRMs according to a tripartite typology of their adherents, as: 1) devotees of a spiritual leader or Truth, 2) disciples of a spiritual discipline, and 3) apprentices of some sorcerer or magic/science.*49* In other words, he based his typology of NRMs "according to the relationship of followers to masters or the relationship of the religious seekers to the sacred power they revere." His threefold classification of NRMs is as follows:*50*

1) Devotee groups
UC, Catholic and Protestant Charismatics, Divine Light Mission, Nichiren Shoshu, ISKCON
2) Discipleship groups
Integral Yoga Institute, Dharmadatu groups
3) Apprenticeship groups
Psychosynthesis, Silva Mind Control, est, Arica, TM, Scientology

According to Bird, 1) members of the *devotee* groups ultimately surrender them-selves to a holy master or ultimate superhuman truth; 2) members of the *discipleship groups* "progressively seek to master spiritual and/or physical discipline in order to achieve a state of enlightenment and self-harmony"; and 3) participants of the *appren-ticeship* groups "seek to master particular psychic, shamanic and therapeutic skills in order to tap and realize sacred powers within themselves." As Bird noted, apprentice-ship groups correspond roughly to what Robbins, Anthony, and Richardson called monistic, one-level, technical groups; likewise, discipleship groups correspond roughly to monistic, two-level, technical groups. Devotee groups, on the other hand, correspond roughly to what the earlier Anthony typology classified as charismatic groups, which in its revised version belong to either monistic or dualistic groups.

I can agree that in Bird's threefold typology the UC should be classified as a devotee group. I have strong misgivings, however, about his sweeping assertion that NRMs of this type "all foster among their participants reduced feelings of moral accountability or enhanced feelings of innocence" *in contrast to* traditional Jewish and Christian denominations that "heighten or at least reinforce feelings of moral account-ability."*51* Many people have come to know that the UC enhances its members feelings, not of innocence, but of *guilt*, especially prior to their marriage under the founder's "Blessing." Furthermore, the UC emphasizes the importance of individual moral responsibility in building a better society, although Bird did not equate moral account-ability with moral responsibility.

I critique Bird's typology, first, because the terms he employs are somewhat ambiguous and not self-explanatory. It is particularly difficult to conceive the differ-ences between the *devotees* and *disciples* of NRMs exactly as proposed by Bird unless told of their distinctions in advance. A second weakness of Bird's typology is that NRMs are classified according to types of followers without reference to the types of their leaders or founders. For example, taking Weber's typology of religious lead-ers/founders into consideration, I can conceive that NRMs where groups of *devotees* follow *ethical prophets* might belong to a different class from NRMs where groups of *devotees* follow *exemplary prophets*. Finally, Bird's sweeping assertion that all contempo-rary NRMs foster among their participants reduced feelings of moral accountability *in contrast to* traditional Jewish and Christian denominations remains very questionable in the absence of any empirical evidence.

6. Hargrove's Typology

Focusing on the function of NRMs and the personality types of their members, Barbara Hargrove proposed a twofold classification of NRMs: *integrative and transfor-mative* religions.*52* She conceptualized conditions leading to susceptibility to NRMs as *alienation* or *anomie*. Furthermore, following Loye, she viewed these two concepts as foci of concern of liberal and conservative personality types, respectively.*53* In other words, *alienation* may be seen as the malady for the liberal personality type, who is concerned for "growth, reaching out, [and] new experience," whereas *anomie* may be seen as the bane of our life for the conservative personality type, who is concerned about a lack, or confusion, of moral codes (norms). Thus, she saw the alienated or liberal personality-type persons as having "growth needs" and often resorting to "anti-institutionalism." In contrast, she discerned the anomic or the conservative personality-type persons as having "identity needs and desire for community."*54*

Hargrove thus classified NRMs attracting the anomic as integrative religions and those attracting the alienated as transformative religions. She also found certain paral-lels between these NRMs and Troeltsch's three types of Christianity: church, sect, and mysticism. She compared the integrative NRMs to his "sect" type, and the transforma-tive NRMs to his "mysticism." In her view, the extreme privatization in the mainline churches facilitated the rise of the integrative NRMs, which offer strict moral codes and a clearly identifiable community. She mentioned the UC as an example of the integra-tive religion. Likewise, she considered secularization or bureaucratization of the main-line churches to be the source of the emergence of the transformative NRMs, which "tend toward celebrating individual awareness and growth."

I agree that by Hargrove's bipolar typology the UC is to be located as one of the integrative NRMs. My criticism is that, in spite of her neat presentation, no bipolar classification of NRMs can avoid the criticism of being excessively reductionistic. There is also a question whether or not alienation and anomie are sufficiently contrastable to serve as the basis for such a bipolar classification.*55*

7. Westley's Typology

Frances Westley presented another bipolar classification of NRMs in her book entitled *The Complex Forms of the Religious Life: A Durkheimian View of New Relig-ious Movements.56* She developed her typology on the basis of where NRMs locate the sacred. One type of NRMs are "those which clearly locate the sacred as lying within the human individual," while the other type are "those which clearly locate the sacred as lying outside the human individual." She regarded these two types as "points at two ends of a continuum" and admitted that there are a variety of NRMs whose view of the sacred is ambiguous. Nonetheless, it is noteworthy that, as her book's subtitle shows, she followed Durkheim and called groups of the first type, which see the sacred exist-ing within the human individual, "cult of man groups" or *cult-of-the-human-person groups.57* These, she noted, are frequently labeled "human potential groups."*58* On the basis of her local research in the Montreal area, Westley classified as cult-of-the-human-person groups six NRMs: Scientology, Psychosynthesis, Arica, est, Shakti, and Silva Mind Control.*59*

Westley treated the UC as not of the cult-of-the-human-person type because in her view the UC is a one of the groups that "see their leaders as incarnate deities."*60* In other words, she regards the UC a group that sees the sacred existing only within the leader and not within the ordinary members. In contrast, in groups classified as cult-of-the-human-person type, members do not regard their leader as being any more divine than the followers.

I question, however, her categorization of the UC as typical of groups not of the cult-of-the-human-person type. It seems that she was not fully informed of the low Christology (emphasizing the humanity of Christ) in the UC, in contrast to the high Christology (emphasizing the divinity of Christ) found in Evangelical and fundamen-talist Christian churches.*61* My contention is that Unification theology gener-ally supports low Christology and high anthropology (i.e., human perfectibility and the divine nature of perfected human beings), and therefore it is possible to find a certain agreement or compatibility between the UC members' view of human beings and what Durkheim termed a cult of the human person.

It is important to note that, as Westley and Lukes described, the mature Durk-heim did not attach any negative connotation to the term "cult of the human person." By cult (Fr. "culte") Durkheim meant not a small deviant religious group, but an act of worship.*62* Cult of the human person meant a religious respect for the innate dignity and worth of each human person. Revising his earlier negative assessment of the cult of the individual,*63* the mature Durkheim reached the conclusion that, far from being detrimental to social solidarity, the cult of the human person "is the only system of beliefs which can ensure the moral unity of the country."*64*

Exposition of the Divine Principle asserts that perfected human beings will acquire "a divine value, comparable to God,"*65* and that all human beings have the potential to reach perfection as Jesus preached in Matthew 5:48, "You must be perfect as your heavenly Father is perfect." Some scholars suggested that Durkheim's concept of the cult of the human person can be viewed as a source for a global civil religion.*66* Mean-while, a number of scholars identified the UC as a promoter of a global civil religion.*67* Therefore, it is natural for us to wonder what kind of relations exists between the UC and the cult of the human person.

Furthermore, given Durkheim's observation that Christian societies more than any other societies have promoted the dignity and worth of individuals-that is, human rights-we must find fault with Westley's quick dismissal of all monotheistic groups (e.g., Christian groups) from consideration as cult-of-the-human-person groups. In *Suicide*, Durkheim noted the rise of the cult of human person in Christian societies as follows:

> If it [disapproving of suicide] has become so formal and severe in Christian so-cieties, this is not because of the idea of the State held by these people but be-cause of their new conception of the human personality. It has become sacred, even most sacred in their eyes, something which no one is to offend.68

In other words, according to Durkheim, mature Christian societies give rise to the cult of human person. There must be something of the cult of human person in the Christian tradition that has promoted the ideal of universal human rights. In my view, it is the Christian teaching of the *imago Dei* (image of God) in every human being. We can regard the Christian teaching that human beings manifest the image of God as the source of the dignity and worth of human beings, that is, the source of "the sacred" in human beings.*69*

Thus, Westley's typology, dichotomizing the existence of the sacred as either within or outside the human individual, is too rigid to explain many new groups of the Christian family, including the UC. Recall that the Bible (e.g., I Corinthians 3:16) calls Christians "God's temple," which means that God's spirit dwells in them. Therefore, we cannot classify all new Christian groups as NRMs that locate the sacred outside the human individual. Moreover, in my view, it is more Durkheimian to acknowledge the existence of the sacred not only within but also outside the human individual. The mature Durkheim regarded society as the real object of worship as well as the real source of the sacred, but came to the view that society exists not only outside the indi-vidual but also within.*70*

8. Lofland and Richardson's Typology

John Lofland and James T. Richardson presented a typology of NRMs as "religious movement organizations."*71* Dissatisfied with the church-sect-cult typology of religious groups, Lofland and Richardson advocated a new classificatory scheme that focuses on the degree of their "corporateness." Their classification focused on NRMs as organizations and distinguished them according to the "degree to which a set of per-sons actively promotes and participates in a shared and collective life."*72* Here we can see the influence of Mary Douglas's typology based on grid control and group commitment.*73*

Lofland and Richardson discerned five basic types of organization in religious movements. In order of their increasing corporateness, they are called *clinic, congrega-tion, collective, corps, and colony*. The degree of their corporateness is measured by the responses to six key questions concerning, 1) income or other sustenance producing work; 2) shelter or residence; 3) food provision and eating organization; 4) family or other emotional support circles; 5) collective promulgation of cognitive orientation; and 6) a belief that the organization itself is ideal. We present Lofland and Richardson's typology of religious movement organizations in Figure 3.*74*

Figure 3: Lofland and Richardson's Typology of Religious Movement Organizations

	Question 1	Question 2	Question 3	Question 4	Question 5	Question 6
Clinic	-	-	-	-	-	+
Congregation	-	-	-	-	+	+

Collective						
Work	+	-	-	-	+	+
Household	-	+	+	+	+	+
Corps	+	+	+	+	+	-
Colony	+	+	+	+	+	+

Question 1. work/income generated?
Question 2. residence organized?
Question 3. organized provision of food and eating?
Question 4. family/support circles organized?
Question 5. collective dissemination of cognitive orientation?
Question 6. arrangement viewed as ideal?

Lofland and Richardson noted that there are various hybrids of these types of the religious movement organization. They referred to the early centers of the UC in America as "hybrids of corps and household collectives." For Lofland and Richardson, the corps is, "not the 'new world in embryo'", but "a stage through which the believer must pass in order to get to the new and qualitatively better new world."*75* Such hybrids of corps and household collectives as were found in the early UC,

□cview themselves as temporary organizations and establish household collec-tives but these households are not viewed as budding, ideal forms of a new world. Like a corps, they are expedient and not "prefigurative." 76

For these reasons, Lofland and Richardson criticized other scholars for describing the UC in the West as a "communal" movement and its centers as "communes." They prop-erly pointed out that "in the literature the term commune is applied indiscriminately to collectives, corps and colonies," and that it is imprecise to use the same word for all three of these very different organizations.*77* I fully agree. Such terms as "commune" and "communal" are ambiguous and misleading labels, especially when applied to the UC even in its early years in Korea. Since Unification theology emphasizes the impor-tance of the family unit (monogamous marriage), the UC centers in the 1970s, with their large number of the live-in single members, must be seen neither as prefigurative of an ideal world nor as an ideal form of living, but as a temporary expedient form that was destined to fade away as the UC developed.

In fact, in its current development, the UC has evolved, using Lofland and Richardson's typology, from a hybrid of corps and household collective to a congrega-tional type. The current diversification of the Unification movement has led many members to pursue various non-religious vocations in business, education, politics, journalism, arts, and entertainment. Moreover, the number of the married members in the UC has increased by leaps and bounds at every mass wedding (e.g., church mem-bers participating in the worldwide blessings of 360,000 couples, 3.6 million couples, 39.6 million couples and 120 million couples between 1995 and 1998). At the same time, the number of members living in centers has decreased. Today, married (Blessed) cou-ples with children who live outside the UC centers are the most common type of mem-bership and constitute a great majority of the local congregations of the UC in Korea, in Japan, in the United States, and in many other nations. As a result of these develop-ments, what Lofland and Richardson would describe as the Congregation has become the mainstay of the UC.
As for the ideal living arrangement of the future Unification movement, Reverend Moon has frequently mentioned that in the future, Blessed families should live as trinities. He envisions housing complexes where groups of three or four Blessed families live in private apartments surrounding a shared common living space, living cooperatively and helping each other in many ways. Among every group of three fami-lies living together there should ideally be families of different races and nationalities. By changing the constituent families of the trinity group every twelve years, families can acquire a record of having truly loved all races and nationalities here on earth.*78* Such a future lifestyle envisioned for the Unification movement would be much closer to the household collective type than to the current congregation type in the Lofland and Richardson typology of religious movement organizations; it may be regarded as a moderate type of communitarian lifestyle. Whether the Unification movement will become such an international and interracial communitarian movement remains to be seen.

Lofland and Richardson's typology and their discussion on the UC thus accu-rately illuminates the nature and characteristics of the UC centers in comparison to other religious movement organizations.

9. Conclusion

In this paper we reviewed most of the prominent typologies of NRMs.*79* By making use of various categories or ideal types set up by these typologies, we have attempted to illuminate the characteristics of the UC. Nevertheless, it is important for us to keep in mind that various categories or ideal types are yardsticks or heuristic tools to understand real movements. We have a tendency to use various types as labels; as soon as we attach a label to a certain NRM, we are liable to read all the attributes of that type into the concrete movement. To avoid this mistake, we should remember that for any defining variable, the two contrasting ideal types are the most extreme cases, while all concrete groups fall somewhere on a continuum between the two ideal types.

I hope that the typological discussions in this paper are helpful in understanding and communicating the characteristics of the UC and of other NRMs. By familiarizing ourselves with pros and cons of each typology of NRMs we will be able to make wise use of these classificatory categories or ideal types as heuristic devices.

Notes

1. Contemporary sociologists of religion have frequently used the term "NRMs." See e.g., David G. Bromley and Phillip E. Hammond, eds., The Future of New Religious Movements (Macon, GA: Mercer Univ. Press, 1987); Eileen Barker, New Religious Movements (London: Her Majesty's Stationery Office, 1989). Many historians of religion, however, prefer to avoid the term because many of what are called NRMs are not really new when seen from a global historical perspective. See e.g., Gordon J. Melton, "Another Look at New Religions," Annals of the American Academy of Political and Social Science 527 (May 1993): 97-112. Many are old traditional religions merely imported from other nations. Some of the terms historians prefer to the "NRMs" are "alternative religions" and "nonconventional religions." See e.g., Timothy Miller, ed., America's Alternative Religions (Albany, NY: State University of New York Press, 1995) and Melton, "Another Look at New Religions." Our review of typologies of NRMs will include not only those labeled NRMs but also what some have labeled religious movements or social movements.
2. For my discussion on other typologies of religion and characteristics of the UC, see the followings: Yoshihiko Masuda, "Typologizing Religious Groups: A Preliminary Presentation Towards a Better Understanding of the Unification Church," Sun Moon Forum 4 (Chonan, Korea: Sun Moon Univ. Press, 1995), pp. 207-36; Yoshihiko Masuda, "Theological Typologies of Religious Groups and the Identity of the Unification Church," Journal of Unification Theology 1 (1996): 318-50; Yoshihiko Masuda, "A Discussion on Miscellaneous Typologies of Religion and the Identity of the Unification Church," Journal of Unification Theology 2 (1997): 398-426.
3 Robert S. Ellwood, Religious and Spiritual Groups in Modern America (Englewood Cliffs, NJ: Prentice-Hall, 1973).
4. It is noteworthy that, introducing the UC Religious and Spiritual Groups (pp. 293-95), Ellwood reprinted a long passage from Arthur Ford, Unknown But Known (New York: Harper & Row; Signet Mystic Book, 1968) pp. 111-12. In this passage, Ford's spirit guide, Fletcher, clearly testified through the mouth of Ford in trance that Reverend Sun Myung Moon is "the voice of this Intelligence-Creative Mind-which you call God," and that "for the present moment he is, in my estimation, a most important spiritual light that shines in the darkness of your confused world." Fletcher further testified that:

Mr. Moon in deep meditation can project himself and be seen just as Jesus has been able to project himself and be seen by the saints. This is one of the marks of the messiahs always.
5. It is important to note that Ellwood did not attach any negative connotation to the term "cult." For his discussion of cults, see Ellwood, Religious and Spiritual Groups; Ellwood, "Several Meanings of Cult," Thought 61 (June 1986): 212-24.
6. Diane Choquette, comp., New Religious Movements in the United States and Canada (Westport, CT: Greenwood, 1985).
7. Gordon J. Melton, Encyclopedia of American Religions, 2d ed. (Detroit: Gale, 1987), attempted to classify all

religious groups in the United States on a basis somewhat similar to Ellwood's classification. Melton presented seventeen large classificatory religious families based on "common heritage, thought world (theology in its broadest sense), and lifestyle" (xiii-xv). Applying this classificatory scheme, Melton classified the UC as one of the groups in "Spiritualist, Psychic, and New Age Family." Julia Corbett called Melton's classificatory scheme a "family grouping" and made a distinction from the so-called "typological classifications" and "choice-point analyses." See Julia Mitchell Corbett, "Religion in the United States: Notes toward a New Classification," Religion and American Culture 3 (Winter 1993): 91-112. If we follow her threefold distinctions of classification, we can also regard Ellwood's scheme of classification as a "family grouping" of NRMs.
8. David F. Aberle, The Peyote Religion among the Navaho, 2d ed. (Chicago: Univ. of Chicago Press, 1982), pp. 315-22.
9. Ibid., p. 316.
10. Ibid., p. 316.
11. For a fine summary and evaluation of Aberle's typology, see John Wilson, Introduction to Social Movements (New York: Basic Books, 1973), pp. 23-27.
12. Bryan Wilson, Magic and Millennium (New York: Harper & Row, 1973), p. 491. Based on a misquotation, Wilson, followed by David Bromley, Anson Shupe, Keith Roberts and Gordon Marshall, renders one of Aberle's typological terms, "alterative" movements, as "alternative" movements.
13. David G. Bromley and Anson D. Shupe, Jr., "Moonies" in America: Cult, Church, and Crusade (Beverly Hills: Sage, 1979), pp. 22-23.
14. Keith A. Roberts, Religion in Sociological Perspective (Homewood, IL: Dorsey, 1984) 204; 3rd ed. (Belmont, CA: Wadsworth, 1995)p. 182.
15. This is a change of my assessment and a departure from my previous uncritical acceptance of their classification of the Unification movement in my Ph.D. dissertation. See Yoshihiko Masuda, "Moral Vision and Practice in the Unification Movement: A Critical Interpretation of the Sociological Literature from a Unificationist Perspective," Ph.D. diss., Univ. of Southern California, 1987.
16. Joseph H. Fichter, "Home Church: Alternative Parish," Alternative to American Mainline Churches, ed. J. H. Fichter (New York: Rose of Sharon, 1983), p. 192; Joseph H. Fichter, The Holy Family of Father Moon (Kansas City: Leaven, 1985), pp. 111-30.
17. [Bo Hi Pak, Thomas Ward and William Lay,] CAUSA Lecture Manual (New York: CAUSA Institute, 1985), p. 242. For a further discussion on the relations between the redemptive (evangelistic) aspect and the transformative or reformative (cultural/social reform) aspect of the Unification movement, see Masuda, Ph.D. diss., pp. 326-30.
18. Aberle, Peyote Religion, p. 317.
19. Charles Y. Glock and Robert N. Bellah, eds., The New Religious Consciousness (Berkeley: Univ. of California Press, 1976).
20. Steven M. Tipton, Getting Saved from the Sixties (Berkeley: Univ. of California Press, 1982).
21. E.g., John Lofland, "The World Savers: A Field Study of Cult Processes," Ph.D. Diss., Univ. of California, Berkeley, 1964; John Lofland, Doomsday Cult: A Study of Conversion, Proselytization, and Maintenance of Faith (Englewood Cliffs, NJ: Prentice-Hall, 1966); John Lofland and Rodney Stark, "Becoming a World-Saver: A Theory of Conversion to a Deviant Perspective," American Sociological Review 30 (December 1965): 862-74.
22. In answer to my question, Professor Bellah confirmed that the omission of the UC from The New Religious Consciousness had not been intentional in the least, but was inadvertent. (Personal conversation, 1983.)
23. Thomas Robbins, Dick Anthony, and James Richardson, "Theory and Research on Today's 'New Religions'," Sociological Analysis 39 (Summer 1978): 95-122. Dick Anthony and Bruce Ecker, "The Anthony Typology: A Framework for Assessing Spiritual and Consciousness Groups," Spiritual Choices, ed. D. Anthony, B. Ecker, and K. Wilber (New York: Paragon House, 1987), pp. 35-105.
24. Anthony and Ecker, Spiritual Choices, p. 94.
25. Robbins et al., "Theory and Research," p. 101.
26. Ibid., p. 101-2.
27. Ibid., p. 101.
28. In the revised version of the Anthony typology, Anthony and Ecker came to employ the terms unilevel versus multilevel instead of one-level versus two-level.
29. Robbins et al., "Theory and Research," p. 105.
30. E.g., Peter Marin, "The New Narcissism: The Trouble with the Human Potential Movement," Harper's (October

1975): 45-56; Edwin M. Schur, The Awareness Trap: Self-Absorption Instead of Social Change (New York: New York Times Book, 1976); Christopher Lasch, "The Narcissistic Society," New York Review of Books, September 30, 1976, pp. 5-12.
31. Robbins et al., "Theory and Research," p. 106.
32. Ibid., p. 100n.
33. Masuda, Ph.D. diss., p. 79.
34. Anthony and Ecker, Spiritual Choices, p. 37
35. Ibid., pp. 60-62.
36 See Zin Moon Kim, The Fountain of Life: Based on the Words of Reverend Sun Myung Moon (New York: HSA-UWC, 1993) p. 231, for an illustrated summary and explanation of Reverend Moon's speeches on the eight stages of restoration.
37. Robbins et al., "Theory and Research," p. 101.
38. Dick Anthony and Thomas Robbins, "Spiritual Innovation and the Crisis of American Civil Religion," Religion and America, ed. M. Douglas and S. M. Tipton (Boston: Beacon, 1983) p. 246.
39. [Eu, Hyo Won,] Exposition of the Divine Principle (New York: HSA-UWC, 1996), pp. 87, 89, 99-103.
40. Eileen Barker, "Living the Divine Principle: Inside the Reverend Sun Myung Moon's Unification Church in Britain." Archives de Sciences Sociales des Religions 45 (January/March 1978): 84.

41. James A. Beckford, "Through the Looking-Glass and Out the Other Side: Withdrawal from the Reverend Moon's Unification Church." Archives de Sciences Sociales des Religions 45 (January/March 1978): 100n. Cf. James A. Beckford, "A Korean Evangelistic Movement in the West," Paper presented at the 12th International Conference for the Sociology of Religion, The Hague, 1973.
42. Dick Anthony and Thomas Robbins, "Cultural Crisis and Contemporary Religion," In Gods We Trust, ed. T. Robbins and D. Anthony (New Brunswick, NJ: Transaction, 1981), pp. 9-31; Dick Anthony and Thomas Robbins, "Spiritual Innovation and the Crisis of American Civil Religion," Religion and America, ed. M. Douglas and S. M. Tipton, (Boston: Beacon, 1983), pp. 229-48.
43. Anthony and Robbins, "Cultural Crisis," p. 17; Anthony and Robbins, "Spiritual Innovation," p. 235.
44. Robert N. Bellah, "Civil Religion in America," Daedalus 96 (Winter 1967): 1-21.
45. For a view of the UC as a promoter of the global civil religion, see e.g., Warren Lewis, "Is the Reverend Sun Myung Moon a Heretic?" A Time for Consideration, ed. M. D. Bryant and H. W. Richardson, 2d ed. (New York: Edwin Mellen, 1978), p. 211; Roland Robertson, "The Sacred and the World System." The Sacred in a Secular Age, ed. P. E. Hammond (Berkeley: Univ. of California Press, 1985), p. 354.
46. Thomas Robbins, Cults, Converts and Charisma: The Sociology of New Religious Movements (London: Sage, 1988), p. 135.
47. Ibid., p. 137.
48. Frederick Bird, "The Pursuit of Innocence: New Religious Movements and Moral Accountability." Sociological Analysis 40 (Winter 1979): 335-46.

49. Frederick Bird, "Charisma and Ritual in New Religious Movements," Understanding the New Religions, ed. J. Needleman and G. Baker (New York: Seabury, 1978), p. 182-83. See also Anthony F. C. Wallace, "Revitalization Movements," American Anthropologist 58 (April 1956): 273, who presented "three orders of personnel: the prophet; the disciples; and the followers" in a campaign organization of what he called "revitalization movements." James A. Beckford, Cult Controversies (London: Tavistock, 1985), combined Bird's threefold typology of the followers of the NRMs and Wallace's "vertical" types of the members within a religious movement, classifying social relationships internal to NRMs in terms of devotee, adept, client, patron, and apostate. In my view, it is wise for him to include patrons and apostates in the discussion on the dynamics of the NRMs. Beckford also classified the external relationships of the NRMs vis-a-vis their host society as retreat, revitalization, and release. Unfortunately, he did not develop his conceptual framework for the purpose of analyzing NRMs in the social contexts into a full-fledged typology of NRMs.

50. Bird, "The Pursuit of Innocence," p. 336.
51. Ibid., p. 343.
52. Barbara Hargrove, "Integrative and Transformative Religions," Understanding the New Religions, ed. J. Needleman and G. Baker (New York: Seabury, 1978), pp. 257-66.

53. See David Loye, The Leadership Passion (San Francisco: Jossey-Bass, 1977).
54. Hargrove, "Integrative and Transformative Religions," p. 262.
55. Cf. Thomas Robbins, Dick Anthony and Thomas Curtis, "Youth Culture Religious Movements: Evaluating the Integrative Hypothesis," Sociological Quarterly 16 (Winter 1975): 48-64., who discuss the relations between "the alienated" and "integration." Robbins and Anthony also discussed integrative, disintegrative and transformative functions of contemporary NRMs in the West. These three categories may be seen as a threefold typology of NRMs, although they did not formally present them as such. See Thomas Robbins and Dick Anthony, "New Religious Movements and Social System: Integration, Disintegration, or Transformation," Annual Review of the Social Sciences of Religion 2 (1978): 1-27.
56. Frances Westley, The Complex Forms of the Religious Life: A Durkheimian View of New Religious Movements (Chico, CA: Scholars, 1983), p. 25.
57. For Durkheim's explanation of the "cult of the human person," see Emile Durkheim, The Division of Labor in Society, trans. G. Simpson (New York: Macmillan, 1964), pp. 172, 407-8; Emile Durkheim, The Division of Labor in Society, trans. W. D. Halls (New York: Free Press, 1984), pp. 122, 338; Emile Durkheim, Suicide, trans. J. A. Spaulding and G. Simpson (New York: Free Press, 1966), pp. 333-336; Emile Durkheim, "Individualism and the Intellectuals," Emile Durkheim, trans. M. Traugott; ed. R. N. Bellah (Chicago: Univ. of Chicago Press, 1973), pp. 43-57. We have avoided the sexist language of Westley's typology by employing "cult of the human person" in place of "cult of man," which she took over from older translations of Durkheim.
58. Because "human potential groups" are sometimes referred to as "humanistic religious groups," Westley's typology is somewhat similar to Fromm's typology of "authoritarian religion" versus "humanistic religion." See Erich Fromm, Psychoanalysis and Religion (New Haven, CT: Yale Univ. Press, 1950).
59. Westley, Complex Forms, pp. 31-34.
60. Ibid., p. 25.
61. For a theological typology of religious groups based on the view of Christ and characteristics of Unification theology, see Yoshihiko Masuda, "Theological Typologies of Religious Groups and the Identity of the Unification Church," Journal of Unification Theology 1 (1996): 318-50.
62. For Durkheim's positive view of the cult of the human person, see Emile Durkheim, "Individualism and the Intellectuals"; Westley, Complex Forms; Steven Lukes, Emile Durkheim: His Life and Work (Stanford, CA: Stanford Univ. Press, 1985), p. 166.
63. Durkheim, Division of Labor in Society, trans. G. Simpson, p. 172.
64. Durkheim, "Individualism and the Intellectuals," p. 50.
65. Exposition of the Divine Principle, p. 164.
66. E.g., Ruth A. Wallace, "Emile Durkheim and the Civil Religion Concept," Review of Religious Research 18 (Spring 1977): 287-90.
67. Lewis, "Is the Reverend Sun Myung Moon a Heretic?" p. 211; Robertson, "The Sacred and the World System," p. 354.
68. Durkheim, Suicide, pp. 333-34.
69. Nonetheless, some Christian theological traditions, notably the Lutheran tradition, emphasized the total loss of the imago Dei in human beings after the fall of our human ancestors. In my view, the Lutheran tradition's teaching of the complete loss of the imago Dei in the fallen human beings, as well as its social ethical theory of two kingdoms, was a factor that had contributed to the Holocaust in Germany during the World War II. On the other hand, the Roman Catholic tradition, which influenced Durkheim, has taught the existence of the imago Dei in all human beings even after the fall and even among non-Christians. Roman Catholic theology considers human reason (rational faculty) and free will to be the essence of the imago Dei in human beings. See Van A. Harvey, A Handbook of Theological Terms (New York: Macmillan, 1964), pp. 125-27; Young Oon Kim, An Introduction to Theology (New York: HSA-UWC, 1983), pp. 47-51; Alister E. McGrath, Christian Theology: An Introduction (Oxford: Blackwell, 1994), pp. 369-71.
70. Emile Durkheim, "The Determination of Moral Facts," Sociology and Philosophy, trans. D. F. Pocock (New York: Free Press, 1974), p. 55, noted, "while society transcends us it is immanent in us and we feel it as such. While it surpasses us it is within us, since it can only exist by and through us□c Thus, to love society is to love both something beyond us and something in ourselves."
71. John Lofland and James T. Richardson, "Religious Movement Organizations: Elementary Forms and Dynamics," Research in Social Movements, Conflicts and Change, ed. L. Kriesberg (Greenwich, CT: JAI, 1984), pp. 29-51; also reprinted in John Lofland, Protest: Studies of Collective Behavior and Social Movements (New Brunswick, NJ:

Transaction, 1985), pp. 179-200; James T. Richardson, ed., Money and Power in the New Religions (Lewiston, NY: Edwin Mellen, 1988), pp. 7-12.
72. Lofland and Richardson, "Religious Movement Organizations," p. 29.
73. See Mary Douglas, ed., Essays in the Sociology of Perception (London: Routledge & Kegan Paul, 1982).
74. Lofland and Richardson, "Religious Movement Organizations," p. 33.
75. Ibid., p. 38.
76. Ibid.
77. Ibid., p. 39.
78. See e.g., Sun Myung Moon, Onna-no Michi [The Way of Women], Malsseum Pockets 2 (Tokyo: Kogensha, 1994); Sun Myung Moon, "Dai Hachikai Sekaitouitu-koku Kaitenbi Keireishiki-go-no Mikotoba [A Speech Delivered after the Pledge Service on the Eighth Foundation Day of the Nation of the Unified World]." Shukuhuku 87 (1995): 10-27.
79. Among prominent typologies of NRMs not discussed in this paper are those by Roy Wallis, Rodney Stark and William S. Bainbridge, and G. K. Nelson.
Roy Wallis, The Elementary Forms of the New Religious Life (New York: Routledge & Kegan Paul, 1984), classified NRMs into three types: 1) world-rejecting NRMs, 2) world-affirming NRMs, and 3) world-accommodating NRMs. Wallis identified the UC as a world-rejecting NRM.

Stark and Bainbridge classified NRMs into three sub-types: 1) audience cults, 2) client cults, and 3) cult movements. They identified the UC in America as a cult movement. See Rodney Stark and William S. Bainbridge, "Of Churches, Sects, and Cults: Preliminary Concepts for a Theory of Religious Movements," Journal for the Scientific Study of Religion 18 (June 1979): 117-31; Rodney Stark and William S. Bainbridge, "Concepts for a Theory of Religious Movements," Alternatives to American Mainline Churches, ed. J. H. Fichter (New York: Rose of Sharon, 1983), pp. 3-25; Rodney Stark and William S. Bainbridge, The Future of Religion: Secularization, Revival, and Cult Formation (Berkeley: Univ. of California Press, 1985).

Geoffrey K. Nelson, "The Concept of Cult," Sociological Review 16 (November 1968): 351-62, also classified NRMs on the basis of their organizational characteristics. Nelson described three types of NRM as 1) cult, 2) permanent cult, and 3) centralized cult. According to Nelson, a cult depends on charisma of its leader and has minimal organization; a permanent cult depends on routinized charisma at a local level and has no national organization or bureaucratic structure; and a centralized cult rests on routinized charisma and has a national office and bureaucratic structure firmly established. Nelson opined that some cults become "new religions." I wonder why we cannot refer to what he called cults as "new religions."

****

4.16 Erskine College and Seminary: McCain Library: Recent Reference Questions

http://www.erskine.edu/library/rrq.htm

October 7th, 2003	Questions on Literature: MLA Bibliography
March 10th, 2003	Robin Wright, Stukes Lecturer: Articles and Books in McCain Library
March 7th, 2003	Faith and Media (Television and Film): Quentin Schultze
March 7th, 2003	Marva Dawn on Christian Worship
March 4th, 2003	Social Research: Body Image Scale, Social Anxiety Scale
February 25th, 2003	Understanding Motivation in Business: Theories X, Y, and Z
February 12th, 2003	Finding Art Images on the WWW
February 5th, 2003	The Black Church and Ministry to People with AIDS
February 3rd, 2003	Space Shuttle Columbia, Lost in February 2003

January 28th, 2003	Footwashing in John's Gospel
January 26th, 2003	Latin America and the United States
October 25th, 2002	"What is justice?"

A seminary student asks about the generation of leaders in ministry who are passing away (Bill Bright of Campus Crusade is a recent example) or moving toward retirement (Billy Graham, James Dobson of Focus on the Family), and wonders "What about the new generation of leaders? What kind of people are they?"
I take this to be a very interesting question, but also one that is very difficult to frame as a question for online searching. We can do a GOOGLE search on the names of the older leaders and find some specifics about each individual ministry or para-church group, but it is somewhat more difficult to draw general conclusions about the new leaders as a group. Christianity Today did several articles in 1996 that address this question, without being able to provide a full answer. These three articles are available through the library's website on INFOTRAC:
"A Letter to Future Church Leaders"(Up & Comers)(Cover Story) by Leighton Ford Christianity Today Nov 11, 1996 v40 n13 p.16-20.
"Fifty Evangelical Leaders 40 and Under" (Up & Comers)(Cover Story) Christianity Today Nov 11, 1996 v40 n13 p.20-31.
"Emerging Values: The Next Generation is Redefining Spiritual Formation, Community, and Mission. (Emerging Leaders). Written by Brian D. McLaren in the journal Leadership (Carol Stream, IL) Summer 2003 v24 i3 p34-40.
To read about Billy Graham and some of the steps he has taken to train new generation of evangelists, try this article:
http://www.beliefnet.com/story/34/story_3480_1.html

I will also quote from an informal "blog" on this subject that raises some interesting questions about the relationship between church and state.
(here is the link if you want the whole bit)
http://markbyron.typepad.com/main/2003/08/theocon_trekthe.html
James Dobson
Chuck Colson
Phyllis Shlafly
Paul Weyrich
Morton Blackwell
Tim & Beverly LaHaye
Pat Robertson
"This list does more than highlight the graying of the movement -- it also reminds us that, for many of the folks listed, there's no clear line of succession within the organizations they lead. There are a handful of younger conservative leaders, to be sure. Yet most of them aren't original-style social conservatives -- instead they're grassroots activists within the party structure.
Many younger evangelicals of a political bent have become political operatives within the Republican party rather than be part of policy-oriented parachurch groups. People like Robertson protégé Ralph Reed and Dobson
http://www.erskine.edu/library/rrqsearch.htm?igor=72 (72)

March 7th, 2003
Marva Dawn was a recent speaker on the Erskine campus, where she addressed both College and Seminary students on worship. Several students have expressed an interest in reading more of her work. An ATLA search leads us to these journal articles in McCain Library.
Beyond the worship wars : Judging style and substance.
Author: Dawn, Marva J. Source: Christian Century 114 Je 4-11 1997, p 550-552.
True worship, real evangelism. Author: Dawn, Marva J. Source: Christian Century 116 Ap 21-28 1999, p 455-458.
Body Building : Worship That Develops Strong Community.
Author: Dawn, Marva J. Source: Reformed Worship no 45 S 1997, p 26-29.
Pop Spirituality or Genuine Story. Author: Dawn, Marva J. Source: Word & World 18 Wint 1998, p 44-56.

"Until Christ Is Formed in You" : Nurturing the Spirituality of Children. Author: Dawn, Marva J. Source: Theology Today 56 no 1 Ap 1999, p 73-85.
Worship and Ethics. Author: Dawn, Marva J. Source: Dialog 32 Aut 1993, p 297-302.
Declaring Peace : What the Bible really says about war.
Author: Dawn, Marva J. Source: Other Side 29 Mr-Ap 1993, p 56-59.
An introduction to the work of Jacques Ellul. Author: Dawn, Marva J. Source: Word & World 9 Fall 1989, p 386-393.

American history. Recently one student chose to do a project on televangelism.

One book that was found to be especially helpful for this project was "Televangelism and American Culture: The Business of Popular Religion" (Grand Rapids, MI: Baker Book House, 1991). The author is Quentin Schultze, who teaches at Calvin College and it turns out that Schultze has written extensively on this subject. Dr. Johnson asks his students to find out something about the author, and I thought it might be useful to link to his personal web page:
Quentin Schultze's Page
and also to list some of his publications here:
Christianity and the Mass Media in America: Toward a Democratic Accommodation (Lansing: Michigan State University Press, forthcoming in 2003).
Habits of the High-Tech Heart: Living Virtuously in the Information Age (Grand Rapids, MI: Baker Academic, 2002).
Communicating for Life: Christian Stewardship in Community and Media (Grand Rapids, MI: Baker Book House, 2000. Translated into Korean.
Internet for Christians (Muskegon, MI: Gospel Films, 1995). Translated into Korean, Spanish, German, Finnish and Japanese. Revised Edition 1996. Third Revised Edition 1997. Also published as a CD-ROM by Logos, Inc.
Winning Your Kids Back from the Media (Downers Grove, IL: InterVarsity Press, 1994). Translated into Korean and Indonesian. Available with a five-part video (Gospel Films, 1995). Note: the video series is available exclusively through Gospel Communications at GospelDirect.com.)
Co-author) The Best Family Videos: For the Discriminating Viewer (Chicago: Northfield, 1994). Second Edition (Minneapolis: Augsburg, 1995).
Redeeming Television: How TV Changes Christians: How Christians Can Change TV (Downers Grove, IL: InterVarsity Press, 1992). Translated into Indonesian and Korean. Book won a national award.
Televangelism and American Culture: The Business of Popular Religion (Grand Rapids, MI: Baker Book House, 1991). Book won two national awards.
(Co-author) Dancing in the Dark: Youth, Popular Culture and the Electronic Media (Grand Rapids, MI: Eerdmans, 1991).
(Editor and Contributor) American Evangelicals and the Mass Media (Grand Rapids, MI: Zondervan/Academie Press, 1990).
Television: Manna from Hollywood? (Grand Rapids,Zondervan, 1986).

March 10th, 2003
To read more Robin Wright, Stukes Lecturer for 2003, try:
Books by Robin Wright in Erskine's McCain Library
Last great revolution : turmoil and transformation in Iran / Robin Wright.
Call Number: DS 318.8 .W75 2001
Sacred rage : the wrath of militant Islam : updated with an epilogue / Robin Wright.
Call Number: DS 63.1 .W75 1986
Full-Text Articles by Robin Wright in InfoTrac and WilsonSelectPlus
What Will Peace Mean To The Middle East? If you think milk and honey, think again: Israel should be fine, but watch out for Syria, Egypt, Saudi Arabia and the other countries that have staved off change. Robin Wright. Time May 22, 2000 v155 i21 p108+
IRAN'S NEW REVOLUTION. (Islamic theocratic government yields somewhat to tolerate more freedoms) Robin Wright. Foreign Affairs Jan-Feb 2000 v79 i1 p133
America's Iraq policy: how did it come to this? Robin Wright. The Washington Quarterly Summer 1998 v21 n3 p53 (18)
The U.S. and Iran: an offer they can't refuse? (expectations of improved relations with the victory of Mohammed

Khatami as Iran's new president) Robin Wright, Shaul Bakhash.
Foreign Policy Fall 1997 n108 p124 (14)
Democracy: challenges and innovations in the 1990s. Robin Wright.
The Washington Quarterly Summer 1997 v20 n3 p23 (14)
Dateline Tehran: a revolution implodes. (Islamic politics in Iran) Robin Wright.
Foreign Policy Summer 1996 n103 p161(14)
"What would the world be like without him?" (Pope John Paul II) Robin Wright.
The Atlantic Monthly July 1994 v274 n1 p24(5)
From Tunisia to Turkey; militant Islam gains ground. Robin Wright. The Nation May 23, 1987 v244 p675(3)
Iran looks beyond Khomeini. (Ayatollah Khomeini) Robin Wright. The Nation Feb 7, 1987 v244 p129(4)
Iran's smiling powerbroker. (Ali Akbar Hashemi Rafsanjani) Robin Wright.
The New Leader Jan 12, 1987 v 70 p5(3)
Iran's greatest political challenge: Abdol Karim Soroush. Wright, Robin. Source: World Policy Journal v. 14 (Summer 1997) p. 67-74 (This item in WilsonSelectPlus from FirstSearch)

February 5th, 2003
Several DMin students at Erskine are working on projects that will try to strengthen the ministry of the Black Church to people with AIDS. Here I want to mention one site that is a very rich resource for this topic. It is a newsletter on the Black Church and AIDS, and has an archive from 1989 - Present.
It frequently features bibliographies that can lead you to many other resources, for example:
HIV/AIDS Resources for People of Faith: An Annotated Bibliography
"HIV/AIDS Focus Paper #26: December 1994" will list

Books and Curriculum Resources for Congregational Study | Books that Give a Biblical, Theological Basis for Ministries to People with HIV/AIDS | Books on Counseling, Social Work, Pastoral Care | Books for or about Women and HIV/AIDS | Videocassettes about HIV/AIDS

January 28th, 2003
From the Reference Desk at Erskine College and Seminary:
Several students in Loyd Melton's class on The Gospel of John are writing papers on John 13, in which Jesus teaches about servanthood and washes the feet of his disciples. The one book that would tell most of the story is:
"Footwashing in John 13 and the Johannine community"
(214 pages) by John Christopher Thomas.
There are several good full-text articles on this topic in the ATLA Religion Database:
"Is Footwashing the Neglected Sacrament? A Theological Response to John Christopher Thomas" by Macchia, Frank D. Source: Pneuma 19 Fall 1997, p 239-249.
"Mandatum novum do vobis : toward a renewal of the Holy Thursday footwashing rite" by Jeffery, Peter. Source: Worship 64 Mr 1990, p 107-141.
Articles in our print collection include:

"From the Upper Room to the Cross: A service including drama, footwashing, and communion" Author: Thompson, Robert Source: Reformed Worship no 50 D 1998, p 10-17.

"Affective content in Jesus' teaching : a closer look at the footwashing in John 13:1-20" Author: Wu, David Source: Christian Education Journal 11 Wint 1991, p 75-85.
http://www.erskine.edu/library/rrqsearch.htm?igor=43 (43)

October 25th, 2002
"What is justice?"
"Justice" – the oldest definition is a good place to start:
"giving every person what is due them."

Justice in this sense of "rendering what is due" can be further broken down into at least four levels:
Retributive justice: "to each according to the harm he has done" (or criminal justice)
Compensatory justice: "to each according to the loss he has suffered" (I'll pay you for the window I broke)
Contractual justice: "to each according to the agreements he has made" (this is what businesses count on)
Distributive justice: "to each according to need OR merit" (slicing a pie or debating a budget for social services)
AND THEN
A different kind of justice: God's act of justice on behalf of the Hebrew slaves, bringing them out of Egypt.
As you might expect, many books and articles have been written on EACH of these questions, and I would be delighted to help Erskine students explore any topicthat interests them...

****

4.17 Guidelines for Church Websites
Teddington Baptist Church

Church Road, Teddington, Middlesex TW11 8PF, UK.
http://ourworld.compuserve.com/homepages/cphicks/tbcweb.htm

Introduction

This page tries to give some guidelines and helpful advice to Churches thinking about having a website. It is based on my experience of running a number of websites since the middle of 1996 and so contains a lot of illustrative links to my own websites. Please forgive me for that - they are the sites whose philosophy I understand best and which I know should still be there as you access this web page!
The online world is developing and changing rapidly. At present only about 5% of British households have Internet access but that proportion is rising fast. A website can serve your existing membership, attract in new members, and change attitudes towards your Church in the surrounding community.
This web page has been specially prepared to support a chapter on "*Websites et Al*" in a book by Rev Richard Littledale published (March 1999) by the Baptist Union on communication techniques for Churches. The book is called "*getting the Message across ... the art of communicating effectively*".
If you want some specific advice on setting up a Church website you can send an e-mail to me at cphicks@compuserve.com

Getting Started

Building a simple site can be quite easy. Most people start with one or two basic pages of information about their Church and then build it up as they learn how to do more. You don't **have** to produce an all-singing and all-dancing site at the outset! I am happy to provide advice (by e-mail), but please read this page first - the answer to your question may be here. In addition, as I am asked further questions which seem likely to be of general interest, I will add the answers to the FAQ section.
Getting Online: If you are reading this, you are presumably already online! However, you may not have realised that most Internet Service Providers offer website facilities free to subscribers as part of the e-mail and Internet access service. I know that CompuServe, AOL, Demon, MSN, Virgin, Dixon's Freeserve and many other providers do this. Many Internet Service Providers, like CompuServe also provide for free the basic software needed to create a web page. Consequently if you are already connected, you can get started very cheaply especially as being connected means you have already all the essential hardware (and possibly the software too). You can get web space of several megabytes (these days even as much as 50 megabytes) bundled (as a "free" offer) with your Internet access subscription costing 15 pounds a month or less for unlimited access at 56K or slightly more for broadband.
Even if your Internet Service Provider does not provide you with free space for a website, you can still get free space from a specialist web service. For example Geocities (http://www.geocities.com) offers space for a free web page to anyone - although the price for this is a series of irritating pop-up boxes which get in the way of your visitors. There are also specifically Christian services offering free web space and help including template services. There are many companies who now offer reasonably priced webhosting and domain registration (especially for .org.uk and .co.uk

domains). Your Internet Service Provider or the company which hosts your website will usually help you register a suitable domain name for a fee!
Since I began writing websites in 1996, I have used CompuServe which gives 5 megabytes (at November 2003). I use about 4 megabyte of that for most of my websites (the LBA website is now on Godsweb). This 5 megabytes of webspace comes "free" for the basic CompuServe subscription of 6-50 pounds a month (Phone bills extra, connect time of more than 5 hours a month charged 1-50 pounds an hour extra.) You can switch to a flat rate payment plan if you use more time than the average user.
Online Time: Maintaining a website requires time on the phone connected to your provider. Apart from anything else, you may want to surf the net to find good graphics and ideas to update your site or provide links. That takes extra time and money but flat rate connection packages are now available from many Internet Service Providers which offer unlimted time online for a fixed monthly price.
Hardware: Most churches coming onto the web are using facilities provided free by a member who (like me) is already into computing in a big way. To do it from scratch would be expensive if you have to buy all the hardware and software (at least 1000 pounds). When I began, I was already on CompuServe and had all the basic software from them. I also had Word 6 and CorelDraw 5 for other purposes. I already had a suitable though aging machine. If you are starting from scratch you will need at least a 486 PC (or Mac equivalent) with a modem and the software capable of connecting you to the Internet.

Why Set Up a Church Website?

Before wasting a lot of time (and possibly money), you need to decide why you are setting up your Church's website - for example whether you want to convey only basic information about the Church or to present more of a *feel* for the Church. Do you want to present your Church as a spiritual and activity resource centre or as a community of people sharing a particular set of beliefs. In deciding this, think about your likely target audience and how to influence them. But do not fall into the trap of presenting your Church as something it is not. It is helpful to describe your typical visitor, in the same way that you would when designing a seeker-service or other outreach event.
Some good basic reasons for setting up a Church website might be as follows (some sites can hit one or more of these targets):

(1) To provide your members with information

The London Baptist Association (LBA) website, for example, is aimed at its own members. It concentrates on providing them with useful information about the LBA. It also signposts them to each other (e-mail addresses, Church websites) and to relevant Christian material on the web.
However, the site inevitably has visitors who stumble on it who may be non-Christians and others who will be Baptists or Christians from outside the LBA. The site recognises that and has a little bit of evangelistic material in case a person stumbles on it who is enquiring about how to become a Christian etc. It also attracts a lot of enquiries from Christians in the USA who are simply browsing the web, sometimes planning to move to or pass through London. It therefore has some additional material aimed at them but that is not allowed to divert the site from its main purpose.

(2) To attract people living in or moving to the area to your Church

At Teddington Baptist Church, we thought our target audience would be the mobile person looking for a Church and either already living in or moving to the neighbourhood. They were likely to have some church background without necessarily being a Christian but interested in seeing what our Church had to offer. We decided to try and convey the Church as a group of interesting people motivated by a belief in Jesus Christ. We set out quite deliberately to dispel the external myth that Christians (and especially Baptists) are boring people who are out of touch with the real world.
We therefore designed the content and presentation of material on our main website to be attractive to the interested outsider. The attractively presented material on the site does contain direct evangelism e.g. Meet Some TBC People as well as the softer evangelism of the Virtual Baptist Church Tour, Views on the News, Leonardo's Notebook (a scientist's jottings on faith), and Our Multimedia History.

(3) To present the Gospel directly to the non-Christian (direct evangelism)

A Church site could be designed at the top level (entry point) for direct evangelism with details of times of service etc at a lower level. Such a site might, for example, try to attract in visitors by using headlines and keywords on currently controversial topics. Then it could turn a initial discusion of them into a Christian challenge.
I do not know how effective that appproach might be for a complete site. People attracted in under false pretences will resent you wasting their time, so always provide full value on the advertised topic as well as any evangelistic spin or

side message. My closest try at this has been with a single site feature on the Teddington Baptist Church site - Bugged by the Millennium? which we have just taken offline. During the year 2000, this offered a choice of links to information on:

- Action 2000 - the Millennium Bug
- Jubilee 2000 - world debt relief
- Greenwich 2000 - celebration details
- Y-2000 - Jesus Christ the reason for the Millennium

It would be possible to set up an entire site around such a theme mixing practical advice with witness and evangelistic messages but I have kept this example down to just two web pages.

(4) To provide a point of contact with the community (soft evangelism)

At Teddington Baptist Church, we set up a second site aimed at a completely different audience - the complete outsider living in the area with no contact or interest in Christian things at all. This site is

Wot? - What's Online for Teddington? which is an Internet information site for the local community.

The only connection with the Church apparent to the casual visitor is that it is sponsored by the Church - and so it has advertising banners for the Church's activities like any other sponsored site on the Internet. It steps right over into the community by carrying information on all local societies, websites etc. Even places to find real ale. We have a clearly stated editorial policy on the website but we have deliberately adopted a non-exclusive stance.

This site takes a lot of work but Wot? has generated a lot of community interest and recognition for the Church. It provides us with a modern image and effectively provides the Church with an advertising bill board in the middle of the local online community. The local library, local voluntary organisations, local Council, and even some local companies send their site visitors to Wot? for local information. Once they are with us, we can present them with our own choice of advertising material.

Other Reasons for Setting up a Church Website

Some might argue that having a website shows that the Church is up-to-date and modern. Just being there is enough. That may be true when someone first comes onto the web - and it is enough reason to have a basic website which takes very little time to set up and maintain.

I believe there are more powerful reasons than that, although they are more to do with future than present impact. The Internet is a new medium for communicating the Gospel. We can only discover how to exploit it by being there. I was inspired to set up Wot? by the wide vision and inspiration on what Church websites can be used for in Patrick Dixon's book called *Cyberchurch: Christianity and the Internet* (published by Kingsway ISBN 0-85476-711-8; RRP 6-99 pounds). This book gives a lot of good ideas on how Churches can develop their use of web sites - visionary stuff!

Existing Church websites can provide you with good ideas for how to identify and reach your target audience. You can find examples of existing London Baptist Church websites on the LBA WWW London page. They range from the very simple and straightforward to quite sophisticated sites.

A very innovative Baptist Church site outside London is that for Sandy Baptist Church which aims to combine a church site with community service.

Who Should Run Your Church Website?

Preferably someone with skill, enthusiasm, and commitment for the long-term. They will need to have, or be provided with, equipment and software. If you are going to entrust the website to a church member, apply the same approach you would to the selection of a newsletter editor. Can this person be trusted to develop and maintain the concept of the website without supervision? Alternatively, are they the kind of person who can perform the necessary technical feats without resenting your intervention and suggestions?

A Basic Website

Creating a Website: Begin by looking at what others have done. There are a number of LBA Churches already on the Web. Have a look at their websites. A list is on the LBA WWW London page. You need to decide what you are going to do before starting to develop your website using any software.

Developing a Style: I always start by developing a style for a new website and setting it out in a "Style Sheet" so I get a reasonably consistent look for all pages on the site. This includes things like how to navigate around the site. Look at what others have done to get some ideas. I hope you have noticed a consistency of style on each my websites. For example, on any of my websites every page has the same top and bottom and may have a similar layout. Again, on every website, each page has a standard way of getting back to the main menu page. For example:

- LBA website - the logo bar to return to the Capital Information Centre is at the top and bottom of every page;
- Teddington Baptist Church - click on any logo to get back to the home page;
- Wot? - click on any logo to get back to the index; standard menu at the top of every page;

These features are deliberate and pre-planned, not an accident. You will find it much easier to develop your site by developing such a standard style and your visitors will find your site much easier to use.
Learning from Others' Code: You can probably learn a lot about how to do the things you see on other people's websites by looking at their HTML code.

- With Netscape you do this by selecting View from the main menu and then selecting Document Source (Version 3) or Page Source (Version 4) from the submenu which appears.
- With Internet Explorer 3/4/5 you do this by selecting View from the main menu and then selecting Source from the submenu.

Copy Others!: It is polite to ask people before you copy their ideas, code, graphics etc. You should also respect copyright.
However, Churches are welcome to copy ideas, code, graphics or any other material from any of my websites in building their own websites. In fact everything on my websites which does not carry a copyright sign is either already in the public domain (and borrowed by me from someone else) or created by me and placed in the public domain. Take care because some items (e.g. music files) may have copyright statements within them.
Basic Editing Software: To start creating a web page, you can use a program like HomePage Wizard (from CompuServe) which does not require you to know any HTML (the language used to write web pages; HTML = HyperText Markup Language). You can spend a lot of money on software (see advanced software) but start small rather than starting by spending money on the best software.
Clip Art and Graphics: I don't like much of the free Christian clip art available on the WWW but by searching you can find some reasonable graphics.
There are also secular sites around like CoolText and Zygraphics which offer free services of generating custom graphics for you - sometimes as samples aimed an encouraging you to visit their site or buy their advanced services.
Template Services: Some companies offer hosting services which may include setting up church websites using a suitable template. These vary from free services which offer a single page on a standard template like Churches dot Net, Find a Church and Netministries to more sophisticated offerings like church123.com and Godsweb which, for a fee, offer flexible templates for church websites which they also host.

An Advanced Website

Advanced Software: I describe below the cost of becoming more sophisticated but don't think you have to spend all the money listed below. I have invested over the years since 1996 as I have built up my understanding. For the first few months of web page design, I used the free software provided by Compuserve, then I started wanting to do things not possible without better facilities. Also I am an experienced computer programmer (since 1966), so have tended to get fairly deeply into coding JavaScript etc. That is not strictly necessary!

If you are more ambitious for your website than can easily be achieved using free software from your Internet service provider, it can cost several hundred pounds to equip yourself with suitable software and information.

Editing Software: I started by using WebEdit (which is a shareware program) to write my HTML code and manage the website files. WebEdit 2.0 Standard Edition cost 40 dollars to register. I later upgraded to WedEdit Pro 3.1 costing a further 40 dollars. The future of WebEdit was uncertain for quite a time because Ken Nesbitt (who wrote it) sold the rights to a company (Luckman) which went out of business in December 1998. However, it has now been acquired by sandiego.com which is promising to keep it updated and is selling the Standard Edition for 80 dollars and the Professional Edition for 130 dollars (at February 2000).

There are many other programs available (e.g. Microsoft Frontpage, Macromedia's Dreamweaver and SoftQuad's HotMetal Pro). These programs can cost 100 pounds or more and can do much of the work for you. They are not strictly necessary - the experts claim to use only Notepad and File Manager - but I would advise buying one if you intend to do serious work on developing and maintaining websites unless you are an experienced programmer. Because I am an experienced programmer and like to work in HTML I still use WebEdit Pro 3.1 but I am also using a similar but more advanced (yet free!) program called HTML-Kit.

HTML and JavaScript: To produce something like the London Baptist Association and Teddington Baptist Church websites, you need to write (or copy and adapt) quite sophisticated HTML code and write (or copy and adapt) JavaScript (I have done all of those). Actually that can all be done with Notepad or a standard wordprocessor but it is easier with a specialist program.

To buy a good book on HTML cost me 47 pounds (*Using HTML* from Que) and a similar good book on Javascript (*Using Javascript* also from Que) cost me another 47 pounds (both including CDROMs).

For very sophisticated sites, you have to find out how to use the latest versions of HTML, JavaScript code, and Java Applets either by studying books, other people's code, or by downloading the latest manual from the Internet. With a good web page authoring program you might not have to learn much HTML but it helps. Netscape has a Javascript Guide and a Javascript Reference site. On the web you can find lots of help: a good advice site for basic HTML is at The Bare Bones Guide to HTML.

I have surfed extensively and downloaded material from a wide range of specialist HTML and JavaScript sites (all free except for connect time). Two excellent JavaScript sites The Javascript Source and JavaGoodies.

Java Applets can be used to generate quite stunning visual and other effects. They can also be found on free sites - see the list at TheFreeSite.com or can be purchased at reasonable prices from sites like AnfyJava.

To find such sites try searching for HTML, Javascript, or Java Applets using search engines like Yahoo and AltaVista.

DHTML: I avoided using Dynamic HTML (DHTML) until late 1999 because it has not been well standardised in its implementation - that is there are big differences between the Internet Explorer and Netscape versions at versions 4/5 of their browsers. If you use it, you need to identify the browser a visitor is using and send them to a page tailored for their browser. See Beginner's Guide to DHTML and also Microsoft's site on DHTML for Internet Explorer.

Creating Graphics: Then, you may also need good graphics software. When I started, to my existing CorelDraw 5 (now selling for less than 100 pounds), I had to add a shareware program called GifWeb to handle transparent Gif89a backgrounds (20 dollars to register) and a shareware program called Gif Construction Set from Mindworkshop to create animated graphics (costing about 30 dollars to register). I also used MapEdit (25 dollars to register) to create the active maps (the graphics and/or maps on which you click to go somewhere).

It is worth putting a lot of effort into getting the graphics on your website as small as possible - designing them to look good on the screen, but still to download quickly as possible.

Music: I also have added music software (Mozart and Digital Studio) which I would not otherwise have bought both to compose music (Mozart is shareware costing 30 pounds to register) and to process it digitally (Digital Studio is shareware costing 30 pounds).

Music Copyright: If you use music still within copyright (within seventy years of the composer's death) you ought to have permission from the composer and/or an online licence. There is now a music licencing scheme for websites (see MCP Media Licensing) which charges £70.50 per quarter (at November 2003) for up to 50 streaming audio clips (for the application form with prices see Application Form. That is expensive for a church website and that is why, at the moment, I am mainly using out of copyright hymn tunes like Amazing Grace or tunes written by people willing to grant free licence to use.

Visitor Counter: Your service provider may give you this facility. Compuserve has only recently starting offering it so to provide a visitor counter I use the following HTML code -

```
<center><h4>You are visitor number: <IMG SRC="http://www.qmw.ac.uk/htbin/counter?mycounter"
ALIGN=center alt="Umpteen"> to this site since 1 January 1997 </h4></center>
```

If you want to use this then replace "mycounter" by a piece of text unique to you (e.g. name or initials of your Church). Note that this counter service is provided free of charge by an academic institution and could be withdrawn at any time. There are now a number of commercial services offering free Visitor Counters including tracking the use of your web pages. A list is at Visitor's Counters.

Visitor Book or Guestbook: There are now a number of websites which offer free Guestbook services. I use the Phaistos Guestbook on the London Baptist Association and Teddington Baptist Church websites. There are a number of other sites offering free services like Visitor's or Guest Books.

Other Sources of Advice

There are various websites designed to help you assemble a church website - have a look at those listed on the LBA WWW Resources page. A UK site to help churches getting onto the Internet is COIN - Christians on the Internet which has various resources to help you get started on the web. Other excellent advisory sites are run by other Christian organisations e.g. SOON Gospel Literature and Gospel.com. In addition you can use a template service to build a simple church website.

There are also secular websites which provide advice on how to build websites to make them easy for visitors to use. TheFreeSite.com lists various free services available for webmasters including Visitor Counters and Guestbooks.

FAQs - Frequently Asked Questions

As webmaster of several Christian websites, I get asked a lot of questions about setting up websites and my experience. Here are some of the questions and the answers I have given.

Colin Hicks

What sort of response have you had from people visiting your Church website?

A very positive one both from Christians and non-Christians. We have had a few people (very few) arrive at the Church having found out about us solely from the website. We get a lot of encouraging e-mails from Christians and non-Christians.

We sometimes get e-mails asking for information. They range from simple enquiries about running a Church website (e.g. what kind of response do you get), to people who want to know about Baptists (e.g. do your members have to be teetotal?), to family history enquiries (e.g. is a named person buried in your graveyard), to rather surprising questions (e.g. I am an American Baptist - do you use the same Bible that we do?). I try to give a positive answer to every enquiry as quickly as possibly with a light and respectful touch remembering that there may be language or cultural difficulties in my understanding the question or their understanding my answer. This can require great diplomacy. I always try to reassure the non-Christian enquirer that we will not take offence at any question they ask because "we do not take ourselves seriously although we do take our faith and our Lord very seriously".

What content have you found has been of most value to those people visiting your Church website?

Obviously you need to have the core information (times of service, address, map, perhaps details of any youth groups). Beyond that we have had an excellent response to a number of our site features, especially to the Virtual Baptist Church Tour. A number of schools and school children all around the country have used our site to get information about the Baptist denomination and we have found the style of that feature attractive to a wide range of age groups.

Our Great Christians web feature has also interested many as it presents aspects of the life of some individual Christians which have inspired some of our own members.
We have some direct evangelistic features on the site into which we try to gather people by softer routes - like Views on the News, Meet some TBC People, Virtual Baptist Church Tour, and Watch a Baptism!.

Are the majority of those visiting your Church website Christians or non-Christians?

We don't know for sure! We know nothing about any visitor unless they choose to tell us by completing the Visitor's Book or sending an e-mail. We get a lot of messages and enquiries from Christians (like yours).
I suspect that for the main Teddington Baptist Church site most visitors are Christians. It has about ten visitors a day (August 2001). I think many are Baptists from the USA because they are much more likely to be online and often want to learn about the UK and London when they are planning a visit to the UK.
For the Wot? site, most visitors will definitely be non-Christians. There is nothing overtly Christian about the site. We have at present (August 2001) an average of about ten visitors a day to Wot? and that number is rising steadily month by month - it was seven a day in the middle of 1999. Visitor numbers peaked at twenty a day for a fortnight in 1999 when Wot? was the featured London site for a major London information site.

How often so you update your Church website?

My main websites are updated at least once a week. Sometimes twice. The core material remains unchanged but there are always minor changes to upcoming events. The monthly features (Views on the News) need to be changed. Wot? is sometimes changed to reflect the seasons. I develop and add a major new feature like Our Multimedia history about once every four months.

What about protecting kids (and others) from bad Internet content?

If you come across any illegal content while browsing the Internet, then report it through the Internet Watch Foundation or by telephone to 01223 236077 and official action will be taken.
A UK based service organised by Christians, **Surfon*the*Safeside**.com, offers a subscription service to block access to offensive sites for £3 a month (November 2003).
Work proceeds on the PICS classification system used to self-rate sites. The PICS system is explained on the W3 PICS page. The system is not yet fully standardised but two of many ratings sites are ICRA and Safesurf. META tags rating this site and/or page as "entirely safe for kids" are at the top of this page's HTML. These were produced by those two ratings systems.
Content Control is already built into Internet Explorer 3 (for Windows 95), Netscape 4 and above, and Internet Explorer 4 and above. They use the ICRA system as standard. Rating systems passed on PICS will be built into other new browsers as they emerge.

To set the Content Control for

- IE3 (Win 95) you use the successive menus: View, Options, Security and then click on Enable Ratings
- IE4 you use the successive menus: View, Internet Options, Content, and then click on Enable in the Content Advisor box
- IE5 and IE6 you use the successive menus: Tools, Internet Options, Content, and then click on Enable in the Content Advisor box

Those working with children and young people also need to take care not to expose them to risk. The Methodist Church has produced some Internet Guidelines (in pdf format) for those working with the internet for children and young people.

****

4.18 Report on Webmaster Survey

Dr. Scott Thumma
Hartford Institute for Religion Research
December 6, 2000
http://hirr.hartsem.edu/bookshelf/thumma_article3.html

In the fall of 2000 students in Hartford's Seminary course on Religion and the Internet electronically surveyed a total of 125 webmasters of U.S. congregational web sites. These sites represented Muslim, Jewish, Catholic, and both conservative and liberal Protestantism congregations.

The surveys were either attached to an email message or directly inserted in the email message to the stated webmaster of these congregational sites. The sites were randomly chosen off search engines and lists of congregational web sites. From the total 125 sent, we received 63 usable responses, almost exactly a 50% response rate. We received surveys from a diversity of types of sites:

- Twenty percent were online a few months while 9.5% were over 4 years (average length of being online was 30 months)
- Twenty six percent were Catholic sites, 15.8% were Southern Baptist, and 13.2% were nondenominational. The remaining 45% were scattered evenly between Evangelical and Mainline Protestant, Jewish and Muslim religious traditions.
- The sites were evenly distributed throughout the country.

Obviously this sample cannot be seen as representative of the nearly 150,000 US religious congregations with some web presence. Nevertheless, even this small number of responses yields several interesting findings about how congregational web sites are created and maintained.

One of the most startling findings is that none of the webmasters surveyed reported that their congregations contracted with professional web design firms outside of their membership to create their sites. This news is both encouraging, since these web sites are "homegrown" grassroots projects of committed and motivated members, and also disappointing, since many of the sites surveyed could have benefited from professional design assistance.

Another significant, but not surprising, finding was the person responsible for the idea to create the web site in the first place. In nearly half the cases a layperson had the original idea for a congregational web site. Pastors were the catalysts for the web site in just 30 percent of the cases, with the remaining 20 percent scattered among either teams of members, committees, and individual staff persons.

The survey yielded interesting insights into the web site planning and construction process as well. As stated above, in the vast majority of cases (75.8%) a skilled member of the congregation was responsible for the site creation, with an additional 21 percent made by congregational staff members. In slightly over half the cases, the congregation as a whole was encouraged to contribute ideas for the site, although a few webmasters confessed that this request for involvement was a big mistake.

A majority (76%) of webmasters, a few of who were not the original creators of their sites, stated that it was relatively easy to get the original material for their sites. Several of those surveyed voluntarily reported that is it a much more difficult task to get continual new material to update their sites. Whatever the case, most of those surveyed didn't spend extensive time planning their sites, with the majority of webmasters (56%) saying it was 2 months or less from the idea of the site to when it went online. Another 30% said they took between 3 to 4 months to bring their sites to actualization.

The responsibility for generating new web content does not rest on the shoulders of the webmaster alone, however. In over half the cases, multiple persons share this task - from a web committee or clergy/staff team to a publications or publicity department. The webmaster is responsible for this effort in a quarter of the sites, a pastor is in 15% and a secretary is in 10% of the sites surveyed. Often these responsible persons garner new information from administrative staff, the newsletter and publicity committee, or from other ministry leaders.

The survey also explored the intended audience of a congregational site. Nearly 50 percent of webmasters said their sites were equally aimed at the general public and at their own members. Another large group of sites (43.5%) were seen as more for the public, with only 7 percent saying they designed their sites mostly for an internal congregational audience. Not surprising, the congregational interest ranged from "very little" to "some" when the web site first was introduced, but most webmasters reported that the congregational interest in the site had increased to at least "some," with 34 percent reporting more than some interest and another eleven percent reporting "a lot of interest."

All the congregations reported publicizing their sites using from 2 to 6 different methods including, in order of mention, search engine submission, bulletins, general congregational literature, public ads, denominational listings, newsletters, brochures, word of mouth, outdoor signs, bumper stickers and radio/TV ads. Interestingly, much of the publicity was equally aimed at external and internal audiences (65%) or internally toward the congregation (23%). Somewhat surprisingly, only 12 percent of respondents stated their publicity efforts were primarily directed at external targets. This seems incongruent with the finding that nearly 44 percent of sites were seen as directed at an external audience.

Webmasters overwhelmingly report a mix of outsiders and congregational members using their sites, although a quarter thought most of their traffic was from nonmember visitors. Nearly a third of webmasters didn't know which pages on their sites were the most popular. Of those who knew the traffic patterns, the pastor's sermons (both audio and in text), newsletters, schedules of events (only if they were kept up-to-date), list of links, and pictures of ministry events drew the most visitors.

As the class members visited the surveyed web sites they noticed that very few of them including interactive features, such as bulletin boards, chat rooms, email listserves or newsletters, downloading of sermon files, hyperlinks to missionaries or interactive schedules and calendars. Many of these interactive features are often available free as downloads from numerous web sites.

One question that was not asked was how successful these sites were at attracting first time visitors and new members. Although not asked, eight respondents (13%) claimed to have gotten first time visitors because of the web site, and all but one of these eight said the congregation gained new members directly as a result of the site.

One methodologically interesting finding from this research effort had to do with email surveying. Our response rate was greatly increased when the survey was inserted in the email rather than sent as an attachment. The response rate for surveys included in the email message was 74.7% while that for surveys sent as attachments was 14 percent. We speculate this difference is due to the recent number of viruses that are broadcast through email attachments. Individuals are less willing to open an attachment from someone they don't know, even if the cover email to which it is attached seems to be from a trustworthy source such as a seminary student doing a class project.

Although this research effort is limited in its scope, it nevertheless offers an interesting glimpse into the process of creating and maintaining a congregational web site. There are many lessons to be learned from the interactions between webmasters, the congregation, its religious leaders and the site that gets created. Often the congregational sites are little more than electronic brochures. Occasionally a site does an excellent job of conveying the culture and character of the congregation in an appealing and inviting manner. In either case, it is certain that congregations are flocking to the web and greater attention needs to be paid to the method and manner by which this process happens.

You might also want to read other online articles about religion and the Internet. They can be found on our section of this site dedicated to the topic.

****

4.19 Research Survey: Sikhs on the net

http://www.mailgate.superva.it.soc.religion.sikhism/msg01345.html

Sikhs on the net: 1st Questionnaire

Hi, This survey is for Sikh Internet Users (survey of 3). All responses will be dealt with in the strictest of confidence. Please complete those questions you are comfortable with. Thanks. Jatinder Singh.

Your E-mail ➢ Required

Your Name ➢ Required

Age

Sex Male Female

Marital Status Married /Not Married
Level of Education
Any Children? Yes No
What work/Study do you do?
When did you first go online (yr)
Where do you most access the Internet?
How much are you online daily (hrs)
Do you go online daily? Yes No
What are the main things you do online?
What Sikh information do you access regularly online (use CTRL to select more than one)
If other, please specify
Your place of residence (town/country)?
Would you like to help me further understand Sikh use of the Net Yes No

Sikhs on the Internet: 2nd questionnaire
Hi, Complete those questions you are comfortable with for this 2nd survey. Thanks. Jatinder Singh.

Your E-mail ➢ *Required*
The Internet provides me with Sangat Agree Disagree
I believe info on the Internet promotes Sikh interests Agree Disagree
The Internet cannot be used to further my development as a Sikh Agree Disagree
I feel the Internet is generally bad for Sikhs Agree Disagree
The combination of the online and offline Sikh world advances my development as a Sikh Agree Disagree
The Internet is not good for my spirituality Agree Disagree
I think the Internet is not good for Sikh politics Agree Disagree
I consider the Internet to be good for Sikh activism Agree Disagree
The Internet does not connect Sikhs in a global manner Agree Disagree
The Internet will affect the Sikh world negatively Agree Disagree
I can gain important Sikh info & knowledge from the Internet Agree Disagree

Questionnaire: Final Survey
Hi. This is the final part of this survey. Complete those questions you are comfortable with. Thanks. Jatinder Singh.

Your E-mail ➢ *Required*
Which Sikh mailing lists (MLs) do you use + why?
Do you promote these MLs? Yes No
Do you contribute to MLs? Yes No
Which Sikh sites do you visit + why?
Do you promote these Sites? Yes No
Your view of Sikh MLs?
Your view of Sikh sites?

Do Sikhs come across well/badly online? Well Badly
When do you surf during the day?
Which Sikh info do you access + why?
Do you read all messages on MLs? Certain All
If certain ones, how do you choose?
Your view of other Sikh ML members?
What religious experience does the web provide?
What do you post/avoid posting to MLs?
What would you miss if the web disappeared tomorrow?
Do you use the Net to communicate privately with Sikhs? Yes No

****

4.20 Islam.com Survey

http://islaam.master.com/texis/master/search/?s=SS&q=islam

Dear Islaam.com visitors:

I am contemplating improving certain aspects of the site. You are the best people to consult in that regard, so I hope you can contribute some of your time to improvement of this da`wah effort by filling out a simple and anonymous survey. Please do that. I truly hope you can complete all of the survey, but if not, do as much as you can and submit your answers.

May Allah count it as a good deed for you and reward you abundantly!

Editor, Islaam.com

1) **How often do you visit Islaam.com?**
   Daily More than once a week Once a week
   Few times a month Once a month or less
2) **How often do you visit the World News section on Islaam.com?**
   Daily More than once a week Once a week
   Few times a month Once a month or less
3) **Are you subscribed to Islaam.com's mailing list?**
   Yes No
4) **What is your overall rating of the site?**
   Excellent Very good Good Fair Poor
5) **How would you rate authenticity/trustworthiness of the information on the site?**
   Excellent Very good Good Fair Poor
6) **How do you find Islaam.com?**
   Extremist Moderate Too liberal
7) **Have you ever recommended Islaam.com to others?**
   Yes No
8) **Relative to other Islamic web sites, Islaam.com is your...**
   Favorite site One of top 3 favorite sites

One of top 5 favorite sites One of top 10 favorite sites
Not really favorite

9) **What do you use Islaam.com for _mostly_?**
Reading new articles advertised through the mailing list
Reading new or old articles
Searching archives
Listening audio lectures
Listening quranic recitations

10) **What type of material do you like best?**
Articles Audio lectures Audio Quranic recitations

11) **What type of topics do you like best for articles/audio lectures?**
Aqeedah Purification of the soul Quran and Tafsir
Sunnah and Hadith Other

12) **What type of articles do you prefer?**
Short Long

13) **How would you rate the design/look of the site?**
Very appealing Somewhat appealing Not appealing Downright ugly

14) **How would you rate the professionalism of the presentation on Islaam.com (given that professionally designed sites communicate trustworthiness of information)?**
Very professional Somewhat professional Unprofessional

15) **How would you rate the frequency of updates?**
Excellent Very good Good Fair Poor

16) **How would you rate the mailing list quality?**
Excellent Good Poor Not a subscriber

17) **How fast do Islaam.com pages load?**
Very fast Fast Average Slow Very slow

18) **How do you find the font size used in articles?**
Too large Just right Too small

19) **What do you think of the site navigation?**
Very easy Easy Somewhat easy Difficult Very difficult

20) **Do you ever use "Email this article" feature?**
Yes No

21) **Do you ever use "Print this article" feature?**
Yes No

22) **How interested are you in ratings given to articles by other visitors?**
Very much Somewhat Not at all

23) **How often do you use the Most Popular Articles feature?**
Very often Often Rarely Very rarely Never

24) **Are you male or female?**
Male Female

25) **In what age group do you belong?**
Less than 20 years old 20-25 years old 25-30 years old
30-40 years old Over 40 years old

26) **How would you best describe yourself?**
Muslim since birth Muslim revert
Non-Muslim contemplating accepting Islam Non-Muslim

27) **What level of education do you have?**
Elementary school High school
2-year or 4-year college degree Master's

Doctorate

28)How active are you in da`wah (call to Islam)?

Very active Active Not very active Not active at all

29)Lastly, what would you do differently on this web site, if you could?

****

4.21 Cyberworship Site Map

www.eattheword.com ©Paul Vickers, 2000
email: webmaster_NOSPAM_@EatTheWord.com

Author
Musings
Links
Music
copyright
Bookshop
Word Study
downloadables/WordStudy.pdf
Introduction
Praise
- Hebrew
  - Barach
  - Hilool
  - Halal
  - Zamar
  - Yadah
  - Shavach
  - Shevach
  - Tehillah
  - Todah
- Greek
  - Aheeneho
  - Aheenos
  - Aretay
  - Doxa
  - Epaheeneho
  - Epaheenos
  - Eulogeo
  - Humneo

Worship
  Hebrew
    Segiyd
    Atsav
    Shachah
  Greek
    Ethelothracekiah
    Eusebeo
    Theosebace
    Therapeuo
    Thracekiah
    Latryooo
    Neokoros
    Proskuneo
    Sebadzomahee
    Sebasma
    Sebomahee
Discussion board
Post
Search
Site Map
Guest book
Search

****

4.22 Religious Resources Theme Map

http://www.religiousresources.org/directory/cat.php?cat_id=85

Worship and Liturgy
Subcategories

Lectionaries and Liturgical Calendars **Pastoral Reference Listings**

... and Dance (details)
A Biblical study of dance as an expression of praise and worship and ministry. Includes a link to Christian video dance instruction and supplies.
A Ten Minute Sermon - Christian Resources (details)

sermon and bible study resources, drama and music including MIDI and tab, prayers and evangelistic material, daily devotionals and humor

Art to Heart (details)
Encounters with God in the world's great art. We offer: 1)Inspiring Christian speaker; 2)Resources for worship leaders to include visual art in worship; 3)Travel to U.S. and European art museums (free travel for tour hosts).
Christian Resource Institute, The Voice (details)
The Christian Resource Institute seeks to provide quality resources for personal study, reflection, teaching, and preaching in the Church

CrossTies Ministries (details)
Crossties Ministries provides educational and training resources to Lutheran Churches in the Houston, Texas area. Based upon the Holy Scriptures, the Lutheran Confessions and psychological studies,
Desperate Preacher Site (details)
Where Pastors and Lay leaders can discuss a variety of topics, to include the Lectionary readings for the current week and also the theological issues of the day.
Expository Sermons and Worship Resources (details)
Teaching by Coty Pinckney of Community Bible Church, Williamstown, Massachusetts. Expository series on Ephesians, Leviticus, marriage, and money, among others. Also worship resources, bible studies, and links.
faith and worship.com (details)
Free resources for Ministry and Worship, with Bibles, Sermons, Commentaries, Christian music and drama, MIDI and tab, faith issues tackled, humor, prayer and Sunday School material.
Family Worship (details)
Worship Resources (Songs, recordings, teaching materials) from Ichthus Christian Fellowship, London, UK, aimed at helping the whole church to worship together. Free monthly newsletter; unique free song-by-email service. Special Kids Zone.
Ken Collins' Web Site (details)
Large web site with worship resources such as daily and topical prayers, a lectionary, and discussions of various Christian topics. All original material.
LifeWayonline.com (details)
LifeWayonline.com is owned by LifeWay Christian Resources. LifeWay has published christian church and family literature for over 100 years. Also operates a large Christian retail chain.
Lift Up Your Hearts (details)
ELCIC worship and spirituality resource site. Large catalogues of annotated links related to liturgy, spirituality, music and the arts.
Methodist Lectionary Cross-reference (details)
A Cross reference between the three lectionaries used by the Methodist Church of UK in recent years. 1975 Service Book, 1992 JLG2 and 1998 RCL. Cross reference by reading or sunday.
Ministry Maker (details)
Provides free church planting resources, sermon outlines, worship ministry helps and links, Christian chat, a new ministry directory, and more.
Revised Common Lectionary, Vanderbilt Divinity Library (details)
A web site that lists the scriptures for each week from the Revised Common Lectionary (Years A and B). Also includes a listing of liturgical colors.
SAMUEL: The Next Generation (Revision 963) (details)
A weekly library of worship resources for congregations using the Revised Common Lectionary - from the United Church of Christ.
Seekers Liturgies (details)
Collection of our inclusive language liturgies that (generally) set the structure and theme of Sunday morning worship.
Sermonhelp.Com (details)
Sermonhelp.Com is a sermon and worship preparation service offering full text sermons, alternate sermon ideas and worship resources for each Sunday. It follows the Revised Common Lectionary used by most mainline denominations.
SermonSeekers.org (details)
Sermonseekers.org includes sermons, Bible teachings, discipleship material, seminary instruction and helpful suggestions to stimulate the practice of Christian truth through the local church and into everyday life.
The Text This Week (details)
Contemporary and Historical study and liturgy links and resources, indexed according to the lessons in the Revised Common Lectionary
Worship Stuff (details)

Here you can find outlines and worship resources to help plan and execute worship experiences for congregations of any size

Worship That Works/Selected Sermons (details)

A weekly sermon series by a wide selection of lay and clergy preachers. The sermons, and a related series of sermon study notes, are available online in advance of use dates based on the Episcopal Lectionary.

WRBC Evangelical Dance Ministry (details)

Ministering in dance under the Anointed Power of God. Changing the world with uplifted hands.

****

4.23 Main Menu, Spiritual Topics:

Religious tolerance, freedom, activities, etc.

http://religioustolerance.org/positive.htm

A Cherokee prayer blessing.

May the warm winds of heaven blow softly upon your house,
May the Great Spirit bless all who enter there,
May your moccasins make happy tracks in many snows,
And may the rainbow always touch your shoulder.

Key spiritual topics:

God, as viewed by many different religions
What is spiritual/religious/scientific truth?
Peace -- Is it attainable?
Recommended books on spirituality, religion and theology

Religious tolerance

What is religious tolerance?
Times and places of religious tolerance in the west
Religious plurality (and exclusivism & inclusivism)

Religiously exclusive passages in the Christian Scriptures
Local groups promoting interfaith dialog
Test your religious tolerance
Tolerance in the Bible
How Christians view non-Christian Religions
Cathedral of the Pines from inclusiveness to intolerance and back
Center for Religious Freedom's book on religious freedom, worldwide

Statements on Religious Freedom and Tolerance

Excerpts:
Excerpts of statements on religious freedom
In the United States:
Williamsburg Charter on the First Amendment (1988)
U.N. report on religious freedom in the U.S. (1998)
Religious rights within the US military
Proclamation on diversity and tolerance by the mayor of Cedar Rapids, IA.
International:
Declaration of a Global Ethic (1993)
Excerpts from *"The Principles of a Global Ethic"*
By UNESCO, on the "Year of Tolerance" (1995)
Statement by Pope John Paul II on the World Day of Peace, (1996)

By the U.N. on freedom of religion in Europe (1999)
The Amman Declaration (1999) on conflicts and religions in the Middle East
The Geneva Spiritual Appeal (1999) on an end to religiously motivated conflict
Other:
Brief quotations about tolerance
Reducing religion-inspired religious conflicts
Religious Tolerance chain letter
See also, religious laws of the U.S., Canada and other nations
Statements of apology for past sins and crimes against humanity:
"*Remorse that ends sin*" A brief essay by the Christian Science Monitor
Roman Catholic apology for past sins and errors issued 2000-MAR-7
Christian apology to Jews and Muslims for the Crusades
Spiritual Activities
"*Salem Day of Contrition,*" 1997-JAN-14
"*Religious Tolerance Day,*" Early FEB
"*National Day of Prayer,*" 1st Thursday in MAY
"*National Day of Reason,*" 1st Thursday in MAY
"*Sabbath of Support*" in Opposition to Racism Late JUN or early JUL
"*Day of Remembrance*" of the evils of slavery. AUG-24
"*International Day of Prayer for the Persecuted Church*" Held in mid-NOV
Online Silence for Religious Tolerance, 1999-NOV-30 at: http://www.angelfire.com/oh2/silence4tolerance/
The "*1000 Lamp Mandala Ceremony for Peace,*" DEC-10
Worldwide prayer and meditation for peace DEC-31
Reconciliation walk: Christian apology to Jews and Muslims for the Crusades
Praying in public schools -- legally
Coming of age rituals for many faiths and countries

Personal Statements on spiritual matters:
Declaration of Peace: A Neopagan statement of personal commitment to peace.
Spiritual Freedom Pledge
Beware the advent virus: Christian thoughts on joy, tolerance, and peace.
The Affirmation of Acknowledgment: A statement of inter-faith tolerance
Statement by President Clinton on Religious Liberty (1995)
A Thanksgiving statement
Quotes: religious, philosophical & humorous
Fun Stuff
A word list of world religions
Humorous quotes from church bulletins
Quotes by children:
About religion
About love

Churches ad hoc, an off-site photo essay which gives an offbeat look at churches in America.Other related menus & topics at this site:

The concept of sin
Religious diversity among the crew of the space shuttle Columbia
Books on spirituality, theology and religion
"Cults" and New Religious Groups (most are quite harmless)
Religious Laws
The national motto: "In God We Trust."
Religious information (membership data, calendars, church attendance...)

Marriage
The use of prayer in the place of medical treatment
Conclusions: which is the "true" denomination or religion; where did we come from; where are we going after death, and other really fundamental questions

Find a faith group which matches your beliefs:
The Belief System Selector by SelectSmart.com tries to match you up with the religion(s) that most closely suit your beliefs, whether it be secular humanism, Unitarian Universalism, Taoism, Hinduism, Easter Orthodox. etc.

SelectSmart.com also has dozens of similar selectors, each dealing with a single religion or spiritual path.

The Beliefnet quiz: "What is your Spiritual Type?" It finds out whether you are a skeptic, spiritual dabbler, questioning believer, confident believer, or another spiritual type.

External Links

1. A group of essays prepared by Sociology classes at the University of Virginia lists many unusual faith groups. See: http://www.religiousmovements.org
2. The Bureau of Democracy, Human Rights, and Labor Affairs of the U.S. government issues an annual report on religious freedom around the world. The 1997-JUL-22 report, *"United States Policies in Support of Religious Freedom: Focus on Christians" is at:* http://www.usia.gov/topical/rights/religion/religion.htm
3. Jewish-Christian Relations site contains statements on Jewish-Christian Relations from Conservative Jewish, Ecumenical, Joint Christian-Jewish, Other Groups Protestant, Roman-Catholic groups, as well as one statement in opposition to inter-faith cooperation. See: http://www.jcrelations.com/
4. A New Millennium's Resolution proposes a resolution for the year 2000 (or perhaps 2001) recognizing humanity's link with the environment. See: http://www.redshift.com/~wsandtt/
5. Chief Arvol Looking Horse of the Lakota, Nakota and Dakota Nation is sponsoring a worldwide day of prayer for global healing on the summer solstice. They occur about JUN-21 each year. See: http://www.worldpeaceday.com/

****

4.24 Worship Map: Site Map & Search

Bruce L. Johnson

http://www.worshipmap.com/sitemap.html

Texis & Texis Webscript Copyright © 2000 Thunderstone

Compass (Teaching)
☐ Biblical Studies--a Theology of Worship
☐ "A Closer Look" at popular songs, Scriptures... about worship
☐ Online articles (index)
☐ Sermons on Worship
  John Piper (index)
  Index to Devotionals (especially on worship)

Resources (Tools)
☐ Main page: favorite tools (often free)
☐ Music
  Main resources: tools, 'traditional' and contemporary worship music
  Hymn history
  Hymn stories (index)
  Psalms Resource Index

Original songs (Bruce L. Johnson) -indexed by lyrics
Advent & Christmas songs

□ Arts (Drama, Banners)
□ Scripture (tools)
□ Liturgy
Prayers
Index to Prayers from Book of Common Prayer
Seasons:
Advent Readings
Advent Materials
Lent: Daily Readings
Lent Materials
Promise of Pentecost
□ Books
□ Software
Music
Bible Study Tools, Reference
□ Training: seminars, worship sites
□ Indexes to worship materials

Pathways (Putting it together)

□ Services (models: with Scriptures, music, prayers)
□ "The Drafting Table" -thoughts, tips, studies on preparing services

Sign In (& Feedback, Questions)

© 1998-2002 Bruce L. Johnson

Produced by Techsys, Inc.

****

4.25 Comparison of God-Centered and Man-Centered Worship

http://www.angelfire.com/nt/theology/godwork2.html

Category	God-Centered Worship	Man-Centered Worship
Goal	Glorifying God by our worship must be our goal, our highest priority. (I Cor. 10:31) It sounds elementary, but the purpose of our corporate worship service is for our congregation to worship God. Evangelism, though important, is secondary.	Bringing people in by our worship service is the highest goal in man-centered worship. Though this seems like a noble goal, it must not be our highest goal. When worship is turned into an evangelistic tool, both worship and evangelism suffer.
Pagan-friendly vs. Seeker-driven	According to Romans 3:10-18, there are none who seek God from their hearts. Though we must show love and concern for the pagans who attend worship, we must be careful not to design the worship service around their desires, but around God's desires. We must remember that the greatest obstacle for the unbeliever is his sinful heart.	In the seeker-driven model, the worship service is adjusted to "meet the needs" [better called 'wants'] of the unbeliever, making it 'relevant' for unbelievers. The theology behind this seeker-driven movement teaches that everyone seeks for God, and all we need to do is take obstacles out of an unbeliever's way in order for them to come to Christ.

Offense	The Gospel is inherently offensive: the spotless Lamb of God who had to undergo hell on the cross for totally depraved sinners. (Romans 1:16) We must share the whole counsel of God, both the offensive and inoffensive parts. (Acts 20:27) Still, we must be careful not to add our own offensiveness to the mix.	Man-centered attempts at worship invariably take out the offense of the Gospel to make it more palatable for so-called seekers. Sermons lack mention of sin, hell, punishment, total depravity... A gospel of salvation has no context apart from salvation from sin by the shed blood of Christ. (Acts 2:36, Heb 9:22c)
Entertainment vs. Worship	Worship is done before an audience of One. We are all the participants, and the desire is that God is pleased with our worship. (Rev. 5:13, Phil 2:10,11) We stand in awe of God, and then our affections are stirred, not vice versa. (Acts 2:43)	Having the goal of 'bringing 'em in' as the top priority will inevitably result in turning the worship hour into an entertainment session. The focus is taken off standing in awe of God and placed, instead, on what the participant will enjoy or how he/she will feel.
Needs vs. Wants	If we focus on what man truly needs, we must understand that our greatest need is for God. When we look to God first and do things His way, the outcome will meet the deepest needs of men. (Matt. 6:33)	In the name of being 'needs-based', the focus actually becomes on what people want. While people's shallow desires are constantly fed, the deepest needs are left unmet. This camp tends to produce rapid quantitative growth and a lack of qualitative growth.
Relevance	Certainly our desire is not to be irrelevant, but the truth of God's Word must never be compromised in the name of so-called relevance.	When relevance is the measure of all things, truth is invariably sacrificed.
Human worth	Human worth is not diminished by being God-centered. Instead, it is established. That is, when we focus on God who alone has worth in Himself, and we understand that we are created in His image, this brings us great worth. (II Samuel 22)	Man has no worth in and of himself, and being man-centered in one's approach to anything is ultimately futile.
Sabbath-worship	God commands us in the fourth commandment to keep the Sabbath holy. In the New Testament, the Sabbath was changed from the 7th day (Saturday) (Exod. 20:8-11) to the 1st day (Sunday). (See Matt. 28:1, Luke 24:1, John 20:19, Acts 20:7, Rev. 1:10) God has given us one day in seven to rest from our worldly labors and feast on Him.	Sunday morning is reserved for the 'evangelistic service', and worship is scheduled for another day. Saturday nights have become popular times for services, with no stress made on the Biblical command and delight of corporate Sunday worship.
Spirit & Truth	God desires worshippers who will worship Him in spirit and truth. (John 4:24) We must know the majestic, holy God and our sinfulness in order to worship Him rightly.	Focus is often on worshipping God 'in the Spirit' with very little emphasis on truth. The problem is that worship without truth, though sincere, is sincerely unpleasing to God.

****

4.26 Denominational Taxonomy

1990 Denominations as Listed by Glenmary Research Center
Coded by the Polis Denominational Taxonomy
www.polis.iupui.edu/RUC/Research/Glenmary_by_Polis_Types_as_table.htm

Glenmary Denominations Reporting for 1990			**The Polis Center Denominational Taxonomy**		
Denomination	**ID**	**Abbrev**	**Level 1**	**Level 2**	**Level 3**
Advent Christian Church	1	advcc	II. Evangelical Prot	C. Evan Prot Other	
American Carpatho-Russian Orthodox Greek Catholic Diocese of the U.S.A.	2	eastor	V. Other Christian	E. Orthodox	
African Methodist Episcopal Zion Church	5	amez	III. Black Protestant	A. Black Mainline	
Albanian Orthodox Archdiocese in America	7	albora	V. Other Christian	E. Orthodox	
Albanian Orthodox Diocese of America	9	albod	V. Other Christian	E. Orthodox	
Allegheny Wesleyan Methodist Connection	11	awmc	II. Evangelical Prot	A. Revivalist/Experiential	1. Holiness
American Baptist Churches in the U.S.A.	19	ambapt	I. Mainline		
Apostolic Christian Church (Nazarean)	39	aposcc	II. Evangelical Prot	A. Revivalist/Experiential	1. Holiness
Apostolic Christian Church of America	40	aposca	II. Evangelical Prot	B. Revivalist/Rational	2. Other
Apostolic Lutheran Church of America	45	aposlu	V. Other Christian	B. Confessional	
Armenian Apostolic Church of Amer Eastern Prelacy	49	arapos	V. Other Christian	E. Orthodox	
Assemblies of God	53	aog	II. Evangelical Prot	A. Revivalist/Experiential	2. Pentecostal
Associate Reformed Presbyterian Church (Gen Synod)	55	arpc	V. Other Christian	F. Mainline Tributaries	
Baptist General Conference	57	baptgc	II. Evangelical Prot	B. Revivalist/Rational	1. Baptist
Baptist Missionary Association of America	59	bmaa	II. Evangelical Prot	B. Revivalist/Rational	1. Baptist
Barren River	60	brnrvr	II. Evangelical	B. Revivalist/Rational	1. Baptist

Missionary Baptists			Prot		
Beachy Amish Mennonite Churches	61	bamish	V. Other Christian	G. Pietist	
Berean Fundamental Church	63	berean	II. Evangelical Prot	B. Revivalist/Rational	2. Other
Bible Church of Christ, Inc., The	66	biblcc	II. Evangelical Prot	B. Revivalist/Rational	2. Other
Brethren Church (Ashland, Ohio)	71	bretas	V. Other Christian	G. Pietist	
Brethren in Christ Church	75	brcc	V. Other Christian	G. Pietist	
Byelorussian Council of Orthodox Churches in North America	80	byelor	V. Other Christian	E. Orthodox	
Catholic Church	81	cathol	IV. Catholic	*A. Latin & B. Other Rites	
Central Baptists	82	cebapt	II. Evangelical Prot	B. Revivalist/Rational	1. Baptist
Christ Catholic Church	83	chrcc	IV. Catholic	B. Other Rites	
Christian and Missionary Alliance, The	89	cmalli	II. Evangelical Prot	C. Evan Prot Other	
Christian Church (Disciples of Christ)	93	discc	I. Mainline		
Christian Churches and Churches of Christ	97	cccc	II. Evangelical Prot	B. Revivalist/Rational	2. Other
Christian Reformed Church	105	chrref	V. Other Christian	B. Confessional	
Church of Christ Scientist	111	ccsci	V. Other Christian	I. Other	
Church of God General Conference (Abrahamic Faith) Oregon, Ill.	121	cggca	II. Evangelical Prot	C. Evan Prot Other	
Church of God (Anderson, Indiana)	123	cgin	II. Evangelical Prot	A. Revivalist/Experiential	1. Holiness
Church of God (Cleveland, Tennessee)	127	cgtn	II. Evangelical Prot	A. Revivalist/Experiential	2. Pentecostal
Church of God (Seventh Day) Denver, Colorado, The	133	cgod7	II. Evangelical Prot	C. Evan Prot Other	
Church of God in Christ (Mennonite)	143	cgodmn	V. Other Christian	G. Pietist	
Church of God of Prophecy	145	cgp	II. Evangelical Prot	A. Revivalist/Experiential	2. Pentecostal

Church of God of the Mountain Assembly, Inc.	146	cgma	II. Evangelical Prot	A. Revivalist/Experiential	2. Pentecostal
Church of Jesus Christ of Latter-Day Saints, The	151	lds	V. Other Christian	D. Latter Day Saints	
Church of the Brethren	157	cob	V. Other Christian	G. Pietist	
Church of the Lutheran Brethren of America	163	lubret	V. Other Christian	B. Confessional	
Church of the Lutheran Confession	164	luconf	V. Other Christian	B. Confessional	
Church of the Nazarene	165	naz	II. Evangelical Prot	A. Revivalist/Experiential	1. Holiness
Churches of Christ	167	cchris	II. Evangelical Prot	B. Revivalist/Rational	2. Other
Churches of God General Conference	171	cggc	II. Evangelical Prot	C. Evan Prot Other	
Congregational Christian Churches, National Assoc of	175	naccc	V. Other Christian	F. Mainline Tributaries	
Congregational Christian Churches Additional	176	cccnot	V. Other Christian	F. Mainline Tributaries	
Conservative Baptist Association of America	179	cbapt	II. Evangelical Prot	B. Revivalist/Rational	1. Baptist
Conservative Congregational Christian Conference	181	ccong	II. Evangelical Prot	B. Revivalist/Rational	2. Other
Cumberland Presbyterian Church	185	cpc	V. Other Christian	F. Mainline Tributaries	
Duck River and Kindred Baptists Associations	189	duckr	II. Evangelical Prot	B. Revivalist/Rational	1. Baptist
Enterprise Baptist	191	eba	II. Evangelical Prot	B. Revivalist/Rational	1. Baptist
Episcopal Church, The	193	episc	I. Mainline		
Estonian Evangelical Lutheran Church	195	eeluth	V. Other Christian	B. Confessional	
Evangelical Congregational Church	199	evancc	II. Evangelical Prot	B. Revivalist/Rational	2. Other
Evangelical Free Church of America, The	203	evfree	II. Evangelical Prot	B. Revivalist/Rational	2. Other
Evangelical Lutheran	207	elca	I. Mainline		

Church in America					
Evangelical Lutheran Synod	209	elsyn	V. Other Christian	B. Confessional	
Evangelical Mennonite Brethren Conference	211	evmenn	V. Other Christian	G. Pietist	
Evangelical Mennonite Church, Inc.	213	emenn	V. Other Christian	G. Pietist	
Evangelical Methodist Church	215	evmeth	II. Evangelical Prot	A. Revivalist/Experiential	1. Holiness
Evangelical Presbyterian Church	216	evpc	II. Evangelical Prot	B. Revivalist/Rational	2. Other
Fire Baptized Holiness Church (Wesleyan), The	217	firebp	III. Black Protestant	B. Black Other	
Free Lutheran Congregations, The Association of	220	freelu	V. Other Christian	B. Confessional	
Free Methodist Church of North America	221	fmeth	II. Evangelical Prot	A. Revivalist/Experiential	1. Holiness
Free Will Baptist, National Association of, Inc.	223	fwbap	II. Evangelical Prot	B. Revivalist/Rational	1. Baptist
Friends	226	friend	V. Other Christian	C. Friends	
Fundamental Methodist Church, Inc.	230	fumeth	II. Evangelical Prot	B. Revivalist/Rational	2. Other
General Conference of Mennonite Brethren Churches	237	gcmenn	V. Other Christian	G. Pietist	
General Six Principle Baptists	241	gensix	II. Evangelical Prot	B. Revivalist/Rational	1. Baptist
Greek Orthodox Archdiocese of North and South America	246	gorth	V. Other Christian	E. Orthodox	
Holy Apostolic Catholic Assyrian Church of the East	249	apcath	IV. Catholic	B. Other Rites	
Hutterian Brethren	257	hutter	V. Other Christian	G. Pietist	
Independent Fundamental Churches of America	259	ifca	II. Evangelical Prot	B. Revivalist/Rational	2. Other
International Church of the Foursquare Gospel	263	foursq	II. Evangelical Prot	A. Revivalist/Experiential	2. Pentecostal
International	265	ipent	II. Evangelical	A. Revivalist/Experiential	2. Pentecostal

Pentecostal Church of Christ			Prot		
Interstate -- Foreign Landmark Missionary Baptists	266	imba	II. Evangelical Prot	B. Revivalist/Rational	1. Baptist
Jasper and Pleasant Valley Baptists	269	jasper	II. Evangelical Prot	B. Revivalist/Rational	1. Baptist
Latvian Evangelical Lutheran Church in America, The	274	latvlu	V. Other Christian	B. Confessional	
Lutheran Church - Missouri Synod, The	283	lcms	V. Other Christian	B. Confessional	
Lutheran Churches, The American Association of	284	aaluth	V. Other Christian	B. Confessional	
Mennonite Church	285	mennt	V. Other Christian	G. Pietist	
Eastern Pennsylvania Mennonite Church	286	epmenn	V. Other Christian	G. Pietist	
Mennonite Church the General Conference	287	menngc	V. Other Christian	G. Pietist	
New Hope Baptist Association	289	nhbapt	II. Evangelical Prot	B. Revivalist/Rational	1. Baptist
Missionary Church, The	291	missnc	V. Other Christian	G. Pietist	
Moravian Church in America Alaska Province	292	morava	V. Other Christian	G. Pietist	
Moravian Church in Amer (Unitas Fratrum) No Prov	293	moravn	V. Other Christian	G. Pietist	
Moravian Church in Amer (Unitas Fratrum) So Prov	295	moravs	V. Other Christian	G. Pietist	
Midwest Congregational Christian Fellowship	296	mwccf	II. Evangelical Prot	A. Revivalist/Experiential	1. Holiness
Netherlands Reformed Congregations	307	nethre	V. Other Christian	B. Confessional	
North American Baptist Conference	313	nabc	II. Evangelical Prot	B. Revivalist/Rational	1. Baptist
Old Missionary Baptists Association	320	oldmba	II. Evangelical Prot	B. Revivalist/Rational	1. Baptist
Old Order Amish Church	323	oamish	V. Other Christian	G. Pietist	

Old Order River Brethren	324	oldrb	V. Other Christian	G. Pietist	
Old Regular Baptists	325	orbap	II. Evangelical Prot	B. Revivalist/Rational	1. Baptist
Open Bible Standard Churches, Inc.	329	opbibl	V. Other Christian	I. Other	
Orthodox Church in America	331	ortham	V. Other Christian	E. Orthodox	
Pentecostal Church of God	339	pentch	II. Evangelical Prot	A. Revivalist/Experiential	2. Pentecostal
Pentecostal Holiness Church, Inc.	349	pentho	II. Evangelical Prot	A. Revivalist/Experiential	2. Pentecostal
Christian (Plymouth) Brethren	353	chrbre	V. Other Christian	G. Pietist	
Presbyterian Church (U.S.A.)	355	pcusa	I. Mainline		
Presbyterian Church in America	356	pcia	II. Evangelical Prot	B. Revivalist/Rational	2. Other
Primitive Advent Christian Church	359	padvcc	II. Evangelical Prot	C. Evan Prot Other	
Primitive Baptists Associations	361	pba	II. Evangelical Prot	B. Revivalist/Rational	1. Baptist
Primitive Methodist Church U.S.A.	363	prmeth	V. Other Christian	F. Mainline Tributaries	
The Protestant Conference (Lutheran)	367	prconf	V. Other Christian	B. Confessional	
Reformed Church in America	371	refch	V. Other Christian	B. Confessional	
Reformed Church in the United States	373	refchu	V. Other Christian	B. Confessional	
Reformed Episcopal Church	375	repisc	V. Other Christian	F. Mainline Tributaries	
Regular Baptists	386	regbap	II. Evangelical Prot	B. Revivalist/Rational	1. Baptist
Romanian Orthodox Episcopate of America	397	romort	V. Other Christian	E. Orthodox	
Salvation Army, The	403	salva	II. Evangelical Prot	A. Revivalist/Experiential	1. Holiness
Schwenkfelder Church, The	405	schewn	V. Other Christian	B. Confessional	
Seventh-Day Adventists	413	sda	II. Evangelical Prot	C. Evan Prot Other	
Seventh Day Baptist General Conference	415	sdbgc	II. Evangelical Prot	B. Revivalist/Rational	1. Baptist

Southern Baptist Convention	419	sbc	II. Evangelical Prot	B. Revivalist/Rational	1. Baptist
Syrian Orthodox Church of Antioch (Archdiocese of the U.S.A. and Canada)	423	syrant	V. Other Christian	E. Orthodox	
Two-Seed-in-the-Spirit Predestinarian Baptists	426	twosed	II. Evangelical Prot	B. Revivalist/Rational	1. Baptist
Truevine Baptists Association	430	truvin	II. Evangelical Prot	B. Revivalist/Rational	1. Baptist
Ukrainian Orthodox Church of Amer (Ecum Patr)	431	ukrort	V. Other Christian	E. Orthodox	
Unitarian Universalist Association	435	unita	V. Other Christian	H. Theologically Liberal	
United Baptists	436	ubapt	II. Evangelical Prot	B. Revivalist/Rational	1. Baptist
United Brethren in Christ	438	ubic	V. Other Christian	G. Pietist	
United Christian Church	441	untchr	V. Other Christian	G. Pietist	
United Church of Christ	443	ucc	I. Mainline		
United Methodist Church, The	449	unmeth	I. Mainline		
Wayne Trail Missionary Baptists Association	466	wayne	II. Evangelical Prot	B. Revivalist/Rational	1. Baptist
the Wesleyan Church	467	wesly	II. Evangelical Prot	A. Revivalist/Experiential	1. Holiness
Wisconsin Evangelical Lutheran Synod	469	wels	V. Other Christian	B. Confessional	
Jewish Estimate	496	jewish	VI. Non-Christian	D. Jewish	
Black Baptists Estimate	497	blbapt	III. Black Protestant	A. Black Mainline	
Independent Charismatic Churches	498	inchar	II. Evangelical Prot	A. Revivalist/Experiential	2. Pentecostal
Independent Non-Charismatic Churches	499	nonchr	II. Evangelical Prot	C. Evan Prot Other	

* Glenmary data for the Catholic Church combines groups coded as "Latin" and "Other Rites" at Level 2 of The Polis Center Taxonomy

****

4.27 Multifaith Taxonomy –A Suggested model using Islamic Transactions in Cyberspace

by Mohamed Taher

Main Facets

A. Traditional Faith's official Web sites
B. Traditional Faith's unofficial Web sites
C. Academic / research institutions' Web sites (with a slant towards Religious / spiritual issues)
D. Faith based Personal Web sites
E. Faith based Meditation Web sites
H. Alternative Traditions official Web sites
I. New age Faith Based independent group Web sites
J. New Age Faith based Personal Web sites
K. New Age Faith based Forums / Club Web sites
L. New Age Faith Based Meditation Web sites
M. Miscellaneous, including pro-religious agencies Web sites
N. Peacekeeping Faith based Web sites
O. Interfaith (inter-denominational) Web sites
P. Multifaith Web sites

Sub Facets

AA. Faith based institutional / officially representing group' Web sites - **Islam**	AB. Faith based institutional / officially representing group' Web sites - **Islam**
1. Online – real-time	2. Offline – non-real time
1.1.Prayer Schedule	1.1.Prayer Schedule
1.11.By day	1.11.By day
1.11.1. Weekdays	1.11.1. Weekdays
1.11.2. Fridays	1.11.2. Fridays
1.11.3. Festivals	1.11.3. Festivals
1.12.By time	1.12.By time
1.12.1. Morning	1.12.1. Morning
1.12.2. Afternoon	1.12.2. Afternoon
1.12.3. Late Afternoon	1.12.3. Late Afternoon
1.12.4. After Sunset	1.12.4. After Sunset
1.12.5. Evening	1.12.5. Evening
1.12.6. Midnight	1.12.6. Midnight
1.13 By Season / Events	1.13 By Season / Events
1.13.1. For rains	1.13.1. For rains
1.13.2. For calamities	1.13.2. For calamities
2. Prayer space	2. Prayer space
2.1. Browser capability	2.1. Browser capability
2.2. Audio / Video capability	2.2. Audio / Video capability
2.3. Religious pre-requisites	2.3. Religious pre-requisites
2.4. Congregation / Group based	2.4. Congregation / Group based
2.5. Private personal	2.5. Private personal
2.6. Monitor resolution	2.6. Monitor resolution
3. Prayer tools	3. Prayer tools
3.1.Submit a prayer request for self	3.1.Submit a prayer request for self
3.1.1.Email	3.1.1.Email
3.1.2.Live requisition	3.1.2. Alternative requisition
3.2. Submit a prayer request for others	3.2. Submit a prayer request for others
3.3. Download a prayer	3.3. Download a prayer
3.4. Live Relay	3.4. Watch a pre-recoded Relay
4. Prayer type	4. Prayer type

4.1. Obligatory Five Prayers 4.2. Non-Obligatory Prayers 4.3 .Haj (Pilgrimage) 4.4. Liturgy - Dhikr 5. Sermon 5.1.Live relay 5.2. Archived 6. Meditate 6.1..Mediator online 6.2. Self-directed 6.3. With tools 6.4. Without tools 7. Buy a product 7.1. Catalog 7.2. Order placing 7.3. Free sample 8. Subscribe or donate 9. Sharing Live Experience 9.1. With text 9.2. During special circumstances, Dua-e-qunoot, qunoot-e-nazila 9.3. While listening to the Quran 9.4. While Seeing the Kaba (Sacred Mosque in Mecca) 9.5. While Seeing the Mosque of the Prophet 9.6. While listening to the litany (Dua) 9.7. While invoking Divine Names (Dhikr) 9.8. While listening to prayer for blessing on the Prophet (Darud)	4.1. Obligatory Five Prayers 4.2. Non-Obligatory Prayers 4.3 .Haj (Pilgrimage) 4.4. Liturgy - Dhikr 5. Sermon 5.1.Live relay 5.2. Archived 6. Meditate 6.1..Mediator online 6.2. Self-directed 6.3. With tools 6.4. Without tools 6.5. The Way: Best Practice 6.5.1. Sufism (Tasawuf, or TSVF) 6.5.1.2. With T: Tark (Abondonment), Taubah (Repentance), Tugha (Virtue) 6.5.1.3. With S: Sabr (Patience), Sidgh (Truthfulness), Safa (Purity) 6.5.1.4. With V: Vud (love), Vird (Remembrance), Vafa'a (Faithfulness) 6.5.1.5. With F: Fard (Solitude), Faqr (Poverty), Fana (Annihilation)** 7. Buy a product 7.1. Catalog 7.2. Order placing 7.3. Free sample 8. Subscribe or donate 9. Sharing Live Experience 9.1. With text 9.2. With Mosque Pictures 9.3. While listening to the Quran 9.4. While Seeing the Kaba (Sacred Mosque in Mecca) 9.5. While Seeing the Mosque of the Prophet 9.6. While listening to the litany (Dua) 9.7. While invoking Divine Names (Dhikr) 9.8. While listening to prayer for blessing on the Prophet (Darud)

****

4.28 Beliefnet Site Map

http://www.beliefnet.com/index/index_172.html

Home > Resources > **Site Map (by topic)**
Looking for an alphabetical listing of topics? Click here.

RELIGIONS

- Baha'i
- Buddhism
  - Dalai Lama
- Christianity

FAMILY & LIFE EVENTS

- Parenting
  - Spiritual Parenting with Mimi Doe

Catholic
Christian Science
Eastern Orthodox
Mormon
Protestant
Quaker

Jesus
Bible

Falun Gong
Hinduism
Islam
Jainism
Judaism
Nation of Islam
Pagan & Earth-Based
Scientology
Secular Philosophies
Shinto
Sikhism
Taoism
Unitarian Universalist
Zoroastrianism

SPIRITUALITY

Meditation & Prayer
Angels & Guides
Astrology
Prayer of the Day
Teachers, Guides & Gurus
Garden & Home
Workplace Spirituality
Gratitude

INSPIRATION
MORALITY
CULTURE

TV & Movies
Books
Music
Humor

Grief & Loss
Life Events

HEALTH & HEALING

Yoga
Illness & Recovery
Caroline Myss
Spiritual Weight Loss

RELATIONSHIPS

Dating
Marriage

NEWS & SOCIETY

Gender & Sexuality
Science & Religion
Politics
Money
Apocalypse

TEENS

CHARITY & SERVICE

Giving
Volunteering

COMMUNITY

Discussions
Dialogue Groups
Celebrations
Memorials
Prayer Circles

SPECIAL FEATURES & TOOLS

Interactive Meditations & Devotionals
Prayer Finder
Quizzes
Sacred Text Searches
Free Newsletters
Belief-O-Matic

BELIEFNET PREMIUM PRODUCTS

In Search of Jesus
Taking Back Islam
The Big Book of Angels
Daily Inspiration Screensaver
Daily Bible Verse Screensaver
Angel Messages

****

4.29 A Taxonomy of Religions according to their Hermeneutics of Fecal Occurrence

by Author Identity Requested
http://dogchurch.org/restroom/feces.html

This has been all over the net in many versions. Feel free to add to it. So far contributors include the world wide web community, John Futterman, Andy Busch, MM, RF, and others.

TAOISM	S__t happens.
CONFUCIANISM	Confucius say: "S__t happens."
BUDDHISM	S__t doesn't really happen. It is only called s__t happening.
Zen	What is the sound of one s__t happening?
SIKHISM	Cut that s__t out, or we'll cut it out of you!
HINDUISM	This s__t has happened before.
PLATONISM	This s__t will happen again.
JAINISM	When it happens, s__t gently. Don't hurt the s__t.
SHINTO	If s__t happens, put a flower in it. Make a pretty offering.
HARE KRISHNA	...s__t happens, s__t happens, s__t happens...
MOONIES	Only happy s__t really happens.
WICCA	S__t happens if you will it to happen.
ISLAM	S__t happens because Allah wills it.
SUFISM	Even though s__t happens, Allah wants you to dance.
PROTESTANTISM	Let s__t happen to someone else.
JUDAISM	Why does this s__t always happen to us?
CATHOLICISM	You deserve this s__t.
Vatican II	If s__t happens, blame the clergy.
PRESBYTERIANISM	S__t should happen decently and in good order.
CALVINISM	S__t is predestined to happen because you don't work hard enough.
7TH DAY ADVENTISM	No s__t on Saturdays.
ANGLICANISM	Scripture contains all things necessary to deal with s__t happening.
ANTIDISESTAB- LISHMENTARIANISM	We still favor happenings of state-supported s__t.
FUNDAMENTALISM	Unless you're one of us, you're s__t.
Baptist	S__t won't happen for you until you're totally immersed in it.
Pentecostal	S__t happens! Hallelujah! Praise the Lord!
METAPHYSICS	In terms of materialistic ontogeny, we're **all** s__t.
NEW AGE	When s__t happens, channel it. Visualise s__t happening.
Feminism	S__t happening is an act of the Goddess.
Feminist Separatism	When s__t happens, blame men.
Men's Movement	Drums & fire make s__t happen hot & loud.
RASTAFARIANISM	Let';s smoke this s__t!
Bud Lightism	S__t happens... I **love** you, man!

EXISTENTIALISM	S__t is, therefore it happens.
JEHOVAH'S WITNESSES	If you just let me in, I'll tell you why s__t happens.
MORMONISM	If s__t happens, make sure you have a 2-year food supply.
RAJNEESH	For $1000, s__t can happen for you, too.
HEDONISM	There's nothing like a good s__t happening!
STOICISM	This s__t is good for me.
ZOROASTRIANISM	Bad s__t happens half the time. The rest of the time, it's good.
Parsi	Don't burn that s__t — fire is sacred!
CHRISTIAN SCIENCE	This s__t is all in your mind.
BAHA'I	S__t happens to everyone alike.
UNITARIANISM	If there is a s__t, let it happen to each in his/her own way.
AGNOSTICISM	Maybe s__t happens, and maybe it doesn't.
Apathy	Who gives a s__t?
ATHEISM	No s__t!

Now this is the variety I like to roll in!
This document is part of the
Virtual Church of the Blind Chihuahua™, www.dogchurch.org

****

4.30 KEY FUNCTIONS OF RELIGION: Sociology of Religion Course Outline

Dr. William Martin

http://www.owlnet.rice.edu/~soci430/outlines/functions.htm

[The Provision of Meaning and Belonging Theodicy: Dealing with Suffering and Evil Meeting Instrumental Needs]

I. WORLD CONSTRUCTION AND WORLD MAINTENANCE

A. INTRODUCTION

1. Peter Berger, *The Sacred Canopy*; also, Berger and Thomas Luckmann, *The Social Construction of Reality.*
2. The Sociology of Knowledge: "Reality" is socially constructed.

B. CONSTRUCTION AND MAINTENANCE OF A SOCIALLY CONSTRUCTED WORLD

1. EXTERNALIZATION
   - a. Human activity is subject to habitualization. Repeated acts become "second nature."
   - b. Habitualization, leads to externalization, or institutionalization.
   - c. By working together, people build a world--culture.
2. OBJECTIVATION
   - a. Though humanly produced, culture takes on an objective character and begins to shape humans.
   - b. The crucial point: passing culture on to new generations. "This is the way it is." Objective.
3. INTERNALIZATION--proceeds by socialization

a. Primary Socialization--parents or parent substitutes.
b. Secondary Socialization--Internalization of institutional or institution-based subworlds. Roles and attitudes of school, occupation, organizations, etc.

4. LEGITIMATION
a. Levels
1) Pre-Theoretical: "I say it is so."
2) Rudimentary Theoretical Propositions: Fairy tales, sagas, legends, fables, conduct books, soap operas.
3) Explicit theories
4) Highest level, overarching system; usually, religion.
b. Supports the ethos. Fills in the gaps left by law.
c. To remind people of the Sacred Canopy, symbols and rituals are employed. Also, a supporting community; e.g., "church."

5. NOMIZATION: The ordering of human experience
a. If canopy in danger, anomie results. To fight anomie, societies have ways of bringing people into line: therapy, sanctions, avoidance.
b. If cannot manage the challenge, religions can fail.

II. THEODICY: DEALING WITH THE PROBLEM OF SUFFERING AND EVIL

A. PROBLEMS REQUIRING EXPLANATION: Death, physical and emotional suffering, collective, adversity, war, success.

B. Types of Theodicy
1. Identification with the Collectivity
2. Karma-Samsara Complex
3. God beyond Ethical Claims
4. Messianism and Millenarianism
5. Other-worldly--dualism, heaven and hell. Zoroastrianism, Christianity, Islam
6. Suffering God
7. Predestination
8. Absurdity/no purpose/chance

III. INSTRUMENTAL RELIGION

A. INTRODUCTION
1. More mundane reasons--tangible material, social, emotional benefits.
2. Clear aspect of primitive religion--ritual for fishing, farming, weather, health, etc. Found in virtually every religion.

B. WORLD RELIGIONS
1. ROMAN CATHOLICISM
2. SHINTO: (An extended example)
a. Distinctly and uniquely Japanese. Earliest knowledge of Japan includes Shinto "The Way of the Kami," (divine spirits).
b. Not in conflict with Buddhism. Buddhism for death, Shinto for Life. Temples often on same grounds.
c. Concerned with adaptation to this life and merging of humans with natural environment.
d. BELIEFS
1) The mysterious at the heart of life. Desire to commune with it, express dependence upon it--the root of all religious experience.
2) Nature beautiful and bountiful. Virtually anything that can inspire feelings of awe, reverence, mystery may be seen has having Kami-nature.
3) Ancestral spirits--From original progenitors of humanity to one's own departed relatives.
4) Also, natural phenomena. Unmistakable animistic aspects.
5) Kami Work in two ways:
a) Take care of specific territorial region--communities, etc.
b) Special spheres of responsibility--insects, passing exams, childbirth, marriage, water supply, money, etc.

6) Essentially optimistic. Human nature not seen as evil.

e. MAIN FORMS

1) IMPERIAL OR STATE SHINTO--Related to Imperial House.
2) SHRINE SHINTO--Practiced at major shrines.
3) MAJOR CULTS: c. 13 officially recognized
4) FOLK SHINTO--everyday Shinto. Superstition, magic.
5) SHRINES--Found everywhere. c. 100,000.

f. RITUALS

1) Purification by water, salt. Particularly when visiting shrines.
2) Rituals of dedication, commitment, requests for help--sprigs of trees, rice, sake, other products. Treat kami as an illustrious guest.
3) Construction rituals. Groundbreaking, framing, finishing off.
4) Shrine Rituals
5) Marriage
6) First shrine visit.
7) Seijin-no-hi (Adult Day). Jan 15. Formal coming-of-age for 21-year-olds.
8) Ema--"horse pictures" or prayer tablets. Various purposes.
9) Special Shrines for money, romance, success in school, etc.

g. SPORT. Especially Sumo

C. MIND CURE

1. Key Figures and Movements
   a. Phineas Quimby
   b. New Thought
   c. Mary Baker Eddy--Christian Science
   d. Unity--Charles and Myrtle Fillmore
2. Theology of Mind Cure
   a. Think the thoughts of God
   b. Humans are individualizations of God (God-in-me)
   c. No demand can outrun supply
   d. Wish projection
   e. Not concerned with limitations
3. Descendants of Mind Cure
   a. Norman Vincent Peale--Power of Positive Thinking
   b. Rabbi Joshua Loth Liebman, Bishop Fulton J. Sheen, Billy Graham
   c. Robert Schuller—Possibility Thinking
   d. Rev. Ike
   e. "Abundant Life" Ministries
4. New Age
5. Pentecostal Instrumentalism
   a. Oral Roberts
   b. Kenneth Hagin
   c. Kenneth Copeland
   d. Bob Tilton
   e. Lakewood Church
   f. Radio/TV Preachers

D. CONCLUSIONS

a. Common idea: Faith Works
b. Materialistic: "All these *things...*"
c. God as resource to be tapped.
d. Can it work for long?

****

4.31 Worship Web Links: Site Map, Synod Resource Centers

(synodresourcenter.org/wma/worship)

Worship

[Worship Web Links <-- Click here]

Synod Resource Centers – Shared Ideas from your resource Center

Worship Services		**Saints/ Festivals**	**Church Seasons**	**Altar Guild**	**Worship Assistants**	**Worship Spaces**	**Sermons**	**Worship Aids**
Baptisms	Matins	Day of Pentecost	Advent	Candles	Lay assistants	Sanctuary	Drama	Bulletins
Children & Youth	Mother's Day	Ascension	Christmas	Paraments	Ushers	Narthex	Text Study	Pew Cards
Clergy	Other	Reformation	Epiphany	Altar appnts	Acolytes	Chapel	Children and Youth	Child Resources
Confirmation	Patriotism	All Saints	Lent	Vestments	Crucifers	Sacristy	Sermons	Other
Dedications	Presentations	Lesser Saints	Holy Week	Communion Supplies	Readers	Nursery		Prayer
Eucharist	Rural	Easter	Pentecost	Sacristy	Greeters			
Funerals	Service of the Word		Easter	Organization of..				
Graduation	Vespers							
Healing	Weddings							
Installations	Anniversary							

****

4.32 www.religion-online.org

Full texts by recognized religious scholars

More than 5,200 articles and chapters. Topics include Old and New Testament, Theology, Ethics, History and Sociology of Religion, Communication and Cultural Studies, Pastoral Care, Counseling, Homiletics, Worship, Missions and Religious Education. Click on a Category. Or Search Religion Online.

THE BIBLE
Authority of the Bibl
Old Testament
New Testament
Bible Commentary

LOCAL CHURCH
Congregational Life
Denominations
Evangelism
Inclusive Language
Megachurch
The Art of Preaching
Women Clergy
Worship/Liturgy

COMMUNICATION
And Religion
And Public Policy
In the Local Church
Media Education

ABOUT RELIGION ONLINE

THEOLOGY
Liberal
Post Liberal/Modern
Evangelical /Conserv
Catholic
Liberation
Women's - Feminist
Process
Indian and Asian
Judaic and Judaism
Dalit
Science and Theology
Miscellaneous
Process Studies Journ

PRACTICAL THEOLOGY
Counseling and Ment
Health
Aging
Illness and Handicapp
Nature of the Church
Prayer and Sacrament
The Christian Life
The Ministry

THEOLOGIANS
Barth
Bonhoeffer
Darwin
Cobb
Kierkegaard
Niebuhr. Reinhold
Niebuhr, H. Richard
Pannenberg
Tillich
Tracy
Wesley
Whitehead
Other Theologians

CULTURE
Religion and the Arts
Architecture
Radio, TV, Movies
Literature, Writers
Music, Composers
Painting, Painters
Cultural Criticism

RECOMMENDED SITES

SOCIAL ISSUES
Abortion
Capitalism/Communism
Church and State
Drugs
Ecology/Environment
Globalization
Homosexuality
Law and Order
Poor and Oppressed
Pornography
Public Education
Public Policy
Terrorism
Other Social Issues

RELIGIOUS SOCIOLOG
Sociology of the Church
Sociology of the Society

EDUCATION
Local Church Education
Higher Education

BOOK LIST (200 online)

HISTORY OF RELIGION
History Before 1900
History After 1900
Civil Rights Movement
The Religious Right

Islam
Comparative Religions
Psychology of Religion

ETHICS
Christian Ethics
Death & Dying
Economic Justice
Genetics
Sexuality
Violence
War and Peace

MISSIONS
The Nature of Mission

INDEX BY CATEGORY

CHURCHES AND SOCIETY
Black Churches
Catholicism
Church in Society
Church in the World
Communities
Ecumenism
Evangelicalism
Family Life
Fundamentalism
Liberalism/Conservatis
Palestine-Israel
Religion and Politics

SEARCH RELIGION ONLINE

INDEX BY AUTHOR

5

Glossary: A Pathfinder for Future History

The literature on the topic of cyber worship is very extensive and continues to explode in every discipline. Future historians are already sensing the direction of Web-based lifestyle:

> "Going beyond TV church and televangelism, today's Web-savvy click-n-brick church, synagogue, temple, and mosque is already delivering words of wisdom in streaming-video format over the Internet to futuristic families at home. "
> "Since the Web mirrors society, it becomes a spiritual manifestation of a new theology. The Web is our theology because the Web is us. It is an extension of our brain-mind consciousness – of our soul – into cyberspace."
>
> Chapter Seven, "Cyber Worship: Congregate Online" in Future Living: The Coming Web Lifestyle, by Frank Feather. (Aurora, On. Warwick Publishing, 2003: 155-160).

The exploding literature on Cyber Worship also comes with a bag full of new jargon. Hence, an attempt is made in this chapter to list the relevant words, in order to save the time of a future historian. Each term in the Glossary is followed by a brief definition. Terms are defined according to their most common usage. The purpose of the glossary is to provide a meaning to words in the context of this book – i.e., terminology does differ in different sources; I have tried to compensate by using terms synonymously, as well as by presenting alternative shades.

How complex is the issue of terminology in this area is obvious from the following:

"Cyber Cemeteries and Virtual Memorials: Virtual Living Monuments as On-line Outlets for Real Life Mourning and A Celebration of Life,"

Hermann Gruenwald and Le Gruenwald,
in *Making Sense of Death: Spiritual, Pastoral, and Perosnal Aspects of Death, Dying and Bereavement,* (Amityville, Baywood, 2003: 113-114)

Cyber cemetreries are being created on-line by individuals and corporations to memorialize loved ones 24/7 worldwide. Virtual memorials offer some of the same features of physical monuments and traditional newspaper obituaries, but they also provide added dimension that can provide help in the grief and bereavement as well as the remembrance and immortalization process. In this chapter, we examine the following dimensions of virtual monuments: accessibility both from a time and distance standpoint; A special place for losses and bereaved with special needs; Building communications and community on-line; Private and Public space, Life and Love—Remembrance and commemoration; Limitation and Control—from VIP to Pets From Obituaries to Monuments; Religion and Culture; Features and Costs; and the Present and the Future.

How to find on-line memorials?

Glossary

The following search words or combinations thereof will help you find what we will call On-line memorials for the purpose of this book. Search words that contain Cyber, Electronic, On-line, Virtual, together with the words such as Cemetery, Grave, Graveyard, Memorial, Mausoleum, Monument. Obituary, Park, Testament, Tribute, result in key words such as Cyber Cemeteries, Virtual Cemeteries, Virtual Monuments, On-line Memorials, On-line Monuments, On-line Obituaries, On-line Memorial Gardens, On-line Graveyards, or On-line Memorial Parks.

When another related term in the glossary is used, it is distinguished by using italics. This is a short list of words used in the book. For more such information one can use the printed dictionaries or online dictionaries.[1]

Print resources include the glossaries in: The Idiot Guide series on major religions, as well as, a generic glossary (pages 249-257) *The Complete Idiot's Guide to The World's Religions*, by Brandon Toropov and Father Luke Buckles, and a more detailed handbook on cyber religion and spirituality, namely, *The Complete Idiot's Guide to Religions Online*, by Prof. Bruce B. Lawrence[2] In addition, there is a specific dictionary of terms that denote a specific object of worship be it saints, snakes or whatever.[3] Too many terms, even in the narrow area of cyber worship, are neither uniform in usage, nor systematically expressive in communicating the idea of sacred cyberspace. And this is true for all religious and spiritual groups that are on the Net. For instance, 'cyber worship' as a term has many variants, including, virtual worship, online worship, digital worship, Internet worship, e-prayer, world wide worship, and so on. There is a need for research in an attempt to streamline the newer words that have appeared in the field of cyber worship. Two key areas of research and study, that may facilitate this desire of Netizens, are business and academia.[4] further, with the emergence of e-commerce the jargon on the Internet has further diversified.[5]

Asynchronous: See *Online*
Alternative Traditions: Alternative Traditions is taking to include, New Age Movements, cults, non-traditional religions, non-religious mystical and non-traditional meditational system, etc.
Asynchronous: See *Synchronous*
Bandwidth: "Think of this as the size of the 'pipe' that the information travels through. A small bandwidth would be represented by a garden hose, a larger bandwidth by a culvert."[6]
Brahmin: Priest, belonging to the upper class. They are considered as elites among the Hindu castes. Only a Brahmin is authorized to perform religious and spiritual rites and rituals. See also *Priest*
Charisma: literally divine grace. Its eastern equivalent (literary, spiritual, mystical, magical) Arabic/ Persian/ Hindu/ Indian traditions is Karishma.
Church: One may wonder why a multifaith space has to be called a Church? The Marriage Act of Ontario (1990), defines: "church" 'includes chapel, meeting-house or place set aside for religious worship.'[7] Incidentally, accepting the growing diversity in the cultures today, the United Religious Initiative has decided to have a common prayer space for all faith groups. [8] What surprises is none has initiated a generic name for the sacred space, housing all or any sacred group. Interestingly, the Western hemisphere (or occident) uses Church as generic term. I quote from a book written by librarian-cum-Webmaster. It opens the Chapter on 'Churches and Religious Groups' with a following disclaimer: "This chapter refers to 'churches' as opposed to saying 'synagogues, churches, mosques, and other religious bodies' simply because it was easier. No slight was intended."[9] In short, a future project must be on developing appropriate terminology, that fits all sizes and that represent the actuality.[10] Ergo, serendipity may take you to a "Temple" (although the organization is a Christian Church not a 'Hindu Temple'), and be prepared for such an odd nametag.[11] And another version of the Church in electronic (read, cyber) space, is here:

> The word "church" can mean a building, or those who congregate and worship there. Here in FECHA, "church" means "community"-one linked by the technology of electro-space. By simply logging on to this site, you have joined our congregation. Feel free to explore the many "rooms" and levels of FECHA, dedicated to the recognition and celebration of the power of focused electrons thru the ages.[12]

Communities: This term relates to social capital, and is not dealt in this book. However, to understand the community framework in worship, and explore its absence and/or existence in the cyber worship this book will talk about congregations, group worship, and such related areas. Also the Web has a large resource on the debate relating to the thesis: Web helps building the social capital or fosters socialization, far better than the traditional methods.[13] In addition, the exclusion in this book, also relates to discussion groups, chat forums. In the context of cyberspace one will not find here an elaborate coverage on congregations as in Christian sense, Jamat or Ummah or community in Muslim sense, Community of faith in Judaism, Sangha or group dynamics that work in Buddhist parlance (Sangha is third Jewel in Buddhism, the other two being, Buddha and Dhamma; etymologically the word Sangha in Pali means the Order or Community of Bhikkhus (monks) and Bhikkhunis (nuns), which by extension and in practice it is considered as the community of the Dharma practitioners).

Comparative religion: In general, the term means, study of world religions to determine their points of similarity and differences. In practice, this is difficult to do on an impartial basis. Students often consider their own branch of their own religion to be "true," and all other branches of their religion, and all other religions to be "false."[14] (See also *Multifaith*)

Congregational Worship: See *Internet Congregation*

Cult: "From the Latin word "cultus," meaning worship. Cult is a word with many religious meanings (and some secular as well) which should be used with great care to avoid misunderstanding. Accommodation calls for a neutral term "new religious movement" be used in its place. Even better is to refer to a religious group by its name:

1. Traditional theological usage: a style of worship and its associated rituals. It can be applied to any faith group.
2. Sociological usage: a small religious group that exists in a state of tension with the predominant religion; e.g. Christianity in Pakistan.
3. General religious usage: a small, recently created religious group; not a variant of an established religion. Often headed by a single charismatic leader.
4. Evangelical usage: a religious group that considers themselves to be Christian but which denies one or more historical beliefs of Protestant Christianity.
5. Counter-cult movement usage: Same as Evangelical usage.
6. Anti-cult movement usage: a small, evil religious group, often with a single charismatic leader, who engage in deceptive recruiting, brainwashing and other mind control techniques
7. Popular belief: A doomsday, dangerous, destructive religious movement whose members risk their life to belong."[15]

There is also a possibility that the traditional mainstream religions may tend to call the non-traditional streams as cult or supernatural.[16] Isn't it worth to quote the Biblical source illustrating this term in a mainstream and traditional sources: "And, in the New Testament, Paul even called a pagan poet a 'prophet.'"[17] Do we still call a pagan by name, or with this much of documentation feel comfortable giving a chance to live and let live, even those that sound as alternative paths? (See also *Occult*, ***Alternative Traditions***)

Customization of Faiths:

> On the eve of Easter weekend, an opinion poll commissioned by two influential publications - the daily Le Monde and the weekly La Vie - revealed that fewer and fewer French citizens, with the exception of Muslims, declared a formal adherence to any religion. Fewer still, again with the exception of Muslims, engaged in regular religious observances. These were reserved for intimate family occasions like baptisms, marriages or funerals. The poll also indicated that belief in the existence of God and in the after-life had declined. And, despite media hype, so had interest in 'parallel faiths' such as astrology, sooth-saying, magic, New Age gurus, faith healing, Shamanism and oriental religions. Paradoxically, however, the French appeared to take a greater interest in the virtues of religious faith provided such virtues were not associated with any given denomination or sanctioned by any scriptural authority.
>
> How does one explain the paradox? Experts writing in the two publications which published the poll results argue that interest in morals rather than in religious dicta or spiritual sermons appears to be staging a come-back.
>
> This is interesting when you consider how at least three generations of French intellectuals denounced all talk of morality as a ploy of the bourgeoisie to detract attention from fundamental issues related to authority, hierarchy and power. The French, the experts claim, are now choosing a custom-made faith for themselves. This 'faith' is deeply 'agnostic' in nature. What this means in practical terms is that it allows French citizens to subscribe to values like fidelity in marriage, respect for the family and generally for order and stability in both private and public life. But at the same time it permits them to take their distance from those claiming to act on behalf of God for, in their view, it is such claims guaranteeing salvation in the next world if not in the here-and-now which give rise to extremism, intolerance, frustration and impatience. Take it for what it is worth but this custom-made faith at least has one redeeming feature: it provides the French with a good enough reason to remain, well, unmistakably French.[18]

Cyber Religion (This term for the purpose of the book is considered synonymous to Online Religion, Religion Online, Virtual Religion, Online Meditation, Online Spirituality, Virtual Meditation, Meditation Online, Virtual Spirituality, etc.): The term Cyber Religion can be viewed in many ways: a) it deals with religious resources on the Web; b) with a

new pattern of religiosity on the Internet, called Cyber religions. Cyber religions gets manifested in two broad types according to Prof. Anastasia: The first type is a completely new phenomenon, with a founder or founders who is /are perceived to introduce a new insight into post-modern religiosity, with examples from Cosmosophy, Digitalism Technosophy and The Church Of MOO; and the second type is 'Cyber religious movements'. Anastasia elaborates: "Because of its structure, the Internet has been beyond the control of any, either political or commercial authority. In the anarchical environment of the Internet, cyber-communities and movements have evolved, having their own rules, agenda, code of practice and communication. All these have been regulated by the members themselves rather than by any outside hierarchical power"[9]; c) "What the Internet will do is spread ideas about religion. In places where society is only familiar with one particular religion, the Internet will allow exposure to other religions and an intermixing of ideas. In areas like Texas where there is very little evidence of any religion other than Christianity, most likely there will be a growth in the number of "minority religions"[20]; and d) What do we mean by Internet? It includes "email, Websites, Discussion Groups, eZines, Chat Rooms" (as described in 'The Internet and the Covenant').[21] Cyber Religion as a theme (and by extension a new emerging interdisciplinary subject of study) then includes Character of cyberspace; the role of multimedia or hypermedia and its postmodernist influences; dynamics of the *community* interactions (or communitas, as is now referred on the Web) as well as the implications (both in its convergence and divergence, or advantages and disadvantages, respectively) on the everyday life and experiences as symbolized by technomystics, technophobes, etc..[22]
Cyberspace: I have come across many definitions of "cyberspace," the word coined in 1984 by science fiction writer William Gibson, but the one I use comes from a two-page list of definitions that Michael Benedikt compiled in his edited volume entitled, Cyberspace: First Steps, states: "Cyberspace: A new universe, a parallel universe created and sustained by the world's computers and communication lines. A world in which the global traffic of knowledge, secrets, measurements, indicators, entertainments, and alter-human agency takes on form: sights, sounds, presences never seen on the surface of the earth blossoming in a vast electronic night" (1992, p.1).[23] Going by different usages, a meaning of the term is: "Cyberspace has a shape. On-line communities, MUDs and Worlds, imply a space inhabited by their citizens. This space, in many cases, is built over time through the dynamic efforts of a domain's administrators and its citizens... The theme common to both "cyber" and "space" is information. With "cyber" information is active. Used in "cybernetics," for instance, it means sounding environments to assess and determine actions. It implies interaction. In contrast, the information of space is passive, its contents less urgent. Space provides a calm backdrop for evaluating and addressing the objects of our interest. It's the foundation for qualitative thought and our subjective world. The space places at our world's center, immersing us, engaging all our faculties. Through sense and cognition we map its places and discover its contents, moment by moment building our space around us. Our presence in this world is entirely artificial, molded by us individually, influenced by our society and culture."[24] Cyberspace and social space may be two sides of a coin. This is the result of a doctoral study by Mark Nunes: 'This dissertation serves as a theoretical foundation for an ongoing study of the spatiality of computer-mediated communication. It also provides a resolution to the problem of space raised by cyberspace, and the tendency to treat cyberspace as separate from the general production of social space within the contemporary developed world.'[25]
Cyber Worship: It is about performing worship on the Internet. Cyber worship is here meant to deal with worship as (prayer, praise, scripture, sacrament, rituals, confessions, Eucharist, rites, pilgrimages, reflection, contemplation, etc.) performed in cyberspace. The term 'cyber worship' includes variants, such as, online worship, virtual worship, electronic prayer, cyber church, e-prarthana, cyber puja, cyber salat, cyber Hajj, cyber synagogue, cyber Minyan, so on and so forth. This book considers cyber worship as synonymous to so many alternative names – summarily all trying to convey probably the same meaning – online worship; online prayer; online spirituality; online meditation; etc. Despite the great glorious features, attributes, dynamism and availability of the Internet and use of the Net for holy activity–anywhere, anytime, and anyhow – the community of believers construe Internet neither as synonymous to omnipresence, or 'worship of the internet' nor 'internet as a new found god'. A few definitions of related terms do exist. The tem 'cyber church' has been coined to refer to churches who live and operate, either partially or entirely, in the connected world of cyberspace, and the church members have been termed cyber-saints

> Cyberchurch is the future?
>
> From Bill Easum's book, Leadership on the Other Side: No Rules, Just Clues:
>
> "Cyberchurches will become some of the largest churches and may be the new form of megachurch."
>
> Mr. Easum has always looked ahead to the future of the church. I wonder what he had in mind when he used the term "cyberchurch." Obviously cyber-communities, like the Ooze, have a number of visitors (Spencer tells me somewhere around

> 75,000 per month). They connect on the discussion boards. Can they be called a church? It is an interesting question....What do you think?[26]

In short, no one knows who started using the term, cyber worship. See Also *Internet Congregation*
Digital Media includes users of the World Wide Web, proprietary online services, and/or other ad- supported digital applications such as e-mail services and CD ROM.[27]
Electronic Worship: Literally, this means using electronic tools for facilitating worship in the traditional prayer space. A transition in the process began with using technology (audio, video and now *Web Cams*, etc.) in worship. By way of progress this led to Wired Church, as well as Media Ministry[28]. See also *Cyber worship,* and *Internet Congregation*
FAQ (Frequently Asked Question): It is a user-friendly feature offered by most websites. Depending on the purpose of the website, the FAQ's offer help-desk substitution. In case the FAQ's don't provide any solution, most websites also offer a point of contact (either one can fill a complaint form or submit question by e-mail).
Faith: "A term which describes the dispositional attitude of the believer towards the object of his belief. It is summed up in the words of St. Paul, 'Now faith is the assurance of things hoped for, the conviction of things not seen' (Hebrews 11.1). Although this is a Christian definition it applies across the spectrum of world faiths."[29]
Faith Healing: "The alleviation of physical and mental ailments by the prayer of a healer relying on a higher source (usually, the power of God) working in response to faith. Known in several religions, the practice is now a major feature of Christian Pentecostal and Charismatic movements, often accompanied by the laying on of the healer's hands, usually in the context of worship."[30]
Filtering: "The setting up of a criteria to select a subset of data from a broad system of it. Filtering information is essential for everyone in daily life. Filtering by parents of small children may be wise. Filtering by others—ISPs or governments is bad, and is called censorship".[31]
FTP (File Transfer Protocol): Noun (computer science) protocol that allows users to copy files between their local system and any system they can reach on the network. Verb. Use the File Transfer Protocol to transfer data from one computer to another; "You can ftp these data".[32]
Guru: Personal spiritual guide in particular, and teacher or mentor in general. It is a preferred usage popular among Hindus. Though among other groups –specifically Sikhs, and in generic sense it has different meaning. "Within Hinduism a spiritual teacher of guide who gives instruction to a disciple or pupil. The pupil in turn treats the Guru with an appropriate reverence and obedience. In Sikhism, Guru is identified with the inner voice of God, of which the Ten Gurus of Sikhism were the human instruments."[33] See also: Priest.
Imam: In sunni traditions, an Imam is a selected Muslim spiritual/religious leader. In Shia thelogy it is a term that is restricted to the descendants of the Prophet Muhammad, with Imam Ali being the first in the chain.
ISP see *Internet service provider.*
Innernet (inner-net): cyber worship here deals with the provision of a virtual wired Web to the basic needs of the human self, that is, the trio: body (physical), mind and soul (metaphysical). In this sense, innernet implies the real-time connectivity with an external world. Most religious and spiritual groups accept these three angles; some faiths consider these three as totally distinct entities, some others don't believe in trifurcation. Furthermore, secularization and de-spiritualization in the modern lifestyle cares more for the physical rather than the metaphysical. Nevertheless, healers, counselors and mentors combine the trio. Such an admixture ensures holistic approach, thereby treating the human personality in a balanced way; and this care goes in to reflect the image of the Creator (in relation to self, in relation to humans and in relation to all other beings). Cyber worship finds its link in this inner circle in the following quote: "The expression of the spirit, the soul, the divine, the universal, is the role of natural religion. Humans have always had the need to connect their external world with an Internal and universal spirit. Because "soul" is immaterial doesn't mean it doesn't exist. It exists as the ether, as emotions, as chemistry, as a lover, as a patriot, as an artist, as a skilled crafts person, being all together inside out with the spirits beyond self and material culture."[34] In short, innernet according to Linda Johnson is a part of self-realization. Linda states in the Chapter on 'Turning on your inner light:

> For most Hindus, Self-realization is God-realization. How can this be? 'The air closed inside a jar is not at all different from the air outside the jar,' said Shankaracharya. 'In exactly the same way, your Inner Self is exactly identical with the Self of all. Smash the jar and the air inside it merges seamlessly with the air outside. Smash the illusion that you exist apart from God, and you merge in that divine reality…Think about it. Just as your five fingers are not really separate because they are linked to the same hand, so the Self in you and the Self in me (and the Self in Lassie the dog for that matter) are not really separate because they are linked in the Supreme Self, the consciousness of God.'[35]

With this wide network connection, innernet (esotericism) is definitely a subject of interest for many disciplines, not just religious and spiritual care providers.[36] Those who are otherwise interested in extranet (outside network in worship context, call it exotericism or outer net), will also find food here.[37] This inclusiveness seems plausible since the twain (esoteric and exoteric esoteric and exoteric) as just two sides of a coin. For more details of the twain see the maps of respective faiths that manifest virtual realities in the quartets: Praise and Prayer, Scripture and Sacrament – separate but inseparable.

Interfaith: "Interfaith is a bridge ...that allows members of all religions and spiritual teachings to reach out across the waters of life, in understanding and communication with each other. Interfaith affirms and supports the underlying goodness of each person, the healing of our planet."[38] And a literary quote, about utility of this connection more so in a networked world, in the messianic words of Whitman summarizes it all (incidentally, *network* is not a new word, it did exist in the past):

> "The earth to be spann'd, connected by net-work...
> The oceans to be cross'd, the distant brought near,
> The lands to be welded together." (Walt Whitman, d. 1892)[39]

Interfaith Internet: "Given the number of religious sites on the Web, surfing the Internet can be like opening your door one Saturday morning to find a representative of every church, synagogue, mosque, or cult group camped out on your front yard, all clamoring for your attention. Not a welcome sight, even for the most devout among us. In order to assist students of religion, or anyone in search of a more thoughtful faith, to separate the wheat from the chaff, we have assembled and reviewed a collection of the more valuable sites on the Internet. We have designated the best of these as ARIL Hot Sites: World Religions, Buddhism, Christianity, Islam, Judaism, and Biblical Resources."[40]

Internet Congregation: Theologically speaking, in a generic sense congregation (communitas) is considered to be possible only in physical environments. This connotation has been always construed to represent a physical prayer space (or in the postmodern lingo, brick and mortar congregations). With the emergence of cyberspace, ideally one expects to have a parallel scenario to find a befitting sacred domain. One such idealistic expressionism comes from a theologian, Prof. Ken Bedell:

> An Internet Congregation is a group of people who intentionally join together to practice their religion on the Internet without gathering for face-to-face meetings. This does not include brick and mortar congregations that conduct ministries such as counseling or religious chat rooms on the Internet. Nor does it include Internet projects that are designed to support or augment congregational life. A religious mailing list or chat room by this definition is not an Internet congregation unless the mailing list or chat room claims to provide a replacement for a traditional congregation. An Internet Congregation is designed to completely replace all of the functions of a traditional congregation.[41]

Rev. Bedell soon realized, during his cyber survey conducted in 1998, that this ideal scenario does not exist at all: "This definition proved to be so restrictive that I was unable to find people who understood themselves to be participants in this kind of an experience."[42] In reality, what he discovered about the virtual space is altogether a different orientation. He found a holy conglomeration of congregational facilitators (supporting, bridging or creating a new spiritual world order with weapons for meditation and devotion) functioning either to disseminate information or as communication channels for sustaining cyber worship. He had hard time coming to terms with those who made high claims (as exclusive cyber congregations), but did not fit his benchmark, or match his definition stated above.[43]

In a multifaith perspective, comparison of three Abrahamic faiths is pertinent. The cyber community representing Judaism did adopt the term, Internet Congregation, but makes no pretensions in admitting what it is and what it is not, implying that 'some conditions and restrictions apply': "Beth Israel - The Internet Congregation: On this site the Congregation Beth Israel community will share information and dialogue about issues and activities of interest to the Congregation and its members."[44] Moreover, we are fortunate that going one-step further, a few members of this community even spelt what it means to congregate and pray on the Web.[45] Contrarily, Muslim Web presence does have many congregational tools (e.g., Cyber Dhikr, Cyber Salat, Cyber Hajj, Cyber Zakat, and Cyber Jihad), but one fails to find a clear pronouncement from authorities to permit or prohibit an Internet Congregation.

Internet Service Provider (ISP): "The party providing one with connectivity to the Internet. Some users have a cable or sort of wireless link to their ISP. For others, their computer may dial an ISP by phone and send and receive Internet packets over the phone lines; the ISP then forwards the packets over the Internet."[46]

Intra-religious Dialogue: "Relations between the world religions (like between historically separated parts of the same religion) vary with the situation and motives of the participants, and may be friendly, hostile, or non-existent."[47]
Liturgy: Public worship or ritual worship of God. "The formal corporate worship of God by a Church. It includes words, music, actions, and symbolic aids, and in Christian form is derived from Jewish ritual. Liturgies exist in a wide variety of prescribed forms, reflecting the needs and attitudes of different religious communities"[48]
Meditation: "Meditation can be considered a technique, or practice. It usually involves concentrating on an object, such as a flower, a candle, a sound or word, or the breath. Over time, the number of random thoughts diminishes. More importantly, your attachment to these thoughts, and your identification with them, progressively become less." [49]
Metadata: Data about data on the Web, including but not limited to authorship, Classification, endorsement, policy, distribution terms, Intellectual Property Rights (IPR), and so on. A significant use for the Semantic Web.[50]
Multifaith: Before dwelling on the definition it is apt to re-iterate, neither, cyber worship is a rival temple, nor Multifaith a new religion. The term Multifaith is not even a counterpart of medieval Indian Mughal monarch, Akbar's attempt to synthesize all religions, called Din-i-Ilahi (Divine Faith, or eclectic religion[51]). Again, Multifaith is NOT a synthesis, bundled spiritual/mystical religion, an attempt at morphing religious beliefs of opposing theology and deities. Here in a broader generic sense, Multifaith is used to signify multiple faiths representing a unity in diversity. It includes first, mainstream religions and spirituality, and second alternative paths of belief and practice—a.k.a. new age movements, non-traditional movements, paganism, etc. "Multifaith is a wide variety of faith traditions presented simultaneously. Multifaith is not a religion, but an approach to living in a religiously and spiritually diverse world that respects the integrity of different faith traditions and promotes diversity.[52] It is not an attempt to convert people from one faith to another or to meld different beliefs and practices into a new faith."[53] "An attempt to initiate dialog, cooperation, and understanding among individuals of many different faiths. It is occasionally used as a synonym for "interfaith." Unfortunately, various religious groups define the term "faith" differently. For example, some conservative Christians regard a person who is not of their denomination to be from a different faith. Other conservative Christians would regard liberal Christians as being of a different faith. Still other Christians interpret "multifaith" as involving other religions, as in a Christian-Jewish-Muslim exchange."[54] In short, there is a subtle difference between interfaith and multifaith, while the former may intersect with faith group, the latter may not intersect at all. Rather multifaith goes parallel among religions/spiritual groups in a vertical matrix.
Mysticism: Pursuing direct inner experience of the Ultimate generally using the vehicle of *prayer*, *meditation*, contemplation, fasting, etc. goes with or without religious traditions. Asceticism is the extreme method of achieving this experience, as commonly adapted in many faiths (Sanyas in Sanskrit as adopted in Hinduism, Buddhism, etc.). Sufism is one form of mystic experience, under the rubric of Islamic way of life. Theologians say, Prophet Muhammad did not approve asceticism as a methodology for this meditational process. A similar variant in Judaism is called kabbala (or "qabbalah").[55] Mysticism, or higher states of consciousness has a common path, among divergent faiths/philosophies, and it is possible to summarily categorize this path into four types, or levels: "Considerable cross-cultural comparisons, taken as a whole, suggest that there are at least four higher or transpersonal states of consciousness, which might be called psychic, subtle, causal and nondual.[56]
Netiquette: "The Internet etiquette. Includes rule like: Be brief, and use both upper and lower case. If you use all upper case, you could be accused of SHOUTING."[57]
Netizens (or Veteran Internet users): "Veteran users, those who have at least three years experience online, are more likely than new comers to have done most Internet activities. The Internet has become an important job-related tool for those with several years' experience. They are much more likely to have done job-related research and use email in job-connected communications than newcomers. In addition, veterans are more likely than newcomers to have performed transactions or managed their money online. These users are disproportionately from higher socioeconomic groups, so education level and household income also show up as important indicators of the things users have done on the Internet."[58]
Network: Three types of networks are included here to indicate a generic meaning of this term, network. First, corporate network (or business, markets, authorities[59]), second, community network (churches, groups, individuals, or social structure[60]) and third, network of computer networks (or computer mediated communication).
Neutrality: Warren A. Nord and Charles C. Haynes in their book Taking Religion Seriously Across the Curriculum (1998), note that: "Neutrality cannot mean hostility or even silence". Neutrality, they believe, requires that we 'must take everyone seriously' as a demonstration of fairness and respect.[61]
Newbies (Newcomers): see *Netizens.*

Occult: "Means hidden or concealed and has come to be applied chiefly to magical arts and practices, as astrology, alchemy or divination."[62] "Thus a number of new religious movements, and some elements of new age religion, are regarded as occult."[63] (see also ***Alternative Traditions***, *Cult, Multifaith*)

Online: (literally, *synchronous*) Connected by computers in a network, especially using Web-based technology. Offline, on the other hand, refers to being disconnected from the network, or not hooked up. *Cyber worship* in this book primarily relates to online religious and spiritual resources, and secondarily to such offline resources. In a broader sense, when we say we are online, we mean that we are in a real-time (or online simultaneously in an interactive situation) virtually linked on the Web to any other computer in the global village (with the help of TCP/IP protocols and networking), whereas the term offline means the opposite scenario. One more definition would make the subject clearer: "In its simplest terms—when something is *synchronous*, we are all there at the same time… and when something is *asynchronous*, we work on our own time (a Web conference is often *asynchronous*)—that is, we read what has been posted—post our thoughts—and maybe come online later and post other thoughts."[64]

Online Religion: See *Cyber Religion*

Online Spirituality: See *Cyber Religion*

Open source: "Software whose source code is freely distributed and modifiable by anyone. W3C sample code is open source software. A trademark of opensource.org."[65]

Pastor: See *Priest*

Prayer: Deepest expression of religious feelings, manifested thro' action and/or intention, vocal and/or silent, etc. It may include worship, adoration, thanksgiving, confession, supplication, as understood in the Christian tradition; meditation in the spiritual and mystical dimensions; puja (worship), prarthana (supplication), shardhanjali (memorial), and prasad (receiving or sharing the sacrament), as in Hinduism; Salat (obligatory or voluntary prayers), (al-Adha) sacrifice, Zakath (obligatory or voluntary charity), and Hajj (pilgrimage) in Islamic way of life; prayer, meditation, and recitation of sutras from scripture as practiced in Jainism; so forth. Like all worship, prayer is both vertical (between the soul and the holy), as well as horizontal (involving the worshiper and the community, kith, kin, relatives, neighbors, etc.). There have been attempts to express prayer viewing it through social and cultural lenses

> Prayer may take the form of petition, adoration, contrition or thanksgiving, but it is always a communication. Since prayer always addresses the person perceived as supporting, maintaining and controlling the order of existence of the one praying, it presupposes a superior/subordinate relationship. Finally prayer aims to have some effect on the person with whom the pray-er communicates, that is, it seeks results.
>
> In this same direction is a classification of the Christian prayer in seven (*relational*) categories, that is, "1. Instrumental ("I want..."); 2. Regulatory ("Do as I tell you..."); 3. Interactional ("me and you..."); 4. Self-focused ("Here I come. . .; here I am..."); 5. Heuristic ("Tell me why...?"); 6. Imaginative ("Let's pretend..."); 7. Informative ("I have something to tell you")."[66] (See also *Worship*)

Priest: Representative of a religion/faith/spirituality/church (synonyms. Pastor, clergy)

Puja: Worship of a deity, image or holy figure performed according to the Hindu practices.

Rabbi (Arabic Rabbani=a holy person): A teacher or leader of worship, connected to a particular synagogue.

Real-time: See *Online*

Religion: It relates to the act of believing and attaching reverence to the Almighty. It is some times difficult to generalize the sub-facets of religions, because of the inherent variations and external manifestations. Some scholars have, however, tried to build a user-friendly thematic structure as part of a course material based on the Key Functions of Religion.[67]

Religious Community: "In every religious tradition there is a notion of religious community. In Christianity it is the Church with its various branches: Orthodox, Roman Catholic and Protestant; in Islam it is the Ummah, with its Sunni and Shiite branches, which often has a close relationship to wider society and politics; in Buddhism it is the sangha with its Theravada and Mahayana branches, which has historically stressed the role of monks; in Judaism there are the modern Orthodox, Reformed and Conservative communities within the wider whole which also emphasizes ethnic factors; and in Hinduism, within the original social framework of the caste system, there are religious communities (sampradayas) centered upon the main deities Shiva, Vishnu, Rama, Krishna, the goddess Devi and so on."[68]

Religious Tolerance: "Religious tolerance is not religious indifference. It is valuing the right of another person to hold beliefs that you know to be wrong". [69]

Rites, Rituals, Sacraments: These three terms refer to a variety of forms, actions, objects, symbols, icons, text, oral message, etc. Two problems emerge in finding a single definition (reflecting religious beliefs and practices) and exactly conveying meaning of these three terms. First, each faith/belief system has its own vocabulary and interpretation, in some cases (for instance, in Islam) rites and rituals cannot be seen as different entities, and in same cases these overlap or intersect. Second, it is difficult to find a single term (in multifaith perspective), exactly corresponding with the Judeo-Christian beliefs (for instance, Baptism, Bismillah and Threading ceremony are all alike superficially, as these are administered in early childhood, but symantically/syntactically they don't have a uniform name). So diverse is this subject that it can emerge with as many details as one wishes, completing information in relation to people, places, time, process and local variations. Similarly, based on the functions and circumstances, one can find more. But, it is, possible to present a generic sense that can convey meaning of rites, rituals and sacraments. By generic, one could see a secular meaning of rituals-cum-sacraments, from a theologian:

> I'm proposing a secular functional definition of a sacrament as "That which acts, in a mysterious or not understood manner, as a catalyst or agent of change transforming a person from one state of being to another". (single to married, non-believer to believer, wounded to healed, distressed to comforted.) [That's really 'wordy'. Any suggestions?]
>
> Sacraments are administered and experienced within the context of a ritual or the ritual itself may constitute the sacrament. It may be or use ceremony (movement), rite (words), symbols (water, oil, a pipe, plant, ceramic dish.....) and signs (directions for living) or complex combinations of all elements. The ritual can be open or closed, formal or informal.[70]

Sangha: Buddhist monastry. Also it refers to a community, party, or an organization in Sanksrit – e.g., Jan Sangh (= peoples' party, the predecessor of currently ruling party in India, i.e., Bharatiya Janata Party).

Secularism: "The term 'secularism' today, whatever its origins and history, describes only a political doctrine, a doctrine about how citizens, even citizens who are devout people, agree to live and try and flourish in a polity that is not governed by religious principles and practices."[71]

Second Information Age: "The first information age was launched by print, and the Bible was its showcase success. The second information age was launched by the Web, and it has no single showcase, but religion is among the many topics that seem to suggest it will be as important for future believers as the printed Bible was for folk in an earlier age."[72]

Spirituality: The state of being spiritual, or in a stage of experience that is primarily a state of mind and influencing the body and thought.[73]

Streaming Technologies: "allows either sound or video to start playing by way of your browser as soon as a sufficient amount of data has arrived. An example of the opposite would be a sound file that loads in its entirety on your computer and then plays."[74]

Synchronous: "The terms 'synchronous' and 'asynchronous' are descriptive, and do not correspond precisely to properties of MEP's (or message exchange patterns)… Many (most?) Web services do not use published MEP's, but instead rely on more or less informal patterns and techniques. In such cases, the terms 'synchronous' and 'asynchronous' are sometimes used to indicate the type of informal pattern being used. They may indicate whether or not coordination and synchronization techniques such as correlation data and particular transport bindings are to be used."[75] See also Online

Techies: Information technology experts.[76]

Video-Conferencing: Using a video-conferencing unit (PictureTel is an example) allows participants to see each other. It needs two special data lines between two sites and needs a video-conferencing bridge for multi-point (more than two sites). It is more expensive than audio-conferencing, but allows two-way picture as well as two-way voice, but is not conducive for really large groups.[77] See also *Web Cams*.

Virtual: "It's the opposite of real, or else it is the really real. Either way, virtual reality, or virtual religion, is another way of talking about the digital divine, a kind of approach to spiritual ideas, persons, and pathways that are expressed, and explored, on the Web. Do they replace other kinds of reality? That is central question of both this book and the second information age."[78] The question that may arise is, whether virtual is tangible or intangible, perceptible or imperceptible? To understand this one must bear in mind that virtual is a subjective issue. Depending on the level (or type) of people's communication system, one perceives what is real and what is virtual. To illustrate this issue of optics, it is appropriate to quote a theological application:

> It is not difficult to pick up what communication channel people are on. Visual people look up to see things. Audio people's eyes bounce between their ears. And kinesthetic people look like they have inferiority complexes. They look down a lot and pull up their feeling from a well inside. So if we are not sensitive to these

three channels when we prepare and deliver homilies, we are losing bunches of people. I really believe that Jesus was visual, audio, and kinesthetic–he told stories that provoked feelings and emotions and that also contained powerful, challenging ideas.[79] See also *Online*

Virtual Religion: See *Cyber Religion*

Web Cams (or Webcam, Web Camera): A webcam is a web page that has live images or even streaming video playing on it from a digital camera attached to the owner's computer, be it in prayer space or meditational area or at any other desired location.[80]

Web. See *World Wide Web.*

World Wide Web: The set of all information accessible using computers and networking, each unit of information identified by a URI (Uniform Resource Identifier).[81] With the popularity of the cyber worship, one need not be surprised to read news headlines, as follows: "When www spells World Wide Worship" appearing on the BBC's website. For that matter a Christian Music book has its title: 'World Wide Worship.' The publisher of this book has a website with this same name (worldwideworship.com) and many others have adopted an extension of this name.[82]

Worship: "Worship involves a diversity of activities such as praise, adoration, confession, thanksgiving, intercession and petition."[83] Worship, as per the current practices does not necessarily relate to the age-old religious or belief system. The new age movements, or alternative religions diversified the meaning as well as its implications.[84] This book does not take sides of any one view point, irrespective of the type of worship, be it traditional worship, my worship (as in MEISM worship) or pagan worship (See also *Prayer*).

Yoga: In Sanskrit it means 'to yoke' or 'join together.' It is based in the religions, languages and cultural history of Indian sub-continent (including religions: Hinduism, Buddhism, and languages: Sanskrit and Pali, etc.). It relates to the converging method of mind-body health, and aims at leading towards a total solution, i.e., self-realization or enlightenment here and in the hereafter. Those who practice are yogi (=male, and yogan=female). The method involves, exercise (physical, mental), concentration, meditation and mystical transcendence. This spiritual context apart, its Western adaptation, influenced largely by the secularization threads, has limited its meaning to physical exercises (minus the spiritual). It is construed as an exercise by way to stretching or relaxing. So what was originally meant as a uniting process toward enlightenment has come to prosper in a different incarnation.

Notes:

1. Online user-friendly tools include, www.divinedigest.com/lexicon.htm,www.webopedia.com, www.spellweb.com/googlewebber.php,www.hyperdictioinary.com, http://whatis.techtarget.com, etc.

2. *The Complete Idiot's Guide to The World's Religions*, by Brandon Toropov and Father Luke Buckles (New York, Alpha Books, 1997). *The Complete Idiot's Guide to Religions Online*, by Bruce B. Lawrence (New Indiana, Macmillan, 2000).

3. "Word List - Forms of Worship and Belief." http://phrontistery.80megs.com/worship.html

4. John Fraim. 'The Promise of Research,' in "WordSpot: Electric Symbols – Internet Words and Culture." www.wordspot.com/electricsymbols.html

5. Dana Hull. It's So E-Verywhere, It's Not E-Xciting Anymore [Sunrise Edition] The Oregonian, Portland, Or. Apr 3, 2000; and Ganesh Markale "The changing face of e-language: The Net and its by-products are fast changing the language we speak and write." Wednesday, April 12, 2000 http://www.ciol.com/content/opinion/tales/100041201.asp (24 February 2004)

6. Badrul Khan. *Web-Based Training* (Englewood Cliffs, N.J., Educational Technology Publications, 2001), 57.

7. "Marriage Act, 1990." www.canlii.org/on/sta/cson/20030812/r.s.o.1990c.m.3/whole.html (10 Oct 2003)

8. "United Religions Initiative," www.uri.org

9. Julie M. Still. The Accidental Webmaster (Medford, N.J., Information Today, 2003),141.

10. 'Thoughts on Internet Naming Systems, by Karl Auerbach.' <www.cavebear.com>.

11. This confusion with nametags may occur at many places, for sure at: The Church of Jesus Christ of Latter-day Saints: "Each temple is dedicated as a house of the Lord Jesus Christ, a place of holiness and peace, set apart from the world." http://www.lds.org/temples/home/0,11273,1896-1,00.html

12. The First Electronic Church of America. "Summaries of World Religions: Church," http://securehosts.com/fecha/religion.htm (22 May 2004)

13. see for instance: Sorin Matei, et al. "Belonging in Geographic, Ethnic, and Internet Spaces." in Wellman, and Haythornthwaite, Eds. *The Internet in Everyday Life*, 404-427; "Set of twins find love and marriage on Internet" http://scout.wisc.edu/Projects/PastProjects/net-news/98-06/98-06-08/0009.html; See also the 'unmarried love story of Jack and Jill', and "Jack and Jill's hill to be restored by UK village" http://scout.wisc.edu/Projects/PastProjects/net-news/98-06/98-06-08/0009.html; etc.

14. "Glossary [A To M] of Religious Terms." http://religioustolerance.org/gl_c.htm

15. "Glossary [A To M] of Religious Terms." http://religioustolerance.org/gl_c.htm

16. "*Cults: An Overview.*" http://www.ex-iwp.org/docs/Cults/Cults-An%20Overview.htm (29 Jan 2004); and Robert Anderson, 'Defining the Supernatural in Iceland,' *Anthropological Forum*, 13 no. 2 (2003), 125. www.trent.ca/~rlohmann.anderson2003.pdf (30 Jan 2004)

17. "Poets and Prophets" in "Post Modern Christianity: The Future of the Church and Post Modern Ministry in the 21st Century." www.futurechurch.net/archives_view.asp/articleid=21

18. Dileep Padgaonkar "Customised faith: Talking Terms," *The Times of India*, May 03, 2003 www1.timesofindia.indiatimes.com/articleshow/45291683.cms (20 May 2004); see also another article on 'audience driven' 'seeker-sensitive' and full service to understand how much of customization is going on: 9Marks Ministries, "The Problem Defined," www.9marks.org (14 April 2004)

19. Anastasia Karaflogka, "Religious discourse and cyberspace" Paper presented in the 18th Quinquennial Congress of the IAHR 512 August 2000 Holiday Inn Durban Elangeni): 11-12.

20. Ryan Willmann "God, The Web, and Nature," October 29, 1999 http://www.mhhe.com/socscience/english/holeton/discussion4/messages/81.html

21. "Unravel the Mysteries," www.bahaiworld.com/conference/ca/unravel

22. Patrick Maxwell, "Virtual Religion in Context." *Religion* 32 (Oct 2002): 343-354; and Wellman , Barry and Haythornthwaite, Caroline. Eds. *The Internet in Everyday Life*.

23. MacWilliams M., "Virtual Pilgrimages on the Internet," http://it.stlawu.edu/~mmac/virtualpilgrimmacpaper.html (inactive link); See also: "Virtual pilgrimage – a rite of cyber-passing," http://www.amen-dir.net/Cybertheology/liminal.htm

24. Peter Anders, 'Moving Vicariously: Tacit embodiment and the shape of On-line Communities' www.mindspace.net/NewPages/Moving2.html (Sept 30, 2003)

25. Mark Nunes, 'Virtual topographies: The Internet and the spaces of everyday life.' Doctoral Dissertation. Emory University, 2002.

26. "Cyberchurch is the future....?" Next Wave: Church & Culture, February 2004, http://charliewear.next-wave.org/2003/11/18

27. "Definitions for Media Metrix Digital Media and Web Ratings," http://www.comscore.com/press/release.asp?press=277 (22 May 2004)

28. United Methodist Church. "Pastors Using Media in Worship Invite Others to Coaching Conference, Oct. 28, Cedar Hill UMC." *Communications* (Oct 4, 2000). www.ntcumc.org/ArcDAC/004q/X001004.html; Gorithians. "Worship (outlines transition in today's worship forms …Sacramental, Experimental, or Sensory Worship… (that manifests in Forms of Worship, Forms of Preaching, etc.)" www.gordy-stith.com/sacramental%20worship.htm; "Electronic Culture: The Call for a New Lutheran Witness (Practices Shape our Life)." (Oct 8, 1999), www.elca.org/eteam/electronicCulture.htm; and "No More Prayer Books? Laptops Only For Church Services? God the Mother With Laptops?" (note: Instead of prayer books, worshipers of the future will be able to download the text onto *laptops* and *palm-held computers*, and scroll their way through the service). www.archbishops.org/cofe1.htm

29. *Larousse Dictionary of Beliefs & Religions* (Edinburgh, Larousse, 1994), 170.

30. *Larousse Dictionary of Beliefs & Religions*, 170.

31. Tim Berners-Lee. *Weaving the Web: The Original Design and Ultimate Destiny of the World Wide Web By its Inventor* (New York, Harper, 1999), 212

32. Source: WordNet 1.7.1 Copyright © 2001 by Princeton University. All rights reserved " Ftp," http://www.websters-online-dictionary.org/definitions/english/ft/ftp.html

33. Laurence Twaddle. *Making Sense of English in Religion* (New York, Chambers, 1992)

34. "This is your brain this is your brain on wiredbrain – Dopamine," http://www.wiredbrain.com/neuro.htm (4 Jan. 2004).

35. Linda Johnson. *Complete Idiot's Guide to Hinduism* (New York, Alpha Books, 2002). 112.

36. To bring architectural harmony: "Temple of Triumph Building Project Overview - A Temple in Celebration of The Heroic Human Spirit." http://www.art-21.org/Temple/Overview.htm; Technological synchronous network in a triangular scenario: "International Unity." *Triangles Bulletin* no. 137 (September 2001) http://www.lucistrust.org/triangles/bulletin/2001/0109_unity.shtml; A global network for intuitive communication purposes: "Soulnet." http://www.dvostrukaduga.hr/page/soulnet.htm; etc. See also: Sharon Janis. "Spirituality For Dummies," (New York, Wiley, John & Sons, 2000) (book and CD).

37. Extranet, intranet and innernet, are not proprietary terms limited to computer world. Don't trust? Read from the following sources: "Lake Avenue Church Extranet" www.lakeave.org/tools/extra/frames/display.asp?id=xwa_main (15 February 2004); Louis Weil. *Sacraments and Liturgy: The Outward Signs – A Study in Liturgical Mentality* (Oxford, England, B. Blackwell, 1983).

38. "What Is Inclusive Christianity and Interfaith Ministry?," http://www.auburn.edu/~allenkc/interfaith/interfaith.html

39. "Welcome to the Quaker Electronic Archive And Meeting Place," http://www.qis.net/~daruma/

40. "Interfaith Internet," http://www.crosscurrents.org/ (22 May 2004)

41. Ken Bedell, "Internet Congregations in 1999," Paper Presented at the 1999 meeting of the Religious Research Association, Boston, Mass. November 4, 1999 http://www.religion-research.org/RRAPaper1999.htm (22 May 2004)

42. Bedell, "Internet Congregations in 1999

43. Bedell, "Internet Congregations in 1999,"

44. "Beth Israel - The Internet Congregation," http://cbi-technology.sharepoint.bcentral.com/default.aspx (22 May 2004); See also "Can a person pray outside a synagogue? There is a statement in the Talmud that a person's prayer is heard "only" in a synagogue, but this is not intended literally; it means only that prayer in a synagogue is especially effective. The halachah about prayer in a synagogue is worded in the Shulchan Aruch (Orach Chayim 90:8) as "A person should try to pray in a synagogue with a congregation". http://torah.org/qanda/seequanda.php?id=798 (22 May 2004)

45. "Wired to the Kadosh Barukh Hu: Minyan Via Internet A Responsum from the Committee on Jewish Law and Standards," http://learn.jtsa.edu/topics/diduknow/responsa/hatesh_internet.shtml (22 May 2004)

46. Berners-Lee. *Weaving the Web*, 214.

47. *Larousse Dictionary of Beliefs & Religions*, 245.

48. *Larousse Dictionary of Beliefs & Religions*, 304.

49. "Glossary [A To M] of Religious Terms." http://religioustolerance.org/gl_c.htm

50. Berners-Lee. *Weaving the Web*, 215.

51. Roderic Vassie. Persian Interpretations of the Bhagavadgita in the Mughal Period with Special Reference to the Sufi Version of 'Abd al-Rahman Chishti. Doctoral Thesis. School of Oriental & African Studies, University of London. 1988. This sample of the syncretism that he followed apart, the Mughal Akbar was also a model for religious accommodation. Non-Muslim subjects in his empire document his generosity: "The Farman2 of Jalaluddin Mohammad Akbar Badshah, Ghazi." www.pushtimarg.net/English/Pushti%20Ashmita/asmita-farmaans.htm

52. What is diversity? "Diversity is 'otherness,' or those human qualities that are different from our own and outside the groups to which we belong, yet are present in other individuals and groups." Business Women's Network. *Diversity Best Practices. WOW! Facts 2002.*" (Washington, Business Women's Network, 2003), 865.

53. "Gathering of Light Multifaith Spiritual Fellowship" gatheringoflight.com

54. "Glossary [A To M] of Religious Terms." http://religioustolerance.org/gl_c.htm

55. "Just What Is the Kabbala?" http://www.meguiar.addr.com/covenant_of_levi_part2.htm; and "Kabbala" http://directory.google.com/Top/Society/Religion_and_Spirituality/Judaism/Online_Jewish_Learning/Kabbala/; See also "Mysticism in World Religions." www.digiserv.com/mystic/F_start.html

56. Ken Wilber. "Waves, Streams, States and Self: Further Considerations for an Integral Theory of Consciousness." [abstract. http://www.csp.org/chrestomathy/cognitive_models.html]

57. Khan. *Web-Based Training*, 56

58. B. Wellman and Caroline Haythornwaite, *The Internet in Everyday Life* (Malden, Blackwell, 2002), 47.

59. "MetaCapitalism" http://www.pwcglobal.com/images/mcs/metacapital.pdf ; Albert-Laszlo Barbasi. "Linked: How Everything Is Connected to Everything Else and What It Means." Plume, 2003; Ralph M. Faris. "Corporate Networks and Corporate Control : The Case of the Delaware Valley." (Greenwood Publishing Group, 1991); Frans N. Stokman, editor. "Networks of Corporate Power: A Comparative Analysis of Ten Countries." (Polity Pr., 1986); Paul Windolf. "Corporate Networks in Europe and the United States." (Oxford University Press, 2002).

60. Joseph Galaskiewicz. Exchange Networks and Community Politics. (Library of Social Research Series # 75) (Beverly Hills, CA., Sage Publications, 1979).

61. in Ronald McCabe, *Civic Librarianship: Renewing the Social Mission of the Public Library* (Lanham, MD., Scarecrow, 2001), 135

62. S. I. Hayakawa, and Eugene Ehrlich. Eds. *Choose the Right Word: A Contemporary Guide to Selecting The Precise Word For Every Situation* (New York HarperPerennial, 1994), 291.

63. *Larousse Dictionary of Beliefs & Religions*. 378.

64. Khan. *Web-Based Training*, 51.

65. Berners-Lee. *Weaving the Web*, 216.

66. This definition and categorization is an idea originally presented by Bruce Malina. Here, the paraphrasing in anthropological and social context is by Jerome H. Neyrey. Jerome H. Neyrey. "Prayer, In Other Words: New Testament Prayers in Social-Science Perspective." http://www.nd.edu/~jneyrey1/Prayer.htm. Speaking in a multifaith vistas, other scholars also view such a social dimension of prayer (as well as worship), and we may cite here, the following for further reference: Boston University School Of Theology: Course Description. "Prayer And Social Engagement." http://www.bu.edu/sth/spirit/prayersocialengage.html; Asghar Ali Engineer. "Haj In Social Perspective." May 2000. www.dawoodi-bohras.com/perspective/haj.htm; Moeslim Abdurrahman. "Fast (Hunger) or Social Asceticism?" www.gusdur.net/english/english_detail.asp?contentOID=303.

Going by the context of cyber worship, an extension of the above social connection can also be seen in popular-culture as spelled by expert in the field of online-religion, namely, Brenda E. Brasher. "The Cyborg: Technological Socialization and its Link to the Religious

Function of Popular Culture." www.religion-online.org/cgi-bin/relsearchd.dll/showarticle?item_id=404. One has to bear in mind that this is all-ado-about a trilogy: theology, human behavior and mass media. Whatever emerges in the penultimate is not always dependant upon such theoretical speculations. The bottom line in such a holy triangle is worth emphasizing:

> "Today, we say unequivocally that there are two major types of theology: (1) academic theology, which concerns itself with critically relating the meanings of sacred texts and traditions to a religious community, and (2) popular theology, which uncritically establishes, maintains, and changes the mythological assumptions of a people, especially through the mass media. Both theologies have cosmological implications and are shaped by anthropological assumptions… It is increasingly clear in the modern world that popular theology has far more direct and immediate influence than academic theology on culture and society." Quentin J. Schultze. "Civil Sin: Evil and Purgation in the Media."
> http://theologytoday.ptsem.edu/jul1993/v50-2-article6.htm

67. "Key Functions of Religion," www.owlnet.rice.edu/~soci430/outlines/functions.html

68. *Larousse Dictionary of Beliefs & Religions*, 435.

69. By Nick Trierweiler, "A Scout is Reverent: A Guide to the Faiths of Other Scouts," http://www.inquiry.net/ideals/faiths/ (Sept 11, 2003).

70. Rev. Howard R. Gorle, "Understanding Ritual," http://www.bereavement.org/ritual.htm (22 May 2004)

71. Akeel Bilgrami, 'The Clash Within Civilizations' *Daedalus* (Summer 2003), 89.

72. Bruce B. Lawrence. *Complete Idiot's Guide to Religions Online,(*Indianapolis, Alpha Books; 1999). 388.

73. "Spirit and Leather," www.westom.com/leather/leatherspirit.com

74. Khan. *Web-Based Training*, 51.

75. W3C Working Draft. "Web Services Glossary." 8 August 2003. www.w3.org/TR/ws-gloss (22 Jan 2004); See also the following article for two inter-related issues, that is an illustration of Jewish adoption of synchronous and asynchronous tools: Barbara Krishenblatt-Gimblett. "The Electronic Vernacular." www.nyu.edu/classes/bkg/issues/electronic-bkg.htm (30 Jan 2004)

76. Judith M. Umbach. "Talking to techies." *Feliciter, journal of the Canadian Library Association* 47 no. 5 (2001), 234-235.

77. Khan. *Web-Based Training*, 58.

78. Lawrence, *Complete Idiot's Guide to Religions Online,* 387.

79. Paul Wilkes, and Marty Minchin, Eds. Best Practices from America's Best Churches (Mahwah, N.J., Paulist Press, 2003), 17.

80. "What's A Webcam?" http://www.halloweenwebcams.com/halloween_webcam_whats.html; "Web Cam Technology." http://ghscomlab.genevacsd.org/theweb/webcams.html

81. Berners-Lee, Tim. *Weaving the Web*, 219.

82. "When www spells World Wide Worship." *BBC NEWS In Depth | dot life,* Monday, 21 May, 2001, http://216.10.26.55/digitalangels/World_Wide_Worship.htm ; Helen Goodall. Ed. World Wide Worship. Kevin Mayhew, 2000; Kevin Mayhew - Worship Resources www.kevinmayhewltd.com/church_music/wwwworres.html ; http://www.worldwideworship.com/listen ;
Caramel Quin. "World Wide Worship,"
www.ivillage.co.uk/computers/int/web/articles/0,,181234_183251-1,00.html ;
"World Wide Worship Team - Equipping Worshipers." http://www.worldwideworshipteam.com ;
Nivedita Mookerji. "World Wide Worship On WWW As Religion Takes E-route."
www.financialexpress.com/fe_full_story.php?content_id=18640

83. *Larousse Dictionary of Beliefs & Religions*, 567

84. "Word List - Forms of Worship and Belief." http://phrontistery.80megs.com/worship.html

#####

5.1. Appendix: Cyber Worship Web Feet

Metadata for Digital Information: Webliography

- *Automatic metadata generation By tom, Section DSpace: General http://scoop.dspace.org/story/2003/10/21/124126/09*
- Automatic RDF Metadata Generator. This form enables you to automatically classify a Web page according to Dewey Decimal Classification (DDC). www.scit.wlv.ac.uk/~ex1253/metadata.html
- Calligraphy Connection http://www.saintjohnsbible.org/news/sj_news.htm
- Cataloguing and metadata for digital images: http://www.slq.qld.gov.au/pub/digital/sd1_meta.htm
- A Comparison of Schemas for Dublin Core-based Video Metadata Representation. Jane Hunter, CITEC, 317 Edward St Brisbane, Qld, 4001, Australia archive.dstc.edu.au/RDU/staff/jane-hunter/ mpeg7/contribution.html
- Digital Video Archives: Managing Through Metadata http://www.clir.org/pubs/reports/pub106/video.html
- Honest" Assessment of Image Formats. JPEG TIFF FPX. Image Quality (general) all very good. File size small large large. Transmission speed fast slow fast. ... apiii.upmc.edu/archive/1998/talks/lieber/tsld017.htm
- Meta Data Issues for Digital Delivery. http://www.saintjohnsbible.org/news/sj_news.htm
- Metabrowser Metadata Editor 1.6 - ZDNet UK Downloads downloads.zdnet.co.uk/0,39025604,39062770s,00.htm
- The MetaWeb Project www.dstc.edu.au/Research/Projects/metaweb
- Review of Visual Art Representation and Communication on the Web www.unisi.it/ricerca/dip/let_mod/ lettura.scrittura/review.pdf
- SOFTWARE Grokking the infoviz Jun 19th 2003 From The Economist print edition. Information visualisation is about to go mainstream. ... www.economist.com/ science/tq/displayStory.cfm?Story_id=1841120
- A Unified Approach to Indexing Multimedia on the Web Lakshman Jayaratne Zhuhan Jiang. Athula Ginige School of Computing and Information Technology University www.research.att.com/~rjana/jayaratne.pdf
- Visual Resources Association. TASI :: Advice - Delivering Digital Images | Metadata and Digital ... www.tasi.ac.uk/advice/delivering/metadata.html
- Visual Arts Data Service. Complex Metadata. http://www.vads.ahds.ac.uk/index.html

5.2. Appendix: Cyber Worship: Web Evaluation

Questionnaire and Survey Results

Dear Sir/Madam Re: my book-writing project, Cyber Worship in Multifaith Perspective
I thank you for the permission given to print the Web page:

So that I may describe the website in your own words, I need your help. I am attaching a questionnaire, and your response will enable me to build a unique profile of websites that exclusively facilitates religious/spiritual activities. While these questions are framed in a generic manner, you are at liberty to respond the way you like. I will be happy to answer any doubts on these issues.

Please complete the questionnaire, A.S.A.P. If it is not too much, may I request you to kindly return the filled in questionnaire as a Word file, via my e-mail: mt2222@yahoo.com.

Cyber Worship Web site's Profile

About the Personality of the Website, Spirit, Minds and bodies…Who:

Author's name, mailing address and e-mail
Creator's name, mailing address and e-mail
Designer's name, mailing address and e-mail
Maintained by: Name, mailing address and e-mail
Webmaster's name: , mailing address and e-mail
Owner's name: if other than the above, mailing address and e-mail

All that matters in a Website… What:

Purpose, goal, mission of the website:
Name of Worship Web page
Linked to how many sites: internally
Linked to how many sites: externally (i.e., websites outside your website)
Which search engines index this site
Categorizing (Is the website for): Prayer, Praise, Scripture, Sacrament, or other (pl. specify)
Website representation by faith/spirituality: Is it mainstream (please specify) or others (please name?)
Is this website approved, if any, by denomination, sect or others (Pl give the name of the body or group.)

Energy, plans, process and prospects How and Why:

What service and products the site offers
Type of audience:
Level of audience:
Is it all free – (that is, no tags attached?)
If for fee, pl. specify the name of the security tool used for e-commerce transactions Please name the brand: Or is it maintained by a different agency (outsourced)?

Space, place and gravity … Where:

URL of the worship Web page
If more than one Web page, please list other URL which your website offers as a facility for worship/religious purpose/spirituality
Host or Web server's name
ISP (Internet Service Provider)'s name
Personal or official website (if official, please give the name of the group, address, and e-mail:
What is your Web page's homepage

Time, linear, cyclical…When:

Date created
Date last modified
Updates: daily, weekly, monthly or when?

Glossary

Daily traffic, unique visitors
Monthly traffic, unique visitors
Do you Maintain web log? (if yes, please specify what tool you use):

Following is a summary of the responses that are analyzed using Web tools:

Table 1 Legend Webwise

Website #	Web site	ISP's Location	Archived Since	Date Last Updated	Link popularity	Link Check (bad links)	Google Page rank Prediction	Position analyzer
1	worldprayers.org	California	May 20, 2000	3-1-2004	Altavista 723; Google 138; Hotbot 739	0	6 / 5	Y=Google Y=Yahoo
2	kashi.org/tour.htm	Florida	Feb 20, 1999	April 2004	Altavista 91; Google 58; Hotbot 130	0	5 / 0	N=Google Y=Yahoo
3	religion-online.org	Texas	Nov 1997	2004 Feb	Altavista 2118; Google 2490; Hotbot 4187	1	7/9	N=Google Y=Yahoo
4	omsakthi.org/worship/prayer_room.html	California	Aug 24, 2000	2-25-2004	Altavista:0 Google:1 Hotbot:0	0	4 / 0	Y=Google Y=Yahoo
5	secweb.org/kiosk.asp	Colorado	1995	April 2004	Altavista 12; Google 259; Hotbot 0	0	6 / 10	Y=Google (Position:03) Y=Yahoo
6	go.to/OnlineWiccanRituals	o	Oct 18, 2001	Jan 2004	Altavista:5 Google:0 Hotbot:0	0	3 / 3	Y=Google Y=Yahoo
7	virushead.net/bdi	California	Jan 11, 2004	3-2-2004	Altavista 101; Google 86; Hotbot 204	0	5 / 4	Y=Google (Position:01) Y=Yahoo
8	enlightenment.com	N/A	1995	2004-04-20	Altavista 562; Google 416 Hotbot 1015	0	6/6	Y=Google Y=Yahoo
9	idsl.net/heather/onlinebuddhistcenter/	Suffolk	1999	Feb 18, 2004	Google:9 Altavista:59 Hotbots:0	0	5 / 5	Y=Google (Position:01) Y=Yahoo
10	dailyzen.com/meditation.asp	Colorado	1998	Mar 25, 04	Altavista:0 Google:1 Hotbot:0	1	7 / 3	Y=Google (Position:02) Y=Yahoo
11	jesuit.ie/prayer/	Dublin, Ireland	Apr 20, 1999	Mar 02, 2004	Altavista:2309 Google:530 Hotbot:0	1	6 / 4	N=Google Y=Yahoo
12	teddingtonbc.org.uk	London	1996	Feb 21, 2004	AltaVista 6 Google 7 Hotbot 5	0	4 / 6	Y=Google Y=Yahoo
13	patriot.net/~bmcgin/chapel.html	New York	Dec 06, 1998	Jan, 2004	Google:12 Altavista:18 Hotbots:0	0	5 / 5	Y=Google Y=Yahoo
14	cyberworship.freeserve.co.uk		Jan 25, 1999	2001	Altavista 2 Google 0 Hotbot 4	2	2 / 2	Y=Google Y=Yahoo
/15	mppc.org/more_about_menlo/Experience_Menlo	California	1995	Apr 2004	Altavista 0; Google 0; Hotbot 0	0	5 / 2	Y=Google Y=Yahoo
16	cathprayer.com	Louisiana	25 Mar 1999	Feb 29, 2004	Altavista:0 Google:0 Hotbot:1	1	4 / 4	Y=Google Y=Yahoo

Table 2 Legend Faithwise

Faithwise	**School / Denomination / Sect**	**Title of activity**	**Contact info**	**Web site ***

Glossary

Faithwise	School / Denomination / Sect	Title of activity	Contact info	Web site *
Multifaith (M)	•	World Prayers	project@worldprayers.org	1
Multifaith (M)	•	Kashi Ashram Tour	kashinfo@kashi.org	2
Multifaith (M)	•	Education	fore@cox.net	3
Alternative Tradition (A)	Om Sakthi	Adhiparasakthi Temple – Virtual Prayer Room	webmaster@omsakthi.org	4
Alternative Tradition (A)	Secular Web Kiosk	Education	iidb@infidels.org	5
Alternative Tradition (A)	Wiccan	Online Wiccan Ritual Education	http://htmlgear.lycos.com/feed/control.feed?a=render&i=1&u=wiccasinovess	6
Alternative Tradition (A)	Virtual Church of Benevolent Deities, Inc.	Education	hnordbe@LearnLink.Emory.Edu	7
Alternative Tradition (A)	•	Enlightenment.com	solstice@enlightenment.com	8
Buddhism (B)	Non-Sectaria	Create An Altar	heather@swsoft.co.uk	9
Buddhism (B)	Zen	Cyber Meditation	www.dailyzen.com/contact.asp	10
Christian (C)	Irish Jesuits	Sacred Space	feedback@jesuit.ie	11
Christian (C)	Baptist	Information	cphicks@compuserve.com	12
Christian (C)	Universalists	Internet Daily Chapel	Bill McGinnis, P.O. Box 2543, Alexandria, VA., 22301. email: bmcgin@patriot.net	13
Christian (C)	○	Praise, Scripture	www.eattheword.com [webmaster_NOSPAM_@EatTheWord.com]	14
Christian (C)	Presbyterian Church U.S.A	Information	950 Santa Cruz Avenue • Menlo Park • California • 94025	15
Christian (C)	Jesuit	Prayer, Information	webmaster@cathnews.com	16

• Not Applicable ○ Data not on the Website *(see Legend) table 1 and table 2

Table 3 Website Design

Consistent	Page Load Time ** In seconds)	Navigational compatibility	Animation / Graphics	Accommodating the user	Documentation	Web site⁺
•	3.29	•	•			1
•	2.39	•	•	•		2
•	2.58					3
•	2.01	•	•			4
	5.10					5
	4.05	•			•	6

Consistent	Page Load Time ** In seconds)	Navi gational compa tibility	Anim ation / Graphics	Accom modating the user	Docum entation	Web site[+]
●	4.65					7
	4.90		●			8
●	2.86	●		●	●	9
	4.87	●	●		●	10
●	2.54	●	●	●	●	11
	2.01					12
●	3.44	●		●	●	13
●	2.74	●			●	14
●	5.18	●	●		●	15
	2.74					16

● Indicates adherence to best practices ** cable (512KB) [netmechanic.com] [+]See Legend (table 1 and table 2)

Table 4 Website Context

Objectives	Content P(rayers), Pr(aise) S(cripture), M(editation), E(ducational)	Link: I(nternal) E(xternal)	Taxonom y compass	Credibilit y	Info type: Media, A(udio), V(ideo), L(ive cam), T(ext), D(igital Imaging)	Products Online: (A)utomated / Onr(on request) / D(ownloads)	Service F(ree) Fe(e-based)	Copyrig ht / disclaimer	Faq / help	Web site*
●	P/M	I	●	●	T	Onr	F	●		1
●	M	I	●	●	T / D	Onr	F			2
●	E/S	I/E	●		T	Onr	F			3
●	P / Pr / M	I / E	●	●	T / A / D	Onr	F		●	4
●	E	I / E	●		T / V	Onr	F		●	5
●	P	I / E			T	Onr	F			6
●	Pr, M	I		●	T	Onr	F	●	●	7
●	M	I	●		D/T	A	F/ Fe	●	●	8
	M	I		●	T / D	A	F			9
	M	I		●	T / D	A	F	●	●	10
●	P / M		●		T	Onr / D	F		●	11
●	E	I/E	●		D / T	C	F	●	●	12
●	P	I/E	●	●	A / T	S	F		●	13
●	Pr	I/E	●		T	S	F	●		14
●	P	I	●		V / D	S	F	●		15

Glossary

Objectives	Content P(rayers), Pr(aise) S(cripture), M(editation), E(ducational)	Link: I(nternal) E(xternal)	Taxonomy compass	Credibility	Info type: Media, A(udio), V(ideo), L(ive cam), T(ext), D(igital Imaging)	Products Online: (A)utomated / Onr(on request) / D(ownloads)	Service F(ree) Fe(e-based)	Copyright / disclaimer	Faq / help	Web site*
•	M	I / E	•		T	S	F	•		16

- Indicates adherence to best practices, *(see Legend) table 1 and table 2

Table 5 Website collaboration

Continuity	Collaboration	Accessibility	Security	Diversity – Multifaith Perspective	Diversity – Multilingual	Web site*
	•	•		•		1
	•			•		2
		•		•		3
•	•	•		•		4
•	•	•				5
	•	•	•			6
		•	•	•		7
•	•	•	•			8
•						9
•		•				10
		•				11
•	•	•				12
	•	•				13
•		•				14
	•					15
						16

- Indicates adherence to best practices, *see Legend table 1 and table 2

Table 6 Profile of Cyber Worship Sites: Who

Author	Creator	Designer	Maintainer	Webmaster	Owner' s name: if other	Website #**
	•		○	•	○	1
•	•	•	•	•		2
•	•	•	•	•		3
•	•	•	•	•		4
○	○	○	○	○	○	5

Author	Creator	Designer	Maintainer	Webmaster	Owner' s name: if other	Website #**
●	●	●	●	●	●	6
○	○					7
●	●	●	○	○	○	8
●	●	●	●	●	●	9
●	●	●	●	○	●	10
○	○	●	○	●		11
●	●	●	●	●	●	12
●	●	●	●	●		13
●	●	●	●	●	●	14
●	●	○	●	●		15
○	●	●	●	●	○	16

**See Websites legend in table 1 and table 2

Table 7 Profile of Cyber Worship Sites: What

Total pages within the site	External Links	Site indexed by	Website representation by faith/ spirituality:	Approved by denomination, …	Websites*
		Google, etc	Interfaith project	Many	1
0	12		Interfaith	Not applicable	2
105	Google= 3,480 Alta Vista= 3,647	Internal Search Engine and Google programmed internally	Many faith		3
500	100	AOL, AlltheWeb, Google, etc	Any Faith	By the Founder of the Om Sakthi Spiritual Movement	4
1000s	A few	Google, etc.	Not applicable	Not applicable	5
Not applicable	Many				6
	80			No	7
	One		Unaffiliated	No	8
112	126	Google, Excite, Lycos, etc	Non-sectarian	Not applicable	9
20	Unknown	Unknown	Buddhism, Zen, Taoism	Not Known	10
6	70	Google, etc.	Catholic, Ignatian		11
0	20	Google, Yahoo	Christian, (Baptist)	Not by outside body	12
		All the big ones	Christian Universalist	No	13
0	5	Google, Yahoo, Lycos, AltaVista	Christian	No	14

Total pages within the site	External Links	Site indexed by	Website representation by faith/ spirituality:	Approved by denomination, ...	Websites*
4	1	Google, Yahoo	Christian Presbyterian Church USA	Presbyterian Church USA	15
Don't Know	Don't Know	Google	Jesuit	Australian Catholic Bishop Conference, Australian Catholic Leaders of Religious Institute	16

*(see Legend) table 1 and table 2

Table 8 Profile of Cyber Worship Sites: How and Why

Service and products	Type of audience	Level of audience	free	fee, tool for e-commerce	Website*
o	Global, all ages, nationalities		Yes		1
o	Spiritual Seekers		Yes	Not applicable	2
o		Pastors, students, "seekers" mostly college level	Yes		3
o	Any	Any	Yes		4
o		Pastors, students, "seekers" mostly college level	Yes		4
o	Persons interested in theism, atheism, agnosticism, naturalism, etc	High school, college, and postgraduate	Yes	Not applicable	5
o	All ages, men, women, teens, all with open mind		Yes	Not applicable	6
o	Human	All, but some religious experience will make it more rewarding	Yes		7
					8
o	Individuals and families interested in Buddhism	Beginners and those experienced, all ages	Yes	No	9
o	Varied	Unknown	Yes		10
o	People of all religious backgrounds	All Levels	Yes		11
o	General public	General public	Yes		12
					13
o	Anyone wanting to find out more about this subject	16+ (because the language is quite formal)	Totally free		14
o	Global audience		No	Charge for sermons MP3 and mpeg downloads	15
o	Catholics	Various	Totally free		16

o Indicates variety of products/services *(see Legend) table 1 and table 2

Table 9 Profile of Cyber Worship Sites: Where

URL of Worship page, if other	If more than one Web page, please list other URL	Host or Web server's name	ISP	Personal or official Website - please give the name of the group	What is your Web page's homepage	Website*
	•				worldprayers.org	1
•	•	Mpinet	Bell South		kashi.org/index.htm	2
		Indconet	Indoconet		religion-online.org	3

URL of Worship page, if other	If more than one Web page, please list other URL	Host or Web server's name	ISP	Personal or official Website - please give the name of the group	What is your Web page's homepage	Website*
•		Interland	AT&T Business Internet Services	Personal but officially sanctioned	omsakthi.org	4
•	•	Subject to change	Not applicable	Internet Infidels	infidels.org	5
•	•	Angelfire		Personal	go.to/ OnlineWiccanRituals	6
•		doteasy.com		Personal	Virushead Eclectic Wave	7
•	•				enlightenment.com	8
•		mailgate.com	Mailgate Ltd.	Personal	idsl.net/heather/ onlinebuddhistcenter	9
•		Data Pipe	Comcaast	Personal	dailyzen.com	10
•		jesuit.ie	Hosting365	Jesuit Communications Centre	jesuit.ie	11
•		Compuserve	Compuserve	Official	TeddingtonBC.org.uk	12
	•	patriot.net	patriot.net	personal	LoveAllPeople.org	13
•	•	Cyberworship hosted by freeserve.com; Eattheword by nightskyhosting .com	Metronet	paulvickers.com	paulvickers.com	14
						15
•		Pair.com	Pair.com	Cathnews.com	cathnews.com	16

Indicates a positive response; *(see Legend) table 1 and table 2

Table 10 Mapping Faiths and Domains Webwise – [See Chapter One for the source of this data]

	.com	.org	.net	.edu	Misc
Online	586	333	112	48	68
Offline	516	225	75	29	83
Home Pages	226	341	45	24	48
Total	1328	899	232	101	199

Table 11 Faithwise Position Analyzer by Search Engines – [See Chapter One for the source of this data]

	google	yahoo
Multifaith	1	3
Alt Trad	4	4
Buddhism	2	2
Christianity	5	6
Total	12	15
	google	yahoo

Table 12 Faith wise Popularity - By Search Engine - – [See Chapter One for the source of this data]

	Altavista	Google	Hotbot
Multifaith	2932	2314	5056
Alt Trad	680	762	1219
Buddhism	9	60	0
Christianity	2335	549	10
Total	5956	3685	6285

Best Practices in Communities of Practice: See what works and what doesn't

Church of Ireland Website Survey

The internet Committee of Central Communications Board of the Church of Ireland.
http://ireland.anglican.org/survey/results.pdf

This report contains the results of the Church of Ireland website survey. The results are written exactly as they were received, except for when they were displayed in a chart. Out of approximately 700 people canvassed in the survey, there were 134 respondents. 118 of these use the website and 16 do not.

Bibliography

Abel-Kops, Chad P., '"What has straw in common with wheat?" A Selective Review of Bibliographical Control in the Field of Homiletics,' firstmonday.org/issues/issue6_7/abel/index.html

Abraham, Lois, "Some religious sites to visit on the Internet Talking about religion in cyberspace Internet: Spirituality online religion: Clergy and laypeople are reaching out to their flocks through the World Wide Web," *The Windsor Star* [Windsor, Ont.] 11 May 1996.

Anderson, Jon W. "Muslim Networks, Muslim Selves in Cyberspace: Islam in the Post-Modern Public Sphere." www.mafhoum.com/press3/102S22.htm

Andres, Hayward P., "Multimedia, Information Complexity and Cognitive Processing." *Information Resource Management Journal* 17, no. 1 (Jan–Mar 2004), 63-78.

Antelman, Kristin, Ed. Database-Driven Web Sites. New York, Haworth, 2002. [Reviewer: Mohamed Taher, in press]

Barclay, R.O. and P.C. Murrary, Virtual Blood, Real Sweat, No Tears: Lessons Learned From Making a Publication About Electronic Publications. (Professional Communication Conference, 1995, IPCC '95 Proceedings, Smooth Sailing to the Future, IEEE International) pages 106-109.

Bauwens, Michel. Edited. 'Religion Online and Techo-Spiritualism,' 1999. cybersociology.com

Becker, Pati Clayton. "In Time of War," *American Libraries* 34 (5) (May 2003) 54-57.

Berners-Lee, Tim. Weaving the Web: The Original Design and Ultimate Destiny of the World Wide Web By its Inventor. New York, Harper, 1999.

Berliner, Barbara. The Book of Answers: The New York Public Library's Telephone Reference Service's Most Unusual and Entertaining Questions. New York, Prentice Hall, 1999.

Beversluis, Joel. Ed. *Sourcebook of the World's Religions: An* Interfatih Guide to Religion and Spirituality. 3rd edition. Novato, CA., New World Library, 2000.

Bibby, Reginald W. Fragmented Gods: The Poverty and Potential of Religion in Canada. Toronto, Irwin Publishing, 1987.

———. Unknown Gods: The Ongoing Story of Religion in Canada. Toronto, Stoddart, 1993.

Brasher, Brenda E. Give Me That Online Religion. John Wiley, 2001. raider.muc.edu/~brashebe/online%20religion.htm

Brockway, Duncan. The Reading and Library Habits of Connecticut Pastors (Summary of the Proceedings of the 28th Annual Conference of the American Theological Association). 1974. 125-127.

Bruce, Harry and Ross Todd, "Cultural dimensions in reference services: Is there unity in diversity?" in Infobridges: Linking Australia and Asia. Proceedings of the Second National Reference and Information Service Section Conference, Darwin 9–11 July 1993. Edited by Murray Maynard. Darwin, N.T., Australian Library and Information Association, 1993: 85-95

Budilovsky, Joan, and Eva Adamson. Complete Idiot's Guide to Meditation. 2nd Edition. Indianapolis, Alpha Books, 2003.

Bunt, Gary R. Virtually Islamic: Computer-mediated communications and Cyber Islamic Environments. Cardiff, University of Wales Press, 2000.

———. Islam in the Digital Age: E-Jihad, Online Fatwas and Cyber Islamic Environments. Virginia, Pluto Press, 2003.

Chepesiuk, Ron, "September 11and its Aftermath: Muslim-American Librarians Reflect" American Libraries (Feb 2002) 40-42.

Chen, Ching-Chih, and Peter Hernon, Information Seeking: Assessing and Anticipating User Needs. New York, Neal-Schuman, 1982.

Chester, Jeff, "The Death of the Internet – How Industry Intends to Kill the 'Net As We Know it," www.jamie.com/archives/000212.html

Cobb, Jennifer J. Cybergrace: The Search for God in the Digital World. Crown Pub., 1998.

"Computer-Assisted Theology Internet Resources." users.ox.ac.uk/~ctitext2/theology/

D'Angelo, John, and Sherry K. Little, "Successful Web Pages: What Are They and Do They Exist?" Information Technology and Libraries, June 1996:71-81.
Davis, Erik. Techgnosis: Myth, Magic+ Mysticism in the Age of Information. Three Rivers Press, 1999.
Davis, Stanley and Bill Davidson. 2020 Vision. New York, Simon & Schuster, 1991.
Dean, Thomas, Ed., Religious Pluralism and Truth: Essays on Cross-Cultural Philosophy of Religion, Albany, State University of New York Press, 1995.
"Deep into the Bone..." in "Re-inventing Rites of Passage." www.gracecathedral.org/enrichment/experts/exc20010516.shtml
Edwards, Mark U, Jr. "Belief.net: an interreligious web site" Christian Century. v.118 no. 16. May 16, 2001: 4.
———. "Virtual worship: a theological challenge." Christian Century. 117 no. 34 D 6 2000: 1262.
Elmasry, Mohamed. Spiritaul Fitness For Life. Kitchener, On., Pandora Press, 2002.
Erdel, Timothy P. *The Reading Habits of Evangelical Mennonite* Ministers. Masters Thesis. University of Chicago. 1978.
———. Bring Also the Books: Studies of Ministers as Readers. Reformed Review, 1982, 136-51.
Etzioni, Amitai. "The Internet versus the Sabbath." Tikkun. 15 no. 1 Ja-F 2000: 30- 31.
Feit, Jonathan Scott. "A (New) Typology of Religious Psychology: Relating Social Context, Attribution, and Affiliation," www.citizenculture.com/about/religiouspsych.pdf
Fierheller, George "A Fabric of Intelligence—How Our Supercomputing Network is Weaving the Next Human Renaissance," Canadian Journal of Information and Library Science 19, no. 1 (April 1994): 31-38.
Fisher Mary Pat. Living Religions/Religion on the Internet. Prentice Hall College Div; 1999.
Fulop, Timothy E. Stephen P. Shoemaker, "Campus Confessions." Christian Century 112 Jl 19-26 1995: 700-701.
Gathering of Light Web site: www.gatheringoflight.org/GOLInfoSheet.htm
Gangler, Daniel R. "Online Dancing: Congregation ministry in a Web world." Christian Ministry. 30 N-D 1999: 16-19.
Goa, David J., "Religion and Public Space," Religious Studies and Theology (Saskatoon) 21 (1) 2002: (26 pages) [David J. Goa, Provincial Museum of Alberta]
God on the Internet, by Mark A. Kellner, Hungry Minds, Inc, 1996.
Gopnik, Adam. "The Virtual Bishop: What does it take to get the French to turn on their computers?" New Yorker 72 Mr 18 1996: 59-63.
Gorman, G. E. "Patterns of Information Seeking and Library Use by Theologians in Seven Adelaide Theological Colleges." Australian Academic & Research Libraries 21 (1990): 137-156.
Greider, Brett "Academic Buddhology and the Cyber-Sangha: Researching and Teaching Buddhism through Multimedia and Internet Sources," www.uwec.edu/greider/BMRB/teach/academic_buddhology.AARpaper.htm
Groothuius, Douglas R. "Christian Scholarship and the Philosophical Analysis of Cyberspace Technologies." Journal of the Evangelical Theological Society 41 D 1998: 631-640.
"Gutenberg Church, Internet World." Christian Century. 117 no. 5 F 16 2000: 173-174.
Hadden , Jeffrey K., Cowan, Douglas E. Editors. Religion on the Internet. JAI Press; (2000).
Hammerman, Joshua. Thelordismyshepherd.Com: Seeking God in Cyberspace. Simcha Press; (2000).
Harris, Roma M. & Patricia Dewedney "Community Information Needs: The Case of Wife Assault." Libraries & Information Science Research 14 (1992): 5-29.
Hawkins, Miriam. An Investigation of the Reading Interests and Habits of Students and Graduates of the School of Medicine and Chandler School of Theology of Emory University. Master's Thesis. Emory University, 1954.
Hayes, Richard P. "The Internet as window onto American Buddhism." American Buddhism, 168-179. London: Curzon Pr, 1999.
Helland, Christopher "Online-Religion/Religion-Online and Virtual Communitas." In Religion on the Internet, Volume 8. Elseview, 2000: 205-233. Abstract, p. 205. http://c.faculty.umkc.edu/cowande/jaitoc.htm
Henderson, Charles. "The Internet as a Metaphor for God?". Cross Currents. 50 no. 1-2 Spr-Sum 2000: 77-83.
"How Much Do Ministers Read?" Christianity Today 15 (24 April, 1961): 647.
Hoyland, Robert G. Seeing Islam as others saw it: A Survey and Evaluation of Christian, Jewish and Zoroastrian Writings on Early Islam. Princeton, N.J., Darwin Press, 1997.
Huseman, Dwight, A. "Books, Periodicals, and the Pastor." Drexel Library Quarterly 6 (1970): 4-26.
"Internet causes divisions, warns French journalist." Christian Century. 116 Ja. 6-13 1999: 12-13.
Judge, Anthony, "Sustainable Internet Penetration of Rural Areas: Reframing the Global challenge of the Digital Divide Through Fruitful Local Metaphors" Prepared for Discussion in Relation to the Preoccupations of the World Summit on the Information Society (Geneva, 2003), 7 March 2003 lactusinpraesens.org/doc00/internet.php
Jungai, Huang, "On Principles of Librarianship," nlc.nlc.gov.cn/newpage/publish/xuebao/2001_2.htm

Karaflogka, Anastasia, "Religious discourse and cyberspace" Paper presented in the 18th Quinquennial Congress of the IAHR 512 August 2000 Holiday Inn Durban Elangeni)

Karahanna, E., and others. "Information technology adoption across time: A cross-sectional comparison of pre-adoption and post-adoption beliefs," MIS Quarterly, 23 (2), 1999:183-213

Katz, James E., and Ronald E. Rice, "Syntopia: Access, Civic Involvement, and Social Interaction on the Net," in The Internet in Everyday Life. Edited by Barry Wellman and Caroline Haythornwaite. Malden, MA., Blackwell, 2002.

Kavanaugh, Andrea L. and Scott J. Patterson, "The Impact of Community Computer Networks on Social Capital and Community Involvement in Blackburg," in The Internet in Everyday Life. Edited by Barry Wellman and Caroline Haythornwaite. Malden, MA., Blackwell, 2002.

Kearns, Grover S., "A Multi-Objective, Multi-Criteria Approach for Evaluating IT Investments: Results from Two Case Studies," Information Resource Management Journal, 17 (1), Jan – Mar 2004, 37-62.

Keene, Michael L. "The church on the Web." Christian Century. 116 Ag 11-18 1999: 774-778.

Kelly, David. "Finding the Path on the Internet: Getting in Touch with the Cyber Sangha and Accessing the Online Resources of the Digital Dharma." Middle Way 74 no 3 N 1999: 185-187.

Kirkwood, Neville A. Pastoral care to Muslims: Building Bridges. Binghamton, N.Y., Haworth, 2002.

Kniffel, Leonard. "Getting into the Spirit," American Libraries 34 (5) (May 2003): 36-40.

Lancour, Haold, "The Reading Interests and Habits of the Graduates of the Union Theological Seminary." Library Quarterly XIV (January 1944): 28-35.

Larousse Dictionary of Beliefs & Religions. Edinburgh, Larousse, 1994.

Lawrence, Bruce B. Complete Idiot's Guide to Religions Online. Indianapolis, Alpha Books; 1999.

Levenson, Jon D. "The Talmud and the Internet: a Journey between worlds." Commentary. 110 no. 5 D 2000: 69- 70.

Levit, Jim. "A Survey of Evangelical Fee Church Pastors on the Ministers' Library." Trinity Journal 5 (1976): 126-134.

Levy, Stephen. "Blaming the Web: The cult used the Internet to spread its weird beliefs and make a living; but fears that the Net is reaching out to grab your kids are exaggerated." Newsweek 129 April 7 1997: 46-47.

McCabe, Ronald. Civic Librarianship: Renewing the Social Mission of the Public Library. Lanham, MD., Scarecrow, 2001.

Mediator's Handbook. (A Friends Conflict Resolution Program of the Philadelphia). Gabriola Island, BC., New Society Publications, 1997.

Main, Linda. Building Websites for a Multinational Audience. Lanham, MD. Scarecrow Press, 2002. [Reviewer: Mohamed Taher in Information Processing Management, in press]

Mintz, Anne P., Web of Deception: Misinformation on the Internet. Cyberage Books. 2002.

Moody, Marilyn, "Every Reader His or Her Access: The First Law of Library Science," Internet Reference Service Quarterly 4(3) 1999: 1-3.

Multifaith Information Manual. Edited by T. Kali Turner. 4th ed. Toronto, Ontario Multifaith Council on Spiritual and Religious Care, 2000.

Munroe, W. Bradley. "On Ethics and the Internet: The Brewing Crisis in Pulpit Ministry." Journal for Preachers 21 no. 1 1997: 48-49.

Nielsen, Jakob. "Ten Usability Heuristics." www.useit.com/papers/heuristic/heuristic_list.html

Nunberg, Geoffrey. Ed. The Future of the Book. Berkeley, CA., University of California Press, 1996.

O'Neill, Edward, T. and Lois Mai Chan. "FAST (Faceted Application of Subject Terminology): A Simplified LCSH-Based Vocabulary," Paper presented at World Library and Information Congress, 69th IFLA General Conference and Council, 1-9 Aug 2003, Berlin www.ifla.org/IV/ifla69/papers/01e-Oneill_Mai-chan.pdf

Ottenhoff, John. "The World Wide Web: Taking the plunge." Christian Century 112 O 11 1995: 939-933.

"Outsted bishop in cyberspace." Christian Century 113 April 10 1996: 390-391.

Perry, Barbara J. "Defenders of the Faith: Hate Groups and Ideologies of Power in the United States." Patterns of Predjudice 32 July 1 1998: 32-54.

Pomerantz, Jeffrey. Question Taxonomies for Digital Reference. Doctoral thesis. Albany, NY., Syracuse University, 2003.

"Praying on the Internet." Christian Century 114 April 16, 1997: 383-384.

Ramji, Rubina. "Building community word by word: religion in the virtual world." God in the Details. New York: Routledge, 2001: 267- 280.

Ranganathan, S. R. Five Laws of Library Science. 2nd ed. Bangalore, Sharda Ranganathan Endowment for Library Science, 1964.
Raschke, Carl. "From Religion to Faith: Levinasian Ethics and the Grammar of Address." www.jcrt.org/archives/04.1/index.html?page=egginton.shtml
Religion on the Internet 2001: Evaluating Online Resources, by STULL, Pearson Professional Education.
Rosen, Jonathan. The Talmud and the Internet: a Journey Between Worlds. New York: Farrar, Straus, and Giroux.
Rosenbush, S., and Einhorn, B., The Talking Internet: Special Report Telecommunications, Business Week, 1 (2000), 174-196.
Rushkoff, Douglas. Nothing Sacred: The Truth About Judaism. New York, Crown Publishers, 2003
Schultze, Quentin J. Internet for Christians: Everything You Need to Start Cruising the Net Today. Gospel Films, Revised edition, 1998.
Sabath, Bob. "community.com" Sojourners 24 S-O 1995: 10-11.
Sarot, Marcel. Michael Scott, and Maarten Wisse. "Philosophy of Religion: a critical survey of online resources." Religious Studies. 36 no. 3 S 2000: 355-366.
Smith, Craig A. "What to Do With Your Church Web Site: Let your light shine, on the Internet. Leadership. 20 Fall 1999: 55-57.
Sood, Gaurav. "Spiritualism online." www.tribuneindia.com/2000/20001225/login/main.htm
'Spiritual World' Special issue of American Libraries 34 (5) (May 2003).
Steinwedel, Stephanie. "The Information Seeking Behavior of Theologians as Humanists: A Review." www.geocities.com/sjsteinwedel/theolog.htm
Taher, Mohamed. "Interfaith Net Resources, What's Hot, What's Not," presentation at An EPIC Conference, February 2003, Toronto, taher.cjb.net
———. Cyber Worship Webliography, 2003 taher.cjb.net
———, and L.S., Ramaiah. Eds. A Dictionary of Library and Information Science Quotations. New Delhi, Aditya Prakashan, 1993.
———.Ed. Encyclopedic Survey of Islamic Culture. New Delhi, Anmol Publications, 1997. 20v.
———.Islamic Studies in India: A Survey of Human, Institutional and Documentary Sources. New Delhi, Concept, 1991.
———. "The Reference Interview Through Asynchronous E-Mail and Synchronous interactive Reference: Does it Save the Time of the Interviewee?" Internet Reference Service Quarterly 7(3) 2002: 22-34.
Taylor, Mark C. About Religion: Economics of Faith in Virtual Culture (Religion and Postmodernism). Chicago, University of Chicago Press, 1999.
Theall, Donald F. and Edmund Carpenter, The Virtual Marshall McLuhan. McGill-Queen's University Press, 2001.
Thistlethwaite, Susan Brooks. "Virtual Reality Christianity." American Theological Library Association Summary of Proceedings 53 1999: 229-237.
Troxel, A. Burge. Personal Computer Applications for the Pastor. Doctoral Thesis. Dallas Theological Seminary. 1987.
Twaddle, Laurence. Making Sense of English in Religion. New York, Chambers, 1992
Wallbridge, John. Sacred Acts, Sacred Space, and Sacred Time. Oxford, G. Ronald, 1996. (An interdisciplinary resource on Bahai Faith)
Wellman , Barry and Haythornthwaite, Caroline. Editors. The Internet in Everyday Life. Malden, MA., Blackwell Publishers, 2003. [Reviewer Mohamed Taher, in press]
Wessles, Mike, "Faith at the Front Desk – Spirituality and Patron Service," American Libraries 34 (5) (May 2003) 42-43.
Wicks, Donald A. 'The Information-Seeking Behavior of Pastoral Clergy: A Study of the Interaction of Their Work Worlds and Work Roles,' Library & Information Science Research 21 (1999): 206-226.
"Wired Religion." Christian Century 114 D 17 1997: 1183.
Wyly, B.J. Overcoming Intellectual and Virtual Access as Barriers to Utilization of Electronic Publications. (Socioeconomic Dimensions of Electronic Publishing Workshop, 1998. Proceedings.) 107-113.
Zukowski, Angela Ann. The Gospel in Cyberspace: Nurturing Faith in the Internet Age. Loyola Press, 2002.
Zaleski, Jeffrey P., and Jeff Zaleski. The Soul of Cyberspace: How New Technology Is Changing Our Spiritual Lives. HarperCollins, 1997

Index

Index

About the Author

Dr. Mohamed Taher is information professional and a former Fulbright alumnus of Rutgers University, New Brunswick, New Jersey, U.S.A. He has master degrees in Library Science (Mysore University, India), and Islamic Studies (Osmania University, India) doctoral degree in Library Science (Calicut University, India) and a post-doctoral degree in History (Agra Univ., India). .

His knowledge gained through formal training combines with 25 years of library work, research, and teaching. This manifests in the roles he has played in knowledge management, assisting in extension of the traditional library frontiers to Web-based development.. As part of his effort to share knowledge he has lectured at Rutgers University, University of Illinois - Urbana-Champaign, University of Toronto, and Seneca College, Toronto. In addition, he is author of many books, articles, reviews and research reports, in multidisciplinary fields with a slant towards area studies (especially religion, culture and society).

He is also a Guest Editor, *Internet Reference Service Quarterly*, Haworth Press; Book Review Editor, *Information Resource Management Journal*, Idea Group Publishing; and Category Editor Visual Information, Internet's DMOZ Open Directory Project.

At present he serves as Information Specialist, Ontario Multifaith Council on Spiritual and Religious Care, Toronto (www.omc.ca).